Post-Reformation
Reformed Dogmatics

Post-Reformation Reformed Dogmatics

The Rise and Development of Reformed Orthodoxy, ca. 1520 to ca. 1725

VOLUME FOUR
The Triunity of God

RICHARD A. MULLER

Baker Academic
Grand Rapids, Michigan

Published by Baker Academic
a division of Baker Publishing Group
P.O. Box 6287, Grand Rapids, MI 49516-6287
www.bakeracademic.com

Second printing, June 2006

Printed in the United States of America

Library of Congress Cataloging-in-Publication Data
Muller, Richard A. (Richard Alfred), 1948–
     Post-Reformation reformed dogmatics : the rise and development of reformed orthodoxy, ca. 1520 to ca. 1725 / Richard A. Muller—[2nd ed.].
         p.   cm.
     Includes bibliographical references and indexes.
     Contents: v. 1. Prolegomena to theology — v. 2. Holy Scripture — v. 3. The divine essence and attributes — v. 4. The triunity of God.
     ISBN 10: 0-8010-2617-2 (v. 1 : cloth)
     ISBN 978-0-8010-2617-1 (v. 1 : cloth)

     ISBN 10: 0-8010-2616-4 (v. 2 : cloth)
     ISBN 978-0-8010-2616-4 (v. 2 : cloth)

     ISBN 10: 0-8010-2294-0 (v. 3 : cloth)
     ISBN 978-0-8010-2294-4 (v. 3 : cloth)

     ISBN 10: 0-8010-2295-9 (v. 4 : cloth)
     ISBN 978-0-8010-2295-1 (v. 4 : cloth)
     1. Reformed Church—Doctrines—History—16th century. 2. Reformed Church—Doctrines—History—17th century. 3. Reformed Church—Doctrines—History—18th century. 4. Protestant Scholasticism. I. Title.
BX9422.3 .M85 2002
230'.42'.09—dc21   2002026165

Contents

PART 2. THE REFORMED ORTHODOX DOCTRINE OF THE TRINITY

Preface

The appearance of this preface indicates the conclusion of a rather long but hopefully fruitful journey. My own interest in post-Reformation Reformed dogmatics has not come to an end, and I have certainly not presented in this and the three preceding volumes an exhaustive overview of the teachings of scholastic Protestantism. I have simply arrived as a conclusion to the plan of study that I undertook some twenty-five years ago, with the intention of producing a monograph on the patterns or trajectories of development of Reformed theology in the sixteenth and seventeenth centuries, with attention to the declared *principia*, or "foundations," of that older theology.

In addition to offering the final section of the proposed study of theological prolegomena and *principia*, the present volume also offers a concluding chapter on the character of Reformed orthodoxy in which an attempt is made to draw together the findings of all four volumes into a more cohesive analysis of scholastic Protestantism than was possible either in the introduction to volume 1 or in the brief concluding sections of volume 2. Themes that appeared in the first and second chapters of volume 1 as theses about the rise and implications of a scholastic and "orthodox" Protestant dogmatics can now be stated as conclusions, in view of the research done in all four volumes.

The concluding chapter will, accordingly, reprise the problems of the relationship of Protestant orthodoxy to philosophy, of the development and alteration of hermeneutics in the course of the sixteenth and seventeenth centuries, and of the impact of these changes on the formulation of doctrine, together with the problem of the transition from the medieval to the early modern era as it had an impact on the theology of the age. The discussion of these problems, in the wake of our detailed exposition of the prolegomena and principia of theology, should lead, finally, to a fuller and clearer definition of the character and significance of scholasticism and orthodoxy in the Reformed tradition.

Finally, to all of the patient (and several impatient) readers who have asked for indices and further apparatus — you will find, at the end of this volume, the promised bibliography. Indices appear in all four volumes.

Richard A. Muller

PART 1

Introduction

1

The Doctrine of the Trinity in the Christian Tradition: The Medieval Background

1.1 The Doctrine of the Trinity in the West

A. Premises and Issues for Charting Its Development from the Twelfth through the Seventeenth Century

1. The trajectory of trinitarian doctrine in relation to issues of continuity and discontinuity in the development of Protestant thought. The trajectory of trinitarian thought in the sixteenth and seventeenth centuries is markedly different from the trajectories of the other issues we have examined in this study (the presuppositional structure of theology as defined in the prolegomena, the doctrine of Scripture, and the doctrine of the divine essence and attributes) — and the scholarly treatment of the doctrine is also quite different in character from the scholarship on prolegomena, Scripture, and the divine essence and attributes. These differences stem from a series of issues and factors that need to be noted from the outset as determinative of the topic and analysis of it.

First, the patterns according to which various doctrines were transmitted from the Middle Ages, through the Reformation, and into the era of orthodoxy remain as varied as the doctrines and many doctrinal nuances themselves. As a result, the patterns of continuity and discontinuity that describe the relationship of the Reformed orthodox to the Reformation and to the Middle Ages are also varied — differing in details from the relationships described in the study of prolegomena, Scripture, and divine essence and attributes. As in the cases of the other doctrinal issues, it is not particularly enlightening to the understanding of the Reformed doctrine of the Trinity to identify one thinker in a given era and one thinker in the next and then determine whether or not their formulations are identical. Given the nature of the development of

Protestant thought in and beyond the Reformation, that sort of continuity will not be found in any case.[1] Nor will the formulae and the patterns of argument found in the Reformed doctrine of the Trinity track through the same thinkers in the same way that the formulae and argumentation tracks in the cases of other shared doctrinal topics. By way of example, the Scotist and nominalist accents that are fairly readily identified in the Reformed prolegomena and in the Reformed discussions of the divine essence and attributes are less clearly marked in the doctrine of the Trinity. Similarly, the fairly clear Calvinian stamp on the shape and topical distribution of the later Reformed doctrine of the inspiration and divine marks of Scripture is not as evident in the Reformed orthodox doctrine of the Trinity — although the exegetical continuities are obvious.

Second, although it is certainly possible to speak of a generally "orthodox" doctrine of Scripture or of the divine essence and attributes, neither of these doctrines stands as a carefully defined dogma of ecumenical orthodoxy — as does the doctrine of the Trinity. Thus, Protestant and Roman Catholic writers of the sixteenth and seventeenth centuries debated the relative authority of Scripture and tradition but did not question either the inspiration or the normative character of Scripture itself. None of the debates over Scripture, moreover, looked to an ancient definition of doctrine and, in fact, there was little precedent for a formal "doctrine of Scripture" in the church prior to the Reformation. The authority of the text as divine Word or revelation only came under attack toward the close of the era of orthodoxy. The doctrine of the divine essence and attributes was, by way of contrast, fully developed as a distinct doctrinal topic long before the Reformation and, in the basic outlines of its orthodox formulations, carried through the Reformation into the era of orthodoxy with little alteration until its encounter with changing philosophical currents in the seventeenth century. But here, too, there was no single dogmatic formula that could be used as a test of orthodoxy; rather, the doctrine contained a series of assumptions, such as eternity, infinity, omnipotence, omniscience, and simplicity, none of which had been the subject of a full creedal definition. The doctrine of the Trinity, by way of contrast, had been closely defined in the patristic era and was ensconced in ecumenical formulae.

The Reformers and the Reformed orthodox, therefore, developed their teaching on the Trinity in conscious dialogue with the patristic and medieval tradition, in overt agreement with the councils of the early church, and in the tradition of the medieval conciliar decisions as well. This broad continuity of churchly doctrine generated the peculiar character of the Protestant development and debate over the Trinity: the Reformed churches and their theologians did not view the traditional dogmas defined by the councils as on a normative level comparable to that of Scripture — that was the assumption held by the Council of Trent. From the Reformers' perspective, the church could not be bound to these formulae in the same way that she was determined

---

1. See Richard A. Muller, "Calvin and the Calvinists: Assessing Continuities and Discontinuities Between the Reformation and Orthodoxy, Part II," in *Calvin Theological Journal,* 31/1 (April 1996), pp. 134-138.

in doctrine by Scripture, but the formulae would stand as normative on a biblical basis. Much of the Reformers' work and by far the greater part of the work of the Reformed orthodox with regard to the doctrine of the Trinity, therefore, was the grounding of the formulae and the traditional language more completely and explicitly on Scripture than had been done for centuries.

Third, whereas assaults on the normative character of Scripture and large-scale alteration of the doctrine of divine essence, attributes, and Trinity were comparatively rare occurrences in Middle Ages (and were typically dealt with very expeditiously), in the sixteenth and seventeenth centuries there was widespread debate over the doctrines of the divine attributes and the Trinity. The churchly theologians of the sixteenth and seventeenth centuries — whether Protestant or Roman Catholic — did not typically formulate their views of Scripture or of the divine essence and attributes over against radical denials of these doctrines, but their doctrine of the Trinity was developed in the context of fairly consistent denial of the doctrine by a number of highly insistent thinkers and groups who became increasingly adept at using both Scripture and early patristic tradition against the church's dogma. To make the point somewhat differently, whereas there was much debate and much very heated polemic in the sixteenth and seventeenth centuries over aspects of the doctrines of Scripture and the divine essence and attributes, the doctrines were not formulated in the context of a large-scale assault on their basic concepts, at least not until the mid-seventeenth century, after orthodox Protestant dogmatics had been fully formulated. Certainly after 1550, the opposite was the case with the doctrine of the Trinity. The seventeenth-century orthodox formulation of the doctrine was accomplished with constant polemic against antitrinitarian views — views that grew out of a highly biblicistic antitrinitarianism such as Christianity had not seen since the patristic period.

2. Drawing out the Protestant orthodox trinitarian trajectory in relation to its antecedents. From the Western catholic perspective, inherited by the Reformation, the development of ecumenical formulae concerning the Trinity did not cease with the close of the patristic era. The Western development of trinitarian doctrine rested not only on the medieval reception of the patristic materials and the subsequent analysis, codification, and expansion of patristic formulae in the schools but also and at least as importantly on the conciliar development of the doctrine in the west following the *filioque* controversy. Sixteenth- and seventeenth-century Protestant discussions of the doctrine of the Trinity are, certainly, the inheritors of this rich medieval development. We must, therefore, distinguish two distinct but not entirely separate tracks of theological development: first, there is the issue of the Western reception of the patristic materials, notably the Western reception of the works of Hilary, Ambrose, Augustine, and Boethius on the Trinity and the process of interpreting the early church's teachings for the sake both of removing potential contradictions and of establishing a clearer set of definitions, now in Latin, over against the historical errors of Sabellianism, Arianism, and Tritheism — errors all too easily repeated, given the difficulties of the trinitarian language of the church. Second, there is the development and defense of the distinctively Western line of trinitarian argument identified by the *filioque* clause of the emended Nicene Creed: when examined from the perspective of the councils, the trajectory of medieval trinitarianism was one of profound and intense ecumenical discussion. The mutual excommunications of the mid-eleventh century did not bring about a silent rupture between east and west but rather stimulated conciliar discussion and, from the Western perspective, the ecumenical establishment of the *filioque* as an article of the creed. From the Western perspective, with which the Reformers of the sixteenth century were in accord, the *filioque* clause and the attendant Western development of trinitarian definition were the final word of ecumenical orthodoxy.

The medieval scholastic development of trinitarian thought is crucial both to an understanding of the impact and implications of Augustinian trinitarian theory and to an understanding of the distinctive character and internal logic of Western trinitarianism, both Roman Catholic and Protestant. With the rise of an early scholasticism in the late eleventh and early twelfth centuries, there was a notable rise in the use of philosophical and linguistic insights in the explanation of Christian doctrine and, consequently, a rise also in debate over the proper explanation of traditional trinitarian language. Both the theologians and the synods of the era addressed a series of significant issues: the rift between East and West over the *filioque*, the nominalism of Roscellin, the problem of the distinction of persons and of attributes brought on by the speculative development of Abelard's trinitarianism, the realism of Gilbert de la Porrée, the divergence between the views of Peter Lombard and Richard of St. Victor, and the virtual tritheism of Joachim of Flora. Roscellin, Abelard, and Gilbert were each responsible for distinct problems in formulation — in the words of Michel, "excesses in dialectic and the intrusion of philosophy into the realm of dogma" led to "three dangerous tendencies" in trinitarian usage, specifically, the overly zealous use of nominalist, conceptualist, and realist philosophical assumptions in explaining the dogma.[2] All of these issued were addressed and, to a large extent, settled by the major conciliar rulings of the councils or synods of Soissons (1092), Bari (1098), Soissons (1121), Sens (1141), and Rheims (1148) and the Fourth Lateran Council in 1215. This conciliar development culminated in the Council of Florence (1438-42), often identified as the seventeenth ecumenical council, at which Latin and many Greek theologians, conjointly recognized the procession of the Spirit from the Father and the Son as a procession from a single *principium* or *arche* and came as close as any council or group in the thousand years of schism to repairing the breach.[3] For convenience in discussion, the medieval development can be divided fairly justly into two distinct periods, the first reaching from the extensive trinitarian meditations of

---

2. A. Michel, "Trinité. II. La théologie latine du VI au XX siècle," in *Dictionnaire de théologie catholique*, vol. 15/2, col. 1713.

3. See Heinrich Denzinger, *Enchiridion Symbolorum, Definitionum et Declarationum de Rebus Fidei et Morum*, 32nd edition, ed. Adolfus Schönmetzer (Barcinone: Herder, 1963), §1300-1302, hereinafter cited as Denzinger-Schönmetzer; cf. L. van der Essen, "Council of Florence," s.v. in *Catholic Encyclopedia*, and Edmund J. Fortman, *The Triune God: A Historical Study of the Doctrine of the Trinity* (1972; repr. Grand Rapids: Baker Book House, 1982), pp. 224-227.

Anselm of Canterbury at the end of the eleventh century to the intense trinitarian meditations of Richard of St. Victor and his contemporaries and the Fourth Lateran Council (1215), and the second from the flowering of high scholasticism in the early thirteenth century to the Council of Florence (1438-39).

3. Issues of Scripture and tradition: patristic study, philosophical issues, and the question of norms. Just as the Reformation and orthodoxy stood in the Western trinitarian tradition, so also did they stand in the Western tradition of the discussion of norms in theology. But here, as we have seen in a previous volume,[4] the magisterial Reformers and their orthodox successors stood in the line, not of the entire tradition of the west, but of that portion of the tradition that understood Scripture as the prior and necessary norm, and tradition as the secondary norm capable of offering probabilities in support of biblical argumentation. In the case of the doctrine of the Trinity, this placement in relation to the earlier tradition became the basis for a complex development of doctrine in the eras of the Reformation and of Protestant orthodoxy. Given their biblical standard, neither the Reformers nor the orthodox could simply reiterate the tradition — rather they saw the need to explain the doctrine of the Trinity in biblical and exegetical terms and to rely on the terms and formulae of the fathers and the councils only as secondary supports of the doctrine. In addition, their wariness of philosophical speculation rendered the more extravagant arguments of the fathers and the scholastics unacceptable to the Reformers and the orthodox. Statement and defense of the doctrine of the Trinity was, moreover, made increasingly difficult by the various antitrinitarian groups that sprang up in the sixteenth and seventeenth centuries, groups that often advocated a starkly rational biblicism over against the tradition, particularly against the views of the Nicene and post-Nicene fathers.

In a sense, the development of the Protestant orthodox doctrine of the Trinity can be described as a battle over the tradition or even as battle between differing modes of reception of the tradition. The rise of patristic scholarship in the era, therefore, also contributes to the picture — as does the rise of critical perspectives on the patristic development, the character of its doctrines, and their relationship to ancient philosophy. It was readily recognized in the seventeenth century that the language and conceptuality of trinitarian doctrine had altered and developed over the course of centuries — and that, if not necessarily different in fundamental intentionality, the teaching of the earliest fathers offered a rather different expression of the triadic nature of the Godhead than the teaching of the Nicene and post-Nicene fathers, and that both appeared rather different from the forms of expression used in the Middle Ages. An eclectic appropriation of this variegated tradition was, moreover, possible both for confessional Protestants, who did not understand tradition as a norm coequal with Scripture, and for the more radical groups, namely, the antitrinitarians, who were often quite willing to discard the tradition entirely.

The Reformed had to contend in particular with the Socinian reception of the church fathers, which not only read the patristic materials as less than normative but

---

4. *PRRD*, II, 1.3 (B.1), 5.5 (A.1-2).

which also read them as representing a steady decline from the purity of the gospel, under the impact of Platonizing philosophical perspectives — as a progress from Arianism before Nicaea, to tritheism after the Nicene formula, to madness in the scholastic era. The Socinian polemic, in turn, brought about a refinement of exegetical argument on the part of the Protestant orthodox and, in addition, a critical assessment of the impact of philosophy, particularly Platonism, on Christian doctrine. The Reformed orthodox also were pressed to choose particular patterns of trinitarian expression that coincided with their reading of the text of Scripture, their understanding of the implications of the philosophical tradition, and with their resultant assumptions concerning the kind of formulations suitable for the affirmation of a trinitarian monotheism over against the monistic and tritheistic patterns that could result from alternative readings of the tradition. In short, the Reformed orthodox doctrine of the Trinity was no simple restatement of the patristic norms — rather it was a complex development of doctrine intended to recover, respect, and use the patristic definitions and arguments insofar as they could be argued anew exegetically, under the authority of the biblical norm. The resultant doctrine stands on trajectories of biblical exegesis and trinitarian formulation that extend from the Middle Ages through the Reformation into the era of Protestant orthodoxy.

B. Scholarly Approaches: A Preliminary Survey of Historiography

1. The historiographical problem and the general histories of doctrine. The doctrine of the Trinity has been the subject of vast but highly focused scholarly discussion, with by far the larger part of the literature examining the patristic period. There is some justice in this emphasis, given the overarching significance of patristic debate and development together with the identification of a full and ecumenical dogmatic conclusion to the debates at Constantinople in A.D. 381. Still, the tendency of the scholarship to emphasize the patristic period and then to manifest a consistent and cumulative diminution of interest in the trajectories of orthodox formulation during the succeeding centuries has created a significant imbalance in the historiography: as scholarship on the Trinity enters the later Middle Ages and the Reformation, the balance has shifted away from the orthodox trajectory to the heterodox trajectory, often leaving the impression that orthodox trinitarianism from the fourteenth through the seventeenth century was a fundamentally uncreative and uninteresting phenomenon and devoted primarily to the refutation of heretical views. As implied in the preceding section, this impression is unfortunate.

Although the doctrine of the Trinity is surveyed and analyzed at length in virtually all of the standard histories of doctrine, this analysis has often been conducted with such emphasis on the patristic development that comparatively little attention is paid to the rich development of the doctrine in the medieval centuries and nearly none to the development in the Reformation and post-Reformation eras.[5] The exceptions

---

5. Thus, e.g., Adolf von Harnack, *History of Dogma*, trans. Neil Buchanan, 7 vols. (repr. New York: Dover, 1961); Jaroslav Pelikan, *The Christian Tradition: A History of the Development of*

to this generalization are few and often relate to the pattern of the older histories of doctrine, written before the time of Harnack and Seeberg, in which all doctrines were sketched out in a more or less systematic pattern for each era of the history— although the discussion of the Reformation and post-Reformation developments are sketchy at best.[6] Of the more recent manuals, only the work of Villanova offers discussions of the doctrine of the Trinity in each era of its development that are suitably proportionate the importance of the doctrine.[7] There are also several topical histories that are devoted entirely to the discussion of the doctrine of the Trinity.[8] In no case, however, do any of these surveys offer detailed discussions the developments in the Reformation and post-Reformation eras.

2. Monographic literature and shorter studies relevant to the later development of the doctrine of the Trinity. There is certainly a vast literature of studies on numerous aspects of the doctrine of the Trinity in the patristic period, much of which has significant bearing on the understanding of later developments, particularly given the close reading of the fathers by both trinitarians and antitrinitarians in the debates of the sixteenth and seventeenth centuries. The standard histories alone amount to a considerable bibliography.[9] By way of contrast, there is a relative decline of scholarly interest in the doctrine of the Trinity during the Middle Ages in the general histories of Christian thought, although several of the manuals of the history of medieval theology offer solid surveys of the materials.[10] There are, moreover, major monographs on various councils and individual thinkers that fill out the history of the medieval development quite adequately.

Doctrine, 5 vols. (Chicago and London: University of Chicago Press, 1971-1989); Reinhold Seeberg, Text-Book of the History of Doctrines, trans. Charles Hay, 2 vols. (1895-98; repr., Grand Rapids: Baker, 1977); also note Barthelemy Haureau, Histoire de la philosophie scolastique, 3 vols. (Paris: Durand et Pedone-Lauriel, 1872-1880) for much collateral discussion.

6. Karl R. Hagenbach, A History of Christian Doctrines, trans. E. H. Plumptre, 3 vols. (Edinburgh: T. & T. Clark, 1880-81); W. G. T. Shedd, A History of Christian Doctrine, 2 vols. (New York: Scribners, 1889; repr., Minneapolis: Klock & Klock, 1978); Henry C. Sheldon, History of Christian Doctrine, 2 vols. (New York: Harper, 1895); Joseph Schwane, Histoire des Dogmas, trans. A. Degert, 6 vols. (Paris: Beauchesne, 1903-4).

7. Evangelista Villanova, Histoire des théologie chréstiennes, 3 vols. (Paris: Éditions de Cerf, 1997).

8. A. Michel, "Trinité. II. La théologie latine du VI au XX siècle," in Dictionnaire de théologie catholique, vol. 15/2, cols. 1702-1830; Robert S. Franks, The Doctrine of the Trinity (London: Duckworth, 1953); Bertrand de Margerie, The Christian Trinity in History, trans. E. Fortman (Still River, Mass.: St. Bede's Publications, 1982); also note, Sidney Cave, The Doctrine of the Person of Christ (New York: Scribners, 1925); Aloys Grillmeier, Christ in Christian Tradition (New York: Sheed & Ward, 1965).

9. Noteworthy among the older works are J. F. Bethune-Baker, Introduction to the Early History of Christian Doctrine (Cambridge: University Press, 1903); J. Tixeront, History of Dogmas, trans. H. L. B., 3 vols. (St. Louis: Herder & Herder, 1910); G. L. Prestige, God in Patristic Thought (London: S.P.C.K., 1952); J. N. D. Kelly, Early Christian Doctrines (New York: Harper & Row, 1960).

10. E.g., Josef Bach, Die Dogmengeschichte des Mittelalters vom christologischen Standpunkte, 2 vols. (Vienna, 1873; repr., Frankfurt: Minerva, 1966); Franz Courth, Trinität. In der Scholastik, Handbuch der Dogmengeschichte, ed. M. Schmaus, A. Grillmeier and L. Scheffczyk, Bd. 2, Faszikel 1b (Freiburg: Herder, 1985).

The problem shifts with the beginning of the sixteenth century. There is no history of the doctrine of the Trinity that covers the era adequately.[11] The trinitarian thought of the Reformers and their orthodox successors has, in fact, received comparatively little treatment, except for a few scattered essays on the views of the more famous Reformers and virtually no analysis of the thoughts on the Trinity among their immediate successors in the late sixteenth century. By way of example, there are several substantial discussions of Luther's approach to the doctrine of the Trinity — and there are several studies of Calvin's teaching.[12] There is, as far as I know, to date, no similar body of literature on the doctrine of the Trinity in the thought of Zwingli, Melanchthon, Bucer, Bullinger, Farel, Viret, Musculus, Vermigli, or other first- and second-generation Reformers. There is, however, a reasonably large body of scholarship dealing with the antitrinitarian thought of the sixteenth and seventeenth centuries, particularly when the extent and impact of the antitrinitarian movements are compared with the development of the theology of the magisterial Reformation.[13]

The same problem appears in the case of the trinitarian theology of the seventeenth-century writers: the heresies have received significant analysis in monograph and scholarly essays, but the orthodoxy, with few exceptions, has been neglected.[14] There is a significant series of essays on seventeenth-century Socinianism,[15] a large body of

---

11. Franz Courth, *Trinitat. Von der Reformation bis zur Gegenwart*, Handbuch der Dogmengeschichte, Bd. 2, Faszikel 1c (Freiburg: Herder, 1996) discusses only Luther and Calvin, and ignores entirely the trajectory of teaching in which they stand, whether with regard to antecedents or later developments. Cf. the exceedingly brief treatment in Fortman, *Triune God*, pp. 239-242.

12. The most significant of these studies are Benjamin B. Warfield, "Calvin's Doctrine of the Trinity," in *Calvin and Augustine*, ed. Samuel Craig (Philadelphia: Presbyterian & Reformed Publishing Company, 1956), pp. 189-284 and, Thomas F. Torrance, "Calvin's Doctrine of the Trinity," in *Calvin Theological Journal*, 25/2 (1990), pp. 165-193. Further bibliography on Calvin's doctrine appears in the following chapter.

13. See Earl Morse Wilbur, *A History of Unitarianism*, 2 vols. (Cambridge: Harvard University Press, 1947-52); idem, *A Bibliography of the Pioneers of the Socinian-Unitarian Movement in Modern Christianity, in Italy, Switzerland, Germany, Holland* (Rome: Edizioni di storia e letteratura, 1950); Joseph Henry Allen, *An Historical Sketch of the Unitarian Movement* (New York: Christian Literature Company, 1894); Stanislaw Kot, *Socinianism in Poland* (Boston: Starr King Press, 1957).

14. Alan Spence, "John Owen and Trinitarian Agency," in *Scottish Journal of Theology*, 43 (1990), pp. 157-173; Carl R. Trueman, *The Claims of Truth: John Owen's Trinitarian Theology* (Carlisle: Paternoster Press, 1998). Reformed sources from the period are excerpted in Heinrich Heppe, *Reformed Dogmatics Set Out and Illustrated from the Sources*, revised and edited by Ernst Bizer, trans. G. T. Thomson (London, 1950; repr. Grand Rapids: Baker Book House, 1978). On the Lutheran development, see Werner Elert, *The Structure of Lutheranism: The Theology and Philosophy of Life of Lutheranism Especially in the Sixteenth and Seventeenth Centuries*, trans. Walter A. Hansen (St. Louis: Concordia, 1962), pp. 217-222; Robert D. Preus, *The Theology of Post-Reformation Lutheranism*, 2 vols. (St. Louis: Concordia, 1970-72), I, pp. 112-163; and the sources excerpted in Heinrich Schmid, *Doctrinal Theology of the Evangelical Lutheran Church*, trans. Charles E. Hay and Henry Jacobs (Minneapolis: Augsburg, n.d).

15. George Hunston Williams, *The Polish Brethren: Documentation of the History and Thought of Unitarianism in the Polish-Lithuanian Commonwealth and in the Diaspora 1601-1685*, 2 vols. (Missoula,

work on the Arianism of the era (particularly that of John Milton),[16] and a sizeable literature on the late seventeenth- and early eighteenth-century British trinitarian controversies.[17]

The reason for the neglect of the Protestant orthodox trajectory is, certainly, the conservatism of the Reformers and their successors, at least with reference to this particular topic: they offer little speculative development of the doctrine and in fact reject most of the speculative trinitarianism of the Middle Ages. In addition, their use of the church fathers tends to be for the sake of defining the terms of orthodoxy rather than for building or developing the doctrinal position. By far the larger part of the doctrine of the Trinity, whether among the Reformers or among their orthodox successors, is exegetical.

1.2 Early Scholastic Examination of the Doctrine of the Trinity: From Anselm to the Fourth Lateran Council (1215)

A. Early Scholastic Developments: From Anselm to Abelard

1. Roscellin and Anselm on the Trinity: the Synod of Soissons (1092). As far as the mind of the late eleventh century was concerned, there could have been no clearer example of the unbridled use of dialectic than the application of a nominalist or, at least, antirealist critique to the doctrine of the Trinity by Roscellin of Compiègne.[18] It is difficult to establish precisely what Roscellin taught, since all his works have been lost or destroyed except for a letter he sent to Abelard. The outlines of his thought have to be reconstructed from comments made in the writings of his

---

Mont.: Scholars Press, 1980); Wilhelmus Johannes Kuhler, Aart de Groot, and Derk Visser, *Het Socinianisme in Nederland* (Leeuwarden: De Tille, 1980); H. J. McLachlan, *Socinianism in Seventeenth-Century England*, (London: Oxford University Press, 1951); Paul Wrzecionko, *Reformation und Frühaufklarung in Polen: Studien über der Sozinianismus und seinen Einfluss auf der westeuropäischen Denken im 17. Jahrhundert* (Gottingen: Vandenhoeck & Ruprecht, 1977).

16. E.g., J. H. Adamson, "Milton's Arianism," in *Harvard Theological Review*, 53 (1960), pp. 269-276; Michael E. Bauman, *Milton's Arianism* (Regensburg: Universität Regensburg, 19); idem, "Milton, Subordination, and the Two-Stage Logos," in *Westminster Theological Journal*, 48 (1986), pp. 173-182; and idem, "Milton's Theological Vocabulary and the Nicene Anathemas," in *Milton Studies*, 21 (1985), pp. 71-92; W. B. Hunter, Jr. "Milton's Arianism Reconsidered," in *Harvard Theological Review*, 52 (1959), pp. 9-35; idem, "Some Problems in John Milton's Theological Vocabulary," in *Harvard Theological Review*, 57 (1964), pp. 353-365.

17. E. Dorothy Asch, "Samuel Clarke's *Scripture-Doctrine of the Trinity* and the Controversy it Aroused" (Ph.D. diss.: University of Edinburgh, 1951); Martin Greig, "The Reasonableness of Christianity? Gilbert Burnet and the trinitarian Controversy of the 1690s," in *Journal of Ecclesiastical History* 44 (1993), pp. 631-651; Thomas C. Pfizenmaier, *The trinitarian Theology of Dr. Samuel Clarke (1675-1729): Context, Sources, and Controversy* (Leiden: E. J. Brill, 1997).

18. On Roscellin, see François Picavet, *Roscelin, philosophie et théologien* (Paris: Alcan, 1911); Eike-Henner Kluge, "Roscellin and the Medieval Problem of Universals," in *Journal of the History of Philosophy*, 16 (1976), pp. 404-414; Jean Jolivet, "Trois variations médiévales sur l'universel et l'individu: Roscellin, Abélard, Gilbert de la Porrée," in *Revue de métaphysique et de morale*, 97 (1992), pp. 97-155; Constant J. Mews, "Nominalism and Theology before Abelard: New Light on Roscellin of Compiègne," in *Vivarium*, 30 (1992), pp. 4-33.

contemporaries, chiefly Anselm, Abelard and John of Salisbury. We can be fairly certain that Roscellin was a confirmed antirealist and that he denied the extra-mental existence of concepts of universals and as a result understood "substances" purely as individuals. This view led him to declare that every existent thing is a unique individual: so-called universals are "mere words." What cannot be ascertained is whether or not Roscellin denied that universals, as such, exist in the mind. Copleston suggests that Roscellin may have assumed, for example, that our idea of "a whole consisting of parts" is a subjective abstraction and that the objective reality is merely a series of discrete individual things — so that ideas of genus and species are also subjective judgments.[19]

The problem with Roscellin's philosophical position was not the position itself — nominalism in the later Middle Ages was perfectly orthodox, as was the conceptualism of Aquinas and Duns Scotus — the problem was, rather, the doctrinal application given by Roscellin to this philosophy. Since all things are individuals and the concepts which link individuals, concepts such as a whole composed of parts, a genus, or a species, the persons of the Trinity must be unique entities. Any words applied to the three — namely, each is a "person", all three are "God" — are merely terms. There is no independently subsistent idea of "person" somehow more real than the three individual persons which can identify them as substantially one. Calling all three "God" is no better solution than calling all three "person": we are left with three discrete individuals and might just as easily speak of three gods. On the one hand, Roscellin could criticize traditional trinitarian language on the ground that, if the three are one substance or thing (*una res*), then the Father and the Spirit will also be incarnate with the Son — or, in what appears to have been Roscellin's own solution to the problem, if they are indeed three persons, they must be three substances or things (*tres res*), existing separately, albeit in accord or united in power and will.[20]

If the unnamed opponent in Anselm's treatise on the incarnation is Roscellin, then Roscellin also argued (in favor of his tritheistic view) that those who claimed that God was "one thing" and that the trinity of persons did not divide the Godhead were unable to explain incarnation. If God is indeed one thing and indivisible, then the entire Godhead, Father, Son, and Spirit, would have to be incarnate. The doctrine of the incarnation demands that God be defined as three numerically discrete individuals.[21] The historical context in which Roscellin wrote is of some interest here — Roscellin was born around 1050 and died in 1120, making him a younger contemporary of Anselm (1033-1109). Both probably accepted the definition of "person" proposed by Boethius in the early sixth century: according to Boethius a person is "an individual

19. Frederick Copleston, A *History of Philosophy*, 9 vols. (Wesminster, Md.: Newman Press, 1946-1974; repr., Garden City: Image Books, 1985), II, p. 144.

20. Roscellin, as reported in Anselm, *On the Incarnation of the Word*, commonly called the *Liber de fide trinitatis et de incarnatione verbi*, ii- iii (PL, 158, col. 266); Michel, "Trinité. II. La théologie latine du VI au XX siècle," col. 1713. Note that Roscellin's result is virtually identical with some forms of modern "social trinitarianism": cf. Jürgen Moltmann, *The Trinity and the Kingdom*, trans. Margaret Kohl (New York: Harper & Row, 1981), pp. 148-150.

21. Cf. Anselm, *On the Incarnation of the Word*, ii-iii (pp. 13-17).

substance of a rational nature." The definition ultimately poses all manner of problems for the doctrines of Trinity and Christ when the concept of individual substance is taken to indicate a unique entity essentially distinct from other similar entities.

Sufficient to make our point here is that Roscellin, as an early nominalist,[22] pressed the Boethian definition in a way that Anselm, the philosophical realist, would not — while neither Roscellin nor Anselm argued the problematic character of the definition itself. The definition itself was first brought into question only after the deaths of Roscellin and Anselm — by Richard of St. Victor in his treatise on the Trinity, ca. 1150. The process of redefinition or clarification continues in the thought of Alexander of Hales, Bonaventure, Thomas Aquinas, and Duns Scotus. In addition, Roscellin — probably on the basis of definition ("person" is an individual substance of a rational nature) — appears to have inferred that a person, as such, could only have one nature. Since Christ obviously has two natures, there must be two persons. We note that traditionally the two-natures doctrine indicated two minds and two wills. Roscellin's nominalist logic dictated that he use the definition to indicate two persons in Christ. His views on the Trinity implied that three "persons" must have three substances, and he appears also to have denied the reality of relations as a way past the problem. The implication, if not the intention, was tritheism.[23]

To this Anselm responded in his *Letter on the Incarnation of the Word* (1092/94) — that "person" and "nature" do not always mean the same thing, even as a "nature" (human nature) is held in common by all human persons.[24] Human nature refers to the conjunction of the several properties and predicates that identify the nature, generally considered, as human — and this is prior to the more particular consideration of the single person as human, as participating in human nature. Moreover, says Anselm, if the individual person is identified as an individual by the conjunction in one thing of several properties, what is to prevent Christ from being identified as an individual, a person, in whom both divine and human properties conjoin? As for the Trinity, since universals or general concepts (*genera*) are real, there can be no objection to identifying the individual persons (*species*) or the Trinity as one God, "God" being the more general concept than "person."[25]

Anselm also insisted that the mystery of the Trinity was not utterly at odds with human reason: the term "nature" indicates what is absolute in God, "person" what

22. Acknowledging the cautions of William J. Courtenay, "Nominales and Nominalism in the Twelfth Century," in *Lectionum Varietates: Hommage à Paul Vignaux (1904-1987)*, ed. Jean Jolivet, et al. (Paris: J. Vrin, 1991), pp. 11-48, that this early "nominalism" did not embody a significant theory of universals and tended to contrast *res* with *voces* rather than *res* with *nomina*. Rather, however, than refer to Roscellin as a "vocalist," I retain the usual usage.

23. Thus, Kluge, "Roscellin and the Medieval Problem of Universals," p. 412; but cf. Picavet, *Roscellin, philosophie et théologien*, pp. 75-80, who affirms Roscelin's intention to submit to ecclesial orthodoxy.

24. On Anselm's theology in general see Jasper Hopkins, *A Companion to the Study of St. Anselm* (Minneapolis: University of Minnesota Press, 1972) — chapter 4 discusses the doctrine of the Trinity.

25. Anselm, *Letter on the Incarnation*, xi (pp. 28-30).

is relative — with the result that the unity of the Godhead belongs to the category of nature or substance, while the plurality of the persons is to be identified as a multiplicity of relations. In this formulation, Anselm points the way to the formulae of the Council of Florence.[26]

Anselm clearly argues in the treatise on incarnation that the notion of a "whole" composed of parts is a reality: a "whole" cannot simply be reduced to three discrete individuals.[27] He draws on the example of the Nile — the great river of Egypt. (The argument, incidentally, draws on the standard patristic metaphors, with one important modification.) We understand, by "Nile" not merely a river, but also the spring from which the river comes and the great lake into which the river flows. The river is not the spring, and neither river nor spring is the lake — but all three are "Nile." "This is the case," concludes Anselm, "in which 'three' is predicated of one complete whole and 'one complete whole' is predicated of three; and yet the three are not predicated of one anther."[28] If this set of relations can be comprehended in nature, it can be comprehended of the transcendent "simple nature" of God, which is beyond time, place, and composition. We do not have a response from Roscellin — but it is clear that we have a fundamental philosophical opposition: Anselm assumes the reality of the "whole" as much as the reality of the "part" and also assumes that the generic whole can subsist, extra-mentally, as one in and through its parts. This is essentially the realist position.

2. Anselm and the Greeks: the Council of Bari (1098). First, out of chronological order, the Council of Bari: in 1098, Anselm attended the Council of Bari and, in a discourse that he delivered before the council, took up a theme that would occupy the attention of many of the major theologians of the Middle Ages — the theme of the *filioque*, or procession of the Holy Spirit from the Son as well as from the Father. Anselm subsequently edited and expanded the discourse and, in 1102, published his treatise *On the Procession of the Holy Spirit*. His support of the *filioque* rested in large part on the Augustinian line of argument that identified the inward procession of persons in psychological terms as a relation of love and held the impossibility of conceiving a loving relation in the Godhead in which one person (namely, the Son) remains separate or inactive. As for the Greek claim that the concept of double procession resulted in the error of two ultimate principles in the Godhead, Anselm could respond that just as the creation of the world by all three persons does not result in a theory of three ultimate principles, so does the procession of the Spirit from the Father and the Son not result in a theory of two principles: for the three persons create as one God, and the Father and the Son are one God in the procession of the Spirit.[29]

3. Abelard and the "conceptualist" model of the Trinity: the Synods of Soissons (1121) and Sens (1141). The early to mid-twelfth century councils, Soissons, Sens,

---

26. Cf. Michel, "Trinité. II. La théologie latine du VI au XX siècle," cols. 1709-10.

27. Anselm, *Letter on the Incarnation*, xiii (p. 31).

28. Anselm, *Letter on the Incarnation*, xiii (pp. 32-33).

29. Anselm, *On the Procession of the Holy Spirit*, ix-x (pp. 113-117); idem, *Letter on the Incarnation*, xvi (pp. 35-36); cf. Michel, "Trinité. II. La théologie latine du VI au XX siècle," col. 1711.

and Rheims (discussed in the following section), reflected the philosophical issues faced by early scholastic trinitarian debate and responded to the conceptualistic approach of Abelard, and the problematic realism of Gilbert de la Porrée.[30] Uniting these conciliar decisions, at least negatively, is the difficulty experienced by the church of the twelfth century in assimilating the results of early scholastic philosophical concerns to trinitarian language. Inasmuch, moreover, as the three councils condemned the trinitarian results of early forms of each of the major medieval epistemological approaches, their decisions signaled the difficulty involved in setting the doctrine of the Trinity into any particular philosophical context.

The trinitarian thought of Peter Abelard was called into question by councils of the church at two points in his career — first at the Synod of Soissons (1121) and later at the Synod of Sens (1141). Our knowledge of the former council is so sketchy that it is impossible to identify the precise points of theology in question or even the book of Abelard that the Council required him to burn, although it appears to have been his *Tractatus de unitate et trinitate divina*,[31] in which Abelard had intended to defend the doctrine of the Trinity against the nominalist tritheism of his former teacher, Roscellin. The long-lived Roscellin returned the favor and, in defense of his own orthodoxy, accused Abelard of reducing the persons to names or aspects of the One God. The charge against Abelard at Soissons, therefore, appears to have been Sabellianism. The charge, moreover, may follow from one place in the work at which Abelard had claimed an analogy between the threeness of the divine persons and the multiplicity of attributes in the divine substance,[32] — it is also possible that he had given his contemporaries offense by his claims that the Trinity had been revealed by the philosophers to the ancient Greeks and by the prophets to the Jews, a point on which he was in fact criticized and which he ultimately retracted.[33] In any case, Abelard's book was condemned by the council and burned. Abelard himself was imprisoned briefly in the abbey of Saint Medard.[34]

At Sens, Abelard was condemned for a set of nineteen propositions elicited from his writings by Bernard of Clairvaux. Prior to the council, Abelard's works, primarily the *Theologia christiana*, had come to the attention of William of Saint Thierry, the friend and associate of Bernard. William appealed to Bernard to address the problems of heresy in Abelard's work, and Bernard expressed his difficulty with elements of

---

30. The trinitarian thought of Abelard and Gilbert as well as the conciliar decision of the era is discussed in Reginald Lane Poole, *Illustrations of the History of Medieval Thought and Learning*, 2nd ed. (London: S. P. C. K., 1920).

31. Peter Abelard, *Tractatus de unitate et trinitate divina*, ed. R. Stölzle (Freiburg, 1891) — the work was unknown until the publication of this manuscript: it can now be recognized as an early version of Abelard's *Theologia christiana*.

32. Abelard, *Tractatus de unitate et trinitate divina*, pp. 61-68.

33. J. Rivière, "Les 'capitula' d'Abélard condamnés au concile de Sens," in *Recherches de théologie ancienne et médiévale*, 5 (1933), pp. 5-8; Eligius M. Buytaert, "Abelard's trinitarian Doctrine," in *Peter Abelard*, ed. E. Buytaert (The Hague: Nijhoff, 1974), pp. 127-152; and Fortman, *Triune God*, pp. 177-181.

34. See the account in Poole, *Illustrations*, pp. 129-132.

Abelard's theology. Abelard, in return, initially promised to correct any errors of doctrine. He subsequently, however, appealed to the bishop of Sens and challenged Bernard to debate on the disputed issues. At Sens, instead of the debate he desired, he found himself condemned by a council. He appealed the council's decision to the pope, only to have the council's condemnation ratified. Abelard died shortly afterward in the spring of 1142.

The issues here too are murky: the nineteen condemned propositions are not precisely found in Abelard's writings, and, indeed, he later denied having held such concepts. The propositions as condemned at Sens contain such curious notions as the claim that "the Father is full of power, the Son [has] some power, the Holy Spirit no power," the denial that the Holy Spirit is of the same substance as the Father, the identification of the Spirit as the soul of the world," and the restriction of omnipotence to the Father alone.[35] Still, it is certain that Abelard did propose similar teachings or at least views that could be treated in an un-nuanced manner and result in something like the teachings condemned by the council. His *Theologia christiana* did identify God the Father as power, the Son as the divine wisdom, and the Spirit as divine "benignity" — and it did go on to indicate that the Son's wisdom was "a certain power" and the Spirit's benignity was neither power nor wisdom. Abelard had also attempted to distinguish generation from procession and had concluded that the Son was "from the substance" of the Father in a "proper" sense (because generated) and the Spirit was not properly "from the substance" of the Father, as proceeded. In the balance, there was certainly no intentional heresy on Abelard's part — his intention was surely to develop the doctrine of the Trinity and to make it intelligible, as was his attempt to distinguish generation and procession, Son and Spirit, a distinction that would be made with relative success by the scholastic teachers of the thirteenth century.

4. Gilbert de la Porrée and the Synod of Rheims (1148). The Synod of Rheims resulted in a series of four propositions that dealt with the unity of divine substance and the threeness, or triplicity, of persons in response to a debate over Boethius' *De Trinitate*, at least as interpreted by Gilbert de la Porrée.[36] The importance of the result stands rather apart from the question of Gilbert's actual guilt or innocence of the charge of "tritheism." Gilbert, the bishop of Poitiers and perhaps the most eminent pupil of Bernard of Chartres, was one of the eminent thinkers of his age. At issue in the controversy was his attempt to refine and explain trinitarian language of Boethius in his *Commentaria in Librum de trinitate*.[37] Gilbert there distinguished, at least logically

---

35. Denzinger-Schönmetzer, §721-739.

36. See the longer discussion of the debate leading to the council in *PRRD*, III, 1.2 (A.1).

37. Gilbertus Porretanus, *Commentaria in Librum de trinitate*, in *PL* 64, cols. 1255-1412; note also the modern edition in *The Commentaries on Boethius by Gilbert of Poitiers*, ed. Nikolaus M. Häring (Toronto: Pontifical Institute of Medieval Studies, 1966). On Gilbert's theology, see Lauge Olaf Nielsen, *Theology and Philosophy in the Twelfth Century: A Study of Gilbert Porreta's Thinking and the Theological Expositions of the Doctrine of the Incarnation during the Period 1130-1180* (Leiden: Brill, 1982); Michael E. Williams, *The Teaching of Gilbert Porreta on the Trinity as Found in His Commentaries on Boethius* (Rome: Gregorian University, 1951); Auguste Berthaud, *Gilbert de la*

and verbally, between God (*Deus*) and divinity (*divinitas*), as well as between person and substance and between the properties or attributes of God, on the one hand, and the simple divine substance or essence, on the other. His intention was to argue the correctness of the orthodox language of Trinity against the three fundamental errors of Arianism, Sabellianism, and tritheism: the Arian mistake was to claim that substantial or essential identity removed all possibility of distinction; the Sabellian error similarly assumed that identity or singularity of substance removed distinction of persons — the former accordingly denied substantial identity in order to distinguish the three, while the latter denied genuine personal distinction in order to confess the one. Tritheists, beginning with the distinction of the persons, assumed different substances. In brief, all of the major trinitarian heresies involved difficulties with the terms "substance" and "person," specifically, a failure to distinguish them properly.

There appear to have been two aspects to Gilbert's teaching on God-language that, at least in the minds of his contemporaries, did not fully cohere. On one hand, Gilbert affirmed the essential divine simplicity and argued that, given the absolute, transcendent unity of God beyond all human comprehension, nothing can be predicated of God as such: the human mind cannot penetrate to the ultimate being of God. On the other hand, Gilbert not only allowed discussion of the divine *substantia*, but claimed that heresies had resulted by not making a proper distinction between the way in which *substantia* was being considered, namely, a distinction between *subsistens* and *subsistentia* understood as a distinction between the object or individual (*id quod est*) and the manner of subsisting by which the object is what it is (*id quo est*).[38] The Arians had rightly held to the doctrine of one God but had concluded that, since the Father is God, the Spirit and the Son could not be — but the orthodox fathers recognized the truth that although the divinity, that by which God is what God is (*id quo est*), is only one, the subsistent individuals who share in the divinity are three. Thus, one can say that the Father is God, with "God" in the predicate, and still rightly identify Son and Spirit as God — whereas one ought not to say that God is the Father, with God as the subject, thereby restrictively identifying "God" as the one individual. According to Gilbert, there were three individuals identified as God in the sense of *id quod est*, but one numerical divine essence considered in the sense of *id quo est*.[39] Gilbert also

---

Porrée, évêque de Poitiers, et sa philosophie, 1070-1154 (Poitiers, 1892; Frankfurt: Minerva Verlag, 1985); also, A. Hayen, "Le Concile de Reims et l'erreur théologique de Gilbert de la Porreé," in *Archives d'histoire doctrinale et littéraire de moyen-âge*, 10 (1935/36), pp. 29-102; Nikolaus M. Häring, "The Case of Gilbert de la Porreé," in *Medieval Studies* 13 (1951), pp. 1-40; idem, "A Commentary on the Pseudo-Athanasian Creed by Gilbert of Poitiers," in *Medieval Studies*, 27 (1965), pp. 23-53; idem, "Notes on the Council and Consistory of Rheims (1148)," in *Medieval Studies*, 28 (1966), pp. 39-59; and Marvin L. Colker, "The Trial of Gilbert of Poitiers, 1148: A Previously Unknown Record," in *Medieval Studies*, 27 (1965), pp. 152-183; and Lambertus Marie De Rijk, "Semantics and Metaphysics in Gilbert of Poitiers: A Chapter of Twelfth Century Platonism," 2 parts, in *Vivarium*, 26 (1988), pp. 73-112, and *Vivarium*, 27 (1989), pp. 11-35.

38. De Rijk, "Semantics and Metaphysics in Gilbert of Poitiers," pp. 75-80.

39. Cf. Nielsen, *Theology and Philosophy in the Twelfth Century*, pp. 143-146, with Williams, *Teaching of Gilbert Porreta*, pp. 59, 63-64.

held that the distinctions among the persons were relational, not substantial, a point quite standard in the tradition of trinitarian orthodoxy, but which, given the character of his other arguments, became a problem in his exposition of the doctrine: his strict sense of divine simplicity coupled with his insistence on the ultimate unknowability of the divine being led him to identify the relational distinction of the persons as "extrinsic" rather than as essential: finite subsistences are essentially or substantially distinct, rendering them different things, whereas the divine subsistences are relationally distinct, extrinsic to their essential identity, given the oneness or singularity of the Godhead.[40]

For his pains, Gilbert was accused of being a tritheist and, alternatively, for positing a divine quaternity. In 1147, a council met at Paris to decide the question. After debating without result, the council adjourned to Rheims in the following year. The nub of the problem, certainly, was his assumption of the unknowability and simplicity of the divine essence coupled with the language of extrinsic relations. On one side, his adversaries believed that he had so separated the ultimate essence or *subsistentia* of the Godhead, the *id quo est*, from the persons that he had posited a quaternity, three persons and, behind them, an ultimate essence; on the other side, if the ultimacy of the essence behind the persons were denied, then it might reduce to a mere generic sense of essence, leaving three gods in the sense of *id quod est*. The Synod of Rheims probably failed to convict Gilbert of heresy — Bernard of Clairvaux and his associate Geoffrey of Auxerre remained convinced of Gilbert's heterodoxy, while John of Salisbury appears to have believed the matter one of misinterpretation of terms on the part of Gilbert's adversaries and a certain opaqueness on the part of Gilbert.

At Rheims, Geoffrey of Auxerre penned a set of articles for use in identifying the heresies of Gilbert. They were used at the council, although not in a binding fashion, and in the aftermath of the debate and the failure to reach a condemnatory verdict, Bernard of Clairvaux offered four heads of doctrine as a positive dogmatic result. They survive in his *Libellus contra capitulum Gilberti*. Their value, certainly, is that they reflect the stable orthodoxy of the day against presumptions of tritheism or divine quaternity:

> I. We believe and confess that there is in God a simple divine nature, and that in no Catholic sense can it be denied that God is divinity and divinity is God. Moreover, if it is said that God is wise by wisdom, great by magnitude, eternal by eternity, one by oneness, God by divinity, and other such things, we believe that He is wise only by that wisdom which is God himself; that he is great only by that magnitude which is God himself; that he is eternal only by that eternity which is God himself; that he is one only by that onenesss which is God himself; that he is God only by that divinity which he is himself; that is, that he is of himself wise, great, eternal, one God.
>
> II. When we speak of the three persons, Father, Son, and Spirit, we confess the same to be one God and one divine substance; and conversely, when we speak of one God or of one divine substance, we confess the same one God and one divine substance to be three persons.

---

40. See Gilbert, *De trinitate*, I.5, 43; Williams, *Teaching of Gilbert Porreta*, pp. 68-70.

III. We believe that God alone, Father, Son, and Holy Spirit, is eternal, and that there are no other things that are from eternity, whether they are called relations or properties, individualities, or unities present with God, that are not God.

IV. We believe that the selfsame divinity, whether it is called the divine substance or [divine] nature, is incarnate, but in the Son.[41]

B. Speculative Development and Conciliar Conclusions, ca. 1150 to 1215

1. The trinitarianism of Richard of St. Victor: Augustinianism, mysticism, and the difficulty of defining "person." Throughout his writings, Richard of St. Victor (d. 1173) emphasized the use of reason in the search for truth. This generalization applies equally to the mystical writings, where the hope is not to transcend reason but that reason, through meditation, should arrive at a purer contemplation of divine truth: "Contemplation," argues Richard, "is the mind's free and clear vision, with admiration, of the wonders of wisdom."[42] Thus, Richard's mysticism never steps outside of the bounds of the Augustinian or Anselmic model of faith in search of understanding — *credo ut intelligam*. The highest step of the mystic, like the work of dogmatic speculation, belongs to the intellect. This means, in turn, that rational argumentation, even rational demonstration, and mysticism are not necessarily opposed to each other.

Richard's great work, *De Trinitate* (ca. 1150), manifests this balance: had its author not inclined toward the contemplative vision of God, the work could not possibly have been written — its central theme, God as love, is profoundly allied to the mysticism of Bernard — yet the assumption of the treatise is that intellect can conceive of the intra-trinitarian logic.[43] Richard indicates that, since God is necessarily three in persons and one in substance, there must be a necessary reason for this fact: there is a necessary reason for everything that exists by necessity. He admits that God is ultimately beyond our comprehension, but this transcendence does not prevent all rational approach to God. It is clear that God is the necessary Being and that this necessity entails the fact that God is necessarily who and what he is — which is to say triune. Richard's study of the Trinity will attempt to show the logic of triunity.[44]

Richard begins by offering, if not a fully logical demonstration of the necessity of the Trinity, then an argument that the One God, if he is indeed the God of love, will be threefold in his nature.[45] This argument rests on a distinction between essence and person: *essence* refers specifically to *what* a thing is — in the world, it relates things to other things of the same type — but *person* refers to *who*, to the individuality, the particular qualities of a thing. The two together, essence and person, constitute the *subsistence* of the thing. In the Godhead, there is one essence, but there are three

---

41. In Bernard, *Libellus contra capitulum Gilberti*, in PL, 185, col. 609; also cited in Schwane, *Histoire des Dogmes*, IV, p. 193.

42. Richard of St. Victor, *De gratia* I.v, in PL, 196, col. 67.

43. Cf. Richard of St. Victor, *De trinitate*, I.v.

44. Cf. Copleston, *History*, II, p. 179.

45. Schwane, *Histoire des dogmes*, IV, pp. 254-255.

distinct modes of existing, defined by particular qualities or properties, namely, their relational distinctions, specifically, distinctions of origin.

This sense of the meaning of person led Richard to reject the usual definition of person, as given in the sixth century by Boethius: "person is an individual substance of a rational nature" (*persona est individua substantia rationalis naturae*) — since it could be applied either to the divine essence or to the persons, if the term *substantia* were not qualified as *subsistentia, modus existendi,* or some other equivalent of *hypostasis.*[46] Richard proposed two alternative definitions: first, of "person" in general: "A person is something that exists through itself alone, singularly, according to a rational mode of existence" (*Persona est existens per se solum juxta singularem quemdam rationalis existentiae modum*); and second, of "person" as one of the divine persons: "A divine person is an incommunicable existence of a divine nature" (*Persona divina est divinae naturae incommunicabilis existentia*).[47]

One of the more interesting elements in Richard's argumentation is his exclusion, based on the relation of the divine persons, of the possibility of a divine quaternity. There is, he argues, a perfection of order and harmony obtaining between the Father, who gives without receiving, the Son, who receives and who also gives, and the Spirit, who only receives (without giving). In this schema, the only possibility remaining is a person who neither gives not receives — but such a person is solitary, not a part of the common life of the three, so that a quaternity is excluded. What is more, only the source of the other divine relations can exist without receiving, so that another being who neither receives nor gives is also utterly excluded on ontological grounds. On the principle of love the same logic obtains — for one is either gracious, as giver, or grateful, as receiver. The Father, who gives without receiving, is the fulness of gracious love; the Son, who gives and receives, is the fulness of gracious love and grateful love in one; and the Spirit, who only receives, is the fulness of grateful love. In the one God, then, there is a fulness and a balance, a harmony of sovereign love — and by extension that which is neither gracious nor grateful has no place in God.

If, on the one hand, Richard added no new dogmatic features to the doctrine of the Trinity, he did succeed in drawing out implications of the trinitarian faith toward a clearer understanding and a more precise conceptualization of the meaning of triunity. He succeeded in developing the doctrine speculatively within the bounds of orthodoxy — and, we note, it was surely not his intention to change doctrine or faith but to understand it. His procedure and his results, therefore, manifest the Augustinian and

---

46. This usage reflects the patristic problem of distinguishing *ousia* from *hypostasis*, both of which had been rendered in Latin as *substantia* and which, after the attempt at differentiation of the terms undertaken by the Cappadocians, were only gradually differentiated in Latin into *substantia* and *subsistentia*. Much of the difficulty with the Boethian definition arises when its use of *substantia* is understood as rendering *ousia* rather than *hypostasis* — whereas Boethius used *essentia* as equivalent to *ousia* and specifically understood *substantia* as rendering *hypostasis*: see Fortman, *Triune God*, p. 163.

47. Richard of St. Victor, *De trinitate*, IV.xi, xxii; cf. Fortman, *Triune God*, pp. 191-192; Schwane, *Histoire des Dogmes*, IV, p. 256.

Anselmic pattern. On the other hand, Richard was more keenly aware than his contemporaries of the problem of the language of essence and person. His argumentation pointed theologians toward more precise and, indeed, more useful definition.

2. The heresies of Joachim and the Fourth Lateran Council. Another option in trinitarian theology was propounded by the mystic chiliast, Joachim of Flora (d. 1202). Joachim had maintained that the emphasis on oneness of essence and "the discrimination of divine substance from the persons"[48] — which was the main point made by Richard of St. Victor in his analysis of the language of Trinity — led to Sabellianism or even to Arianism. Joachim appears to have proposed a divine triad of persons who together constitute one God, denying the identity of the persons as Lombard had defined it, "one supreme reality (res),"[49] and instead insisting on a generic unity. Joachim, accordingly, used as analogies the oneness of a "herd" or of a "populace," allowing oneness of essence or substance only in the sense of a secondary substance of genus.[50]

The full content of Joachim's trinitarian thought is notoriously difficult to recover. The condemnation of Joachim indicates that his heterodox views were contained in "a small book or tractate ... against master Peter Lombard concerning the unity or essence of the Trinity (de unitate seu essentia Trinitatis)" — but the book itself has not survived. To complicate matters further, other surviving works of Joachim appear to offer fairly orthodox statements of the doctrine of the Trinity. Modern scholarship has, accordingly, asserted his orthodoxy[51] and reaffirmed his heresy,[52] although all agree that Joachim opposed Lombard's teaching on the ground that it introduced a quaternity. Scholars are also divided on the background of Joachim's objections, with several arguing that he drew on Greek or Byzantine trinitarianism.[53] Leaving aside the modern debate, it remains the case that Joachim's counter to Lombard embodied a view that, as far as the theologians of the early thirteenth century were concerned, was unmistakably tritheistic, inasmuch as it removed all hint of quaternity by defining the unity of divine essence generically rather than numerically.

The Fourth Lateran Council (1215), known also for establishing transubstantiation as dogma, propounded the trinitarian norm for the medieval church in two fundamental definitions. The first of these is found in the creedal affirmation of the council, intended

---

48. Seeberg, History, II, p. 108.

49. Cf. the discussion in Ebeling, "Hermeneutical Locus of the Doctrine of God," pp. 73-83.

50. Denzinger-Schönmetzer, §803; translated in The Christian Faith in the Doctrinal Documents of the Catholic Church, ed. J. Neuner and J. Dupuis, 2nd ed. (Dublin: Mercier Press, 1976), §317.

51. Thus, Delno C. West and Sandra Zindars-Swartz, Joachim of Fiore: A Study in Spiritual Perception and History (Bloomington: Indiana University Press, 1983), pp. 53-56.

52. Morton W. Bloomfield, "Joachim of Flora: A Critical Survey of His Canon, Teachings, Sources, Biography, and Influence," in Traditio, 13 (1957), pp. 249-311; also see his "Recent Scholarship on Joachim of Fiore and His Influence," in Prophecy and Millennarianism (Essex: Longman, 1980), pp. 23-52.

53. Cf. Paul Fournier, Études sur Joachim de Flore et ses doctrines (Paris: Picard & Fils, 1909), pp. 14-16; cf. Seeberg, History, II, p. 108; Bloomfield, "Joachim of Flora," pp. 284-285, disagrees.

primarily as a full statement of the faith against the heresies of the Albigenses and the Cathars. Here the council presents an affirmation of the one God against the dualistic heresies, carefully relating the language of three persons to the identification of God as one simple essence and also defining the work of the Godhead *ad extra* as one work, at the same time clearly distinguishing God from the creation, both spiritual and material. The formula also includes the doctrine of double procession but, sensitive to the Greek critique of the *filioque*, adds by way of clarification that the three divine persons "are ... the one principle of the universe, the creator of all things, visible and invisible." Echoing the Athanasian Creed, the council also declares that the three persons "are consubstantial and fully equal, equally almighty and equally eternal."[54]

Against the tritheism of Joachim of Flora, the council declared the unique reality of the divine essence, undivided in three persons:

> We ... believe and confess with Peter Lombard, that there is a certain single Being (*una quaedam res*), something incomprehensible and ineffable, which truly is the Father, the Son, and the Holy Spirit, three persons at once, and individually each of them. And thus in God there is a only Trinity and not a quaternity; because any one of the three persons is that Being (*res*), namely, substance, essence or divine nature, which alone is the ground (*principium*) of things, outside of which nothing can be found; and that Being (*res*) is not begetting, nor begotten, nor proceeding; but it is the Father who begets, the Son who is begotten, and the Spirit who proceeds, that there may be distinctions in persons and unity in nature.[55]

It is important to underscore this definition, inasmuch as it represents the fundamental distinction between the divine essence as such, belonging in common to all three persons, and the divine persons themselves, understood as relations within the essence: the divine essence that is the Son is not begotten, rather the Son, considered as Son and person, is begotten. Thus, the Son, as God, possesses such attributes as *aseity*, being underived or "from himself." The point is fundamental, given that a notion of an ultimate essence as the *principium* of the Godhead and of the persons as generated or emanated essences, as opposed to the doctrine of the Father as *principium*, yields, not Trinity, but quaternity.[56] This line of argument will pass directly into the Reformed tradition.

The council clarified the point by citing Gregory of Nazianzen to the effect that "the Father is one (*alius*), the Son another (*alius*), and the Holy Spirit another (*alius*), yet there is not another thing (*aliud*)" given that the Father, the Son, and the Spirit are the same *res*, namely, the same reality or "thing."[57] It is, thus, not the divine essence that generates divine essence, but the Father that generates the Son:

---

54. Denzinger-Schönmetzer, §800; Neuner and Dupuis, §19.

55. Denzinger-Schönmetzer, §804; Neuner and Dupuis, §318.

56. Cf. Alfonso Maieru, "À propos de la doctrine de la supposition en théologie trinitaire au XIVe siècle," in *Medieval Semantics and Metaphysics*, ed. E. Bos (Nijmegen: Ingenium, 1985), pp. 221-222.

57. Denzinger-Schönmetzer, §805; Neuner and Dupuis, §319, citing Gregory of Nazianzen, *Epistle to Cledonius*.

One cannot say that [the Father] gave [the son] a part of his substance and retained a part for Himself, since the substance of the Father is indivisible, being entirely simple. Nor can one say that in generating the Father transferred His substance to the Son, as though he gave it to the Son in such a way as not to retain it for Himself.... It is therefore clear that the Son, being begotten, received the substance of the Father without any diminution, and thus the Father and the Son have the same substance. Thus, the Father and the Son, and the Holy Spirit who proceeds from both, are the same *res*.[58]

1.3 The High and Late Scholastic Development of Trinitarian Doctrine

A. The Scholastic Doctors of the Thirteenth Century

1. Foundational formulations: William of Auvergne, Alexander of Hales, and Albert the Great. Although these contributions of Anselm and Richard of St. Victor to the development of the Western doctrine of the Trinity were considerable, it was left to various teachers of the thirteenth century, William of Auvergne,[59] Alexander of Hales, Bonaventure, Albert the Great, Thomas Aquinas, and Duns Scotus, to give the doctrine its definitive scholastic form.[60] These thinkers again took up the problem of "person" language, giving clearer expression to the issues raised by Richard of St. Victor and arriving at a far more viable solution than he.[61] They also addressed two other major problems of trinitarian thinking: the problem of the identity or meaning of the intra-trinitarian emanations, specifically in relation to the debate over the "*filioque*," and the problem of the reflex or passive relations of the Son and the Spirit. In the former discussion, the medieval doctors affirmed the distinct subsistence of Son and Spirit by distinguishing between the begottenness of the Son and the procession of the Spirit in terms of the nature, intellect, and will of the Godhead. In the latter, they carefully refined the language of circumincession by noting how the two emanations were not merely active but also passive relations — thereby describing the roles of Son and Spirit in the inner trinitarian life and avoiding the impression given particularly in Greek patristic theology of an emanation out of the Father toward externals. What is more, beginning with William of Auvergne's *De trinitate* (ca. 1223) these theologians of the thirteenth century evidence the impact of Aristotelian thought

---

58. Denzinger-Schönmetzer, §805; Neuner and Dupuis, §319; also see the text and translation in Norman P. Tanner, *Decrees of the Ecumenical Councils*, 2 vols. (Washington, D.C.: Georgetown University Press, 1990), I, p. 231.

59. William of Auvergne, *De trinitate, seu de primo principio*, ed. with an intro. by Bruno Switalski (Toronto: Pontifical Institute of Medieval Studies, 1976); also *The Trinity, or the First Principle*, trans. Roland J. Teske and Francis C. Wade (Milwaukee: Marquette University Press, 1989).

60. A. Krempel, A. *La doctrine de la Trinité chez Saint Thomas: Exposé historique et systematique* (Paris: J. Vrin, 1952); Joseph Butterworth, "The Doctrine of the Trinity in St. Thomas Aquinas and St. Bonaventure" (Ph.D. diss.: Fordham University, 1985).

61. Cf. M. Bergerson, *La Structure du concept latin de personne*, in *Études d'histoire littéraire et doctrinale du XIIIe siécle*, first series, vol. II (Paris and Ottawa: Pontifical Institute of Medieval Studies, 1932).

— which had not, of course, touched the earlier Western discussion of the doctrine of the unity and trinity of God.

As Teske indicates, William of Auvergne's *De trinitate* "is not all of one piece," at least by later systematic standards for defining the limits of the dogmatic treatise on the Trinity.[62] William's work begins with a discussion of primary and secondary being and of possibility, offers a proof of the doctrine of the Trinity, presents a massive discussion of the doctrine in critical dialogue with the Aristotelian metaphysics of Avicenna, and concludes with three chapters on the problems of God-language. When, however, William's *De trinitate* is set against the background of earlier medieval discussion, including Anselm's *Monologion* and *Proslogion* and Richard of St. Victor's *De trinitate*, this concatenation of topics evidences a certain degree of continuity with earlier medieval tradition. Anselm's two treatises, after all, move from proofs to the being of God, meditate on the relationship between the necessary being of God and the contingent being of the world order, and conclude with presentations of the doctrine of the Trinity — and Richard had offered a proof of the doctrine of the Trinity, indicating the necessity of three persons and the impossibility of four (or more!) on the basis of the logic of the *filioque*. In addition, both Anselm and Richard understood their treatises, at least in part, as essays in the logic of God-language.

Alexander of Hales, a somewhat neglected figure in modern studies of medieval theology and philosophy, was one of the truly formative thinkers of his age and, undeniably the source of many of the distinctive features of later Franciscan theology. One of the characteristics of his thought, as distinct from the line of Dominican theology established by his contemporary Albert the Great, was his reluctance to move away from a more Augustinian line of philosophy toward rapprochement with the new Aristotelianism.[63] From one perspective, the whole of Alexander's theology flows out of the assumption that the good is self-diffusive, *bonum est diffusivum sui*.[64] This principle applies, of course, most fully to the absolute Good, which is God — and it can be understood either essentially or personally: the former is the "communication of divine goodness to creatures," the latter the act by which "one person diffuses himself in the procession of another."[65] Still, however important the principle is to understanding Alexander's thought in general or his trinitarianism in particular, it remains the case that Alexander also insisted that the doctrine of the Trinity, unlike the truth of the existence of God, was a mystery inaccessible to human reason.[66]

Alexander also provided a set of definitions which provide the primary reference of the Franciscan school on the doctrine of the Trinity. His definitions of the persons draws on the traditionally accepted language of Boethius, but modifies it in view of the work of redefinition and refinement found in Richard of St. Victor and Peter

---

62. Roland J. Teske, Introduction, in William of Auvergne, *The Trinity*, p. 53.
63. Cf. the discussion in Copleston, *History of Philosophy*, II, pp. 232-239.
64. Thus, Fortman, *Triune God*, p. 211.
65. Alexander of Hales, *Summa theol.*, pars I, [n. 330, ad. 4]
66. Alexander of Hales, *Summa theol.*, pars I, [n. 10]

Lombard.[67] Like Richard, Alexander defined the divine "person" as a particular mode of existence within the divine essence, a mode perfect and incommunicable, which constituted each person as complete and distinct. Also like Richard, he saw the need to go beyond Boethius to establish essence as the general category, person as the particular and therefore within the essence. Thus, the "distinction" of the persons in the one divine essence is the "difference of relation or of mode of existing" that arises "by reason of origin."[68] Alexander also saw the danger of separating essence and person so far that essence could become a fourth thing, a Godhead prior to the persons. "Mode of existing," argued Alexander, differentiates the persons from one another, but not from the divine essence. Thus, according to Alexander, distinction in God between essence and person is not a real distinction (*secundum rem*), but only a distinction of the rational intellect (*secundum intelligentiam rationis*); nonetheless, the distinction between persons is real even in God.[69]

Alexander objects to the claim that the distinction between persons and essence or between relations and the divine substance must either be according to substance or such as subsists between a thing and another thing (*secundum rem*) or merely according to our intellect (*secundum intellectum solum*). The first distinction would rule out divine simplicity, the latter would render the Trinity a doctrine fashioned in the human mind. Alexander responds that, in its inward economy, the one and same divine essence, is disposed as Father, who is neither generated nor proceeded from another; as Son, who is generated from another; and as Spirit, who proceeds from both — and that this manner or mode of being is "not merely according to the acceptation of out understanding, but in fact according to the thing itself." Thus the Godhead must be considered both in terms of "the identity of substance" and in terms of "a disposition according to the consideration of origin or first principle" — in the first instance, there is the essential identify of the divine persons, in the second, there is the disposition or plurality of the Godhead according to "the predicament of relation."[70]

Alexander can argue from this basis that the relations of generation and procession do not apply directly to the essence: that is, there is no generation or procession of the essence. In order to explain these relations, Alexander recalls in part the logic of Richard of St. Victor but adds a modification typical of the Augustinian-Franciscan theology: the goodness of God is communicable in two ways, by the generation of a person and by the working of divine love — either by nature or by will. The Son is begotten of the Father as an act of love; the Spirit proceeds from the will of the Father and the Son. Like Lombard and in opposition to the recently condemned heresies of Joachim, Alexander declares that the divine essence is common to the persons, is entire in each, and is not divided in the begetting or proceeding.

---

67. Schwane, *Historie des Dogmes*, IV, p. 260.

68. Alexander of Hales, *Summa theol.*, pars I, [n. 312, ad. 1]

69. Schwane, *Historie des Dogmes*, IV, p. 261, summarizing Alexander of Hales, *Summa theol.*, pars I, inq. II, tract. 2, q. 1, memb. 1, cap. 7, art. 3.

70. Alexander of Hales, *Summa theol.*, pars I, inq. I, tract. 2., q. 2, ad 3.

Albert the Great, in contrast to Alexander of Hales, saw the need to introduce Aristotelian philosophy more fully into a dialogue with Christian theology — not, however, to the loss of the Augustinian tradition and its transmission of a more Platonic philosophical model. So, too, did Albert draw heavily not only on Augustine but also on the neoplatonic approach of Pseudo-Dionysius.[71] Albert's doctrine of the Trinity, like that of his predecessors and contemporaries, assumes that the doctrine is inaccessible to reason — to the point that he even notes the patristic claim that Plato learned of the Mosaic revelation in order to explain the vestigial trinitarianism of Platonic thought.[72]

Albert is also one of the major medieval theologians who expressed dissatisfaction with the Boethian definition of person, in fact, noting four possible definitions — namely, one from Boethius, two from Richard of St. Victor, and one from Abelard — and arguing that all needed modification and qualification. He did, insist, moreover, on the basic Anselmic point that a divine person was to be distinguished by a relation of opposition, specifically a "relation of origin." His understanding of the personal relations of generation and procession adumbrated Aquinas inasmuch as Albert argued an intellective procession of the Son as Word and a volitional procession of the Spirit as love, although more than Aquinas, Albert understood the generative procession of the intellect as a natural mode of emanation.[73]

2. Bonaventure. Bonaventure's distinctive contribution to trinitarian theology occurs in his *Breviloquium*, in his commentary on the *Sentences* of Lombard, and in the well-known spiritual treatise, the *Itinerarium mentis ad Deum*.[74] Particularly in the *Breviloquium*, Bonaventure's description of the Triune God as "first principle" becomes central to the explanation of all divine life and activity, particularly the multiform revelation of God as three in the light of essential oneness. There can, of course, be no purely rational discussion of the Trinity:

> The trinity of persons in the unity of essence cannot be naturally known through creatures, for this is proper to the divine nature alone, and its like neither is nor can be found in creatures, nor can it be rationally excogitated ... So the philosophers never knew it.[75]

Faith alone knows this truth, but reason can confirm and explicate it from the doctrines of divine simplicity, primacy, perfection and blessedness. Nonetheless, just as there

---

71. See Copleston, *History of Philosophy*, II, pp. 293-299.

72. Albert the Great, *In Sent.*, I, d. 3, a. 18.

73. Fortman, *Triune God*, pp. 203-204.

74. See Fortman, *Triune God*, pp. 203-204; Konrad Fischer, *De Deo Trino et Uno: das Verhältnis von productio und reductio in seiner Bedeutung für der Gotteslehre Bonaventuras* (Göttingen: Vanderhoeck & Ruprecht, 1978); John P. Dourley, "The Relationship between Knowledge of God and Knowledge of the Trinity in Bonaventure's *De mysterio trinitatis*," in *San Bonaventura Maestro*, ed. A. Pompei (Rome: Pontifica Facolta Teologica San Bonaventura, 1976), vol. II, pp. 41-48.

75. Bonaventure, *In Sent.*, I, d. iii, a. 1, q. 4; cited in Fortman, *Triune God*, pp. 212-213.

is a certain triformity belonging to natural conceptions of the divine,[76] there is also a certain logic to the doctrine of the Trinity and that, specifically, given that there are only "two noble modes of producing," there must be three persons, and there can be only three persons.[77]

In the *Breviloquium*, Bonaventure divides his treatise on the Trinity into three major topics: the basic topic of the unity of substance and plurality of persons; the problem of the "plurality of apparitions" or manifestations of God in the temporal world; and last, the problem of the "multiplicity of appropriations" or attributes which seem to be predicated more "appropriately" to one divine person than to the others. Bonaventure emphasizes throughout the unity of God as first principle of all things and therefore the unity of all divine manifestations.[78] Trinity or triunity, rightly understood, allows the affirmation of the attributes of oneness (unity, simplicity, immensity, eternity, immutability, necessity, and primacy), but also of such attributes as "perfect fecundity," love, liberality, equality, interrelationship, likeness, and inseparability, which do not follow logically from perfect unity and which would not at all be characteristic of the primary One of a monistic philosophy.[79] Bonaventure does not propose to prove his doctrine rationally, but rather to develop its implications in the context of faith, following out the Augustinian and Victorine teaching "that God communicates Himself in the best manner by eternally having a loved one and another beloved of these two, and hence God is one and triune."[80]

> For an understanding of this belief, sacred doctrine teaches that in the divine persons there are two emanations, three hypostases, four relations, and five notions, but there are only three personal properties.[81]

The logic of this teaching comports with the assumption that God is the first and highest being. From the fact that God is first it follows that God is perfect and noncomposite or simple — since there is something prior to every imperfect or composite being.[82] On the one hand, we know that the self-communication of the Godhead, in the generation of the Son and the procession of the Spirit, accounts for a certain threeness in the one God, while, on the other hand, we know that God is the first and highest and therefore the most simple and most perfect being. The self-communication and threeness of the first and highest being will accord with its

---

76. Cf. Dourley, "The Relationship between Knowledge of God and Knowledge of the Trinity in Bonaventure's *De mysterio trinitatis*," pp. 43-44.

77. Bonaventure, *In Sent.*, I, d. ii, a. 1, q. 4, citing Aristotle, *Physics*, ii.6, on the modes of production.

78. J. Guy Bougerol, *Introduction to the Works of Bonaventure*, trans. José de Vinck (Paterson: St. Anthony Guild, 1964), pp. 110, 112; Zachary Hayes, *The Hidden Center: Spirituality and Speculative Christology in St. Bonaventure* (New York: Paulist Press, 1981), pp. 56-57.

79. Cf. Bonaventure, *Breviloquium*, I.ii.2.

80. Bonaventure, *Breviloquium*, I.ii.3.

81. Bonaventure, *Breviloquium*, I.iii.1.

82. Bonaventure, *Breviloquium*, I.iii.2.

simplicity and perfection: the self-communication will therefore be perfect and will not violate the divine simplicity by producing three separate things or substances. In addition, given that the Father is considered ingenerate or innascible, the Son generated, and the Spirit proceeded, the divine self-communication involves only two activities or emanations, one terminating on the Son and the other terminating on the Spirit.

Further, these emanations are in two modes, the mode of nature and the mode of will.[83] Granting that "generation" means specifically the production or begetting of something of the same *genus* or nature, the correlation of generation with an emanation according to the mode of nature has a certain logic to it. Similarly the term "procession," indicating movement or progress, correlates with the faculty of will, just as the root verb of *processio, cedere,* "to give," relates to volition or will. The inclusiveness of the concept of an emanation of nature has also the effect of ratifying the procession of the Spirit from the Son as well as from the Father, since the common nature of the generated Son with the ungenerated Father would indicate a common willing and a common emanation according to the mode of will.[84] Two hypostases emanate, Bonaventure notes, and one does not: the one is the necessary source of the others by means of a "substance-producing emanation" in order that there not be an infinite series (as in Neoplatonism), but three hypostases only, as required in Christian thought, with no source external to the three. The divine self-communication by way of emanation indicates, therefore, three hypostases, or *supposita,* in the Godhead, a *suppositum* being, simply, an independent subsistence. Because, moreover, the terms of the emanation (generation and procession) indicate only the relation of the Father to the Son, the Father to the Spirit, and the Son to the Spirit, but not the relation of the Son to the Father, the Spirit to the Father, and the Spirit to the Son, there are more relations than there are emanations. Relations, unlike emanations, imply reciprocity — and, therefore, imply a number exactly double that of the emanations — but since Bonaventure accepts "double procession" the relations between Son and Spirit are identical to those between Father and Spirit, yielding four and not six relations. These relations are exhaustively descriptive of the Son and Spirit as emanations, but not of the Father, who is not emanated — so that the total description demands a fifth notion or concept, the "innascibility" or ingenerate nature of the Father.

From this logical paradigm Bonaventure returns to the doctrinal side of the question, showing how his language of emanation, hypostases, relations, and notions conjoins with the scriptural language of Father, Son, and Spirit.[85] Father, Son, and Spirit indicate the personal properties of the three hypostases, three only corresponding to the pattern

---

83. Bonaventure, *Breviloquium,* I.iii.2; cf. Bonaventure, *In Sent.,* I, d. 2, a.1, q.2. Thomas Aquinas will agree that there are only two possible modes of emanation but will refer them to intellect and will rather than nature and will, because intellect and will are mutually exclusive and nonconvertible functions: see Aquinas, *Summa theol.,* I, q. 27, art. 2, 3.

84. Fortman, *Triune God,* p. 214.

85. Bonaventure, *Breviloquium,* I.iii.6.

of emanation which results in the three persons. The personal property of the Father, which distinguishes him from Son and Spirit, is innascibility, or ingenerability: the Father is the "beginning without a beginning." This is a negative property which indicates the Father's position in the Trinity — "Father," however, implies not only the negative of innascibility but also the relation of the Father, as person, to Son and Spirit.[86]

The second hypostasis has several doctrinal titles — primarily Image, Word, and Son. These terms indicate three ways of understanding the personal property of the second hypostasis or person. "Image" expresses the similitude or likeness of the Son to the Father, as in Hebrews 1:3; "Word" the intellective or expressive character of the similitude, the Son as revealer; and "Son" the natural similitude of the Son to the Father. Since the similitude of nature most fully refers to the subsistence of the Son as God, Bonaventure calls it the "hypostatic" similitude.[87] The Spirit or third hypostasis is both the nexus or bond of love between the Father and the Son and the one sent by, the gift of, both Father and Son. The sending or gift of the Spirit corresponds with the voluntary mode of the Spirit's emanation — the "love" manifest in the Spirit renders the voluntary gift "especial" and the name Holy Spirit, as indicating a substantial emanation or individual subsistence, indicates also the hypostatic character of the Spirit — thus the Spirit is a "voluntary, especial, and hypostatic gift."[88] This language assumes distinctions in the Godhead, such that do not disturb its simplicity — in fact, three modes of differentiation corresponding with the basic differentiation of the persons from the essence as "modes of existence or emanation" (i.e., the "plurality of persons"); the differentiation of the persons from one another but as having the same essence (i.e., the "plurality of the substantial and relative predications"); and finally, the differentiation of substantial properties or "essential properties and notions" which, as the attributes of the essence as such, belong to all the persons.[89]

In all of these modes of differentiation there are only two categories of predication or two "predicaments" (praedicamenta), substance and relation. In order to establish this point,[90] Bonaventure lists the ten categories of predication as set forth by Aristotle: substance, quantity, relation, quality, activity, passivity, place, time, position, and habit. The last five belong to the corporeal world and are only figuratively applied to God. The former five can be predicated of God, but, clearly, in the case of God all but "relation" merge with the category of substance and are defined by it — leaving only two categories, substance and relation, which correspond to the divine essence and the divine persons: that is, there is one divine substance or essence and there are a series of relations which refer to the persons without dividing the essence.

---

86. Bonaventure, Breviloquium, I.iii.6.

87. Bonaventure, Breviloquium, I.iii.6; cf. Bonaventure, I Sent, dist. 31.2, art. 1, and Hayes, Hidden Center, p. 58.

88. Bonaventure, Breviloquium, I.iii.6.

89. Bonaventure, Breviloquium, I.iv.6.

90. Bonaventure, Breviloquium, I.iv.2.

Bonaventure's discussion of the "apparitions" and "appropriations" addresses crucial issues concerning the manifestation and attributes of the persons *ad extra*:

> although God is infinite, invisible, unchangeable, nevertheless He dwells particularly in holy men, He appears to patriarchs and prophets, He descended from heaven, He even sent the Son and the Holy Ghost for the salvation of the human race. Although in God there are the individual nature, virtue and operation of the Trinity, yet the sending or apparition of one person is not the sending or apparition of the other. Although there is in the Trinity the greatest equality, nevertheless it is the function of the Father alone to send and not to be sent.[91]

The "sending" of divine persons is rooted in the intra-trinitarian relations of generation and procession: the Son and the Spirit are sent whereas the unregenerate or innascible Father only sends but never is sent — and the Son, who is generated but who is also a source of the procession of the Spirit, not only is sent but also sends. The Spirit, who is not a source of another person within the Trinity, is sent but does not send. When this model is applied to *ad extra* acts of the Godhead, such as the incarnation of the Son and the gift of the Spirit, it overcomes the possible implication of mutability: the "descent from heaven" cannot be physical descent from one place to another — after all, God is not physical and does not occupy space — rather it indicates God's gracious acts toward sinners. When God manifests himself in grace and knowledge, he is said to descend, even though "He is not changed in Himself."[92] Even in incarnation, the issue is not that the Son becomes present where he was not present before, but that he becomes "present to us through knowledge or grace," as sent by the Father, from whom he is generated.

3. Thomas Aquinas. In the *Summa theologiae* Aquinas makes the comment, "Jerome says that heresy comes from undue prolixity; therefore we should address ourselves to discuss the Trinity with care and modesty."[93] Or, as he declared in the commentary on the *Sentences*,

> Our profession is uncomplicated, that in God exists a plurality of persons in unity of nature; we are convinced on account of the witness of faith, not for the reasons given above.[94]

---

91. Bonaventure, *Breviloquium*, I.v.1.

92. Bonaventure, *Breviloquium*, I.v.4.

93. Aquinas, *Summa theol.*, 1a, q. 31, art. 2. On Aquinas' doctrine of the Trinity, see Fortman, *Triune God*, pp. 204-210; Robert L. Richard, *The Problem of an Apologetical Perspective in the trinitarian Theology of St. Thomas Aquinas* (Rome: Gregorian University, 1963); Horst Seidl, "The Concept of Person in St. Thomas Aquinas," in *The Thomist*, 51 (1987), pp. 435-460; Brian Davies, *The Thought of Thomas Aquinas* (Oxford: Clarendon Press, 1992), pp. 185-206.

94. Aquinas, *I Sent.*, dist. 2, art. 1, 4, in *St. Thomas Aquinas, Theological Texts*, selected and trans., with notes by Thomas Gilby (Durham, N.C.: Labyrinth Press, 1982), § 380 (hereinafter cited as Gilby).

Aquinas' clearly chooses not to follow the more speculative path of Richard of St. Victor and Bonaventure, although he expresses a deep appreciation of the logic of triunity once confessed:

> A thing may be reasonably proved either by going to the root of the matter and producing a cogent demonstration ... or by accepting it and then showing how the consequences fit the evidence. ... The second must be adopted when we would show forth the truth of the Blessed Trinity. We start with acceptance, and then afterwards may give recommending reasons, not that they sufficiently demonstrate the mystery.[95]

Or, as he indicated in his commentary on Boethius' *De trinitate*, this doctrine is "uniquely an object of belief" that cannot be proven by demonstrations: all arguments or reason fall short of yielding necessary conclusions; indeed, the arguments only create probability, and that only for a believer.[96] Whereas, therefore, the philosophers knew something about the oneness of God and the divine attributes, including some of the attributes, like power, wisdom, and goodness, that belong peculiarly to the persons of the Trinity, they could know nothing concerning the personal relations in the Godhead.[97]

In his own exposition of the Trinity, Aquinas was as concerned as Bonaventure to outline the terms of the doctrine as one essence, two processions, and therefore only three persons, four real relations, and five notions or concepts.[98] In contrast to Bonaventure's understanding of processions of nature and will, Aquinas interpreted the two processions (i.e., the generation of the Son and the procession of the Spirit) as acts of understanding and will or processions of the Word and of Love, respectively. Given, moreover, that God is a being of an "intellectual nature," there can be only two basic acts — one of intellect or understanding, the other of will — and there cannot be any further multiplication of acts, given that "the procession which is accomplished within the agent in an intellectual nature terminates in the procession of the will."[99] These two processions also fall within the explanatory model of Augustine's metaphor of the lover and the beloved — given that the intelligible or intellective procession of the Word is the procession of the only beloved Son, the object of the Father's love, that this procession is not an act directed *ad extra*, but one that terminates *ad intra*, and given that in an "intellectual nature" such acts involve both intellect and will. "The operation of the will within ourselves involves also another procession, that of love, whereby the object loved is in the lover."[100] Like Bonaventure, Aquinas resonates with the Augustinian and Victorine language concerning the logic of the Trinity as an expression of divine love:

---

95. Aquinas, *Summa theol.*, 1a, q. 32, art. 1, ad 2 (cited from Gilby, §79); cf. the comments of Davies, *Thought of Thomas Aquinas*, pp. 188-191.

96. Aquinas, *In Boetius De trinitate*, I.4

97. Aquinas, *Summa theol.*, 1a, q. 32, art. 1, ad 1.

98. Aquinas, *Summa theol.*, 1a, qq. 27, 28, 29, 30, 32.

99. Aquinas, *Summa theol.*, 1a, q. 27, a. 3, ad 1.

100. Aquinas, *Summa theol.*, 1a, q. 27, a. 3.

Goodness is generous. God is supremely good. Therefore supremely generous. But he cannot supremely give himself to creatures, for they cannot receive his entire goodness. The perfect gift of himself is not to another diverse by nature. Therefore within him there is distinctness without division. ... Sheer joy is his, and this demands companionship. ... Perfect love must be matched. Charity is unselfish love. But creatures cannot be loved above all; they are not attractive enough. Therefore in the divine begetting is there perfect lover and perfect beloved, distinct, but of one nature.[101]

Neither Aquinas nor Bonaventure elaborates the point — they assume that Augustine's and Richard's *De Trinitate* are known to their audience. In accord with the earlier usage, Aquinas declares that this is a complete and perfect "fecundity": there can be no further processions, given that the two kinds of procession, intellect and will, are completely fulfilled in the *ad intra* procession of "one perfect Word, and one perfect Love."[102]

Thomas was also profoundly concerned to argue the primacy of the Father as the *principium* of the Son and the Spirit, but at the same time to highlight the dangers inherent in identifying the Father as the "cause" of the other two persons. On this point he noted an important difference between the Greek and the Latin fathers on the issue of intra-trinitarian relationships: Athanasius, Basil, and Theodoret spoke of the Father as the "cause" of the other persons; the Latin fathers preferred forms like "principle" or "author," an issue that would be raised in the later medieval councils. In Aquinas' view, the Latin usage is preferable inasmuch as the Father is neither final, material, nor formal cause of Son or Spirit — what remains is the notion of "efficient cause" as the sole applicable concept. But an efficient cause is conceived as a different substance than its effects: God is substantially different from the world of which he is the efficient cause! Clearly, however, the Son is one with the Father in substance:

to avoid reckoning the Son as of different substantial nature from the Father, we prefer to use, instead of *cause*, such terms as *fount*, *head*, and so forth, which signify both origin and identical substance.[103]

In addition, speaking of the Father as "cause" implies that the Son is "effect" and belongs to the created order: the terminology is unacceptable.

On the other hand, the Latin fathers' language is not only more adequate, it is scriptural. Here Aquinas posits a rule for theology that takes our minds back to the Nicene debate and the early patristic warnings against excessive speculation:

we should not be freer than Holy Scripture in attributing terms to God. There the Father is called the principle or beginning: "in the beginning was the Word."[104]

---

101. Aquinas, *Summa theol.*, 1a, q. 32, art. 1, ad 2

102. Aquinas, *Summa theol.*, 1a, q. 27, a. 5, ad 3; cf. Aquinas, *Compendium*, I.56.

103. Aquinas, *Contra errores graecorum*, I, as cited in Gilby, § 98; cf. *Summa theologiae*, Ia, q. 33, a. 1.

104. Aquinas, *Contra errores graecorum*, I, as cited in Gilby, § 98.

Scripture never speaks of the Father as cause of the Son or of the Son as caused —
principle, *principium*, is the better term as more scriptural and also as more general
in scope than cause: "since divine truths are incomprehensible and beyond definition,
it is more appropriate to keep to broad terms . . . when speaking about God."[105]

Note that Aquinas here not only retains but utilizes substantively the reading of
John 1:1 that we noted early on in patristic theology as crucial to the philosophical
appropriation of Christianity in the ancient world but as lost to the modern reader,
whose vision has been overly influenced by the traditional English versions. Aquinas,
of course, receives his insight from the Latin of Jerome: "*In principio erat verbum*," which
renders the Greek *arche* more accurately than the English, "In the beginning...." The
text can mean "In the divine first principle, that is, the Father, was the Word" — a
reading in perfect conformity with v. 18 of the prologue, where the Son is said to be
in the bosom of the Father, and 17:21, where Jesus says he is in the Father and the
Father in him.

In treating of the divine persons, unlike his teacher Albert, who saw the value in
several of the available definitions of person, Aquinas, both in his commentary on
the *Sentences*, where Lombard provided him with the definition, and in the *Summa
theologiae*, where, presumably, he could have exercised more freedom in argument,
advocated the definition of Boethius, "an individual substance of a rational nature."
Still, as Fortman comments, after Aquinas has explained the definition and added
his own qualifications on all the terms, "it can seem that he has corrected rather than
approved it," a conclusion justified by the alternative definitions provided elsewhere
by Aquinas — "a relationally distinct subsistent in the divine essence" and "a distinct
subsistent in the divine nature."[106] Aquinas also anticipates the problem faced by the
Reformers — namely, that the term "person" is not found in either the Old or the
New Testament and ought therefore not be applied to God. Aquinas answers that
"although the word *person* is not found applied to God in Scripture ... nevertheless
what the word signifies is found to be affirmed of God in many places of Scripture;
as that he is the supreme self-subsisting being, and the most perfectly intelligent
being."[107]

An important element of Aquinas' doctrine of the Trinity is his fairly traditional
identification of the personal relations of paternity, filiation, and procession as
constitutive of real distinctions in the Godhead while at the same time insisting on
the simplicity of God. This pairing of the two arguments is sometimes missed or
misinterpreted in discussions of Aquinas' doctrine: it has been claimed, for example,
that "classic Latin statements of Trinity doctrines are complicated (some would say
muddled) at crucial places by simplicity theory, i.e., by the notion that in God there
are really no distinctions at all — not even between the divine relations and the divine

---

105. Aquinas, *Contra errores graecorum*, I, as cited in Gilby, § 98.

106. Fortman, *Triune God*, p. 208, citing Aquinas *De potentia.*, ix.4; cf. Horst Seidl, "The Concept
of Person in St. Thomas Aquinas," in *The Thomist*, 51 (1987), pp. 435-460.

107. Aquinas, *Summa theologiae*, Ia, q. 29, a. 3, ad 1.

essence."[108] The muddle, however, is not on the part of Aquinas. Arguably, it arises out of a loss of clear understanding of the traditional notion of simplicity compounded by a confusion over the meaning of "real distinction." Aquinas' denial of a "real distinction" between essence and persons is hardly a denial of all distinctions in the Godhead, but only and quite specifically a denial of any substantial distinction between essence and person, in other words, the denial of any distinction that would render the essence one "thing" and the divine persons other "things": affirmation of a real distinction between essence and persons would be the affirmation of a divine quaternity.[109]

Aquinas, thus, does deny that there is a real distinction between the divine relations and the divine essence, but only because, with the entire orthodox tradition, he assumes that the essence is not divided by the persons or personal relations in the Godhead and that the essence belongs entirely to each of the persons. In the very same article, Aquinas quite clearly indicates that although a relation (i.e., a relation such as unbegottenness, begetting, or proceeding) does not differ from the essence as a thing from another thing — there can be no distinction of person or relation from the divine substance according to substance (secundum rem) — relation and essence do differ conceptually, "according to the consideration of the understanding" (secundum intelligentiae rationem). As in the discussion of the distinction of attributes where he rules out real distinctions between essence and attributes or between the attributes themselves,[110] he here denies a real distinction between essence and person, thereby ruling out composition, but (as in the discussion of the attributes) he does not rule out a conceptual or rational distinction between essence and person. The language here echoes that of Alexander of Hales in his argument for the identity of substance and distinction of relations in the Godhead. Furthermore, Aquinas continues, in the very next article, to argue that there not only must be distinctions in God, but that the distinctions between the persons are "real distinctions."[111]

To this argument, it might be objected that the distinction between persons is no different from the distinction between attributes — both are distinctions made "according to consideration of names" or "term" (secundum nominis rationem) — with the result that the persons cannot be really distinct. Aquinas responds by clarifying the difference between a distinction between attributes and a distinction between relations: attributes, such as power and goodness, do not result in any conceptual opposition and, therefore, cannot be distinct secundum rem — but relational distinctions, namely, ingenerate and generate, do stand in conceptual opposition and are therefore to be understood as distinct: since the relations are in God realiter and are in relative (but not essential or substantial) opposition to one another, there is

---

108. Cornelius Plantinga, Jr., "Gregory of Nyssa and the Social Analogy of the Trinity," in The Thomist, 50/3 (July 1986), pp. 342-343.

109. See the discussion of medieval doctrine of simplicity in PRRD, III, 1.2 (A.3, B.4).

110. See Aquinas, Summa theol., I, q. 3, a. 7; cf. PRRD, III, 1.2 (B.4), and cf. ibid., 4.3, B-D.

111. Aquinas, Summa theol., I, q. 28, a. 3: Plantinga, "Gregory of Nyssa and the Social Analogy," cites only article 2.

a real distinction in God, albeit one that is not according to the thing or substance absolutely considered (*secundum rem absolutam*) but according to the thing or substance relatively considered (*secundum rem relativam*).[112] It is, thus, fundamentally incorrect to claim that for Aquinas "there are really no distinctions at all" in God: what is ruled out are real distinctions that are absolute or substantial, such as subsist between things and other things.

4. The Council of Lyons (1274). The Council of Lyons was the first major attempt of the Latin and Greek churches to mend the breach occasioned by the *filioque* controversy of the tenth and eleventh centuries. Its formulae stand on the intellectual ground gained both in earlier Western councils like Soissons, Sens, Rheims, and Fourth Lateran and in the development of the broader outlines of the Western doctrine of the Trinity at the hands of the scholastic teachers of the thirteenth century.[113] The relevant documents of the council are the formal letter containing the Profession of Faith of Michael Paleologus and the council's own Constitution of the Holy Trinity and the Catholic Faith. The former document, presented to the council by the representatives of the eastern emperor and the Greek church as an official letter of the Greek church, was understood by Pope Clement IV as a basis for discussion at the council and it was written with the specific intention of representing a favorable Greek view of the Latin church's theology — in fact, it appears to have been little more than a transcription of Clement IV's own proposals, the trinitarian portion of which reproduced the formulae of Leo IX on the eve of the schism, sent to the emperor for his approval. The Profession of Faith, thus, does not indicate any genuine acknowledgment of the validity of the *filioque* on the part of the eastern emperor. Nor does the Profession of Faith belong to the actual decisions of the council. Still, the Profession of Faith was read at the council, and it contains a notable expression of the Western trinitarian perspective, identifying Father, Son, and Spirit as "one omnipotent God ... coessential, consubstantial, co-eternal and co-omnipotent" and arguing that "each individual person in the Trinity is the one true God, complete and perfect." The Holy Spirit, moreover, is "complete, perfect, and true God, proceeding from the Father and from the Son, co-equal, consubstantial, co-omnipotent, and co-eternal with the Father and the Son in all things." The Trinity, therefore, "is not three gods but one God."[114]

---

112. Aquinas, *Summa theol.*, I, q. 28, a. 3, corpus & ad 2; Note that the point again closely parallels Alexander of Hales, *Summa theol.*, pars I, inq. I, tract. 1, q. 3, cap. 2. What is at stake here is the levels of distinction that can be predicated of the Godhead: there can be no real or substantial distinction between the essence and the persons, given that this would make the persons substantially different from the divine substance. There can be a real but relational, not substantial, distinction between the persons, given that although the persons are substantially identical, there is a genuine opposition of relationality. This represents a higher level of distinction between persons than between attributes, given that the attributes are properties of the essence that belong equally to each of the persons and that the attributes do not stand in relational opposition to one another, as would be the case if God were both powerful and not powerful, good and not good.

113. See F. Vernet, "Lyon, Concile de," in *Dictionnaire de théologie catholique*, IX, cols. 1379ff.

114. The Profession of Faith of Michael Paleologus, in Denzinger-Schönmetzer, §851-853.

The second major document, the Constitution of the Holy Trinity and the Catholic Faith, is the decision of the council. It too offers a definition of the relationship of the Holy Spirit to the Father and the Son — and it reiterates the *filioque*, but with the very precise modifier that "the Holy Spirit proceeds eternally from the Father and Son, not as from two principles but from one, not by two spirations but by one only."[115] This, the *Constitution* continues, is the faith of the whole church, of all the "fathers and doctors, both Latin and Greek." And then, to make the definition utterly clear, the *Constitution* concludes in the negative:

> Therefore, in order to forestall such errors, with the approval of the holy Council, we condemn and disapprove those who presume to deny that the Holy Spirit proceeds eternally from the Father and the Son, or who rashly dare to assert that the Holy Spirit proceeds from the Father and the Son as from two principles, not from one.[116]

This final condemnation, with its specific denial that the double procession can be taken to mean two first principles, or *principia*, in the Godhead is as close as Lyons comes to a concession to the Greek church's long-standing critique of the *filioque*. The doctrinal explanation is, however, a considerable development over the formula of the Fourth Lateran Council, given the clear statement that there is a single divine *principium* and only one "spiration" and that, given this understanding, the *filioque* must be understood as the doctrine of all the Fathers, whether Western or Eastern. The formulae produced at Lyons did serve to consolidate the Western understanding of trinitarian orthodoxy but, despite the representation of the Eastern church and the apparent acceptance of the conciliar result by the Greeks, including the emperor, Michael Paleologus, the ecumenical effect of the council was limited: the Greek orthodox ultimately denied the validity of both formulae.

B. Late Medieval Developments

1. Peter Auriole and Durandus of Sancto Porciano. The rise of a more critical approach to metaphysics and epistemology, associated with what has (rightly or wrongly) been classified as "nominalism," led to further debate over the doctrine of the Trinity in the early fourteenth century.[117] Peter Auriole (d. 1322) is often counted among the predecessors of Ockham, or at least of those developments of the fourteenth and fifteenth centuries that restricted the impact of philosophical speculation on formulations of revealed doctrine such as the Trinity. Still, he did develop a perspective on trinitarian statement that drew on his predecessors' meditations on the nature of the procession of persons. In agreement with the decisions of the preceding centuries, he insisted that the divine essence is itself ingenerate and that the begetting of the

---

115. Constitution on the Holy Trinity and the Catholic Faith, in Denzinger-Schönmetzer, §850; Neuner and Dupuis, §321.

116. Constitution on the Holy Trinity and the Catholic Faith, in Denzinger-Schönmetzer, §850; Neuner and Dupuis, §321.

117. See: Hester Goodenough Gelber, "Logic and the Trinity: A Clash of Values in Scholastic Thought, 1300-1335" (Ph.D. Dissertation, University of Wisconsin, 1974).

Son and the spiration of the Spirit are not essential but personal generations or emanations. Perhaps reflecting on the divergence of the Latin and Greek fathers on the matter of procession, Auriole grounded the distinction of persons not in their relations but in their persons: specifically, he argued that generation and procession differ not as actions but in their object or result. He also insisted that the personal relations are distinct not essentially or *realiter* but only rationally, a point of difference with the greater part of the tradition and a step toward the dilemma of Ockham's definition.[118]

Durandus of Sancto Porciano (d. 1334) is remembered as a philosophical and theological renegade among the Dominicans who frequently set aside the arguments of Albert and Aquinas. In the case of the doctrine of the Trinity, he argued, in opposition to the teachings of his order, that it was possible to offer a rational demonstration concerning the procession of the divine persons. He began on the assumption, contra Thomas Aquinas, but held by some Dominicans (notably, Robert Fishacre, Ulrich of Strasbourg, and James of Metz) as well as by Alexander of Hales and Bonaventure, that the procession of the Word was a procession of "nature" — indeed, he argued that this was not a "generation" but an "emanation" of a superabundant nature. Given the same explanation for the procession of the Spirit, Durandus may have obscured the difference between filiation and spiration that so occupied the thirteenth century. More significant for later developments — including those in Reformed orthodoxy — Durandus departed from Aquinas in his language of the distinction of persons, in fact, pressing further away from the "real distinction" proposed by Alexander: the distinction between essence and relation, he indicated, was not merely a rational distinction, but a distinction approaching the real distinction, not between things but between modes or ways of possessing a particular reality. Thus a person is constituted as a distinct individual in a way different from the constitution of an essence as individual.[119] Durandus argued a variety of modal distinction between the divine persons — and he concluded that the foundation of the subsistence of each person was, therefore, the divine essence itself and not the personal relation.[120] Arguably, this view is a precise extension of the decision of the Fourth Lateran Council and a more adequate rendering of both the Cappadocian *tropos hyparxeos* and its Augustinian equivalent, *modus subsistendi*, as it is also a view that will carry forward into the sixteenth and seventeenth centuries whether in Calvin's views on divine *aseitas* or in van Mastricht's approach to the distinction of persons.

2. Duns Scotus and William of Ockham. Duns Scotus intended to carry forward the basic Franciscan model of the doctrine of the Trinity — certainly in accord with the conciliar formulae of Fourth Lateran and Lyons, but in terms of the specifically Halesian and Bonaventuran understanding of the intra-trinitarian emanations or

---

118. Michel, "Trinité," cols. 1750-1751.

119. Durandus, *In Sent.*, I, d. 33, q. 1, n. 33; cf. Michel, "Relations divines," in *DTC*, XII, col. 2146.

120. Durandus, *In Sent.*, III, d. 1, q. 2, n. 7; cf. Michel, "Relations divines," in *DTC*, XII, cols. 2153-2154.

processions. Specifically, he argued that the processions are two, of nature (the begetting of the Son) and of will (the procession of the Spirit). In accord with the fundamental assumption that the inward distinction of the persons rests on relations of opposition, Scotus indicated that these processions of nature and will are opposites inasmuch as the former is "determined toward its object," given its grounding in nature, the latter free, given its grounding in will.[121] Still, in Scotus' view, both processions are necessary, given that they belong to primary actuality of the divine faculties, intellect and will. Scotus can identify the Son's procession as natural and intellective, given his definition of *natura*, drawing on both of the traditional senses of the term: *natura* can simply indicate "the divine essence itself, in which the three persons consist," or it can indicate a generative power belonging to an individual in its primary actuality. The latter sense of *natura* corresponds to the productive capacity of the divine intellect, understood as memory — as distinct from its operative function of knowing objects, common to all three persons of the Godhead. The divine memory, as a function of the Father, is productive *ad intra* naturally, specifically, having a perfect, natural inclination to produce its object or determination toward its object, namely, the Son. Given, moreover, this natural determination of the divine intellect, it does not belong to the power or will of the Father either to produce or not produce the Son. The generation of the Son is "involuntary."[122]

Scotus describes the procession of the Spirit in a similar manner, but in relation to the divine will. Like intellect, will can be understood as both productive and operative, both in primary and in secondary actuality. In its secondary or operative actuality, the divine will is common to all three persons of the Godhead. In its primary or productive actuality, however, it arises out of the divine essence considered as loving power and as a lovable object — the Father and the Son, in the traditional Augustinian language of the lover and the beloved — and is therefore the principle productive of the Holy Spirit. Given that this is a volitional act of the Godhead, it is a free act, neither natural, nor necessary, nor contingent — but since it is the divine will in *actu primo*, it is the will itself producing, not the result of an act of willing (which would be the will *in actu secundo*). Scotus differs categorically with Aquinas, moreover, in the understanding of this volitional act: according to Aquinas it is a natural act that proceeds "by mode of the will."[123] Scotus views this formulation as not doing justice to the freedom of the divine will and insists that it cannot be called a natural procession — the persons of the Father and the Son must be entirely free in the determination of the production of the Spirit and in no way determined, not even in the sense that the Father is determined to produce the Son.[124]

In Scotus' version of the *filioque*, the Father and the Son together are the one *principium* and the one spirative power that is productive of the Spirit, but the Father

121. Minges, *Scoti doctrina philosophica et theologica*, II, pp. 203, 209.
122. Minges, *Scoti doctrina philosophica et theologica*, II, pp. 201-203.
123. Aquinas, *Summa theologiae*, Ia, q. 41, a. 3, ad 3.
124. Minges, *Scoti doctrina philosophica et theologica*, II, pp. 207-208, 211.

spirates of himself (*ex se*), while the Son spirates from the Father from whom he has the power of spiration. Put in another way, the Father retains a radical primacy inasmuch as he has or is, in a prior sense, both the intellective and the volitional fecundity of the Godhead in their primary actuality — by the former he generates the Son and communicates to the Son the latter. It is by this generation that the Father communicates to the Son all that the Son has, according to which the Son is of one will with the Father and therefore with the Father spirates the Holy Spirit. The Spirit thus proceeds from both Father and Son but the *principium* of the Spirit remains unitary inasmuch as it is one fecundity of will that the Father has and has communicated to the Son.[125]

As to the definition of person, Scotus places himself clearly in the line of Richard of St. Victor's definition, "an incommunicable existence of an intellectual nature," and rejects the Boethian definition, "individual substance of a rational nature."[126] Scotus' intention is to focus on the identification of personal properties as incommunicable in the divine essence over against the essential properties which are communicated from the Father to the Son and from the Father and the Son to the Spirit. This basic definition yields Scotus' sense that the distinctions among the divine persons are not "real" but "formal distinctions." The personal properties do not agree in a formal sense with the essence as such, given that the essence itself "is one thing" that neither generates nor is generated — "a thing that generates," Scotus argues, "generates an other thing that is really distinct, for no thing generates itself."[127] Were the persons really distinct from the divine essence, it would be one thing and they three others, which is patently false. The persons ought therefore to be understood as "formally distinct" from the divine essence, inasmuch as according to its own "formal concept," each person is not identical with the divine essence considered as a unity: the divine essence is absolute, the persons relative; the divine essence is unconstituted, the persons constituted; the essence is communicable and is communicated from the Father to the other persons, the persons or personal properties are not communicable. Nonetheless, there are real distinctions among the persons: "that which produces is necessarily distinguished *realiter* from what is produced by it."[128] Scotus' trinitarian formulations not only justify his title, *Doctor subtilis*, they also stand on a sure trajectory toward the conciliar formulae of Florence and the final shape of medieval trinitarian orthodoxy. The point will be most clearly illustrated in the Scotist explanation of the primacy of the Father, the single *principium* of the spiration of the Spirit, and the *filioque*.

---

125. Minges, *Scoti doctrina philosophica et theologica*, II, pp. 210-211.

126. Scotus, *Opus Oxoniense*, I, d. 23, n. 4; cf. Minges, *Scoti doctrina philosophica et theologica*, II, pp. 222-223.

127. Scotus, *Opus Oxoniense*, I, d.5, q.1, n.4; as cited in Minges, *Scoti doctrina philosophica et theologica*, II, p. 223. On the various kinds of distinction and their significance, see the discussions in *PRRD*, III, 4.3 (C-D.1); and below, 3.2 (B).

128. Scotus, *Opus Oxoniense*, I, d.26, n.8; as cited in Minges, *Scoti doctrina philosophica et theologica*, II, p. 225; cf. Petrus Chrysologus Botte, "Ioannis duns Scoti doctrina de constitutivo formali personae Patris," in *De Doctrina Ioannis Duns Scoti*, edited by C. Balic, III, pp. 85-104.

In the theology of Ockham, a nominalistic denial of formal or real relational distinctions led to a profound difficulty in defining the doctrine of the Trinity. Thus, at the same time that he recognized the need of trinitarian language to speak of real relations or formal distinctions in the divine essence, Ockham indicated that it was rationally or philosophically impossible to conceive of a plurality of relations or formalities when an identity of essence was also assumed.[129] Although Ockham was clear in his affirmation of the doctrine and its mystery, he was unable to present a clear philosophical basis for its vocabulary, leading to the censure of his teaching at the papal court in Avignon in 1326. Specifically, Ockham was criticized for holding that everything conceptually true concerning the divine essence was also conceptually true concerning the divine persons and for holding that there was no difference between the correspondence of the essence with the divine attributes and the correspondence of the essence with the personal relations in the Godhead.[130] In Ockham's defense, one must note a consistency in his thought on the question of the rationality of the faith: he also assumed that the divine existence and unity were indemonstrable, even as he held firmly to belief in the one God. With specific reference to the doctrine of the Trinity, moreover, Ockham endeavored to work within the bounds of the Fourth Lateran Council, so that his discussion of the question, "*Utrum ... Deus generat Deum?*" distinguished between an essential and a personal usage of "Deus": in the essential sense, the persons are to be considered one *realiter* and God, as essence, cannot be said to be generated; in the personal sense, where "Deus" indicates a person or *suppositum*, then God can be said to generate God, inasmuch as God the Father generates God the Son.[131]

Ockham did uphold the normative doctrine, albeit without much development of the more speculative language. Against Scotus, Ockham had generally denied the formal distinction — but he admitted it in one place only, namely, among the persons of the Trinity, and only in a limited sense. He allowed no broad sense of formal characteristics or properties that might be identified *ad intra*, but rather in the sense that the divine "essence is three persons and a person is not three persons."[132] Ockham was drawn to this conclusion because he viewed the traditional language of a real distinction between persons as untenable, indeed, self-contradictory, inasmuch as the standard syllogistic argument based on the real distinction was inapplicable to God. Thus: "all 'a' is 'b'; 'c' is not 'b'; therefore 'c' is not 'a'" — but "the divine essence is the Son; the Father is not the Son; nonetheless, the Father is the divine essence." The Father is, thus, identical *realiter* with the divine essence but distinguished *formaliter* within it by "paternity" — the Son and the Spirit, identical with the essence *realiter* but distinguished formally by filiation and spiration. There is a unity or simplicity of

129. Vignaux, "Nominalisme," in *DTC*, XI, col. 777.
130. Cf. Amann, "Occam, Guillaume de; V. L'Église et la Doctrine d'Occam," in *DTC*, XI, col. 892.
131. Maieru, "À propos de la doctrine de la supposition en théologie trinitaire au XIVᵉ siècle," pp. 227-228.
132. Fortman, *Triune God*, pp. 223-224, citing Ockham, *Summa logicae*.

divine essence but a multiplicity of relations. Ockham concurred with Scotus that the divine will is the principle according to which the Spirit is emanated.[133] Later medieval theologians were pressed by such argumentation to affirm that the orthodox dogma of the Trinity did not contain contradictory propositions, either in a purely verbal or in a fully logical sense.[134] Nor ought it to be concluded from the technical nature of the late medieval discussions and debates that the doctrine had become merely a matter of speculation. There is abundant evidence that these late medieval trinitarian discussions had a consistent relation to the piety of the era and could serve as a foundational theme in preaching.[135] And, of course, the doctrine remained a primary point of ecumenical discussion with the eastern orthodox.

3. **The Council of Florence (1438-1442).** Less than a century before the Reformation, the lengthy proceedings of the Council of Ferrara-Florence (usually simply called the Council of Florence) were themselves a continuation of the Council of Basel (1431). The council, convened by Pope Eugenius IV, had as its fundamental purpose the healing of the schism with the Eastern Orthodox on such issues as papal primacy, purgatory, the use of unleavened bread in the Eucharist, and the *filioque*.[136] Eastern delegates included the patriarchs of Antioch, Alexandria, and Jerusalem, plus the metropolitan of Moscow as the representative of the Russian Orthodox. The eastern emperor came from Constantinople for the sake of reunifying Christians in the face of the Islamic threat.

On the specific point of the *filioque*, there was an extended debate over the doctrinal question, led, among others, by Bessarion the Archbishop of Nicaea, Markus Eugenicus of Ephesus, and Isidore of Kiev, arguing the Greek position, and Giovanni Montenero the Dominican provincial general of Lombardy, the Archbishop of Rhodes, and Giovanni di Ragusa arguing the Latin view. From the Greek perspective, the Latin position not only violated the canons of Nicaea and Constantinople, but also stood contrary to the New Testament and the Greek Fathers. In particular, the Greeks assumed that the language of double procession indicated two *principia* or sources in the Godhead, in short, a denial of the primacy of the Father. Montenero gained considerable respect from the Greeks through his mastery of the Fathers, Latin and Greek. In particular he was able to argue the proximity of the Latin tradition's language of a procession of the Spirit from the Son, given the primacy of the Father, with the Greek tradition's language of a procession through the Son.[137] In the same vein, Giovanni di Ragusa argued that it was the Latin tradition to insist on the primacy of the Father and the Father's sole ultimate causality in the procession of the Spirit, while

---

133. Vignaux, "Nominalisme," in *DTC*, XI, col. 778-779.

134. Cf. Alfonso Maieru, "Logique et théologie trinitaire: Pierre D'Ailly," in *Preuve et raisons*, ed. Z. Kaluza and P. Vignaux (Paris: J. Vrin, 1984), pp. 253-268.

135. Thus, e.g., Gabriel Adrianyi, "Pelbart von Temesvar (ca. 1435-1504) und seine trinitarischen Predigtvorlagen," in *Im Gespräch mit dem dreieinen Gott*, ed. M. Boehnke and H. Heinz (Düsseldorf: Patmos Verlag, 1985), pp. 276-284.

136. J. Gill, *The Council of Florence* (Cambridge: Cambridge University Press, 1959).

137. Gill, *Council of Florence*, pp. 229-231.

at the same time insisting that the Son, as begotten of the Father, is also God from whom the Spirit proceeds. The argument came to a conclusion after nine sessions, with a somewhat equivocal result. A formula was agreed on by the Latin representatives and many of the Greeks, as well as Isidore of Kiev. There was no final ratification of the decrees of the council in either Constantinople or Moscow.

The decrees of the Council of Florence both extended a fairly refined basis for reunion or at least the removal of mutual excommunication to the Greek and Russian churches and, at the same time, defended the *filioque* clause as "added into the Symbol legitimately ... for the sake of clarifying the truth."[138] Still, the formula represents the Latin view as the primary model and offers the Greek language as a matter of clarification, in fact, assimilating the Greek view of a procession of the Spirit from the Father through the Son to a theory of double procession. It is not remarkable that the Greek theologians were not entirely convinced. The Decree for the Greeks in fact begins with a formal declaration of the truth of the *filioque*, offering only the common faith in a single *principium* as an element of doctrine shared with the Greeks:

> we define that this truth of the faith must be believed and received by all and that all must profess: the Holy Spirit is eternally from the Father and the Son; he has his nature and subsistence at once (*simul*) from the Father and the Son; he proceeds eternally from both as from one principle and through one spiration.[139]

Next, the Decree offered its explanation of the agreement of the Greek with the Latin view:

> we declare: when the holy doctors and fathers say that the Holy Spirit proceeds from the Father through the Son, this must be understood in the sense that, as the Father, so also the Son is what the Greeks call "cause" and the Latins "principle" of the subsistence of the Holy Spirit.[140]

This clarification of argument is a step past the conciliar formulation of Lyons a century and a half before in that it identifies the Greek language of the Spirit's procession through the Son with the equally Greek trinitarian identification of causality of subsistence and, by way of that identification, the equivalence of the Greek and the Latin teaching. As if this statement were not a clear enough Westernization of the Greek view, the Decree continues, "since the Father has through generation given to the only-begotten Son everything that belongs to the Father, except being Father, the son has also eternally from the Father, for whom he is eternally begotten, that the Holy Spirit proceeds from the Son."[141] The procession of the Spirit, which is from the Father, is bestowed on the Son in the begetting of the Son — leaving the Father the ultimate *principium*, and maintaining his primacy, but understanding the procession

---

138. Decree for the Greeks, in Denzinger-Schönmetzer, §1302; Neuner and Dupuis, §324.
139. Decree for the Greeks, in Denzinger-Schönmetzer, §1300; Neuner and Dupuis, §322.
140. Decree for the Greeks, in Denzinger-Schönmetzer, §1301; Neuner and Dupuis, §323.
141. Decree for the Greeks, in Denzinger-Schönmetzer, §1301; Neuner and Dupuis, §323; cf. Fortman, *Triune God*, p. 225.

as given to the Son in virtually the same way that it can be said that the Father gives to the Son to have life in himself.

After the departure of the Greek delegates, the Latin bishops and theologians continued to meet in order to present formulae of reunion with the Syrian church with their delegates. The Decree for the Jacobites or the Syrian church, dating from the closing sessions of the council (1442), elaborates in detail the divinity and distinction of the persons, echoing the Athanasian Creed and clearly enunciating the oneness and unity of the essence over against the distinction of the persons as an "opposition of relationship."[142] Thus, the church confesses

> one true almighty, unchangeable and eternal God, Father, Son, and Holy Spirit, one in essence, trine in persons: the Father not begotten, the Son begotten from the Father, and the Holy Spirit proceeding from the Father and the Son. ... the Father is only the Father, the Son only the Son, the Holy Spirit only the Holy Spirit. The Father alone begot the Son out of his substance; the Son alone was begotten from the Father alone; the Holy Spirit alone proceeds from both the Father and the Son. These three persons are one God and not three gods, for the three are one substance, one essence, one nature, one Godhead, one infinity, one eternity, and everything (in them) is one where there is no opposition of relationship.[143]

This way of construing the intra-trinitarian relations reflects the teaching of Anselm as mediated through the major teachers of the high scholastic era, notably Aquinas.[144] This doctrine, the Decree continues, makes clear that the unity of the Godhead is such that the persons are "wholly in" one another — a perfect and complete co-inherence or perichoresis — and that, therefore, "none precedes the other in eternity, none exceeds the other in greatness, or excels the other in power." The begetting and the procession are eternal and without beginning.[145]

The Decree for the Jacobites also makes clear, in order to meet eastern objections, that the *filioque* does not imply two ultimate sources or *principia* in the Godhead — in fact, the *filioque* contravenes both a notion of two *principia* and any division of the divine essence. First, the primacy of the Father: the Father "is the origin without origin" and "all that the Son is or has, he has from the Father" but defined in such a way as to provide a foundation for the *filioque*, "he is the origin from origin." Then, the definition of the Spirit's procession in terms of the *filioque*: "all that the Holy Spirit is or has, he has at once (*simul*) from the Father and the Son." But this doctrine does not undermine either the primacy of the Father or the sense, now carefully nuanced, of the single *principium* of the Spirit's procession, given that "the Father and the Son

---

142. Decree for the Jacobites, in Denzinger-Schönmetzer, §1330; Neuner and Dupuis, §325.

143. Decree for the Jacobites, in Denzinger-Schönmetzer, §1330; Neuner and Dupuis, §325.

144. Cf. Anselm, *On the Procession of the Holy Spirit*, i (pp. 86-88); Aquinas, *Summa contra gentiles*, IV.xiv.15.

145. Decree for the Jacobites, in Denzinger-Schönmetzer, §1331; Neuner and Dupuis, §326.

are not two origins of the Holy Spirit, but one origin, just as the Father, the Son, and the Holy Spirit are not three origins of creation but one origin."[146]

In its fundamental teaching, the Council of Florence reiterated the results of the earlier medieval councils — Bari, Fourth Lateran, and Lyons — with at least two significant further nuances. First, as already noted, the formula ensconces in Western trinitarian doctrine the Anselmic notion, taken up so clearly by Aquinas, that the only real distinctions in the Godhead arise from the opposition of relations in the emanations of Son and Spirit from the Father. All other distinctions belong to the essence itself and must be understood as other than real or substantial — and the real or substantial distinctions among the persons are relational and within the "thing," and are therefore of a sort that they do not compromise the unity of the divine essence: they are not distinctions from the essence or distinctions of essence, but distinctions within the one indivisible essence.

The second highly significant nuance points toward the congruence of the *ad intra* life of the Godhead with the *ad extra* manifestation and work, namely, that the relation between the Father and the Son is such that, given the character of the Father's primacy, the Son in unity with the Father is, with the Father, the *principium* of the Holy Spirit — and that this single *principium* in the inner life of the Godhead mirrors the way in which the *ad extra* work is also one, the three persons together being the sole *principium* of creation.

---

146. Decree for the Jacobites, in Denzinger-Schönmetzer, §1331; Neuner and Dupuis, §326; cf. Paul Henry, "On Some Implications of the 'Ex Patre Filioque tamquam ab uno Principio,'" in *The Eastern Churches Quarterly*, Supplement 19 (1948), pp. 19-20.

2

The Doctrine of the Trinity
from the Sixteenth to the Early
Eighteenth Century

2.1 Scripture and Traditional Trinitarian Language in the Era of the Reformation

A. The Reformers from the Time of Luther to the Mid-Sixteenth Century, ca. 1520-1565

1. Prologue: the problem of the history of the doctrine of the Trinity in Reformation and post-Reformation Reformed thought. The history of the doctrine of the Trinity in the sixteenth and seventeenth centuries is, from one perspective, little more than the history of the defense of traditional orthodox formulations against a variety of resurgent patristic heresies — indeed, this is the perspective taken by most of the works dealing with the problems confronting trinitarian doctrinal formulation between the Reformation and the Enlightenment and written contemporaneously with the debates, notably, the histories by Maimbourg and Berriman,[1] the heresiological works by writers like Hoornbeek, Cheynell, and Edwards,[2] and the historical sections

---

1. Louis Maimbourg, *Histoire de l'Arianisme depuis sa naissance jusqu'à sa sin: avec l'origine & le progrés de l'heresie des Sociniens* (Paris: Sebastien Mabre-Cramoisy, 1683); idem, *The history of Arianism, by M. Maimbourg; shewing its influence upon civil affairs: and the causes of the dissolution of the Roman empire. To which are added, two introductory discourses. With an appendix containing an account of the English writers in the Socinian and Arian controversies*, by William Webster (London, Printed by W. Roberts, 1728-1729); William Berriman, *An Historical Account of the Controversies that have been in the Church, concerning the Doctrine of the Holy and Everblessed Trinity. In Eight Sermons preached at the Cathedral Church of St. Paul, London, in the years 1723 and 1724* (London: T. Ward & C. Rivington, 1725).

2. Johannes Hoornbeek, *Summa controversiarum religionis, cum infidelibus, haereticis, schismaticis* (Utrecht, 1653); Francis Cheynell, *The Rise, Growth, and Danger of Socinianisme together with a plaine*

of various eighteenth-century theological systems, like those of Stackhouse and Knapp.[3] The point can easily be made that the orthodoxy of the era, insofar as it rested overtly on the patristic definitions and never advanced speculatively even as far as the conclusions of the medieval doctors, did not represent a development of doctrine.

If, however, one looks to the question of the extent and manner in which the theologians of the Reformation and Protestant orthodoxy received and used the materials of the tradition, the ways in which they dealt with the problems of antitrinitarian heresies, and the patterns of stress and strain on both language and exegesis caused by the philosophical and critical changes that took place in the course of the sixteenth and seventeenth centuries, then a rather different picture emerges. We can distinguish between an early Reformation phase, extending as far as 1535 or 1540, during which the Reformers were hesitant to use traditional trinitarian language in normative confessional statements and compendia of basic doctrines, given their assumption of the subordinate status of tradition, and a later stage, beginning around 1540, during which the rise of antitrinitarian teachings demanded response from the Reformers and the usefulness of traditional dogmatic language became increasingly evident. Characteristic of this second phase of development is a renewed emphasis on the usefulness of the patristic language in the defense of the biblical doctrine of the Trinity against various heretics and an increased emphasis on the development of an exegetically based trinitarianism.

The Protestant view of Scripture also caused a series of difficulties for dogmatics or doctrinal theology in the sixteenth century, particularly in relation to the Reformation and post-Reformation critique of tradition and the gradual shift in hermeneutics from the more typological forms of precritical exegesis to an emphasis on the literal sense of the text, construed in an increasingly historical and critical way — difficulties that were not immediately obvious to all of the parties involved in theological debate or that at least did not become pressing problems at the very outset of the Reformation. The doctrine of the Trinity is a case in point. The magisterial Reformers were orthodox in their trinitarian formulations, even though, at the outset of the Reformation, they frequently expressed a sense of the limitation of the traditional trinitarian vocabulary. Still, the Reformers placed particular emphasis on the triune identity of God as the ultimate truth of God known only in and through the Christian revelation; and they were concerned, as the sixteenth-century debate progressed, over

---

discovery of a desperate designe of corrupting the Protestant religion, whereby it appeares that the religion which hath been so violently contended for (by the Archbishop of Canterbury and his adherents) is not the true pure Protestant religion, but an hotchpotch of Arminianisme, Socinianisme and popery (London: Samuel Gellibrand, 1643); Thomas Edwards, The first and second part of Gangraena: or A catalogue and discovery of many of the errors, heresies, blasphemies and pernicious practices of the sectaries of this time, vented and acted in England in these four last years. Also a particular narration of divers stories ... an extract of many letters, all concerning the present sects; together with some observations (London: T. R. and E. M. for Ralph Smith, 1646).

3. Thomas Stackhouse, A Complete Body of Speculative and Practical Divinity, 3 vols. (Dumfries, 1776), I, pp. 236-241; Georg Christian Knapp, Lectures on Christian Theology, trans. Leonard Woods (New York: Tibbals, 1859), I.iv.2, pp. 144-162.

the character and right use of the traditional language of substance and person against the various antitrinitarian thinkers of the day — specifically, over the question of whether the language of patristic orthodoxy, not taken directly from the text of Scripture, could in fact be an accurate representation of the biblical message.

The early orthodox development of Reformed trinitarianism assumes the appropriation of patristic norms in confessional documents and is characterized by a flowering of large-scale theological treatments of doctrines like Trinity and the Person of Christ. Not only did the theologians of the later sixteenth and early seventeenth century recognize the usefulness of the traditional language and definition, they also felt the need, already identifiable in such Reformation era documents as Calvin's *Reply to Sadoleto*, to insist on the catholicity of the Reformation and, as a result, in their dogmatic works to evidence the Protestant reliance on the tradition. Early orthodoxy, as evidenced in works like Zanchi's *De tribus Elohim* and Polanus' *Syntagma theologiae*,[4] drew on ancient materials in even more depth and detail than had the Reformers. A characteristic of the early orthodox discussion of the doctrine of the Trinity is the various theologians' consistent reference to the terminology of the early church in detailed discussions of the doctrine. It is also fairly clear that the early orthodox reception of scholastic method together with the early orthodox critical appropriation of the Christian Aristotelianism of the older dogmatic tradition provided a methodological and philosophical context within which traditional trinitarian language well served the needs of orthodoxy in the face of continuing pressure from the antitrinitarian arguments of Socinus and other critics of patristic dogmas.

Protestant orthodox adherence to traditional categories, both doctrinal and philosophical, came under increasing strain during the era of high orthodoxy, given the changes in philosophical language that characterize the second half of the seventeenth century. Whereas the early orthodox writers could assume a relatively stable usage of terms like "substance," "essence," "person," and "subsistence," their high orthodox successors had to contend with new rationalist philosophies that embodied radically altered assumptions concerning substance, causality, and individual existence — and, in addition, they had to contend with an increasingly rationalistic antitrinitarianism that drew on or at least profited from these altered assumptions and could, far more convincingly than the antitrinitarianism of preceding generations, argue the impossibility of three persons or subsistences having the same essence. The trinitarian controversies of high orthodoxy, therefore, take on a rather different tone than those of the Reformation and the early orthodox era, particularly to the extent

---

4. Jerome Zanchi, *De tribus Elohim, aeterno Patre, Filio. Et Spiritu Sancto* (Frankfurt am Main: Georgius Corvinus, 1573), also in vol. 1 of the *Operum theologicorum D. Hieronymi Zanchii*, 8 vols. (Heidelberg: Stephanus Gamonetus and Matthaeus Berjon, 1605) and *Operum theologicorum D. Hieronymi Zanchii*, 10 vols. in 9 (Geneva: Samuel Crispin, 1617-1619); Amandus Polanus von Polansdorf, *Syntagma theologiae christianae*, 2 pts. (Hainau, 1609); ibid, in folio (Geneva, 1617); also idem, *Partitiones theologiae christianae*, pars I-II (Basel, 1590-1596) and *The Substance of the Christian Religion* (London, 1595), a translation of part I of the *Partitiones*.

that the language and conceptual framework of Christian Aristotelianism was no longer universally accepted, even among the orthodox writers.

The problem of antitrinitarian exegesis was, certainly, the most overtly intense of the issues faced by the Reformers and their successors, given the Protestant emphasis on the priority of the biblical norm. For the various antitrinitarians consistently rejected tradition in the name of their own exegesis of Scripture. In addition, in the seventeenth century, there was a partial coincidence, given the textual problems of such texts as 1 John 5:7 and 1 Timothy 3:16, between the Socinian position and the views of various text-critical scholars. The orthodox found themselves in the very difficult position of arguing a traditional view of the Trinity against an antitrinitarian exegesis that appeared, in a few instances, to represent the results of text criticism and, in a few other instances, to represent a literal exegesis of text over against an older allegorism or typological reading — at the same time that, in many of its readings, it appeared to be a contorted and rationalizing attempt to undermine not only the traditional but also the basic literal sense of the text. This latter characteristic of Socinian exegesis cut in two directions: on the one hand, it could be presented, as was typical of the Socinian argumentation, as on a par with the text-critical results used in the Socinian reading of other passages, giving warrant to the antitrinitarian reading at least by association; on the other hand, it could be seen as an excessive result of the newer hermeneutical approaches, creating an otherwise unwarranted suspicion of certain kinds of textual criticism on the part of the orthodox. In either case, the orthodox task of building the primary justification of the doctrine of the Trinity on exegesis was made more difficult.

There were, therefore, three basic issues to follow in the discussion of the trinitarian thought of the Reformers and the Reformed orthodox — namely, the careful use of a well-defined patristic vocabulary, increasingly tuned to the particular needs and issues of Reformed thought, the intense battle over the exegetical ground of the doctrine in both testaments in view of the biblicistic assault on the doctrine from Socinians and other antitrinitarians, and the struggle to find a suitable set of philosophical categories for the understanding and explanation of the doctrinal result, given the alteration or at least the fluidity of the conception of substance. At the heart of these lay the exegetical issue, given the Reformation emphasis on the priority of Scripture over all other norms of doctrine and alteration of patterns of interpretation away from the patristic and medieval patterns that had initially yielded the doctrine of the Trinity and given it a vocabulary consistent with traditional philosophical usage.

2. The doctrine of the Trinity in the thought of the earliest Reformers. The early Reformers proposed no variation in the received trinitarian orthodoxy except in relation to the more speculative elements of the medieval scholastic doctrine. Luther's basic expressions of the doctrine, as found in the two catechisms, simply reiterate the normative doctrine in its most basic form, without any technical terms or elaboration. Luther clearly upheld the traditional symbols, the Apostles' Creed, the Niceno-Constantinopolitan formula, the Athanasian Creed, and the Te Deum.[5] In his comments on these creedal forms Luther notes that "belief that the three Persons are one God takes nothing whatever away from the single true Godhead" and that "we have indications in Scripture that there are three persons in the divine substance." Luther was also quite adamant that the entire Scripture, in both Old and New Testaments, spoke this truth and that the use of the plural *Elohim* to indicate the one God identified God as "single in substance" but distinguished into "three Persons."[6] In his more detailed comments, moreover, Luther reflects the medieval development of trinitarian language that affirms the primacy of the Father in the order of persons while at the same time insisting on the fulness of the divine essence or nature in each of the persons, the simplicity of the divine essence, and the common work of the persons *ad extra* — at the same time that he avoided abstruse questions concerning the kind of distinction that obtained between persons and disputed the validity of Lombard's argument that the essence is neither begotten nor proceeded, but only the persons.[7] The latter point is one on which Calvin would differ sharply with Luther, albeit without mentioning Luther's name.[8]

---

5. See especially, Martin Luther, *The Three Symbols or Creeds of the Christian Faith* (1538), trans. Robert Heitner, in *Luther's Works*, ed. Jaroslav Pelikan and Helmut Lehmann, 56 vols. (St. Louis: Concordia / Philadelphia: Fortress, 1955-86), hereinafter, *LW*, 34, pp. 197-229, where Luther notes as his topic the Apostles' and the Athanasian Creed, and the Te Deum, but adds, at the end of the Treatise, the Nicene Creed. Cf. Fortman, *Triune God*, p. 239, who does not note the Nicene Creed.

6. Luther, *Three Symbols*, in *LW*, 34, pp. 223, 226-227.

7. Luther, *WA*, 39, 2.287-288; see the discussion of Luther's doctrine in Julius Köstlin, *The Theology of Luther in its Historical Development and Inner Harmony*, trans. Charles E. Hay, 2 vols. (Philadelphia: Lutheran Publication Society, 1897), II, pp. 310-318; also note Reiner Jansen, *Studien zu Luther's Trinitätslehre* (Bern and Frankfurt: Lang, 1976); Christine Helmer, *The Trinity and Martin Luther: A Study on the Relationship between Genre, Language and the Trinity in Luther's Works, 1523-1546* (Mainz: P. von Zabern, 1999).

8. John Calvin, *Institutio christianae religionis, in libros quatuor nunc primum digesta, certisque distincta capitibus, ad aptissimam methodum: aucta etiam tam magna accessione ut propemodum opus novum haberi possit* (Geneva: Robertus Stephanus, 1559), I.xiii.25; cf. the comments in François Wendel, *Calvin: The Origins and Development of His Thought*, trans. Philip Mairet (New York: Harper & Row, 1963), p. 167, n. 54. In citing the 1559 *Institutes*, I have consulted both *Institutes of the Christian Religion*, trans. Henry Beveridge, 2 vols. (Edinburgh, 1845; repr. Grand Rapids: Eerdmans, 1994) and *Institutes of the Christian Religion*, ed. John T. McNeill, trans. Ford Lewis Battles, 2 vols. (Philadelphia: Westminster, 1960), hereinafter referenced as "Calvin, *Institutes*." Calvin's shorter tracts and treatises are cited from *Selected Works of John Calvin: Tracts and Letters*, ed. Henry Beveridge and Jules Bonnet, 7 vols. (Grand Rapids: Baker Book House, 1983). I have cited Calvin's commentaries from *Commentaries of John Calvin*, 46 vols. (Edinburgh: Calvin Translation Society, 1844-55; repr. Grand Rapids: Baker Book House, 1979), hereinafter abbreviated as CTS, followed by the biblical book and, when applicable, the volume number of the commentary on that particular book. I have also consulted John Calvin, *Sermons of Maister Iohn Calvin, upon the Book of Iob*, trans. Arthur Golding (London: George Bishop, 1574; repr. Edinburgh: Banner of Truth, 1993); *Sermons of M. John Calvin, on the Epistles of S. Paule to Timothie and Titus*, trans. L. T. (London: G. Bishop, 1579; repr. Edinburgh: Banner of Truth, 1983); and *The Sermons of M. Iohn Calvin upon the Fifth Booke of Moses called Deuteronomie*, trans. Arthur Golding (London: Henry Middleton, 1583; repr. Edinburgh: Banner of Truth, 1987). Latin and French texts of Calvin's commentaries, sermons, and

Melanchthon was perhaps the most radical of the Reformers in his early willingness to exclude not only traditional language but also older dogmas from the essentials of the faith. In the 1521 edition of his *Loci communes*, Melanchthon could polemicize against the introduction of non-biblical categories such as trinitarian vocabulary into the standard or basic *loci* of Christian theology, while the Schwabach Articles introduce the standard creedal vocabulary of the essence and persons of the Godhead, and the Augsburg Confession offers explicit reference to "the decree of the Nicene Synod," which is "without doubt to be believed."[9] As subsequent editions of the *Loci communes* demonstrate, Melanchthon quickly recognized the need to offer an explicit and fully developed doctrines of the Trinity, grounded in examination of texts in both Testaments.

This concern over the biblical grounds of theological language, coupled with an assumption concerning the clarity and simplicity of the biblical Word, is characteristic of Bucer's work, including the Tetrapolitan Confession: unlike many of the major Reformed confessions, particularly the great national confessions of the mid-sixteenth century like the Belgic and Gallican Confessions and the Thirty-Nine Articles, the *Tetrapolitan* offers no acknowledgment of the Apostles' Creed or the great ecumenical creeds of the early church. Bucer had complained, before the writing of the Tetrapolitan Confession, against the use of traditional trinitarian vocabulary in Schwabach Articles. His reaction to this internal Protestant quandary is significant, particularly granting his training in scholastic theology. Bucer recognized that the language, although not strictly biblical, was certainly a valid means for stating and codifying the biblical revelation concerning the identity of God. He commented that he found no fault in the Schwabach Articles and "personally could accept all these articles as they stand" and would even be willing to defend the very words and phrases of the document.

Nonetheless, when Bucer commented on the Schwabach Articles, he found certain points lacking "clarity" and "simplicity" and felt that some revision was required if Protestants were to be expected to act with a unity of theological purpose.[10] "Doctor Luther," writes Bucer,

> thinks that the word *"trinitas"* should not be used; others object to the word *"persona"* because the ordinary man — to the offense of the Jews and all others who have not yet joined our religion — uses the word "person" in the ordinary sense and speaks of the three Persons as though they were three separate beings (an error which is also

treatises, unless otherwise noted will be cited from *Ioannis Calvini opera quae supersunt omnia*, ed. G. Baum, E. Cunitz, and E. Reuss (Brunswick: Schwetschke, 1863-1900), hereinafter, *CO*.

9. Cf. Melanchthon, *Loci communes* (1521), in *Opera quae supersunt omnia*, ed. C. G. Bretschneider and H. E. Bindseil, *Corpus Reformatorum*, vols. 1-28 (Brunswick: Schwetschke, 1834-1860), 21, col. 83-84 (hereinafter *CR*); cf. Schwabach Articles, I, in Johan Michael Reu, *The Augsburg Confession: A Collection of Sources with an Historical Introduction* (Chicago: Wartburg, 1930; repr. St. Louis: Concordia, 1983), pp. *40-*44; Augsburg Confession, I.i, in Philip Schaff, *The Creeds of Christendom, with a History and Critical Notes*, 6th ed., 3 vols. (New York, 1931; repr. Grand Rapids: Baker Book House, 1983), III, pp. 7-8.

10. *Bucer's Critique of the Schwabach Articles*, in Reu, *Augsburg Confession*, p. *49.

suggested by the word "trinity"). It is also known how many quarrels have arisen over the *"processionibus"* and *"notionibus"* which are not mentioned in the Scriptures at all. Now it would be proper to speak of such a high and incomprehensible mystery in the clearest, that is, most scriptural manner; this would be the best way of preventing godless quarrels.[11]

Bucer's comments concerning the term *persona* are particularly significant, granting both the long history of medieval discussion and debate over the theological definition of the term,[12] and the concern of the Reformers to hold as closely as possible to the language of Scripture and to shun the niceties of scholastic distinctions. After Schwabach, and perhaps in the light of his own caveat, Bucer appears to have concluded that his goal of "scriptural" clarity could only be achieved through a limited use of the traditional terminology of Trinity and Christology: he avoided reference to the early creeds as norms — while at the same time introducing into the Tetrapolitan Confession the Latin terms "substance," "nature," "person," and "trinity," but not noting any of the more technical terms, like "filiation," "procession," and "circuminces-sion" or the Greek terms "hypostasis," and "ousia." This limited and somewhat critical use of the traditional trinitarian language carried over into the thought of the second generation Reformers and became a staple of Reformed orthodoxy — causing, among other variations and alterations in the doctrinal discussion, an increasingly exegetical approach to the doctrine of the Trinity, at least in Protestant circles.

3. Reappropriation of traditionary norms in the doctrinal treatises of the Reformers. From the third or fourth decade of the sixteenth century onward, there was a development in Protestant approaches to the doctrine of the Trinity — on the one hand, the Reformers became more and more willing to accept the traditional terminology as normative, while, on the other, they distanced themselves from the increasingly loud, albeit never very large, chorus of antitrinitarianism. These two sides of the development were, of course, related.

If Melanchthon must be cited as the Reformer most opposed to the inclusion of traditional dogmas and churchly dogmatic developments in a basic statement of Christian belief, he is also the Reformer who must be identified as most sensitive to the ecclesial need to state doctrines in a more elaborate form. The successive editions of his *Loci communes* well illustrate the point: if Melanchthon declaimed against the inclusion of the doctrine of the Trinity in 1521, by 1543 he had recognized the importance of a well-developed trinitarianism to the statement of Christian doctrine — in part due to the presence of heathens at the boundaries of Christendom, in part due to the presence of heretics within.[13]

The early Reformation wrestling with the problem of trinitarian vocabulary and the consequent worry over the interpretive question of using such language to explain

---

11. *Bucer's Critique of the Schwabach Articles,* in Reu, *Augsburg Confession,* pp. *49-*50.

12. Cf. Fortman, *Triune God,* pp. 191-192, 203-204, 208-209, and *passim.*

13. Cf. Melanchthon, *Loci communes* (1521), in CR 21, col. 83-84, with idem, *Loci communes* (1543), in CR 21, col. 607-637.

the biblical text is evident also in the development of and debate over Calvin's trinitarian formulae. In the first edition of the *Institutes*, Calvin had attempted to deal, on the one hand, with the demands of the biblical language and, on the other, with the complaints of more radical Protestants of the day, who objected on biblical grounds to the use of the language of Nicene orthodoxy:

> Persons who are not contentious or stubborn see the Father, Son, and Holy Spirit to be one God. For the Father is God; the Son is God; and the Spirit is God: and there is only one God. ...three are named, three described, three distinguished. One therefore, and three: one God, one essence. ... Not three gods, not three essences. To signify both, the ancient orthodox fathers said that there was one *ousia*, three *hypostaseis*, that is, one substance, three subsistences in one substance.[14]

"The heretics bark," Calvin comments,

> that *ousia, hypostaseis*, essence, persons, are names invented by human decision, nowhere read or seen in the Scriptures. But since they cannot shake our conviction that three are spoken of, who are one God, what sort of squeamishness is it to disapprove of words that explain nothing else than what is attested and sealed by Scripture. ...what prevents us from explaining in clearer words those matters in Scripture which perplex and hinder our understanding, yet which faithfully serve the truth of Scripture itself, and are made use of sparingly and modestly and not at the wrong occasion?[15]

Calvin further justified the language by arguing in return that no one would claim that all theological or religious "discourses" ought to be "patched together out of the fabric of Scripture": it is, after all, legitimate to use words not found in Scripture to explain the meaning of Scripture.[16]

Calvin's trinitarian thinking developed quickly and polemically in the face of a series of accusations leveled against his doctrine. Calvin's initial reluctance to use the traditional trinitarian language with regularity, coupled with his insistence on the doctrine of divine aseity, had brought early accusations of heresy from two pastors of Neuchâtel, Chapponeau and Courtois. These two churchmen accused Calvin of denying the Trinity — largely on the ground of Calvin's seeming hesitancy concerning the orthodox terminology in the 1536 *Institutes* and the entire absence of the traditional terminology from the *Confession of Faith* issued by Calvin and Farel in 1537, as it was from Farel's *Sommaire* of 1525.[17] Calvin's friend and ally Viret faced similar charges

---

14. Calvin, *Institutes* (1536), II.7.

15. Calvin, *Institutes* (1536), II.8.

16. Calvin, *Institutes* (1536), II.8.

17. Farel did ultimately introduce the traditional terminology in the final edition his *Sommaire* of 1552. See Guillaume Farel, *Sommaire et briefve declaration* [1525] Fac-similé de l'edition originel, publié ... par Arthur Piaget (Paris: Droz, 1935); and idem, *Sommaire: c'est une brieve declaration d'aucuns lieux fort necessaires à un chacun Chrestien* [1552], cap. I, III, in *Du Vray usage de la croix de Iesus-Christ par Guillaume Farel suivi de divers écrits du même auteur* (Geneva: J. G. Fick, 1865), p. 209: "nous confessons ... un seul Dieu en trois personnes ... en unité d'Essence & de nature, confessons la Trinité des personnes en vraye distinction personelle & parfaite union d'Essence"; and p. 212:

for his confession of 1534, in which there was no use of the traditional terminology of Trinity, substance, and person.[18] Calvin added to the controversy by refusing to subscribe to the Athanasian Creed at the Synod of Lausanne, held later in 1537 — at which point he and the other Genevan pastors were accused of Arianism and Sabellianism by Pierre Caroli.[19]

In response to his accusers, Calvin did confess the "distinction of persons in the one God" as the "orthodox consensus of the church" in the prefatory epistle to the 1537 and 1538 catechisms, but significantly, he did not add the language to the text of either the catechism or the confession.[20] Relatively complete statement, albeit still brief by most standards, appears finally in the creedal section of Calvin's 1539 *Institutes*. The underlying motive for full and correct statement of the doctrine was, therefore, on Calvin's part, more a clarification and defense of orthodoxy and of the orthodoxy of the Genevan Reformation than it was intense theological interest in the traditional terminology. His hesitance regarding the normative use of traditionary terminology — even the language of the Nicene and Athanasian Creeds — echoed that of Luther and Melanchthon.[21] In addition, Calvin's approach to the traditional language evidences his clear sense of literary genre: such language as not necessary in basic confessions of faith, but it was required in more advanced works, particularly those designed to train clergy. As in the parallel case of Melanchthon's theology, Calvin's published writings, notably the *Institutes*, evidence a fairly rapid expansion of trinitarian discussion under the impact of the polemic to the point that the patristic doctrine, which had initially received minimal treatment but had certainly never been denied, became a stated foundation of the faith.[22]

"Iesus Christ, vray fliz de Dieu ... estant un avec luy en essence, vray Dieu ... & vray homme...." The statement in Wilbur, *History of Unitarianism*, I, p. 16 that Farel made "not the slightest reference to the Trinity or the dual nature of Christ" is misleading inasmuch as Wilbur cites only the 1524 edition of the *Sommaire* and then reads the problem in terms of the typical seventeenth-century Socinian argument that the magisterial Reformers failed to take the Reformation to its logical conclusion, namely, to the Socinian removal of all traditionary accretions, including Trinity and incarnation.

18. Cf. Abraham Ruchat, *Histoire de la Réformation de la Suisse* (Noyon, 1836), V, pp. 27-29. Viret's major theological essays are Pierre Viret, *Exposition familière de l'oraison de nostre Seigneur Jésus Christ* (Geneva, 1548); *Disputationes chrestiennes* (Geneva: J. Gérard, 1552); *Exposition de la doctrine de la foy chrestienne, touchant la vraye cognoissance & le vraye service de Dieu* (Geneva, 1564); *Instruction chrestienne en la doctrine de la Loy et de lÉvangile*, 2 parts (Geneva, 1564); and the *Exposition familière sur le Symbole des Apostres*. Geneva, 1560), translated as *A Verie familiare Exposition of the Apostles Crede* (London, n.d.).

19. See E. Bachler, "Petrus Caroli and Johann Calvin," in *Jahrbuch für schweizerische Geschichte* 29 (1904), pp. 41-169.

20. Calvin, *Catechismus* (1538), p. iv; cf. Stephen Reynolds, "Calvin's View of the Athanasian and Nicene Creeds," in *Westminster Theological Journal*, 23 (1960/61), pp. 33-57.

21. Cf. the comments of Willem Nijenhuis, "Calvin's Attitude towards the Symbols of the Early Church during the Conflict with Caroli," in *Ecclesia Reformata: Studies on the Reformation* (Leiden: Brill, 1972), I, pp. 82, 85-86, 90-92.

22. It is clearly an error to speak of a "latent antitrinitarianism among the early Reformers" as in Wilbur, *History of Unitarianism*, I, pp. 12-18.

Calvin could argue quite pointedly that, beyond the doctrine of the unity or oneness of divine essence,

> God also designates himself by another special mark to distinguish himself more precisely from idols. For he so proclaims himself the sole God as to offer himself to be contemplated clearly in three persons. Unless we grasp these, only the bare and empty name of God flits about in our brains, to the exclusion of the true God. Again, lest anyone imagine that God is threefold, or think that God's simple essence be torn into three persons, we must here seek a short and easy definition to free us from all error.[23]

The point is, therefore, very clearly made that the dogmatic definition of Trinity concurs with and, in some sense, completes and clarifies the doctrine of the divine essence and attributes. Contrary to the statement occasionally made about the doctrine of God in the early Reformation, Calvin cannot be seen as moving away from a classical doctrine of divine simplicity or from a strong emphasis on the problem of the divine essence and attributes — his purpose is rather to place the language of Trinity properly into the context of the doctrine of God as the final identification of God in the Christian revelation. For Calvin, it is quite enough to note the distinction of Father, Son, and Spirit and to recognize that the distinction, albeit necessary to the right understanding of God, "is not a distinction of essence, which it is unlawful to make manifold." The divine essence must always be regarded as "simple and undivided."[24] The classical terms, "person" and "substance," give definition to the truth that "three are spoken of, each of which is entirely God, yet ... there is not more than one God."[25]

Once having acknowledged the usefulness and rectitude of the traditional trinitarian language, Calvin also expressed a strong antagonism to any further speculation. Nor did he simply argue that the scholastic attempts to develop analogical language for understanding the internal divine emanations were illegitimate; he went so far as to criticize severely Augustine's speculative discussion:

> Augustine, beyond all others, speculates with excessive refinement, for the purpose of fabricating a Trinity in man. For in laying hold of the three faculties enumerated by Aristotle, the intellect, the memory, and the will, he afterwards out of one Trinity derives many.[26]

Somewhat less pointedly, Calvin wrote in his *Institutes*,

> I really do not know whether it is expedient to borrow comparisons from human affairs to express the force of this distinction [among the divine persons]. Men of old were indeed accustomed sometimes to do so, but at the same time they confessed that the analogies they advanced were quite inadequate. Thus it is that I shrink from all rashness

---

23. Calvin, *Institutes*, I.xiii.2.

24. Calvin, *Institutes*, I.xiii.2

25. Calvin, *Institutes*, I.xiii.3.

26. Calvin, *Commentaries on Genesis*, (CTS Genesis, I, p. 93) and cf. the similar remarks in *Institutes*, I.xv.4, on the Augustinian conception of the *imago Dei*.

here: lest if anything should by inopportunely expressed, it may give occasion either of calumny to the malicious, or of delusion to the ignorant.[27]

Such reservations would remain characteristic of Reformed theology throughout the era of orthodoxy.

Calvin nonetheless insists on a biblical expression of the distinction among the divine persons and goes on to frame it in a manner that reflects some of concerns behind the rejected patristic metaphors and even some of the logic underlying medieval scholastic discussion of the character of the divine begetting and proceeding: "to the Father is attributed the beginning of the activity, and the fountain and wellspring of all things; to the Son, wisdom, counsel, and the ordered disposition of all things; but to the Spirit is assigned the power and the efficacy of that activity."[28] The disputative structure of Calvin's trinitarian discussion, moreover, which moves from an initial definition of the subject, through an extended discussion of the divinity of the Son, to the arguments for the divinity of the Spirit before concluding his definition and examining the various heresies both ancient and modern,[29] points toward the structure of later orthodox argument.

Similar cautions are noted by Bullinger,[30] Musculus,[31] Hyperius,[32] and Vermigli,[33] who were considerably less concerned than Calvin with the problem that the terms of traditional trinitarianism did not arise directly out of Scripture and considerably more ready to present a traditionary doctrine. Thus, after having defined the various means by which we come to a genuine knowledge of God, Bullinger addressed at length the "doctrine of the prophets and apostles, which teaches that to be the true knowledge of God, that acknowledges God to be one in essence and three in persons."[34] Scripture abounds in testimonies to the unity of the divine essence, which Bullinger cites at

---

27. Calvin, Institutes, I.xiii.18.

28. Calvin, Institutes, I.xiii.18.

29. Calvin, Institutes, I.xiii.14-15, on the divinity of the Spirit. As in the case of his proofs of the divinity of the Son, here also Calvin offers no extended exegesis, but rather a dogmatic disputatio: a full view of his doctrine of the spirit, therefore, must look to his commentaries and treatises as well as to the Institutes.

30. Heinrich Bullinger, The Decades of Henry Bullinger, trans. H.I., edited by Thomas Harding, 4 vols. (Cambridge University Press, 1849-52), IV.iii (III, p. 154); also note, as sources of Bullinger's more formal theological definitions, Confessio et expositio simplex orthodoxae fidei (Zürich, 1566), text in Schaff, Creeds, III, pp. 233-306; and idem, Compendium christianae religionis (Zürich, 1556).

31. Wolfgang Musculus, Loci communes sacrae theologiae (Basel, 1560; third edition, 1573); in translation, Commonplaces of Christian Religion (London, 1563; 1578). I have used the Basel, 1560 edition and the London, 1578 translation.

32. Andreas Hyperius, Methodus theologiae, sive praecipuorum christianae religionis locorum communium, libri tres (Basel: Froschauer, 1568).

33. Peter Martyr Vermigli, P. M. Vermilii loci communes (London: Kyngston, 1576; editio secunda, London: Vautrollerius, 1583); in translation, The Common Places of Peter Martyr, trans. Anthony Marten (London: H. Denham, et al., 1583).

34. Bullinger, Decades, IV.iii (III, p. 154).

length,[35] and it also consistently testifies to the Trinity, in both the Old and the New Testament.[36] Bullinger is concerned, in particular, to draw these latter trinitarian testimonies into relation to the issue of the divine threeness and moreover to state the issue at a moderately technical level, using the scholastic terminology of distinction without division or separation:

> Now I suppose these divine testimonies are enough, and do sufficiently prove that God in substance is one, of essence incomprehensible, eternal, and spiritual. But under that one essence of the Godhead, the holy scripture shows us a distinction of the Father, of the Son, and of the Holy Spirit. Now note here, that I call it a distinction, not a division or a separation. For we adore and worship no more Gods but one: so yet that we do neither confound, nor yet deny or take away, the three subsistences or persons of the divine essence, nor the properties of the same.[37]

Hyperius provides an even more traditional pattern of argument, providing a positive, albeit brief, discussion of patristic metaphors for the doctrine of the Trinity, drawn from Basil the Great and Augustine.[38] Musculus also manifests a highly traditionary pattern of exposition and, at least in this place, echoes the original shape of Lombard's *Sentences* in the virtual identification of the doctrine of God with the doctrine of the Trinity. Also of interest, in the flow of Musculus' argument is his adoption of the scholastic order of discussion — *An, Quid,* and *Qualis sit?* — with the understanding of the doctrine of the Trinity as corresponding to the question of "what sort?" or *qualis.*[39]

Also of considerable significance as an indication of the direction taken by the Protestant doctrine of the Trinity during the era of the Reformation is Hutchinson's *The Image of God, or laie mans booke,* published in London in 1550.[40] In his dedicatory epistle to Archbishop Cranmer, Hutchinson explains that the first part of the title, "Image of God," is a direct reference to Christ, "the lively image of the divine majesty." The treatise is intended as an instruction in the truth of God, given that "this is eternal life, to know thee and Jesus Christ whom thou hast sent, to be the true God" (Jn. 17:3). He subjoins the phrase "the laie mans booke," inasmuch as "images were wont to be named *Libri Laicorum,* 'the books of the laity,'" and this image or book is intended for their edification.[41] Rather than present either a book simply about Christ as image

---

35. Bullinger, *Decades,* IV.iii (pp. 154-156): e.g., Deut. 6:4-5 (cf. Mark. 12:29-30); Exod. 20:2-3; Deut. 32:39; Ps. 18:30-31; Is. 42:8; 44:6; 45:6-7; 1 Tim. 2:5; Eph. 4:5-6; 1 Cor. 8:4-6.

36. Bullinger, *The Old Faith, an Evident Probacion out of the Holy Scripture, that the Christen Fayth ... hath Endured sens the Beginning of the Worlde* (1547), trans. Myles Coverdale (Cambridge: Cambridge University Press, 1844), pp. 53, 57.

37. Bullinger, *Decades,* IV.iii (p. 156).

38. Hyperius, *Methodus theologiae,* I (pp. 109-111).

39. Musculus, *Loci communes,* i-iii (*Commonplaces,* pp. 1-18); cf. the discussion in *PRRD,* III, 3.1 (A.2).

40. Roger, Hutchinson, *The Image of God, or Laie Mans Book, in whych the Right Knowledge of God is Disclosed* (London: John Day, 1550); also, in *The Works of Roger Hutchinson* (Cambridge: Cambridge University Press, 1842), pp. 1-208.

41. Hutchinson, *Image of God,* pp. 2-3.

of God or a broad primer of all things having to do with Christ and salvation, Hutchinson's focus is on the true doctrine concerning God, specifically, the God revealed in Christ, namely, the Trinity. The volume serves as an introduction to the doctrine of God, in which an initial series of nineteen chapters deal with God and his attributes and then a set of eleven subsequent chapters present, in order, a definition of "person," an argument "that there be three [divine] persons," and a conclusion teaching "that all three are but one God." The whole work is characterized by consistent and massive biblical referencing of the doctrine and by recourse to patristic definition and terminology concerning the Trinity. Equally of interest is Hutchinson's assumption, clarified in detail throughout the book, that all of the major heresies are rooted in misunderstandings of the doctrine of the Trinity — whether Arianism, Manicheeism, transubstantiation, the mass, "popish" priesthood, the Libertines, anthropomorphism, Origenistic apocatastasis, Epicureanism, astrology, or a host of others. In contrast to works from the earliest stages of the Reformation, this is a major elaboration of doctrine, as well as a significant testimony to Protestant appropriation of the tradition of the church.

The documents and the dogmatic queries of the Reformation, therefore, stand in a direct and positive relationship to the later development of a traditional or classical trinitarian theory by the Protestant orthodoxy. In fact, the statements of Bullinger concerning the difference between attributes relating to the divine operations *ad extra* and the personal characteristics of the Father, Son, and Spirit clearly presume a larger systematic context, such as would later be developed by the early orthodox writers. Still, the Reformers' doctrine of the Trinity is characterized more by a fundamental biblicism than by an overt recourse to traditionary norms. Despite the genuine connections between the Reformers' views on the Trinity and the earlier Western tradition of trinitarian theology, their primary point of reference in arguing the doctrine of the Trinity was Scripture, not tradition. Thus, the various elements of trinitarian theology that the Reformers drew from the tradition were nevertheless justified by them, not on the basis of the tradition, but on the basis of the exegesis of Scripture. This approach is, of course, precisely what ought to be expected, given the biblical norm argued by the Reformers — but it still marks a shift in the argumentation of doctrine, given the Reformers' heightened sensibility concerning the potential disagreement between the tradition (or aspect of it) and the text of Scripture.

The character of early Reformation trinitarianism, then, as defined by the Reformers sense of the subordination of tradition to the scriptural norm, creates difficulties for the analysis of the doctrine and its development — difficulties that become all the more apparent when studies of the issue take on a dogmatic form. Thus, the hesitance of the Reformers concerning doctrines and terms that were not explicitly announced in the pages of Scripture speaks against the attempt of recent writers like Torrance and Butin to understand Trinity as the central motif of Calvin's theology.[42] Similarly,

---

42. Thomas F. Torrance, "Calvin's Doctrine of the Trinity," in *Calvin Theological Journal*, 25/2 (November 1990), pp. 165-193; Philip W. Butin, *Revelation, Redemption, and Response: Calvin's*

the vagueness and the hesitance of the Reformers concerning the adoption (or adaptation) of patristic language as absolutely normative, coupled with their stated abhorrence for the kind of speculation implied by patristic trinitarian metaphors, renders nearly impossible any attempt to classify their trinitarian theology as either largely Latin or largely Greek in its patristic models. Of course, on this latter point, two opposing viewpoints are found in the literature. The classic essay by Warfield places Calvin very much in the line of Western, Latin trinitarianism, particularly in the line of Hilary and Augustine.[43] Others have voiced the thesis that Calvin's teaching had a modalistic tendency.[44] More recently, Torrance has attempted to identify Calvin as holding a fundamentally Greek patristic perspective, in the line of Athanasius and the Cappadocian fathers, notably, Gregory of Nazianzen. The connection, however, is tenuous; Torrance even tries to argue that Calvin's use of Augustine draws on places in Augustine's *De trinitate* where the influence of Nazianzen must be hypothesized.[45]

Trinitarian Understanding of the Divine-Human Relationship (New York: Oxford University Press, 1995).

43. Benjamin B. Warfield, "Calvin's Doctrine of the Trinity," in *Calvin and Augustine*, ed. Samuel Craig (Philadelphia: Presbyterian & Reformed Publishing Company, 1956), pp. 189-284; similarly, Shedd, *History of Christian Doctrine*, I, p. 380. Also see Allan M. Harman, "Speech about the Trinity, with Special Reference to Novatian, Hilary, and Calvin," in *Scottish Journal of Theology*, 26 (1973), pp. 385-400; B. Engelbrecht, "The Problem of the Concept of the 'Personality' of the Holy Spirit According to Calvin," in *Calvinus Reformator: His Contribution to Theology, Church and Society* (Potchefstroom: Potchefstroom University, Institute for Reformational Studies, 1982), pp. 201-216; and David J. Engelsma, "Calvin's Doctrine of the Trinity," in *Protestant Reformed Theological Journal*, 23 (1989), pp. 19-37.

44. Thus, Karl Barth, *The Theology of John Calvin*, trans. Geoffrey W. Bromiley (Grand Rapids: Eerdmans, 1995), pp. 310-313, 326-328; Werner Krusche, *Das Wirken des Heiligen Geistes nach Calvin* (Göttingen: Vandenhoeck & Ruprecht, 1957), pp. 5-10; Courth, *Trinität. Von der Reformation bis zur Gegenwart*, pp. 24, 28. The issue is taken up and the scholarship surveyed in Hans Esser, "Hat Calvin eine 'leise modalisierende Trinitätslehre'?" in *Calvinus theologus: Notes of the European Congress on Calvin Research*, ed. Wilhelm Neuser (Neukirchen: Neukirchner Verlag, 1974), pp. 113-129, with the conclusion that the contention lacks merit.

45. Torrance, "Calvin's Doctrine of the Trinity," pp. 165-193, especially p. 179, and idem, "The Doctrine of the Holy Trinity: Gregory of Nazianzen and John Calvin," in *Calvin Studies V*, ed. John H. Leith (Davidson, N.C.: Davidson College, 1990), pp. 7-19; also printed in *Sobornost*, 12 (1990), pp. 7-24. Cf. the similar conclusion in Christoph Schwöbel, "The Triune God of Grace: The Doctrine of the Trinity in the Theology of the Reformers," in *The Christian Understanding of God Today*, ed. James M. Byrne (Dublin: Columbia Press, 1993), p. 51. Torrance's arguments ought to be regarded more as an attempt to claim a particular theological heritage for twentieth-century neoorthodoxy than as serious historical scholarship. Typical is his claim that "It was well known during the Reformation that in his doctrine of the Trinity Calvin took his cue from Gregory the Theologian — that is why Melanchthon nicknamed Calvin 'the Theologian' after Gregory" (T. F. Torrance, "The Distinctive Character of the Reformed Tradition," in *Reformed Review*, 54/1 (Autumn, 2000), p. 7; cf. "Calvin's Doctrine of the Trinity," p. 179): these assertions amount to little more than wishful thinking on Torrance's part. The Melanchthonian reference to Calvin as "Theologian" comes from Beza's *Life of Calvin*, with reference to the Ratisbon Colloquy of 1541, and offers no reason for the title other than Melanchthon's respect for Calvin — there is no evidence that this was a reference to Gregory as there is no evidence that anyone during the Reformation understood Calvin as resting

The difficulty here is in ascertaining Calvin's underlying patristic preference (if indeed there is one to be found) from a pattern of citation intended, most probably, to cite authorities for the sake of establishing orthodoxy rather than for the sake of identifying or defining a distinct trajectory of thought within the broad spectrum of orthodox statement. If, moreover, the explicit use of a particular father or set of fathers indicates any particular preference in patristic thought, Calvin is certainly Western, Latin, and Augustinian in his perspective. The parallel between Augustine and Nazianzen, rather than indicating a hidden reliance on the latter, documents a greater continuity between Augustine and the Greek fathers than some writers, including Torrance, would like to allow.

There is a similar problem in the identification of the medieval background: the Reformers, as explicitly indicated by Bucer in his comments on the Schmalkald Articles, tended to reject the language of medieval theologians like Aquinas and Bonaventure, who attempted to clarify the doctrine of the Trinity by adding terms like *processiones* and *notiones*. Neither the terminological developments nor the speculative elaboration of Augustinian metaphors characteristic of the medieval doctors' approach to the doctrine of the Trinity carried over into the Reformation, and although the scholastic terminology reappears among the Reformed orthodox, very little of the medieval speculation ever made its way into the Protestant orthodox doctrine. It is, therefore, virtually impossible to identify medieval antecedents to Protestant trinitarianism: Torrance's attempts to associate Calvin's work with the thought of Richard of St. Victor, merely on the basis of Calvin's apparently non-Boethian understanding of *persona*, are particularly vacuous:[46] Calvin does not, after all, use Richard's (or Scotus') definition of person as "divinae naturae incommunicabilis existentia," nor does his text offer any explicit or implicit indications of an attempt to read the Victorine model through the thought of Athanasius, Gregory of Nazianzen, and Cyril of Alexandria. It is a far more likely explanation of Calvin's usage that it represents a combination of his association of *persona* with the preferred Augustinian term, *subsistentia*, and his encounter with late medieval and early sixteenth-century theological language, of unspecified origin, in which the medieval debates over the implications of *persona* were reflected.

It is highly probable that the immediate source of Calvin's definition of *persona* (first found in the 1559 *Institutes*) was the *Loci communes* of Melanchthon, where (from 1543 onward) the traditional Latin definition of "person" as "substantia individua" is noted and then immediately qualified with the explanation of the "hypostases" or persons as "three genuine subsistences."[47] Calvin's own definition of person as "a subsistence in God's essence, which while related to the others, is distinguished by an incommunicable quality," avoids the difficulty of the Boethian definition and

---

his trinitarian theology primarily on Gregory of Nazianzen.

46. See Torrance, "Calvin's Doctrine of the Trinity," p. 172.

47. Melanchthon, *Loci communes* (1543), in CR, 21, col. 613. On Calvin's method and on the impact of Melanchthon on Calvin, see Richard A. Muller, *The Unaccommodated Calvin: Studies in the Formation of a Theological Tradition* (New York: Oxford University Press, 2000), pp. 99-158.

consistently uses *essentia* rather than *substantia* to indicate the oneness of God. Calvin also declares categorically "by the term 'subsistence' we would understand something difference from 'essence.'" Calvin goes on to argue that each of the subsistences is "related to the others" but "distinguished by a special quality."[48] Calvin reinforces this latter point in a subsequent comment on the relationships between the Father, the Son, and the Spirit:

> in each hypostasis, the whole divine nature is understood, with this qualification — that to each belongs his own peculiar quality. ... And ecclesiastical writers do not concede that the one is separated from the other by any difference of essence. By these appellations which set forth the distinction (says Augustine) is signified their mutual relationships and not the very substance by which they are one.[49]

Calvin thus, arguably, reflects much of the distinctively Western or Latin development of the doctrine of the Trinity and in fact offers a definition that is as much or more like the variant definitions provided by Aquinas than any of the Victorine or Scotist definitions.[50]

There is also, embedded in Calvin's definition, a strong reflection of the dictum, characteristic of Western trinitarianism since Anselm, that the distinctions between the persons are relations of opposition — as also the assumption, emphasized by Lombard and ensconced in the formula of the Fourth Lateran Council, that divine essence is unoriginated and unbegotten.[51] What is more, given Calvin's adherence to the *filioque* and his impassioned defense of the aseity of the Son, his trinitarian thought, like that of the Reformed tradition in general, follows out a fully Western or Latin paradigm, in the trajectory of the decisions of the several medieval councils and the later medieval writers, but lacking any interest in the more speculative elements of the medieval development. The hypothesis of Torrance that Victorine and Scotistic conceptions were mediated to Calvin by John Maior and then revised or modified by specifically Greek trinitarian notions is indefensible — as is the contention that there are modalistic tendencies in Calvin's thought.

B. Antitrinitarianism in the Era of the Reformation

1. The sources and context of sixteenth-century antitrinitarianism. Over against the magisterial Reformers and the Roman Catholic theologians of the day, theologians like Michael Servetus, Giovanni Blandrata, Valentine Gentile, and Laelius and Faustus Socinus examined the text of Scripture in a strictly linguistic and non-traditionary exegesis and found no doctrine of the Trinity: on the one hand, in the name of a return to the original message of Jesus they and their followers leveled a biblical critique against

---

48. Calvin, *Institutes*, I.xiii.6.
49. Calvin, *Institutes*, I.xiii.19.
50. Cf. the observations in Villanova, *Histoire des théologie chréstiennes*, II, p. 379.
51. Calvin, *Institutes*, I.xiii.25; cf. the comments in Shedd, *History of Christian Doctrine*, I, p. 381; this is also the conclusion of Wendel, *Calvin*, p. 167, n. 54.

the traditional churchly doctrine of the one divine essence and three divine persons. On the other hand, looking at the writings of the earliest church fathers, they could argue no clear doctrine of the Trinity. Servetus in particular argued the case for a pre-Nicene, non-trinitarian view — with the result that his theology and that of other antitrinitarians looked like nothing so much as a reprise of ancient heresies. It is difficult to identify the sources or grounds for these views. On the one hand, they can be explained as a coalescence of the humanistic philological techniques of the Renaissance with the rather typical Renaissance humanistic polemic against the scholastic tradition, here extended to the more intricate dogmatic developments of the late patristic period — and with a radical, a-traditional version of the Renaissance *ad fontes* and the Reformers' *sola Scriptura*. That scholarly advocate of the antitrinitarians, E. M. Wilbur, could claim that their theology was merely a natural outgrowth of early Reformation thought and, in fact, evidence that the antitrinitarians, unlike the Reformers, followed out the implications of their reformist position to its logical conclusions.[52] Certainly, the antitrinitarian position is characterized by a radical biblicism coupled with a renunciation of traditional Christian and philosophical understandings of substance, person, subsistence, and so forth, as unbiblical accretions. Yet, it is also hardly the case that the antitrinitarian stress on the utter and absolute unity of God to the exclusion of personal distinctions in the divine essence was utterly a-philosophical and simply a return to the basic biblical message, as one recent writer has proposed.[53]

2. The theology of Michael Servetus. Although not the earliest of the sixteenth-century antitrinitarians, and not the inspiration of what could be called a "movement," Michael Servetus was certainly the most significant early exponent of the teaching.[54] A Spaniard by birth, Servetus was highly educated, competent in the classical and biblical languages, and well versed in the writings of the fathers. He studied law at Toulouse. His chief work, the *Christianismi restitutio*, in which he offered a biblical and patristic exposition of his teaching, presented for the sake, as his title indicates, of restoring Christianity to its pristine form, together with a series of letters arguing his views against Calvin.[55] Servetus' *Restitutio*, a vast work of over seven hundred pages,

---

52. Wilbur, *History of Unitarianism*, I, pp. 12-18.

53. Antonio Rotondo, *Calvin and the Italian Anti-trinitarians*, trans. John and Anne Tedeschi, vol 2 of *Reformation Studies and Essays* (St. Louis: Foundation for Reformation Research, 1968), pp. 21-25; cf. the balanced assessment in Aart de Groot, "L'antitrinitarisme socinien," in *Études theologiques et religieuses*, 61 (1986), pp. 55-56.

54. Wilbur, *History of Unitarianism*, I, pp. 49-75; 113-212; also, Jerome Friedman, *Michael Servetus: A Case-Study in Total Heresy* (Geneva: Droz, 1978); Francisco Sanchez-Blanco, *Michael Servets Kritik an der Trinitätslehre: philos. Implicationen u. histor. Auswirkungen* (Frankfurt: Lang, 1977); also, among the older literature, Émile Saisset, "Doctrine philosophique et religieuse de Michel Servet," in *Revue des deux mondes*, 21/4 (1848), pp. 586-618; idem, "Le procès et la mort de Michel Servet," in *Revue des deux mondes*, 21/5 (1848), pp. 818-848; L. Cologny, *L'antitrinitarisme à Genève au temps de Calvin: étude historique* (Geneva: Tappoiner & Studer, 1873); and Jean Geymonat, *Michel Servet et ses idées religieuses* (Geneva: Carey, 1892).

55. Michael Servetus, *Christianismi restitutio. Totius ecclesiae apostolicae est ad sua limina vocatio, in integrum restituta cognitione Dei, fidei Christi...* (Vienne: s.n., 1553); also see *The Two Treatises of*

proposed the entire recasting of Christianity — the doctrines of God, Christ, justification, regeneration, baptism, and the Lord's Supper. The first portion, a discourse and dialogues against the Trinity, in seven books, echoes and expands an earlier work of Servetus.[56]

The roots of Servetus' doctrine of God are not only in his revisionist reading of Scripture and the fathers, but also and perhaps preeminently in his nearly pantheistic philosophy, drawn in part from a reading of the Hermetica — which, it should be noted, represent an ante-Nicene form of classical religious philosophy, akin in many ways to middle Platonism, although in the sixteenth century, typically understood as contemporary with Moses.[57] Servetus describes God as incomprehensible, radically transcendent, imparting existence to all things by communicating his essence to them and containing them in himself. There is a divine trinity of sorts in Servetus' theology — the Father alone is truly God, Jesus of Nazareth is the Son of God, given his supernatural origin, and the Holy Spirit is the power of God directed toward human beings. Servetus denies the appropriateness of the terms Trinity, person, essence, and hypostasis in describing the Godhead and speaks only of a threefold manifestation of God as Father, God in Christ, and God as the power of the Spirit. Beyond the fundamental resemblance between Servetus' view of the Trinity and the doctrines soon to be developed by the Socinians, there is a highly significant appropriation of patristic and classical materials implied in these teachings: Servetus, like later Socinians, held to an erosion of biblical truth during the patristic period and gravitated toward the pre-Nicene fathers as a source for his doctrine of God. Servetus marks, therefore, not only the beginnings of the sixteenth and seventeenth-century dogmatic battle over the Trinity but also the beginnings of the debate over the assessment and appropriation of the early tradition.

3. The "Italian antitrinitarians." A group of Italian antitrinitarians, Blandrata, Gentile, and Alciati, all took some inspiration from the humanist and jurist Matteo Gribaldi as well as from Servetus.[58] The nature of the connection between Gribaldi and the other "Italian antitrinitarians" is unclear: Gribaldi had been in contact with the Italian refugee congregation in Geneva and had expressed his views on the unity of God to members of the congregation, and he was certainly well known to Blandrata, Gentile, and Alciati, whose antitrinitarian speculations followed on his own within a few years. After serving on the law faculty at Padua from 1548 to 1555, Gribaldi

---

Servetus on the Trinity, trans. E. M. Wilbur (Cambridge, Mass.: Harvard University Press, 1932). Servetus' doctrine is summarized in R. Willis, *Servetus and Calvin* (London: Henry King, 1877).

56. Michael Servetus, *De Trinitatis erroribus, libri septem* (N.p.: s.n., 1531).

57. Saisset, "Doctrine philosophique et religieuse de Michel Servet," pp. 586-618. On the history of reception of the Hermetic literature, see Brian P. Copenhaver, *Hermetica* (Cambridge: Cambridge University Press, 1992), pp. xlvii-li.

58. See Rotondo, *Calvin and the Italian Anti-trinitarians*, and Wilbur, *History of Unitarianism*, I, pp. 211-38, where the impact of Servetus is minimized; and note the critique in Jerome Friedman, "Servetus and Anti-trinitarianism: à propos Antonio Rotondo," in *Bibliothèque d'Humanisme et Renaissance*, 35 (1973), pp. 543-545.

left Italy under suspicion of Protestant sympathies for his estate at Farges in the canton of Bern and, eventually, a post at the University of Tübingen. As early as 1553, while living on his Swiss lands, Gribaldi had expressed sympathy with Servetus' theology. On a visit to Geneva in 1554, he was suspected of antitrinitarian views. The Genevan consistory questioned him but, because his estate was in Bernese territory, merely criticized his views and proceeded no further. He appears to have held that the Father alone was self-existent God, while the Son and the Spirit subsist as distinct persons by reason of their derivation from the Father. Gribaldi concluded, moreover, that each of these "persons" was divine and therefore God, with the Father as the head or primary deity of the three. The unity of God was maintained by Gribaldi in a generic sense, given the unity of power and wisdom in all three persons.[59]

Gianpaulo Alciati, Giorgio Blandrata, and Giovanni Valentin Gentile were all educated Italians who fled to Geneva to avoid persecution, Alciati arriving in 1552, the others in 1556. By 1558, the Consistory was troubled enough by their views that it demanded that all members of the Italian congregation sign a confession of faith. Alciati is reported to have identified the persons of the Trinity as "three devils ... worse than all the idols of the papacy."[60] With the norm of the confession in place, Alciati, Blandrata, and Gentile were condemned and forced to leave Geneva. Calvin published a short treatise responding specifically to Blandrata's questions.[61]

Gentile, whose trial had been longer and more complex than Alciati's or Blandrata's, criticized the trinitarianism of Calvin's *Institutes* in 1559 — Calvin replied with his *Impietas Valentini Gentilis detecta*, in which Calvin not only responded to Gentile's theology but also recounted the debates of 1558. Gentile's doctrine was very much like that of Gribaldi — asserting the self-existence of the Father alone and the derivation of the other persons from the Father. Gentile also believed that any assertion of the ultimate sharing of a single essence by the persons led to the conclusion that there was a divine quaternity, namely, the ultimate essence itself, distinct from the persons, and then the three persons partaking of the essence, a view that he ascribed to Calvin. Gentile's doctrine of God, by contrast, argues three distinct persons, each identified as divine, but differing in order, rank, and individual properties.[62] Thus, the Father alone is *autotheos* (God of himself), *agennetos* (unbegotten), and the ultimate *essentiator* or giver of being. The Son is *deuterotheos* and *heterotheos* (a second or other God), not of himself but of the Father, and therefore not *essentiator* but *essentiatus*, made or created. The Spirit, similarly, is distinct and derived — so that there is not

---

59. Wilbur, *History of Unitarianism*, I, p. 222.

60. Cited in Wilbur, *History of Unitarianism*, I, p. 227.

61. Jean Calvin, *Responsionum ad quaestiones Georgii Blandratae* (Geneva, 1558); and see Joseph Tylenda, "The Warning That Went Unheeded: John Calvin on Giorgio Biandrata," in *Calvin Theological Journal*, 12 (1977), pp. 24-62.

62. Gentile's trials and teachings are summarized in Benedict Aretius, *Valentini Gentilis iusto capitis supplicio Bernae affecti brevis historia & contra eiusdem blasphemias defensio articuli de sancta Trinitate* (Geneva, 1567), translated as *A Short History of Valentinus Gentilis the Tritheist* (London, 1696); see pp. 40-41.

"one God" (*unus Deus*) in the numerical sense, but rather a generic oneness of nature, given the source of the Son and Spirit in the work of the Father. Gentile could write of a single divine nature or essence, a single generic Godhead, but his sense of the term did not allow any conception of an indivisible divine substance held in common by the three persons.[63] Gentile was executed for heresy in Bern in 1566.

By far the greater development of sixteenth-century antitrinitarianism took place in Poland, where the influence of the Italian antitrinitarians was most strongly felt. Blandrata, Alciati, and Gentile all journeyed there, as did Laelius Socinus and Bernardino Ochino. In addition, Petrus Gonesius (ca. 1530-ca. 1571), author of the first significant antitrinitarian confession to be presented in Poland, is thought to have been associated with Gribaldi in Padua.[64] Gonesius confessed the authority of Scripture as the norm for Christian doctrine and insisted that Scripture taught the oneness of God. This God, who is one in essence and person, created the world by means of his Son, who was created by him out of his essence for the sake of his creative work. The Son is, therefore, distinct from and subordinate to the Father and not, in the strictest sense, God. As Wilbur points out, Gonesius' doctrine is not exactly Arian, inasmuch as he does not teach the creation of the Son out of nothing.[65]

The theology of the two Socini, Laelio and Fausto, needs also to be considered here.[66] Laelio Socinus, an Italian refugee and correspondent with Bullinger and Calvin, may have been connected with radical theologies in Italy prior to his flight to Switzerland and was, in 1555, while in Zürich, accused of false teaching. He then wrote a confession of faith, on the basis of which he was exonerated.[67] He subsequently visited Poland with the written recommendations of Calvin and Bullinger to various supporters of reform, including Johannes à Lasco. His connection with the antitrinitarian movement and identification as its founder rests with the work of his nephew, Fausto Socinus, who inherited his uncle's unpublished manuscripts and eventually provided the foundational theology for the Polish Unitarians of the late sixteenth and seventeenth centuries.

Like the other Italian antitrinitarians and like Servetus, Fausto Socinus insisted on the radical oneness of God — one in essence and in person — and viewed the doctrine of the Trinity as without any biblical foundation. Still, as several recent scholars have pointed out, Socinus distanced himself and his views enough from the teachings of Servetus and of Gentile, and the notion of a simple linear historical development from Servetus, to Alciati, Blandrata, and Gentile, to Lelio Socinus, and

---

63. Aretius, *Short History*, pp. 42-46.

64. Cf. Wilbur, *History of Unitarianism*, I, p. 286; also see Nancy Conradt, "John Calvin, Theodore Beza, and the Reformation in Poland" (Ph.D. diss.: University of Wisconsin, 1974).

65. Petrus Gonesius (Conedzius), *Doctrina pura et clara* (Kiszka, 1570), summarized in Wilbur, *History of Unitarianism*, I, pp. 291-292.

66. See Wilbur, *History of Unitarianism*, I, pp. 239-247 (Lelio); 387-395 (Fausto), 408-419 (Racovian Catechism).

67. See the translation in Edward M. Hulme, "Lelio Sozzini's Confession of Faith," in *Persecution and Liberty: Essays in Honor of George Lincoln Burr* (New York: Century, 1931), pp. 211-225.

then to Fausto Socinus, is an oversimplification of the history — just as there is, early on in the antitrinitarian movement of the sixteenth century, reason to distinguish between the quasi-trithesitic views of Gentile and the radically monotheistic adoptionism of the Socini.[68]

Perhaps because of very specified acceptance of the Boethian definition of person, Socinus held that inasmuch as a person is "an indivisible, intelligent essence," unity of essence implies singleness of person.[69] So also did he identify the Holy Spirit as the power of God and not as a distinct person. Where he offered a teaching that was original was in his Christology: he understood Jesus Christ as fully human but miraculously conceived by the divine Spirit. This conception is the ground of our identification of Christ as the Son of God. Socinus steps beyond the other early antitrinitarians in denying even a subordinate deity to Christ, offering a radically consistent monotheism of God the Father.

Despite differences in doctrinal result, a common thread runs through the various antitrinitarian arguments. The theology of these antitrinitarians must not be confused, as it frequently has been in the past, with an incipient rationalism. Virtually all of the sixteenth century antitrinitarians were biblicists. They lacked not a reverence for the text as the norm of doctrine but rather a traditionary norm for the regulation of their exegesis. They believed quite strongly that they had simply taken the next logical step beyond that of the Reformers: they accepted the Reformers' attack in the name of *sola Scriptura* on the doctrinal accretions characteristic of medieval theology and turned the new, non-allegorical, textual, and literal exegesis on a wider array of traditional dogmas, most notably, the doctrine of Christ and the doctrine of the Trinity. Like the early Reformers, moreover, they were reluctant to use non-biblical language in the formulation of normative doctrine — although they invariably radicalized the point: whereas Calvin, for example, readily admitted that the trinitarian vocabulary was not strictly biblical while at the same time recognizing its usefulness against heresy, the antitrinitarian writers, from Servetus and Gentile to the Socini, were convinced that the non-biblical language was to be utterly excluded and, by way of extension of the point, that several of the early heresies were closer to the truth than Niceno-Constantinopolitan orthodoxy.

---

68. Cf. R. Friedmann, "The Encounter of Anabaptists and Mennonites with Anti-trinitarians," in *Mennonite Quarterly Review*, XXII (1948), pp. 139-162 and Rotondo, *Calvin and the Italian Anti-trinitarians*, pp. 5-10.

69. *The Racovian catechisme: wherein you have the substance of the confession of those churches, which in the kingdom of Poland and Great Dukedome of Lithuania, and other provinces appertaining to that kingdom, do affirm, that no other save the Father of our Lord Jesus Christ, is that one God of Israel, and that the man Jesus of Nazareth, who was born of the Virgin, and no other besides, or before him, is the onely begotten Sonne of God* (Amsterdam: For Brooer Janz, 1652), qq. 21-23. Also note, *The Racovian Catechism*, with notes and illustrations, trans. Thomas Rees (London: Longman, Hurst, 1818). The Rees edition is useful inasmuch as it gathers into its apparatus various seventeenth-century additions to the text from the Socinian literature of the day.

C. In Debate with the Antitrinitarians: Further Developments in Reformation-Era Trinitarianism

The fully developed use of traditional trinitarian language in the work of second-generation Reformers like Calvin, Musculus, Vermigli, and Bullinger must also be understood against the background of the problem of antitrinitarianism. So also, in the development of Reformed theology, the model of development found in Melanchthon's *Loci communes* remains highly significant — Melanchthon's work was certainly of considerable influence on the expansion of Calvin's *Institutes*, and his theology was nearly as important to Reformed thought as was the work of any of the second-generation codifiers. Melanchthon's *Loci communes* of 1543 was one of the first Protestant systematic works to incorporate polemic against the antitrinitarians, specifically Servetus, into its definition and justification of the term "person."

One highly significant element of Calvin's trinitarian theology, enunciated primarily in polemic, whether early on defending his own orthodoxy against Caroli, Chapponeau, and Courtois or, in one of his last controversies, defending the trinitarianism of the Reformation against Blandrata and Gentile, is his understanding of the generation or origination of the Son from the Father in terms solely of the intra-trinitarian relation of begottenness and not in terms either of time or of being.[70] Calvin first argued this view in response to the critique of two pastors of Neufchâtel, Chaponneau and Courtois. From Calvin's perspective, these two pastors had not only misunderstood his teaching, they had also denied a fundamental premise of trinitarian orthodoxy, the self-existence or aseity of the Son.[71]

In response, Calvin interpreted the words of the Apostle Paul, "in Him dwelleth the fulness of the Godhead" (Col. 1:19), to mean that "Christ, insofar as he is God" partakes fully of the divine essence.[72] Calvin certainly allowed some subordination in the order of the persons — but in order only, as indicated by the generation of the Son from the Father and by the procession of the Spirit from the Father and the Son, but he adamantly denied any subordination of divinity or essence. There is, after all, only one divinity, one divine essence, that belongs indivisibly and fully to each of the persons.[73] The only conclusion capable of being drawn from this doctrine is the self-existence, or aseity, of Christ insofar as he is divine — and the consequent distinction between speech about the Son as person and speech about the Son as God:

---

70. Calvin, *Institutes*, I.xiii.17-18.

71. Warfield, "Calvin's Doctrine of the Trinity," p. 237.

72. CO, XI, 560: "Quantum ad locum illum ubi quasi ex tripode haereticos pronunciat qui dicunt Christum, in quantum Deus est, a se ipso esse, facilis est responsio. Primum mihi respondent annon verus et perfectus Deus sit Christus? Nisi Dei essentiam partiri velit, totem in Christo fateri cogetur. Et Pauli expressa sunt verba: quod in eo habet plenitudo divinitatis. Iterum rogo, a se ipsane an aliunde sit illa divinitatis plenitudo? At obiicet, filium esse a patre. Quis negat? Id ego quidem libenter non modo semper confessus sum sed etiam praedicavi."

73. Calvin, *Institutes*, I.xiii.17-18; cf. Wilhelm Niesel, *The Theology of Calvin*, trans. Harold Knight (London: Lutterworth, 1956; repr. Grand Rapids: Baker Book House, 1980) p. 59; also note T. H. L. Parker, *Calvin: An Introduction to His Thought* (Louisville: Westminster/John Knox, 1995), pp. 31-32.

Truly this is where these donkeys are deceived: since they do not consider that the name of the Son is spoken of the person, and therefore is included in the predicament of relation, which relation has no place where we are speaking simply (*simpliciter*) of the divinity of Christ.[74]

This perspective on trinitarian language, identified by Calvin's use of such terms as *autotheos* and *aseitas* with reference to the divinity of Christ, remained a prominent feature of Calvin's trinitarianism as he continued to debate the issue of orthodoxy with Caroli.[75]

Calvin repeated his point with emphasis in a debate of 1558, in response to the anti-trinitarianism of Blandrata and Gentile. Gentile insisted that the begetting of the Son and the procession of the Spirit amounted to a radical subordination of the second and third persons, with the result that the Father alone is truly God: "The Father is a unique essence ... the Father is the only true God; it is he who gives his essence to the other persons of the Divinity."[76] Against Calvin's conception of full essential equality of the persons, Gentile argued that any such sharing of essence amounted to such an abstraction of essence from person that it implied a quaternity rather than a Trinity. Of course, Gentile was not defending a conception of divine Trinity: rather he argued that the unity of God and the distinction of the Persons could be maintained only by rejecting the notion of "Trinity" as unbiblical and by recognizing the subordination of the Son and Spirit to the Father.[77] Calvin's response not only affirmed the traditional doctrine of the Trinity, it also argued against any essential subordination of persons by allowing that the Father is the source only of the emanation of persons. Thus, "as to his essence, the Son is *absque principio*, while considered as to his person, he finds his *principium* in the Father."[78] This insistence on the begetting and procession of personal relations but not of divine essence became characteristic of a Calvinian line of Reformed orthodoxy, maintained in the next generation by Beza.[79]

---

74. CO, XI, 560: "Verum hoc est in quo asini isti falluntur: quia non considerant nomen filii dici de persona ideoque in praedicamento relationis contineri, quae relatio locum non habet ubi de Christi divinitate simpliciter agitur." Cf. Warfield, "Calvin's Doctrine of the Trinity," p. 238.

75. See John Calvin, *Pro G. Farello et collegis eius adversus Petri Caroli calumnias*, in CO 8, col. 289-340.

76. Cited by J. Gaberel, *Histoire de l'Église de Génève depuis le commencement de la Reformation jusqu'a nos jours*, 3 vols. (Geneva, 1858-1862), II, p. 227. A survey of these controversies is available in Rotondo, *Calvin and the Italian Anti-trinitarians*.

77. Gaberel, *Histoire*, II, p. 227.

78. *Expositio impietatis Valen. Gentilis* (1561), in CO, IX, 368: "Et certe non aliud fuit patrum consilium, nisi manere originem quam ducit a patre filius, personae respectu, nec obstare quominus eadem sit utriusque essentia et deitas: atque ita quoad essentiam, sermonem esse Deum absque principio: in persona autem filii habere principium a patre."

79. See Theodore Beza, *Quaestionum et responsionum christianarum libellus, in quo praecipua christianae religionis capita kat epitome proponunter* (Geneva, 1570; second part, Geneva, 1576), in translation, *A Booke of Christian Questions and Answers* (London, 1572) and *The Other Parte of Christian Questions and answeres, which is Concerning the Sacraments* (London, 1580); also note Beza's *Confession de la foy chrestienne* (Geneva, 1558), in Latin, *Confessio christianae fidei, et eiusdem collatio*

D. The Trinitarian Orthodoxy of the Reformed Confessions

Given the orthodox and catholic intentions of the Reformation and the intense debate with antitrinitarians, the first codifiers of Reformation theology were drawn, at the confessional level, to the traditional trinitarian vocabulary and, in order to manifest the place and relation of trinitarian language in the doctrine of God, to fairly traditional language of the divine essence as well. Even more important to the issue of doctrinal formulation, moreover, is the assertion, repeated in the doctrinal writings of the individual authors and in the confessional documents as well, that these dogmatic concepts are eminently biblical in their meaning and intention despite the non-biblical origins of the language of person and substance or essence.

The Belgic Confession, like the Gallican, offers a full statement of the doctrine of the Trinity, under the rubric, "God Is One in Essence, yet Distinguished in Three Persons":

> According to this truth and this Word of God, we believe in one only God who is one single essence, in which are three persons, really (*réellement*), and in truth (*à la vérité*), and eternally distinguished (*éternellement distinguées*) according to their incommunicable properties; namely, the Father, and the Son, and the Holy Spirit. The Father is the cause, origin, and beginning of all things visible and invisible. The Son is the word, wisdom, and image of the Father. The Holy Spirit is the eternal power and might, proceeding from the Father and the Son. Nevertheless, God is not by this distinction divided into three, since the Holy Scriptures teach us that the Father, and the Son, and the Holy Spirit each has his person [rendered] distinct by their properties; but in such manner, always, that these three persons are but one only God. It is therefore evident that the Father is not the Son, nor the Son the Father, and likewise the Holy Spirit is neither the Father nor the Son. Nevertheless, these persons thus distinct are not divided, nor confounded, nor mingled; for the Father has not assumed the flesh, nor has the Holy Spirit, but the Son only. The Father has never been without His Son, or without His Holy Spirit. For They are all three co-eternal and co-essential. There is neither first nor last; for they are all three one, in truth, in power, in goodness, and in mercy.[80]

From a purely doctrinal perspective, the Second Helvetic Confession offers a similar basic statement of the doctrine, following a brief declaration of oneness of the divine essence and the unity of God over against the "multitude of gods" worshiped by the pagans. Bullinger did not hesitate present the standard language of patristic and medieval orthodoxy — namely distinction of persons without the division of the essence and the coequality, consubstantiality, and coeternity of the persons. As Staedke

cum Papisticis Haeresibus ... adjecta est altera brevis eiusdem Bezae fidei Confessio (Geneva, 1560; London, 1575). A further index to Beza's teaching can be found in *Propositions and Principles of Divinitie Propounded and Disputed in the University of Geneva.under M. Theod. Beza and M. Anthonie Faius*, trans. John Penry (Edinburgh, 1595).

80. Belgic Confession, VIII; cf. Gallican Confession, VI (in Schaff, *Creeds*, III, pp. 389, 362-363).

remarked, there are reminiscences of the Athanasian Creed in the Second Helvetic Confession and there is a clear declaration of the *filioque*.[81]

Not content with the basic doctrinal statement, the Belgic Confession continues its trinitarian exposition with an entire chapter devoted to the biblical foundations of the doctrine, another concerning the divinity of Christ, and yet another on the divinity of the Holy Spirit.[82] The biblical argumentation of the Belgic Confession is significant not only for its presence as a characteristic Reformation-era biblicism, indicating the unwillingness of the Reformers to confess as their fundamental faith a doctrine evidenced only by way of the probabilities of the tradition, but also given the confession's assumption that the doctrine of the Trinity belongs to both Testaments, having been given in a "somewhat obscure" form in the Old Testament and very plainly in the New Testament. The exposition is not lengthy: only two Old Testament passages are cited, namely, Genesis 1:26-27, with its divine plural, "Let us make man," and Genesis 3:22, "Behold the man has become as one of us." Of the numerous New Testament passages cited, it is worth noting that the Belgic Confession offers 1 John 5:7, the Johannine Comma, assuming its legitimacy as a canonical text.[83] Debate over the antiquity of the doctrine is not as evident in the Second Helvetic Confession, which does not cite Old Testament trinitarian texts — or, incidentally, the Johannine Comma.[84]

2.2 Formulation and Defense of the Doctrine of the Trinity in the Era of Protestant Orthodoxy

A. The Development of the Doctrine of the Trinity in Early Orthodoxy, 1565-1640

1. Positive doctrinal developments in the early orthodox era. As noted at the beginning of this chapter, the early orthodox development of the doctrine of the Trinity evidenced several major features: the ongoing and, in fact, intensifying debate with antitrinitarians; an increasingly exegetical approach to the doctrine; a pronounced identification of the doctrine of the Trinity as a "necessary" or "fundamental doctrine," both in relation to confessional or dogmatic concerns and in relation to piety; a broadened sense of the significance of the doctrine as a basis for understanding the divine operation in other doctrinal topics (notably predestination, the *ordo salutis*, and covenant); and the large-scale reception of the patristic tradition. The early orthodox development of the doctrine of the Trinity, then, continued the tendency of the Reformers to adopt and appropriate traditionary, particularly patristic materials and definitions in the exposition and defense of orthodoxy, in conjunction, however,

---

81. Second Helvetic Confession, III.iii; cf. Joachim Staedke, "Die Gotteslehre der *Confessio Helvetica posterior*," in *Glauben und Bekennen: Vierhundert Jahre Confessio Helvetica Posterior, Beiträge zu ihrer Geschichte und Theologie,* edited by J. Staedke (Zürich: Zwingli Verlag, 1966), pp. 253-256.

82. Belgic Confession, IX, X, and XI, respectively (in Schaff, *Creeds,* III, p. 390-395).

83. Belgic Confession, IX (in Schaff, *Creeds,* III, p. 390-391).

84. Second Helvetic Confession, III.4 (in Schaff, *Creeds,* III, p. 241)

with the reformulation of doctrine in a highly exegetical manner. In the compendia of the era, by such writers as Polanus, Ames, Bucanus, Ainsworth, Wollebius, and Alsted,[85] the definitions and structure of the doctrine are outlined and the exegetical background indicated by masses of references to the text of Scripture. In the larger dogmatic works, by writers like Zanchi, Ursinus,[86] and Polanus, both exegesis and patristic referencing are evident, given in full, in the body of the argument.

The Reformed orthodox, following out the lines of argument already established for Protestantism by the Reformers, adopted the basic positions of the Western trinitarian tradition, positions that assume the essential equality of the divine persons, double procession, and the removal of all subordination except in the order of the procession and operation of the persons. This fundamentally Augustinian model, ensconced in the medieval conciliar tradition and refined by the medieval doctors, can be found in short form in the thought of Calvin and his contemporaries and, much expanded and developed in the seventeenth-century debates, in the writings of the Reformed orthodox.

If the polemic against the various sixteenth-century antitrinitarians rested primarily on contention for traditional exegesis of trinitarian passages, the positive development of the doctrine, reaching perhaps its most elaborate formulation in Zanchi's *De tribus Elohim*,[87] brought with it also a return to the theological tradition, to the fathers and to the medieval theologians — and even to the classical philosophers — in the interest

---

85. William Ames, *Medulla ss. theologiae* (Amsterdam, 1623; London, 1630); also note, idem, *The Marrow of Theology*, trans. with intro. by John Dykstra Eusden (Boston: Pilgrim, 1966; repr. Durham, N.C.: Labyrinth Press, 1984); Gulielmus Bucanus, *Institutiones theologicae seu locorum communium christianae religionis* (Geneva, 1602); in translation, *Institutions of the Christian Religion, framed out of God's Word*, trans. R. Hill (London: G. Snowdon, 1606; London: Daniel Pakeman, 1659); Henry Ainsworth, *The Orthodox Foundation of Religion, long since collected by that judicious and elegant man Mr. Henry Ainsworth, for the benefit of his private company: and now divulged for the publike good of all that desire to know that Cornerstone Christ Jesus Crucified*, edited by Samuel White (London: R. C. for M. Sparke, 1641); Johannes Wollebius, *Compendium theologiae christianae* (Basel, 1626; Oxford, 1657); idem, *The Abridgement of Christian Divinitie*. Trans., with annotations by Alexander Ross (London: T. Mab and A. Coles, 1650); Johann Heinrich Alsted, *Methodus sacrosanctae theologiae octo libri tradita* (Hanau, 1614); idem, *Theologia catechetica, exhibens sacratiaaimam novitiolorum christianorum scholam, in qua summa fidei et operum ... exponitur* (Hanau, 1622); and idem, *Theologia didactica, exhibens locos communes theologicos methodo scholastica* (Hanau, 1618; second edition, 1627).

86. Most of Ursinus' works are gathered in *Opera theologica quibus orthodoxae religionis capita perspicue & breviter explicantur*, ed. Quirinius Reuter, 3 vols. (Heidelberg, 1612). The major doctrinal works are *Loci theologici*, in *Opera*, vol. 1; and the lectures on the Heidelberg Catechism. These lectures were first published as *Doctrinae christianae compendium* (Leiden: Iohannes Paetsius, 1584; also, Oxford, 1585), edited for inclusion in the *Opera* as *Explicationes catecheseos*, in *Opera*, vol. 1; and in translation, *The Commentary of Dr. Zacharias Ursinus on the Heidelberg Catechism*. Trans. G. W. Williard, intro. by John W. Nevin (Columbus, Ohio, 1852; repr. Phillipsburg, New Jersey: Presbyterian and Reformed Publishing Co., 1985), hereinafter cited as Ursinus, *Commentary*.

87. Jerome Zanchi, *De tribus Elohim*; also found in volume I of *Operum theologicorum D. Hieronymi Zanchii*, 8 vols. (Heidelberg: Stephanus Gamonetus and Matthaeus Berjon, 1605) and of *Operum theologicorum D. Hieronymi Zanchii*, 10 vols. in 9 (Geneva: Samuel Crispin, 1617-1619): part, book, and chapter citations apply to all three editions; pages are cited from the Geneva edition.

of establishing a correct use of the terminology of trinitarian doctrine in the exposition of its scriptural foundations. The work is significant for its exegetical (as opposed to more speculative) emphasis and for the fact that Zanchi placed it first in order in the model for his massive (and, unfortunately, never fulfilled system), before his discussion of the essence and attributes in the *De natura Dei*. This point is, unfortunately, ignored by most of the writers who have examined Zanchi's thought.[88] The work is divided into two parts, the former consisting in eight books, the latter in five. The exegetical emphasis immediately appears in the way in which Zanchi sets forth first his premises concerning the examination of the doctrine of God and his basic trinitarian definitions — deriving the unity of God from Jehovah, the Trinity from Elohim, presenting a series of texts from both Testaments that indicate the plurality of the Godhead as Father, Son, and Spirit, and then passing on in the six chapters of book one to traditionary trinitarian language. The remainder of the first part is fundamentally exegetical, reviewing the biblical basis for understanding the divinity and personhood of the Son (books II-VI) and the Spirit (book VII), followed by a concluding positive doctrine of the Trinity (book VIII). The second part of the treatise engages in debate with the ancient contemporary heretics and the antitrinitarians.

The large-scale development of the doctrine, with detailed recourse to Scripture and to the church fathers is also characteristic of Polanus' *Syntagma theologiae*, which (of the full-scale systematic works of the era) certainly contains the most extensive presentation of the doctrine of the Trinity. Polanus' work is notable for its grasp of the older tradition, both patristic and medieval. In its doctrine of the Trinity, the *Syntagma* draws most heavily on the church fathers, but it also evidences knowledge of the medieval discussion of the Trinity, notably the discussion of the concept of person.[89]

Bartholomaus Keckermann, one of the eminent philosophers and architectural framers of Reformed doctrine in the early orthodox period,[90] even went so far as to develop on Augustinian and Thomist lines a series of rational metaphors or arguments for the triune nature of God in his theological system. His approach was to draw on the view of God as exercising intellect and will and to associate Word with intellect and Spirit with will, particularly the will as exercised in an act of love. Few of the thinkers of the era of orthodox chose to follow Keckermann — with only the semi-Cartesian federalist Burman and the profoundly Cartesian Poiret building their

---

88. E.g., Otto Gründler, *Die Gotteslehre Girolami Zanchis und ihre Bedeutung für seine Lehre von der Prädestination* (Neukirchen: Neukirchner Verlag, 1965), a translation of Gründler's "Thomism and Calvinism in the Theology of Girolamo Zanchi (1516-1590)" (Th.D. diss., Princeton Theological Seminary, 1961).

89. Polanus, *Syntagma theologiae*, II.ii.

90. Bartholomaus Keckermann, *Systema sacrosanctae theologiae, tribus libris adornatum* (Heidelberg, 1602; Geneva, 1611) is also found in Keckermann's *Opera omnia quae extant*, 2 vols. (Geneva, 1614), appended to vol. II, separate pagination. On Keckermann's theology, see W. H. Zuylen, *Bartholomaus Keckermann: Sein Leben und Wirken* (Leipzig: Robert Noske, 1934); also see Richard A. Muller, *After Calvin: Studies in the Development of a Theological Tradition* (New York: Oxford University Press, 2003), pp. 122-136.

doctrines of the Trinity around a rational argument for divine threeness.[91] Still, Keckermann's reappropriation of the Augustinian and Thomistic lines of argument on the nature of the intra-trinitarian relations had a broader impact than merely the question of the rationality or provability of divine threeness — the language of the divine as mind considering itself as object and of the divine love as generating and contemplating its own image became fairly common among the later Reformed, and extended meditations on the divine love and on the identity of the Son as the object of God's love appear in Owen's trinitarian theology.[92]

Even though the larger number of theologians chose not to develop the more speculative trinitarian metaphors or rational arguments for the Trinity, the patristic materials became of increasing interest and were more closely scrutinized as sources of dogma and of dogmatic problems than they had been in the sixteenth century. This development, moreover, proceeded in two directions: it was both a characteristic of the Reformed assumption of catholicity as evidenced in the study and appropriation of patristic materials and a sign of engagement with the patristic (especially the pre-Nicene) argumentation of the various antitrinitarians of the age.[93] Thus, patristic meditation on the eternal Word, or Logos, in relation to the Father and, specifically, to the notion of an inward generation of begetting, becomes a major feature of the Reformed orthodox trinitarian definition, as found, for example in Polanus and the *Synopsis purioris theologiae*.[94]

In addition, following out the line of classical linguistic scholarship begun in the Renaissance and Reformation, the orthodox could not simply return to the uncritical use of patristic and scholastic terminology — rather the incorporation of terms like *ousia, hypostasis,* and *prosopon* in the Greek and *essentia, subsistentia,* and *persona* in Latin demanded careful etymological and philosophical analysis of the exact meaning of the words. This etymological interest remained typical of theologians of the seventeenth century like Polanus and Gomarus,[95] and in the era of high orthodoxy, Leigh, Marckius and Rijssen.[96] Beyond the etymological issues, early orthodox thinkers

---

91. See further below 3.1 (C.3-4).

92. Thus, John Owen, *ΧΡΙΣΤΟΛΟΓΙΑ*, in *The Works of John Owen*, ed. William H. Goold, 17 vols. (London and Edinburgh: Johnstone and Hunter, 1850-53), I, pp. 144-159.

93. On the Reformed orthodox use of patristic sources (with further bibliography) see Muller, *After Calvin*, chap. 3.

94. Polanus, *Syntagma theol.*, III.v (p. 206); *Synopsis purioris theologiae, disputationibus quinquaginta duabus comprehensa ac conscripta per Johannem Polyandrum, Andream Rivetum, Antonium Walaeum, Antonium Thysium* (Leiden, 1625; editio sexta, curavit et praefatus est Dr. H. Bavinck, Leiden: Donner, 1881), VIII.xvii; and see below 5.2 (B.2); 6.1 (B.2).

95. Franciscus Gomarus, *Disputations theologicae*, in *Opera theologica omnia*, 3 vols. (Amsterdam, 1644).

96. Edward Leigh, *A Treatise of Divinity* (London, 1646); idem, *A Systeme or Body of Divinity* (London, 1662); Johannes Marckius, *Christianae theologiae medulla didactico elenctica* (Amsterdam, 1690); idem, *Compendium theologiae christianae didactico-elencticum* (Groningen, 1686); Leonardus Rijssenius, *Summa theologiae didactico-elencticae* (Amsterdam, 1695; Edinburgh, 1698; Frankfurt and Leipzig, 1731).

like Polanus also drew heavily on patristic sources in order to define and nuance the doctrinal discussion of the generation of the Son and the Spirit.[97]

At the beginning of the seventeenth century, the doctrine of *aseitas* of the second person of the Trinity was an initial point of contention in the Arminian controversy,[98] and it remained a significant point of difference between Reformed and Remonstrant theology as the Remonstrants became increasingly subordinationistic in their views of the Trinity. The brief controversy over the Son's aseity between Arminius and his colleague Lucas Trelcatius, Jr., often forgotten because of the larger predestinarian debate of the era, registers how much in continuity the early orthodox writers were with the Reformers, specifically with Calvin, in their trinitarian thinking — just as it also measures the variety of formulation that could arise in the context of an early orthodoxy examining not only its immediate roots in the theology of the Reformers but also its more remote roots in the older tradition of doctrine, including the patristic period.

Arminius defined his trinitarian views more after the model of Greek patristic theology than after the Latin, Augustinian model. Arminius understands the *vita Dei*, or life of God, as the "very nature and form" of the divine essence and argues that God has life in himself, that is, has *aseitas* or is *autotheos*. The begetting of the Son by the Father should be understood as a generation of the Son's person by communication of essence and that, therefore, the attribute of self-existence, or *aseitas*, belonged to the Father exclusively. The Son, as derived, cannot be *autotheos*, except in the limited sense that the Son is "one who truly and in himself" is God — any claim that the Son is "one who is God from himself" is unacceptable.[99] A doctrine that makes such a claim implies three deities.[100] This charge, leveled against Trelcatius, resembles the complaint leveled by Gentilis against Calvin's doctrine of the aseity of the Son considered as to essence — and it also resembles Joachim of Flora's attack on Lombard. Trelcatius, by way of contrast, had affirmed that the begetting of the Son was a begetting or generation of sonship, so that the Son had his sonship from the Father — but he also had argued that the divine essence, belonging to the three persons in common, was itself ingenerate, and that the Son, considered essentially as God has the attribute of *aseity* as well.[101]

---

97. Polanus, *Syntagma theol.*, III.v, vi.

98. Cf. Richard A. Muller, "The Christological Problem in the Thought of Jacobus Arminius,"in *Nederlands Archief voor Kerkgeschiedenis*, vol. 68 (1988), pp. 145-163; cf. below 6.3 (B).

99. Jacob Arminius, *Apologia adversus articulos XXXI. in vulgos sparsos*, xxi, in Jacob Arminius, *Opera theologica* (Leiden, 1629), pp. 164-166.

100. Arminius, *Declaratio sententiae*, in *Opera*, pp. 100-102; cf. George P. Fisher, *History of Doctrine* (New York, 1896), p. 341.

101. Calvin argued in his *Expositio impietatis Valen. Gentilis* that, considered according to his essence, the Son is "absque principio" but considered according to his person, he has his *principium* in the Father (in *CO*, 9, col. 368); Ursinus similarly states that the divine essence, as possessed by each of the divine persons is from itself, whereas the persons of the Son and the Spirit are from the Father: see *Loci theologici*, in Zacharias Ursinus, *Opera theologica quibus orthodoxae religionis capita perspicue & breviter explicantur*, 3 vols., ed. Quirinius Reuter (Heidelberg, 1612), I, col. 540. Jerome

The controversy that ensued in the faculty at Leiden not only offered a prelude to the even more bitter debate that would arise shortly over grace and predestination, it also offered a prelude to the century-long debate between Reformed and Remonstrant over the doctrine of the Trinity. The question underlying the assignment of *aseitas* to the Father and the Son or, on the other side of the debate, strictly to the Father, was the question of precisely what is generated in the generation or begetting of the Son. In the traditional Western model, as argued by Peter Lombard and ratified in the Fourth Lateran Council, the divine essence neither generates nor is generated; rather the person of the Father generates the person of the Son — with the result that the Son, considered as to his sonship, is generated, but considered as to his essence is not. Or, to put the point another way, there is no essential difference between the Father and the Son, the only difference being the relation of opposition, namely, the begottenness of the Son. The Son, therefore, has all of the attributes of the divine essence, including aseity. The early orthodox Reformed maintained, in accord with Trelcatius, and with considerable nuance, this characteristic feature of Calvin's trinitarianism, the identification of the second person of the Trinity, considered as to essence, as *authotheos* or having the attribute of *aseitas*. Their doctrinal formulations of the point, moreover, evidence the early orthodox effort to reappropriate the teaching of the fathers in some depth as a basis for orthodoxy, despite their insistence that the patristic materials were not normative in any final sense.[102]

As in the case of other doctrinal *loci*, the *locus de Deo* and, specifically, the portion of the *locus* dealing with trinitarian issues was argued in a highly exegetical fashion by the early orthodox writers. Their use of exegetical argumentation, moreover, was grounded either in their own work as linguists and commentators or in the expanding exegetical tradition of Reformed Protestantism. Thus, among the British writers of the era, Ainsworth (already noted as the author of a short compendium of doctrine) worked primarily as an exegete.[103] Perkins, most significant for his doctrinal and casuistical treatises, was also a substantial commentator.[104] A similar pattern is

---

Zanchi makes the point that the Son is "autotheos" according to essence inasmuch as the divine essence is one and the same in all of the persons: see *De tribus Elohim*, in *Opera*, I, col. 540; and cf. the similar formulations in William Perkins, *A Golden Chaine*, in *The Workes of ... Mr. William Perkins*, 3 vols. (Cambridge, 1612-1619), I, pp. 14-15; idem, *An Exposition of the Symbole or Creed of the Apostles*, in *Workes*, I, pp. 176-177, 282; and Polanus, *Syntagma theologiae*, III.v, as discussed in Richard A. Muller, *Christ and the Decree: Christology and Predestination in Reformed Theology from Calvin to Perkins* (Durham, N.C.: Labyrinth Press, 1986; repr. Grand Rapids: Baker Book House, 1988), pp. 30-31, 100-101, 113-114, 152-161. Also see Warfield, "Calvin's Doctrine of the Trinity," pp. 233-243.

102. On this issue, see Jean Daillé, *De usu patrum* (1636), translated as *A Treatise of the Right Use of the Fathers in the Decision of Controversies Existing at this Day in Religion*, trans. T. Smith, edited, with a preface by G. Jekyll, 2nd ed. (London: Henry Bohn, 1843).

103. Henry Ainsworth, *Annotations upon the Five Books of Moses, the Book of Psalms, and the Song of Songs*, 7 vols. (London: Miles Flesher, 1626-27); reissued in 2 vols. (Edinburgh: Blackie & Sons, 1843), hereinafter cited as *Annotations upon Genesis*, *Annotations upon Exodus*, etc.

104. William Perkins, *A Clowd of Faithfull Witnesses ... a Commentarie Upon the Eleventh Chapter to the Hebrews* [and] *A Commentarie Upon Part of the Twelfth Chapter to the Hebrews*, in *Workes*, vol.

identifiable in the work of Franciscus Junius, who was known in his time both as a major linguist and exegete and as an eminent teacher of doctrinal theology.[105] As far as general method is concerned, the early orthodox commentators evidence, as did the Reformers before them, a sense of the relationship between the *sacra doctrina*, or sacred teaching, in Scripture and the task of doctrinal formulation that consistently asked the exegetical question of the precise, literal meaning of the text, but did so in the context of the broader scope of books in Scripture and of the Bible as a whole and of a concept of the analogy of faith. The result of this approach to the text, given the patterns of Renaissance logic and rhetoric in which the Reformed writers of the era were trained, led to the elicitation of topics or *loci* in which theological themes were elaborated based on exegetical collations from various places in Scripture.[106] With specific reference to the doctrine of the Trinity, the Reformed orthodox consistently raised broader doctrinal questions in their exegesis of texts that had, in the Christian tradition, become the basis for trinitarian formulation. Their exegesis manifests differences in the reading of Old Testament texts, differences relating to use of typological and figurative readings and to relative willingness to apply the broader results of the analogy of faith and the sense of the scope of the whole of Scripture, differences in the ways in which linguistic tools (including the use of Judaica) were drawn into the work of interpretation, and, therefore, as well, differences in the trinitarian understanding of the Old Testament, a matter of major debate during the seventeenth century. So also, in their approach to various New Testament texts, varied patterns of textual and exegetical analysis yielded differing readings and, in particular, varied approached to disputed texts.[107]

2. Early orthodoxy and the antitrinitarians. The attack leveled upon the doctrine of the Trinity, beginning with Servetus, Blandrata, and Gentile and developed further in the thought of the two Socini, brought increased dogmatic attention to the doctrine of the Trinity in the latter half of the sixteenth century. The character of the orthodox Protestant formulation, therefore, altered in this new context: the trinitarian theology of codifiers of the Reformation, like Calvin, Musculus, Bullinger, Vermigli, and Hyperius, had been formulated in the context of the beginnings of antitrinitarian debate and the need for Protestants to argue their own catholicity — but the trinitarian views of the next generations, the founders of early orthodoxy, was formulated not merely

---

III; idem, *An Exposition of the Five first Chapters of the Epistle to the Galatians: With the Continuation of the Commentary Upon the Sixth Chapter*, in *Workes*, vol. II.

105. FranciscusJunius, *Sacrorum parallelorum libri tres: id est comparatio locorum Scripturae sacrae, qui ex testamento vetere in Novo adducuntur*, second edition (London: G. Bishop, n.d.); idem, *The Apoclayps, or Revelation of S. John with a Brief Exposition* (Cambridge: John Legat, 1596).The major dogmatic works are *De vera theologia*; idem, *Theses theologicae quae in inclyta academia Ludgunobatava ad exercitia publicarum disputationum* [*Theses Leydenses*]; and idem, *Theses aliquot theologicae in Heidelbergensi academia disputatae* [*Theses Heidelbergenses*], in *Opuscula theologica selecta*, ed. Abraham Kuyper (Amsterdam: F. Muller, 1882), pp. 39-101, 103-289, 289-327, respectively. More detail on the commentators and their work can be found in *PRRD*, II, 7.1 (A.2).

106. See the discussion in *PRRD*, II, 7.4 (C.3-4); 7.5 (A-B).

107. See below 4.2 on the exegesis of various trinitarian texts.

over against the views of individual antitrinitarians but also over against the rise of antitrinitarian churches or movements in Poland and Hungary and against a major alteration of God-language that, in the seventeenth century, generated a host of speculative rejections not only of the traditional conception of God but also of the doctrine of the traditional forms of the Trinity.

Shortly after the middle of the century, as the Reformed church in Hungary was beginning to establish itself confessionally over against the Lutherans, debate began within the Reformed church over the doctrine of the Trinity. In 1561, a formal disputation on the doctrine was held between Peter Mélius, the Reformed pastor of Debreczen, and a minister, Thomas Aran, who had written an antitrinitarian book and had preached overtly against the Trinity in Debreczen. Suspicions were also raised concerning the views of one of the Hungarian church's own luminaries, Francis Dávid, who had engaged in theological conversations with Giovanni Blandrata, already known as an antitrinitarian. Peter Caroli, already known for his doubts about Calvin's orthodoxy, began to doubt Dávid's trinitarianism and, in 1565, found his suspicions confirmed in a brief debate.[108] In February of the following year, at the Synod of Torda, the trinitarian conflict came to the fore, beginning a debate that lasted until the Unitarians were granted ecclesial status by the Hungarian crown in 1571. Wilbur indicates that it was in the course of these debates that the term "Unitarian" arose as a name for the antitrinitarians, spreading to Polish Socinian and to English antitrinitarians only in the latter half of the seventeenth century, by way of Hungarian students in the Netherlands.[109]

The primary points in debate were the contentions of Blandrata and Dávid that the doctrines of the Trinity and of the deity of Christ were not biblical — as had been argued in a theological treatise written largely by Blandrata and Dávid.[110] In their view, Christ ought to be reverenced and even "adored" as the "Lord of all" who gives access to God the Father and who bestows the blessings of salvation on those who are his, yet not understood as essentially divine. Only the Father is the "Most High" God.[111] This approach still stood in close relation to that of the Polish antitrinitarians, who followed Socinus' teaching that, in view of the New Testament witness in such texts as Matthew 28:18, John 5:22-23, and Philippians 2:9-11, we may pray to Christ — although it is only commanded that we pray to God the Father. In the fully developed Unitarianism of his 1582 *Defensio*, Dávid argued, against Blandrata and Socinus, that

108. Peter Caroli, *Brevis explicatio orthodoxae fidei de uno Deo et Spiritu Sancto adversos blasphemos G. Blandratae et F. Davidis errores* (Wittenberg, 1571).

109. See the survey of the history in Wilbur, *History of Unitarianism*, II, pp. 28-49; on the term "Unitarian," see pp. 47-48, note 12.

110. Francis Dávid, et. al., *De falsa et vera unius Dei Patris, Filii et Spiritus Sancti cognitione libri duo* (1568), intro. Antal Pirnát, ed. Robert Dán (Budapest: Akadémiai Kiadó, 1988). Also see Mihály Balázs, *Early Transylvanian Antitrinitarianism (1566-1571): From Servet to Palaeologus* (Baden-Baden: Koerner, 1996).

111. Dávid, et. al., *De falsa et vera unius Dei Patris*, II.iv.

only God the Father is to be invoked or addressed in prayer, as Christ himself taught, because Christ is not divine.[112]

Whereas the treatment of the doctrine of the Trinity in the earlier Reformed systems — including Calvin's *Institutes* — was comparatively brief, highly scriptural, and not overly burdened by the technical aspect of theologizing, theologians of the age of orthodoxy found it increasingly necessary to develop trinitarian arguments both polemically and positively. On the polemical side, response to the Hungarian antitrinitarians contributed considerably to the development of detailed Protestant discussion: from the Lutheran camp, Georg Maior responded to Dávid and then sharply answered Dávid's rejoinder.[113] Among the Reformed, both a vast positive development of the doctrine and polemical rejoinder combined in Zanchi's *De tribus Elohim*. The heated trinitarian debates of the seventeenth century focused on the continuing presence of the Socinian or antitrinitarian side of the Reformation — in a far more organized, articulate, and exegetically sophisticated form than was found in the sixteenth century — and on the related and rising tide of trinitarian subordinationism associated with the continental Arminians, Episcopius, and Curcellaeus and with Arian, semi-Arian, and Socinian theologians in England.

B. Socinianism in the Seventeenth Century

1. Continental developments. The impact of the Italian antitrinitarians on the Protestant churches in Poland was considerable. The decade following 1560 saw intense debate between the antitrinitarians and the Reformed which, rather than stifling antitrinitarianism, led to a crystallization of the movement as a distinct church.[114] By the middle of the next decade, the Polish antitrinitarians had their first major exposition of doctrine in Georg Schomann's catechism and confession. The work includes a declaration of the oneness of God and of the humanity of Jesus Christ, whose sonship consists in his subjection to God the Father in the work of salvation.[115]

The arrival of Fausto Socinus in Poland in 1580, after an unsuccessful attempt to find a common ground between himself, Blandrata, and the Hungarian antitrinitarians under the leadership of Francis Dávid, marks the beginning of his formative influence on the theology of the Unitarian movement. That debate concerned the propriety of invoking Christ's name in prayer and worship — a point that Dávid and his associate Christian Franken denied and Socinus affirmed. Socinus, given his own umwillingness

---

112. Francis Dávid, *Defensio Francisci Davidis; and, De dualitate tractatus Francisci Davidis*, Cracoviae, 1582, intro. by Mihály Balázs (Budapest: Akadémiai Kiadó, 1983), p. 3; cf. Wilbur, *History of Unitarianism*, II, pp. 71-4.

113. Georg Maior, *De uno Deo et tribus personis, adversus Franc. Davidis et Georg. Blandratam* (Witenberg, 1569), followed by Francis Dávid and Giovanni Blandrata, *Refutatio scripti Georgii Majoris* (Kolosvár, 1569), and Georg Maior, *Commomefactio ad Ecclesiam Catholicam ... contra Blandratam* (Wittenberg, 1569??).

114. See the historical narrative in Wilbur, *History of Unitarianism*, I, pp. 307-355.

115. George Schomann, *Catechesis et confessio fidei, coetus per Poloniam congregati, in nomine Jesu Christi* (Crakow, 1574).

to claim the essential divinity of the Son, was unable to convince the Hungarians to include Christ's name in invocation.[116] In Poland, Socinus' views were more readily accepted, at least on christological issues. His relationship to the Polish antitrinitarian church remains a conundrum, given that he rejected its doctrine of adult baptism and was probably never admitted to full communicant membership, but still served for more than two decades as one of the church's major theological advisors.[117]

During the era of relative peace and toleration under the rule of Sigismund III and his immediate successor, Socinianism flourished in Poland, leading to a large-scale development and systematization of doctrine. Socinus' *Christianae religionis institutio*, left unfinished at the time of his death, became the basis for the Racovian Catechism, written out by the leading antitrinitarians of the next generation, Valentinus Smalcius, Hieronymus Moscorovius, and Johannes Völkel and first published in 1605 (Polish) and 1609 (Latin). From the perspective of orthodox writers of the age, this Socinian system was little more than a combination of elements from various patristic heresies, specifically Sabellianism, Arianism, and the dynamic monarchianism of Artemon.[118] In any case, the basic premises of the Socinian theology were an insistence that God is both essentially and personally one; that Christ, the Son, is not "God over all"; that the Holy Spirit is a power or divine influence, not a person; and that Christ had no existence before his conception and birth.

The presence of this ongoing debate created a difficult situation for nominally orthodox Protestant theologians who developed ideas at odds with traditional perspectives, even when their intention was not to alter fundamental doctrines. Thus, the appearance in 1645 of Calixtus' treatise *De trinitate* and in 1649 of his more elaborate *De mysteria trinitatis, anex solius V.T. libris possit demonstrare* aroused a storm of protest, not only from his Lutheran brethren,[119] but from the Reformed as well. It was Calixtus' contention that the assumption, held by the church since the time of Justin Martyr, Irenaeus, and Tertullian, that the doctrine of the Trinity was enough revealed in various verses in the Old Testament that the ancient Israelites had some, albeit vague, understanding of it, was in error — and that the doctrine of the Trinity could not be argued on the basis of the Old Testament alone. Unfortunately for Calixtus, not only did his arguments undermine an exegetical argument that had

---

116. See Fausto Socinus, *De Jesu Christi Invocatione Disputatio ... cum Francisco Davidis*, in *Opera*, II, col. 709ff.; and Fausto Socinus, *Disputatio inter Faustum Socinum Senensen & Christianum Franken, de honore Christi*, in *Opera*, II, col. 767ff.

117. Wilbur, *History of Unitarianism*, I, pp. 394-395.

118. Thus, William Berriman, *An Historical Account of the Controversies that have been in the Church, concerning the Doctrine of the Holy and Everblessed Trinity*. (London: T. Ward and C. Rivington, 1725), p. 411.

119. See the *Consensus repetitus fidei vere Lutheranae* (1666), art. I, §14.

belonged to basic Lutheran theological education since Melanchthon's *Loci communes* and Chemnitz's expansion of it,[120] his views were also echoed by the Socinians.[121]

The publication in 1656 of the *Bibliotheca Fratrum Polonorum* also marks a significant point in the development of seventeenth-century antitrinitarianism, for although many of the Socinian works had already appeared in print separately, they were not universally accessible.[122] The appearance of the *Bibliotheca* in six folio volumes not only made the Socinian materials available more broadly, it also exhibited the scope and skill of the Socinian exegetes and theologians, placing together for the first time the most substantial antitrinitarian theology of the era and its extensive exegetical foundation. A major reversal of fortune for the Socinian movement also occurred at this time — the new ruler of Poland, Casimir, was able to battle his Cossack and Swedish adversaries to a stalemate and then to turn from war to matters of religion. At the Diet of Warsaw in 1658, he decreed that all antitrinitarians were either to recant their views or to leave Poland within three years, leading to the dispersion of the Polish Unitarian churches following 1560.

In striking parallel with the Socinian assault on trinitarian exegesis, the Socinian and Arian writers of the seventeenth century applied an increasingly historical and critical method of interpretation to the documents of the early Christian tradition and argued with increasing cogency that the standard, orthodox terminology of Nicea was not only opposed to the language of Scripture but was also quite at odds with the theology of the pre-Nicene church. The opening salvo in the late seventeenth-century debate and a major inspiration for Bull's treatise were the work of Christophoros Sandius, the *Nucleus historiae ecclesiasticae, exhibitus in historia Arianorum* (1668) — referred to by Bull as "poisonous"[123] — and the *Irenicum irenicorum* published anonymously by Daniel Zwicker, or Zuicker, in 1658.[124] These works, together with

---

120. Cf. Melanchthon, *Loci communes* (1543), locus 1, with Chemnitz, *Loci theologici*, I, pars. 2, cap. ii.

121. Cf. Francis Turretin, *Institutio theologiae elencticae*, 3 vols. (Geneva, 1679-85; a new edition, Edinburgh, 1847), III.xxvi.

122. *Bibliotheca fratrum polonorum quos Unitarios vocant*, 6 vols. (Irenopolis [Amsterdam]: s.n., 1656).

123. George Bull, *Defensio fidei nicaenae. Defence of the Nicene Creed, out of the Extant Writings of the Catholick Doctors, who Flourished during the First Three Centuries of the Christian Church* [1685], a new translation, 2 vols. (Oxford: Parker, 1851), vol. I, p. ix, with reference to Christophorus Chr. Sandius, *Nucleus historiae ecclesiasticae, exhibitus in historia Arianorum, tribus libris comprehensa* (Cologne, 1668; second edition, 1676); also idem, *Bibliotheca anti-trinitariorum, sive catalogus scriptorum, et succincta narratio de vita eorum auctorum..., opus posthumum Christophori Chr. Sandii; accedunt alia quaedam scripta, quorum seriem pagina post praefationem dabit, quae omnia simul juncta compendium historiae ecclesiasticae Unitariorum, qui Sociniani vulgo audiunt, exhibent* (Freistad: Johannam Aconium, 1684).

124. Daniel Zwicker, *Irenicum irenicorum, seu, Reconciliatorus Christianorum hodiernorum norma triplex: sanaomnium homnium ratio, scriptura sacra & traditiones* (London: n.p., 1658); also, idem, *Irenicomastix iterato victus & constrictus, imo obmutescens, seu Novum & memorabile exemplum infelicissimae pungnae J.A. Comenii contra Irenici irenicorum auctorem. Id ostendente Irenici irenicorum auctore* (Amsterodami: n.p., 1662).

the writings of earlier critics of traditional trinitarianism, had a major impact on the thought of the Remonstrant theologians Episcopius and Curcellaeus. Episcopius declared that the Nicene Creed and the subsequent standards of patristic orthodoxy had been "precipitously framed" out of an excited "party spirit."[125] Curcellaeus went so far as to recommend the historiography of Zwicker's *Irenicum*, noting that it contained "unshakeable testimonies and arguments" to the effect that Nicaea had propounded a new doctrine.[126]

2. Socinianism and antitrinitarianism in seventeenth-century Britain. The English trinitarian controversy of the second half of the seventeenth century was only partially rooted in the continental debate over Socinianism. After two antitrinitarians, Bartholomew Legate and Edward Wightman, were burned at the stake in 1612, charged with Arianism, the Latin Racovian Catechism was ordered burned in London in 1614, and its publication in England banned, there was little open advocacy of variant doctrines of the Godhead in England until the beginning of the 1640s. Still, antitrinitarian books published in the Netherlands and in Poland made their way to England — in 1640, Archbishop Laud issued a series of Constitutions and Canons Ecclesiastical, the fourth of which suppressed Socinianism, without, however, specifying the actual doctrinal points at issue. Rather it "decrees that no persons shall import, print, or disperse any of their books, on pain of excommunication, and of being farther punished in the Star Chamber."[127]

The sense of a Socinian menace, particularly as hidden under an appeal to Scripture alone against tradition, was registered also in a series of works written between 1637 and 1644 against Chillingworth's *Religion of Protestants*, the most elaborate being Francis Cheynell's *Rise, Growth, and Danger of Socinianism* (1643). The beginning of controversy over indigenous Socinianism in England, however, awaited another event: it can be traced to the work of John Biddle, an Oxford tutor who, in 1644, was accused of heresy after having told his colleagues that his biblical studies had led him to deny the traditional doctrine of the Trinity.[128] Biddle has been called the father of English Unitarianism and can certainly be credited with the introduction of a positive statement of Socinian teaching into English theology, prior to the arrival of exiled Polish Socinians in England after their expulsion from Poland (1660) — although, at least according to the published testimony of his followers, he had read only Scripture and had no knowledge of the writings of the Socinians.[129]

---

125. Simon Episcopius, *Institutiones theologicae*, IV.xxxiv.2, in Episcopius, *Opera theologica*, 2 vols. (Amsterdam, 1650), vol. I.

126. Stephanus Curcellaeus, *Quaternio dissertationm theologicarum adversus Samuelem Maresium ... opus posthumum* (Amsterdam: Ioannes Henricus, 1659), I.118.

127. Cited in Daniel Neal, *The History of the Puritans, or Protestant Nonconformists; from the Reformation in 1517, to the Revolution in 1688*, 2 vols. (New York: Harper, 1844), I, p. 346; the entire text of the Constitutions and Canons is found in ibid., pp. 345-347.

128. See the detailed account in Wilbur, *History of Unitarianism*, II, pp. 193-208.

129. See "A Short Account of the Life of John Bidle," in John Biddle, *The Apostolical and True Opinion concerning the Holy Trinity* (London: s.n., 1691), pp. 4-5; not found in the original edition, *The Apostolical and True Opinion concerning the Holy Trinity* (London: s.n., 1653). Biddle's teaching

In Biddle's view, the Father alone is God: Biddle identified essence, individuality, and person to the point that any distinction in number or person demanded a distinction in essence. According to Biddle, removal the difference in number yields not equality but identity — assertion of the difference in number yields difference in essence. Inasmuch as two persons are different in number, they must be, in Biddle's logic, difference in essence. In his "XII Arguments drawn out of the Scripture," Biddle set himself to the task of offering syllogistic arguments against the divinity of the Spirit: "He that is distinguished from God is not God: The Holy Spirit is distinguished from God: Ergo. ... He that hath a will distinct in number from that of God is not God: The Holy Spirit hath a will distinct in number from that of God, Ergo."[130] Biddle denied the divinity of Christ and of the Spirit but affirmed, on the grounds of their distinct wills, their personal identity or subsistence — arguing Christ to be an inspired human being and the Spirit to be an angel.[131] This, he held, was the simple meaning of Scripture. It was the latter assumption that caused both Cloppenburg and Owen to identify him with the fourth-century heresy of Macedonianism or Pneumatomachianism.[132] As Owen pointed out, moreover, Biddle's views on the Spirit distinguished him from "his new masters the Socinians, who deny [the Spirit] his personality, and leave him to be only the efficacy or energy of the power of God."[133] This teaching, together with his christological heresy, led to his condemnation and imprisonment by Parliament. His book was ordered burned.[134]

Biddle's initial defense, XII arguments drawn out of the Scripture (1647), and his Confession of Faith (1648) were immediately attacked.[135] The first response was an

----

is also found in John Biddle, A Twofold Catechism: the one simply called A Scripture-catechism; the other, A brief Scripture-catechism for children ... Composed for their sakes that would fain be meer Christians, and not of this or that sect (London: J. Cottrel, for R. Moone, 1654); in Latin, Duae catecheses: quarum prior simpliciter vocari potest catechesis scripturalis posterior, brevis catechesis scripturalis pro parvulis ... primum quidem a Johanne Biddello; in Latinam linguam translatæ per Nathanaelem Stuckey (London: s.n., 1664).

130. Biddle, Apostolical and True Opinion (1691), pp. 1, 6.

131. John Biddle, A Confession of Faith Touching the Holy Trinity, According to the Scriptures (London: s.n., 1648), pp. 5-6.

132. Johannes Cloppenburg, Vindiciae pro deitate Spiritus Sancti adversus Pneumatomachum Johannem Biddellum Anglum (Franecker, 1652); John Owen, Vindiciae Evangelicae; or, the Mystery of the Gospel Vindicated and Socinianism Examined (Oxford, 1655), also in Works, XII, pp. 74, 82, 334; note the similar accusation in Berriman, Historical Account, p. 423.

133. Owen, Vindiciae Evangelicae, in Works, XII, p. 334; cf. Stephen Nye, A Brief History of the Unitarians, called also Socinians (London: s.n., 1687), p. 33.

134. See the accounts in Neal, History of the Puritans, II, p. 157, and the life of Biddle in Apostolical and True Opinion.

135. John Biddle, XII arguments drawn out of the Scripture: wherein the commonly-received opinion touching deity of the Holy Spirit is clearly and fully refuted: to which is prefixed a letter tending to the same purpose, written to a member of the Parliament (London: s.n., 1647); reprinted with Apostolical and True Opinion (1691).

anonymous tract,[136] followed rapidly by several learned treatises, perhaps the most notable by Matthew Poole, the exegete.[137] Biddle briefly obtained release from prison, but was sentenced again on the basis of a restatement of his views in his *Catechism* (1654).[138] During the next decade, Biddle's arguments continued to be attacked in England and were also addressed by several continental theologians, one of whom, Maresius, went so far as to argue that England had become the new center of antitrinitarianism.[139] At about the same time, new editions of the Racovian Catechism and several continental Socinian works — the latter probably translated by Biddle — also saw the light of day in England, licensed by John Milton to be published by Dugard, printer to the Council of State.[140]

Nor was Biddle the lone English antitrinitarian of his day or the only one to raise questions about the legitimacy of the traditional trinitarian vocabulary: Thomas Lushington,[141] Paul Best, Thomas Webb, John Fry, John Knowles, and John Goodwin were also accused of various trinitarian heresies following 1640.[142] Moreover, as the English controversy developed and widened to include Arian, semi-Arian, and other non-Nicene options for trinitarian formulation, it acquired dimensions not precisely paralleled in the continental debate. To be sure, there was a strongly subordinationistic line of trinitarian argumentation found among the continental Arminians, but nowhere on the continent were Arian and semi-Arian views espoused as normative theology by so many and so eminent a group of theologians. In addition, nowhere on the continent were theologians so pressed to extremes of formulation as to generate, within the church, so many accusations of tritheism and Sabellianism.

---

136. *Gods glory vindicated and blasphemy confuted: being a brief and plain answer to that blasphemous book intituled, Twelve arguments against the deity of the Holy Ghost, written by Tho. Bidle, Master of Arts ... : wherein the arguments of the said book are set down together with proper answers thereto, and twelve anti-arguments proving the deity of the Holy Ghost* (London: William Ley, 1647).

137. Matthew Poole, *Blasphemoktonia: The Blasphemer Slain; or, a Plea for the Godhood of the Holy Ghost, vindicated from the Cavils of J. Bidle* (London, 1648; 2nd ed., 1654); also note Nicolas Estwick, *Pneumatologia: or, A Treatise of the Holy Ghost, in which the Godhead of the third Person of the Trinitie is ... defended against the sophisticall subtleties of John Bidle* (London, 1648).

138. John Biddle, *A Twofold Catechism: the one simply called A Scripture-catechism; the other, A brief Scripture-catechism for children ... Composed for their sakes that would fain be meer Christians, and not of this or that sect* (London: J. Cottrel, for R. Moone, 1654).

139. Thus, Samuel Maresius, *Hydra Socinianismi Expugnata* (Groningen, 1654); also note Nicolaus Arnoldus, *Atheismus Socinianus à Johanne Bidello Anglo, nuper sub specioso Scripturae titulo orbi obtrusus. Jam assertâ ubique Scripturarum Sacrarum veritate detectus atque refutatus* (Franeker: Johannes Wellens, 1659). Among the English responses are William Russell, *Blasphemoktonia: the Holy Ghost Vindicated* (London, 1648); Francis Cheynell, *The Divine Triunity of the Father, Son, and Holy Spirit* (London, 1650); and Edward Bagshawe, *Dissertationes duae Antisocinianianae, in quibus probatur Socinianos non debere dici Christianos* (London, 1657).

140. See Wilbur, *History of Unitarianism*, II, pp. 201-202.

141. Thomas Lushington was the translator and editor of Johann Crell, *The Expiation of a Sinner in a Commentary upon the Epistle to the Hebrewes* (London, 1646).

142. See David Masson, *The Life of John Milton*, 7 vols. (1877-1896; reprint, New York: Peter Smith, 1946), III, pp. 157-159.

John Goodwin certainly ought not to be grouped too quickly with the antitrinitarians, for his polemic was not so much against the doctrine as against the legitimacy of the civil authorities acting to punish antitrinitarians! Goodwin's point was that Scripture used neither the term "Trinity" not the term "person": Scripture indicates neither that God is one person nor that God is three persons. In the absence of clear biblical grounds for the approval or denial of a doctrinal point, Goodwin contended that there ought to be toleration.[143] Yet, protest on the basis of Scripture, against the terminology of orthodoxy, was characteristic of the antitrinitarianism of the era: as Thomas Edwards commented of Best,

> that fearfull Blasphemer ... hath been ... excused ... that he was not guilty of blasphemy, that he denied only the tripersonality, not the Trinity, *Athanasius* Trinity, not the Scripture Trinity, that he denies not the operation of the Persons, but only the name of the Persons.... The questioning of the doctrine of the three Persons hath been excused, that the Persons were Schoole notions, that came not into the Church till some hundreds of yeers after Christ.[144]

These debates were echoed in the theology of John Milton, whose views on tolerance echo precisely those of Goodwin, and whose trinitarian theology has excited considerable controversy in the twentieth century. In recent studies, the teaching of Milton's *De Doctrina Christiana* has been described both as an "orthodox" pre-Nicene subordinationist and as a "classic example of Renaissance antitrinitarianism."[145] As examination of the sources clearly indicates, Milton's trinitarianism did not follow the recognized patterns of orthodoxy in his own day — and although (for reasons that will appear presently) it does not precisely fit into any one patristic heresy , Milton's doctrine of God shares fundamental premises with ancient Arianism and, in fact, can be seen to modify them in accord with philosophical currents of the seventeenth century. Characteristic of Milton's discussions of the Godhead is his assumption of the radical oneness and ultimacy of God and his declaration that Scripture alone must be the norm for discussion, to the exclusion of traditionary creeds. Milton also drew

---

143. John Goodwin, *Theomachia, or, The grand imprudence of men running the hazard of fighting against God in suppressing any way, doctrine or practice concerning which they know not certainly whether it be from God or no* (London: Henry Overton, 1644); cf. John Hunt, *Religious Thought in England, from the Reformation to the End of Last Century, a Contribution to the History of Theology*, 3 vols. (London: Strahan & Co., 1870-1873), I, p. 261.

144. Edwards, *Gangraena*, III, p. 235.

145. Cf. J. H. Adamson, "Milton's Arianism," in *Harvard Theological Review*, 53 (1960), pp. 269-276; Michael E. Bauman, "Milton's Arianism: 'Following the way which is called Heresy'" (Ph. D. diss., Fordham University, 1983); idem, "Milton, Subordination, and the Two-Stage Logos," in *Westminster Theological Journal*, 48 (1986), pp. 173-182; and idem, "Milton's Theological Vocabulary and the Nicene Anathemas," in *Milton Studies*, 21 (1985), pp. 71-92; W. B. Hunter, Jr. "Milton's Arianism Reconsidered," in *Harvard Theological Review*, 52 (1959), pp. 9-35; idem, "Some Problems in John Milton's Theological Vocabulary," in *Harvard Theological Review*, 57 (1964), pp. 353-365; and W. B. Hunter, Jr., C. A. Patrides, and J. H. Adamson, *Bright Essence* (Salt Lake City: University of Utah Press, 1971).

the conclusion from his conception of the unity and singularity of the divine essence that there could only be one fully divine "person."[146] This identification of singularity of essence with singularity of person was, of course, characteristic of the seventeenth-century Socinian argument.[147] Milton also consistently denied the traditional trinitarian formulae and noted that "Trinity" was not a biblical term or concept. He argued that the Son was begotten or made in time according to the eternal will or decree of God, and that the incommunicable essence of the Father alone possesses the divine attributes.[148] Given Milton's argument that the Son is, in effect, an exalted creature, begotten or made of the Father before all worlds, his theology is not in the strictest sense Socinian — rather as various scholars have argued, it is Arian, including its further identification of the essentially distinct and subordinate Son as "God." There is, however, one major exception to the generalization that this view is "Arian." Milton's notion of a primary generic material substance that initially or eternally belongs to God alone and out of which God makes all things (without, however, imparting his essential attributes to creatures)[149] is rather different from the historical Arian assumption of a creation ex nihilo and its attendant ontic divide between God and world, and belongs instead to divergent trajectories of seventeenth century metaphysics, perhaps to the materialism of Thomas Hobbes.[150]

It was, certainly, after 1660 that the spread of Socinianism did have its greatest impact on England, as witnessed by the publication of Crell's *Two Books ... touching one God the Father* in 1665.[151] The "two books" of the work derive from the structure of its argument: in the first book, Crell mounts a scriptural refutation of the doctrine of the Trinity, and in the second he argues that the doctrine cannot be sustained by reason but is in fact rationally unsupportable: following out the view of the Racovian Catechism, Crell insisted that "a person is in vain distinguished from his own essence," with the result that a distinction of person implies a distinction of essence.[152] What is notable here, beyond the attack on orthodoxy, is the shift in meaning of the terms — and it is difficult to determine which term has shifted the most, given that in

---

146. John Milton, *Complete Prose Works*, ed. Don M. Wolfe, 7 vols. in 10, to date (New Haven and London: Yale University Press, 1953-), XIV, p. 202.

147. Cf. Biddle, *A Confession of Faith Touching the Holy Trinity*, pp. 5-6.

148. Milton, *Works*, XIV, p. 42ff.

149. See the discussion in Baumann, "Milton's Theological Vocabulary," pp. 73-74 and John Peter Rumrich, "Milton's Concept of Substance," in *English Language Notes*, XIX (1982), pp. 218-233; and note Hunter, "Milton's Arianism Reconsidered," p. 12-13.

150. Thomas Hobbes, *The English Works of Thomas Hobbes of Malmesbury*, ed. Sir William Molesworth, bart., 11 vols. (Darmstadt: Scientia Verlag Aalen, 1962), IV, pp. 306-313. On Hobbes attribution of corporeality to God, see Copleston, *History of Philosophy*, V, ch. 1.2 and Jean-Luc Marion, "The Idea of God," in *Cambridge History of Seventeenth-Century Philosophy*, ed. D. Garber and M. Ayres (Cambridge and New York: Cambridge University Press, 1998), p. 289.

151. Johannes Crellius, *The Two Books of John Crellius Francus, touching one God the Father wherein many things also concerning the nature of the Son of God and the Holy Spirit are discoursed of*. Kosmoburg [London: s.n.], 1665.

152. Crellius, *Two Books*, p. 140; cf. *Racovian Catechism*, III.i (Rees, p. 33).

traditional Christian Aristotelian philosophy, all individual human persons have the same "essence." Crell's language, like Socinus' and Biddle's, has strong affinities with nominalism and with the trinitarian difficulties encountered by early medieval nominalism in the person of Roscellin.

One attempt to create a reconciliation among British Protestants over against the continued threat of "popery," a treatise entitled *The Naked Truth* and published anonymously in 1675 by Herbert Croft, bishop of Hereford, only served to identify the depth of the controversy. The treatise proposed Protestant reconciliation on the basis of the Apostles' Creed — a proposal not unlike Calixtus' concept of constituent articles of the faith derived from the consensus of the first five centuries — and thereby to include even the Arians and Socinians of the era in the Protestant consensus. Even the moderate Gilbert Burnet refused to set aside the normative status of the Nicene Creed and criticized the Remonstrants, Episcopius and Curcellaeus for doing so.[153]

C. The New Philosophies and the Problem of God-Language

The rise and development of Socinianism in the seventeenth century cannot entirely account for the variant trinitarianisms of the age, including the English debates of the 1640s and 1650s, the variant language and historical perspectives of the Cambridge Platonists, and the doctrinal alternative proposed by Milton. In addition to the spread of a rational and biblicistic Socinian critique of traditional dogmatic language, the antitrinitarianism of the era was also fueled by developments in philosophy that challenged either the Christianized versions of Aristotelianism that had been the norm in theological usage or the older Aristotelian models themselves. The new philosophies of the seventeenth century tended to detach themselves from traditional conceptions of essence, substance, and individuality and, in so doing, critiques not only the older philosophy but also the theology that had grown attached to it and had reached, during the course of centuries, a linguistic concordat with traditional philosophical vocabulary.

Notable here is the alteration in meaning of such terms as "substance" and "essence" that can be traced among the various philosophical schools of the seventeenth century.[154] In 1611, Randle Cotgrave defined the French *substance* as "substance, matter, stuffe," *substanciel* as "substantiall, stuffie," and *essence* as "an essence or being, the nature or subsistence of things" — perhaps reflecting a movement away from the older dual philosophical usage of "essence" to mean both the individuality and the quiddity, or whatness, of a thing, toward understanding the term in a more material and exclusively individual sense, perhaps more as *haeccitas* than as *quidditas*. His

---

153. Gilbert Burnet, A *Modest Survey of ... the Naked Truth* (London, 1676), pp. 5-6; and see Ethyn W. Kirby, "'The Naked Truth': A Plan for Church Unity," in *Church History*, 7 (1935), pp. 45-61.

154. See the discussion in R. S. Woolhouse, *Descartes, Spinoza, Leibniz: The Concept of Substance in Seventeenth-Century Metaphysics* (London and New York: Routledge, 1993); cf. Farrer's introduction to G. W. Leibniz, *Theodicy: Essays on the Goodness of God, the Freedom of Man, and the Origin of Evil*, intro. by Austin Farrer, trans. E. M. Huggard (London: Routledge & Kegan Paul, 1951; repr. Chicago: Open Court, 1985), pp. 13-21; and Copleston, *History of Philosophy*, IV, passim.

definition of *substance*, moreover, carries only the connotation of primary substance, the actual stuff or material identity of a thing, and not the connotation of secondary substance, the species or genus of a thing.[155] Of course, when one looks to the technical manuals, there is little difference on the point between Thomas Wilson's *Rule of Reason* (1551/52) and Thomas Spencer's *Art of Logick* (1628): both offer the identification of "first" or primary substance as the individual thing and "second" or secondary substance as the kind of thing, namely, the species or genus.[156]

There is evidence, moreover, that the newer philosophies of the day tended to identify substance much in the way we have seen Cotgrave's dictionary tend — toward the identification of substance with the individual thing rather than the species or genus. Descartes, for example, proposed a definition of substance that, in its strictest sense applied only to God and in its looser sense only to individual beings:

> By substance we can understand nothing else than a thing which exists so that it needs no other thing in order to exist. And in fact, only one single substance can be understood which clearly needs nothing else, namely God. ... Created substances, however, whether corporeal or thinking, may be conceived under this common concept; for they are things which need only the concurrence of God to exist.[157]

In opposition to Descartes' mechanical view of the universe, Henry More and Ralph Cudworth argued the genuine interaction between spiritual and material being and concluded that all spiritual being, including God, must be understood as having the attribute of extension as a necessary predicate. Having made the point, however, More recognized the immediate necessity of qualifying it: the attribute of extension was the only way in which he could conceive of divine omnipresence, given that the normal sense of the word implied embodiment. Yet, God does not have a body, strictly so-called, but rather God, as a spirit, is an indivisible entity capable of penetrating bodies.[158] More and Cudworth argued the emanation of being from the divine and, drawing on the Platonic tradition, held the creation of the material world by the instrumentality of the World Soul, which not only produces the being of the world but also infuses

---

155. Randle Cotgrave, A *Dictionarie of the French and English Tongues* (London: Adam Islip, 1611), s.v., *essence, substance, substanciel*.

156. Thomas Wilson, *The Rule of Reason, Conteinyng the Arte of Logique*, newely corrected, London: R. Grafton 1552), fol. C vi; Thomas Spencer, *The Art of Logick, Delivered in the Precepts of Aristotle and Ramus*, (London: John Dawson, 1628), p. 129.

157. Descartes, *Principles of Philosophy*, I.li-lii.

158. Henry More, *An Antidote against Atheisme*, 2nd ed. (London: J. Flesher, 1655), I.iv (pp. 16-17); cf. Amos Funkenstein, *Theology and the Scientific Imagination from the Middle Ages to the Seventeenth Century* (Princeton: Princeton University Press, 1986), pp. 23-24, 77. Further see, Lydia Gysi, *Platonism and Cartesianism in the Philosophy of Ralph Cudworth* (Bern: Herbert Lang, 1962) and Amos Funkenstein, "The Body of God in 17th Century Theology and Science," in *Millenarianism and Messianism in English Literature and Thought, 1650-1800*, ed. R. Popkin (Leiden: Brill, 1988), pp. 149-175.

it with life — a premise directed not only against Cartesian dualism but also against Hobbesian materialism.[159]

The Platonic or platonizing approach also held several difficulties for seventeenth-century trinitarianism.[160] First and foremost, as the Cambridge Platonists themselves recognized, the concept of an emanation of being from the ultimate Monad, or One, characteristic of the Platonic tradition and followed, with modification, by various of the church fathers, was not a suitable foundation for trinitarian monotheism, given its view of the emanated *Nous*, or divine Intellect, and the emanated *Psyche*, or World Soul, not only as lower than the Monad but also as separated from it was more readily understood as a form of tritheism than as monotheism. Cudworth recognized, moreover, that even a highly subordinationistic Platonic Trinity could identify the three hypostases as *homoousios*, given a generic understanding of *ousia*, or essence (opposed to the tendency of various forms of seventeenth-century rationalism). Second, this reading of the implications of Platonism in turn led Cudworth, following Petavius, to conclude that the post-Nicene fathers generally and the Cappadocians in particular held a generic and not a numerical unity of divine essence, leaving Athanasius as the sole significant representative of a fully developed trinitarian monotheism — a point appropriated directly by the late seventeenth-century antitrinitarians in their polemic against orthodoxy. The antitrinitarians were able to argue, using Petavius and Cudworth, that the patristic solution was a form of tritheism and, therefore, utterly unbibilical.[161]

---

159. See: *The Cambridge Platonists in Philosophical Context: Politics, Metaphysics, and Religion*, ed. G. A. J. Rogers, J. M. Vienne, and Y. C. Zarka (Dordrecht and Boston: Kluwer Academic Publishers, 1997); Geoffrey P. H. Pawson, *The Cambridge Platonists and their Place in Religious Thought*, foreword by Alexander Nairne (London: S. P. C. K., 1930); Mother Maria, *Platonism and Cartesianism in the Philosophy of Ralph Cudworth* (Bern: H. Lang, 1962); Frederick James Powicke, *The Cambridge Platonists, a Study* (Cambridge, Mass.: Harvard University Press, 1926); James Deotis Roberts, *From Puritanism to Platonism in Seventeenth-Century England* (The Hague: Martinus Nijhoff, 1968).

160. Cf. Sarah Hutton, "The Neoplatonic Roots of Arianism: Ralph Cudworth and Theophilus Gale," in *Socinianism and its Role in the culture of the XVIth to XVIIth Centuries*, ed. L. Szczucki, Z. Ogonowski, and J. Tazbir (Warsaw: PWN, Polish Scientific Publisher, 1983), pp. 139-145. On the varied relationship between the seventeenth-century platonists and the classical Platonic tradition, see Copleston, *History of Philosophy*, V, pp. 54-66. Also see Ernst Cassirer, *The Platonic Renaissance in England*, trans. James P. Pettegrove (Edinburgh: Nelson, 1953).

161. Ralph Cudworth, *The True Intellectual System of the Universe: the first part; wherein, all the reason and philosophy of atheism is confuted; and its impossibility demonstrated* (London: Printed for Richard Royston, 1678), following the later edition, 2 vols. (Andover, Mass., 1837-38), I, pp. 777-778, 791-804; and cf. Anon., *Defense of the Brief History of the Unitarians* (London: s.n., 1691), p. 5 and the anonymous treatise, attributed to Thomas Smalbroke, *The judgment of the fathers concerning the doctrine of the Trinity opposed to Dr. G. Bull's Defence of the Nicene faith: Part I. The doctrine of the Catholick Church, during the first 150 years of Christianity, and the explication of the unity of God (in a Trinity of Divine Persons) by some of the following fathers, considered* (London: s.n., 1695), p. 66; and see below 3.2 (A.3). Note also that patristic scholarship has tended away from Cudworth's conclusion and understood the Cappadocians as arguing a sole, indivisible divine *ousia*: cf. Kelly, *Early Christian Doctrine*, pp. 268-269; Prestige, *God in Patristic Thought*, pp. 242-245, 256-261. Although the Cappadocians do not speak specifically of a "numerical unity of divine essence" they arguably make the same point in different language, namely, in their consistent affirmation of divine

Turning from the rationalist idealism of Descartes and the English Platonists to the rationalist materialism of Hobbes yields, interestingly enough, a similar difficulty for traditional theology. Hobbes assumes that, rightly understood, the terms "substance and body signify the same thing."[162] "In the most general acceptation," Hobbes indicates, a body is "that which filleth, or occupieth some certain room, or imagined place; and dependeth not on the imagination, but is a real part of that which we call the universe." Insofar as bodies are the subjects of various predications and alterations of properties, they are called "substances" as distinct from "accidents" or the properties that inhere in them. Given this identification of "body" with "substance," the notion of an "incorporeal substance" is a contradiction in terms: what we call "spirit" is "either a subtle, fluid, and invisible body" or "a ghost, or other idol or phantasm of the imagination."[163] Hobbes, quite willingly, draws the corporeal conclusion concerning the substance or "spirit" of God. Citing Genesis 1:2, "the Spirit of God moved upon the face of the waters," he argues, "Here if by the *Spirit of God* be meant God himself, then is *motion* attributed to God, and consequently *place*, which are intelligible only of bodies, and not of substances incorporeal."[164] The implications of this vocabulary for trinitarian theology are clearly negative — and point toward a strongly heterodox, perhaps Socinian, perspective on Hobbes' part.[165]

The alteration of substance-language typical of the developments in seventeenth-century thought would cause inordinate difficulty for the traditional doctrine of God, especially for the doctrine of the Trinity. The older orthodoxy had been able to focus on the notion of a primary spiritual substance as suitable to the discussion of God: secondary substance, denoting species or genus, was, of course, excluded, given the existence of one sole God — primary substance, the individual, functioned well, given the ability of the traditional philosophical perspective to speak of spiritual substance and to identify levels of distinction within that substance that did not constitute divisions and/or indicate composition. When substance is redefined, whether in the Cartesian or the Hobbesian manner, it becomes quite impossible to imagine three subsistents sharing one indivisible substance — indeed, we have returned to the problem encountered at the beginning of the scholastic era in the thought of Roscellin, where a nominalistic understanding of language and reality led to the identification of all substances as individuals and to a fundamental problem in expressing the doctrine of the Trinity. Nor is the association between the Socinian trinitarian language or Hobbes' understanding of substance and the medieval nominalist approach to language and reality merely incidental: Ockham continued to be seen as a significant thinker throughout the seventeenth century, and an Ockhamist or nominalist epistemology

---

simplicity — given that simplicity means non-composite and that a genus is, by definition, a composite: see further, in this volume, 3.2 (A.2-3).

162. Hobbes, *Leviathan*, II, xxxiv.

163. Hobbes, *Leviathan*, II, xxxiv.

164. Hobbes, *Leviathan*, II, xxxiv.

165. Cf. C. A. J. Coady, "The Socinian Connection: Further Thoughts on the Religion of Hobbes," in *Religious Studies*, 22 (1986), pp. 277-280.

remained in the philosophical curriculum of the universities throughout the period and was consistently recognized as both a viable perspective and a significant opponent by various thinkers of the era.[166]

D. Orthodox Trinitarian Formulation in the High Orthodox Era, 1640-1685

1. The confessional foundation: the Declaration of Thorn and the Westminster Standards. By the beginning of the high orthodox era, the Reformed confessional theology had been fully established and the need to write new confessions was no longer pressing. Still, two of the symbols of the high orthodox era are noteworthy for their churchly trinitarianism: the *Declaratio Thoruniensis* (1645), or Declaration of Thorn, and the Westminster Standards (1647). Both documents are thoroughly trinitarian, the former presenting the doctrine of the Trinity as a foundation of catholic orthodoxy, the latter confessing it as a fundamental doctrine resting on the biblical norm.

The *Declaratio Thoruniensis*, does not offer a full doctrine of the Trinity but rather, in an initial section, presents a declaration of the full agreement of Reformed doctrine with the traditions of the first five centuries, affirming the priority of Scripture while also acknowledging the authority of the ecumenical creeds.[167] The second section of the *Declaratio* defines the Reformed faith and notes points of difference with the Roman and Lutheran confessions, specifically commenting that the "we acknowledge and believe that the Holy Trinity and the Person of our Lord Jesus Christ, the *theanthropos*, are the articles most fundamental to the Christian faith" and find "no dissensions between our churches and the Roman." The *Declaratio* goes on to comment on the excessive speculative development of the doctrine at the hands of the medieval scholastics.[168] From the perspective of definition and formulation, therefore, the *Declaratio* is not of particular importance for the Reformed doctrine of the Trinity — whereas from the perspective of the identification of teachings fundamental to the Reformed faith, it makes clear the Reformed adherence to the orthodox doctrine of the Trinity as a fundamental of the faith.

The Westminster Confession provides as brief, normative statement of the doctrine of the Trinity that emphasized both the language of substance and person and the personal properties and relations:

> In the unity of the Godhead there be three persons, of one substance, power, and eternity; God the Father, God the Son, and God the Holy Ghost [1 John 5:7; Matt. 3:16, 17; Matt. 28:19; 2 Cor. 13:14]. The Father is of none, neither begotten, nor

---

166. Dorothea Krook, *John Sergeant and His Circle: A Study of Three Seventeenth-Century English Aristotelians*, ed., with an intro. by Beverley C. Southgate (Leiden: E. J. Brill, 1993), pp. 6, 36-37, 98-101.

167. *Declaratio Thoruniensis: Generalis declaratio*, in H. A. Niemeyer, ed., *Collectio confessionum in ecclesiis reformatis publicatarum*, 2 parts. (Leipzig: J. Klinkhardt, 1840), pp. 669-670.

168. *Declaratio Thoruniensis: Specialis declaratio*, II.1, in Niemeyer, *Collectio confessionum*, p. 671. For a discussion and analysis of the orthodox Lutheran doctrine of the Trinity, see Robert D. Preus, *The Theology of Post-Reformation Lutheranism*, I, pp. 112-163; and Schmid, *Doctrinal Theology of the Evangelical Lutheran Church*, pp. 129-159.

proceeding: the Son is eternally begotten of the Father [John 1:14, 18]: the Holy Ghost eternally proceeding from the Father and the Son [John 15:26; Gal. 4:6].[169]

The Larger Catechism offers a bit more detail, but nothing of a speculative nature:

Q. 8. Are there more Gods than one?
A. There is but one only, the living and true God.
Q. 9. How many persons are there in the Godhead?
A. There be three persons in the Godhead, the Father, the Son, and the Holy Ghost; and these three are one true, eternal God, the same in substance, equal in power and glory; although distinguished by their personal properties.
Q. 10. What are the personal properties of the three persons in the Godhead?
A. It is proper to the Father to beget the Son, and to the Son to be begotten of the Father, and to the Holy Ghost to proceed from the Father and the Son from all eternity.
Q. 11. How doth it appear that the Son and the Holy Ghost are God equal with the Father?
A. The Scriptures manifest that the Son and the Holy Ghost are God equal with the Father, ascribing unto them such names, attributes, works, and worship, as are proper to God only.[170]

2. The continental writers. The early orthodox trinitarian development, whether in its defensive or polemical form, its patristic interest, or its broader dogmatic forms continued during the era of high orthodoxy, both among the continental and the British Reformed writers.[171] Nearly all of the major continental Reformed writers of the era wrote full theological systems — with the result that the method as well as the content of their doctrine of the Trinity is readily available, as is the relationship between their doctrine of the Trinity and the larger topic, the doctrine of God, as well as that between their doctrine of the triune God and the remainder of the theological system.

Inasmuch as all of the reformed writers, however much they may have differed on narrower matters of form and definition, consistently identified the Trinity as one of the necessary doctrines or fundamental articles of the faith, the doctrine stands as of primary importance in their systems. It is noteworthy — and certainly contrary to the reputation of these writers in the older scholarship — that for all the debate of the era over the doctrine of the divine essence and attributes, that doctrine was never accorded the status of fundamental article, necessary for salvation. Indeed, given the importance of the doctrine of the Trinity to the orthodox, both confessionally and structurally in relation to the rest of their theology, it comes as close to being the "central dogma" of Reformed orthodoxy as any doctrine: although it did not provide a basis for deducing other doctrines, it certainly did offer a basic guideline for the formulation of other doctrinal issues.

Among other major expositions found in the works of orthodox writers of the mid-seventeenth century, the doctrine of the Trinity found in Johannes Cocceius' *Summa*

---

169. Westminster Confession of Faith, II.iii.
170. Westminster Larger Catechism, qq. 8-11.
171. The British writers will be surveyed below, 2.2 (D.3).

theologiae certainly exemplifies these generalizations.[172] Cocceius, moreover, is a useful example, both given the breadth of his exposition — easily comparable to the trinitarian discussions of contemporaries, whether non-federalist like Maccovius, Maresius, and Voetius,[173] or federalist, such as Heidanus, and Burman[174] — and given the tendency of some of the older scholarship to understand him as virtually a theologian of one doctrine, namely, covenant, and to view his covenant theology as a biblicistic alternative to the scholasticism of his era.[175] Not only has recent scholarship set aside this stereotype, it has also placed Cocceius more fully and definitively into his seventeenth-century context as sharing a variant scholastic method with his contemporaries and as standing in the central development of Reformed orthodox theology on doctrinal topics other than covenant.[176]

Like his Reformed contemporaries, Cocceius was concerned, first and foremost, to argue that the doctrine of the Trinity was a necessary doctrine, over against the Socinians and the Remonstrants. That there is one God in three persons is a matter of the deepest faith — and the usage "person" with reference to the Godhead is justified

---

172. Johannes Cocceius, *Summa theologiae ex Scriptura repetita* (Geneva, 1665; Amsterdam, 1669); also found in Cocceius, *Opera omnia theologica, exegetica, didactica, polemica, philologica,* 12 vols. (Amsterdam, 1701-1706), VII, pp. 131-403; also note Cocceius's shorter theological compendia, *Aphorismi per universam theologiam breviores,* in *Opera,* vol. 7, pp. 3-16; and *Aphorismi per universam theologiam prolixiores,* in *Opera,* vol. 7, pp. 17-38.

173. Cf. Johannes Maccovius, *Collegia theologica quae extant omnia* (Franecker, 1641); idem, *Distinctiones et regulae theologicae et philosophicae* (Amsterdam, 1656); and idem, *Loci communes theologici* (Amsterdam, 1658); Samuel Maresius, *Collegium theologicum sive systema breve universae theologiae comprehensum octodecim disputationibus* (Groningen, 1645; 1659); Gisbertus Voetius, *Selectae disputationes theologicae,* 5 vols. (Utrecht, 1648-1669; idem, *Syllabus problematum theologicorum, quae pro re natâ proponi aut perstringi solent in privatis publicisque disputationum, examinum, collationum, consultationum exercitiis* (Utrecht: Aegidius Romanus, 1643); and idem, *Catechesatie over den Heidelbergschen Catechismus,* ed. Abraham Kuyper, from the 1662 edition of Poudroyen, 2 vols. (Rotterdam: Huge, 1891).

174. Abraham Heidanus, *Corpus theologiae christianae in quindecim locos digestum,* 2 vols. (Leiden, 1687); idem, *Disputationes theologicae ordinariae repetitiae,* 2 parts (Leiden, 1654-1659.); and idem, *Fasciculus disputationum theologicarum de Socianismo* (Leiden, 1659); Franz Burman, *Synopsis theologiae et speciatim oeconomiae foederum Dei,* 2 parts (Geneva, 1678; Den Haag, 1687).

175. E.g., Albertus Van der Flier, *Specimen historico-theologicum de Johanne Cocceijo anti-scholastico.* (Utrecht, 1859); Charles S. McCoy, "The Covenant Theology of Johannes Cocceius" (Ph.D. diss., Yale University, 1956); idem, "Johannes Cocceius: Federal Theologian," in *Scottish Journal of Theology,* XVI (1963), pp. 352-370; and Heiner Faulenbach, "Johannes Cocceius," in *Orthodoxie und Pietismus,* ed. Martin Greschat (Stuttgart: W. Kolhammer, 1982), pp. 163-176; and idem, *Weg und Ziel der erkenntnis Christi. Eine Untersuchung zur Theologie des Johannes Cocceius* (Neukirchen: Neukirchner Verlag, 1973).

176. Thus, Willem J. Van Asselt, *The Covenant Theology of Johannes Cocceius (1603-1669),* trans. Raymond A. Blacketer (Leiden: E. J. Brill, 2001); idem, "The Doctrine of the Abrogations in the Federal Theology of Johannes Cocceius," in *Calvin Theological Journal,* 29/1 (1994), pp. 101-116; idem, "Johannes Cocceius Anti-Scholasticus?" in *Reformation and Scholasticism: an Ecumenical Enterprise,* ed. Willem J. Van Asselt and Eef Dekker (Grand Rapids: Baker Book House, 2001), pp. 227-251; and idem, *Johannes Coccejus: Portret van een zeventiende-eeuws theoloog op oude en niewe wegen* (Heerenveen: Groen en Zoon, 1997).

by its applicability to the biblical materials. Cocceius also was concerned to define the terms "essence" and "person" in such a way as to maintain the utter simplicity of the Godhead and at the same time avoid the Sabellian implication of a single divine person.[177] These concerns led him — again, like many of his Reformed contemporaries — to a careful examination of the patristic materials and the controversy between the Latin and the Greek churches over the *filioque*. These concerns yielded, in Cocceius' *Summa theologiae* and in his sets of *Aphorismi*, a nuanced trinitarianism that drew on traditional concepts of the order of the persons — with the Father understood as having primacy and standing as the *fons deitatis* and with each of the persons understood as identified and distinguished by an incommunicable personal property. Cocceius even echoes the older tradition in his identification of these personal characteristics as *notiones* — namely, *paternitas, filiatio*, and *processio*. Still, like most of his Reformed predecessors and contemporaries, Cocceius chose not to follow the medieval tradition further in identifying the generation of the Son as an act of intellect and the procession of the Spirit as an act of love or will.[178]

Cocceius also stands in clear relation to the earlier Western tradition in his appreciation of and rapprochement with the Greeks over the question of the *filioque*. He cautions advocates of the *filioque* that the doctrine is not directly available from Scripture, but rests on a series of conclusions drawn from various readings of the text — and he warns the opponents that their language of the Father as "cause" and "principium" of the Son holds difficulties as well.[179] He also stands ready to acknowledge the lack of propriety in the original Western emendation of the Niceno-Constantinopolitan formula, at the same time that he argues the assimilation of the Eastern formula (procession of the Spirit from the Father through the Son) to the Western language of procession from the Father and the Son, much in the sense of the formulae of the Council of Florence. Thus, the Spirit is the Spirit of both the Father and the Son, given that both Father and Son send the Spirit. Still, in this twofold sending, there remains only one *fons deitatis*, the Father, who is the source of both Son and Spirit.[180]

Among the major Reformed treatises on the Trinity produced by continental authors is Amyraut's *De mysterio trinitatis*, an exhaustive examination of the various trinitarian texts found in Scripture and of the writings of the fathers, in which the exegetical and traditionary grounds of the doctrine are upheld against the heresies of the time, particularly against the increasingly subordinationist trinitarianism of the Remonstrants.[181] In its form and content, moreover, the treatise manifests a profound

---

177. Cocceius, *Aphorismi breviores*, VI.3-4.

178. Cocceius, *Aphorismi prolixiores*, VII.1-4; cf. Van Asselt, *Covenant Theology*, pp. 177-179.

179. Cocceius, *Summa theologiae*, XII.3-18; and cf. Van Asselt, *Covenant Theology*, pp. 180-184.

180. Cocceius, *Summa theologiae*, XII.7-14.

181. Moyse Amyraut, *De mysterio trinitatis, deque vocibus ac Phrasibus quibus tam Scriptura quam apud Patres explicatur, Dissertatio, septem partibus absoluta* (Saumur: Isaac Desbordes, 1661). Also note the Salmurian theology synopsized in Moyse Amyraut, Louis Cappel, and Josue La Place, *Syntagma thesium theologicarum in Academia Salmuriensi variis temporibus disputatarum*, editio secunda, 4 parts

continuity with the broad Reformed orthodox sensibility of a unified *locus de Deo* and illustrates the placement of Amyraut *within* the bounds of confessional orthodoxy in polemic against its standard opponents, despite the intensity of the conflict over his own doctrine of the hypothetical efficacy of Christ's satisfaction.[182] Amyraut does not begin with the discussion of the three persons typical of the *de trinitate* sections of a full system — rather, he begins his *De trinitate* where the theological system begins the *locus de Deo*, with the unity of the divine essence, follows this discussion with a disputation on the infinity of God, and proceeds, third in order, to a disputation on the vestigial revelation of the Trinity in nature, including here discussion of the "Platonic trinity."[183] The treatise then moves on to examine the "primordial" revelation of the Trinity in the Old Testament, the New Testament revelation, the biblical words and phrases requiring trinitarian explanation, and the language of the fathers.[184] Amyraut argues, in sum, that the biblical revelation "wondrously agrees" with "right reason" and at the same time vastly transcends it: in their proper use, reason and metaphysics do not plumb the mystery, but rather help to explain and defend it — particularly against the improper use of Boethian and scholastic definitions by Arminius and Curcellaeus.[185]

The historical aspect of the debate was complicated when the Jesuit dogmatician and historian Dionysius Petavius (1583-1682) wrote his vast and erudite *De theologicis dogmatibus* (1644-50) from the perspective of a churchly and normative development of doctrine: he accepted the historical point that ante-Nicene doctrine was substantively different from Nicene orthodoxy — but argued that the church, having the authority to determine true doctrine, could develop and change its formulae.[186] Bull and various other Protestants found the work dangerous because Petavius saw nothing wrong in the assertion that the Nicene definition stated a doctrine not known to earlier fathers: whereas Petavius could argue the normative authority of the church in establishing doctrine, Bull, resting on the Thirty-nine Articles, could not. The solution, for Bull, was to refute Petavius. On the other hand, many among the Reformed orthodox saw harmonization of the fathers as needless, given that the fathers were not understood to be an infallible norm for doctrine — indeed, prior to Petavius, the Reformed theologian Jean Daillé had argued not only that even the nominally orthodox fathers had often disagreed among themselves, but, specifically, they had disagreed over the

---

(Saumur: Joannes Lesner, 1664; second printing, 1665).

182. See the argument in *PRRD*, I, 1.3 (B.2-3)

183. Amyraut, *De mysterio trinitatis*, pars I: *De unitate essentiae Dei* (pp. 3-37); pars II: *De infinitate Dei* (pp. 38-108); pars III: *De revelatione istius Mysterii in Dispensatione Naturae* (pp. 109-163). See the discussion of the structure of the *locus* in *PRRD*, III, 3.1 (A-B).

184. Amyraut, *De mysterio trinitatis*, pars IV: *De primordiis revelationis illius in Veteri Testamento* (pp. 163-241); pars V: *De revelatione mysterii illius in Evangelio* (pp. 242-323); pars VI: *De vocibus & phrasibus quibus explicatur in Scriptura sacra* (pp. 324-407); pars VII: *De vocibus & phrasibus quibus explicatur apud Patres* (pp. 408-546).

185. Amyraut, *De mysterio trinitatis*, VII, pp. 541, 542-544.

186. Cf. Petavius, Dionysius, s.v. in *RED* and *NCE*.

conception of the Trinity and over the unity of substance in the Godhead.[187] The problem here, as in the contest between the Protestant and Roman churches over the doctrine of Scripture, arose directly out of the confrontation of a rising textual and historical approach to the materials of the canon and of the tradition — in the absence of an overarching allegorizing and, therefore, harmonizing hermeneutic. Indeed, the seventeenth-century debate over the Trinity, both in relation to the text of Scripture and in relation to the historical materials of the early church, stands as a primary example of the great hermeneutical problem of orthodoxy.

A second focus of continental orthodox debate was the developing Remonstrant theology in the generations after Arminius. Against the tendencies of orthodox Protestantism, Episcopius and Curcellaeus, echoed in England by the semi-Arians like Thomas Emlyn and James Pierce, argued that the history of the first five centuries manifest considerable variety of trinitarian formulation and, in particular, that the ante-Nicene theologians held to a subordination of the Son that was both different from the Nicene teaching and acceptable as a foundation for a form of contemporary orthodoxy. Episcopius and Curcellaeus, in particular, were singled out by Reformed orthodox writers like Francis Turretin for refutation — the former for arguing in what appeared to be agreement with the Socinians that the "mystery of the Trinity" was not a fundamental article of the faith and the latter for his historical arguments on the problem of the Nicene and post-Nicene concepts of the *homoousios* and *perichoresis*, which he identified as ambiguous and unbiblical concepts.[188]

Cloppenburg's several systematic essays and his lengthy series of polemical treatises against the enemies of orthodoxy confront the trinitarian heresies of the day directly and evidence the theological commerce between England and the continent. His positive doctrine, albeit not without polemical overtones, is found in his *Syntagma exercitationum selectarum, Exercitationes ad locos communes theologicos, Protheoria theologiae christianae; quo agitur de theologiae & religionis definitione, partitione & distributione*, and the *Disputationes XV de canone theologiae*.[189] His polemics attacked the Remonstrants, the Anabaptists, the Socinians, with treatises singling out the Socinian Christology of Valentinus Smalcius and views expressed by the English anti-trinitarian John Biddle on the Holy Spirit.[190] This latter point of reference is significant inasmuch as it once again indicates the close relationship between theological developments on the continent and those in England. Similarly, the defensive treatises of Nicolaus Arnold rebuffed the Socinian readings of Christian doctrine both in their continental form

---

187. Daillé, *Treatise on the Right Use of the Fathers*, I.v (pp. 80-81).

188. Cf. Turretin, *Inst. theol. elencticae*, III.xxiii.10, 11, 13; xxiv.1, 19.

189. All in Johannes Cloppenburg, *Opera Theologica*, 2 vols. (Amsterdam, 1684).

190. Johannes Cloppenburg, *Compendiolum Socinianismi* (Franeker Idzardus Balck, 1651); *Anti-Smalcius, de divinitate Jesu Christi: Pars prior, De munere Christi prophetico. Pars posterior, De munere Christi regio* (Franeker: Idzardus Balck, 1652); *Kort begrijp van de opkomste ende leere der Socinianen, kortelick vervat in 11 capittelen, by een gebracht ende grontelick wederleyt in de Nederlantsche tale* (Dordrecht: Vincent Caimax, 1652); *Vindiciae pro deitate Spiritus Sancti adversus Pneumatomachum Johannem Biddellum Anglum* (Franecker, 1652).

and in the works of Biddle. Arnold was particularly important for his nearly line-by-line refutation of the Racovian Catechism.[191]

The massive polemical efforts of Hoornbeeck not only included a major attack on the Socinians in his systematic survey of all religious and theological deviations,[192] they also include what is perhaps to most intense and extended of the continental Reformed efforts to refute the antitrinitarians.[193] In the line of Hoornbeeck among the continental Reformed in the assault on Socinianism was Andreas Essenius, who recognized the "popular" character of the problem and wrote against the heresy in the vernacular.[194]

Among the high orthodox writers who developed significant trinitarian conceptions, Francis Turretin sums up the polemical development of the doctrine. As is the case with all of the doctrines in his *Institutio*, the doctrine of the Trinity as presented by Turretin is not the full Reformed orthodox doctrine — rather it is the polemical or elenctical aspects of the doctrine, set forth for the defense of orthodoxy. Turretin divides his discussion into nine chapters, the first five arguing the doctrine of the Trinity in general, followed by two chapters on the Son and two on the Spirit, in both cases arguing the deity and the personhood, respectively. The specific adversaries are the Remonstrants and the Socinians — the former for denying the status of the doctrine as a fundamental or necessary doctrine, the latter for denying the doctrine altogether. Against the former, Turretin argues the necessity of the doctrine to salvation, including the possibility of arguing the doctrine from the Old Testament as necessary to the salvation of the patriarchs and prophets. Against the latter, Turretin defends, principally, the full divinity and distinct personhood of the Son and Spirit, revealing the extent to which the doctrine had become an exegetical task, linked to the work of late seventeenth-century biblical interpreters. A positive, relatively non-polemical exposition was presented by Turretin's Genevan successor, Benedict Pictet.[195]

---

191. Nicolaus Arnold, *Religio Sociniana seu Catechesis Racoviana maior publicis disputationibus (inserto ubique formali ipsius catecheseos contextu) refutata* (Franeker: Idzardus Albertus & Joannes Jansonus, 1654); and *Atheismus Socinianvs à Johanne Bidello Anglo, nuper sub specioso Scripturæ titulo orbi obtrusus. Jam assertâ ubique Scripturarum Sacrarum veritate detectus atque refutatus* (Franeker: Johannes Wellens, 1659).

192. Johannes Hoornbeeck, *Summa controversiarum religionis, cum infidelibus, haereticis, schismaticis* (Utrecht, 1653).

193. Johannes Hoornbeeck, *Socinianismus confutatus*, 3 vols. (Utrecht, 1650-64).

194. Andreas Essenius, *Christelike en een-voudige onderwyzing tegens de Sociniaensche en zommige daer aen grenzende dwalingen, gesteld* (Amsterdam: Johannes van Waesberge, 1663) also note his *Synopsis controversiarum theologicarum, et index locorum totius s. scripturae, quibus adversarii ad errores suos confirmandos, et veritatem impugnandum vel declinandum, praecipue abuti solent: ubi tum adversarii, qui iis abutuntur, tum singulae eorum collectiones brevi methodo proponuntur* (Utrecht: Meinardus a Dreunen, 1677).

195. Benedict Pictet, *Theologia christiana ex puris ss. literarum fontibus hausta* (Geneva, 1696); the translation, *Christian Theology*, trans. Frederick Reyroux (Philadelphia: Presbyterian Board of Publication, n.d.), is reasonably accurate for what it offers, but it omits passages, rearranges text, and removes all of the numbers identifying distinct propositions and paragraphs.

Mastricht, by way of contrast, offers a full discussion of the doctrine, running from an initial exegetical argumentation for the truth of the Trinity based on 2 Corinthians 13:14, "the grace of the Lord Jesus Christ, and the love of God, and the communication of the Holy Spirit, be with all of you, Amen," in collation with a series of other texts — to a doctrinal formulation, a refutation of the various heresies, and a practical application in which he argues the importance of the doctrine for faith and the ways in which the doctrine supports piety.[196] Here we see the full expansion of the doctrine, together with the broad sense of its implications for other *loci* in the body of Reformed doctrine, notably election and the covenant, as witnessed both in the trinitarian aspects of the doctrine of the eternal decree and in the *pactum salutis*. In Mastricht's exposition, not only do trinitarian elements appear in the other *loci*, but elements of the other *loci* have a substantive presence in the doctrine of the Trinity. This doctrinal interpenetration is perhaps most evident in the discussion of the second Person of the Trinity, where Mastricht rests his doctrine primarily on Psalm 2:7-8, "Thou art my Son, this day have I begotten thee," understood as a revelation of the intra-trinitarian economy as well as the foundation of the plan of salvation and, therefore, of the covenantal relationship between the Father and the Son.[197]

Among Mastricht's contemporaries, a related *Nadere Reformatie* approach is evident in the theology of Wilhelmus à Brakel, where two portions of the four-part model are given prominence, namely the doctrinal or dogmatic and the practical. Brakel's *Redelijke Godsdienst* offers a vernacular version of the orthodox theology, buttressed with biblical citations and, as necessary, rebuttals of the heresies of the era, followed by carefully-defined statements of the relationship of the doctrine to practice or Christian "use."[198] In both cases, Mastricht and Brakel, we have examples of the confluence of scholastic training and piety that is characteristic of the movement inspired by the work of the Utrecht professors Gisbertus Voetius and Johannes Hoornbeeck.[199] A detailed theology, with considerable emphasis on the Trinity, written out in the form of extended catechetical exercises on the Apostles' Creed and Lord's Prayer was produced in the

---

196. Petrus van Mastricht, *Theoretico-practica theologia, qua, per capita theologica, pars dogmatica, elenchtica et practica, perpetua sumbibasei conjugantur, praecedunt in usum operis, paraleipomena, seu sceleton de optima concionandi methodo*, 2 vols. (Amsterdam: Henricus & Theodorus Boom, 1682-1687); subsequent editions, in one vol. folio (Utrecht: van de Water, Poolsum, Wagens & Paddenburg, 1714; editio nova, 1724), II.xxiv.1, citing 2 Cor. 13:13, according to the *Statenvertaling* versification, 13:14 in the KJV.

197. Mastricht, *Theoretico-practica theol*, II.xxvi.2.

198. Wilhelmus à Brakel, *ΛΟΓΙΚΗ ΛΑΤΡΕΙΑ, dat is Redelijke Godsdienst in welken de goddelijke Waarheden van het Genade-Verbond worden verklaard ... alsmede de Bedeeling des Verbonds in het O. en N.T. en de Ontmoeting der Kerk in het N. T. vertoond in eene Verklaring van de Openbaringen aan Johannes*, 3 parts (Dordrecht, 1700; second printing, Leiden: D. Donner, 1893-94); in translation, *The Christian's Reasonable Service in which Divine Truths concerning the Covenant of Grace are Expounded, Defended against Opposing Parties, and their Practice Advocated*, translated by Bartel Elshout, with a biographical sketch by W. Fieret and an essay on the "Dutch Second Reformation" by Joel Beeke, 4 vols. (Ligonier, PA: Soli Deo Gloria Publications, 1992-95).

199. For a discussion and further bibliography on Voetius, see Muller, *After Calvin*, pp. 110-116, 227-228.

same era by the Utrecht covenant theologian Herman Witsius.[200] Witsius' expositions evidence the *Nadere Reformatie* interest in piety, just as they also demonstrate the breadth of his biblical and patristic learning.

3. **Major British thinkers and doctrinal developments.** In separating the British development of doctrine from the continental development of Reformed thought, we in no wise indicate a major difference in doctrine from the continental Reformed, only a difference in ethos identifiable in the less-systematic character of the British Reformed approach and the tendency of the British, at least in the beginnings of seventeenth-century Puritan and Reformed theology, to be more attentive to the relationship between piety or spirituality and doctrinal statement than the continental thinkers. Throughout the seventeenth century, the British writers and the continentals were fully aware of each others' works and the mutual influences are obvious.

Quite significant, both in England and for the development of continental orthodoxy was the *Instructiones historico-theologiae de doctrina Christiana* by John Forbes of Corse, professor at Aberdeen. The work appeared at Amsterdam in 1645 with prefatory letters of commendation from Polyander, Triglandius, Spanheim, and Rivetus of Leiden, Voetius, Maresius, and Hoornbeeck of Utrecht, Cloppenburg, and Cocceius of Franecker, Alting of Groningen, and Vossius, then of Amsterdam.[201] The various books or parts of the volume present biblical-historical statements of the doctrines of God such as Trinity, incarnation, sects within the church, and various heresies such as adoptionism and Pelagianism, together with topics of polemic and debate like Mohammedanism, the sacraments, purgatory, and the chair of Peter. The work is noteworthy for its gathering of sources and texts: thus, on the Trinity, it surveys the history of heresies, offers copious excerpts from Ignatius, Justin, Athenagoras, and Irenaeus, provides texts of the Antiochene Creed against Paul of Samosata, the Nicene, Constantinopolitan, and Athanasian Creeds, gives selections from Athanasius and the Cappadocians, and presents a series of topical chapters, again based on historical sources. Forbes argued the orthodoxy of the ante-Nicene tradition, but allowed for the development of language, recognizing the relative fluidity of terms prior to councils and other moments of dogmatic definition. He could, therefore, argue against the various trinitarian heretics of the day who had claimed, for example, that the doctrine of the Trinity was a late patristic invention.[202]

From Forbes, the Protestant orthodox of the late sixteenth century also received a catalogue of patristic *regulae* "useful for understanding the ways of speaking

---

200. Herman Witsius, *Exercitationes sacrae in symbolum quod Apostolorum dicitur. Et in Orationem dominicam* (Amsterdam, 1697); in translation, *Sacred Dissertations on what is commonly called the Apostles' Creed*, trans. D. Fraser, 2 vols. (Edinburgh: A. Fullarton / Glasgow: Kull, Blackie & Co., 1823) and *Sacred Dissertations on the Lord's Prayer*, trans., with notes, by William Pringle (Edinburgh: Thomas Clarke, 1839). There is also significant trinitarian meditation in Witsius' *De oeconomia foederum Dei cum hominibus libri quattuor* (Leeuwarden, 1685; Utrecht, 1694), II.ii-iv, relative to the *pactum salutis*.

201. John Forbes, *Instructiones historico-theologicae de doctrina christiana* (Amsterdam, 1645).

202. See further, in this volume, 3.2 (A.2).

(*loquutiones*) about the trinity of God;" first and foremost of which, for Forbes, was the Augustinian dictum that wherever one of the persons is named in relation to a particular work, the operation of the entire Trinity is understood. The multiplicity of works terminating on particular persons does not disrupt or compromise the unity of knowledge and will in the Godhead.[203] Thus, too, Forbes indicates, Athanasius had insisted that the Trinity is "undivided and united in itself, so that when the Father is named, his Word is with him and his Spirit is in the Son." The Spirit is not to be understood as *extra Verbum*. And Gregory of Nyssa is seen to concur in his declaration that there is no variation in glory between the Father, the Son, and the Spirit.[204]

The virtue of Forbes' work lies in its cogent and broad gathering of materials indicative of the orthodox trajectory of doctrine — although its tendency is to see the history not as a development of new concepts but as an increasingly explicit defense of a relatively stable doctrinal point. Still, Forbes' work, unlike Bishop Bull's more famous *Defense of the Nicene Faith*, did not rest its claims of patristic truth on a radical harmonization of ante-Nicene with post-Nicene doctrinal statements. Forbes, like Daillé, was willing to recognize differences of opinion among the fathers and to recognize that, given the fathers lack of uniformity, they could not function as a unified, final authority in doctrinal matters.

The doctrine of the Trinity also received concentrated attention from several of the major English Puritan divines: John Arrowsmith, Regius Professor of Divinity at Cambridge and a member of the Westminster Assembly, wrote a massive treatise on the divinity and humanity of the Son based on the Johannine prologue.[205] Perhaps the clearest British expression both of the positive doctrine of the Trinity and of the orthodox polemic came from Francis Cheynell, who was, like Arrowsmith, a Westminster divine: *The Rise, Growth, and Danger of Socinianism* (1643) and, after the Socinian controversy broke in earnest, *The Divine Triunity of the Father, Son and Holy Spirit* (1650). In the former treatise, Cheynell argued the weakness of the trinitarian theology of the Anglican church and accused both Laud and Chillingworth of tending toward Socinianism — he was certainly correct in noting the Arianizing direction of much theology in his time, a problem that would become apparent in the latter decades of the seventeenth century.[206] The Quaker George Whitehead produced a treatise — with specific reference to the much-disputed "Johannine comma" (1 John 5:7) — on *The Divinity of Christ, and the Unity of the Three that Bear Record in Heaven* (1669). Nor ought the more catechetical and homiletical developments to be neglected:

203. Forbes, *Instructiones hist.*, I.xxi.1, citing Augustine, *Enchiridion*, 28.

204. Forbes, *Instructiones hist.*, I.xxi.1, citing Athanasius, *Ad Serapionem*; Nyssa, *Lib. de differentia essentiae & hypostaseos*.

205. John Arrowsmith, *Theanthropos, or, God-Man: being an Exposition upon the First Eighteen Verses of the First Chapter of the Gospel according to St. John, wherein is most accurately and divinely handled, the divinity and humanity of Jesus Christ, proving him to be God and Man, coequall and coeternall with the Father* (London: Humphrey Moseley & William Wilson, 1660).

206. Cf. McLachlan, *Socinianism*, pp. 52-62, on Laud, Chillingworth, their use of Acontius' *Stratagematum Satanae*, and Cheynell's critique.

British thinkers like Flavel, Vincent and Watson produced significant catechetical discussions of the doctrine of the Trinity in commentaries on the Westminster Shorter Catechism.[207] Among the Anglican divines of the era, moreover, John Pearson stands preeminent as an exegete and theologian, serving as a major collaborator in the *Critici sacri* (1660).[208] Pearson's *Exposition of the Creed* (1659) evidences his grasp of biblical, patristic, medieval, and early modern materials and his *Lectiones de Deo* offer a more scholastic approach to theological definition.[209] The former work is particularly important for its exposition of the doctrines of the Trinity and the person of Christ.

Perhaps the greatest of the English Puritan authors of the era, both for his massive works on Christian communion with God as Trinity, on the doctrine of the Holy Spirit, and on the glory of Christ, and for his detailed grasp of the history and problem of Socinianism, was John Owen.[210] Against the Socinians and in response to the English antitrinitarian developments of the mid-seventeenth century, he penned *Vindiciae evangelicae; or, the Mystery of the Gospel Vindicated and Socinianism Examined* (1655) and *A Brief Declaration and Vindication of the Doctrine of the Trinity: as also of the Person and Satisfaction of Christ* (1669).[211] The trinitarian foundation of his theology is evident in his *Communion with God the Father, Son, and Holy Ghost* (1657), while his most enduring contribution to trinitarian theology is certainly the *Pneumatologia or, A Discourse Concerning the Holy Spirit*, a treatise that occupied Owen during the last decade of his life and that fills two volumes in his collected works. The first portion of the *Pneumatologia* appeared in 1674, with successive parts published in 1677, 1678, 1682 and (posthumously) 1693: the work is perhaps the most exhaustive analysis of

207. John Flavel, *An Exposition of the Assembly's Catechism, with Practical Inferences from Each Question*, in *The Works of John Flavel*, 6 vols. (London: Baynes and Son, 1820; repr. Edinburgh: Banner of Truth, 1968), VI, pp. 138-317; Thomas Vincent, *An explicatory catechism, or, An explanation of the Assemblies Shorter catechism: wherein all the answers in the Assemblies catechism are taken abroad in under questions and answers, the truths explained, and proved by reason and scripture, several cases of conscience resolved, some chief controversies in religion stated: with arguments against divers errors, itself, for the more and clear and through understanding of what is therein learned* (London: George Calvert et al., 1673); Thomas Watson, *A Body of Practical Divinity* (London, 1692).

208. *Critici Sacri: sive doctissimorum virorum in SS. Biblia annotationes, & tractatus*, 9 vols. (London, 1660).

209. John Pearson, *An Exposition of the Creed by John, Lord Bishop of Chester* (London, 1659; third edition, with additions, 1669); I have followed *An Exposition of the Creed*, with an analysis by Edward Walford, M.A. (London: Bell and Sons, 1887); also John Pearson, *Lectiones de Deo et attributis* (ca. 1661), in *The Minor Theological Works of John Pearson, D.D.*, now first collected, with a memoir of the author ... by Edward Churton, 2 vols. (Oxford: Oxford University Press, 1844), I, pp. 1-267.

210. I have consistently followed John Owen, *The Works of John Owen*, ed. William H. Goold, 17 vols. (London and Edinburgh: Johnstone & Hunter, 1850-53), and idem, *An Exposition of the Epistle to the Hebrews*, ed. William H. Goold, 7 vols. (London and Edinburgh: Johnstone and Hunter, 1855). On Owen's theology, see Carl R. Trueman, *The Claims of Truth*; Sebastian Rehnman, *Divine Discourse: The Theological Methodology of John Owen* (Grand Rapids: Baker Book House, 2002); and idem, "John Owen: A Reformed Scholastic at Oxford," in *Reformation and Scholasticism*, ed. Van Asselt and Dekker, pp. 181-203.

211. John Owen, *A Brief Declaration and Vindication of the Doctrine of the Trinity: as also of the Person and Satisfaction of Christ* (1669), in *Works*, vol. 2, pp. 365-439.

the Person and Work of the Spirit ever produced.[212] It is both a positive and a polemical exposition of doctrine, with arguments against the Socinians, the Quakers, and the various impieties of the era of the Restoration. Moreover, in his works against the Socinians and his review of Grotius' *Annotationes*, and, in addition, in his major commentary on the Epistle to the Hebrews, Owen defended the traditional trinitarian and christological exegesis of Scripture.

Had Owen not written so expansively on the doctrine of the Trinity and particularly on the person and work of the Holy Spirit, his contemporary Thomas Goodwin would certainly be remembered as having produced one of the most exhaustive treatises on the work of the Holy Spirit in the seventeenth century. This posthumously published work, gathered together from manuscripts into a fairly cohesive treatise in ten books by Goodwin's son, focuses on the work of the Spirit in the salvation of human beings.[213] The work is largely a work of piety and non-polemical in its argument. Still, it presents numerous reflections on the place of the Spirit in the Trinity and on the unity of the divine work as distributed among the persons, and it reflects the orthodox doctrine of the Trinity as developed by the Reformed and Puritan divines during the seventeenth century. Similar comments can also be made concerning Goodwin's posthumous *Discourse of Christ the Mediator*, noteworthy for its presentation of the doctrine of the work of Christ both in a language suitable for piety and in the light of the carefully tooled scholastic distinctions of the era. Goodwin was particularly sensitive to the trinitarian issues underlying christological discussion, notably the issues of the intra-traintarian foundation of Christ's work (described by Goodwin in terms of the *pactum salutis*) and of the *opera appropriata* of the persons as personal works nonetheless indicative of the unity of the divine work *ad extra*.[214]

If Owen and Goodwin offered largely nonspeculative expositions of the doctrine of the Trinity, Christ, and the Holy Spirit, intended, on the one hand, for basic edification and, on the other, for the refutation of trinitarian errors, their contemporary and sometime opponent in polemic Richard Baxter produced a more speculative doctrine of the Trinity — an irony given Baxter's reputation as an author of works on piety. Baxter held a fundamentally trinitarian or triadic view of the universe in general: he held that the mark of the divine Trinity had been impressed on all things and was profoundly attracted to the triadic models in the philosophy of Campanella.[215] Taking this triadic model of reality as his foundation, Baxter could conclude that the

---

212. John Owen, ΠΝΕΥΜΑΤΟΛΟΓΙΑ *or, a Discourse concerning the Holy Spirit* (1674-1693) in *Works*, vols. 3-4.

213. Thomas Goodwin, *Of the Work of the Holy Ghost in our Salvation*, in *Works*, 5 vols. (London, 1681-1704), as vol. V; also *Works*, 12 vols. (Edinburgh and London: Nichol & Nisbet, 1861-1866), as vol. VI.

214. Thomas Goodwin, A *Discourse of Christ the Mediator*, in *Works* (1861-1866), vol. V.

215. Carl R. Trueman, "A Small Step Toward Rationalism: The Impact of the Metaphysics of Tommaso Campanella on the Theology of Richard Baxter," in *Protestant Scholasticism: Essays in Reassessment*, ed. Carl R. Trueman and R. Scott Clark (Carlisle: Paternoster Press, 1999), pp. 181-195.

triadic nature of human beings, made in the image of God, provided the best metaphor for the Trinity: the Godhead was to be best understood in terms of its life, intellect, and will — the Father, as the living principle; the Son, as intellect understanding itself (*intellectus se intelligens*); the Spirit as will loving itself (*voluntas se amans*). In the eternal act of the Godhead, the Father by knowing generates the Son, and the Father and the Son by the communication of divine love produce the Spirit. These internal relations of the Godhead, moreover, according to Baxter, provide the foundation of the relationship of the Godhead to the world: the Father is the power of the Godhead manifest in the creation of things, the Son is the wisdom of the Godhead manifest in the ordering of things and in the gift of grace, and the Spirit is the love of the Godhead manifest in end or goal of all things.[216]

In addition, as evidenced clearly by the exegetical side of the Socinian assault, the sixteenth- and seventeenth-century revolution in hermeneutics together with the Protestant loss of the normative functions of tradition and churchly magisterium rendered the doctrine increasingly difficult of easy proof. Socinian exegesis could, for example, wax eloquent over the subordinationist implications of texts like 1 Cor. 15:28, "And when all things shall be subdued unto him, then shall the Son also himself be subject unto him that put all things under him, that God may be all in all" or John 14:28, "... I go unto the Father, for my Father is greater than I." Orthodox Protestant exegetes held fast to traditional patristic and medieval distinctions concerning such texts, so that the "the Son's subjection to his Father" is argued not to "prove his inequality of essence or power with his Father" but only "that he should deliver up his mediatory kingdom to his Father."[217] Or, in the case of the latter text, "my Father is greater than I," the words indicate that the Father is "not greater in essence, (as the Arians and Socinians would have it,) ... but greater, 1. Either as to the order amongst the Divine Persons ... Or, 2. As a Mediator sent from the Father ... in the form of a servant."[218] The orthodox exegetes were also still able to argue, albeit with

---

216. Richard Baxter, *Methodus theologiae christianae* (London, 1681), I.ii (pp. 34-37); cf. Fisher, "Theology of Richard Baxter," p. 155.

217. Matthew Poole, *Annotations on the Holy Bible*, 2 vols. (London, 1683-85); reissued as *A Commentary on the Holy Bible*, 3 vols. (London: Banner of Truth, 1962), III, p. 595, hereinafter cited as Poole, *Commentary*; cf. Hilary, *De trinitate*, IX.51, 54-55; Augustine, *De trinitate*, I.vii.14; xi.22; II.i.3; VI.ix.10.

218. Poole, *Commentary*, John 14:28, in loc. (III, p. 357). Other major commentaries of the era offer the same conclusions: see JeanDiodati, *Pious and Learned Annotations upon the Holy Bible, plainly Expounding the Most Difficult Places Thereof*, third edition (London: James Flesher, 1651), in loc.; John Trapp, *Annotations upon the Old and New Testaments in Five Distinct Volumes* (London: Robert White, 1662), in loc., reissued as *A Commentary on the Old and New Testaments*, 5 vols. (London: Richard Dickinson, 1856-1868), V, p. 397; *The Dutch Annotations upon the Whole Bible: Or, All the holy canonical Scriptures of the Old and New Testament ... as ... appointed by the Synod of Dort, 1618, and published by authority, 1637*, 2 vols., trans. Theodore Haak (London, 1657), in loc.; and *Annotations upon all the Books of the Old and New Testament, wherein the Text is Explained, Doubts Resolved, Scriptures Parallelled, and Various Readings observed*, by the Joynt-Labour of certain Learned Divines (London, 1645; 2nd ed., 1651; 3rd ed. 1657) in loc., hereinafter cited as *Westminster Annotations*, from the 1645 edition, unless otherwise noted.

ever-decreasing grounds, even in the late seventeenth and early eighteenth centuries, that warrant still existed for the inclusion of disputed passages like the so-called "Johannine comma" (1 John 5:7) or of the word "God" in 1 Tim. 3:16 in the authoritative text.[219] Such debates, moreover, spawned an entire genre of treatises in which orthodox writers presented a verse-by-verse refutation of the Socinian exegesis.[220]

The high level of polemic and the technical character of scholastic debate should not lead to the conclusion that the trinitarian interests of the seventeenth century were ever far removed from the context of piety: just as the "scholastic" theology of the age was the technical form, paralleled at less-technical levels by "positive" and "catechetical" theology, so too were the debates fought at every level. And it must also be observed that the level of theological technique found in tracts and treatises written by laity was very high — as is demonstrated by the trinitarian, christological, and covenantal argumentation found in the tracts of the self-educated John Bunyan. He expressed major concerns over the errors of his day, particularly "taking a part of the word only" and, for example, concluding from a text like Deuteronomy 6:4, "The Lord our God is one Lord," that "there are not three persons in the godhead."[221] In addition, as Bunyan's tracts demonstrate, not only doctrinal knowledge but also the need for precision in one's orthodoxy was also assumed: thus, on the subject of the Trinity, Bunyan confessed "three persons or subsistences" in the Godhead and indicated that "these three are in nature, essence, and eternity, equally one."[222]

Some of the orthodox writers of the era noted that there were adumbrations of the doctrine of the Trinity in the works of Plato: Plato indeed speaks of three principles, goodness or being; the word or reason of that supreme being; and the spirit "which diffuses its influence throughout the whole system of beings ... the soul of the world." His followers speak of these principles as "three hypostases."[223] These Platonic

---

219. Cf. Poole, Commentary, 1 John 5:5 and 1 Tim. 3:16, in loc. with Matthew Henry, An Exposition of the Old and New Testament: wherein each chapter is summed up in its contents: the sacred text inserted at large, in distinct paragraphs; each paragraph reduced to its proper heads: the sense given, and largely illustrated; with practical remarks and observations, New edition, revised and corrected, 6 vols. (London: James Nisbet, n.d.), 1 John 5:5 and 1 Tim. 3:16 in loc. Note that this edition of Henry's commentary is unpaginated and must be cited by the book, chapter, and verse. On the debate over the "Comma," see below, 4.2 (C.3).

220. E.g., Paul Jasz-Berenyi, Examen doctrinæ ariano-socinianæ à quodam anonymo sub hoc titulo evulgate, Doctrina de Deo, & Christo, & Spiritu Sancto, ipsis scripturae verbis, ante paucos annos, à quodam divinæ veritatis confessore, in sermone Germanico concinnata, nunc vero, in gratiam exterorum, Latine edita (London: Samuel Brown, 1662); H. C. De Luzancy, Remarks on several late writings publish'd in English by the Socinians wherein is show'd the insufficiency and weakness of their answers to the texts brought against them by the orthodox. London: Tho. Warren, 1696.

221. John Bunyan, Of the Trinity and a Christian, in The Whole Works of John Bunyan, Accurately Reprinted from the Author's Own Editions, with editorial prefaces, notes, and life of Bunyan by George Offor, esq., 3 vols. (1875; reprint, Grand Rapids: Baker Book House, 1977), II, p. 387.

222. John Bunyan, A Confession of Faith, §4-5 in Works (Offor), II, p. 594.

223. Cf. Thomas Ridgley, A Body of Divinity: Wherein the Doctrines of the Christian Religion are Explained and Defended, being the Substance of Several Lectures on the Assembly's Larger Catechism, 2

adumbrations of divine triunity received their most exhaustive seventeenth-century exposition at the hands of the Cambridge Platonist Ralph Cudworth.[224] And although his work lies outside of what can be properly called either Reformed orthodoxy or English Puritanism, the scope and impact of the work is such that some notice must be taken of it here. Cudworth's *True Intellectual System of the Universe* (1678) was written as a quasi-historical refutation of atheism and determinism in which the "true intellectual system" was identified as having classical philosophical and patristic roots.

Granting the character of the Platonic models themselves and the use to which they had been put both by theologians of the early church like Eusebius of Caesarea[225] and by trinitarian apologists of the seventeenth century, the Reformed orthodox raise questions concerning both the origin of these concepts in Plato and the advisability of their use in the cause of Reformed trinitarianism. Such arguments, argues Ridgley, do not derive from "the light of nature": their source ultimately is the Bible. Plato traveled in Egypt and his followers, Plotinus, Proclus, and Porphyry, most certainly borrowed their trinitarian metaphysics from their Christian adversaries.[226]

The possible Judaeo-Christian origins of Platonic trinitarianism did not, however, give universal credence to the use of Platonic argumentation in the orthodox doctrine of the Trinity. Cudworth's highly philosophical understanding of the Trinity, particularly given the context of debate with Socinian theology, was rapidly pronounced heretical, albeit without any great precision: Turner pronounced him to be a "Tritheist" and subsequently, in the same treatise, identified Cudworth as "an Arian, a Socinian, or a Deist."[227] Like the historical work of Petavius, Cudworth's *True Intellectual System* served to identify for its age the diversity of ancient trinitarian expression, a point that had been taken up in far less detail and with far less erudition by antitrinitarians of the sixteenth and seventeenth centuries. The accusations of heresy were, therefore, largely a matter of guilt by association. Yet Cudworth's work certainly fueled the fires of late seventeenth-century trinitarian debate, particularly as it touched on the problem of pre-Nicene and non-Nicene expressions of the doctrine. Unlike church historians of the nineteenth century like Newman, the theologians of the seventeenth century well recognized that the division of patristic debate between Arian and Nicene parties

---

vols. (London, 1731-33), p. 111, col. 1, citing (Pseudo) Plato, *Second Epistle to Dionysius*; note the later edition, *Commentary on the Larger Catechism; Previously Entitled A Body of Divinity*, revised, with notes by John M. Wilson (1855; reprint, Edmonton: Still Waters Revival Books, 1993) also note Marckius, *Compendium*, V.xxviii.

224. Cudworth, *True Intellectual System of the Universe*, I, pp. 759-791.

225. Eusebius of Caesarea, *Preparation for the Gospel*, trans. Edwin Gifford, 2 vols. (Oxford: Clarendon Press, 1903; repr. Grand Rapids: Baker Book House, 1981), XI.xvii-xxii; idem, *The Proof of the Gospel*, trans. W. J. Ferrar, 2 vols. (London: S.P.C.K., 1920; reprint, Grand Rapids: Baker Book House, 1981), IV.i-v. On Eusebius' theology, see Colm Luibhéid, *Eusebius of Caesarea and the Arian Crisis* (Dublin: Irish Academic Press, 1981).

226. Ridgley, *Body of Divinity*, p. 111, cols. 1-2.

227. John Turner, *Discourse on the Messiah* (London, 1685), pp. 17, 19.

was simplistic — and several authors, perhaps with reliance on Cudworth, sought to find non-Arian but also non-Nicene options for theological expression.[228]

Mastery of ancient texts is also apparent in the work of George Bull, bishop of St. David's. Like John Forbes' earlier *Instructiones historico-theologiae*, Bishop George Bull's *Defense of the Nicene Faith* is noteworthy for its erudite (if ultimately unsuccessful) attempt to show that historically the church had always taught the same doctrine, albeit in varying terms, and that the ante-Nicene and Nicene doctrines were identical in substance. Bull published his *Defensio Fidei Nicenae* (1685) just prior to the outbreak of the late seventeenth-century English trinitarian controversy. The work began as a defense of his own orthodoxy against charges of Socinianism and developed into an elaborate historical proof that the theology of Nicaea had preceded the council and was, in fact, the norm of earliest Christianity. Bull, who ended his days as bishop of St. Davids, was a high Anglican and, as far as the English debates of the seventeenth century frame his work, no ally of the Puritans or English Reformed tradition. Nonetheless, his work was of massive significance for the orthodoxies of his day and respected by Puritan and Reformed alike. Bull's *Defense* not only assessed evidences from the fathers but also developed arguments against Petavius, Sandius, Zwicker, Episcopius, and Curcellaeus.

There is some irony, but considerable justice, in the fact that the central logical pivot of Bull's argument earned him the praise of the Roman Catholic Bossuet — for Bull had argued that Christ's promise to be with the church always, even to the end of the world, could only be true if the church was preserved without error in the doctrines of Nicaea. Bossuet applauded the argument and extended it to the Council of Trent. Bull's method was to gather statements of the ante-Nicene church concerning Christ's divinity and preexistence and then read them in the light of Nicene doctrine. The result of this rather ahistorical method was a doctrine of the Trinity which, though staunchly anti-Arian, tended to interpret the creedal language of "God of God, Light of Light, Very God of Very God" as an indication of derivation of the Son and therefore also of the Spirit from the Father. The tendency, then, even in Bull's defense of Nicaea is toward a subordinationist doctrine of the Son and the Spirit. Bull also published a treatise against the subordinationistic tendencies in the Christology of Episcopius and the Remonstrants,[229] demonstrating that his own subordinationist tendencies were hardly as great as those of many of his contemporaries. The later Reformed, including

---

228. Cf. Pfizenmaier, *Trinitarian Theology of Dr. Samuel Clarke*, pp. 89-142. Newman's understanding of the Arian controversy can be found in John Henry Newman, *The Arians of the Fourth Century, their Doctrine, temper, and Conduct, chiefly as Exhibited in the Councils of the Church, between A.D. 325, and A.D. 381* (London: J.G. & F. Rivington, 1833; 2nd ed., 1878); the return to a scholarly perception of varied parties in the debate is magisterially surveyed in R. P. C. Hanson, *The Search for the Christian Doctrine of God: The Arian Controversy, 318-381* (Edinburgh: T. & T. Clark, 1988).

229. George Bull, *Judicium Ecclesiæ Catholicæ trium primorum seculorum, de necessitate credendi quod Dominus noster Jesus Christus sit verus Deus, assertum contra M. Simonem Episcopium aliosque.* (Oxford: George West, 1694); also *The Opinion of the Catholic Church for the First Three Centuries, on the Necessity of Believing that our Lord Jesus Christ is truly God*, trans. T. Rankin (London, 1825).

De Moor, cite Bull's work well into the eighteenth century, noting both its massive documentation of the fathers against various heretics, but also arguing against its fairly radical subordination of the Son, a point of doctrine inimical to Reformed trinitarianism.[230]

Bull offered what became, for many orthodox writers of the seventeenth century, a definitive proof that the doctrine of the Trinity had been believed "everywhere, always, and by all" in precisely the form given it by the council of Nicaea. Bull's *Defense* was viewed by many in its own time as a definitive rebuttal and was accepted as a standard proof of the historical error of seventeenth- and eighteenth-century Arianism in general and of Sandius' work in particular long into the Age of Reason, at least by the proponents of orthodox doctrine, as Stackhouse's laudatory remarks indicate.[231] Here, too, however, we encounter the problem of the late orthodox inability to cope with the new historical method and what might be called "critical exegesis." As in the case of the exegesis of Scripture, so also in the case of Sandius' and Zwicker's exegesis of the ante-Nicene theology, the opponents of orthodoxy were able to show that the documents, understood in their historical context, did not easily produce the doctrines of later Christian orthodoxy — while the orthodox theologians of the day tended to avoid issues of history and development and to look at the documents from the point of view of the later dogmatic result, a method in the history of doctrine not unlike the use of the *analogia fidei* in the exegesis of Scripture. Bull, in other words, assumed the universal harmony of orthodox Christian doctrine throughout the centuries and, when he examined the ante-Nicene sources, found that they all stood in agreement with Nicaea.

Bull subsequently penned a brief defense of his great treatise and a second, very short, discourse against the heretical tendencies in late seventeenth-century England.[232] In the latter treatise, he identified what he saw as a problem of Sabellianism latent in many of the orthodox responses to the Arianism and subordinationism of the late seventeenth century. Like Arminius, some eight decades earlier, Bull identified a problem in the various seventeenth-century identifications of the Son as *autotheos*. In Bull's view,

> there is but one fountain or principle of Divinity, God the Father, Who only is Αὐτόθεος, God of and from Himself; the Son and the Holy Ghost deriving their

---

230. See Bernhard de Moor, *Commentarius perpetuus in Joh. Marckii compendium theologiae christianae didactico-elencticum*, 7 vols. in 6 (Leiden, 1761-1771), I.v.7, citing Bull favorably as a source of materials.

231. Stackhouse, *Complete Body of Divinity*, vol. I, p. 240.

232. Geroge Bull, *The Consubstantiality and Coeternity of the Son of God with God the Father, Asserted; or, some few Animadversions on a trretise of Mr. Gilbert Clerke, entitled, AnteNicenismus*, in *The English Theological Works of George Bull, D.D., sometime Bishop of St. David's* (Oxford: J. H. Parker, 1844), pp. 409-44; idem, *The Doctrine of the Catholic Church for the First Three Ages of Christianity, concerning the Blessed Trinity, considered, in opposition to Sabellianism and Tritheism* [1697], in *English Theological Works*, pp. 371-82.

Divinity from Him; the Son immediately from the Father, the Holy Ghost from the Father and the Son, or from the Father by the Son.[233]

Bull did not accept the distinction between the consideration of the second Person of the Trinity as the begotten Son and consideration of the second Person of the Trinity according to the fulness of his essence, the essence itself (which the Son has) being *a se ipso*. Bull continues his argument by noting, in support of Sherlock and, by implication, against South, that they "are very near unto this heresy [of Sabellianism], who acknowledge only a modal distinction between the Father, Son, and Holy Ghost."[234]

2.3 The Doctrine of the Trinity in the Late Seventeenth and the Early Eighteenth Century

A. Perspectives on the Trinitarian Problem in a Time of Transition, 1685-1725

The transformation of Christian doctrine that took place at the end of the seventeenth and in the early eighteenth century under the impact of rationalist philosophy and altered patterns and models of exegesis is nowhere more apparent than in the doctrine of the Trinity. Here, as in the doctrine of the divine essence and attributes, nominally orthodox writers strained under the loss of much of the exegetical basis of the doctrine as they did under the problem of the increasingly problematic character of traditional philosophical and theological vocabulary.

Some nominally orthodox writers drew upon the new philosophies for the sake of developing and defending traditional theism, while others turned away from the traditional alliance of theology and philosophy and attempted to develop theological systems and doctrinal statements without overt recourse to any philosophical perspective. The result of their efforts was either the maintenance of orthodox teaching without its traditional exegetical and philosophical underpinnings or a development of doctrine away from traditional norms. The former model is apparent in the so-called transitional or latitudinarian theologies of J. A. Turretin, Osterwald, and Burnet in which the "orthodoxy" of the writer is occasionally open to question and, in the mid-eighteenth century, in the late orthodox works of writers like Venema,[235] De Moor, and Gill.[236] The latter development is manifest in the mathematical trinitarianism

---

233. Bull, *Doctrine of the Catholic Church*, p. 371.

234. Bull, *Doctrine of the Catholic Church*, p. 373.

235. Herman Venema, *Exercitationes de vera Christi Divinitate, ex locis Act. XX: 28, I Tim. III:16, I Joh. V: 20 et Col. I:16, 17: quibus de vera lectione et genuio sensu eorum accuratius disseritur* (Leovardiae: Gulielmus Coulon, 1755), and idem, *Institutes of Theology*, part I, trans. Alexander Brown (Edinburgh: T. & T. Clark, 1850).

236. John Gill, *Complete Body of Doctrinal and Practical Divinity: or A System of Evangelical Truths Deduced from the Sacred Scriptures*, with *A Dissertation Concerning the Baptism of Jewish Proselytes*, 2 vols. (1769-1770; reissued, London: Tegg & Company, 1839; reprint, Grand Rapids: Baker Book House, 1978). Gill's theology was rooted in his exegetical efforts: *An Exposition of the New Testament*, 3 vols. (London, 1746-1748); and *An Exposition of the Old Testament*, 6 vols. (London, 1748-1763);

of Darjes and Wallis, the proof of the Trinity from the principle of sufficient reason by the Wolffian Reinbeck; the quasi-Cartesian "tritheism" of Sherlock, the seeming "Arianism" of Whiston, Clarke, and Newton; and the apparent modalism of some of their opponents.[237]

Not to be underestimated here is the impact of patristic scholarship in the seventeenth century. If the Reformation altered the balance of Scripture and tradition by declaring that, although tradition stood as a subordinate norm identifying probabilities, it still could err (as demonstrated by the experience of the later Middle Ages), the antitrinitarian debate of the late seventeenth century altered the balance once more. The antitrinitarians claimed a biblical foundation that was radically anti-traditionary — to the point that writers like Nye and Smalbroke argued the biblical rectitude of views expressed by early heretics like the Ebionites and Nazarenes.

The last decades of the seventeenth and the beginning of the eighteenth century saw such a vast alteration of the exegetical and philosophical framework of explanation that the attempts at trinitarian discussion of a whole generation of writers failed to produce a statement of doctrine that was at the same time philosophically contemporary and theologically orthodox. In addition, these English Socinians claimed to be truly Protestant and fundamentally biblicistic, true heirs of the Reformation — noting that the Reformation proclaimed the correct biblical standard but did not go far enough in rooting out the problematic elements of the tradition (among which the doctrine of the Trinity held a place of prominence).[238]

B. Trinitarian Debate in Britain

1. From Bull's *Defense* (1685) to *The Naked Gospel* (1690). Coincident with the debate over Bull's work was the revival of Socinianism in England. The heresy had not died with Biddle in his prison — it was too much a characteristic of the rationalizing and ethicizing mind of the time to pass easily out of existence. In 1687 Stephen Nye published the apologetic treatise *A Brief History of the Unitarians,*[239] announcing the beginning of the great trinitarian controversy of the end of the seventeenth century. Shortly thereafter, Nye began to issue a series of tracts, republishing several of Biddle's works and augmenting them with essays of his own. The link between Nye and Biddle was the London merchant Thomas Firmin, who financed the publication of Nye's history. Firmin had befriended Biddle some three decades earlier, prior to Biddle's trial and exile, and had adopted Unitarian views. Beginning in 1662, Firmin had undertaken a series of charitable ventures, particularly

---

hereinafter cited by book of the Bible, e.g., *Exposition of Genesis*, etc.

237. Note Thomas C. Pfizenmaier, "Was Isaac Newton an Arian?" in *Journal of the History of Ideas*, 58 (1997), pp. 57-80, for a significant discussion of Newton's place in the seventeenth-century discussion of Nicaea and a cogent argument for Newton as a non-Arian *homoiousian*; cf. the discussions in Fortman, *Triune God*, p. 245; and Franks, *Doctrine of the Trinity*, pp. 149-151.

238. Anon., *Defense of the Brief History*, p. 3.

239. Stephen Nye, *A Brief History of the Unitarians, called also Socinians* (London, 1687).

with a view to helping refugees of religious persecution in Poland.[240] In a similar gesture, Firmin underwrote the publication of antitrinitarian theology. Together with the *Brief History*, Firmin also issued *Brief Notes on the Athanasian Creed* and shortly thereafter an expanded version of the *Brief Notes* in an ironically entitled diatribe against Athanasius, *The Acts of the Great Athanasius*.[241]

The *Brief History* provides a carefully argued antitrinitarian doctrinal statement, gathers a mass of texts from Scripture (in canonical order), and uses the writings of the early fathers to argue a scriptural and ante-Nicene consensus concerning the subordination of the Son to the Father and the absence of any positive identification of the Spirit as a "person." Jesus could properly be titled "Minister" or "Messenger" of God and called "Son of God" insofar as he had been conceived by the divine power or "Spirit." Clearly, Jesus was a creature and not the equal of the Father. In addition to citing the works of Petavius, Sandius, and Episcopius in favor of Unitarianism, other great names were enlisted as antitrinitarian allies: Erasmus was praised as an Arian, Grotius as a Socinian.[242]

One little-noted aspect of the English controversy is the difficulty caused in the seventeenth century by the traditional trinitarian vocabulary, particularly by the term "person." As an examination of Nye's writings indicates, the traditional dogmatic understanding of "person" as *hypostasis* or *subsistentia* was increasingly less understood, and the identification of individual human beings as "persons" left the doctrine easy prey to those who viewed it as tritheistic. He insisted that "Jesus Christ is in Holy Scripture always spoken of, as a distinct and different Person from God; and described to be the Son of God and the Image of God."[243] Scripture, however, consistently "speaks of God as but one Person; and speaks of him and to him by singular Pronouns, such as *I, Thou, Me, Him, &c*" — the existence of three divine "persons" would necessarily indicate "three Gods."[244]

The *Brief Notes* and *Acts* take the Athanasian Creed as the point of departure for a polemic against all who would view right teaching rather than right living as necessary to salvation: by way of arguing the Unitarian case, it poses an attack on the very idea

---

240. See Wilbur, *History of Unitarianism*, II, p. 217.

241. See *The faith of one God, who is only the Father; and of one mediator between God and men, who is only the man Christ Jesus; and of one Holy Spirit, the gift (and sent) of God; asserted and defended, in several tracts contained in this volume; the titles whereof the reader will find in the following leaf. And after that a preface to the whole, or an exhortation to an impartial and free enquiry into doctrines of religion* (London: [s.n.], 1691). This is the first in a series of five antitrinitarian anthologies published between 1691 and 1703, the first three were sponsored by Firmin, beginning with a republication of tracts by Biddle, superintended and augmented by Nye: see the discussions of these collections and their contents in Hunt, *Religious Thought*, II, pp. 273-278; III, 604-607; and in Herbert McLachlan, "Seventeenth-Century Unitarian Tracts," in *The Story of a Non-Conformist Library* (Manchester: University of Manchester Press, 1925), pp. 53-87.

242. Nye, *Brief History of the Unitarians*, pp. 31-32 (Erasmus, Grotius, and Petavius); 34-35 (Episcopius and Sandius).

243. Nye, *Brief History of the Unitarians*, p. 11.

244. Nye, *Brief History of the Unitarians*, pp. 19, 24.

of an orthodoxy. The Athanasian Creed identifies its own teaching with the "Catholic Faith" and arbitrarily anathematizes any and all who depart from its norm. Yet its doctrine of the double procession of the Spirit excludes the whole Greek Church in the present and virtually all of the fathers up to and including those at the time of Nicaea. Athanasius himself was hardly regarded as orthodox in his own time: the majority of bishops, in accord with the ante-Nicene church, were Arian and saw to the condemnation of Athanasius at the Councils of Milan and Ariminum. The Athanasian Creed is contradicted by the Nicene view of the Son as "God of God" and by the infallible testimony of Scripture to the subordination of the Son. How then can the Athanasian Creed be identified as catholic — and how can such a distorted "orthodoxy" be required of anyone as a ground of salvation? The Unitarian position, according to the *Brief Notes* and *Acts*, relied on Scripture and not on subsequent rationalization.

Theological debate was intensified early in 1690 by the anonymous publication of *The Naked Gospel* by Arthur Bury.[245] The work was not, strictly speaking, either Socinian or directly supportive of the Socinian doctrinal program, but it offered such a blistering attack on the Christian tradition, whether of the later fathers or of the orthodoxy of the late seventeenth century, that it was easily associated with some of the arguments of the Socinians. Specifically, Bury argued that "scholastic" thinking, particularly the use of logic and metaphysics, had created a grand and confusing edifice of "new doctrines" not found in the gospel. It was the task of his book to criticize the rational or "natural" religion of the church in his time and propose a return to the original, simple, "naked" gospel of Christ and the apostles.[246] Bury attacks the ecumenical councils, particularly Nicaea, blaming them for creating a false and highly rationalized christology instead of more simply and directly the high "dignity" and "divinity" of Christ's person and his divine sonship in the office of mediator. As for the doctrine of the Trinity, Bury indicates that it is ultimately confusing, inasmuch as the identification of three divine "persons" in no way indicates three Gods and the language of the traditional doctrine, therefore, has no good analogy to typical usage.[247] Bury was suspended from the university.

2. William Sherlock and the broadening debate. The subsequent British debate is particularly significant in view of the philosophical diversity of its participants.[248] With the publication of William Sherlock's *A Vindication of the Holy and Blessed Trinity*

245. *The Naked Gospel, discovering I. What was the gospel which our Lord and his apostles preached, II. What additions and alterations latter ages have made in it, III. What advantages and damages have thereupon ensued : Part I. Of Faith, and therein, of the Holy Trinity, the incarnation of our Blessed Saviour, and the resurrection of the body* (London : s.n., 1690; London: Nathanael Ranew, 1691).

246. Bury, *Naked Gospel*, fol. G2r.

247. Bury, *Naked Gospel*, fol. E1v-E2r.

248. See the accounts of the debate in Roland N. Stromberg, *Religious Liberalism in Eighteenth Century England* (Oxford: Oxford University Press, 1954) and Martin Greig, "The Thought and Polemic of Gilbert Burnet, c. 1673-1704 (Ph.D. diss., Cambridge University, 1991) and idem, "Reasonableness of Christianity? Gilbert Burnet and the trinitarian Controversy of the 1690s," in *Journal of Ecclesiastical History*, 44/4 (October, 1993), pp. 631-651.

(1690), the character of the debate changed. Sherlock intended his treatise as a refutation of the Socinian teachings of Biddle, Nye, and Firmin and as a clarification of the orthodox definition of the Trinity for the sake of its better defense. Sherlock's intention has been to reassert orthodoxy specifically by offering explanations of the traditional trinitarian vocabulary suitable to the philosophical assumptions of his time. Given the variant views of substance and individuality we have seen from the earlier debates, Sherlock's approach did in fact address a major linguistic and philosophical issue. In Sherlock's estimation, the older formulations of one God in three persons which had for so long been supported by an Aristotelian definition of substance did not fare particularly well in a universe where all is either thought or extension. He offered, therefore, a somewhat Cartesian redefinition of the doctrine.[249] He was almost immediately accused of tritheism.

In accord with the Cartesian assumption that the starting point of certainty and therefore of philosophical discourse is the individual self-consciousness and that this self-consciousness is the fundamental identifier of the individual existent, Sherlock put forth the rather novel theological point that the fundamental, threefold existence of God was the existence of three individual centers of divine self-consciousness. As centers of consciousness, the three are numerically distinct, but as infinite and omniscient mind, each knowing totally the other, they are essentially identical. He accordingly described the divine unity as consisting in the divine persons' unique knowledge of one another's thoughts, a knowledge impossible for finite spirits. There are, then, three infinite minds, distinct from one another yet united in their mutual self-understanding. The essential distinction between individual human "persons" can be recognized in their inability to be totally and intimately conscious of and in communion with the thoughts of one another: in the case of the persons of the Trinity, this communion is complete, granting the identity of God as simple or single act or, as Sherlock preferred (drawing on the theology of the Cappadocian fathers), a single energy.[250]

Sherlock claimed not that he had fathomed the mystery of the Trinity in this theory, but that he had shown the doctrine to be logically possible. In matters of salvation, however, faith in the mystery, and not logical exposition, was required: the doctrines of the Athanasian Creed represent the faith of the church, the essential condition for adult baptism into the communion of the saved. Since no one would claim that Jews or Turks could be saved by their personal righteousness apart from Christian faith, none ought to assume that heterodox Christians who refuse the faith of the church can be saved by works. In essence, Sherlock's answer to the *Brief Notes* was the declaration, typical of the seventeenth-century orthodox, that orthodox doctrine was necessary, as the proper object of faith, for salvation.

---

249. William Sherlock, *A vindication of the doctrine of the holy and ever blessed Trinity and the incarnation of the son of God: occasioned by the brief notes on the creed of St. Athanasius, and the brief history of the Unitarians, or Socinians, and containing an answer to both* (London: William Rogers, 1690).

250. Cf. Franks, *Doctrine of the Trinity*, p. 149.

At least two prominent dissenters were convinced by Sherlock to abandon their orthodoxy. William Manning adopted a fully Socinian view of God and Christ while his friend Thomas Emlyn adopted an Arian subordination of the Son to the Father rather than give up the doctrine of Christ's pre-existence.[251] Emlyn's *An Humble Inquiry into the Scripture Account of Jesus Christ* (1702) placed traditional trinitarian and christological dogmas under such withering scrutiny that Emlyn earned two years in prison for his pains.[252] As the controversy continued, moreover, it became painfully obvious to churchly defenders of orthodox trinitarianism that Sherlock's teaching was more dangerous than useful.

Sherlock's attempt to use the language of self-consciousness as the foundation of trinitarian formulae was attacked immediately by Robert South and eventually condemned as heresy by the Heads of Colleges at Oxford. South's *Animadversions upon Dr. Sherlock's book* (1693) protested against the "new notions and false explications" employed by Sherlock in defense of orthodoxy.[253] South was dissatisfied with what he felt was a reductionistic definition of God as infinite Mind and by the identification of a Person as a self-consciousness: Mind is not to be equated with substance — and for God to exist he must be substantial. Furthermore, self-consciousness is a characteristic of a person, not the entirety of a person and — again — not a substance in and of itself. South obviously was unconvinced by the Cartesian claim of two substances in the universe, thought and extension. South also queried of Sherlock how this view of personal distinctions in God indicated threeness — why was there a limit on the number of self-consciousnesses?

In response to these theories, South accused Sherlock of tritheism.[254] South viewed the doctrine of the Trinity as a "mystery" which lay beyond the powers of natural reason. Sherlock had argued against Socinianism in the name of Scripture but had rested his primary doctrinal argument upon philosophy. South pilloried Sherlock for his philosophizing and then himself set out to refute Sherlock's rather Cartesian language by opposing it with the older Aristotelian scholastic language of essence, substance, existence, and subsistence, the latter term indicating the mode of existence by which a thing has its own individuality. South argued that the being and essence

---

251. Cf. Michael R. Watts, *The Dissenters*, 2 vols. (Oxford: Clarendon Press, 1978), I, p. 372.

252. Thomas Emlyn, *An humble enquiry into the Scripture account of Jesus Christ, or, A short argument concerning his deity and glory, according to the gospel* (London, 1702; reissued, Frankfort, Ky.: James M. Bradford, 1803).

253. Robert South, *Animadversions upon Dr. Sherlock's book, entituled A vindication of the holy and ever-blessed Trinity, &c,: together with a more necessary vindication of that sacred and prime article of the Christian faith from his new notions, and false explications of it humbly offered to his admirers, and to himself the chief of them, by a divine of the Church of England* (London: Randal Taylor, 1693). South's positive theological formulations are found in Robert South, *Sermons Preached upon Several Occasions*, 5 vols. (New York: Hurd & Houghton, 1866-1871).

254. Robert South, *Tritheism charged upon Dr. Sherlock's new notion of the Trinity and the charge made good: in an answer to the defense of the said notion against the Animadversions upon Dr. Sherlock's book, entituled, A vindication of the holy and ever-blessed Trinity, &c. by a divine of the Church of England* (London: John Whitlock, 1695).

of God were one and that, therefore, there was but one existent God. The three persons are identical as God, having one being, essence, and existence — yet they are three distinct subsistences. Loss of this language South viewed as the path to heresy: when Sherlock spoke of God as infinite mind and three centers of consciousness, he lost the idea of divine substance and with it the ability to identify God as something rather than as nothing! South also insisted that personal subsistence preceded the possibility of individual consciousness as much as substantial existence preceded necessarily any mental function: consciousness cannot be the ground for identifying personality. Sherlock's response to South accused the latter of Sabellianism.[255]

The Unitarian writers of the era, gathered together by Firmin in A Second Collection of Tracts (1693), proceeded to have a field day with the theorizations of Sherlock and South. Sherlock was nothing more than a Cartesian tritheist. South simply revived Aristotelian scholasticism and with it the dead theories of Peter Lombard, Innocent III, and the Fourth Lateran Council. Other trinitarian authors were identified as Sabellians and modified Arians. The entire attempt to argue a divine Trinity was proved absurd by its proponents![256] A Third Collection of Tracts, issued in 1695, launched refutations of all the leading trinitarians of the age — not only of philosophical or scholastic thinkers like Sherlock and South but also of less-dogmatic writers like Bishops Tillotson, Stillingfleet, and Burnet, and offered an erudite rebuttal of Bishop Bull's interpretation of the doctrines of the Fathers.[257]

The outcome of the initial controversy, as generated in part by Bull and in part by Nye, was summed up, from the Socinian or Unitarian side, by Nye: "upon the whole, we may say, There is now no Socinian controversy," given that "the misunderstanding that was common to both parties, the Church and the Unitarians, is annihilated."[258] In his own analysis of the debate, Nye had distinguished the orthodox writers and their responses into two basic categories, the "Real trinitarians" and the "Nominal trinitarians" — indicating a differentiation between those writers who claimed a "real" distinction between the persons of the Trinity (and, who, in Nye's view, advocated

255. William Sherlock, A defence of Dr. Sherlock's notion of a Trinity in unity: in answer to the animadversions upon his vindication of the doctrine of the holy and ever Blessed Trinity: with a post-script relating to the calm discourse of a Trinity in the Godhead: in a letter to a friend (London: William Rogers, 1694).

256. A Second Collection of tracts proving the God and father of our Lord Jesus Christ the only true God, and Jesus Christ the son of God, him whom the father sanctified and sent, raised from the dead and exalted, and disproving the doctrine of three almighty and equal persons, spirits, modes, subsistences, or somewhats in God, and of the incarnation (London?: s.n., 1693?).

257. A Third Collection of tracts: proving the God and father of our Lord Jesus Christ the only true God, and Jesus Christ the Son of God, him whom the Father sanctified and sent, raised from the dead and exalted, and disproving the doctrine of three almighty, real, subsisting persons, minds, or spirits: giving also an account of the nominal Trinity, that is, three modes, subsistences, or somewhats in God, called by schoolmen Persons, and of the judgment of the Fathers and Catholick Church for the first 150 years (London?: s.n., 1695).

258. Stephen Nye, An account of Mr. Firmin's religion, and of the present state of the Unitarian controversy (London: s.n., 1698), p. 48.

tritheism) and those who held a "nominal" or terminological distinction between the persons of the Trinity (and whose views on the unity of the Godhead could be accepted by the Unitarians). The origin of Nye's approach was probably the debate between Sherlock and South — with Sherlock being identified in debate as a tritheist, from Nye's perspective, a "real trinitarian"; and South being identified as a Sabellian, from Nye's perspective, a "nominal trinitarian."

As indicated by the title to the third collection of tracts, in which Nye's discussion of the "real" and "nominal" trinitarians appeared, the Unitarians could argue against "the doctrine of three almighty, real, subsisting persons, minds, or spirits," which they took to be tritheism, and allow the validity of "an account of the nominal Trinity, that is, three modes, subsistences, or somewhats in God, called by schoolmen Persons."[259] Under the latter language, both orthodox trinitarianism and various forms of trinitarian subordinationism, including both Arianism and what, for lack of a better term, has been called "semi-Arianism," could gather. And with their position thus defined as "nominal trinitarianism," most English Unitarians were willing to acknowledge the Thirty-nine Articles as confessing a Trinity of "mode of appearance or manifestation."[260] The result of this partial resolution was, on the one hand, the inclusion of a refined Unitarianism within the ranks of the Church of England and, on the other, far from the end of debate, the inauguration of a new phase of controversy, in which some of the attempts at orthodox solution, notably those of Sherlock, South, and Clarke, themselves came under attack alongside of the Socinian or Unitarian position.

The closing years of the century saw the bishops Stillingfleet and Burnet defending in a nondogmatic and nonphilosophical language the doctrine of the Trinity as the best use of the language of Scripture.[261] In addition, the nonhistorical approach of Bull to the defense of traditional trinitarianism came under increasing attack,[262] and — at the same time — became in the view of others, the palladium of trinitarian orthodoxy.[263] There was also a notable rise in interest in the history of the doctrinal

259. See Stephen Nye, A Discourse concerning the Nominal and Real trinitarians, in A Third Collection (London?: s.n., 1695).

260. Berriman, Historical Account, p. 427.

261. Edward Stillingfleet, A discourse in vindication of the doctrine of the Trinity with an answer to the late Socinian objections against it from Scripture, antiquity and reason, and a preface concerning the different explications of the Trinity, and the tendency of the present Socinian controversie (London: Henry Mortlock, 1697); Gilbert Burnet, An Exposition of the Thirty-Nine Articles of the Church of England (London, 1699; revised and corrected, with notes by James R. Page, New York: Appleton, 1852).

262. Gilbert Clerke, Tractatus tres: quorum qui prior ante-Nicenismus dicitur, is exhibet testimonia patrum ante-Nicenorum, in quibus eluct sensus ecclesiæ primævo-catholicæ, quoad articulum de Trinitate: in secundo, Brevis responsio ordinatur ad D. G. Bulli defensionem synodi Nicenæ authore Gilberto Clerke ...; Argumentum postremi, vera & antiqua fides de divinitate Christi, explicata & asserta, contra D. Bulli, judicium ecclesiæ catholicæ &c. per anonymum (London?: s.n., 1695?); The judgment of the fathers concerning the doctrine of the Trinity opposed to Dr. G. Bull's Defence of the Nicene faith: Part I. The doctrine of the Catholick Church, during the first 150 years of Christianity, and the explication of the unity of God (in a Trinity of Divine Persons) by some of the following fathers, considered (London: s.n., 1695).

263. Thus, J. Deacon, The fathers vindicated, or, Animadversions on a late Socinian book entitul'd The judgment of the Fathers touching the Trinity, against Doctor Bull's Defence of the Nicene faith by a

problem of the Trinity, both recent and ancient. In the midst of the fray, Aretius' *History of Valentinus Gentilis, the Tritheist* appeared in print, with the rather pointed rebuke on its title page that the translator intended it "for the use of Dr. Sherlock," whose doctrine was identified with that of a "noted Tritheist" of the preceding century.[264] So, too, was patristic doctrine a significant issue, even at the relatively popular level of vernacular tracts on the ancient heresies.[265] A massive discourse by Pierre Allix on the potential Jewish backgrounds to the Trinity, specifically with reference to language of distinction in the Godhead found in Judaica, also appeared to strengthen the orthodox cause.[266]

At the same time, the argument between South's old scholasticism and Sherlock's new Cartesian Trinity came to a head at the University of Oxford. After a polemical university sermon delivered by South in November 1695, the university declared Sherlock a heretic. Sherlock replied with a refutation of the decree against him and preached a sermon vindicating himself and the Scriptures (25 April 1697) at the London Guildhall, before the Lord Mayor. The result of the controversy was more the diffusion of doctrinal dissension than the victory of any party: South's scholasticism alone received university sanction, but there was no definitive condemnation of Sherlock by the church and, in addition, no settlement of the question of the Trinity. Unitarianism was not silenced, and Arianism — as a doctrinal possibility within the established church — was about to rear its head.

If South objected, in the name of orthodoxy, to the potential tri- (or poly) theism of Sherlock's Cartesian trinitarianism without proposing a new philosophical or linguistic solution, Wallis, a mathematician at Cambridge, proposed an alternative view to Sherlock's that looked in the other direction, toward a modalistic solution to the trinitarian problem. Wallis proposed that all language of mind and self-consciousness be set aside on the ground that the term "person" as used in trinitarian language stood in no relation to the term "person" as applied to human beings: the term, in its trinitarian usage, indicated simply a distinction in the divine essence. (Of course, on this point, Wallis was entirely correct and was simply registering both the age-old problem of the Boethian definition of person and the increasing difficulty of adapting that or similar definitions to the altered perception of human beings as persons in the early modern era.) Wallis noted, not without echoes of the Augustinian psychological metaphors of the Trinity, that the human soul is and knows and acts

---

presbyter of the Church of England (London: R. Chiswell, 1697).

264. Benedictus Aretius, *A Short History of Valentinus Gentilis the Tritheist* (London, 1696); the original Latin edition was published in Bern, 1567.

265. E.g., Anonymous, ΧΡΙΣΤΟΣ ΑΥΤΟ ΘΕΟΣ *or an Historical Account of the Heresie Denying the Godhead of Christ* (London: Thomas Hodgkin, 1696).

266. Pierre Allix, *The judgement of the ancient Jewish church, against the Unitarians: in the controversy upon the holy Trinity, and the divinity of our Blessed Saviour* (London: R. Chiswell, 1699). Given Allix's teaching in this treatise and his position in the French Reformed church, it is difficult to accept the usual attribution of *A Defence of the Brief History of the Unitarians, Against Dr. Sherlock's Answer* (London: s.n., 1691) to him.

— three distinct aspects of soul — but remains one soul; just as a cube has length, height, and depth — three distinct dimensions — and yet is one cube.[267] A similar tendency toward modalism, albeit without Wallis' mathematical metaphors, can be detected in the nominally orthodoxy theology of Thomas Ridgley, even as he protests against the overt Sabellianism of some of his contemporaries.[268] Throughout the period, moreover, orthodox divines continued to wrestle with the difficulties of person-language.

3. Renewed debate: Whiston and Clarke on the Trinity. In the second decade of the eighteenth century, debate resumed in earnest when William Whiston and Samuel Clarke revived the question of ante-Nicene orthodoxy and precipitated a major controversy over Arianism in the Anglican and the dissenting churches. Quite literally, the rise of a scholarly Arianism in the English church at the beginning of the eighteenth century can be traced, formally, to three substantial essays: William Whiston's *Primitive Christianity Revised* (1711-12), his *Athanasius Convicted of Forgery* (1712), and Samuel Clarke's *Scripture Doctrine of the Trinity* (1712).[269] The accusation of Arianism was frequently made by the high church party of the Church of England against latitudinarian bishops and clergy, but there was little solid evidence to support the change until the publication of these works and the controversy which developed around them. The works, moreover, are very different. Whiston's are historical essays by a highly scrupulous churchman concerned to define his orthodoxy according to the earliest patristic witness. Clarke's work is a theological essay resting on Scripture and the fathers but striving on the basis of reason to derive a valid doctrine of God.

Whiston was hardly a rationalist: he attempted to rest his doctrine on patristic authority and called himself a "Eusebian" because he believed the consensus of the early fathers to be contrary to Athanasian teaching, in particular, contrary to the Athanasian Creed, which he (on good linguistic grounds) pronounced to be a forgery. For all the historical flaws in Whiston's labors — like his contention that the long recension of Ignatius' letters was genuine and the shorter version a later epitome or his claim that the so-called Apostolic Constitutions were truly apostolic[270] — his work

---

267. John Wallis, *The doctrine of the blessed Trinity, briefly explained in a letter to a friend* (London: Tho. Parkhurst, 1690); and *A second letter concerning the Holy Trinity: pursuant to the former from the same hand: occasioned by a letter there inserted from one unknown* (London: Tho. Parkhurst, 1691).

268. Cf. Ridgley, *Body of Divinity* (1855), I, pp. 153-159.

269. William Whiston, *Primitive Christianity reviv'd*, 5 vols. (London: Printed for the author, 1711-12); idem, *Athanasius convicted of forgery: in a letter to Mr. Thirlby of Jesus-College in Cambridge* (London: A. Baldwin, 1712); Samuel Clarke, *The Scripture Doctrine of the Trinity*, in *The Works of Samuel Clarke*, 4 vols. (London, 1738; repr. New York: Garland, 1978), vol. IV. For a discussion of the controversy and of Clarke's doctrine, see E. Dorothy Asch, "Samuel Clarke's *Scripture-Doctrine of the Trinity* and the Controversy it Aroused" (Ph.D. diss., University of Edinburgh, 1951) and Pfizenmaier, *Trinitarian Theology of Dr. Samuel Clarke*.

270. William Whiston, *An essay upon the Epistles of Ignatius* (London: Benjamin Tooke, 1710); idem, *St. Clement's and St. Irenaeus's vindication of the apostolical constitutions, from several objections made against them. As also an account of the two antient rules thereunto belonging, for the celebration of Easter. With a postscript on occasion of Mr. Turner's Discourse of the apostolical constitutions* (London:

does represent an advance over the rather dogmatic reading of the ante-Nicene fathers by Bishop Bull some four decades earlier. Whiston easily demonstrated that ante-Nicene theology was not of a piece with Athanasian and Nicene "orthodoxy" and that the Nicene theology itself was different from what could be elicited from the so-called Athanasian Creed — where he is unconvincing is in his declaration that something akin to Arianism represented the normative theology of the New Testament and the early fathers.[271]

Clarke's theology was the epitome of rational supernaturalism: he gathered textual evidence but rested primarily on reason — and, what is more, denied that he was an Arian on the ground that his doctrine was his own and quite different from patristic formulations. Of the two writers, therefore, Clarke is better representative of the theological tendencies of the time and of the effect of rationalist philosophy upon doctrinal formulation. Clarke was, moreover, quite accurate in denying that he was a historical Arian: he has been described as occupying "a position of indecision between Origen and Arius."[272] In his treatise, Clarke assessed texts from Scripture and the fathers, with his primary emphasis upon the authority of Scripture. The fathers were far from infallible, though it was clear to Clarke that the ante-Nicene fathers were distinctly less metaphysical in their doctrines than the fathers after Nicea. In addition, Clarke, like Whiston, argued that virtually all the ante-Nicene fathers were Arian in their theology.

Clarke drew copious texts from the New Testament to demonstrate that the doctrine of Scripture pronounced the Father only to be fully and absolutely divine in himself and the bearer of all the attributes of duty. He cited, comparatively, the texts "There is none good but One" (Mark 10:18) and "I and the Father are one" (Jn. 10:30), arguing that the masculine "one" of the former text indicated the "person" of the Father as absolute God while the neuter "one" of the latter denoted a oneness of power exercised alike by Father and Son. This reading Clarke supported from Tertullian and buttressed with the declaration of Origen that the Father is self-existent and the fountainhead of the deity. Since Scripture does not explicitly deny that the Son is self-existent substance or explicitly state that the substance of the Son is derived from nothing, the Arian reading must be rejected as well as the Nicene: Clarke rejects both the claim that there was a time when the Son was not and the teaching that the Son is coeternal with the Father.

Of the Son, we can say that he was before the creation of the world and that he existed before the beginning. The Son is the instrumental cause in the Father's work of creation and is the revealer of the Father's will in the work of salvation. This indicates not only the agreement of the Son with the Father but also his subordination to the

---

J. Roberts, 1715).

271. William, Whiston, *Three essays, I. The council of Nice vindicated from the Athanasian heresy. II. A collection of ancient monuments relating to the Trinity and incarnation and to the history of the fourth century of the church. III. The liturgy of the Church of England reduc'd nearer to the primitive standard* (London: Printed for the author, 1713).

272. Henry C. Sheldon, *History of Christian Doctrine*, 2 vols. (New York: Harper, 1895), II, p. 99.

Father. Having made these points, Clarke turned to texts which seemed to favor Nicene "orthodoxy," in particular to John 1:1, "the Word was God." This passage, he noted, is in the past tense: it does not say that the Word *is* God. The text is, therefore, consistent with the views of Philo, Justin and Irenaeus, who view the Word as the revealer of the Father. He "was God" insofar as he appeared in the form and with the revelation of God. Since the text also declares that the Word was "with God" rather than "in God," the distinction of the Son, as person, from the Father is guaranteed and the coeternity of the Son clearly denied.

Clarke hypothesized that the Son was begotten by an act of will and not by necessity. As for the Spirit, it is nowhere given the divine name and is subadviate not only to the Father but also to the Son — as both Scripture and the fathers indicate. Clarke insisted that the idea of coequal and coeternal persons was necessarily tritheistic. He also denied the idea of one indivisible divine substance or essence: the essence was divisible and the three persons all partook of it, the Son and Spirit being derived from the Father and therefore subordinate to him. The view was not tritheism, since it allowed that the Father alone was truly God. Clarke's theism, like that of his close friend and associate Isaac Newton, was highly influenced by new perceptions of the implications of space and time, and — like Henry More and, indeed, like the Cartesians, Spinozists, and Hobbsians against whom he wrote — had considerable difficulty understanding the infinitude of divine being apart from assumptions of extension.[273] More importantly, Clarke's trinitarianism was grounded in the historical insights of Petavius and Cudworth, both of whom had begun to question, from a perspective of relative orthodoxy, the ahistorical assumption that all of the church fathers from Ignatius of Antioch to Athanasius held trinitarian views commensurate with the Nicene formula. Clarke clearly recognized that the fathers offered other options than the Sabellian, Arian, and Athanasian — indeed, as Pfizenmaier has demonstrated, Clarke's trinitarianism echoes the conservative, post-Nicene thought of Eusebius of Caesarea and Basil of Ancyra and can hardly be identified as Arian.[274]

Clarke's theology indicates that the issue of the relationship between fourth century controversy and eighteenth-century debate may be quite subtle and that the gradual perception of the diversity of patristic trinitarianism (contra Bishop Bull) in fact belongs to the rising historical-critical consciousness and to the latitudinarianism of the day (which themselves are related!). Of course, few in that time were prepared to allow for the relative "orthodoxy" of the Eusebian and homoiousian positions as non-Arian alternatives to Nicaea; and, unfortunately for Clarke, the Socinians of the day appeared to reflect the historical-critical conclusions, and the historical-critical conclusions, in turn, looked all too much like an outgrowth of radical Reformation antitrinitarianism, going all the way back to Servetus' *Restitutio*. All the same, the fact remains that, at the beginnings of Western historical consciousness and historical-critical method

273. Cf. Edwin A. Burtt, *The Metaphysical Origins of Modern Science*, revised ed. (New York: Humanities Press, 1951), pp. 135-150, 258-262, with Funkenstein, *Theology and the Scientific Imagination*, pp. 77-97.

274. See Pfizenmaier, *trinitarian Theology of Dr. Samuel Clarke*, pp. 89-141, 217-220.

(paralleling the work of Richard Simon in the biblical field), *some writers* who were not Socinian or strictly heretical did see the problem and saw it more clearly than either their own "orthodox" contemporaries or nineteenth-century theologians and historians like Newman.

Clarke was almost immediately charged with heresy in the Lower House of the Convocation of the Church of England and attacked forcefully in pamphlets. The case against Clarke in the Convocation of the Church of England came to no result: the Lower House demanded a retraction from Clarke and received only an explanation that Clarke's beliefs were not at all Arian — inasmuch as Clarke assumed that the Son was more than a creature begotten in time. The case was further complicated when, after the Lower House refused the explanation, the Upper House, where the bishops sat, accepted it. Where the convocation failed to convict, the pamphleteers succeeded, with the most important refutation and condemnation coming from the pen of the eminent Daniel Waterland, *A Vindication of Christ's Divinity* (1719).[275]

Waterland insisted on a doctrine of the coeternity of the three persons in order to assert the full divinity of the Son and the Spirit. He took his stand firmly on the ground of Old Testament monotheism, which declared the existence of one God and one God only. These declarations, according to Waterland, completely refuted Clarke's attempt to identify the Father as God in an absolute sense and the Son and Spirit as God in a derivative sense. Scripture allows no derivative gods! Waterland objected to Clarke's language of a personal God on the grounds that it claimed "a personal supreme Deity, but ... added two other deities, who were also persons."[276] Such a doctrine would relegate Son and Spirit to the status of inferior deities — such as are explicitly denied in Scripture and cannot properly be called "God." Christ is either fully God, Waterland could argue, or not God at all, but simply a creature. Both Scripture and the fathers, however, assume that Christ is truly divine and that the Word was begotten before the creation of the world. The Arian doctrine, therefore, must be ruled out as heretical.

In reply to Waterland, Clarke argued on two fronts. First, he noted that Scripture demands not that we subscribe to a metaphysical construction like the doctrine of the Trinity, but that we simply acknowledge Father, Son, and Spirit to be God. It ought to be clear, Clarke argued, that the prologue to John uses the word "God" in two different senses, as does Paul when he writes concerning the Father "of whom are all things" and of the Son "through whom are all things": two distinct personal beings,

---

275. The pamphlet war is too elaborate to survey: Clarke was attacked by Thomas Bennet, John Edwards, Francis Gastrell (bishop of Chester), James Knight, Robert Nelson, John Potter (bishop of Oxford), Daniel Waterland, Edward Welchman, and Edward Wells. Clarke was defended by John Jackson, Arthur Ashley Sykes, Daniel Whitby, and several anonymous pamphleteers — and, of course, in a series of treatises, by Clarke himself. A useful summary from the time is available in Thomas Hearne, *An Account of all the Considerable Books and Pamphlets, that have been wrote on either side, in the Controversy concerning the Trinity, since the year 1712* (London, 1720); and see the excellent survey of the debate in Pfizenmaier, *Trinitarian Theology of Dr. Samuel Clarke*, pp. 179-196.

276. Hunt, *Religious Thought in England*, III, p. 25.

one subordinate to the other are being termed "God," yet only one, the Father, may be identified as the Jehovah of the Old Testament. Second, Clarke noted that the use of the word "person" advocated by Waterland was utterly inadequate. Since a person is to be identified as an intelligent agent, quite obviously God, as intelligent agent, could not be one God and three persons at the same time.

The debate between Samuel Clarke and his opponents, most notably Thomas Bennet, manifested the increasing difficulty of maintaining traditional trinitarian person-language in the early modern era. Clarke had defined God as the "One Supreme Cause and Original of Things" and as the "One simple, uncompounded, undivided, intelligent Agent, or Person; who alone is the Author of all Being, and the Fountain of all Power."[277] Clarke continued with his basic trinitarian definition by stating that "with this First and Supreme Cause or Father of all things, there has existed from the Beginning, a Second Divine Person, which is his WORD or Son."[278] The problem in the definitions was obvious to Clarke's objectors. Bennet replied that the biblical usage of "Word" did not imply "a distinct Being from that God *with* whom he existed from the Beginning."[279]

The problem with Clarke's language arose directly out of his interpretation of the term "person" as an "intelligent Being" — an interpretation, we note, that was resident in the Western doctrine of the Trinity from the moment that it began to wrestle with the problematic of Boethius' definiton — and his subsequent identification of three divine intelligent Beings, one primary and the other two subordinate. As Bennet wrote, with obvious irritation both at Clarke's arguments and at the limitations of his own usage, "The WORD is ... not a *second* Divine Person in my sense of the word *Person*."[280]

A subcontroversy, typical of the eighteenth century, was the debate between Clarke and his opponents over Arian subscription to the Thirty-nine Articles. Clarke had contended in his *Scripture Doctrine of the Trinity* that subscription was a matter of accepting the articles in the light of one's reading of Scripture and that, therefore, he could subscribe to the article on the Trinity: the sense of the article was indeterminate, he noted, not clearly Arian, Nicene or Sabellian! Waterland argued that the sense of the authors of the Thirty-nine Articles was intrinsic to their correct interpretation, that the authors were Nicene trinitarians, and that, therefore, no Arian or Sabellian could in good conscience subscribe. Waterland was, unfortunately, Arminian in his soteriology. It was quickly pointed out by Arthur Ashley Sykes that the authors of the articles and the original intent were Calvinist. If Waterland's logic concerning Arianism and subscription were correct, then the same logic would prevent Waterland, as an Arminian from subscribing to the articles! This subcontroversy represents but one aspect of the gradual shift away from serious dogmatic subscription

---

277. Clarke, *Scripture Doctrine*, proposition 1.

278. Clarke, *Scripture Doctrine*, proposition 2.

279. Thomas Bennet, A *Discourse of the Everblessed Trinity in Unity, with an Examination of Dr. Clarke's Scripture Doctrine of the Trinity* (London, 1718), p. 232.

280. Bennet, *Discourse*, p. 232.

to articles and creeds that was characteristic of the eighteenth century in its tendency toward rational rather than traditional doctrinal theology.

Fiddes' *Theologia speculativa* (1718) appears to be almost oblivious to the British trinitarian debates of the late seventeenth century while, at the same time, quite sensitive to problems raised during the somewhat earlier debates over Socinianism. Fiddes draws on the fathers in order to argue — as had Forbes and Bull before him — a consistent patristic testimony, whether pre-Nicene or Nicene, to "a co-essential and co-eternal Trinity," granting that "the titles and attributes ascrib'd to the Son expressly and frequently, (and sometimes, tho' not so often, to the Holy Ghost; but always understood and implied) are demonstrative proofs that all three Persons are suppos'd to be comprehended in the idea of the one God."[281] Fiddes' stated adversaries are Arius, Socinus, and Crellius, who exclude "the other two Persons from the Godhead" by identifying the Father solely as God.[282] Fiddes does, indeed, recognize a difference in language between the ante- and post-Nicene fathers: he notes that an eternal generation of the Word was taught by Ignatius, Irenaeus, Origen, Constantine the Emperor, Eusebius, and others, while a temporal and "improper" generation or efflux for the creation of the world and another for the sake of the incarnation were taught by the Apologists, Tertullian, Hippolytus, and, indeed, also Constantine — but he distances this view from Arianism (and Socinianism) inasmuch as the second and third concepts in no way negate the first "proper and eternal generation" by which the Son is understood as fully divine in terms equivalent to those of Nicaea.[283]

The movement from confessional orthodoxy toward deism or rational supernatural-ism, encouraged by the works of Locke, Toland, Clarke, and Whiston and by the rather successful encounter of the new Socinianism with orthodox opponents, was nowhere more clear than among the Presbyterians. Watts notes the opinion of James Pierce, a Presbyterian clergyman of Exeter, inspired by a reading of Clarke on the Trinity that he must "part with some beloved opinions, or else quit my notion of the authority of the Holy Scriptures."[284] In September of 1718, Pierce declared his new faith to his brother clergy: he held for a subordinate deity of the Son and the Spirit. The clergy of Exeter appealed for advice to the dissenting clergy of London.

In three meetings of Salters' Hall in London (19 and 24 February and 3 March 1719), the dissenting clergy of London were unable to muster a majority vote in favor of subscription to the older confessional standards with their traditional trinitarianism. An anonymous pamphlet chronicling the meetings, *An Account of the Late Proceedings of the Dissenting Ministers at Salters' Hall* (1719), records the resolution of the ministers to exclude "human ... interpretations" from articles on the Trinity. At the final meeting, the minority subscribed to an orthodox statement of the doctrine of the Trinity those

---

281. Richard Fiddes, *Theologia speculativa: or, The First Part of a Body of Divinity ... wherein are Explain'd the Principles of Natural and Revealed Religion* (London, 1718), IV.i.2 (p. 392).

282. Fiddes, *Theol. spec.*, IV.i.2 (p. 385).

283. Fiddes, *Theol. spec.*, IV.ii.2 (pp. 434-35).

284. Watts, *Dissenters*, I, p. 374.

who refused to sign — the "Non-Subscribers" — protested their orthodoxy, denied all charges of Arianism, and rested their non-subscription upon the "Protestant principle" of Scripture as the sole norm of Christian faith. Just as the antinomian controversy of the 1690s had divided Presbyterians and Congregationalists, with the Congregationalists maintaining a fairly traditional Calvinist orthodoxy, so did the Salters' Hall meeting divide them again, with the majority of Congregationalists and Particular Baptists subscribing to traditional trinitarianism and the Presbyterians and General Baptist tending toward non-subscription. The theological pattern of the century was set: Presbyterianism in England would fall away from its confessional standards toward Unitarianism or toward the refined semi-Arianism of the day.

C. Patterns of Trinitarian Orthodoxy in the Eighteenth Century

1. Changing exegetical perspectives. It would be difficult to underestimate the impact of changing patterns of exegesis on the understanding of the doctrine of the Trinity. By the early eighteenth century, the trinitarian heresies had infiltrated both trajectories of English Protestantism, whether Anglican or dissent — on the Anglican side a fair number of churchmen and theologians tended toward various forma of Arian and semi-Arian thought, while on the dissenting side, there were both Socinian and Sabellian tendencies in addition to the Arianistic development.[285] In addition, not only did the results of textual criticism appear to stand firmly on the side of the Socinians with regard to such texts as 1 Timothy 3:16 and 1 John 5:7, the new construal of the "literal sense" of texts also had ruled out much of the traditionary trinitarian reading of the Old Testament for which the Protestant orthodox had fought so hard — again, against the Socinians.

The noted Anglican latitudinarian theologian and bishop Gilbert Burnet identified the doctrine of the Trinity as a mystery of the faith inaccessible to reason: it was a doctrine "that we should have had no cause to have thought of ... if the scriptures had not revealed it to us." He then went on to note that the doctrine had little foundation in the Old Testament: "take the Old Testament in itself without the New, and it must be confessed that it will not be easy to prove this article by it."[286] Having given up the Old Testament grounds of the doctrine — a point very dear to the seventeenth-century orthodoxy — Burnet proceeded to develop the doctrine on New Testament grounds alone, making no reference to disputed texts such as 1 Timothy 3:16 or Titus 2:13 and concluding with a dismissal of 1 John 5:7 as a "contested passage" unnecessary for the proof of the doctrine of the Trinity.[287] Clearly, the lines of battle had shifted, and not in a direction favorable to the older orthodox model.

---

285. Cf. W. G. T. Shedd, A *History of Christian Doctrine*, 2 vols. (New York: Scribners, 1889), pp. 385-386 with Sir Leslie Stephen, *History of English Thought in the Eighteenth Century*, 2 vols., preface by Crane Brinton (New York: Harcourt, Brace and World, 1962), I, pp. 356-359, 361-364.

286. Burnet, *Exposition of the Thirty-Nine Articles*, pp. 42-43.

287. Burnet, *Exposition of the Thirty-Nine Articles*, pp. 46-47.

Similarly, although offering a stronger form of the argument, the moderate Anglican and professedly orthodox Thomas Stackhouse, vicar of Beenham, Berkshire, and the author, by his own admission, of one of the rare English systems of theology in his time, the *Complete Body of Divinity* (1729), identified the doctrine of the Trinity as biblical, indeed, but also "purely Christian," resting entirely on the New Testament witness. Stackhouse, a committed, creedal trinitarian, is quite convinced that "the Jews themselves never had any express revelation of this matter" and that, specifically, the plural *Elohim* conjoined to a singular verb "is a common idiom of the Hebrew tongue, and cannot be supposed to import a plurality of persons in the divine essence." Similarly, phrases like "Let us make man" or "the man is become like one of us" are plurals of majesty "as is customary for kings" and therefore "do not imply the plurality of the speaker, nor any consultation among the several persons of the Godhead." The expression "Holy, holy, holy" is merely an emphatic form "common to all languages" and hardly a trinitarian text. Stackhouse does not, however, regard this exegetical result as a major problem — merely as a demonstration that the doctrine of the Trinity is "the Shibboleth of the christian church, and that wherein the professors of christianity are distinguished from all other worshippers in the world."[288]

Of course, it would be incorrect to conclude that the majority of Reformed orthodox theologians gave up the Old Testament foundations of the doctrine of the Trinity. Rather, the defense became more philological, focusing on the irregularities of the usages and denying the applicability of a plural of majesty as a suitable explanation — given, among other things, the lack of use of such a plural in other instances of kingly decree in the Old Testament. In addition, many of the orthodox were quite willing to press the point of a gradual revelation, drawing on the extant sense of a movement from promise to fulfillment and from shadow or type to reality and antitype: the trinitarian understanding of Old Testament texts, they could argue, not only supplies a partial doctrine of the Trinity, it also is an understanding that would not easily result were it not for the continuation and fulfillment of the revelation in the New Testament.[289] Wyttenbach, for one, following out the Wolffian interest in natural religion and in the elements of truth lodged in religions other than Christianity, remarks that since the doctrine of the Trinity is necessary to salvation, it was also necessary that it be revealed to the faithful under the Old Testament. Not only can the doctrine berse found expressed in Ps. 33:6; Isa. 48:16 and 61:1, it was also the conclusion of the later Jewish doctors, writing in the Cabbala and the Zohar, that there were three divine hypostases.[290] The doctrinal point of an ancient revelation of the Trinity did not disappear, but the orthodox exegesis became increasingly distanced from what an increasing number of critical exegetes viewed as an "assured result."

---

288. Stackhouse, *Complete Body of Divinity*, I.vi (I, pp. 188-189).

289. Thus, De Moor, *Commentarius perpetuus*, I.v, §13-16; cf. Salomon Van Til, *Theologiae utriusque compendium cum naturalis tum revelatae* (Leiden, 1704; 2nd ed., 1719), II.iii (pp. 43-44).

290. Daniel Wyttenbach, *Theses theologicae praecipua christianae doctrinae capita ex primis principiis deducta continentes ... publicé defenderunt Isaacus Sigfrid ... & Daniel Wyttenbach* (Frankfurt, 1747), xxxvi.

2. Major doctrinal models. Perhaps the single most important point that can be made concerning the major doctrinal statements of the transitional thinkers and the late orthodox is that they offer a fundamentally stable doctrine of the Trinity. This relative exegetical and dogmatic stability is manifest in such diverse continental writers of the early to mid-eighteenth century as Francken, Van der Kemp, van Til, Vitringa, Gürtler, Wyttenbach, Stapfer, Comrie, Venema, De Moor, and Klinkenberg.[291] Of the group, Wyttenbach stands out as attempting to accommodate the orthodox model to a more rationalist (in his case, Wolffian) philosophical approach. He assumes that a foundation for theology needs to be developed rationally, with a natural theology preceding his supernatural theology: in the former, he offers a rationally argued doctrine of the divine essence and attributes built on cosmological proofs; in the latter, following his doctrine of Scripture, he produces a full statement on the divine essence and attributes, followed by a doctrine of the Trinity. The doctrine of essence and attributes, he argues, is more clearly and fully offered by revelation, but also utterly confirmed by its rational foundation, whereas the doctrine of the Trinity is available through revelation alone. Beyond this, the doctrine of the Trinity is necessary for salvation inasmuch as it reveals the Son and the Spirit as the foundation of the divine work of saving humanity from sin.[292]

In the case of Klinkenberg, who was perhaps more exegete than dogmatician, the trinitarian formulations of the theological system are directly related to a cautious trinitarian and christological reading of Scripture, continuing the precritical hermeneutic long into the eighteenth century. By way of example: Klinkenberg makes no trinitarian comments either in Genesis 1 or 18, as would have been typical of a more typological example of the older exegesis, but he does understand Exodus 3:2,

---

291. Aegidius Francken, Stellige god-geleertheyd: dat is, De waarheden van de hervormde leer: eenvoudig ter nedergestelt, en met de oeffening der waare Godsaligheyd aangedrongen, 3 vols. (Dordrecht: J. Van Braam, 1712); idem, Kern der Christelijke leer: dat is de waarheden van de Hervormde godsdienst, eenvoudig ter nedergesteld, en met de oefening der ware Godzaligheid aangedrongen (Dordrecht: J. van Braam, 1713; Groningen: O.L. Schildkamp, 1862); Johannes van der Kemp, De Christen geheel en al het Eigendom van Christus. Rotterdam: R. van Doesburg, 1717); in translation, The Christian Entirely the Property of Christ, in Life and Death, Exhibited in Fifty-three Sermons on the Heidelberg Catechism, trans. John M. Harlingen, 2 vols. (New Brunswick: Abraham Blauvelt, 1810; repr. Grand Rapids: Reformation Heritage Books, 1997); Campegius Vitringa, Doctrina christianae religionis, per aphorismos summatim descripta, 8 vols. (Arnheim, 1761-1786); idem, Korte stellingen: in welke vervat worden de grondstukken van de christelyke leere (Amsterdam: Balthazar Lakeman, 1730); Nicholaus Guertlerus, Institutiones theologicae ordine maxime naturali dispositae ac variis accessionibus auctae (Marburg, 1732); idem, Synopsis theologiae reformatae (Marburg: Müller, 1731); Johann Friedrich Stapfer, Institutiones theologiae polemicae universae, ordine scientifico dispositae, fourth edition, 5 vols. (Zurich, 1756-57); Alexander Comrie, Stellige en praktikale verklaring van den Heidelbergschen catechismus, volgens de leer en de gronden der reformatie (Amsterdam and Leiden, 1753); Jacob van Nuys Klinkenberg, Onderwys in den godsdienst, 11 vols. (Amsterdam: J. Allart, 1780-1794); and Jacob van Nuys Klinkenberg and Ger. Joh. Nahyus, De Bijbel, door beknopte Uitbreidingen, en ophelderende Aenmerkingen, verklaerd, 27 vols. (Amsterdam: Johannes Allart, 1780-1790), after Exodus, entirely the work of Klinkenberg, hereinafter cited as Klinkenberg, Bijbel verklaerd.

292. Wyttenbach, Tentamen theol., I, locus iii, §336-337.

with its reference to the Angel of the Lord, in a trinitarian sense, as also the threefold benediction of Numbers 6:24-26.[293] He also typically begins each book of the Bible with a lengthy introduction, setting forth the history, addressing problems in the text, and identifying the scope of the book, often addressing critical issues as well as maintaining the broader interpretive patterns of the older exegesis. Where he departs from the older orthodox model is in the apologetic and rationalistic form of the theological instruction or system, where Trinity has disappeared from the initial doctrine of God even as the discussion has become a natural theology — only to appear in the course of the biblical history and the discussion of salvation.

Paralleling the shifts in exegetical method and the loss of numerous biblical texts, particularly from the Old Testament, that once served to argue the doctrinal point, there was an increased interest in metaphors and logical arguments for the doctrine — whether ancient or modern in origin. Metaphors like the Augustinian model of divine loving and its objects or of one mind endowed with memory, understanding, and will, or the medieval variant, favored by the Thomist tradition, of a mind or spiritual being in its two faculties of intellect and will, used seldom in the early and high orthodox eras, became rather popular in the late orthodox era, together with newer mathematical or geometrical metaphors, like the triangle or the three dimensions of a cube. Throughout his career, Leibniz had insisted, against various Socinian adversaries, that the Trinity could be defended, if not demonstrated, logically.[294] Among the British, John Edwards and Stackhouse allowed logical arguments for the doctrine of the Trinity.[295]

This logical or philosophical interest was not, however, universal: its rise was countered in the later orthodox era by a consistent disdain on the part of other Reformed writers for the use of philosophical argumentation in defense of the Trinity. Ridgley identifies the doctrine of the Trinity as "a subject of pure revelation," incapable of being "learnt from the light of nature,"[296] and explicitly opposes the tendency observable in the work of many of his contemporaries to argue the doctrine rationally — to engage in "incautious" use of "dark hints" in ancient philosophy and poetry.

---

293. Klinkenberg, *Bijbel verklaerd*, Gen. 1:1, 27; 18:1-2; Exod. 3:2; Num. 6:24-26, in loc. It is possible that the absence of trinitarian referencing in Genesis was due to the influence of Klinkenberg's coauthor, Nahuys, who died at the conclusion of the work on Exodus.

294. Leibniz, *Defensio trinitatis per nova reperta logica* (1669), in *Sämtliche Schriften und Briefe*, (Berlin: Deutschen Akademie der Wissenschaften, 1923-), series 7, vol. 1; and see the discussion in Maria Rosa Antognazza and Howard Hotson, *Alsted and Leibniz on God, the Magistrate and Millennium* (Wiesbaden: Harrassowitz, 1999), pp. 36-44.

295. John Edwards, *Theologia Reformata: or, the Body and Substance of the Christian Religion, comprised in distinct discourses or treatises upon the Apostles Creed, the Lord's Prayer, and the Ten Commandments*, 2 vols. (London: John Lawrence, et al., 1713); idem, *Theologia reformata, or, Discourses on those graces and duties which are purely evangelical : and not contained in the moral law, and on the helps, motives, and advantages of performing them, being an entire treatise in four parts, and if added to the two former volumes, makes a compleat body of divinity* (London: T. Cox, 1726); and see below, 3.1 (C.4).

296. Ridgley, *Body of Divinity* (1855), pp. 135, 145.

Similar reservations must be put forth with regard to the standard similes and metaphors used to explain the doctrine: those who use them are well intentioned, but they fail to recognize that virtually all of the metaphors and similes are based on physical analogies in which some object is divided into three parts — precisely what the orthodox doctrine of the Trinity strives to avoid. "Who are these," Ridgley queries, "that, by pretending to illustrate the doctrine of the Trinity by similitudes, do that, which, though very foreign to their design, tends to pervert it?"[297] The lesson of these "similitudes" is that they are not enlightening and ultimately undermine the doctrine! Ridgley also mentions, with considerable disapprobation, the use of Plato in answer to the antitrinitarian claim that the doctrine of a divine Trinity is "unintelligible" — he notes the Roman Catholic Pierre Daniel Huet's *Concordia rationis et fidei* as a contemporary example and comments that "what they call an advantage to the doctrine, has been certainly very detrimental to it; and, as a late learned divine observes, has tended only to pervert the simplicity of the Christian faith with mixtures of philosophy and vain deceit." Against such use of philosophy, Ridgley cites Colossians 2:8.[298] In the next generations, neither Boston, Gill, nor Brown refers to the logical arguments or the Augustinian metaphors, and all three understand the doctrine of the Trinity as grounded on revelation alone.[299]

In the increasingly rationalistic context of late orthodoxy, however, quite a few Protestant thinkers followed a line of argument more akin to Huet's than Ridgley's: they continued the emphasis, already found among various of the seventeenth-century philosophers and theologians, on the presence of trinitarian concepts of the Godhead in Platonic and Neoplatonic philosophy. Wyttenbach, for example, argued apologetically that not only did ancient Israel know of the Trinity and witness to it in the Old Testament, so also did the ancient gentiles know of the Trinity, as can be seen from the oracles of Zoroaster and the teachings of Plato.[300]

Paralleling the shift in exegetical method (which was marked by the beginnings of a more historical-critical approach to the text) there was also a shift, in the latter part of the seventeenth century, to a more historical and contextual reading of the church fathers.[301] As noted in the previous section with reference to Petavius and Cudworth, this more historical reading of the materials also fueled the fires of variant

---

297. Ridgley, *Body of Divinity* (1855), p. 147.

298. Ridgley, *Body of Divinity*, p. 111, col. 2-p. 112, col. 1 (1855, p. 146); citing Huet, *Concordia rationis et fidei*, II.iii.

299. Cf. Thomas Boston, *An illustration of the doctrines of the Christian religion, with respect to faith and practice, upon the plan of the assembly's shorter catechism. Comprehending a complete body of divinity. Now first published from the manuscripts of ... Thomas Boston*, 2 vols. (Edinburgh: John Reid, 1773; reissued, 1853), hereinafter cited as Boston, *Commentary on the Shorter Catechism*; Gill, *Body of Divinity*, I, pp. 187-245; John Brown, *A Compendious View of Natural and Revealed Religion. In seven books* (Glasgow: John Bryce for J. Matthews, 1782; 2nd ed. revised, Edinburgh: Murray and Cochrane, 1796; reissued, Philadelphia: David Hogan, Griggs & Co., 1819).

300. Wyttenbach, *Theses theologicae*, xxxvi.

301. See D. W. Dockrill, "Authority of the Fathers in the Great trinitarian Debates of the Sixteen-Nineties," in *Studia Patristica*, 18/4 (1983), pp. 335-347.

trinitarianism, particularly given the ability of theologians, on historical grounds, to identify patterns in nominally orthodox patristic trinitarianism that were either pre-Nicene or non-Nicene. There are, for example, peculiarities, arising from the context of debate with Arians and Socinians, in Ridgley's trinitarian language. Although Ridgley confesses the full divinity of Father, Son, and Spirit and argues pointedly the Reformed doctrine of the deity of the Son and the Spirit, he hesitates to identify the term "Son" as the ultimate and proper designation of the divine second person. "Son," according to Ridgley, even when used of the second person of the Trinity in his eternity, properly indicates his mediatorial office, in the fulfillment of which Christ is both fully divine and fully human. In brief, the logic of his argument must be traced to his debate with the Socinians, who assigned sonship entirely to the human Jesus: in response, Ridgley argues that sonship properly indicates divinity and humanity together in the person of the Mediator, while never setting aside the extended usage of "Son" as rightful title of the second person of the Trinity.[302]

Among the British writers of the late orthodox era, the Particular Baptist John Gill stands out as a defender of the doctrine of the Trinity as "a doctrine of pure revelation" to the setting aside of all but biblical argumentation and patristic usage. Gill argued and defended the doctrine both in his famous *Body of Divinity* and in a separate, extended treatise on the subject.[303] The treatise (1731) preceded the theological system (1769-70) and appears to have been, in large part, the basis of Gill's exposition in the *Body of Divinity*. What is characteristic of both works, although more evident in the treatise, are Gill's distance from any particular philosophical models of the era, his reliance on a traditionary exegetical-topical exposition, and, within that exposition, his impressive use of Judaica, particularly rabbinic exegesis, as a support of his interpretation of the Old Testament, including its trinitarian implications. In addition, Gill evidences a significant awareness and use of the theological works of Reformed and, occasionally, Lutheran orthodox predecessors in the seventeenth century.[304] A generation past Gill, the outlines of the older orthodoxy mingled (as previously noted of the Dutch exegete and theologian Klinkenberg) with a somewhat more rationalist, apologetic model that moved from natural to revealed theology the outlines of a fully orthodox trinitarianism, alive to the problems of definition in the eighteenth century, can be found in the theology of John Brown of Haddington.[305]

---

302. Ridgley, *Body of Divinity* (1855), I, pp. 135-163.

303. John Gill, A *Treatise on the Doctrine of the Trinity* (London, 1731).

304. For a discussion of Gill's relationship to the Reformed tradition, see Richard A. Muller, "John Gill and the Reformed Tradition: A Study in the Reception of Protestant Orthodoxy in the Eighteenth Century," in *The Life and Thought of John Gill (1697-1771): A Tercentennial Appreciation*, ed. Michael A. G. Haykin (Leiden: E. J. Brill, 1997), pp. 51-68.

305. Cf. Brown, *Compendious View*, II.ii (pp. 128-146).

PART 2

The Reformed Orthodox Doctrine of the Trinity

3

The Doctrine of the Trinity in Reformed Orthodoxy: Basic Issues, Terms, and Definitions

3.1 The Trinity as a "Fundamental Article" of Faith

A. The Place, Order, and Importance of the Doctrine

1. Views of the Reformers. Whether positively in their creedal and catechetical expositions and their various manuals or bodies of doctrine or in their responses to the early antitrinitarians, the Reformers uniformly gave testimony to the importance of the doctrine of the Trinity in their theology and to the necessity of respecting the mystery of the doctrine. The doctrine of the Trinity, according to the Reformers and their successors, belonged to the category of fundamental and necessary articles.[1] Even Melanchthon's early exclusion of the doctrine from his set of treated *loci* (albeit not from his listing of foundational topics) had more to do with issues related to speculation than with the question of necessary beliefs for Christians. When Melanchthon added an exposition of the doctrine to later editions of his *Loci communes*, the trinitarian model became the central issue of his doctrine of God, given far greater detail than the unity of essence and the attributes, for, as Melanchthon testifies, although the mystery of the Trinity is beyond all human comprehension, some attempt at expressing the doctrine must be made in order to distinguish Christian worship from that of the pagans.[2]

In the confessions and theological systems of the Reformers the doctrine of the Trinity is almost invariably placed in the creedal or catechetical order, early on in the

---

1. On fundamental articles, see *PRRD*, I, 9.1 (A-B).
2. Melanchthon, *Loci communes theologici* (1543), locus 1.

order of doctrines, preceded only by preliminary matters and the discussion of Scripture, and followed immediately by creation and providence. Insofar as many of these works do not have extended discussions of the divine essence and attributes, the doctrine of the Trinity receives the central place in the doctrine of God. Thus, Calvin's *Institutes* offer a long paragraph on issues relating to essence and attributes and then engage directly and at length in the discussion of the Trinity. For Calvin, the doctrine of the Trinity was "another special mark" beyond the revealed attributes by which God makes his identity and intention known to us — and without the knowledge of the three persons, we can "have only a bare and empty name of God floating in our brains" and no "idea of the true God."[3] Calvin's placement and understanding of the doctrine, at least as far as the order and arrangement of the *Institutes* are concerned, remained highly influencial by the initial catechetical model of the *Institutes* and by the dispersal of the creedal portion of the catechism into the four books of the 1559 edition: thus, he comes to the doctrine of the Trinity after his initial discussion of the knowledge of God and of human beings and his discussion of Scripture and God's revelation in it.[4] The pattern, albeit far more discursive, is virtually identical in implication to the dominant model of the later orthodox: prolegomena, Scripture, and God. Calvin also assumes that the order proceeds from discussion of the one God and his attributes to the discussion of the Trinity.[5] (Given that the arrangement of the Vermigli-Massoinius *Loci communes* was patterned on Calvin's *Institutes*, the same arrangement obtains there and Vermigli's theology had its impact in the Calvinian form.)

Bullinger identifies the Trinity as clearly taught in Scripture, together with the unity of God, and he counsels that believers "simply rest therein, and not curiously search or lust after any further knowledge in this life than what God has revealed."[6] In the *Decades*, his approach to the Trinity occurs precisely where one would expect, in his sermon on the first article of the Creed. As for the arrangement of the doctrine of God itself, Bullinger's *Compendium* and *Decades* broach both topics together, given the creedal model of both documents at this point, and in the *Compendium*, the recounting of the attributes follows the definition of the Trinity.[7]

Perhaps the clearest statement of the place of the doctrine found among the second generation of the Reformed comes from Hyperius, who identified *Deus* as the first *locus* to be treated in the order of six basic *loci* (following an introductory discussion of Scripture as the basis of doctrine): God, Creatures and Human Beings, the Church, the Doctrine of the Law and the Gospel, the signs or Sacraments, and the

---

3. Calvin, *Institutes*, I.xiii.2.

4. On the order and arrangement of the *Institutes*, see Muller, *Unaccommodated Calvin*, pp. 118-139.

5. Cf. Calvin, *Institutes*, I.x.1-3; xiii.1, where the oneness of God and the attributes are discussed, albeit briefly. Also note the comments in *PRRD*, III, 3.1 (A.2); 3.3 (B.1).

6. Bullinger, *Compendium*, II.ii.

7. Cf. Calvin, *Institutes*, I.xiii.2.; Bullinger, *Compendium*, II.ii; Bullinger, *Decades*, I.vii (I, pp. 124-126).

Consummation. Within the doctrine of God itself, Hyperius assumes that the proper order is to move from the divine oneness to the divine threeness.[8]

Musculus' model has much in common with these other second-generation efforts, but it also has some rather distinctive features. We have already noted his extensive presentation of the divine attributes.[9] In his order and arrangement of the *loci*, Musculus places first a set of preliminary remarks concerning the existence and nature of God and then, prior to his discussion of the Creation, Fall, and work of redemption, addresses the doctrine of the Trinity and the works or operations of God. He is then able to offer, when he returns, some thirty-eight chapters later, to the nature and attributes of God, to offer a trinitarian and often highly soteriological understanding of the attributes at various crucial places in his lengthy discussions of each attribute. This arrangement, by the way, can be missed in a perusal of the contents of the sixteenth-century English translation of the *Loci communes*, in which "Of God" appears as the first *locus* and "Of the Works of God" as the second: in the Latin editions, the *loci* stand as (I) *De Deo*, (II) *De divinitate Christi*, (III) *De divinitate Spiritus sancti*, and (IV) *De operibus Dei*. The material is not missing from the English translation, but only gathered into a three-part chapter under one heading.

2. The Reformed orthodox approach to the doctrine of the Trinity. The doctrine of the Trinity occupies a crucial position both in the scholastic Protestant system and in the exegesis and piety of the era of orthodoxy as well.[10] Beginning with Zanchi, who registered Ochino's suggestion that the Trinity be viewed as a doctrine not necessary to salvation, the Reformed consistently state the contrary: the Protestant orthodox place the doctrine of the Trinity among the "fundamental" or "necessary articles" and, against both Socinian denial of the doctrine and Remonstrant denial of its fundamental character, argue its necessity to the salvation of believers. The doctrine is taught in Scripture and, therefore, ought to be understood as pertinent to salvation! Moreover, the doctrine is necessary, given the consistent reference of Scripture to the Son and the Spirit of God, to the right confession of the one God, which is clearly necessary to salvation.[11] One of the great errors of modern writers has been their claim that the Reformers did not emphasize the doctrine of the Trinity sufficiently and that the Protestant scholastics devalued the doctrine of the Trinity because of an emphasis on the essence and attributes of God.[12] This error arises out of two misapprehensions

---

8. Hyperius, *Methodus theologiae*, pp. 12, 91-92.

9. See *PRRD*, III, 2.1 (B.2); 3.3 (B.1-2), et passim.

10. Cf. the comments in Muller, *Christ and the Decree*, pp. 35, 37-38, 113-115, 136-138, 143-145, 149-152, 156-159, 164-167, 181.

11. Cf. Zanchi, *De tribus Elohim*, pt. 2, V.ix (cols. 561-564); Voetius, *Selectarum disputationum theologicarum*, I, xxviii; with Turretin, *Inst. theol. elencticae*, III.xxiv; Mastricht, *Theoretico-practica theol.*, II.xxiv.20; Ridgley, *Body of Divinity* (1855), I, pp. 136-137; Van der Kemp, *Christian Entirely the Property of Christ*, I, p. 183; Boston, *Commentary on the Shorter Catechism*, I, p. 143; Heppe, *Reformed Dogmatics*, p. 105; and with the Lutheran dogmaticians in Schmid, *Doctrinal Theology of the Evangelical Lutheran Church*, pp. 137-138

12. Most pointedly, Karl Barth, *Church Dogmatics*, ed. G. W. Bromiley and T. F. Torrance, 4 vols. (Edinburgh: T. & T. Clark, 1936-1975), I/1, pp. 300-304, II/1, pp. 261, 287-288, where the density

concerning the form and method of scholastic system. On the one hand, it assumes that the comparatively greater space allotted to the doctrine of the essence and attributes of God is a sign of its greater importance to the system. Quite to the contrary, extent of exposition is not a sign of importance or lack thereof — instead, the extent of any discussion in a scholastic system is primarily a function of the number of parts or divisions of a topic and of the ease or difficulty of the argument. The doctrine of the essence and attributes of God, which is to say, the doctrine of the divine oneness or unity, is neither more nor less important than the doctrine of the Trinity: it simply contains more topics for discussion and definition.

The comparative brevity of the positive, systematic presentations of the doctrine can be explained, moreover, by the assumption of the Reformed orthodox that the doctrine of the Trinity is not a proper place for extensive rational demonstration and argumentation. Owen refers to the reverence with which "these awful mysteries" ought to be presented.[13] Turretin begins his discussion with the assertion that the "sacred mystery of the Trinity" can "neither be grasped by reason nor demonstrated by example" but can be discussed "only on the authority of revelation as received by faith, and respected by piety"[14] — while Marckius, Pictet, and Rijssen warn against the temptation to follow the medieval scholastics into speculation concerning the *opera ad intra*.[15]

On the other hand, it is sometimes argued in modern discussions of the subject — perhaps on the basis of one of Luther's early complaints against late medieval commentaries on Lombard's *Sentences* — that the treatment of the Trinity following the doctrine of the essence and attributes indicates a subordination of the doctrines concerning the personal God of the Bible to metaphysical concerns. Here, too, we must dissent and for a variety of reasons. Not only is the primary testimony of Scripture to the oneness of God, it is also the case that nearly all of the modern reflection on the biblical God as personal refers to the will and affections of the one God — namely, to the attributes of that God — in his relation to his creation, and not specifically to the Trinity or to the divine subsistences traditionally denominated "persons." In addition, the placement of the doctrine of the Trinity second in order arises, in the first place, out of the need to set the doctrine against the background of divine oneness and to argue the predication of all the divine attributes equally of each of the persons on the grounds of the full possession of the divine essence by each of the persons. The logic of the discussion demands prior definition of oneness, essence, and attributes.

---

of the contrary evidence forces Barth to comment on the scholastic Protestant understanding of the Trinity as the deep mystery of the faith as an instance that makes one question "whether or not they knew what they were saying" (I/1, p. 303). Also note Otto Weber, *Foundations of Dogmatics*, *Foundations of Dogmatics*, trans. Darrell Guder, 2 vols. (Grand Rapids: Eerdmans, 1981-82), I, pp. 349-352, 397-398 and the comments of Emil Brunner, *The Christian Doctrine of God; Dogmatics: Volume I*, trans. Olive Wyon (Philadelphia: Westminster, 1950), pp. 205-206, 242-243; and see the discussion of this problem in PRRD, III, 3.1 (A-B).

13. Owen, *Brief ... Doctrine of the Trinity*, in *Works*, II, pp. 367.

14. Turretin, *Inst. theol. elencticae*, III.xxiii.1.

15. Marckius, *Compendium*, V.xii; Pictet, *Theol. chr.*, II.xii (pp. 111-112); Rijssen, *Summa theol.*, IV.xiii-xiv.

In the second place, it is the discussion of the work of the three persons, first in their relationships *ad intra* and then in their common work *ad extra*, that provides the point of transition from the doctrine of God to the rest of the system — that is, to the doctrines of the works of God. Thus, again, the logic of discussion provides the reason for the order of the doctrine: first the doctrine of God, then the doctrine of God's works. The issue is one of the flow of theological system, not of greater or lesser importance of doctrinal *loci*.

The intimate relation between the *loci* is apparent, moreover, in the occasional variations of order and arrangement that occur in the Reformed orthodox doctrine of God. Thus, Wendelin makes the classic division between the doctrine of the essence and attributes and the doctrine of the trinity, but he reserves his discussion of the divine unity for the *locus* on the Trinity, thereby establishing the intimate relationship of the topics and emphasizing both the monotheistic context of Christian trinitarianism and the connection between trinitarian statements and the assumption of divine simplicity, infinity, perfection, omnipotence, and sufficiency — all of which can be understood only in the context of divine oneness. His basic thesis on the Trinity, that "there are, in the one and simple nature of God, distinct persons who possess [it] in common," leads him to place all discussion of divine threeness into the context of divine oneness. God, therefore, is one with respect to nature, plural with respect to person — and we are bound to recognize, Wendelin continues, that the word "God" is used in two ways in Scripture, essentially, with reference to oneness, and personally, with reference to the plurality pf persons. We see, therefore, a distinction of topics for the sake of exposition, not a radical separation of issues.[16]

Finally, the assumption of a lessening of interest in the doctrine of the Trinity in comparison with the doctrine of the divine attributes is clearly refuted by examination of the polemical treatises, independent theological essays, and sermons of the orthodox, as distinct from their systems of theology. A vast amount of energy was expended throughout the seventeenth century in the defense of the Trinity against both Socinian and Arminian views — while the arrival of modern forms of Sabellianism and Arianism in the latter half of the seventeenth century elicited a significant historical and dogmatic literature from orthodox Protestants.[17] A more churchly and practical concern for the doctrine of the Trinity is manifest, moreover, in the numerous sermons and positive treatises on the subject, in which the orthodox demonstrate their belief that the doctrine was a primary foundation of faith and life with strong soteriological implications.[18]

---

16. Wendelin, *Christianae theologiae libri duo*, I.ii.1 (1-2).

17. E.g., Owen, *Brief ... Doctrine of the Trinity*; Bull, *Defensio fidei Nicaenae*; William Berriman, *An Historical Account of the Controversies that have been in the Church, concerning the Doctrine of the Holy and Everblessed Trinity. In Eight Sermons preached at the Cathedral Church of St. Paul, London, in the years 1723 and 1724* (London: T. Ward and C. Rivington, 1725).

18. E.g., John Owen, *ΧΡΙΣΤΟΛΟΓΙΑ: or, a Declaration of the Glorious Mystery of the Person of Christ* (1679), in *Works*, vol. 1, pp. 2-272; idem, *ΠΝΕΥΜΑΤΟΛΟΓΙΑ or, a Discourse concerning the Holy Spirit* (1674-1693) in *Works*, vols. 3-4.

The importance of the doctrine to Reformed orthodoxy is perhaps nowhere more forcefully and eloquently stated than in Owen's treatise on *The Divine Original of Scripture*, in which Owen offers as an argument for the divine purpose in Scripture that it presents "some revelations ... so sublimely glorious, of so profound and mysterious an excellency" that they are beyond reason to the point of confounding it at first glance, and yet, when rightly contemplated, reason itself must recognize "that unless they are accepted and submitted unto, although unsearchable, not only all that hath been received must be rejected, but also the whole dependence of the creature on God be dissolved, or rendered only dreadful, terrible, and destructive to nature itself."[19] The doctrine of the Trinity, Owen continues, is just such a doctrine: "take away ... the doctrine of the Trinity, and ... there can be no purpose of grace by the Father in the Son — no covenant for the putting of that purpose in execution: and so the foundation of all fruits of love and goodness is lost to the soul."[20]

3. The order and arrangement of the *locus*. As is to be expected, the order and arrangement of the *locus de Deo* varies in its presentation of the Trinity, albeit not as much as in its presentation of the attributes. Among the theologies of the second-generation Reformers, Calvin's *Institutes* stands out as more detailed and precise in its outline, particularly in the form understood by the sixteenth-century editors, who offered the following description of the arrangement of the chapter:

> This chapter consists of two parts. The former delivers the orthodox doctrine concerning the Holy Trinity. This occupies from sec. 1-21, and may be divided into four heads; the first, treating of the meaning of Person, including both the term and the thing meant by it, sec. 2-6; the second, proving the deity of the Son, sec. 7-13; the third, the deity of the Holy Spirit, sec. 14 and 15; and the fourth, explaining what is to be held concerning the Holy Trinity. The second part of the chapter refutes certain heresies which have arisen, particularly in our age, in opposition to this orthodox doctrine. This occupies from sec. 21 to the end.[21]

Calvin thus introduces the topic, defines "person" and other traditional trinitarian terms, discusses the divinity of the Son and the Spirit, and concludes his positive exposition with a statement of the full doctrine of the Trinity, framing it as a result of the more or less exegetical exercise of proving the deity and persons of the Son and the Spirit. Only after fully defining the doctrine does he address the heresies. Notably absent here is a distinct discussion of God as Father in the trinitarian sense.

In the early orthodox era, Polanus offered a well-designed ordering of the *locus* that stood in basic continuity with Calvin's model, but added a separate discussion of the Father. The chapter heads are "I. Concerning the term person, whether it may be used with reference to God, and how it is distinguished from other related terms; II. What is a divine person; III. On the number of divine persons; IV. On God the Father; V.

---

19. John Owen, *Of the Divine Original, Authority, Self-evidencing Light, and Power of the Scriptures*, in *Works*, XVI, pp. 339-40.

20. Owen, *Divine Original*, p. 341.

21. As given in Calvin, *Institutes*, I.xiii (Beveridge).

On the Son of God; VI. On the Holy Spirit; VII. Concerning the Holy Trinity; VIII. Axioms concerning the Holy Trinity, or concerning the three persons in the unity of the Godhead; IX. Refutation of objections against the *homoousion* of the Father, the Son, and the Holy Spirit; X-XI. Refutation of objections against the distinction of persons."[22] The patterning is very much like Calvin's — an introduction to the terms, particularly "person," followed by the identification of the persons, demonstrating their distinction and divinity, concluding with the definition of the Trinity, and then passing on to objections. Similarly, from the same era, Alsted's *Theologia didactica* discusses the doctrine under the following heads: "Concerning the persons of the Trinity in their relation to one another; Concerning the persons of the Trinity in their distinction; Of God the Father; Of the Son of God; Of the Holy Spirit."[23] The absence of chapters refuting heresies stems from the "didactic," as distinct from "scholastic" or "polemical," model of the treatise.

Among the high orthodox theologians, similar models and orders appear, albeit with some minor alterations of argument, largely for the sake of clarification of issues and definitions. Thus, Maresius begins the *locus de Sacro-sancta Trinitate* of his *Collegium theologicum* with a declaration of the "excellency" of the doctrine and a brief definition (i-ii); he then proceeds to an extended set of definitions of terms (iii-x), a discussion of the threeness of person and unity of essence (xi-xiii), an analysis of the distinction of the persons (xiv-xx), a discussion of the personal properties (xxi-xxiii), a statement of the *opera trinitatis ad intra* emphasizing the primacy of the Father (xxiv-xxv), the generation of the Son from the Father (xxvi), and procession of the Spirit from the Father and the Son (xxvii), the distinctions between generation and procession, their order, and the modes of operation *ad intra* and *ad extra* (xxviii-xxxiv). All this leads to an extended definition of the Trinity and unity of God (xxxv-xl), the identification of the Trinity as a necessary doctrine beyond but not contrary to reason (xli-xliii). Maresius then comes to the demonstration of the doctrine from the Old (xliv-xlv) and New (xlvi-xlviii) Testaments, followed by specific biblical arguments for the divinity and person of the Son and the divinity and person of the Spirit (xlix) from their names (l-li), their attributes (lii), their works (liii), and the honors accorded them (liv-lvi). Finally, against various heresies ancient and modern, Maresius stresses the divinity and distinct personality of the Spirit (lvii-lix), and concludes with a comment on the practical use of the doctrine (lx).[24] Like Calvin, Maresius offers no separate discussion of God the Father — and in accord with nearly all the theologies examined, he moves from introductory comment to definitions of terms, full definition, arguments from Scripture for the deity and persons of the Son and Spirit, and a conclusion. Unlike the early orthodox, but quite like other high orthodox theologies, Maresius lines out the topics according to which the divinity of the Son and Spirit are demonstrated — divine names, divine attributes, divine works, and divine honor. This latter elaboration

22. Polanus, *Syntagma theol, Index capitum, lib. III.*
23. Alsted, *Theologia didactica,* I.xxx-xxxiv.
24. Cf. Maresius, *Collegium theologicum,* III (pp. 44-66)

is simply that, a more detailed topical division of material already found in the order and arrangement of Reformed theologies looking back to Calvin's *Institutes*.

In Turretin's *Institutio*, the arrangement is somewhat different, given the fundamentally polemical approach of the treatise. He begins with a series of definitions of the terms — essence, substance, subsistence, person, Trinity, *homoousios* — and then discusses the doctrine as a mystery and a fundamental article, against the Socinians and the Remonstrants.[25] Turretin next defines the doctrine, against the Socinians, as referring to one divine essence in three persons, and then, also against the Socinians, argues that the doctrine can be demonstrated from the Old Testament.[26] Then follows a discussion of the distinction of the persons, the deity and eternal generation of the Son, and the deity and procession of the Spirit.[27] Again, the model moves from definition of terms to the demonstrations of the divinity of the Son and Spirit, given that these are the controverted topics — with the omission of separate discussion of the Father, as Van Til would later comment, the personality of the Father is evident and the deity of the Father beyond controversy.[28]

A noteworthy, largely non-polemical doctrinal model is found in Brakel's *Redelijke Godsdienst*, where the doctrine of God is discussed in two extended chapters, *Van God* and *Van de Goddelijke Personen*. Here the statement of the mystery is presented first and foremost, against the various heretical objections, as a biblical doctrine available only through revelation (i-ii). Next there is a juxtaposition of the unity of the divine essence with the threeness of the persons (iii-iv). There follows an extended discussion of the plurality of divine persons in the biblical revelation (v-viii), a discussion of the eternal generation of the Son (ix-xxv), of the person of the Holy Spirit as "spirit," as "holy," as a "person," and as divine (xxvi-xxxiii), of the "practical" use of the doctrine, with significant emphasis on the work of the Spirit (xxxiv-xlix).[29] Nearly all of the major systematic works from the era of orthodoxy discuss, somewhere in the *locus*, the mystery of the Trinity and define the doctrine as resting on revelation alone, having a status beyond reason, although not unreasonable. This set of assumptions yields a doctrine that is grounded primarily on the biblical text and, in its use of exegetical materials, follows out the typical hermeneutical pattern of the Reformed orthodoxy, namely, the use of explicit statements of Scripture, the use of conclusions drawn from individual texts or collations of texts, and the assumption of an overarching scope of Scripture that permits broad-ranging conclusions resting on the entirety of the revelation.

---

25. Turretin, *Inst. theol. elencticae*, III.xxiii-xxiv.

26. Turretin, *Inst. theol. elencticae*, III.xxv-xxvi.

27. Turretin, *Inst. theol. elencticae*, III.xxvii-xxxi.

28. Salomon Van Til, *Theol. revelata compendium*, III (p. 45).

29. Brakel, *Redelijke Godsdienst*, I.iv.1-49.

B. The Trinity of God as a Mystery beyond Reason

1. Views of the Reformers. The Reformers tended not only to defend the traditional doctrine of the Trinity as biblical but also to deemphasize the authority of the traditional trinitarian terminology — particularly the more speculative language of the medieval scholastics concerning the character of the trinitarian emanations in the Godhead. The patristic metaphors and various references to *vestigia trinitatis*, whether in the human frame or in the world at large, never became major elements in the doctrinal expositions of the Reformers.

In the first edition of his *Loci communes*, Melanchthon chose to note the doctrine of the Trinity among the standard topics belonging to theology — and then chose not to discuss it in his largely Pauline survey of the basic theological *loci*, commenting that, together with such topics as "the mystery of creation" and the "manner of incarnation," it was better left undiscussed than speculated on: "we do better to adore the mysteries of the Deity than to investigate them." "What is more," he added, "these matters cannot be probed without great danger."[30] As the shape and content of his *Loci communes* developed, Melanchthon added a lengthy discussion of the doctrine of God, focused largely on the doctrine of the Trinity and its biblical foundations, but he did so in the recognition that the doctrine remained a mystery, albeit one that needed statement and even doctrinal elaboration in the church:

> although all the minds of men and of angels stand in wonderment in admiration of this mystery, that God has begotten a Son and that the Holy Spirit, the Sanctifier proceeds from the Father and the Son, yet we must concur in this, because, as has already been said so many times, we must believe concerning God as He has revealed Himself. ... Although we cannot probe this mystery to the depths, yet in this life God has willed that there be at least a beginning of knowledge of this subject.[31]

Calvin indicates the vast difference between Christian views of God and those based solely on human "imaginations" and identifies the "unity ... existing in three persons" as a most "intimate knowledge" of God's nature belonging only to the Christian revelation.[32] Calvin also went to great pains to identify the proper use of the traditional trinitarian language and its limits: the terms essence, person, subsistence, and so forth, are useful as guides or boundaries to expression, keeping the church from heresy, but they are no more than a set of "clearer terms" by which we explain the "dark and intricate" places of Scripture that lie beyond the human capacity to penetrate. Such terms must be "kept in reverent and faithful subordination to Scripture truth, used sparingly and modestly."[33] In keeping with this limitation of the use of churchly language concerning the Trinity, Calvin avoided all but the basic patristic terms and spoke quite negatively of the more speculative Augustinian metaphors drawn from

---

30. Melanchthon, *Loci communes* (1521), p. 21.
31. Melanchthon, *Loci communes* (1543), p. 21.
32. Calvin, *Institutes*, I.xiii.1-2.
33. Calvin, *Institutes*, I.xiii.3.

human nature.[34] Viret, by way of contrast, perhaps because of the more popular nature of his writings, did use metaphors — notably the patristic metaphor of the sun, its rays, and the heat; the Augustinian metaphor of understanding, memory, and will; and a metaphor of the three persons of Adam, Eve, and Seth, drawn out of Justin Martyr. Of the latter, Viret appreciated the fact that Eve came forth from Adam and that both together begat Seth (indicating double procession!), but he also noted the problem of using human persons in a metaphor, given the tritheistic implication of identifying the divine essence as secondary essence or genus. Viret, departing considerably from Calvin, evidenced a particular fondness for the Augustinian metaphor.[35]

Bullinger offered an assessment of metaphors and similes applied to the Trinity similar to Calvin's. Some would attempt to explain the mystery of the Trinity by "similitudes," he writes, "but in all the things that God hath made ... there is nothing which can properly be likened to the nature of God: neither are there any words in the mouth of men that can properly be spoken of it: neither are there any similitudes of man's invention that can rightly and squarely agree with the divine Essence." Therefore, "injury is done to the majesty of God, if it be compared with mortal things."[36] Nevertheless, since Scripture itself speaks in such a way as to accommodate its truth "to our infirmity," a few parables or similitudes, if taken with caution, are not out of place in a reverent discussion of the Trinity.

> As the sun is the headspring of the light and the heat, so is the Father the headspring of the Son, who is light of light: and as of the sun and the beams together the heat doth come, so of the Father and the Son together the Holy Ghost proceedeth. But now put case or imagine that the sun were such as never had beginning, nor ever shall have ending; and should not then, I pray you, the beams of this everlasting sun be everlasting too? And should not the heat, which proceedeth of them both, be everlasting, as well as they? Finally, should not the sun be one still in essence or substance, and three by reason of the three subsistences or persons?[37]

Finally, writes Bullinger, one must pass from such parables and similies to the recognition that, insofar as this mystery lies beyond human comprehension, it is a matter for faith alone.[38]

2. Approaches of the Reformed orthodox. Echoing the Reformers, the Reformed orthodox almost invariably comment that the doctrine of the Trinity is the sublime and sacred mystery of the Christian faith "which can neither be grasped by reason nor demonstrated by example, but is offered by divine Revelation alone to be received

---

34. Calvin, *Institutes*, I.xv.4; cf, similarly, Calvin, *Commentary on Genesis*, Gen. 1:26 (CTS *Genesis*, I, p. 93).

35. See Georges Bavaud, *Le Réformateur Pierre Viret (1511-1564); Sa théologie* (Geneva: Labor et Fides, 1986), pp. 60-66.

36. Bullinger, *Decades*, IV.iii (p. 165).

37. Bullinger, *Decades*, IV.iii (p. 166).

38. Bullinger, *Decades*, IV.iii (p. 167).

by faith and contemplated with reverence."[39] Brakel begins his discussion of the Trinity with the remark that, "having spoken of the name, the being and the personal properties of God, we turn to the profoundest mystery of the holy Triunity (*de allerdiepste geheimenis van de heilige Drieëenheid*)."[40] Indeed, so far does the mystery of the Trinity "transcend reason" that it can be "demonstrated from the revealed word alone."[41] Zanchi can be said, perhaps, to have set the tone for the Protestant scholastic discussion by stating categorically that "we can neither know nor speak anything of this mystery, except to the extent that it is supported by Scripture." Second, he comments, the only way to develop the doctrine is by close examination of Scripture, specifically interpreting the text by "the analogy of faith."[42]

The British divines express nearly identical sentiments: Owen denominates the doctrine of the Trinity "unsearchable" to the point that "at the first proposal" of such a teaching, the unassisted rational faculty "startles, shrinks, and is taken with horror, meeting that which is above it, too great and too excellent for it." This is a doctrine, Owen concludes, that is "above and beyond the reach of reason."[43] Citing Exodus 33:18-23, Owen comments that we are able to know "external representations of God" and "created appearances of his glory" akin to the "back parts" of a man who passes us by, "but as to the being of God and his subsistence in the Trinity of persons, we have no direct intuition into them, much less comprehension of them."[44] Similarly, Manton indicates that the doctrine of the Trinity "is a mystery proper to the scriptures." "Other truths," he continues, "are revealed in nature, but this is a treasure peculiar to the church."[45]

The orthodox, thus, feel that dogmatic discussion of the Trinity is mandated by revelation even though the doctrine be an impenetrable mystery — and that, further, the revelation, insofar as it can be understood, must be illustrated or explicated with the tools of reason. The illustrations, however, cannot be considered any more than very limited aids to understanding: here the epistemological side of the Reformed *non capax* comes to the fore. Why, then, the discussion, if it must necessarily be imperfect — why the attempt at rational, doctrinal statement if reason must fail before the mystery? The answer for the seventeenth-century Protestant mind was simple:

---

39. Turretin, *Inst. theol. elencticae*, III.xxiii.1; Amyraut et al., *Syntagma thesium theologicarum*, I.xv.1-2; cf. Heppe, *Reformed Dogmatics*, pp. 105-110.

40. Brakel, *Redelijke Godsdienst*, I.iv.1; cf. Beza et al., *Propositions and Principles*, II.i-ii.

41. Turretin, *Inst. theol. elencticae*, III.xxv.4; cf. Maresius, *Collegium theologicum*, iii.41; Mastricht, *Theoretico-practica theol.*, II.xxiv.21, and note the statement found in Heppe, *Reformed Dogmatics*, pp. 105-10.

42. Zanchi, *De tribus Elohim*, pt. I, I.i.2 (col. 3).

43. Owen, *Divine Original*, pp. 339-340.

44. Owen, *ΧΡΙΣΤΟΛΟΓΙΑ*, p. 67.

45. Thomas Manton, *Sermons upon John XVII*, in *The Complete Works of Thomas Manton*, 22 vols. (London: J. Nisbet, 1870-1875), X, p. 158; cf. Ridgley, *Body of Divinity* (1855), I, pp. 138-143.

The mystery of the Trinity is necessary to be known and believed of all that shall be saved; it was not so plainly revealed to the Jews of old, as it is to us in the new Testament. A perfect and full knowledge of this mystery is not attainable in this life.[46]

This is a wonderful mystery rather to be adored and admired than inquired into; and yet every one is bound to know it with an apprehensive knowledge, though not with a comprehensive. No man can be saved without the knowledge of the Father; he hath not the Father who denieth the Son; and he receives not the Holy Ghost who knows him not, John 14:17 (cf. 1 John 2:23).[47]

This characterization of the doctrine of the Trinity was, of course, a matter of controversy: the Socinians and the Remonstrants both denied that the Trinity could be a fundamental article of the faith — a claim that the orthodox were quick to point out was, in itself, a fundamental error. In Hoornbeeck's view, the biblical basis for the Reformed position was offered by 1 John 2:23, "he who denies the Son, has denied the Father," as well as by the baptismal formula of Matthew 28:19. What is more, Hoornbeeck could argue, the Socinians themselves confirm the point, as seen in Schlichting's attack on Meisner: in attempting to undermine the Lutheran Meisner's arguments concerning fundamental articles, Schlichting had stated that if the doctrine of the Trinity were true, it would be fundamental and had then concluded that, given its falsity, it could not be. Hoornbeeck concludes that even the adversaries admit the fundamental nature of the doctrine, and given its truth, it therefore must be understood as necessary to salvation.[48]

3. **The practical use of the doctrine of the Trinity.** Thus the orthodox not only state the doctrine of the Trinity as the ground of all other Christian doctrine — they also state it as an eminently practical doctrine, as illustrated by the practical sections of Mastricht's analysis and by Owen's trinitarian treatise, *Of Communion with God ... or, the Saints' Fellowship with the Father, Son, and Holy Ghost Unfolded* (1657).[49] The Reformed orthodox theologians' profound sense of the ultimate and foundational nature of the doctrine of the Trinity for faith and worship and for the architecture and content of theological system frequently leads them to discuss at length the "practical use" of the doctrine in the church. For the late orthodox, even this point has become a matter of debate, given the tendency of the Remonstrant theologians to argue both

---

46. Leigh, *Treatise*, II.xvi (p. 127): insistence upon the fundamental character of the doctrine and of its inclusion in doctrines necessary to salvation is characteristic of orthodoxy, both Reformed and Lutheran; cf. Schmid, *Doctrinal Theology of the Evangelical Lutheran Church*, pp. 137-138, citing König, *Theologia positiva acroamatica*: "Whoever is ignorant of the mystery of the Trinity does not acknowledge God as He has revealed Himself in His Word, and is ignorant of the definition of God given in the Scriptures. The mystery of the Trinity being either ignored or denied, the entire economy of salvation is ignored or denied."

47. Leigh, *Treatise*, II.xvi (p. 140).

48. Hoornbeeck, *Socinianismus confutatus*, I.ix (pp. 218-219).

49. John Owen, *Of Communion with God the Father, Son, and Holy Ghost, each person distinctly, in Love, Grace, and Consolation; or, the Saints' Fellowship with the Father, Son, and Holy Ghost Unfolded* (1657), in *Works*, II, pp. 1-274.

a more subordinationistic view of the Trinity and the inadvisability of focusing too much attention on the difficult nuances of the topic. Thus, Brakel comments that

> the Remonstrants, who make no effort to deny the Trinity, still attempt to demean it by indicating that it is unprofitable. But the Word testifies to the contrary.[50]

Witsius commented, still more pointedly, that "nothing is more false than that calumny of the Remonstrants, by which they deny that the article of the holy Trinity has any practical use." Inasmuch as the Trinity is a "fundamental" article of the faith, the general character of Christian truth that it "is according to godliness" (Titus 1:1) all the more belongs to the doctrine of the Trinity: this doctrine, continues Witsius, is "the source of all genuine faith" and "of all true religion" since "he cannot have Christian faith, who does not believe that a person in the Godhead could have been given ... to be a successful Mediator with God; but this would have been impossible, if the Godhead had subsisted only in one person."[51] Indeed, the Reformed orthodox are unanimous in declaring that the doctrine of the Trinity is necessary to salvation and, therefore, an integral part of the faith and piety of the church: as Calvin commented, "unless we grasp" the revelation of God as three persons, "only the bare and empty name of God flits about in our brains, to the exclusion of the true God."[52] Witsius echoes Calvin precisely: "He who does not adore the Father, the Son, and the Holy Spirit, as equal in divine majesty, worships not the true God, but a creature of his own imagination."[53]

There is, of course, variety of formulation in the Reformed orthodox discussion of the practical use of the doctrine of the Trinity: Turretin states quite simply and briefly that

> the article of the Trinity is not only theoretical, but also practical, since it conduces to gratitude and worship of God — to the end that we may devote our faith and service to the Triune God who has revealed himself to us. And [it conduces] to consolation inasmuch as [by it] we may know that Christ has truly redeemed us and that our salvation has been made secure.[54]

Witsius offers three basic uses, adding admonition to the instruction and consolation indicated by Turretin.[55] More elaborately, Mastricht divides the topic into seven practical uses ranging from the reproof of "atheistical antitrinitarians," to the support of worship and to the communion of saints. Ridgley, too, offers seven, the majority

---

50. Brakel, *Redelijke Godsdienst*, I,.iv.35; cf. Limborch, *Theologia Christiana*, II.xii.2, 27, 29.

51. Witsius, *Exercitationes*, VI.xxiv.

52. Cf. Calvin, *Institutes*, I.xiii.2, with Ursinus, *Commentary*, p. 138; Turretin, *Inst. theol. elencticae*, III.xxiv.11-14; Brakel, *Redelijke Godsdienst*, I.iv.34; Ridgley, *Body of Divinity* (1855), I, pp. 135-37.

53. Witsius, *Exercitationes sacrae in symbolum*, VI.xxiv.

54. Turretin, *Inst. theol. elencticae*, III.xxiv.17.

55. Witsius, *Exercitationes sacrae in symbolum*, VI.xxv-xxvii.

of which focus on redemption and the prayerful contemplation of God.[56] For Owen, the great practical use of the doctrine of the Trinity — to which he devoted some three hundred pages of exposition — is that "the saints have distinct communion with the Father, and the Son, and the Holy Spirit" in the order of "the dispensation of grace": every gift and beneift of God "groweth originally from the Father, and cometh not to us but by the Son, nor by the Son, to any of us in particular, but through the Spirit."[57]

Heppe, unfortunately, virtually omitted this aspect of the doctrine and thereby obscured perhaps the most fundamental intersection of the "speculative" or "contemplative" side of orthodox or scholastic theology with the practical dimension.[58] These various "uses" of the doctrine of the Trinity bear detailed examination, given their significance to the Reformed exposition of the doctrine of the Trinity and, in addition, given the light that they shed on the fundamentally trinitarian character of orthodox Reformed theology as a whole: if there is a single central dogma in the Reformed system, not in the sense of a deductive principle, but in the sense of a foundational premise for the right understanding of all other doctrine, the Trinity is most surely that central dogma. This centrality, moreover, can be seen in the breadth and scope of the uses, which extend from preliminary discussions of revelation, to Christology, to the order of salvation, to the church, and to the last things.

For Ridgley, the first (albeit not the primary) use of the doctrine of the Trinity concerns the distinction between natural and revealed religion. Natural religion

> respects the knowledge of God, so far as it may be attained without help of divine revelation, and the worship which the heathen, who have nothing else to guide them but the light of nature, are obliged to give to the divine Being. [Revealed religion,] which is founded on scripture, contains a personal display of the glory of the Father, the Son, and the Holy Ghost. This is necessary to be known and believed; as it is the foundation of all revealed religion. The sum of Christianity consists in our subjection to, and adoring the Godhead, as subsisting in the Father, the Son, Holy Spirit.[59]

Significantly, Ridgley points directly to the uniqueness of the biblical revelation of God as "personal" — Father, Son, and Spirit — in contrast to the revelation of God as Being that is available in nature. We remember that Scotus, long before, had distinguished between metaphysics and theology on the ground that the former understands its object as *Deus qua Ens*, while the latter understands it object as *Deus qua Deus*. The doctrine of the Trinity, then, is the fundamental article of the faith inasmuch as it provides the fundamental distinction between Christianity and other religion and inasmuch as it presents the primary and central focus both of subjection

---

56. Cf. Mastricht, *Theoretico-practica theol.*, II.xiv.22-28, with Ridgley, *Body of Divinity* (1855), I, pp. 239-241.

57. Cf. Owen, *Of Communion with God*, in *Works*, II, p. 9; Owen, *Vindication of ... Communion with God*, in *Works*, II, p. 281.

58. Heppe, *Reformed Dogmatics*, p. 105.

59. Ridgley, *Body of Divinity* (1855), I, p. 240.

and adoration — obedience and faith. This latter point must certainly be understood in terms of the traditional definition of religion as consisting in the worship and knowledge of God and its reflection in the architectonic description of all theology, introduced into Reformed orthodoxy primarily by Ramists like Polanus, Wollebius, and Ames, as consisting in articles concerning the faith and articles concerning our obedience.[60]

C. Rational Argumentation for the Doctrine of the Trinity

1. The *vestigia trinitatis*: Reformed approaches. As implied in the discussion of the mystery of the Trinity, many of the Reformed orthodox, like the Reformers themselves, distanced themselves from all forms of rational argumentation *toward* the doctrine of the Trinity and allowed only limited use of traditional metaphors and similes in their expositions. Others, however, broached the question of the traditionary rational argumentation more positively. As with other doctrinal topics, one is impressed by the variety of formulation within confessional limits — belying the understanding, typical of the older scholarship, of Reformed orthodoxy as "rigid" and monolithic.

The concept of *vestigia trinitatis*, "vestiges" or "marks of the Trinity" stamped on the created order and, specifically, on human nature, was, therefore, noted by the orthodox with widely varying degrees of receptivity. The assumption of *vestigia* stands in direct relationship to the doctrine of the works of the triune God *ad extra* and rests on the same logic as attends the concept of a natural revelation: the impress of the maker remains on that which is made.[61] Furthermore, the creation not only contains within it various signs of the identity and attributes of the creator, it also bears a closer resemblance to the Creator in the higher levels of the hierarchy of being, granting that the higher the order of creature, the closer it stands to the divine being. Patristic and medieval exegesis had found significant ground for the doctrine, moreover, in the opening chapter of Genesis, where the entire Trinity was revealed in the texts concerning the God whose Spirit "moved upon the face of the waters," whose Word was spoken in the work of creation, and who, in the creation of human beings at the apex of the temporal order could declare in the plural, "Let us make man in our image."[62] Medieval writers, moreover, who had followed out the Augustinian line of

60. Polanus, *Syntagma theol.*, II.1; idem, *Substance of the Christian Religion*, p. 1; Wollebius, *Christianae theol. comp.*, praecognita, §2; Ames, *Medulla theologica*, I.ii.1-2; cf. PRRD, I, 3.4 (B.1-2).

61. See Dennis R. Klinck, "*Vestigia Trinitatis* in Man and His Works in the English Renaissance," in *Journal of the History of Ideas*, 42 (1981), pp. 13-27.

62. Cf. Genesis 1:2, 3, 26 with Augustine, *The Literal Meaning of Genesis*, trans. John Hammond Taylor, 2 vols. (New York: Newman Press, 1982), I.v.11-vii.13; II.vi.10-14; III.xix.29; and with Nicolaus of Lyra, *Biblia sacra cum Glossa interlineari, ordinaria, et Nicolai Lyrani Postilla*, 7 vols. (Venice, 1588), in loc.; and note Cornelius à Lapide, *Commentaria in Scripturam Sacram R. P. Cornelii a Lapide, e Societate Jesu ... accurate recognovit*, editio nova, 27 vols. (Paris: Vives, 1866), in loc., for a synoptic view of the patristic and medieval exegesis used in the sixteenth century.

a trinitarian *imago Dei*, could argue that there was a vague and imperfect capacity within the natural knowledge of God for a trinitarian apperception of the divine.[63]

This older pattern of interpretation carried over with mixed reception into the Protestant exegetical tradition, given the tendency of Protestant exegesis toward a denial of allegory. Calvin had tended to deemphasize this traditionary approach to the impress of the Trinity on human nature, remarking in his commentary on Genesis that "Augustine, beyond all others, speculates with excessive refinement, for the purpose of fabricating a Trinity in man," and commenting only that "I acknowledge, indeed, that there is something in man which refers to the Father, and the Son, and the Spirit,"[64] but not specifying what. Several of Calvin's contemporaries, however, as well as many later Reformed theologians, offered broader discussion of the subject or, at least, an acknowledgment of the Augustinian view without, however, major elaboration of Augustine's more speculative metaphors. Viret, by way of contrast, developed patristic metaphors at some length, with a particular affection for Augustine's language of understanding, memory, and will and for the medieval language of emanations of intellect and will.[65] The early orthodox similarly employed patristic language concerning the begetting or emanation of the Word *ad intra* and *ad extra*, and the standard metaphors of a fountain and stream, the sun and its rays, water and rising vapor, tree and branches, the mind and its inward word — usually expressing the need for caution with such forms of discourse.[66]

Amyraut and Leigh also note "adumbrations" or "resemblances" by which the concept of triunity may be understood from the natural order, specifically from the cosmos itself, the sun, and the human soul, from which the ancient pagans perhaps gathered some sense of the tridaic nature of God.[67] These analogies do not serve as proofs, given the inability of the finite creature to rise by analogy from the finite to the infinite:

> Two resemblances are much used in Scripture, the Light and the word. The Light which was three days before the Sun, Gen. 1. and then condensed into that glorious body, and ever since diffused throughout the world, is all one and the same light. So the Father of lights which inhabiteth light which none can approach, Jas. 1:17. and the Sun of righteousness, Mal. 4:2. in whom the fulness of the Godhead dwelleth bodily [Eph. 1:17,18], and the holy Ghost the Spirit of illumination are all one and the same God.[68]

---

63. Cf. Dourley, "Relationship between Knowledge of God and Knowledge of the Trinity in Bonaventure's *De mysterio trinitatis*," pp. 44-45.

64. Calvin, *Commentary on Genesis*, Gen. 1:26 (*CTS Genesis*, I, p. 93).

65. Pierre Viret, *Exposition familière de l'oraison de nostre Seigneur Jésus Christ* (Geneva, 1548), p. 165; idem, *Exposition familière sur le symbole*, pp. 63-64, 73-74, 297; Bavaud, *Pierre Viret*, pp. 60-64.

66. E.g., Beza et al., *Propositions and Principles*, III.iv; *Synopsis purioris theol.*, VIII.xvi-xvii.

67. Amyraut, *De mysterio trinitatis*, III, pp. 132, 135-149.

68. Leigh, *Treatise*, II.xvi (p. 126).

Amyraut also notes the metaphor of the triangle, which became quite popular among late seventeenth- and eighteenth-century writers.[69] So also, without mentioning their source in Augustine, Leigh and Amyraut offer the spiritual or mental analogies for the Trinity:

> Again it is the same thing that the mind thinketh, and the word signifieth, and the voice uttereth: so is the Father as the mind conceiving, the Son as the word conceived or begotten, the holy Ghost as the voice or speech uttered and imparted to all hearers; and all one and the same God.[70]

Ainsworth (also following Augustine) drew out the metaphor biblically, commenting that the "image" of Genesis 1:26 indicates the "image of the holy Trinity; whereby man in nature, knowledge, righteousness, holiness, glory, &c. resembled God his maker."[71]

2. Seventeenth-century scholastics and the ancients: partial trinitarian conceptions granted to reason in classical philosophy. Equally significant to the question of legitimacy of rational arguments for the Trinity of God are the Reformed orthodox discussions of vestigial or partial trinitarian conceptions found in ancient philosophy. Given the extensive knowledge both of the classical and of the patristic heritage characteristic both of the Reformers and of the Protestant orthodox, these discussions are relatively frequent in the older dogmatics, and they consistently raise the question of the uniqueness of the Christian revelation. In addition, when paired with the issue of partial or incomplete revelations of the Trinity in the Old Testament, these reports of ancient philosophical trinitarianism allowed some of the orthodox dogmaticians cautiously to argue a progressive character to revelation, with the fullness of God's truth being manifest in the New Testament only.[72] The Platonic "triad" in Plato himself, Plotinus, and Proclus, the Parmenidean "trinity," and the emanation of Mind and Word from the ultimate deity in the Hermetica were noted by the Reformed as primary examples of the vague notions of the Trinity found among the ancient pagan philosophers.[73] These trinitarian or triadic elements of ancient philosophy were, moreover, debated by various writers in the seventeenth century, as they had been by the church Fathers, as the source of altered, often heretical, views of the doctrine of the Trinity — notably by Amyraut and Cudworth.[74]

Among the Puritans, Manton noted that Plato spoke of the divine as *nous*, *logos*, and *pneuma*, while Trismegistus used *prota*, *theos*, and other terms for the deity. Such

---

69. Amyraut, *De mysterio trinitatis*, III, p. 157.

70. Leigh, *Treatise*, II.xvi (p. 126); cf. Amyraut, *De mysterio trinitatis.*, III, pp. 146-149.

71. Ainsworth, *Annotations upon Genesis*, Gen. 1:26 in loc.

72. Cf. *Synopsis purioris theol.*, VII.xxxvi-xxxvii; Amyraut, *De mysterio trinitatis*, pars III, passim and VII (p. 531).

73. Among the Reformers, note Musculus, *Loci communes*, i (*Commonplaces*, p. 13, col. 1); cf. Amyraut, *De mysterio trinitatis*, III, pp. 117-122; Cudworth, *True Intellectual System*, I, pp. 728-798.

74. Amyraut, *De mysterio trinitatis*, III, pp. 127-128; Cudworth, *True Intellectual System*, I, pp. 756-757, 778-780, with Cudworth denying the Platonic origins of Arianism.

adumbrations of the Trinity were most probably "general notions" gathered by the ancient philosophers through contact with the Jews, or perhaps the passages in which these concepts are found are additions to the text made at a later date by well-meaning Christians "who counted it a piece of their zeal to lie for God."[75] Edwards and Ridgley, similarly, comment on the adumbrations of the doctrine of the Trinity found in Plato and later Platonists: Plato speaks of three principles, namely, goodness or being, the word or reason of the supreme being, and the spirit "which diffuses its influence throughout the whole system of beings ... the soul of the world" — while Plato's followers speak of these ultimate principles as "three hypostases."[76] These views, Ridgley argues, do not derive from "the light of nature" — rather their ultimate source was the Bible. Like Manton and, moreover, like the fathers, Ridgley assumes that this ancient philosophical trinitarianism were the result of Plato's contact with Jews during his travels in Egypt. Later Platonists, like Plotinus, Proclus, and Porphyry, borrowed their trinitarian metaphysics from their Christian adversaries.[77]

The possible Judaeo-Christian origins of Platonic trinitarianism did not, however, give easy credence to the use of Platonic argumentation in the orthodox doctrine of the Trinity in the seventeenth century. Samuel Parker questioned the entire project, doubting that Plato's thought evidenced any knowledge at all of ancient Hebrew wisdom and specifically arguing against any genuine resemblance between the "Platonick Triad" and the Christian Trinity. The first and second persons of the Christian Trinity, he noted, are Father and Son, of the Platonic, *monas* and *nous*: there is not even a superficial resemblance! Beyond this, the Platonic Triad continues in the emanation of the human soul, so that it represents a descending order or ranking of "Intellectual Beings," not a Trinity of three coessential and coequal persons.[78] Gale, writing a decade later from the perspective of his own attempt to create a theologically acceptable "Reformed" Platonism, acknowledged the problem, noting the "dark notices of the Trinitie" in Platonic philosophy, particularly among the later Platonists. Like Parker, he noted the emanationistic assumptions of Platonism and argued that the triadic model of the ultimate Monad, the eternal intellect, or *Nous*, and the World-soul indicated three essentially distinct hypostases, not to be assimilated to the Christian Trinity. To the argument, Gale added the arguments of Cyril of Alexandria to the effect that the Platonic model was the seed of Arianism. Gale also concluded, with specific reference to Cudworth's massive analysis of the problem, that any attempt

---

75. Manton, *Sermons upon John XVIII*, in *Works*, X, p. 158.

76. Ridgley, *Body of Divinity*, p. 111, col. 1, citing Plato, *Second Epistle to Dionysius*; cf. Edwards, *Theologia Reformata*, I, p. 324; also Marckius, *Compendium*, V.xxviii. N.B.: the authenticity of the letter is disputed; see W. K. C. Guthrie, *A History of Greek Philosophy*, vols. (Cambridge: Cambridge University Press, 1962-19), IV, pp. 65-66; V, pp. 399-401.

77. Ridgley, *Body of Divinity*, p. 111, cols. 1-2.

78. Samuel Parker, *A Free and Impartial Censure of the Platonick Philosophie* (Oxford: W. Hall, 1666), pp. 108-115.

to reconcile the Platonic with the Christian Trinity would "be of most dangerous consequence."[79]

Ridgley mentions, with considerable disapprobation, the use of Plato in answer to the antitrinitarian claim that the doctrine of the Trinity is unintelligible. He goes on to cite Pierre Huet's *concordia rationis et fidei* as a contemporary example of this technique, commenting that "what they call an advantage to the doctrine, has been certainly very detrimental to it; and ... has tended only to pervert the simplicity of the Christian faith with mixtures of philosophy and vain deceit."[80] At very best, comments Ridgley, these "similitudes" only illustrate: they cannot prove the doctrine. At worst they subvert the doctrine and give it into the hands of heretics.[81] For example, the use of divine power, goodness, and wisdom to illustrate the creative, conserving, and governing work of God supports Sabellianism and also fails to limit the number of persons to three — there might be as many persons as there are divine perfections! Analogies from the human soul, from "efficient, constitutive, and final causes," from the light, heat, and motion of the sun, from a fountain as source, water, and stream are also defective:

> These, and many other similitudes of like nature, we find in the writings of some, who consider not what a handle they give to the common enemy. There are, indeed, in most of them, three things, which are said, in different respects, to be one ... all these similitudes ... lead us to think of the whole divided into those parts, of which they consist ... or they speak of three properties of the same thing.[82]

The use of reason in arguing the doctrine of the Trinity should therefore be restricted to a close examination of Scripture.[83]

Reason does show that Scripture admits of only one God and that the meaning of the word "God" in Scripture is sufficiently clear. Nor does Scripture allow one being to be the supreme God by nature and another, lesser, being to be God according to his office. Similarly, examination of Scripture does not yield

> any notion of a middle being between God and the creature, or one that is not properly God, so as the Father is, and yet more than a creature, as though there were a medium between finite and infinite; neither are we led, by scripture, to conceive of any being,

---

79. Theophilus Gale, *The Court of the Gentiles. Part IV. Of Reformed Philosophie. Wherein Plato's Moral and Metaphysic or Prime Philosophie is reduced to an useful Forme and Method* (London: J. Macock, 1677), II.vi.3 (p. 382); cf. Hutton, "Neoplatonic Roots of Arianism," pp. 143-145. Note that Gale's *Court of the Gentiles*, IV/1-3, was published a year before Cudworth's *True Intellectual System*, to which Gale here refers. Cudworth's work had, however, already passed the censor, Samuel Parker, in 1671 — and, presumably, Gale had access to the text of the work.

80. Ridgley, *Body of Divinity*, p. 112, col. 1, citing Col. 2:8.

81. Ridgley, *Body of Divinity*, p. 112, cols. 1-2.

82. Ridgley, *Body of Divinity*, p. 112, cols. 1-2.

83. Ridgley, *Body of Divinity*, pp. 112-113.

that has an eternal duration, whose eternity is supposed to be before time, and yet not the same with the eternal duration of the Father.[84]

What cannot be found, before the era of Rationalism in the late seventeenth and eighteenth century, is the assumption that the doctrine of the Trinity can be rationally demonstrated without recourse to the materials of revelation. Noteworthy here, particularly as an index to the initial impact of Cartesian thought on seventeenth-century Protestantism, is the argument of the mystical Cartesian theosopher Poiret that the doctrine of the Trinity can be illustrated rationally.[85] (Of course, Poiret stands outside of the boundaries of Reformed orthodoxy, not only on the ground of his Cartesianism, but also on the grounds of his radical — and rationalistically deductive — soteriological universalism.)[86]

3. Keckermann, Ainsworth, and Burman on the logic of the divine emanations. Some of the Reformed did identify rational arguments or a posteriori confirmations for the trinitarian nature of God and employ elements of the medieval vocabulary concerning the inward emanations of the Godhead,[87] and others, while excluding rational or natural demonstration, indicate that reason can confirm the biblical arguments by way of showing the doctrine to be in agreement with what is known of God's essence and attributes.[88] Ames and the theses presented at Saumur offered a short statement of the logic of the Trinity that reflected the medieval language of the Son and Spirit as processions of intellect and of will or love, respectively.[89] Voetius notes these more speculative points — whether the Word proceeds as a divine cognition or an intellective generation, whether the Spirit is produced *per modum amoris*, and whether *Amor* is the proper name of the Holy Spirit — identifying the questions as "doctè ignoratur," a matter of beyond knowing, or "quaestio curiosa," an excessively inquisitive question.[90] Baxter, on the other hand, expressed appreciation for such discussion of the logic of the trinitarian emanations.[91] Ridgley, in turn, noted the danger of using the metaphors and unintentionally fostering error.[92]

By way of contrast, Keckermann, Ainsworth, and Burman went so far as to offer discussions of the logic of the divine emanations that could stand as a kind of proof in its own right — and then, of course, there is the extended Cartesian argumentation

---

84. Ridgley, *Body of Divinity*, p. 113, col. 1.

85. Cf. Pierre Poiret, *Cogitationum rationalium de Deo, anima et Malo* (Amsterdam, 1677) and idem, *L'oeconomie divine*, 7 vols. (Amsterdam, 1687).

86. See Richard A. Muller, "Found (No Thanks to Theodore Beza): One 'Decretal' Theology," in *Calvin Theological Journal*, 32/1 (April 1997), pp. 145-51.

87. Cf. Polanus, *Syntagma theol.*, III.4; Ames, *Medulla*, I.v.16; Leigh, *Treatise*, II.xvi (p. 126).

88. Mastricht, *Theoretico-practica theol.*, II.xxiv.9; cf. Turretin, *Inst. theol. elencticae*, III.xxv.4, 14ff.

89. Ames, *Medulla*, I.v.16; Amyraut et al., *Syntagma thesium theologicarum*, I.xvii.22.

90. Voetius, *Syllabus problematum*, II.iv (fol. I1v, I2v).

91. Cf. Baxter, *Catholike Theologie*, I.iii. 25-27; idem, *Methodus theologiae*, I.ii, q. 5-6 (pp. 82-87); with Trueman, "A Small Step Towards Rationalism," pp. 186-187.

92. Ridgley, *Body of Divinity* (1855), I, p. 147.

offered late in the seventeenth century by Sherlock.[93] Still, none, to my knowledge, attempted to revive the kind of rational argumentation that medieval authors like Richard of St. Victor developed on the basis of the Augustinian metaphor of the lover, the beloved, and the bond of love uniting the two.

Keckermann and Ainsworth argued at length for the logic of divine triunity on grounds drawn perhaps out of the Thomistic tradition, given its parallel emanations of intellect and will — or perhaps evidencing a Scotist accent in its double procession language of the conjunction of intellect and will in the Son's spirating of the Holy Spirit. He was attracted to this particular model because of his strong advocacy of the identification of divine persons as "modes of existing" or subsisting.[94] Given his understanding of a mode of existing as capable of being predicated of a thing in order to identify distinctions in the thing that were neither substantial nor essential and did not result in rendering the thing composite, Keckermann took the notions of an intellective generation and mode of the divine existence and a volitional procession or mode of divine existence as an ideal way of arguing the unity of essence and distinction of persons against the various antitrintarians of this time.[95]

It cannot be denied, Keckermann continues, that God has understanding or intellect and that this intellect is the actuality of the divine essence itself and is, therefore, both infinite and eternal. Moreover, given its actuality, the eternal divine intellect must eternally have an object that it knows or understands. Since the divine intellect is most perfect, so also must its eternal object be most perfect — and since there can be nothing more perfect than God, the object of the divine intellect can be none other than God himself. Thus, the divine intellect eternally reflects upon itself, indeed, has for its eternal object the "most perfect image of itself."[96]

Such an image is "rightly called" a "production, conception, and generation" in the divine essence — indeed, most properly called a"generation." Generation "is nothing other than the act of a substance, by which it produced from itself a like substance; when therefore God by conceiving of himself produces a substantial image of himself, this is rightly called the generation of that self-same image." There is an analogy, Keckermann continues, between this divine generation and the thinking or conceiving of an image in the human mind — even as learned persons view their mental images as "conceptions" and then, when they publish books, think of the ideas as having been given birth or generated. Of course, beings that have entirely different natures will be characterized by differing modes of generation, and the most perfect being will have the most perfect mode of generation. Moreover, inasmuch as "the generations and conceptions of the intellectual or rational life are interior," the generation or conception that takes place in the most perfect life of God, "whose entire life is intellect," will necessarily be "the most conjoined and utterly intimate

93. Keckermann, *Systema ss. theologiae*, I.iii. (pp. 10-33); Burman, *Synopsis theologiae*, I.xxxii.48; Sherlock, *Vindication of the doctrine of the holy and ever blessed Trinity*, pp. 48-69.

94. On this terminology, see below 3.2 (A.6).

95. Keckermann, *Systema theologiae*, I.iii (p. 20); cf. Ainsworth, *Orthodox Foundation*, pp. 11-13.

96. Keckermann, *Systema theologiae*, I.iii (pp. 20-22).

conception." Given its perfection, this perfectly generated inward image of God's self is set forth as a divine "mode of existing, or second person, rightly called either the image of the son of God," as the apostle teaches, Hebrews 1:3, calling the Son the "image of the father's subsistence." Since, moreover, "in God, understanding and being are the same (*intelligi & esse idem sint*)," it is necessary that God and the Son of God be the same in essence and existence.[97]

To this argument, at comparable length, Keckermann conjoins a rational argument for the Holy Spirit as the perfectly proceeded volitional object of the love of the Father and the Son. Keckermann argued that where there is intellect, there is also will — where a most perfect intellect, a most perfect will. There is also a necessary order of the faculties that will yield the Spirit as third of the divine persons, given that God does not will anything except insofar as he knows it. And just as the divine intellect takes as its object the ultimate truth, so the will takes as its object the highest good. Accordingly, the divine will is necessarily reflexive in its ultimate willing, taking the divine essence itself, the ultimate knowable good, as its object.[98] Since, moreover, the Father eternally both conceives the Son, his image, and wills to love the Son perfectly, the love of the Father in the Son and the Son in the Father results in the procession of "third mode of existing" as an image proceeding from its archetype, by the conjunction of intellect and will.[99]

Burman similarly noted — at far less length — that the Trinity might be argued from the intellectual nature of God: for all intelligent beings have in their mind certain ideas (i.e., as objects of comprehension) but the wisdom in the mind of God must be a perfect wisdom representing all things, in short, the Word or Son of God. The infinite intellect also expresses itself as will or (in the case of an eternal being that has himself as object) the inclination toward itself as the sole good: this inclination is understood to be the Holy Spirit.[100] But since these three modes of subsisting do not differ as to essence, they are to be understood as Trinity in unity. Similarly, God can be conceived as three in one according to his power; for in eternity God is not unoccupied (*otiosum*) but producing and self-productive and thus again in himself threefold but coeternal and coequal.[101]

These arguments, although not widely used among the Reformed, were not utterly excised from Reformed dogmatics by objections from various of the high orthodox theologians. They appear, as noted, in Baxter, and they recur in the early eighteenth-

---

97. Keckermann, *Systema theologiae*, I.iii (pp. 22-26); cf. Ainsworth, *Orthodox Foundation*, pp. 11-12. Note George Bull, *The Doctrine of the Catholic Church for the First Three Ages of Christianity, concerning the Blessed Trinity, considered, in opposition to Sabellianism and Tritheism* [1697], in *English Theological Works*, p. 374, who insists that this argumentation is "no novel subtlety of the schools, but a notion that runs through all the Fathers."

98. Keckermann, *Systema theologiae*, I.iii (pp. 28-29); cf. Ainsworth, *Orthodox Foundation*, pp. 12-13.

99. Keckermann, *Systema theologiae*, I.iii (p. 30).

100. Burman, *Synopsis theologiae*, I.xxxiii.1: the language of intellect and will follows the Thomist pattern, as distinct from the Franciscan language of nature and will; see above, 1.3 (A.2-3).

101. Burman, *Synopsis theolologiae*, I.xxxiii.1.

century English theologies of John Edwards and Thomas Stackhouse, the former a Reformed member of the conforming clergy, the latter a moderate Anglican. Edwards, after defining the doctrine and showing its biblical and historical foundations, offers comments on the ability of reason to discuss the mystery. At this point, he summarized some of the arguments of the "schoolmen," commenting that readers may accept or reject them as they choose — namely, the argument that "God the *Father* is *Original Wisdom*; his *Reflex* Act of *Knowledge* is his *Son*, his *Loving* himself, and the Son, is the *Holy Ghost*." He also cites the Augustinian metaphor of "understanding will, and memory."[102] Stackhouse, quite carefully, states that the metaphor of "infinite rational Mind" that contemplates itself in the "perfection of understanding" and takes pleasure in the contemplation in an "act of love and volition" is a "distant resemblance" of the Godhead:

> To help our apprehensions a little farther in the conception of this great mystery, let us (with the schoolmen) see whether, upon the grounds and notions of reason, we can frame to ourselves any thing that may carry in it some shadow and resemblance of one single undivided nature's casting itself into three subsistences without receding from its own unity.[103]

Stackhouse and Edwards also favor the patristic metaphor of the sun and its rays — and, in addition, the more modern metaphor of "a triangle, consisting of equal sides, whose substance or matter is the same."[104]

4. Trinitarian logic, Cartesianism, and reaction in the late seventeenth and early eighteenth centuries. A more cautious approach became a model for later writers, most of whom, like Leigh, noted the limitation of rational and philosophical tools in discussion of the mystery of the Trinity:

> We cannot by the light of nature know the mystery of the Trinity, nor the incarnation of Jesus Christ. But when by faith we receive this doctrine we may illustrate it by reason. The similes which the Schoolmen and other Divines bring, drawn from the creature, are unequal and unsatisfactory, since there can be no proportion between things Finite and Infinite.[105]

Moreover, given the state of the controversies of the day, some demonstrative discussion was viewed as useful by several of the seventeenth-century writers. Thus, after setting forth the basic concept of the Trinity of God as positive doctrine, Burman states that knowledge of this doctrine and the faithful confession of its sublime and sacred mystery are necessary to salvation — and he proceeds to pronounce anathema upon the Remonstrants, Socinians, and other antitrinitarians.[106] The existence of controversy

---

102. Edwards, *Theologia Reformata*, I, pp. 322-323.
103. Stackhouse, *Complete Body of Divinity*, I.vi (I, pp. 214-215).
104. Stackhouse, *Complete Body of Divinity*, I.vi (I, pp. 214-215), citing Edwards, *Body of Divinity*, i.e., *Theologia Reformata*, I, pp. 322-323.
105. Leigh, *Treatise*, II.xvi (p. 126).
106. Burman, *Synopsis theologiae*, I.xxxii.48.

leads him to devote an entire chapter to the "demonstration" of the doctrine of the Trinity. Like Turretin and Pictet, he declares all proffered rational proofs of the doctrine to be insufficient confirmation — and he will devote most of the chapter to proofs drawn from Scripture. Nevertheless, Burman does state three arguments drawn from reason. The first of these follows upon the attribution of goodness to God: of its very nature goodness is self-communicative, and God could, therefore, be considered perfectly good in his eternity only if his essential goodness were eternally communicated. Thus, from eternity, God must be considered as *persons*, equal and associated with one another (*personas aequales & socias*) in this essential self-communication.[107]

Nonetheless, some of the orthodox writers were willing to develop some rational argumentation concerning the internal logic and meaning of the doctrine of the Trinity — not to prove the doctrine from reason, but to show in almost Thomistic fashion that the doctrine, once held, was not unreasonable. Ridgley devotes some space in his exposition of the Trinity to an excursus on "the use of reason in proving or defending the doctrine of the Trinity, or any other doctrines of pure revelation."[108] This doctrine and those like it could not have been "at first discovered by reason," nor, once revealed, can they be totally comprehended. Nevertheless, reason does not become totally useless but stands as a servant to faith. Revelation provides knowledge of necessary doctrines and "reason offers a convincing proof" of the truth of doctrine:

> in order to reason's judging of the truth of things, it first considers the sense of words; what *Ideas* are designed to be conveyed thereby, and whether they are contrary to the common sense of mankind; and if it appears that they are not, it proceeds to enquire into those evidences that may give conviction, and enforce our belief thereof; and leads us into the nature of the truths revealed, receives them as instamped with the authority of God, and considers them as agreeable to his perfections, and farther leads us into his design of revealing them.... Now this may be applied particularly to the doctrine of the Trinity; for it contains no absurdity contradictory to reason ... and the evidences on which our faith herein is founded, will be farther considered, when we prove it to be a scripture doctrine, by the express words thereof, agreeable to the mind of the Holy Ghost, or by just consequences deduced from it; by which it will farther appear, that it is necessary for us to use our reason in stating those doctrines, which are neither founded on, nor can be comprehended by it.[109]

Reason enters here as a tool to be employed in exegesis — not as a basis of the doctrine itself. Even so, the doctrine of the Trinity "cannot be learned from the light of nature": it cannot be known from the creation and providence of God. That God "made all things by his essential word" belongs to the truths of revelation, as does the place of the Spirit in the work of creation:

---

107. Burman, *Synopsis theologiae*, I.xxxiii.1.
108. Ridgley, *Body of Divinity*, p. 110, col. 1.
109. Ridgley, *Body of Divinity*, p. 110, cols. 1-2.

The light of nature could discover to us, indeed, that God, who is a Spirit, or incorporeal Being, has produced many effects worthy of himself; but we could not have known hereby, that the word *Spirit* signifies a distinct person.[110]

Similarly, "the work of our redemption" is known only through revelation.

The rejection by many of the Reformed orthodox of rational and philosophical proofs of the Trinity extends even to those arguments set forth by Augustine in his *De Trinitate*: the Reformed respect for Augustine cannot dissuade them on this point. Augustine, they were convinced, had pressed rational investigation beyond its proper bounds. Marckius even cites Augustine specifically — arguments from the intellect, will, power, goodness, and blessedness of God, the simile of a triangle, or the threefold form of the soul, light, the rainbow, trees, and so forth fall short in many ways, since they either presuppose knowledge of revelation, or can be frustrated by numerous exceptions, or inasmuch as similes that illustrate but do not prove a point often obscure it by dissimilarity, or finally because they do not remove all doubt — all of which, Marckius indicates, are true even of those similes offered by Augustine.[111]

This rejection of rational argumentation concerning the Trinity — and the general failure of Reformed theologians to duplicate Keckermann's arguments or Augustine's — demonstrate the effects of the epistemology outlined in the *loci de theologia* and of the *duplex cognitio dei* theme in particular.[112] Natural knowledge of God is not rejected, and in those places where the soteriological connection of a doctrine is not particularly stressed, reason may take on a powerful function coordinate at times with revelation; but into the mysteries of the faith, particularly those which relate to the work of Christ, reason and rationalism dare not intrude. The exposition of the doctrine of the Trinity is, in most of the orthodox systems, exceedingly brief in comparison to the exposition of the unity, essence, and attributes of God.

3.2 The Terms of Trinitarian Orthodoxy

A. Reformed Definition in the Scholastic Era

1. Reformed orthodox reception of traditional trinitarian terminology. The Reformed orthodox were consistently aware of the difficulties of traditional trinitarian language — given the ultimately unfathomable mystery of the Godhead; the relative complexity of post-Nicene explanation, particularly with reference to the meaning of "essence" or "substance" and "hypostasis," "subsistence," or "person"; the post-biblical provenance of the dogmatic terms in the context of the assumption of an

---

110. Ridgley, *Body of Divinity*, p. 110, col. 2.

111. Marckius, *Compendium*, V.xxviii.

112. Cf. Rijssen, *Summa theol.*, IV.xvi: margin, "*Mysterium hoc non ex lumine naturae probatur,*" and text, "*Unde nullus hic rationi, sed sola revelationi locus.*" Rijssen notes similitudes in nature and the threefold principle of Platonism, "mind, word, and spirit": the former do not constitute proof, and the latter rests on a reading of Moses and the prophets and is, at best, secondary; similarly Marckius, *Comp. Theol.*, V.xxviii. None of the rational arguments are developed at any length.

ultimate biblical norm;[113] the enormous exegetical pressure of the heresies, both ancient and modern; and the increasingly historical sensibility (on the part of orthodox and antitrinitarian alike) of difference or at least distinction between the language of Scripture, the language of the earliest fathers, the post-Nicene formulae, and the medieval terminology. The era of orthodoxy was, after all, an era of rising patristic scholarship. In the second half of the seventeenth century the diversity of patristic trinitarianisms had become particularly apparent, with the result that theologians were pressed to identify which trajectory of meaning among the nominally orthodox church fathers led to the proper result — namely, to a trinitarian monotheism as distinct from either a refined form of monism or an implied tritheism.

Explanation of the doctrinal terms, their precise meaning, and their limitation was therefore a significant element of the *locus de Deo uno et trino* in the dogmatic theology of the late sixteenth and the seventeenth century. Precedent can be found in Calvin's *Institutes* and also in Zanchi's *De tribus Elohim*.[114] The Reformed and the Lutherans were in nearly complete agreement on this issue: Witsius could cite both Gomarus and Johann Gerhard as sources for the best definitions of trinitarian vocabulary — with Gerhard offering the "more copious" discussion.[115] The question *de personarum divinarum trinitate* was stated concisely in both its polemical and positive aspect by Gomarus in a preface to the theses of his sixth *disputatio*:

> Whereas "it is the catholic faith" (as solemnly and gravely indicated by Athanasius), "that we ought to honor a Unity in Trinity and a Trinity in Unity": it will be suitable for us to adjudge, before we proceed from the topic just now concluded to the next issue, whether this doctrine can be illustrated from the divine words of Scripture and protected against the poisonous machinations of the heretics. "For there is nowhere more dangerous to err, nowhere more toilsome to seek, nothing more fruitful to attain."[116]

Gomarus' references indicate that the two quotations derive, respectively, from the Athanasian Creed and Augustine's *De Trinitate* (I.iii); a third reference points the reader toward John of Damascus' *On the Two Natures of Christ*. The citation from Augustine not only evidences Gomarus' considerable interest in the patristic roots of doctrine, but also his reverence, shared by the orthodox of his day, for the doctrine itself. Gomarus notes also the "manifold ambiguities of the words *hypostasis, prosopon, and persona*, caused by abuse" both by "the inexperienced who are overwhelmed" by

---

113. Beza et al., *Propositions and Principles*, II.iii.

114. Calvin, *Institutes*, I.xiii.2-6; Zanchi, *De tribus Elohim*, pt. I, I.ii.2 and I.ii-vi.

115. Witsius, *Exercitationes*, vi.4, citing Gomarus, *Disputationes* and Gerhard, *Loci communes*, iii.2. Gerhard was recognized as one of the significant seventeenth-century scholars of patristic theology: note Johann Gerhard, *Patrologia, sive de primitivae ecclesiae christianae doctores vita ac lucubrationibus* (Jena, 1653) and see the discussion in Muller, *After Calvin*, pp. 52-53; and cf. Schmid, *Doctrinal Theology*, pp. 140-46 with Heppe, *Reformed Dogmatics*, pp. 111-118.

116. Gomarus, *Disp. theologiae*, VI (p. 19); Amyraut et al., *Syntagma thesium theologicarum*, I.xvii.2.

the difficulties of the problem and by "the experienced who are wearied" by the continued debate over the terms.[117]

Ridgley notes that the Socinian and Remonstrant objections to traditional trinitarian language are not altogether groundless: the doctrine is a difficult one, and the basic terms, "person" and "hypostasis" are to some degree problematic. The Socinian and Remonstrant remedies are, however, "worse than the disease." Citing the *Institutes*, Ridgley praises Calvin's ability to cut through the problems of terminology to the idea of "the Father, Son, and Spirit, being the one God, but distinguished by their personal properties." Nevertheless, "person" needs to be carefully defined in order to formulate the threeness as over against the oneness of God.[118]

This need for precise definition becomes even more obvious when one recognizes that the words "person" and "nature," or "essence," are applied differently to God than to human beings: for individual human beings also have individual and separate natures,

> but when we speak of the Persons in the Godhead, as having the divine nature and perfections, we say that this nature is the same individual nature in all of them, though the Persons are distinct, otherwise the Father, Son, and Holy Ghost, could not be said to be truly and properly God, and to have the same understanding, will, and other perfections of the divine nature.[119]

The three persons thus are "the same in substance, ... the one only living and true God."[120] This language of essence, existence, subsistence, *suppositum*, person, personhood (*personalitatis*), and the use of this language in presenting the mystery of the Trinity must be carefully defined.[121]

2. Trinitas. In the title and first sentence of his *locus, de S.S. Trinitate*, Marckius speaks both *de Personarum Trinitate* and *de Trinitate Personarum*, which is to say, of the persons of the Trinity and of the trinity of persons. These phrases, he argues, make clear from the outset that the term *Trinitas* is equivalent to *Trium Unitas*: the subject itself, in its primary definition, denies composition in the Godhead and speaks of a divine Trinity *in simplicibus suis*. The point is of utmost importance, given the fact that a definition of Trinity that respected the full divinity of the persons in their distinction and then "severed or divided" them, not indicating the numerical unity of divine substance would be tritheism.[122] The Greek patristic writers, notes Marckius, made this very clear in associating with the term *triada* such declarative and restrictive epithets as *hagias, theias, proskunetes,* and *homoousiou,* and by speaking in such carefully

---

117. Gomarus, *Disp.theologiae*, VI (p. 19).

118. Ridgley, *Body of Divinity*, p. 115, col. 2, citing Calvin, *Institutes* I.xiii.5.

119. Ridgley, *Body of Divinity*, p. 116, col. 2.

120. Ridgley, *Body of Divinity*, p. 116, col. 2.

121. Cf. Marckius, *Compendium*, V.iii. use of the term *suppositum* here indicates the contact of orthodoxy with the terminology of medieval scholasticism. A *suppositum* is "a complete being, incommunicable by identity, incapable of inhering in anything, and not supported by anything" (Ockham, cited in Copleston, *History of Philosophy*, III, pp. 100-101).

122. Downame, *Summe*, i (p. 33).

defined phrases as *triauges tes mias theotetos*.[123] In Latin the term *trinitas* indicates a threefold or ternary distributive number (*usurpata pro numero distributivo ternario*) and in its theological usage is applied "*ad pluralitatem personarum in unitate Essentiae*."[124] Rijssen notes that the word "Trinity" — which the papists would lock within the tradition — derives not in the abstract but in the concrete from Scripture. Rijssen here refers to the disputed text, 1 John 5:7; others among the early orthodox would simply refer to the threefold designation of God as Father, Son, and Holy Spirit in the New Testament and argue, as Bucanus did, that "Trinity" is found in Scripture not "according to the letter" but "according to the sense" of the text and that, in the case of 1 John 5:7, where the "three" are "one," the terms "trinity" and "unity" are rightly inferred from the sense of the passage.[125]

Forbes attempted to define the doctrine more precisely by arguing that "in the trinity of God there is both unity and distinction, not however by composition, or division, or diversity, or differentia properly so called, or discrepancy, or dissimilarity; neither triplicity, nor singularity, neither solitude nor confusion." God is "not unitary (*unicum*) but one (*unum*), not triple (*triplex*) but trinitary (*trinum*)": thus Gregory of Nazianzus speaks of "unity in Trinity, and Trinity in unity."[126] Thus, the essential simplicity of God is retained, and theology recognizes that there is nothing either prior or posterior to God, who is *actus purus*,[127] while nonetheless understanding a modal distinction between the essence and the persons of the Trinity and a real distinction between the persons, albeit not in an essential or absolute, but in a personal and relative sense.[128] There is, therefore, no *distinctio realis absoluta* in God, nor is there a *distinctio formalis* as if between gradations of the divine essence — granting that the divine essence is single, simple, perfect, and subject to no gradations. Forbes adds, by way of qualification, that the Scotist formal distinction between the persons, which argues the nonidentity of the persons in a formal sense, falls outside of stricture and should be understood as a virtual or modal distinction.[129]

First, the names, Father, Son, and Holy Spirit, indicate the mutual relations in God — not as if the Godhead were "collected together from several parts," but rather distinguished into the three. Second, the order of the persons (first, Father; second, Son; third, Holy Spirit) indicates the manner in which the divine essence is distributed; while the third distinction, between modes of operation, follows directly from the order of persons — so that the Father's operation is *à se*, from the Father himself, but through the Son and the Spirit. Similarly, fourth, the *opera ad extra* are understood as the indivisible work of the entire Trinity, working as one God, but "according to the order

---

123. Marckius, *Compendium*, V.i.
124. Marckius, *Compendium*, V.i; Beza et al., *Propositions and Principles*, II.iv.
125. Rijssen, *Summa theol.*, III.iii, controversia I; Bucanus, *Institutions*, i (p. 9); cf. Turretin, *Inst. theol. elencticae*, III.xxiii.9; Amyraut et al., *Syntagma thesium theologicarum*, I.xv.1.
126. Forbes, *Instructiones hist.*, I.xxxiii.1, 3, citing Nazianzus, *Oratio* 23.
127. Forbes, *Instructiones hist.*, I.xxxiv.3.
128. Forbes, *Instructiones hist.*, I.xxxv.19
129. Forbes, *Instructiones hist.*, I.xxxv.20, citing Scotus, *I Sent.*, d. 2, q. ult.; d. 8, q. 4.

of the persons" and according to the special economy or arrangement of the divine work as it terminates upon an individual divine person: thus "there is but one God, the Father, *of whom* are all things ... and one Lord Jesus Christ *by whom* are all things" (1 Cor. 8:6) or again, "ye are justified in the name of the Lord Jesus, and by the Spirit of God" (1 Cor. 6:11). Fifth, the persons are distinguished by the "properties" or "personal operations" that are also sometimes called "characteristic, diacritic, or gnoristic": these "pertain neither to the essence nor to the persons considered in the abstract, but to the persons considered in the concrete." Further, these personal operations are not absolute but relative perfections — which is to say they are different from the absolute perfections or attributes that belong to the divine essence: they are perfections that are really distinct and that are predicated of the persons individually, in the passive voice: thus the Father is unbegotten, the Son is begotten, and the Spirit is sent or proceeded.[130]

3. *Substantia, essentia, ousia,* and related issues. The theological language of substance and essence, which had proved from its beginnings prior to the time of the council of Nicaea to be both a necessity and a fundamentally problematic aspect of the Christian doctrine of the Trinity, continued to be a source of orthodox formulation and of profound debate in the seventeenth century. On the one hand, Reformed orthodoxy inherited the traditional language of divine essence and attributes, of one divine essence or substance and three divine subsistences or persons, and sought to maintain and defend it as the basic language of orthodoxy.[131] On the other hand, Reformed orthodoxy both inherited and encountered a series of problems with the traditional language that, by the end of the era of orthodoxy, rendered the maintenance of the tradition difficult at best. First, the Reformed orthodox inherited a variety of ancient, patristic, and medieval qualifications concerning the use of essence and substance that were particularly relevant to the notion of divine persons — and they inherited the further qualifications of the Reformers concerning the normative use of traditionary, but non-biblical terms in the doctrine of the Trinity. Second, the orthodox encountered a series of objections unique to their own time, arising out of antitrinitarian heresies and out of variant forms of the new rationalism. On the one hand, the antitrinitarians tended to argue a radical identity of substance or essence with person, while on the other, the rationalists offered definitions of substance that proved incompatible with the definitions of traditional Christian theism.

Already in antiquity, the term *ousia*, despite its original Aristotelian distinction into πρώτη οὐσία (primary substance) and δευτερα οὐσία (secondary substance), had developed a series of related but rather distinct meanings: Stead suggests seven — existence, category or status, substance, stuff or material, form, definition, and truth.[132] This variety of usage immediately renders the discussion of divine *ousia* somewhat problematic, as did the Platonic assumption that God is beyond essence

---

130. Marckius, *Compendium*, V.vi.

131. Beza et al., *Propositions and Principles*, II.v.

132. See Christopher Stead, *Divine Substance* (Oxford: Clarendon Press, 1977), pp. 132-156.

or substance. Nonetheless, as Stead points out, none of the other categorical terms (quantity, quality, relation, etc.) is helpful. and when one asks the question of what God is like or what God *has* in the sense of properties, attributes, or qualities, *ousia* is the rather natural term, given that it refers, in its primary sense of an individual, to that in which properties inhere.[133]

The basic Aristotelian understanding of essence and substance was reflected in the philosophical language of the seventeenth century: Spencer's logic defines substance as indicating either a "singular & individuall being" or a "genus and species" of being — the initial sense, the individual being, is the proper one, often identified as "first" or "primary substance"; the second, the genus or species, the improper or figurative sense of the term, often identified as "second" or "secondary substance."[134] Not only is the individual primary and the genus secondary in an ontic sense, this is also the case in logic: the individual or primary substance is the subject of a sentence and the primary "seat of argument" — the secondary substance or genus and species of a thing can function as either predicate or subject and, of course, will be the predicate of the primary substance (one can state, e.g., that "Simon is a man"; one would not say that "Man is a Simon").[135]

So also, however, were several of the ancient limitations and variations of the language of essence and substance reflected in the seventeenth-century usage. Keckermann defines substance as "Being subsisting through [or by] itself" (*Substantia est Ens per se subsistens*), namely, individual being not inhering or subsisting in another — a definition having both some possible application to God but also posing some difficulty for trinitarian application.[136] Keckermann immediately notes the question whether "substance" is a term common to God and creatures, but is best illustrated by examples drawn from the creatures — yielding the further definition "substance (*substantia*) is a being (*ens*) that has its own existence (*proprium esse*), and supports incidental properties." Substance, then, divides into a series of categories and subcategories: first, it is either infinite or finite, referring either to God or to creatures; next, finite substance is either spiritual or corporeal — the spiritual either good or evil, the corporeal either simple or mixed; finally, the simple refers either to the heaven itself or to the various irreducible elements, the mixed to individuals compounded of the elements.[137]

In his metaphysics, however, in order to safeguard the doctrine of God from speculative reason or at least to reject the Suárezian notion of the univocity of being, Keckermann follows the Platonic tradition and argues that God is not properly spoken of in terms of substance and accident, given that God is *supra Ens*, "beyond Being" in the normal sense of the word, "beyond all Substance and Accident." He therefore understands substance primarily as finite substance, the individual, composed of form

133. Stead, *Divine Substance*, pp. 160-162.
134. Spencer, *Art of Logicke*, I.iii.3 (p. 16).
135. Spencer, *Art of Logicke*, I.iii.4, 7; I.xxvii.1 (pp. 17, 21, 129).
136. Keckermann, *Systema logicae minus*, I.iii, in *Opera*, I, col. 175.
137. Keckermann, *Systema logicae minus*, I.iii, in *Opera*, I, cols. 175-176.

and matter. In this context, he defines essence as form independent of individual existence: "Essence is the primary internal principle of Substance, by which a thing can exist in a certain place and time, although it may not yet exist. ... For when God first willed that something exist, it at once had essence, even thought it did not yet have existence."[138] "Essence," then, strictly speaking, is the whatness or quiddity, whereas "substance" identifies the existent individual — and, by definition, in the finite order, essence and existence are separable, with essence standing prior to existence. Essence, therefore, with reference to finite things, in the most strict usage of the era, refers to what Aristotle would have called the secondary *ousia*, whereas substance indicates, strictly, the primary *ousia*.

Given the doctrine of divine simplicity and its implicates, the inseparability of essence and existence in God and the essential identity of the divine attributes, the seventeenth-century orthodox were pressed to define substance and essence with great care in their theology — apart from any problems caused by the new rationalism and its variant understandings of substance. Since God is one, sole, and absolute, and since there is but a single, undivided divine essence or substance, there can be no genus "god." There is no divine "essence" apart from the one, individual divine "substance." The distinction between primary and secondary *ousia* does not apply: understanding "god" as indicating a secondary essence is characteristic of polytheism, where an essence is shared by various divine beings. Therefore, the terms "substance" and "essence" are roughly equivalent in their application to God: the individual being (substance) of God is inseparable from the identity or whatness (essence) that God is. Also used in an equivalent sense are the terms "nature" and, in the case of British divines, "Godhead," both of which can also be used to indicate what God is in the concrete: "by *the* Godhead," Boston comments, "is meant the nature or essence of God."[139]

The terms, therefore, were in need of precise definition. According to Aretius, *ousia* derives from the Greek word for Being, ὁ ὤν, just as *Jehovah* derives from *Ejeh* and *Deus* is etymologically related to *deitas*. Given that God is referred to by Scripture as ὁ ὤν (Rev. 1:7), *ousia* is a term legitimately used to refer to God. There was, however, in the course of the trinitarian tradition, debate over the meaning and rendering of the term *ousia*: Aretius notes that the term was rendered *essentia* or *substantia*, with *essentia* as the generally preferred translation — particularly given that its etymological rootage in *esse* parallels that of *ousia*. The underlying problem of determining the language arises from the fact that God is ultimately incomprehensible and, therefore, incapable of being described — as Evagrius Ponticus said, the ineffable mystery of the Godhead is to be adored in silence rather than dogmatically explained — but the word *substantia*, as used in philosophy, indicated precisely something "capable of being defined," indeed, of being distinguished from an accident or incidental property.[140]

---

138. Keckermann, *Scientiae metaphysicae brevis synopsis et compendium*, I.ii, in *Opera*, I, col. 2015; on form and matter, cf. Keckermann, *Gymnasium logicum*, II.iii, in *Opera*, I, col. 431-432.

139. Boston, *Commentary on the Shorter Catechism*, I, p. 143.

140. Aretius, *History of Valentinus Gentilis*, VII (pp. 52-53, 56)

From the same era, Zanchi notes the patristic debate over *ousia* and *hypostasis*: given that the former denoted *essentia* and the latter *substantia*, creating a near contradiction if both terms were used, the former to indicate the oneness of God, the latter the threeness. However, the use of *hypostasis* to indicate the individual divine persons or subsistences points toward resolution of the debate.[141]

Witsius indicates, citing John of Damascus, the terms "essence, nature, and form" are synonymous in the trinitarian vocabulary.[142] The word *ousia*, rendered in Latin as *substantia* or *essentia*, correctly reflects the scriptural ascription to God of such terms as *theotes* (Col. 2:9), *physis* (Gal. 4:8), and *theia physis* (2 Peter 1:4).[143] Indeed, whether one uses *essentia* or *substantia* as the proper rendering of *ousia*, both terms denote "something *Absolute*, not *Relative*.[144] Turretin identifies *ousia* as indicating, in Latin, either *essentia* or *natura*, with both Latin terms quite specifically indicating the "whatness" or "quiddity" of God. This usage is, moreover, applied to God both in the concrete and in the abstract — namely, both with reference to the being of God and also to the deity or divinity of God's nature. Thus, in the concrete, God is called ὁ ὤν in Exodus 3:14 and Revelation 1:4, 7 — while in the abstract, both "deity," *theotes* (Col. 2:9), and "divine nature," *theia physis* (2 Pet. 1:4), are ascribed to God.[145]

Turretin also notes differences among the church fathers over the use of the term *substantia*. The more typical patristic usage of *substantia*, comments Turretin, does not relate to the sense of the word as that which "stands under" the accidents or incidental properties of a being, given that the concept of divine attributes does not identify the attributes as incidental properties and does not imply a separability of attributes from the divine essence. Rather this typical patristic usage points toward the divine self-existence or subsistence — *substantia*, in this sense, translates *hypostasis* and not *ousia*. Hilary, accordingly, identified *substantia* as the translation of *hypostasis*, and spoke of three "substances" in the Godhead.[146] Others, notably Tertullian and Augustine, used *substantia* as a synonym for *essentia* or *natura* and indicated a single divine substance. Turretin appears to recognize the fairly pointed patristic debate over the term and to recognize as well that the use of the new term, *subsistentia*, as the translation of *hypostasis* was the result of the debate.[147]

The difficulty in using *substantia* in discussions of the Trinity was exacerbated by the Boethian definition of "person" as an "individual substance of a rational nature." In this form, *substantia* either is taken to mean *subsistentia* or the definition leads to

141. Zanchi, *De tribus Elohim*, pt. I, I.ii.3 (cols. 10-11).

142. Witsius, *Exercitationes*, VI.iv, citing John of Damascus, *De fide*, I.

143. Rijssen, *Summa theol.*, III.iii, controversia I; cf. Zanchi, *De tribus Elohim*, pt. I, I.ii.5 (col. 13).

144. Aretius, *History of Valentinus Gentilis*, VII (p. 54), citing Augustine, *De Trinitate*, V. ii.8.

145. Turretin, *Inst. theol. elencticae*, III.xxiii.3.

146. Turretin, *Inst. theol. elencticae*, III.xxiii.4, citing Hilary, *De synodis*, 32 (cf. *NPNF*, 2 ser., IX, p. 13).

147. Turretin, *Inst. theol. elencticae*, III.xxiii.4, citing Tertullian, *Against Praxeas*: see cap. 9, 11, 18-19, 21-22 (cf. *ANF*, III, pp. 603-606, 613-618); and Augustine *De trinitate*, V.ix (*NPNF*, 2 ser., III, p. 92).

a form of tritheism: there cannot be three rational essences or natures in the Godhead. Such language — which understands substance as the equivalent of person in the sense of the Aristotelian "primary substance" — would reduce the unity of the Godhead to a generic unity, with the term "God" indicating a genus or class of beings rather than a single or sole divine Being. Specifically, *ousia* or *theotes* refers to the unity of the Godhead in a manner different than the reference of the common essence of humanity to individual human beings — whereas divinity, as Father, Son, and Spirit, is numerically one God, human beings, one in essence, are numerically many. The difference is illuminated in part by the infinitude and immensity of the divine essence, which is incapable of division (*impartibilis*). Zanchi dwells on the issue at length — the divine oneness is such that, as is also indicated in many passages of Scripture, there cannot be "a plural number of Gods." By implication, an infinite essence or being can only be one — a denial of numerical oneness would result in the attribution of infinite essence to each one of three separate individuals, clearly an impossibility.[148] This last point, of course, echoes the Athanasian Creed: *Immensus Pater: immensus Filius: immensus Spiritus Sancti ... sicut non ... tres immensi.*"[149]

4. Homoousios. The Nicene term *homoousios* also received considerable attention from the Reformers and the Reformed orthodox given, on the one hand, its dogmatic significance and, on the other, its absence from the text of Scripture. The term was used by the Nicene fathers against the Arian heresy, the orthodox writers note, to prevent an erroneous interpretation of the person of Christ.[150] The fathers, Vermigli notes,

> of set purpose disputed against those who denied the Godhead of the holy Ghost and equality of the three divine persons: as we see by the strife over the word *Homoousion*, of like substance, from which many of the Catholics at the beginning did restrain themselves, because it seemed to be but new, and that it was not had in the holy Scriptures: and yet they nevertheless did embrace and most willingly admit the thing signified. Howbeit we strive not about these things, but grant first and chiefly whatsoever is in the holy Scriptures: and then whatsoever is necessarily and manifestly derived out of them.[151]

The orthodox typically recognized *homoousios* as the most suitable term for indicating the identity of essence and the distinction of divine persons. The term is certainly preferable to possible alternatives such as *monousios* or *tautousios*. These alternatives are ambiguous in their implications, and, in addition, they are not applicable to the case of the three persons in the one divine essence. *Tautousios*, Turretin comments, can be used to designate one who has his essence from himself alone — and therefore, "with respect to person," applies to the Father alone. The term does not well designate

---

148. Zanchi, *De tribus Elohim*, pt. I, I.ii.5; iii.1-2 (cols. 13-16).
149. Symbolum Quicunque (Athanasian Creed), 9, 11 (in Schaff, *Creeds*, II, pp. 66-67).
150. Rijssen, *Summa theol.*, III.iii, controversia I.
151. Vermigli, *Commonplaces*, I.xii.18.

several persons partaking of one essence.[152] *Monousios* is even more problematic, inasmuch as it could be used to identify the Sabellian notion of a single divine *hypostasis*: the term indicates a being that is unitary or singular in essence. The sun, comments Turretin, is *monousios*, given that it is a unitary thing alone in its species: God also can be rightly called *monousios*, without reference to the divine persons, given the unity of the divine essence, but the persons cannot be called *monousioi*, "because they are three persons, not one only."[153] We know from Scripture that the number of persons in God is three (Matt. 28:19) and that we also assume that God is one — so that the language of orthodoxy rightly expresses the truth that "as they are persons, truly distinct, as one and another; all however *homoousioi*, having the same essence."[154] Positively, the declaration that the divine persons are *homoousios* indicates that they are *coessentiales* or *consubstantiales*, meaning that they together have "a sole (*unicus*) and utterly the same (*eius demque plané*) essence or nature," against those who would claim that the divine persons are *homoiousios*, of a like nature or essence only.[155]

Controversy was intensified by the claims of antitrinitarians from Servetus and Socinus onward that the terms themselves were problematic and not representative of the earliest witness. In the late seventeenth-century controversy, antitrinitarians pointed out that even the purportedly orthodox terms militated against the doctrine, inasmuch as the ancient definitions of *ousia* and *homoousios* offered by orthodox writers of the era, like Bishop Bull, indicated generic unity (with *ousia* understood as secondary substance), not the numerical unity (with *ousia* understood as primary substance) of God. "Dr. Bull hath incontestably proved," one opponent argued,

> by a great Number of Quotations, and might have proved by a great many more; that by consubstantial, or *of the same Substance*, the Fathers meant not the same substance *in Number*, but the same *in Properties*. As Stars are consubstantial to Stars, and the Bodies of Men to the Bodies of Beasts; because they are Substances *of the same kind* (that is, corporeal) and *of the same Properties*.[156]

If this is all that *homoousios* means, however, the three Persons would be three Gods.[157]

This issue, with specific reference to the understanding of *ousia* in its primary or secondary sense, was raised by various seventeenth-century writers with reference to the teaching of the Cappadocian fathers and Athanasius. Cudworth argued quite pointedly that the Cappadocian fathers' analogy of three human beings, coupled with a restrictive definition of *ousia* as secondary essence, would yield a definition of the

---

152. Turretin, *Inst. theol. elencticae*, III.xxiii.12.

153. Turretin, *Inst. theol. elencticae*, III.xxiii.12.

154. Rijssen, *Summa theol.*, IV.iii: "quatenus personae sunt, vere distinctae, ut alius & alius; omnes tamen homoousioi, eandem numero Essentiam habentes."

155. Amyraut et al., *Syntagma thesium theologicarum*, I.xvii.8; Beza et al., *Propositions and Principles*, II.ix.

156. [Smalbroke?] *Judgment of the Fathers*, p. 66, referring to Bull, *Defense of the Nicene Creed*, II.i (pp. 53-85).

157. [Smalbroke?] *Judgment of the Fathers*, pp. 68-70.

three divine hypostases as essentially one in the generic, but not the numerical, sense. If this were the direction of the Cappadocian argument, Cudworth argued, we would be left with tritheism. He saw the way to a solution, however, in the thought of Athanasius: for although, as far as Cudworth could see, Athanasius understood *ousia* in the generic sense, Athanasius also insisted that God was "one thing" and not a group of things or hypostases.[158] Amyraut, similarly, citing Athanasius against the subordinationistic tendencies of Arminius and Curcellaeus, argues that in the Godhead, as distinct from the case of Peter and James, there is not merely a generic but, necessarily, a numerical unity of substance. The Son could not be equal to the Father in all things were not the substance "absolutely one." Indeed, the relationship between "the Father generating (*generantem*) and the Son generated (*genitum*)" cannot be understood in a "human manner," inasmuch as "in their consubstantiality no partitions or divisions of divinity are to be conceived" — with the result that *homoousios* must be understood as indicating a "numerical identity" of essence.[159] This, moreover, was the conclusion of the medieval councils — namely, that God was one *res*, numerically a single deity — and that discussion of the relationship between divine "essence" language and the philosophical issue of primary and secondary essences must respect the singularity of God and not understand "God" as the name of a genus of beings. This linguistic problem and its monotheistic solution were inherited by the Reformed orthodox.

5. *Persona*. The problem entailed on "person" language, as noted in the introductory chapter, was recognized by the medieval scholastics, who attempted to offer a series of variations on and modifications of the traditional Boethian definition.[160] The Reformers and Protestant orthodox were not unaware of this older problem, nor were they unaware of the increasing difficulty in the use of the term in the seventeenth century — as registered in the writings of various antitrinitarians. As a result, the orthodox offered their own variations and modifications of the definition, frequently with some relationship to the struggles of the medieval scholastics. A useful and fairly standard set of definitions related to the issue of divine persons in the unity of the essence appears in the early orthodox works of Perkins and Polanus.[161] In Polanus' words, "a person of the Deitie is a subsistence in the Deitie, having such properties as cannot be communicated from one to another."[162]

The word "persona," comments Marckius, is susceptible of various derivations. It might come form the Chaldaic roots *prm*, "a garment," or *prs*, "to divide or make distinct"; or from the Greek *perizonnuo*, or *prosopon*, or *peri soma*; or it might simply be a Latin term formed from the phrases *per se una* or *per se sonas* or even more simply from *personando*. The theological use of the term, notes Marckius, begins with

---

158. Cudworth, *True Intellectual System*, I, pp. 793-797; II, pp. 7-12.

159. Amyraut, *De mysterio trinitatis*, VII (pp. 518-521); cf. the rather nicely stated definition of Brown, *Compendious View*, II.i (pp. 128-129).

160. Cf. above, 1.2 (B.1); 1.3 (A.2-3).

161. Perkins, *Golden Chaine*, V (p. 14, col. 1); Polanus, *Partitiones*, I.iv.

162. Polanus, *Substance*, I.iv (p. 13).

Tertullian, who is generally credited with the introduction of the word into trinitarian debate.[163] A distinction needs to be made between the Greek *hypostasin*, which relates to *essentia*, and *prosopon*, which indicates *substantia* or *persona*: here the orthodox have recourse directly to Tertullian's determination of the issue — a *persona* is identified as one who has *substantia*.[164] Turretin specifically denies that the term is to be understood as being taken from the context of drama, where actors are *personati*, or "impersonators," and the term *persona* can indicate the mask worn to portray a character. Nor, indeed, does the theological usage of the term indicate "some quality or external appearance which adds nothing to the importance of a cause" or merely an "office or function."[165] The definition of "person" and particularly of "person" in relation to "essence" became, in fact, a focal point of the debate with the Socinians, who consistently offered a different understanding of the terms, according to which "essence" and "person" were united rather than distinguished in meaning. Thus, the Racovian Catechism:

> The essence of God is one, not in kind but in number. Wherefore it cannot, in any way, contain a plurality of persons, since a person is nothing else than an individual intelligent essence. Wherever, then, there exist three numerical persons, there must necessarily, in like manner, be reckoned three individual essences; for in the same sense in which it is affirmed that there is one numerical essence, it must be held that there is also one numerical person.[166]

In the Socinian understanding, "person" is identified with primary essence — yielding a numerical threeness of essence with reference to Father, Son, and Spirit, and, as a result, excluding the Son and the Spirit from the category of God.

By contrast, a "person" in the language of orthodoxy indicates an individual or independent subsistence; it in no way implies a different essence:

> in order for something to be called a "person" the following criteria must be met: 1. that it be a substance. 2. that it be intelligent. 3. that it is not part of another. 4. that it is not sustained [in its existence] by another; "*persona*," therefore, indicates the undiminished condition (*statum completum*) of an intelligent substance.[167]

What is significant here is that the Reformed orthodox writers, without overtly citing the medievals, clearly reflect the medieval wrestling with the difficulties of inherited definitions of person, notably the Boethian definition, "an independent substance of a rational nature," and, like many of the medieval thinkers, move past Boethius while at the same time retaining key terms of the definition. Wendelin, similarly, attempted to avoid entirely the toils of the Boethian definition by adapting one of the alternative definitions, namely, the one we have encountered already in Aquinas and in Calvin:

163. Cf. Calvin, *Institutes*, I.xiii.6.
164. Marckius, *Compendium*, V.ii.
165. Turretin, *Inst. theol. elencticae*, III.xxiii.7.
166. *Racovian Catechism*, p. 33; cf. Crellius, *Two Books*, p. 140.
167. Rijssen, *Summa theol.*, IV.i; similarly, Ridgley, *Body of Divinity*, p. 116.

"A divine person is usually described as an incommunicable subsistence of the divine essence."[168] He then went on to note that "in general *persona* is usually defined" as "an individual subsistence, living, intelligent, incommunicable, not sustained by another, not part of another."[169] Turretin also avoids the identification of "person" as an individual substance and speaks of an individual "intellectual *suppositum*."[170] This, of course, again raises the problem of the meaning of the term "substance" — which Rijssen assumes here to have the sense of a *suppositum*, given the numerical unity of the divine essence. Thus, says Rijssen, "a divine Person signifies not only Essence, nor only a mode of subsisting, but such a mode as belongs to the Essence itself."[171] The words God, Father, and Spirit are used in Scripture both essentially (cf. John 3:16: "for God so loved the world") and personally (cf. Acts. 20:28: "God redeemed the Church with his blood").[172]

As defined by Leigh, "a person is one entire, distinct subsistence, having life, understanding, will and power, by which he is in continual operation."[173] Turretin indicates that a "person," or *hypostasis*, in the proper and most strict sense of the term, is an "intellectual *suppositum*," a usage that is found in fact in Scripture, in 2 Corinthians 1:11.[174] Yet, the understanding of the Son and the Spirit as "person" does not indicate a separate intelligence or an intelligent being separate from the Father — so that "the three Persons of the Godhead are not three Persons in the same sense in which three Men are three Persons."[175] As for the Socinian objection that a single essence implies a single person, Owen responds, "that in one essence there can be but one person may be true where the substance is finite and limited, but hath no place in that which is infinite."[176] This latter point is significant to the Socinian definition, inasmuch as the Socinian doctrine of God assumed a limited God and, certainly in the case of Biddle's teaching, an essentially finite deity as well.[177] As the Reformed orthodox recognized, the divine persons — however one defines the distinctions made among them — are distinct *within* the one primary essence that is God. To argue otherwise, specifically, to identify a person as the primary essence, is to claim real or substantial distinctions between the persons, to reduce the unity of the persons to a generic unity of secondary

---

168. Wendelin, *Christianae theologiae libri duo*, I.ii.2.

169. Wendelin, *Christianae theologiae libri duo*, I.ii.2; cf. Amyraut et al., *Syntagma thesium theologicarum*, I.xvii.10.

170. Turretin, *Inst. theol. elencticae*, III.xxiii.7.

171. Rijssen, *Summa theol.*, IV.ii: "Persona divina nec solam Essentiam, nec solum subsistendi modum significat, sed Essentiam tali modo se habentem."

172. Rijssen, *Summa theol.*, IV.iv.

173. Leigh, *Treatise*, II.xvi (p. 129).

174. Turretin, *Inst. theol. elencticae*, III.xxiii.7; Amyraut et al., *Syntagma thesium theologicarum*, I.xvii.9.

175. Bennett, *Discourse of the Everblessed Trinity*, p. 218.

176. Owen, *Vindiciae evangelicae*, in *Works*, XII, pp. 170-171.

177. See *PRRD*, III, 4.4 (C.3).

essence, and to produce either a form of tritheism or a radical subordinationism, akin to the *homoiousian* or *homoian* theologies of the fourth century.[178]

With specific reference to the text of Hebrews 1:3, Gouge could pose the definition, presumably against early Socinian exegesis of the text, that

> *Essence* or nature, importeth a common being: as *Deity* or God-head, which is common to the *Father, Sonne, holy Ghost.* For the *Father* is *God,* the *Sonne* is *God,* and the *holy Ghost* is *God.* But *subsistence* or *person* implieth a different, distinct, individual, incommunicable, property; such are these three, *Father, Sonne, holy Ghost.* For the *Father* is different from the *Sonne* and *holy Ghost*: so the *Sonne* from the *Father* and the *holy Ghost*: and so the *holy Ghost* from the *Father* and the *Son*: and every of those distinct in himself, and so incommunicable, as neither of these persons is, or can be, the other.[179]

Pictet, in a similar argument, concludes his discussion with a justification of the traditional language reminiscent of Calvin: the word "person" as applied "by theologians" to each of these "three in whom the divine essence subsists ... is not so apposite, but in the absence of other terms, we accept it, together with the entire Christian church."[180] As will appear below, in the discussion of *subsistentia*, the orthodox insist that "person" is not applied to God in the way it is applied to human beings — given that, although human beings are also independent subsistences, their individuality is not understood as a real relation or a relation of opposition within a single being.

These definitions, Wendelin and Leigh argue, meet the several requirements for the consideration of an individual as "person" — that is, since not all individual things are persons. By individual, Wendelin comments, is meant a singular thing, *res singularis*, inasmuch as universals, such as indicate genus and species, cannot be persons. The term "subsistence" indicates, moreover, an independent *individuum*, inasmuch as it is distinct from an "accident," which has no independent subsistence, but inheres in something else. In short, a person must be an individual "substance" or "subsistence" insofar as "accidents are not persons" but "inhere in another thing: ... a person must subsist." Even so, "living" must be added to the definition, inasmuch as an "inanimate individual," like a stone or a statue, is not a person — similarly, "intelligent," since brute creatures are not persons.[181]

This "lively and intelligent substance endued with reason and will," must also be "determinate and singular, for mankind is not a person, but John and Peter." The attribute of incommunicability, thus, indicates that "a person is not an essence, which is capable of being communicated to many individuals," while the qualifier that a person is not part of another being sets persons apart from entities such as souls, which are

---

178. Cf. Pfizenmaier, "Was Isaac Newton an Arian?" pp. 73-79.

179. William Gouge, *A Learned and very Useful Commentary on the Whole Epistle to the Hebrews* (London: A.M., T.W. and S.G., 1655), 1:3, §21 (p. 18); Beza et al., *Propositions and Principles*, II.vi-vii.

180. Pictet, *Theol. chr.*, II.xiii.11.

181. Wendelin, *Christianae theologiae libri duo*, I.ii.2 (1); cf. Leigh, *Treatise*, II.xvi (p. 129).

part of a human being.[182] Human nature, thus, is not a person insofar as it is "communicable to every particular man," while the individual or particular recipient of that nature is a person, incapable of communicating his nature as he has it in its particularized form to any other. A person is not directly or immediately sustained by another but is an independent subsistence — in scholastic terms, a *suppositum*: "The human nature of Christ is not a person, because it is sustained by his deity"; nor is the soul in man a person, because it is a part of the whole.[183] Whereas finite human nature is one in species (or genus) and plural in persons or individuals, the infinite divine nature is one without qualification, there being no genus or species "god," the plurality of persons in no way removing the numerical unity of essence.[184] Or, to make the point somewhat differently, Peter, James, and John "were three persons" and, as such "were separated one from the other," but in the Godhead, the divine persons, "however distinguished by their characters and properties, are never separated, as having the same divine essence or nature."[185]

It might also be argued, logically (if one followed the famous Boethian definition to the letter), that *Omnis persona est substantia intelligens, ubi ergo tres personae, ibi tres substantiae*. Rijssen denies this, arguing that the definition of person as *substantia intelligens* does not carry with it the conclusion that the three persons in God are different in essence.[186] This problem arises linguistically from the two rather different uses of the word *substantia* in the writings of the Latin fathers of the fourth and fifth centuries — as the translation of *ousia*, roughly synonymous with *essentia*, and as a translation of *hypostasis*: as Turretin comments,

> the ancients sometimes ... take *substance* for *subsistence*, like Hilary, who acknowledges *three substances of the Godhead* in [his] *De synodis*. Others, apparently understanding *substantia* as nature and essence, recognize only one [*substantia*] and deny that there are three, such as Augustine in *De trinitate* and Tertullian in *Adversus Praxean*.[187]

A final objection takes much the same point of departure as the previous — the problem of identity and plurality: "The one God is three in persons: the Father is the one God; Ergo, the Father is three in person." Here, too, the logic of the argument misunderstands the logic of trinitarian language, for "the word God in the major is taken essentially, in the minor, personally." "The Father," notes Rijssen, "is not the one God, when the word *God* is understood as the essence common to the three persons."[188]

---

182. Wendelin, *Christianae theologiae libri duo*, I.ii.2 (1); cf. the virtually identical (probably derivative) discussion in Leigh, *Treatise*, II.xvi (p. 129).

183. Leigh, *Treatise*, II.xvi (p. 130); cf. Amyraut et al., *Syntagma thesium theologicarum*, I.xvii.1.

184. Amyraut et al., *Syntagma thesium theologicarum*, I.xvii.11.

185. Ridgley, *Body of Divinity* (1855), I, p. 151.

186. Rijssen, *Summa theol.*, IV.ix, controversia I, obj. 7 & resp.

187. Turretin, *Inst. theol. elencticae*, III.xxiii.4.

188. Rijssen, *Summa theol.*, IV.ix, obj. 8 & resp.

Marckius qualifies carefully the meaning of the traditional philosophical terms used to define the Trinity, with particular attention to the term "person." It is not the case, he writes,

> that "personality" (*personalitas*) indicates a genuine something or a distinct Being (*verum aliquod & reale Ens*), having its own essence; nor is it to be inferred that there is in God a fourfold essence, one divine plus a threefoldness of person.[189]

Nor is *personalitas* merely a negation of actual or real communication of characteristic properties on the part of an essence, in order that it might be distinct from other essences: for it is the person of the Logos, and not the divine essence, that is incarnate. The correct understanding of "person" in this specifically trinitarian sense takes a middle course between these extremes, where "person" is understood as an incommunicable "mode" of subsistence that limits and completes a substantial nature.[190]

A divine person, then, can be identified as "an incommunicable subsistence of the divine essence," granting that the divine essence is possessed in common by the three persons, while the persons represent incommunicable characteristics: Father, Son, and Spirit are God, but the Father is not the Son, the Son not the Spirit, and so forth. The essence is one, the persons several: thus,

> essence is absolute, person relative: the persons of the Son and Spirit have an origin, the essence does not. Person generates and is generated: essence neither generates nor is generated.[191]

The persons, therefore are identified according to what they have in common and how they are distinct: they have in common the numerically singular and indivisible divine essence, the essential properties, the works, dignity, and honor of God. They are distinct, however, in origin, in order, and in manner of operation, inasmuch as the Father is from himself (*a se*), the Son from the Father, and the Spirit from the Father and the Son; the Father is first, the Son second, and the Spirit third in order; and in internal operation, the Father acts *a se*, the Son from the Father, and the Spirit from the Son and the Father.[192]

6. Hypostasis, subsistentia, and modus subsistendi. As already indicated in the discussion of trinitarian texts in the exegetical tradition, the term *hypostasis* is distinguished from the other trinitarian terms by its presence in the text of the New Testament. Noting the identification of the Son as "the brightness of [the Father's] his glory," Calvin continues,

> The fair inference from the Apostle's words is, that there is a proper subsistence (hypostasis) of the Father, which shines refulgent in the Son. From this, again it is easy to infer that there is a subsistence (hypostasis) of the Son which distinguishes him from

---

189. Marckius, *Compendium*, V.iii.
190. Marckius, *Compendium*, V.iii.
191. Wendelin, *Christianae theologiae libri duo*, I.ii.2 (2).
192. Wendelin, *Christianae theologiae libri duo*, I.ii.2 (3).

the Father. The same holds in the case of the Holy Spirit; for we will immediately prove both that he is God, and that he has a separate subsistence from the Father. This, moreover, is not a distinction of essence, which it were impious to multiply. If credit, then, is given to the Apostle's testimony, it follows that there are three persons (*hypostases*) in God. The Latins having used the word *Persona* to express the same thing as the Greek *hypostasis*, it betrays excessive fastidiousness and even perverseness to quarrel with the term."[193]

Reflecting the heated debates with Socinus and other antitrinitarians over the term, Gomarus begins his thesis on the Trinity with a lengthy clarification of the term "hypostasis," which he understands not in its early signification as similar to "ousia," but in the later signification as determined by the Cappadocian fathers: *hypostasis* is derived from *hyphestanai, subsistere* and therefore "*significat autem (ut loquuntur) subsistentiam: & quidem abstracte, vel concrete*" — whether taken abstractly or concretely, *hypostasis* refers to subsistence.[194] Thus, in the key biblical *locus*, Hebrews 1:3, *hypostasis* is rightly rendered "subsistence" or "person" and not "essence," given that here the Son is distinguished from the Father as type from archetype, produced from producer, while at the same time the essential identity of the Father and the Son is clearly indicated.[195]

Rijssen similarly appeals to the theological (and philosophical) use of the term *hypostasis* to indicate *subsistentia*, which he defines as an "entity," the "ultimate *terminus* and completion of a substantial nature" which is by nature "singular, ... complete, and incommunicable."[196] Taken abstractly, *hypostasis* can indicate the action or actuality of subsisting (*actus subsistendi*) and, by synechdoche, something that stands, remains, or occupies a place. In a less strict manner of speaking, taken actively, *hypostasis* indicates the "constitution" of something, as, for example, the constitution of a human being (*hominis constitutio*), or, taken passively, the "existence" or "substance" of a living thing and even the manner in which it, as a subject, subsists, in short, its *modi existendi*.[197] Concretely, the word *hypostasis* means a subsistent thing (*rem subsistentem*).[198] After a lengthy etymological analysis, Gomarus turns to the scriptural usage and to his final theological determination of *hypostasis*.[199] He notes that in Job 22:20, "Whereas our *substance* is not cut down, but the remnant of them the fire consumeth," the Hebrew word *kim*, from the verb meaning "to stand or stand up," indicates *substantiam* or *subsistentiam* and has been rendered as *hypostasis* by the Septuagint and as *persona* by Kimchi — not, of course, that the text of Job can be used

---

193. Calvin, *Institutes*, I.xiii.2.

194. Gomarus, *Disp. theol.*, VI.i; cf. Walaeus, *Loci communes*, X, N.B., pp. 235-236. For the antitrinitarian view, see Racovian Catechism, p. 140; Milton, *Christian Doctrine*, I.ii, v (in *Complete Prose Works*, VI, pp. 140-142, 223-225).

195. Gomarus, *Disp. theol.*, VI.xiv; cf. Zanchi, *De tribus Elohim*, pt. I, I.iv.3 (col. 18).

196. Rijssen, *Summa theol.*, III.iii, controversia I.

197. Gomarus, *Disputationes*, VI.ii.

198. Gomarus, *Disputationes*, VI.iii.

199. Gomarus, *Disputationes*, VI.iv-xiii.

to justify trinitarian language, but that the term *hypostasis* is clarified in its churchly significance by its use in the passage.[200]

Many of the orthodox attempt further to describe this plurality in the Godhead as distinct modes of subsisting or existing. A "mode of subsistence" or "mode of existence" — *modus subsistendi*, or τρόπος ὑπάρξεως — in the Godhead "is a relation inhering in the existence of God," that is usually identified with the term "person," given that the modes of subsisting in the Godhead are identified not by essential but by "personal properties." This truth, comments Keckermann, is a mystery such that the contemplation of it by the intellect is comparable only to the eye of a bat smitten by the sun![201] Still, some definition is necessary, if only for the sake of stating the doctrine without error. A subsistence, strictly speaking, is "a Mode of Being, by which a thing exists by itself, without existing in another, either as a part in a whole, or an *Adjunct* in the *Subject*."[202] Subsistence, therefore, indicates something very different from "essence" and "existence" — subsistence is what distinguishes the divine persons one from another, whereas essence and existence refer to their unity as God. The orthodox follow the traditional definition of "subsistences" in the Godhead as real relations or relative properties, modes of the divine being — which, in the Godhead can be called persons, as distinct from usages applicable in the creaturely order, where relative properties or real relations in a being cannot be understood as "persons."[203]

Among the early orthodox, Keckermann and Ames in particular preferred the term *modus* or *modus subsistendi* as a precise description of the way the persons related to the essence of God — and despite the problem caused by Sabellianism for this type of theological language, the terminology remained with the orthodox, especially with those who had a strong interest in philosophical usage.[204] The definition of the terms of trinitarian language thus indicates the utter unity of the divine being while at the same time safeguarding with precision the way in which the one essence is also three — leading many of the orthodox to adopt the Augustinian distinction between the oneness of essence and the threenesss of its "modes of subsistence":

> Although Trinity in its native signification signifies the number of any three things, yet by Ecclesiastical custom it is limited to signify the three Persons in the Trinity. This is not meant as if the Essence did consist of three Persons as so many parts; and therefore there is a great difference between Trinity and Triplicity. Trinity is when the same Essence hath divers ways of subsisting; and Triplicity is when one thing is compounded of three as parts. They are three not in respect of Essence or Divine attributes, as three Eternals, but three in respect of personal properties, as the Father

---

200. Gomarus, *Disputationes*, VI.xiii.

201. Keckermann, *Systema theologiae*, I.iii (p. 16); cf. Amyraut et al., *Syntagma thesium theologicarum*, I.xvii.15; on the Cappadocian use of τρόπος ὑπάρξεως, see Kelly, *Early Christian Doctrine*, pp. 265-266; Prestige, *God in Patristic Thought*, pp. 245-246.

202. South, *Animadversions upon Dr. Sherlock's Book*, p. 34.

203. Ames, *Medulla*, I.v.9.

204. Keckermann, *Systema theologiae*, I.iii (p. 19), citing a definition from Ursinus, *Exercitationes catecheticae*, p. 173 (cf. *Commentary*, p. 130); Ames, *Medulla*, I.v.1-10.

is of none, the Son of the Father, and the Holy Ghost of both; three Persons but one God, as to be, to be true, to be good, are all one, because Transcendents.[205]

From the basic understanding that the one, undivided divine essence is "common to the three subsistences," the Reformed orthodox draw a set of interrelated conclusions: since the three subsistences have the essence in common, each is properly said to exist of itself, as far as its essence is concerned.[206] This follows from the fact that all attributes or properties belonging to the divine essence must also belong to each of its modes of subsisting. Nonetheless, the distinct or personal properties that identify each subsistence individually cannot be predicated of the essence as such.[207]

As late as Gill, who had to contend with the revival of Arianism in England, we find the language of "mode" employed and the attempt made to define the term and its use very precisely:

> nor is the distinction merely modal; rather real modal; for though there are three modes of subsisting in the Deity, and each Person has a distinct mode, yet the phrase seems not strong enough; for the distinction is real and personal; the three in the Godhead are not barely three modes, but three distinct Persons in a different mode of subsisting, who are really distinct from one another.[208]

This use of *modus subsistendi*, or "way of subsisting," stands in contrast to the pattern of definition typically adopted by Lutheran orthodoxy. It was typical of the Reformed to use the term *modus subsistendi* when discussing the persons of the Godhead essentially and to argue that the "persons are distinguished from the essence, not *sola ratione* nor by a real distinction, nor even formally, as the Thomists claim, but modally or by a modal distinction, which is between the *ens* and the order or mode of the *ens*."[209] Turretin comments that, although no human language can do justice to the mystery of the Trinity, the notion of a modal distinction between the persons in the essence best serves the needs of the doctrine.[210]

7. *Circumincessio, perichoresis, emperichoresis.* Supplementing the term *homoousios*, but more firmly grounded in Scripture, is the term *perichoresis* or *emperichoresis*, usually rendered into Latin as *circumincessio*. The term is also rendered *mutua circumplexio*, indicating the ultimate, mutual interrelation of the persons, as appears from John 10:38 and 14:10-13 where the Son states that he is in the Father and the Father in him.[211] The persons also conjoin with one another in "their equal participation in the dignity and honor that flow forth from the one supreme nature" — although not in such a

205. Leigh, *Treatise*, II.xvi (p. 127).

206. See further below 6.3 on the aseity of the Son.

207. Ames, *Medulla*, I.v.1-4.

208. Gill, *Complete Body of Divinity*, I, pp. 201-202: the term "real modal" strongly echoes Mastricht, *Theoretico-practica theol.*, II.xxvii.9.

209. Keckermann, *Systema ss. theologiae*, p. 59; cf. the similar language of Rijssen, in Heppe, *Reformed Dogmatics*, p. 114.

210. Turretin, *Inst. theol. elencticae*, III.xxvii.3.

211. Rijssen, *Summa theol.*, III.iii, controversia I.

way as to render impossible the superiority of the Father as evidenced in the economy of redemption, where the Son is subordinate by reason of his office. Even so, their conjunction *ad intra* is understood as an *emperichoresis* or *mutua inexistentia* flowing from the unity of essence, as indicated by John 10:38, "the Father is in me and I in him."[212]

Granting this essential conjunction and "mutual inexistence," the persons must also be carefully distinguished. Here the Reformed orthodox offer different approaches. Marckius comments that the standard metaphysical terms used to indicate distinctions between beings, "real, modal, rational, personal and so forth" — the distinctions typically argued by the medieval scholastics — only cause confusion and debate, so that it is better to distinguish the persons in name, order, mode of operation, works *ad extra*, and personal operations.[213]

8. *Proprietates, relationes,* and *notiones.* The relationships drawn between the Father and the Son, together with the idea of a divine Trinity, demand a further set of descriptive terms that allow identification of *proprietates, relationes,* and *notiones.* The orthodox discussion of the Trinity offers a direct analogue to the discussion of the divine attributes in the differentiation between *proprietates essentiales* and *proprietates personales,* the former category of "property" referring to the divine attributes that the persons of the Trinity hold in common and that identify them each as fully and equally divine, the latter category referring to the distinctive characteristics of the persons individually that serve to identify them as persons within the Godhead.

> The personal property of the Father is to beget, that is, not to multiply his substance by production, but to communicate his substance to the same. The Son is said to be begotten, that is, to have the whole substance from the Father by communication. The Holy Ghost is said to proceed, or to be breathed forth, to receive his substance by proceeding from the Father and the Son jointly; in regard of which he is called the Spirit of the Father, and the Spirit of the Son both, Gal. 4:6. The Father only begetteth, the Son only is begotten, and the Holy Ghost only proceedeth. Both procession and generation are ineffable. In the manner of working they differ, for the Father worketh of himself, by the Son, and through the Holy Ghost; the Son worketh from the Father by the Holy Ghost; the Holy Ghost worketh from the Father and the Son by himself. There is so one God, as that there are three persons or divers manners of being in that one Godhead, the Father, Son, and the Holy Ghost.[214]

Here we see the return of the medieval scholastic terminology (although not of the extended speculative use of Augustinian metaphor characteristic of much medieval trinitarianism). This terminology, as noted above, was not seen as useful by the Reformers and had been rejected as unnecessary by some.[215] Reformed orthodox

212. Marckius, *Compendium,* V.v; Amyraut et al., *Syntagma thesium theologicarum,* I.xvii.14.

213. Marckius, *Compendium,* V.vi.

214. Leigh, *Treatise,* II.xvi (pp. 128-129); cf. Beza et al., *Propositions and Principles,* II.x-xi; Amyraut et al., *Syntagma thesium theologicarum,* I.xvii.15.

215. Cf. Bonaventure, *Breviloquium,* I.iii.1-6, and above, 1.1 (A.2).

reappropriation of the language was, arguably, for the purpose of providing a full Latin trinitarian vocabulary that could do justice to the complexity of the patristic development, particularly given the context of new and sophisticated debate over the doctrine of the Trinity.

The sequence of terms defines the intratrinitarian unity and distinction. *Proprietas* indicates a distinguishing characteristic of a subsistence not shared with other subsistences: in the trinitarian vocabulary, it indicates, in other words, the "peculiar mode of subsisting" belonging so a person, according to which the person "is constituted in his personal being and is distinguished from others."[216] Thus, in God there are three *proprietates* — *paternitas, filiatio,* and *spiratio. Relatio* also refers to personal properties but in the very specific sense of the way in which the distinct subsistences (and their *proprietates*) relate to one another: in God there are four *relationes* — *paternitas, filiatio,* and *spiratio,* both *activa* and *passiva. Notio* designates the way in which the three persons are distinct from one another: and there are five *notiones* — *agenesia, paternitas, filiatio, spiratio,* and *processio* — which identify all of the trinitarian concepts, whether active or passive. From this latter category comes the distinction between *actus notionales,* which flow from the essential properties of God and have their *terminus ad extra,* namely, in the common work of the three persons, and the *actus essentiales,* which flow from the personal *proprietates* of God and have their *terminus ad intra* — generation and filiation.[217] In the series, "property," "relation," and "notion," there is an increasingly "wider extension" of meaning, so that there are three properties, but four relations, and five notions or concepts.[218]

All these terms, Turretin and Rijssen conclude, are justified by their utility in discourse and their necessity in the fight against heresy.[219] The heretics of the seventeenth century, Socinians and Arminians, like the heretics of old, either deny the usefulness of the terms outright or make an appeal for "return to the simplicity of the sacred writings." The Arminians specifically argue that no one ought to be compelled to prove their orthodoxy by subscription to "words invented by human beings."[220] The problem, in Turretin's view, is that the new heretics, like the ancient ones, condemn the words in order to deny the truths indicated by them — which is, of course, the reason not only for retaining the terms but also for defining them precisely.[221]

The "*proprietates*" of the persons of the Trinity are the "*characteristica idiomata,*" or "limiting Attributes, which coming from the persons, are not only limited in the persons, but also do limit the persons, both in themselves and among themselves."[222]

---

216. Turretin, *Inst. theol. elencticae,* III.xxiii.14.
217. Rijssen, *Summa theol.,* III.iii, controversia I.
218. Turretin, *Inst. theol. elencticae,* III.xxiii.14.
219. Rijssen, *Summa theol.,* III.iii, argumenta; Turretin, *Inst. theol. elencticae,* III.xxiii.16-17.
220. Turretin, *Inst. theol. elencticae,* III.xxiii.16.
221. Turretin, *Inst. theol. elencticae,* III.xxiii.17.
222. Trelcatius, *Schol. meth.,* I.iii (p. 60).

The essential *proprietates*, however, apply to the entire Godhead as one and may be defined as

> attributes of God, essential to God, whereby both the verity of the Essence clearly appears in itself, and is distinguished from others; yet so, that they really differ neither from the Essence, nor among themselves: not from the Essence, because they are so in one Essence as that they are the very essence: for God is a simple working power; not among *themselves*: for that which is in God is one, and from this primary unity, every difference and every number ought to be far removed.[223]

This is the case since God cannot be characterized as having "composition of matter or form." God is

> good, true, just, & c. without quality or bound, exceeding great and incomprehensible, without motion or action, without passion, ... without time ... habit, or addition; the Lord of all things: for all the properties are affirmed of God Essentially, and that both formally and in the abstract, because of the individual perfection of the Essence, as also subjectively, and in the concrete, because of the verity of God existing.[224]

The distinction between the persons of the Trinity is a distinction in number, insofar as the three subsist "truly, distinctly, and *per se*" and are distinguished by their relations and personal properties, which are incommunicable, internal works of the Godhead proper to the persons.[225] In addition,

> there follows an external distinction in respect of effects and operations which the persons exercise concerning external objects, namely the creatures; for though the outward works are undivided in respect of the Essence, yet in respect of the manner and determination, all the persons in their manner and order concur to such works. As the manner is of existing, so of working in the persons.
>
> The Father is the original and principle of action, works from himself by the Son, as by his Image and wisdom, and by the Holy Ghost. But he is said to work by his Son, not as an instrumental but as a principal cause distinguished in a certain manner from himself, as the Artificer works by an Image of his work framed in his mind, which Image or Idea is not in the instrumental cause of the work ... [1 Cor. 8:6; Rom. 11:36; Heb. 1:2, 3].[226]

Thus, the personal works of the Trinity testify to the unity and the trinitarian interrelationship of circumincession of the persons:

> To the Son is given the dispensation and administration of the action from the Father by the Holy Ghost, 1 Cor. 8:6; John 1:3 & 5:19.
>
> To the Holy Ghost is given the consummation of the action which he effects from the Father and the Son, Job 26:13; 1 Cor 12:11.

---

223. Trelcatius, *Schol. meth.*, I.iii (p. 61).
224. Trelcatius, *Schol. meth.*, I.iii (p. 62).
225. Cf. Leigh, *Treatise*, II.xvi (p. 138).
226. Leigh, *Treatise*, II.xvi (pp. 138-139).

The effects or works which are distinctly given to the Persons, are, Creation ascribed to the Father, Redemption to the Son, Sanctification to the Holy Ghost; all which things are done by the Persons equally and inseparably in respect of the effect itself, but distinctly in respect of the manner of working.[227]

B. Trinitarian Distinctions in the Godhead: Between Essence and Persons — Among the Persons

1. The distinction between essence and person — rational or modal? The basic definitions of the Trinity and of the divine persons return us to the question of the nature of the distinctions in the Godhead, given the unity of the divine essence. As Turretin comments, "the persons are manifestly distinct from the essence because the essence is one and while the persons are three."[228] The very establishment of the doctrine of the Trinity demands some further clarification of the manner in which the persons may be said to be distinct: after all, the persons are surely distinct from the essence, inasmuch as the persons are three and the essence is one — and the persons are also surely distinct inasmuch as they are differently named and inasmuch as their names indicate something of the relationships that identify them as individuals. Thus, with regard to "essence" and "person," Turretin notes, "The former is the common principle of external operations, which are undivided and common to the three persons; the latter are the principle of internal operations, which belong to the single persons mutually related to each other."[229]

In drawing together the themes of oneness of essence and threeness of person, we observe that the divine nature common to the three persons alone is God even as the three persons alone are God and that the unity and equality of the persons does not stand in contradiction to their distinct personal properties or to their order of operation in the work of the Godhead. Thus,

> a person is such a subsistence in the Divine nature, as is distinguished from every other by some special or personal property, or else it is the God-head restrained with his personal property. Or it is a different manner of subsisting in the Godhead, as the nature of man doth diversely subsist in *Peter, James, John*, but these are all not one. It differs from the essence as the manner of the thing from the thing itself, and not as one thing from another; one person is distinguished from another by its personal property, and by its manner of working.[230]

The essence of God produces neither another divine essence nor the divine persons; nor does a person produce the essence; rather both the one producing and the one produced are persons.[231] Thus, as implied by the definition of person as one not

---

227. Leigh, *Treatise*, II.xvi (p. 139).
228. Turretin, *Inst. theol. elencticae*, III.xxvii.1.
229. Cf. Turretin, *Inst. theol. elencticae*, III.xxvii.1.
230. Leigh, *Treatise*, II.xvi (p. 128).
231. Rijssen, *Summa theol.*, IV.v: "Essentia neque essentiam, neque personum produxit, ut nec persona essentiam, sed producens & productum nonnisi persona est."

sustained by another, the divine persons have their essence and existence from themselves, at least in the sense that the divine essence is neither multiplied not divided, but rather possessed entire and without division by each of the persons: it is not the essence that is generated or spirated, but the persons themselves.[232] They differ from the divine Essence not *realiter* — that is to say, not *essentialiter, ut res & res* — but *modaliter, ut modus à re:* "the personal properties by which the persons are distinguished from the Essence, are modes of a sort, by which they are characterized, not formally and properly as in creatures who are affected in certain ways by their properties, but eminently and analogically, rising beyond all imperfection."[233]

Having defined the distinctions between the persons of the Trinity in terms of incommunicable properties which belong to the persons individually and which thus show why one person is not to be confused with the others, the orthodox take considerable pains to argue that the distinction between the persons is not "merely by negation."[234] The incommunicable properties are founded upon a positive distinction between persons and a positive and formal constitution of each person: if this were not so the several *modus subsistendi in divinis* would merely be categories superadded to the unity of the divine essence. In order truly to speak of persons in the Godhead, we must recognize positive distinction.[235] This leads to the controversy with the antitrinitarians and to various arguments in favor of a positive distinction of persons in the divine essence.

Rijssen notes that the problem of distinguishing between the persons of the Trinity has bred two extremes of doctrine. The first of these is Sabellianism, named for Sabellius Pentapolitanus, who was born in Egypt and introduced his ideas ca. 200 A.D. He was followed in his heresy by "Praxeas Asiaticus and Hermogenes Afer, and in more recent times M. Servetus, who have stated the distinction between persons as a purely rational distinction, as if there were only one person, which according to its various effects is said to be in the manner of the Father, or the manner of Son, or the manner of Spirit."[236]

The second extreme of trinitarian heresy is tritheism, put forth by Philoponus and Valentinus Gentilis, "who from the three persons devise three eternal and unequal spirits, essentially distinct from one another."[237] The orthodox stand between these two extremes, acknowledging a modal distinction between the persons insofar as the persons are constituted by personal properties which are to be conceived as incommunicable modes of subsisting. This distinction is "less than real" but nonetheless not merely rational: "the orthodox take a middle position, and confess a modal

---

232. Cf. Wendelin, *Christianae theologiae libri duo*, I.ii.3 (3).

233. Rijssen, *Summa theol.*, IV.vi; cf. Amyraut et al., *Syntagma thesium theologicarum*, I.xvii.12.

234. Rijssen, *Summa theol.*, IV.ix, margin: "Subsistentia in divinis non dicit meram negationem."

235. Rijssen, *Summa theol.*, IV.ix.

236. Rijssen, *Summa theol.*, IV.vii; very similarly, Leigh, *Treatise*, II.xvi (p. 131) and Turretin, *Inst. theol. elencticae*, III.xxvii.9.

237. Rijssen, *Summa theol.*, IV.vii: "qui extribus personis tres fingit Spiritus aeternos & inaequales, essentialiter inter se distinctos."

distinction between the persons, inasmuch as the personal properties of the persons [of the Godhead] are established as incommunicable modes of subsistence, by which the persons are distinguished."[238] Since the "persons" are understood as "modes of subsistence," the distinctions between them are "modal." The following personal distinctions, therefore, are observed: "1. In order, since the Father is the first, the Son the second, and the Holy Spirit the third person; 2. of properties, inasmuch as *agennesia* is attributed to the Father, *gennesia* to the Son, and *ekporeusis* to the Spirit; 3. in mode of operation, since the Father operates *a se*, the Son from the Father, and the Spirit from both [the Father and the Son]."[239]

These basic patterns of argumentation became a matter of controversy with the antitrinitarians of the seventeenth century who argued pointedly against the identification of the divine persons as modes of subsistence and held that, given the real, personal distinctions between the Father and the Son, or among the Father, Son, and Holy Spirit, the only way to salvage monotheism was the radical subordination of the Son and the Spirit. "If the Fathers had held," one antitrinitarian of the era argued,

> that the three Persons are but one only (numerical) Substance, one infinite Spirit, one omniscient Mind and energy; and that they are called Persons, only because the one (numerical) substance subsists *in three Modes*, that is, *after three several manners*: I say, if this had been the Opinion of the Fathers, the Question would not have been, how *three* Persons can be but one God, but *how they be called Hypostases or Persons?* As at this day, no Man is so foolish as to charge the Nominal trinitarians with Tritheism ... in calling *Modes* (or a Substance subsisting in three manners) *Persons*, when it is so obvious that Modes are not Persons, but certain Affections and accidental Denominations belonging to Persons.[240]

The distinction of the persons must be considered in two ways — first, the way in which the divine persons are distinct from the divine essence and, second, the way in which they are distinct form one another. The distinction between the persons and the essence is not a distinction between genus and species, since there is no genus "god": "god" does not indicate a class of beings, of which there are three instances. There is, moreover, no real distinction between the three persons and the divine essence, as if the essence were one thing (*res*) and the three persons each another thing, for God is a simple or noncomposite being. Rather the persons are rationally or conceptually (*ratione*) distinct, not merely in the mind of the finite knower but *in ipsa re*, that is, in the Godhead or divine essence itself.[241] Or to make the point in another form, "we do not have [in the Godhead] a thing and another thing, but a thing and the modes of a thing by which it is not compounded but distinguished."[242]

---

238. Rijssen, *Summa theol.*, IV.vii.
239. Rijssen, *Summa theol.*, IV.viii.
240. [Smalbroke?] *Judgment of the Fathers*, p. 67.
241. Mastricht, *Theoretico-practica theol.*, II.xxiv.8.
242. Turretin, *Inst. theol. elencticae*, III.xxvii.4.

2. The distinctions between the persons — modal or real? It was, moreover, entirely to be expected that the Reformed would use language of modal distinctions in their discussions of the Trinity, given their tendency to follow the Western, Augustinian concept of the persons as modes of subsistence in the Godhead. As Keckermann noted at the beginning of his discussion of the Trinity, the identity of essence and existence in God can be stated as an identity of *modus* or manner: the divine "mode of essence and of existence in no way differ: but what this *modus* is, is very difficult for the intellect to conceive."[243] Still, in finite things, we can distinguish aspects or degrees, such as degrees of heat, that do not imply the addition of a new thing or part to the thing originally under consideration and that are not the thing itself, but modes of the thing. By the same token, when we wish to discuss something in God that is not a thing or substance (*res*) separate from God and is also neither another God nor a divine essence, we speak of a mode of divine existence — as was proposed by John of Damascus, who drew on Justin Martyr's language and spoke of the divine persons as "τρόπος ὑπάρξεως, *modos existentiae* in Deo," a definition, Keckermann notes, that was approved by Ursinus in his catechetical lectures and used also by Zanchi. The notion of "modal distinction," Keckermann concludes, is therefore to be used to distinguish the person from the divine essence and to distinguish among the persons.[244]

This seemingly simple solution, however, was not universally adopted among the Reformed, partly because of the strong traditionary attraction of another usage, namely, the real distinction, partly because of the difficulties attendant on the use of modal terminology in the context of the various dogmatic and philosophical battles of the seventeenth- and early eighteenth centuries. Zanchi, it should be remembered, had echoed the main line of the *via antiqua* and argued pointedly for the real distinction of relations in the Godhead.[245] This model was argued early on and quite forcefully by Zanchi, who defined the persons as "distinct truly and really (*verè & realiter*)" but not "essentialiter" given that they are subsistents in the one divine essence: the persons are distinct but not divided (*distincti ... non autem divisi*).[246]

A summary of the argument, noting the views of Arnold, Mastricht, Maresius, Lampe, and Spanheim, with some attempt at resolution, is found as late as De Moor's *Commentarius perpetuus*. It provides a useful set definitions prefatory to discussion of the high orthodox resolution of the question of the interpersonal distinctions in the Godhead. De Moor notes five possible ways of arguing the distinction: First, *ratio ratiocinatae*, by reason of rational analysis, defined specifically as having a foundation in the thing (*res*) that is the object of the reasoning. Second, *formaliter*, in the sense that "the essence is formally constituted in personal existence" by the distinctions between the persons. Third, *modaliter*, in the sense that a mode or manner of a thing's

---

243. Keckermann, *Systema theologiae*, I.iii (p. 16).
244. Keckermann, *Systema theologiae*, I.iii (pp. 17, 19).
245. Zanchi, *De natura Dei*, II.ii (col. 69).
246. Zanchi, *De tribus Elohim*, pt. I, I.v.2 (col. 21).

subsistence can distinguished from the thing itself — reflecting the identification of the persons as "modes of subsistence." In this sense, "the persons are distinguished from the divine essence and among themselves not *realiter* or *essentialiter*, as a thing from a thing, but modally as a mode from a thing and modes of a thing from one another." Fourth, *realiter*, which, De Moor notes, is the distinction favored by the "Auctor," Marckius, in an attempt to state a distinction that is neither merely rational nor essential. Such a real distinction, De Moor adds, is not what the scholastics call *distinctio realis maior*, such as can be made between a thing and a thing (*inter res & res*), as if there were in the Trinity distinctions between one and another thing (*aliud & aliud*) or between one and another essence — this would violate the unity of God. Rather it is a *distinctio realis minor*, such as can be made between "a thing and the modes of a thing, or between the modes themselves," in short, a restatement of the modal distinction. (Arguably, this *distinctio realis minor* is precisely what Aquinas indicated by a real distinction of relational opposition.)[247] Fifth, drawing on Maresius, De Moor notes that one can also speak of a *distinctio personalis*, given the grounding of the distinction in the personal properties of the Father, Son, and Spirit — but here, again, De Moor understands the point to be identical with the modal distinction or the *distinctio realis minor*.[248]

Discussion of the proper use of these distinctions relative to the Trinity was offered, among the high orthodox, by Mastricht, Turretin, and Marckius. This distinction between the persons, comments Mastricht, is a difficult matter that has been typically framed either against the Sabellians or against various tritheists. On the one hand, the Sabellians admit no difference between the persons other than a purely rational or nominal distinction; on the other hand, a tritheist like Valentin Gentile would claim three beings or essences, one primary, the *essentiator*, the other two secondary or *essentiati*. Against the Sabellians, some have argued that the persona are distinct *realiter*, as *res & res* — really, as one thing from another thing — but this view verges on tritheism.[249] Here, we must place many of Reformed who adopted the traditional language that began at least as early as Alexander of Hales: that the persons are really distinct from one another as *res* and *res*, although not in such a way as to render them separate essences — indeed, the persons are understood as distinct only rationally from the essence.[250]

Others, Mastricht indicates, primarily against the tritheists, have argued that the persons are distinct modally (*modaliter*), as one manner of subsisting from another. This language consciously echoes Augustine. Turretin is perhaps the most eminent example of its use.[251] (It is important to note, over against a particular twentieth-century confusion of terms typical of "social trinitarians," that this use of the language of "modal distinction" or of divine "modes of subsistence" does not amount to the heresy of

---

247. See above 1.3 (A.3).
248. De Moor, *Commentarius perpetuus*, I.v.5; cf. the discussion in *PRRD*, III, 4.3 (C-D).
249. Mastricht, *Theoretico-practica theol.*, II.xxiv.9.
250. Alting, *Methodus theol*, III (p. 77B).
251. Turretin, *Inst. theol. elencticae*, III.xxvii.3.

Sabellianism or "modalism": the reference here is to *ad intra* "modal" distinctions, not, as in the heresy, to *ad extra* roles or modes of self-presentation.) As the Reformed orthodox note, the Sabellians did not argue a modal distinction between the persons in the Godhead but rather a purely rational distinction of persons in their outward manifestation or role coupled with an insistence that the persons were not distinct *ad intra*.[252]

If the divine persons can be said to be distinct from the divine essence *modaliter*, a somewhat different language must be used to indicate their distinction from one another — given, as Turretin remarks, that the essence can be predicated of the persons and that there is no "opposition" between essence and person *in concreto*, but that the persons are opposed to one another and "cannot be mutually predicated of each other."[253] This difference raises a problem in the language of distinction, given that the distinction between the persons is greater than what some have called modal, but still not as great as what is usually indicated by a "real distinction." Thus, some of the Reformed prefer simply to state that the persons are distinct modally, whereas others indicate that the persons are distinct *realiter* — although, as Turretin indicates, this real distinction must be understood as a "minor real distinction" such as exists not between things and other things but such as exists between a thing and its modes or between the modes of a thing. And, in fact, such a definition is found in Owen:

> this God is the Father, Son, and Holy Ghost; which are not diverse names of the same person, nor distinct attributes or properties of the same nature or being, but one, another, and a third, all equally that one God, yet really distinguished between themselves by such incommunicable properties as constitute the one to be that one, and the other to be that other, and the third to be that third. Thus the Trinity is not the union or unity of three, but it is a trinity in unity, or the ternary number of persons in the same essence.[254]

It is also found in the theses published at Saumur, where the persons are said to be distinguished *realiter* "as a mode of a thing from another mode."[255] This kind of definition, Turretin comments, corresponds with the modal distinction made by the other Reformed, so there is no great difference in substance between the variant definitions.[256] Mastricht notes that he prefers to indicate a "really modal" (*realiter modaliter*) distinction to press the point that the modal distinction is not merely rational but is made "in truth" (*revera*) and bears therefore a truth value or genuineness akin to the real distinction. To avoid all problems of language, one may simply state that

252. Turretin, *Inst. theol. elencticae*, III.xxvii.9.
253. Turretin, *Inst. theol. elencticae*, III.xxvii.8.
254. Owen, *Divine Original of Scriptures*, in *Works*, XVI, p. 340.
255. Amyraut et al., *Syntagma thesium theologicarum*, I.xvii.12.
256. Turretin, *Inst. theol. elencticae*, III.xxvii.11.

the persons are distinct not *realiter* but personally (*personaliter*) and that in a supernatural, not a natural sense.[257]

At somewhat greater length and with perhaps greater use of technical language, Marckius thus summarizes the problem under four heads: first, there is in God one single, most simple, and most singular essence — a point that must be made strongly against all "three-formists" (*Triformianos*) and tritheists (*Tritheistas*), both ancient and modern. Second, there are three genuine persons (*tres personas veras*) which, considered "abstractly," are understood as "incommunicable modes of existence of the divine essence."[258] The relationship of the persons to one another and to the essence are explained usually in metaphysical terms concerning distinctions — *rationis ratiocinatae*, *formalis*, *modalis*, and *realis* — all of which, Marckius notes, are suited to the consideration of finite and imperfect things and must be used carefully. The terms are necessary, however, in order to maintain right doctrine against such heretics as "Servetus, Sabellius, Noetus, Praxeas, the Patripassians, and the Simonians" who understand the persons as merely names of the one divine essence.[259] Third, "the persons agree or conjoin with one another (*convenire inter se*) in one essence, which was well expressed at Nicaea with the term *homoousion* as opposed to such terms as *homoiousion*, *heterousion*, *synousion*, *tautoousion*, *monoousion*, and *henousion*": for the essence is one in number, without division or multiplication, and threeness is "predicated of it not in terms of genus or species, but analogically." Thus it is not incorrect to say both that "persons" are "in the divine nature" and that "the nature is in the persons."[260] In sum, the distinction of persons must be identified either as a modal or formal distinction or as a *distinctio realis minor* in order that the individual persons not be identified as, individually, the primary essence of the Godhead and the unity of divine being reduced to a generic unity of secondary essence. There is a fundamental coherence between the arguments leading to a refined sense of the distinction of persons — neither a *distinctio realis maior* such as stands between distinct things, distinct substances, or distinct realities; nor a distinction of reason or of concept such as stands between the essentially and subsistentially identical inseparable attributes of a thing — and the insistence, along the traditional patristic lines of argument, that the persons do not divide the divine primary essence or substance but are instead distinct modes of subsistence within that essence.

---

257. Mastricht, *Theoretico-practica theol.*, II.xxiv.9: "non quidem oer solam ratiocinationem, sed revera."

258. Marckius, *Compendium*, V.v, citing only the first two of four arguments; cf. Downame, *Summe*, i (p. 33).

259. Marckius, *Compendium*, V.v.

260. Marckius, *Compendium*, V.v.

4

The Trinity of Persons in Their Unity and
Distinction: Theology and Exegesis in the
Older Reformed Tradition

4.1 The Trinity of Persons according to the Reformers

A. The Continuity of Precritical Exegesis and the Biblical Norm: Protestant Trinitarian Formulation and the Interpretation of Scripture

1. Shared perspectives: Trinity and precritical exegesis. The exegetical foundations of the doctrine of the Trinity were of profoundest importance to the Reformers and the Protestant orthodox, given their understanding of the secondary and defensive value of the traditional trinitarian language. As noted in the historical survey found in the preceding chapter, the received doctrine itself and its largely patristic vocabulary could not be normative in the ultimate sense — its traditionary heritage alone did not justify its presence in the confessions. This issue was made abundantly clear in the earliest Reformed confessions and in Calvin's *Institutes*. The Reformers and the orthodox, therefore, had to outline the biblical foundations of the doctrine in far greater detail than the medieval doctors, and they were bound to rest their teachings on exegesis rather than on the repetition of traditionary norms. This characteristic of Protestant doctrine became a major point of issue in the development of a Protestant doctrine of the Trinity, given the alternative exegesis found in the writings of the highly biblicistic antitrinitarians of the age.

The Reformed orthodox, despite the changing patterns of exegesis and hermeneutics that affected their theology and, specifically, their ability to formulate cherished dogmas inherited from previous ages, continued to assume, as had the Reformers, that the broader theological scope of the text of Scripture and the method of interpretation by means of the *analogia Scripturae* offered not only warrant for traditional trinitarianism but also a series of clear trinitarian references throughout the text of Scripture. Given the shift in exegesis and hermeneutics that began to take place toward the close of the seventeenth century and culminated in the eighteenth, examination of the way in which the older orthodoxy conjoined the exegesis of text to the formulation of doctrine becomes highly significant for an understanding of their theology.

Beyond the importance of the Old as well as the New Testament to the exegesis of the doctrine of the Trinity in the eras of the Reformation and orthodoxy lies the further issue of the continuity of precritical exegesis. The Reformers and the Protestant orthodox inherited several interpretive approaches to work with in their reading of the texts: as noted in general in the preceding volume, Protestant exegesis in the eras of the Reformation and orthodoxy did not entirely set aside a series of fundamental assumptions of patristic and medieval exegesis and, in fact, stood in the center of a developing line of literal, grammatical exegesis that included such luminaries of the medieval period as Thomas Aquinas and Nicholas of Lyra.

2. The Reformers and trinitarian exegesis. From the lineage of Lyra in particular, the Reformers inherited a highly useful model of a twofold literal reading of texts in the Old Testament. In this view, the literal sense of an Old Testament text could be read in a more historical, contextual manner and also in a spiritual, prophetic manner. In addition to this double literal sense of the text, the Reformers also had access to a hermeneutic of movement from promise to fulfillment, shadow to full revelation, type to antitype that understood the differences between the Old and the New Testament primarily in terms of the movement of revelation as focused on Christ and redemption.[1] This model served well in the understanding of the covenant history in the Bible, given (in Calvin's words) the unity of the covenant of grace in "substance" from Abraham to the last days, but its difference in "administration."[2]

These differences in covenantal administration or economy not only account for the different understandings of the law, particularly, the abolition of the ceremonial law of the Old Testament in the New Testament and the extension of the covenant of grace to the Gentiles in the New Testament, but also for differences in the extent of the revelation of God and Christ. Thus, Christ and his offices were often revealed under figures and types in the Old Testament, only to be manifest fully in the New — and the threeness of the one God was revealed vaguely in the plurality of reference to the one God, in references to the Redeemer in divine terms and as having divine attributes, and in references to the Spirit of God, only to be fully identified in the New Testament as the one God who is Father, Son, and Spirit. From the perspective of the hermeneutic inherited by the Reformers and the orthodox from the church's tradition, it did not appear at all curious that God was revealed as Father, Son, and

---

1. On the medieval background to this model, see James S. Preus, *From Shadow to Promise: Old Testament Interpretation from Augustine to the Young Luther* (Cambridge, Mass.: Harvard University Press, 1969), and idem, "Old Testament *Promissio* and Luther's New Hermeneutic," in *Harvard Theological Review*, 60 (1967), pp. 145-161. Also note the discussion of Reformation and post-Reformation patterns of interpretation in *PRRD*, II, 7.3-7.4.

2. Calvin, *Institutes*, II.x.2.

Spirit in the New Testament but that these crucial terms did not appear in regular conjunction throughout the Old Testament: in fact, this difference in language appeared as a fundamental instance of the movement from promise to fulfillment.

3. Trinitarian exegesis in the era of orthodoxy. The exegetical approaches of the Reformed orthodox illustrate exceedingly well the patterns of continuity and discontinuity that characterize the development of Reformed theology in the sixteenth and seventeenth centuries. Identifying these patterns and trajectories of interpretation is, in the first place, not a matter of examining the exegetical results of Bucer or Calvin or Bullinger and then searching out identical formulations or identical answers to all questions in the writings of an individual seventeenth-century thinker. Among the Reformers themselves as among the Reformed orthodox, there were differences of interpretation and of emphasis in the exegesis of particular texts. The continuities in interpretation, whether in general or with specific reference to the doctrine of the Trinity, ought to be sought in the common set of hermeneutical and doctrinal questions addressed to the text of Scripture and in the common assumption that the text, interpreted correctly, does in fact yield the right doctrine of the church, freed from the abuses and excesses of the later Middle Ages and of the Roman Church, and therefore fundamentally catholic. The discontinuities appear largely in the shifting methods of the seventeenth century, brought on by increasing expertise in the biblical and cognate languages and in the realm of textual criticism — and they register in the debates of the Reformed orthodox with alternative exegesis of the Socinians and Remonstrants and, perhaps most clearly, in the orthodox response to text-critical exegetes like Grotius, whose advocacy of a highly literalistic approach, increasingly approximating the eighteenth-century beginnings of higher criticism, led them to results suspiciously like the results of the heretics.

As might be expected, the Reformed orthodox approach to the trinitarian and christological reading of the Scripture carried forward both the more literal and the more allegorical or typological approaches of the sixteenth-century Reformers. Thus, the more literal-grammatical approach represented by Calvin finds its analogue in such exegetes as Calvin, Beza, Perkins, Ainsworth, Willet, Rivetus, Diodati, and Poole. Although these exegetes identify many of the traditional types, tropes, and doctrinal associations, their emphasis usually falls on the text and its literal meaning, often on issues of philology and right translation, and on those figures that, arguably, are intrinsic to the text and therefore provide firm ground for the drawing of doctrinal conslusions. By contrast, the more allegorized or typological approach found in Vermigli carried forward in such Reformed exegetes as Piscator, Cocceius and his various followers in the Federal School, Dickson, and Matthew Henry.[3]

---

3. Cf. Richard A. Muller, "William Perkins and the Protestant Exegetical Tradition: Interpretation, Style and Method in the Commentary on Hebrews 11," in William Perkins, *A Cloud of Faithful Witnesses: Commentary on Hebrews 11*, edited by Gerald T. Sheppard, *Pilgrim Classic Commentaries*, vol. 3 (New York: Pilgrim Press, 1991), pp. 71-94. On the exegetical tendencies of the Federal School, see Ludwig Diestel, *Geschichte des Alten Testamentes in der christlichen Kirche* (Jena: Mauke's Verlag, 1869), pp. 527-534; and Wilhelm Gass, *Geschichte der Protestantischen Dogmatik in*

Protestant theologians, after all, were unable to claim the authority of the early church as an absolute support for the doctrine of the Trinity as were Roman theologians after the Council of Trent. Nor, of course, would they need to argue, in the wake of Petavius, the fundamental authority of the church's *magisterium* to indicate the correct teaching. The sole ultimate norm for doctrine was the Holy Scripture, albeit as read and interpreted in the context of the believing community, guided by the testimony of the Spirit.

B. The Order and Distinction of the Persons: Views of the Reformers

1. The Reformers and trinitarian definition: general considerations. The doctrine of God remains incomplete until the concept of the unity and simplicity of the divine essence is drawn into relation with the concept of the Trinity of persons. Contrary to the frequently noted caveat that the doctrine of the essence and attributes stands as a philosophical discussion of "what" God is over against the doctrine of the Trinity as a biblical and "personal" statement of "who" God is, it must be recognized that the lines between these two parts of the doctrine of God are not so easily or neatly drawn. Not only did the medieval scholastics, the Reformers, and the Protestant orthodox recognize the necessity of a profound interrelationship between these two parts of the *locus de Deo*, they also were aware of the biblical, traditionary, and philosophical dimensions both of the doctrine of God as one in essence and of the doctrine of God as three persons. Indeed, the great problem confronting the doctrine of the Trinity as it passed through the Reformation into orthodoxy was the problem of the traditionary and philosophical usages necessary to the doctrine of the Trinity and their relationship both to changing patterns of exegesis and to changing approaches to philosophy and its problems. Like the Cappadocian fathers and Augustine, and in the tradition of the medieval doctors, the Reformed orthodox recognized that the doctrine of the Trinity could only be supported in the context of a carefully enunciated monotheism — as argued in the doctrine of the divine essence and attributes and quite specifically in the doctrine of divine simplicity.[4]

From the time of the initial codification of Reformed theology onward, the major expositors of Reformed theology tended to offer lengthy discussions of the language of the Trinity and of the individual divine persons, accompanied by proofs of their divinity and coequality. Similar doctrinal presentations (albeit resting on different exegetical and hermeneutical approaches) are offered by Calvin, Vermigli, Musculus,

---

ihrem Zusammenhange mit der Theologie überhaupt, 4 vols. (Berlin, 1854-67), II, pp. 289-290.

4. A point not sufficiently grasped by contemporary proponents of so-called social trinitarianism, who attempt to find antecedents for their position in patristic theology: cf. Gregory of Nyssa, *Answer to Eunomius*, I.19; and idem, *Answer to Eunomius' Second Book*, II in NPNF, 2 ser. V, pp. 57, 254-255; idem, *Great Catechism*, I, in ibid., pp. 474-476; Basil the Great, Letter 134 (to Amphilochius), in NPNF, 2 ser., VIII, p. 274; Augustine, *De Civitate Dei*, XI.10; idem, *De Trinitate*, VI.7, 8; Rufinus, *On the Apostles' Creed*, 4, in NPNF 2 ser. III, p. 544; cf. W. J. Hill, "Simplicity," s.v. in NCE, vol. XII; Eric Osborne, *The Beginnings of Christian Philosophy* (Cambridge: Cambridge University Press, 1981), pp. 31-78.

Hyperius, and Bullinger: each accepts the normative status of the language of traditional orthodoxy while at the same time offering reflection on the limits of such extra-biblical terminology, and each notes how the language ought to be understood in the context of Scripture. There is a double burden identifiable in nearly all of these Reformation-era discussions of the Trinity: on the one hand, the Reformers evidence the need to distance themselves from the various heresies, while, on the other, they evidence an equal need to set themselves apart from the Roman Catholic claim that the traditionary language of the doctrine takes its authority from the church. The problem of using the orthodox language was complex: the Reformers were constrained to uphold the priority of Scripture and at the same time argue the language of the tradition at the very moment that more radical writers were discarding the tradition in the name of Scripture and Roman Catholic opponents were upholding the tradition as valid in relative independence from Scripture.

Despite a certain hesitance on the part of the Reformers to accord normative status to traditional trinitarian language, the pressure of antitrinitarianism, on the one hand, and of accusations of heresy from Roman Catholics, on the other, led to fairly full discussions of the order and relationships of the persons in the theological systems of the second generation of Reformers. Calvin, thus, confesses that he is not quite sure "whether it is expedient to borrow comparisons from human affairs" to explain the doctrine of the Trinity, but he is certain that Scripture identifies the Father as "the beginning of activity" in the Godhead and as "the fountain and wellspring of all things," attributes to the Son "wisdom, counsel, and the ordered disposition of all things," and to the Spirit "the power and efficacy" of the divine activity. In addition, although there can be no "before" or "after" in God's eternity, "the observance of an order" in the Godhead "is not meaningless or superfluous, when the Father is thought of as first, then from him the Son, and finally from both the Spirit."[5] Even so, the mind is led to conceive of God in an ultimate sense, of the wisdom that issues forth from God, and of the "power by which he executes the decrees of his plan": because of this order, the Son is understood "to come forth from the Father alone; the Spirit from the Father and the Son."[6]

Characteristic of the trinitarian expositions found in the works of their generation, the Reformers pass on, after their basic trinitarian formulations, to the examination of various Old and New Testament texts that witness to the distinction between the Father, the Son, and the Spirit and that "demonstrate" the full divinity particularly of the Son and Spirit.[7] Old Testament reference to the Trinity is an assumption that

---

5. Calvin, *Institutes*, III.xiii.18.

6. Calvin, *Institutes*, I.xiii.18: note that the distinction between the decree and its execution, sometimes described as a speculative notion absent from Calvin's thought, is in fact resident in Calvin's view of the trinitarian activity and is hardly a speculative concept; cf. Muller, *Christ and the Decree*, pp. 20-22.

7. Cf. Bullinger, *Decades*, IV.iii, with Calvin, *Institutes*, I.xiii; Musculus, *Loci communes*, i-iii; and note Vermigli, *Commonplaces*, (where the same pattern is followed, courtesy of Vermigli's editor, Massonius).

they share with the fathers, the medievals, and the later Protestant orthodox — and Old Testament texts are consistently integrated into arguments for the divinity and the distinction of the Son and the Spirit. Thus, against sixteenth-century antitrinitarians like Blandrata, Gentile, and Servetus, the Reformers argued that the *doctrine* of the Trinity, unlike the *term* "Trinity," is not an invention of human beings — not of the fathers or bishops of the early Church; nor was it originated following Christ's ascension. Rather, it belongs to the entire revelation of God, including that in the Old Testament.[8]

Bullinger indicates that the mystery of the Trinity was known to the patriarchs and prophets of the Old Testament insofar as they speak of "the promised Seed" and write the word for God, *Elohim*, in the plural with a singular verb. Even so God speaks in the plural in the first chapter of Genesis but tells us in Isaiah 44:24 that he alone is creator.[9] Many other citations of the prophets substantiate this argument.[10] Calvin, of course, did not favor the interpretation of *Elohim* as a trinitarian reference, but he is quite at one with Bullinger in identifying the references to the "Mighty God" in Isaiah 9:6, to the "branch of David" as "Jehovah our Righteousness" (Jer. 23:5-6), and to the "Angel of the Eternal God" (Judg. 6:11-12, 20-22) as prophetic proofs of Christ's divinity.[11] The faith in God as Father, Son, and Holy Spirit is thus received by us from God himself, delivered by the prophets, confirmed by the Son of God and the apostles, and therefore taught by the whole church. Vermigli cites several instances in the Old Testament in which God is spoken of in the plural. These, he says, are an embarrassment to the Jews, who "will not acknowledge three persons in the divine nature."[12] These passages cannot be said to represent the opinion of men, as when Paul writes, "There be many gods and many lords," because, as in the instance of 2 Samuel 7:23, these texts can only refer to the "true God" and therefore indicate "the Father, the Son, and the Holy Ghost: which being three persons, yet are they conjoined as one substance."[13] Bullinger concludes his argument by noting sharply that, in the Old Testament, bounds were set on conduct and knowledge and enforced by the death penalty: "and we also have certain appointed bounds about the knowledge of God, which to pass is hurtful to us; yea, it is punished with assured death."[14] Here again, we have an adumbration of the seventeenth-century debates between the orthodox and the Socinians: it remained typical of Reformed orthodox theology to argue adumbrations of the Trinity in the Old Testament.[15]

2. The views of Calvin and Bullinger. Citing Seneca, Calvin places his doctrine of the Trinity into the context of an expostulation on the profound contrast between

---

8. Calvin, *Institutes*, I.xiii.3-4; cf. Bullinger, *Decades*, IV.iii (III, pp. 158, 160-165, 169-172).
9. Bullinger, *Decades*, IV.iii (III, pp. 169-170).
10. Bullinger, *Decades*, IV.iii (III, pp. 170-172).
11. Calvin, *Institutes*, I.xiii.9-10.
12. Vermigli, *Commonplaces*, I.xii.3.
13. Vermigli, *Commonplaces*, I.xii.3.
14. Bullinger, *Decades*, IV.iii (III, p. 173).
15. See Turretin, *Inst. theol. elencticae*, III.xxvi.

pagan philosophical conceptions of God and the biblical teaching concerning the "infinite and spiritual essence" of God. There is nothing here like the modern contrast between the Christian notion of the Trinity and a supposedly "Greek" conception of infinite essence — Calvin quite explicitly couples the statement of essence and attributes with the doctrine of the Trinity as essential to the Christian view over against the pagan. We are forbidden by the language of Scripture to imagine God as in any way earthly or carnal: Scripture teaches that he dwells in the heavens and fills all things. Calvin singles out the Manichees, whose dualism attempted "to destroy [God's] unity and restrict his infinity."[16] This ultimate unity and infinity distinguishes the true God from all idols — but, Calvin adds, there is another aspect of the divine revelation that even "more precisely" sets God apart from the idols, namely, the revelation that God is three in person.[17]

This truth of the divine threeness is necessary if believers are to have more than a "bare and empty" conception of the divine. Clear definition is necessary, moreover, if believers are to be preserved from two particular errors, the understanding of God as a threefold being and the conception of God as three beings. These two heresies are, moreover, the reason that Christians ought to follow the wisdom of the church in its use of the terms "essence" and "hypostasis" or "substance" and "person." That these terms are not words drawn from the Bible, moreover, ought not to distract Christians from their usefulness in combating error: after all, Scripture itself indicates that the Son is the "express image" of the Father's "hypostasis," and thereby teaches that the Father's subsistence differs in some way from that of the Son. It is wicked, Calvin concludes, to complain about the terms when they merely serve to explain the truths of Scripture![18]

Calvin and Bullinger both trace the development of patristic trinitarian language to the pressures of heresy. Early on in the history of the church, Bullinger argues, "pestilent men" made the "perverse" claim that the three divine persons could not have the same essence and nature. Both Bullinger and Calvin take pains to deny the heresy of Noetus and Sabellius — patripassianism — according to which the Father, the Son, and the Holy Spirit are simply representations of the "diverse attributes of God" and of the threefold operation of creating, redeeming, and sanctifying.[19] Thus, the names Father, Son, and Holy Spirit do not simply refer to attributes: rather they "show to us what God is in his own proper nature":

> For naturally and eternally God is the Father because he did from before beginnings unspeakably beget the Son. The same God is naturally the Son, because he was from before beginnings begotten of the Father. The same God is naturally the Holy Ghost,

---

16. Calvin, *Institutes*, I.xiii.1.
17. Calvin, *Institutes*, I.xiii.2.
18. Calvin, *Institutes*, I.xiii.2-3.
19. Bullinger, *Decades*, IV.iii (III, p. 156); Calvin, *Institutes*, I.xiii.4..

because he is the eternal Spirit of them both, proceeding from both, being one and the same God with them both.[20]

In refutation of those, like the Arians, who would apply certain attributes to the title of Father in isolation from the names of Son and Spirit, Bullinger argues, "And when in the scriptures he is called a gentle, good, wise, merciful, and just God, it is not thereby so much expressed what he is in himself, as how he exhibits himself to us."[21] Such attributes, therefore, do not identify distinctions between the persons, inasmuch as those distinctions are internal rather than external to the Godhead.

It was these controversies that brought into use a set of terms necessary to maintain the truth of the Scriptures:

> Therefore immediately after the beginning there sprang up the terms of Unity, Trinity, essence, substance, and person. The Greeks for the most part used *ousia*, *hypostasis*, and *prosopon*: which we call essence, subsistence, and person.[22]

Calvin, even more directly than Bullinger, moves toward the identification of "subsistence" as the proper equivalent of *hypostasis*, and therefore as the technical term used to express what, less technically, had been identified under the Latin term *persona*:

> By *person*, then, I mean a subsistence in the Divine essence — a subsistence which, while related to the other two, is distinguished from them by incommunicable properties. By *subsistence* we understand something other than *essence*. For if the Word were God simply and had not some property peculiar to himself, John could not have said correctly that he had always been with God. When he adds immediately after, that the Word was God, he calls us back to the one essence. But because he could not be with God without dwelling in the Father, hence arises that subsistence, which, though connected with the essence by an indissoluble tie, being incapable of separation, yet has a special mark by which it is distinguished from it.[23]

Calvin thus clearly preferred the Augustinian approach to the definition of "person" as a "subsistence" in the divine essence rather than as some had understood the term, a "substance": whereas *substantia* and *essentia* are very similar in meaning, *subsistentia* and *essentia* are relatively easily distinguished. They both rightly interpreted *persona* and also permitted the three persons to be distinguished within the Godhead, each having its own distinctive characteristic or "incommunicable quality." This, Calvin adds, is clearly the sense intended in the first chapter of John's Gospel:

> For if the Word were God simply and had not some property peculiar to himself, John could not have said correctly that he had always been with God. When he adds immediately after, that the Word was God, he calls us back to the one essence. But because he could not be with God without dwelling in the Father, hence arises that

---

20. Bullinger, *Decades*, IV.iii (III, p. 156).
21. Bullinger, *Decades*, IV.iii (III, p. 157).
22. Bullinger, *Decades*, IV.iii (III, p. 158); cf. Calvin, *Institutes*, I.xiii.4; cf. xiii.21-24.
23. Calvin, *Institutes*, I.xiii.6.

subsistence, which, though connected with the essence by an indissoluble tie, being incapable of separation, yet has a special mark by which it is distinguished from it. Now, I say that each of the three subsistences while related to the others is distinguished by its own properties. Here relation is distinctly expressed, because, when God is mentioned simply and indefinitely the name belongs not less to the Son and Spirit than to the Father. But whenever the Father is compared with the Son, the peculiar property of each distinguishes the one from the other. Again, whatever is proper to each I affirm to be incommunicable, because nothing can apply or be transferred to the Son which is attributed to the Father as a mark of distinction.[24]

Nor is this discussion restricted to the *Institutes*: Calvin, very much in the spirit of Bucer's remarks on the same text, understands the distinction and full divinity of the Son as clearly indicated exegetically: on the text of John 17:5, he comments, "a manifest distinction between the person of Christ and the person of the Father is here expressed; from which we infer, that he is not only the eternal God, but also that he is the eternal Word of God, begotten by the Father before all ages."[25]

Bullinger also evidences extensive recourse to patristic language, commenting on the ancient debate over the use of *ousia* and *hypostasis* and, by extension, over the proper rendering of *hypostasis* into Latin. Citing Rufinus of Aquilea, Basil the Great, Sozomen, and Socrates, Bullinger shows that there was some question as to whether or not the words had in fact any difference in meaning and whether or not they should be used in theology.[26] The result of the patristic debates was, ultimately, that a difference in meaning was identified between *ousia* and *hypostasis* and between *substantia* and *subsistentia* — "substance denotes the nature of a thing and the foundation (*ratio*) on which it stands ... but subsistence ... indicates the individual that exists."[27]

Calvin similarly notes with some sarcasm the patristic debate over the translation of *hypostasis* either as *substantia* or *subsistentia* — he cannot make too much of the value of the terms themselves when the fathers could not agree, but he pledges himself to echo the "modesty" of Hilary and Augustine.[28] But he also assumes the doctrinal consensus of the fathers despite the terminological debate — and he argues, against Servetus use of the pre-Nicene tradition, that the distinction between Father and Son in Irenaeus and Tertullian cannot be understood as an essential subordination of the Son. Adumbrating later debate between orthodox writers like Forbes and Bull and the Socinians, Calvin indicates that the pre-Nicene theology leads to Nicaea, not to Arius.[29]

---

24. Calvin, *Institutes*, I.xiii.6.

25. Calvin, *Commentary on John*, 17:5 (CTS *John*, II, p. 169); cf. Martin Bucer, *Enarratio in Evangelion Iohannis*, ed. Irena Backus (Leiden: E. J. Brill, 1988), John 17, sect. 1 (pp. 473-474).

26. Bullinger, *Decades*, IV.iii (III, pp. 158-160); cf. Calvin's discussion of the patristic debate in *Institutes*, I.xiii.5.

27. Bullinger, *Decades*, IV.iii (III, p. 158), citing Rufinus' *Ecclesiastical History*.

28. Calvin, *Institutes*, I.xiii.5.

29. Calvin, *Institutes*, I.xiii.27-28.

At best, then, such terms should be used cautiously in opposition to error, but never elevated to the level of biblical authority. "Therefore," concludes Bullinger,

> away with the pope's champions to the place whereof they are worthy, which, when we teach that all points of true godliness and salvation are fully contained and taught in the canonical scriptures, by way of objection do demand; in what place of the scripture we find the names of Trinity, person, essence, and substance; and finally wherein we find that Christ hath a reasonable soul? For although those very words consisting in those syllables are not to be found in the canonical books ... yet the things, the matter, or substance, which those words signify, are most manifestly contained in those books.... Neither is it greatly material whether they are called substances, or subsistences, or persons, as long as the distinction among them is plainly expressed, and each one's several properties; confessing so the unity, that yet ye confound not the Trinity, nor despoil the persons of their properties.[30]

The unity and distinction of the three persons is the crucial point to which Scripture testifies.[31]

> The Father is not the Son; the Son is not the Father; neither is the Holy Ghost the Father, or the Son: but the Father is the Father of the Son, the Son is the Son of the Father, and the Holy Ghost proceeds from them both; and yet those persons are so joined and united, that he who denies one of them hath in him none of them. Yea, whosoever denies this Trinity is pronounced to be Antichrist: for he denies God, which is one in Trinity and three in Unity; and so consequently confounding or taking away the properties of God, he denies God to be such a one as he is in very deed.[32]

3. Musculus on the distinction and order of the divine persons. Following the examination of the nature of God according to his essence, Musculus turns to God considered as person and as substance.[33] He differentiates between *ousia* and *hypostasis* — "essence" and "substance" — a unity of essence does not presuppose a unity of substance or person. Essence signifies "that which was common to all persons in the Holy Trinity" while substance "that which is proper to every person in the Trinity" and which "so appertained to one person, that it could not be attributed unto the other two persons." Thus,

> To be unbegotten, is not applied to the Son, but to the Father & the Holy Spirit. To proceed forth, is not said of the Father, nor of the Son, but only of the Holy Spirit, who proceeds from the Father and the Son. So the substance or property of the Father is, that he is the Father and unbegotten: the substance of the Son, that he is the only begotten Son: the substance of the Holy Spirit is contained under this voice Spirit, and is expressed by his proceeding forth.[34]

---

30. Bullinger, *Decades*, IV.iii (III, p. 160).
31. Bullinger, *Decades*, IV.iii (III, pp. 160-165: numerous citations).
32. Bullinger, *Decades*, IV.iii (III, p. 165).
33. Musculus, *Loci communes*, i (*Commonplaces*, p. 11, col. 2).
34. Musculus, *Loci communes*, i (*Commonplaces*, p. 12, col. 2).

Those things which were previously stated of God's essence Musculus now expressly affirms of each of the persons. (Musculus follows the usage of "substance" found in Latin patristic writers like Hilary and Jerome, where it is the equivalent of *hypostasis* rather than of *ousia*, and avoids the usage of "subsistence" in place of "substance.")[35]

In the Old Testament these "three substances" were given by the words *Jahweh*, *dabar*, and *ruah*. "That is to say, the existent, the word, and the spirit: as in the 33. Psalm. 'By the word of God the heavens were settled, and by the spirit of his mouth all the powers of them.'" The Greeks expressed the "property of the substances in God by this word *prosopa*, that is, a countenance or face, the Latins by the word person, by which words every substance might be set forth to be known and understood."[36]

> So that God in essence is one, as in nature and godhead, in substance or person, three, which trinity not only the holy scriptures do set forth, but also some of the Books of the Philosophers, and the Sybil's verses. The school of Plato also acknowledged to be in God *nous*, *logos*, *kai pneuma*: that is to say, the understanding, the word, and the spirit.[37]

Musculus here reflects the assumptions of the church fathers, notably Eusebius of Caesarea, who cited Plato and others, notably Numenius of Apamaea, as having adumbrated the Trinity. Nonetheless, Musculus continues,

> this knowledge of the holy trinity was somewhat hidden, till the revelation of the word that took flesh, when the holy spirit began more especially to work. Then this mystery of the trinity in God was openly set forth by Christ, when he said: Go, teach all people, baptizing them in the name of the father, & the son, and of holy spirit.[38]

Christ might have spoken of the unity of God, writes Musculus, but he chose to speak of something less known rather than of a point generally agreed upon: he thus reveals the mystery of the Trinity to the world.

> These things be manifest and must with a simple and clear faith be believed, that God is one in essence, nature, and godhead, will, moving and working; three in persons, of which every one hath several substance and property, which for all that be so in God, that the essence, nature, godhead, Majesty, working, will, power, honor, and continuance forever, is common to them all, all coessential, all coeternal.[39]

---

35. Musculus, *Loci communes*, i (*Commonplaces*, p. 12, col. 2).

36. Musculus, *Loci communes*, i (*Commonplaces*, p. 12, col. 2), citing Psalm 33:6. Calvin is somewhat more cautious, noting that reference to "the word" of God certainly allows the inference that the "Eternal Word" or "only-begotten Son" created the world, but that "the breath of his mouth," often used by the fathers as a reference to the Spirit, is only a metaphor for God's speech and thus synonymous with "word": see Calvin, *Commentary on the Psalms*, 33:6 (CTS *Psalms*, I, p. 543).

37. Musculus, *Loci communes*, i (*Commonplaces*, p. 13, col. 1).

38. Musculus, *Loci communes*, i (*Commonplaces*, p. 13, col. 1); cf. Eusebius, *Preparation for the Gospel*, XI.xvii-xxii.

39. Musculus, *Loci communes*, i (*Commonplaces*, p. 13, col. 2).

Thus, the doctrine does not imply three gods "but three unsearchable substances or persons in one true God set forth for the knowledge of Christ, his only begotten son, and for the increase of his glory, according to the measure of his revelation." These three substances are not diverse in nature or in being. Musculus gives, by way of clarification, the similitude of the Sun — "a fountain of light never ceasing," the brightness that comes forth from it, and the heat that proceeds out of it; but farther than this, he refuses to speculate:

> Now how the father from ever and evermore begat the son, and the holy spirit from both not begotten but proceeding, doth as we may say breathe forth, so that he may particularly be called the Spirit, not withstanding that Christ commonly called God a Spirit, it is too obscure for any man's understanding to conceive, much less may it be plainly expounded. Neither is it meet that we should search this secret of our Lord God.[40]

Doctrine here depends entirely on Scripture, Musculus insists, and therefore needs to follow it closely without speculation.

C. The Order and Distinction of the Persons: Views of the Reformed Orthodox

1. Positive definition among the Reformed orthodox. The orthodox presentations of the doctrine of the Trinity are considerably more elaborate than those offered by the Reformers, but they can hardly be viewed either as speculative or overly rationalistic. The Reformed orthodox attempted to reproduce the basic arguments offered by the Reformers in the context of a far more detailed analysis of trinitarian language. This detail arose in part because of the detail already present in the tradition and in part because of the rise of Socinianism. Indeed, the basic concern of the Reformers, so well enunciated by Calvin, to use the terms of patristic orthodoxy as guides to the interpretation of Scripture while at the same time recognizing the difficulty of applying and using words to the text that are not found in it, remained a concern of the orthodox, as did the use of rational argumentation in a *locus* that taught so great a mystery. More than the Reformers, the early orthodox writers borrow technical language from the older scholastic tradition and treat the doctrine of the Trinity as integral to their doctrine of God, albeit typically without the more speculative aspects of the medieval doctrine, such as elaboration of the Augustinian metaphors or use of the "proofs" of divine Trinity developed by Richard of St. Victor.

Perkins thus concludes his discussion of God with a fairly representative early orthodox definition of trinitarian terms:

> The persons are they, which subsisting in one Godhead, are distinguished by incommunicable properties.... They therefore are coequal and are distinguished not by degree, but by order. The constitution of a person is, when as a personal property, or the proper manner of subsisting is adjoined to the Deity, or the one divine nature.

---

40. Musculus, *Loci communes*, i (*Commonplaces*, p. 14, col. 1).

Distinction of persons, is that, by which albeit every person is one and the same perfect God, yet the Father is not the Son or the holy Ghost, but the Father alone; and the Son is not the Father or the holy Ghost, but the Son alone; and the H. Ghost is not the Father or the Son, but the Holy Ghost alone: neither can they be divided, by reason of the infinite greatness of that most simple essence, which one and the same, is wholly in the Father, wholly in the Sonne, and wholly in the Holy Ghost: so that in these there is diversity of persons, but unity in essence. The communion of the persons, or rather union, is that by which each one is in the rest, and with the rest, by reason of the unity of the Godhead: and therefore each one doth possess, love and glorify another, and work the same thing.[41]

Following out this traditional pattern of argument, an early orthodox formulator like Keckermann could pay considerable attention not only to the doctrine of the divine essence and attributes and to the doctrine of the Trinity, but also to the way in which the doctrines related to one another. Keckermann notes that the former presents the *essentia Dei absolutè spectata*, the essence of God absolutely considered, while the latter discusses the manner or disposition of the divine essence or existence (*modus essentiae sive existentiae*).[42] Nonetheless, God has chosen to reveal to the human race that he is at once one and three (*unum simul ac trinum patefacere*) — and the mystery ought therefore to be studied soberly in faith. Since the existence of God is identical with the divine essence, Keckermann continues, it must be fundamental rule of trinitarian doctrine that the mode or manner (*modus*) of God's existence does not differ from the mode of his essence. It is not as if there can be diverse "things" in God — rather the divine *modi existentiae* must be God himself.[43]

What is characteristic of the Reformed scholastics is an interest (echoing that of the medieval doctors) to establish a suitable definition of *persona* for trinitarian theology, given the imprecision of the Latin word over against the Greek term *hypostasis* and given the relatively greater precision of such Latin terms as *substantia*, *subsistentia*, and *individuum*. According to Trelcatius, the names of the persons signify three things:

first the *Individuum* itself or singular thing subsisting, intelligible, incommunicable, and not sustained of another: secondly, the very properties of every *Individuum*, by which they are distinguished from others, and which also the Schoolmen have called *Principia Individuantia*: lastly, these both together, they are called subsisting *Individua*, together with their properties and the manner of being, because they signify nothing else than the Essence subsisting in some one *Individuum*, and by the property thereof severed and limited.[44]

The persons of the Trinity, Father, Son, and Holy Ghost, are "distinct, not by degree, or state, or dignity, but by the order, number, and manner of doing."[45] For in order

---

41. Perkins, *Golden Chaine*, V (p. 14, col. 1).
42. Keckermann, *Systema*, I.iii (col. 72).
43. Keckermann, *Systema*, I.iii (col. 73).
44. Trelcatius, *Schol. meth.*, I.iii (p. 56).
45. Trelcatius, *Schol. meth.*, I.iii (p. 56).

the Father is just and of himself "not in regard of Essence, but in regard of person existing." The Son is second in respect of person, since as person he exists by eternal generation from the Father: yet in terms of his Essence "he is of himself and God himself." Even so the Holy Ghost, third in order, since he proceeds from the Father and the Son, is "God of himself, with the Father and the Son, in regard of Essence."[46]

Echoing many in the Reformed tradition, Pictet repudiates the "unbridled audacity of the vain and speculating schoolmen" who only open the door to heresy by their "dangerous subtleties" of explanation. Perhaps with Augustine and with an early Reformed orthodox writer like Keckermann in mind, he notes that "distinguished men, both in this and former ages, have attempted to render this mystery plain by many examples" — these arguments captivate the mind momentarily only to fade into oblivion before the incomprehensible mystery of the Trinity and unity of God. Faith alone receives this doctrine.[47]

Pictet's preference, reflecting both the decline of the older Christian Aristotelianism and a distaste for the theological results of the new rationalist philosophies, is to offer no arguments from reason but only from the Scripture — nor is there any attempt to make the Trinity of God reasonable. Pictet insists that the Trinity is a mystery which must be accepted on faith. Indeed, he denies the efforts of those who have tried to explain the mystery: the intellectual audacity of the scholastics, their "specious arguments" and "dangerous locutions," have only served to breed heresies.[48]

"Scripture," he notes, "names three to whom the divine nature is ascribed, specifically, the *Father*, the *Son*, and the *Holy Ghost*" — in the baptism of Christ, the great commission (Matt. 28:19) and the Pauline benediction (2 Cor. 13:14).[49] "Not only in the New Testament is mention made of these three together, but in the Old Testament also ... 'the Spirit of the Lord God is upon me (the Son), because the Lord hath anointed me (by his Spirit) to preach the gospel to the poor'" (Isaiah 61:1). Nor must we omit those passages in which the plurality of persons appears to be pointed out, such as, "Let us make man in our own image."[50] Thus, as Wendelin comments, "Throughout Scripture, there are three to whom the name of God, the properties of God and the work of God are ascribed: God the Father, God the Son, and God the Holy Spirit," and these three are distinct "in number, order, manner of working, proper names, and personal properties."[51]

2. **Definition over against fundamental objections.** Some argue that the conception of God as one is a complete view of God — to which Rijssen replies the concept of God as one *concipit completum quoad complementum essentiae, non personalitatis*

---

46. Trelcatius, *Schol. meth.*, I.iii (pp. 56-57).

47. Pictet, *Theol. chr.*, II.xiii.8.

48. Pictet, *Theol. chr.*, II.xiii.7; cf. Rijssen, *Summa theol.*, IV.xvi.

49. Pictet, *Theol. chr.*, II.xiii.1-2, citing but not quoting John 14:16; 1 Cor. 12:3; Gal. 4:6, and elaborating on the use of the names in Rev. 1:4-5. Cf. Rijssen, *Summa theol.*, IV.ix, controversia I, argumenta 1-2 (N.T.).

50. Pictet, *Theol. chr.*, II.xiii.3.

51. Wendelin, *Christianae theologiae libri duo*, I.ii.3 (1).

— the discussion of God as one attains a certain completeness in the discussion of the essence absolutely considered, but this does not amount to a complete view of God or, indeed, a complete view of the divine essence, which must also be considered, relatively or relationally, with regard to the divine persons.[52]

More serious are objections such as the claim that essential identity demands personal identity: "The divine essence is the Father; the divine essence is the Son; Ergo, the Son is the Father." The logic of the syllogism is fallacious, comments Rijssen, inasmuch as the subjects of both major and minor are particulars: it is not as if the divine essence, understood universally, can be called simply "Father," without further qualification of meaning.[53] Similarly, one could argue that the divine essence is incarnate, the Father as well as the Son has the divine essence, therefore the Father must be incarnate. Such arguments are fallacious — they are not logic but paralogism, given that essence and person (or one person and another person) are not identical absolutely or *simpliciter*.[54]

Yet there remains the problem, raised by antitrinitarians in both the late sixteenth and the seventeenth centuries, that a single essence, merely from the fact that it is single, cannot be three persons: to say that one is three implies a contradiction and, inasmuch as both essence and person indicate individual existence, there appears to be no rational way of holding to the doctrine of the Trinity. The objection is strengthened in some of the antitrinitarian writers by a reversion to the ancient problem of the terms *ousia* and *hypostasis*, which (even in the original Nicene anathemas) were understood as synonymous:

> neither *substance* nor *subsistence* can add anything to an utterly complete essence, and the word *person*, in its more recent use, means any individual thing gifted with intelligence, while *hypostasis* means not the thing itself but the essence of the thing in the abstract. *Hypostasis*, therefore, is clearly the same as essence, and in the passage cited above [Heb. 1:3] many translate it by the Latin word *essentia*. Therefore, just as God is an utterly simple essence, so he is an utterly simple subsistence.[55]

Furthermore,

> it is quite impossible for any entity to share its essence with anything else whatsoever, for it is by virtue of its essence that it is what it is, and is distinguished numerically from everything else.[56]

According to this logic, if the Son is identical in essence to the Father, he is either "no entity at all or the same entity as the Father."[57] Or, to make the point another

---

52. Rijssen, *Summa theol.*, IV.ix, cont. I, objectio 4 & resp; cf. Turretin, *Inst. theol. elencticae*, III.xxiii.1.

53. Rijssen, *Summa theol.*, IV.ix, obj. 6 & resp.

54. Zanchi, *De tribus Elohim*, pt. 2, V.vi.8 (col. 547).

55. Milton, *Christian Doctrine*, I.ii (in *Complete Prose Works*, VI, pp. 142-143).

56. Milton, *Christian Doctrine*, I.v (in *Complete Prose Works*, VI, p. 225).

57. Milton, *Christian Doctrine*, I.ii (in *Complete Prose Works*, VI, p. 225).

way, the fact that the Son is incarnate and the Father is not determines them to be of differing essences.

Such arguments were not unique to Milton and were answered by various writers from the early orthodox era onward. Ursinus, Beza, Zanchi, and other Reformed orthodox reply that the argument may carry for a finite essence, which cannot be an individual essence or substance and three persons at the same time, given that not only its distinct properties but also its subsistence as a "separate thing" (*res separatae*) give it its hypostatic character. Thus, Peter, Paul, and Timothy share in the essence of humanity and its essential properties, but they are not one human, inasmuch as they are three separate things. The divisibility of the essence "humanity" renders it impossible for there to be one human essence, in the strictest sense, as a single, unitary primary substance, and at the same three human persons: the common humanity of the three human persons does not indicate, as it must in God, a numerical unity of essence, only a generic unity. There is no genus "God."[58] The argument, however, does not apply to the infinite, simple, and individual essence of the Godhead: for here is a single essence or substance that cannot be separated or divided, but in which there are distinct incommunicable properties, three in number, that identify distinct, but not essentially separate hypostases.[59] Identity of essence in no way implies the removal of variations or distinctions. Thus, the one divine essence is incarnate, but only in one of its hypostases or persons.[60]

The orthodox argument was not in fact as simplistic as Milton and other seventeenth-century antitrinitarians appear to have assumed. The antitrinitarian claim was posed against the traditional orthodox view that Trinity or triunity did not involve a logical contradiction. It remained within the realm of logic to claim divine oneness and divine threeness, given that the divine oneness referred to essence and the threeness to person. If essence and person were equated, then the orthodox doctrine would amount to a claim that God is one in the same way that God is three, which would amount to a contradiction. But this, the orthodox counter, is precisely the limitation of the old metaphor of three persons, Peter, James, and John, having the same essence — if "essence" or "substance" refers to individual existence, then the statement is impossible, because, clearly, the individuality that Peter has cannot be communicated to or shared with James. This assumption, however, "is the constant fallacy that runs through all the arguments of the Socinians ... all that they urge against a triple subsistence of the divine nature is still from instances taken from created natures, and applied to the divine."[61] The fallacy involves an illegitimate transition from genus to genus, from one kind to another kind, concluding "because this holds

58. Venema, *Inst. theol.*, V (p. 137).

59. Beza, *Theses seu axiomata de Trinitate*, in *Tractationes*, I, p. 652; cf. Ursinus, *Commentary*, p. 138.

60. Zanchi, *De tribus Elohim*, V.vii.4 (col. 555).

61. South, *Doctrine of the Blessed Trinity Asserted*, in *Sermons*, II, p. 405.

true in things of this nature ... that therefore the same must be true in things that are of a clean different nature; which is a manifest paralogism."[62]

Similarly, it may be objected that when three things are one and the same, they must be the same as each other and in no way distinct: "a most simple essence cannot be the essence of three persons," given that the persons, as distinct and divided, remove the simplicity of the essence. Ursinus indicates that the argument would be correct in the case of an essence that would have to be divided or multiplied in order to produce multiple persons. In the Trinity, however, the three are distinct in one respect, that is, as persons, and the same in another respect, that is, as regards essence. The persons are united in one essence and yet are not the same as one another — or, more precisely against the argument, the claim "is false when understood of such an essence as that which is the same and entire in each single person."[63] The orthodox point is not merely that the divine essence is infinite in contrast to the finitude of created natures and that infinity accounts for the possibility of one essence being in three persons, but rather that, as seen from the differences between God and creatures — such as infinity, simplicity, and other divine attributes, not to mention the way in which all the attributes are predicated of God — the point concerning the Trinity is not irrational, but in fact, it is "agreeable even to the notions of bare reason to imagine, that the divine nature has a way of subsisting very different from the subsistence of any created being."[64]

So also, the objection that the distinction of the three persons from the essence constitutes a quaternity — namely, the three persons and the essence itself — and that therefore are three deities or three distinct things in God is fallacious because the essence is not distinct from the persons as a thing (res). Thus,

> there is in the Trinity *alius & alius*, another and another, but not *aliud & aliud*, another thing and another thing, as there is in Christ; the Father is another person from the Son, but yet there is the same nature and essence of them all. They differ not in their natures as three men or three Angels differ, for they differ so as one may be without the other; but now the Father is not without the Son, nor the Son without the Father, so that there is the same numerical Essence.[65]

The persons are not distinct *realiter*, as separate "things," from the divine essence, but "differ from it, and from each other, only in the mode of subsisting."[66]

Yet, insofar as each person is fully divine, there is a sense in which, considered as God, each person has the divine essence *a se ipso*. Accordingly, the Father, the Son, and the Holy Spirit are one in that they share the "perfections of the divine nature" and that the Son and the Spirit both "have the divine nature in the same sense in which the Father is said to have it."[67]

---

62. South, *Doctrine of the Blessed Trinity Asserted*, in *Sermons*, II, p. 405.

63. Ursinus, *Commentary*, p. 138; cf. Rijssen, *Summa theol.*, IV.xi, obj. 5 & resp.

64. South, *Doctrine of the Blessed Trinity Asserted*, in *Sermons*, II, p. 405.

65. Leigh, *Treatise*, II.xvi (p. 128).

66. Ursinus, *Commentary*, p. 138.

67. Ridgley, *Body of Divinity*, p. 117, cols. 1-2.

Inasmuch as they are said to be equal in power and glory, we may observe; that there are two expressions, which we often use, to set forth the deity of the Son and Spirit; sometimes we say that they are God, equal with the Father; at other times, that they have the same essential perfections. To which, it may be, some will reply, that if they are equal, they cannot be the same; or, on the other hand, if they are the same, they cannot be equal. For understanding what we mean by such-like expressions, let it be observed, that when we consider them as having the divine essence, or any of the perfections thereof, we do not choose to describe them as equal, but the same; we do not say that the wisdom, power, holiness, & e. of the Son and Spirit, are equal to the same perfections, as ascribed to the Father: but when we speak of them as distinct Persons, then we consider them as equal. The essential glory of the Father, Son, and Spirit, is the same; but their personal glory is equal; and in this sense we would be understood, when we say the Son and Holy Ghost are each of them God, or divine Persons, equal with the Father.[68]

The persons of the Trinity are thus distinct in number in the sense that their relations and the names which signify their relations — Father, Son, and Holy Spirit — are incommunicable. The personal properties of the Father, Son, and Holy Ghost, "paternity, or not being begotten; a being begotten; and a proceeding" are distinct internal works of the Trinity and proper, incommunicably, to each person individually. The eternal works of the Trinity, however, are indivisible, though the manner of execution relates to the order of the persons.[69] "These three persons are God; three in unity unconfusedly, and one in Trinity indivisibly."[70]

All men confess the divinity of the Father. That of the Son follows from his essential equality with the Father: his works are one with the Father (John 5:18) and Paul states expressly his divinity (Phil. 2:6 and Col. 2:9). Furthermore the divine names are given to Christ as are the divine attributes of eternity, omnipresence, omniscience, omnipotence (Rev. 1:17; Matt. 28:20) and the divine work of Creation and Redemption.[71]

The same arguments prove the divinity of the Holy Ghost: thus, the Holy Ghost's works are one with those of the Father and the Son; his divinity is expressly stated in Scripture, and he is revealed to have both divine attributes and a role in the work of creation and redemption.[72] Thus, in conclusion, there is a unity of divine essence, or as can be said, one divine *res*, yet there are three distinct persons:

And these three persons are one God, for although personally the Father be one; the Son be another; and the holy Ghost another person: yet Essentially the Father is not one thing, the Son another thing, and the holy Ghost another thing. The truth and

---

68. Ridgley, *Body of Divinity*, p. 117, cols. 1-2.
69. Trelcatius, *Schol. meth.*, I.iii (pp. 52-58).
70. Trelcatius, *Schol. meth.*, I.iii (p. 58).
71. Trelcatius, *Schol. meth.*, I.iii (pp. 58-59).
72. Trelcatius, *Schol. meth.*, I.iii (p. 59).

perfection of this both Unity and distinction, is seen in the knowledge of the Attributes or proprieties both of the Essence and the persons.[73]

4.2 Exegetical Issues and Trajectories: Reformation and Orthodoxy

A. The Trinitarian Exegesis of Scripture: Hermeneutical Assumptions

The Reformers and, subsequently, the Reformed orthodox appealed directly to specific texts in Scripture as teaching the doctrine of the Trinity directly — by presenting each of the three divine persons as God. These texts, such as Genesis 1:1-3, 26-27; 11:7; Psalm 33:6; Isaiah 6:3, 8; 61:1-3; 63:7-12; Haggai 2:4-5; Matthew 28:19; Luke 3:22; John 1:32-33; 3:34; 14:16-17, 26; 15:26; Galatians 4:4-6; 2 Thessalonians 2:13-16; 1 Peter 1:2; and 1 John 5:7, were typically referenced in the basic expositions and definitions of the doctrine of the Trinity as explicit biblical statements of the three persons in the one God. Interpretation of these texts, however, did not completely present the biblical foundation for the Trinity any more than the texts identifying God specifically as eternal or everlasting offered the complete ground for the doctrine of divine eternity: the Reformers and the orthodox both assumed that their interpretive method indicated use not only of texts that provide direct statement of a doctrine but also texts that, taken together or juxtaposed with one another, permit a conclusion to be drawn. This is only to say that, in examining the Reformers' and, later, the Reformed orthodox exegesis of specifically trinitarian texts, we have not exhausted their biblical argumentation and that the biblical demonstration of the doctrine of the Trinity is complete only after other texts that individually or together argue the divinity and personality of the Son (and still others, the divinity and personality of the Spirit) have been presented.

In addition, the Reformers, as later the orthodox, assumed a hermeneutic of movement from shadow and promise in the Old Testament to fulfilment in the New, and accordingly held a partial revelation of the Trinity in the Old Testament, a complete revelation in the New.[74] This hermeneutical assumption yielded an entire class of texts beyond what might be called the standard series of juxtapositions for the sake of drawing conclusions. Each of these additional sets of texts consisted in a text or texts from the Old Testament in which God was unmistakably referenced, particularly texts in which God was identified as Jehovah that was also cited in the New Testament with specific reference to one of the divine persons, either the Son or the Spirit. The necessary conclusion was that Scripture, in its larger expanse, explicitly identified either the Son or the Spirit as Jehovah, and therefore as the one God, demanding a trinitarian reading. The exegetical argumentation, therefore, spans both the entire Bible and the entire *locus*.[75]

---

73. Trelcatius, *Schol. meth.*, I.iii (p. 60).

74. Amyraut et al., *Syntagma thesium theologicarum*, I.xv.3, 24-26.

75. In what follows, I have been selective, citing only a few of the major arguments for the Trinity, leaving aside numerous texts cited by both orthodox and Socinian. I also reserve discussion of texts related to the divinity and personhood of the Son and the Spirit for later chapters.

That this pattern of argument had been relatively successful in the exegetical establishment of trinitarian doctrine can be inferred from the direct attack on it by the Socinians. Nye thus gathered his antitrinitarian arguments based on the Old Testament into two divisions — namely, an examination either of those texts that were used singly or directly to argue the doctrine of the Trinity or the divinity of the Son or the Spirit, and those texts that "perhaps would not, if alone considered, prove the Orthodox Doctrine; but do it sufficiently when compared *with*, and interpreted *by* some Texts of the New Testament."[76] Of course, it was Nye's intention to deny the interpretations, or at very least, to show them either very obscure or highly figurative — on the ground that a doctrine so supposedly important as the Trinity ought to appear by direct statement or evident logic from the texts. In addition, the Jews never concluded a Trinity, despite their detailed reading of the Old Testament — and various theologians of the church, whether in the era of the fathers, in the Middle Ages, or in the sixteenth and seventeenth centuries, have occasionally admitted that the doctrine of the Trinity belongs to the New Testament only.[77] This latter datum is sufficient for the beginning of Nye's argument, given the orthodox insistence on the presence of the doctrine in the Old Testament.

B. Exegetical Issues and Trajectories: Old Testament

1. Trinity in the Old Testament: issues in debate in the sixteenth and seventeenth centuries. The Reformed orthodox insisted — against the Socinians — that plurality of persons is proved not only from the New but also from the Old Testament.[78] On this point, their assumptions were fully in accord with the teachings of all centuries of Christianity, from the patristic period and the Middle Ages through the Reformation. In particular, the Reformed orthodox concern to identify a trinitarian faith in the Old Testament echoes the traditional assumption, emphasized by early Reformed tradition, of the unity of the faith and of the promise of salvation from the beginnings of the biblical narrative, an assumption that included the claim that fundamental teachings of Christianity were available to the patriarchs.[79]

The continuity with Reformation-era exegesis, moreover, is quite striking, as are the various trajectories, from the more literal, less christological approach of Calvin to the more allegorical and typological approach of other Reformed exegetes, like Vermigli and Musculus: the trajectories continue into the era of orthodoxy, often with the added feature of a polemic against those antitrinitarians who point to the Old Testament as a disproof of the doctrine or against the Remonstrants, who denied that the doctrine was fundamental or had any practical significance. What becomes apparent in tracing out some of these lines of interpretation is that the Reformed of the sixteenth and seventeenth centuries did not, in a simplistic and rigidly eisegetical manner, impose

---

76. Nye, *Brief History*, p. 42.
77. Nye, *Brief History*, pp. 67-68.
78. Cf. Turretin, *Inst. theol. elenctica*, III.xxvi.
79. Thus, Bullinger, *Old Faith*, pp. 13-14, 24-27, citing Eusebius, *Ecclesiastical History*, I.iv.

dogmatic categories on a set list of texts. Rather, they worked through a series of traditionally identified texts, with varied results — recognizing with consistency that the whole of Scripture, both Old and New Testament, spoke to the fundamental articles of the faith, notably, in this instance to the doctrine of the Trinity, but often arguing different exegetical nuances and sometimes widely differing results of particular texts, despite the intensity of the polemic. The polemical issue was nicely summarized by Turretin:

> From what was previously indicated by us concerning the necessity of this doctrine as a fundamental article, it might be satisfactorily gathered that it was revealed and known under the Old Testament, since fundamentals are the same among all believers, and cannot be either augmented or diminished: but the Socinians, in order to destroy faith in this mystery on whatever ground, typically argue that it is a new doctrine invented after the time of Christ and the apostles, a point mimicked by the Arminians. It is therefore necessary to assert our faith in the mystery against both of these adversaries, not only from the New, but also from the Old Testament.[80]

The difficulty of finding references to the Trinity of God in the Old Testament was explained by the orthodox much as they explained the movement from unwritten to written Word and the movement from "promise" in the Old Testament to "fulfillment" in the New: "in the Old Testament the Doctrine of the Trinity of persons in the unity of the God head was more obscurely taught: but in the New Testament we are clearly and most comfortably assured, that the Father, Son, and holy Ghost do sweetly conspire to perfect the Salvation of the Faithfull, and confirme unto them the promises of the Covenant."[81] In addition, the orthodox assumed, in all of the divine work of revelation, the point noted above in our preliminary discussion of the order of system: the fundamental revealed truth of God is his unity or oneness both in being and in governance. Thus, Owen could argue:

> From the foundation of the world, the principal revelation that God made of himself was in the oneness of his nature and his monarchy over all. And herein the person of the Father was immediately represented with his power and authority; for he is the fountain and original of the Deity, the other persons as their subsistence being of him: only, he did withal give out promises concerning the peculiar exhibition of the Son in the flesh in an appointed season, as also of the Holy Spirit, to be given by him in an especial manner.[82]

In the work of the seventeenth-century exegetes and theologians, moreover, the identification and explication of these traditional trinitarian passages — like the creation narrative of Genesis 1 — was not merely a matter of citing the text into a dogmatic system. Proofs of the Trinity taken by the orthodox from the Old Testament and other Jewish sources were not a set of simple or fideistic readings of text to conform

---

80. Turretin, *Inst. theol. elencticae*, III.xxvi.1.
81. John Ball, *A Treatise of the Covenant of Grace* (London, 1645), II.i (p. 201).
82. Owen, *ΠΝΕΥΜΑΤΟΛΟΓΙΑ*, in *Works*, III, p. 43.

to a prior opinion: on the first level, these interpretations are all accomplished within the bounds of orthodox hermeneutic, usually by the method of interpreting Scripture by means of Scripture — and in a large number of instances by the conference of Old Testament with New Testament. There is an often subtle hermeneutic exercised in the light both of the best textual tools then available and of a study of traditionary materials, including Hebraica — and there was also reflection on texts in view of various traditionary hermeneutical understandings, including the movement from prophecy to fulfilment and the related double literal sense associated with Nicholas of Lyra. On the second and more exegetically detailed level we have such works as Pierre Allix's *Judgment of the Ancient Jewish Church Against the Unitarians* and, in the late orthodox era, Gill's treatise on the Trinity. The argument of Allix's and Gill's treatises was of importance to orthodoxy in view of the Socinian contention that the idea of a Trinity in God was inimical to biblical monotheism and therefore to the theological context of the gospel.

2. Divine threeness in the exegesis the Pentateuch and the historical books. In the story of creation (Genesis 1:1-3, 26-27), the Reformed note, the plural noun *Elohim* is used of the one God (Gen. 1:1), and God speaks of himself in the plural: "*Faciamus hominem ad imaginem nostram*" (Gen. 1:26). Yet, whether in the era of the Reformation or that of orthodoxy, the Reformed are less than unanimous concerning the implication of the text. Thus, according to Bullinger, the "*bara Elohim*" of Genesis 1:1 might be translated "*creavit Dii*" as a sign of the oneness and plurality of God.[83] Calvin, by way of contrast, comments that although "the inference is drawn" from the conjunction of the plural noun with the singular verb, "that the three Persons of the Godhead are here noted," the direct use of the text as an argument for the doctrine of the Trinity "appears to me to have little solidity."[84]

> Readers [ought] to beware of violent glosses of this kind. They think that they have testimony against the Arians, to prove the Deity of the Son and of the Spirit, but in the meantime they involve themselves in the error of Sabellius, because Moses afterwards subjoins that the Elohim had spoken, and that the Spirit of the Elohim rested upon the waters. If we suppose three persons to be here denoted, there will be no distinction between them. For it will follow, both that the Son is begotten by himself, and that the Spirit is not of the Father, but of himself. For me it is sufficient that the plural number expresses those powers which God exercised in creating the world. Moreover I acknowledge that the Scripture, although it recites many powers of the Godhead, yet always recalls us to the Father, and his Word, and spirit, as we shall shortly see. But those absurdities, to which I have alluded, forbid us with subtlety to distort what Moses simply declares concerning God himself, by applying it to the separate Persons of the Godhead.[85]

---

83. Bullinger, *Decades*, IV.iii (III, p. 135).
84. Calvin, *Commentary on Genesis*, 1:1 (*CTS Genesis*, I, pp. 70-71).
85. Calvin, *Commentary on Genesis*, 1:1 (*CTS Genesis*, I, p. 71).

Nonetheless, Calvin does view the fact of creation by means of the Word implied by God's speaking in Genesis 1 and confirmed by the text of John 1:1-3 — and he can conclude from Genesis 1:3 that "since ... by the Word of God things which were not came suddenly into being, we ought ... to infer the eternity of His essence." Thus, too, "the Apostles rightly prove the Deity of Christ from hence, that since he is the Word of God, all things have been created by him." Servetus is therefore in error when he "imagines a new quality in God when he begins to speak."[86]

Among the early orthodox exegetes, Ainsworth finds the trinitarian reference in Genesis 1 not by a simple and rather non-exegetical statement that the God who speaks his Word and whose Spirit hovers on the face of the waters must be a Trinity or by a simple reference to the plural form of Elohim and the phrase "Let us make man." This exegetical conclusion is reinforced through a study of Hebraica: Ainsworth could note that in "the Chaldee paraphrase called *Jerusalemy*", the first verse of the chapter had been rendered, "In wisdom...." "So," Ainsworth continues,

> sundry Hebrews apply this mystically to *the wisdom of God, whereby the world was created, as it is written, the Lord by wisdom, founded the earth*, Prov. 3:19. *and, in wisdom hast thou made them all*, Ps. 104:24. R. Menachem on Gen.1. Many Christian writers also, apply it unto Christ, the *wisdom of God by whom he made the world*, 1 Cor. 1:24; Heb. 1:2; Prov. 8:27-30.[87]

Here, by way of the biblical hypostatization of Wisdom, the text of the paraphrase, rabbinic argument, and an oblique reference, probably to the fathers, Ainsworth finds ground in the Hebrew text and the Hebrew language for the beginning of his trinitarian argument. Clearly God does not here speak of himself and his angels, since the image indicated is the image of God himself, and neither are angels God nor are men created in the image of angels.[88] This argument concerning the plurality of Elohim became of increasing importance to the trinitarian exegesis of the Old Testament and the related identification of Trinity as a fundamental doctrine of the faith, given the seventeenth-century Socinian denial of any plural references to the Godhead anywhere in the Bible.[89]

The same truth is clearly manifest in the references to God and his work throughout Genesis, chapter 1: following out a traditional pattern of exegesis found earlier in Zanchi's vast *De tribus Elohim*, Rijssen comments that the Trinity is demonstrated "from the history of creation" where Moses distinctly speaks of Elohim creating, the Spirit of Elohim moving on the waters, and the Word producing all things. This interpretation of the text cannot simply be asserted; it must be argued because "our adversaries do not deny that Elohim is God," rather they deny the genuine significance of the plural noun and its singular verb. This is not merely the plural *honoris causa*

---

86. Calvin, *Commentary on Genesis*, 1:3 (*CTS Genesis*, I, p. 75).

87. Ainsworth, *Annotations upon Genesis*, Gen. 1:27 in loc.; cf. Christopher Cartwright, *Electa thargumico-rabbinica; sive Annotationes in Genesin* (London, 1648), p. 3, citing the Jerusalem Targum.

88. Rijssen, *Summa theol.*, IV.ix, controversia I, argumenta 1-2 (O.T.).

89. Nye, *Brief History of the Unitarians*, p. 19.

employed by kings and princes — for we have no further examples of this manner of speech in relation to God. Rijssen also argues that the name of God, Jehovah, when juxtaposed with other designations of God, implies a distinction that is personal and not essential.[90] By Spirit, moreover, "it is impossible to understand air or wind, since no such thing had yet been created, and no separate things had been made"; nor can Spirit here (Gen. 1:2) mean an angel, inasmuch as God uses no intermediaries in creation; nor is it the power or efficacy of God that brings about the life and fruitfulness of the created order, since this nurturing of the world order is distinguished from the Spirit as an effect from its cause or an action from its foundation. Thus, by Spirit or Spirit of Elohim, we understand a person or individual (suppositum) who concurs in the work of the God, Elohim.[91]

Of course, the concept of divine speech ("the Lord said"), uttered "objectively and terminatively" for the production of creatures, indicates the effective command of God in creation — and not directly and precisely the second person of the Trinity. Here, however, the second person, the eternal Word, understood ad intra et originaliter, is the foundation or principium quod of the command. Even so, when Scripture states explicitly that it is the "Word of the Lord" (Verbum Jehovae) by which the heavens were formed, the text implies a distinction between Jehovah, the Word, and the Spirit.[92]

The point is quite easily made that this argument is not a matter of dogmatic proof-texting,[93] but instead a direct use of the then "assured result" of exegesis, as presented by a grammatical-critical and even text-critical but not yet historical-critical method. Poole and other exegetes of the day continued, like the fathers, the medieval doctors, and the Reformers, to find allusions to the Trinity in the first chapter of Genesis: the "Spirit of God" that moved on the face of the waters (Gen. 1:2) could not have been "the wind, which was not yet created, as is manifest, because the air, the matter or substance of it, was not yet produced; but the Third Person of the glorious Trinity, called the Holy Ghost, to whom the work of creation is attributed, Job xxvi.13, as it is ascribed to the Second Person, the Son, John 1:3; Col. 1:16, 17; Heb. 1:3; and to the First Person, the Father, everywhere."[94] Similarly, the creation by means of spoken word (v. 3), elicits the comment,

> He commanded, not by such a word or speech as we use, which agreeth not with the spiritual nature of God; but either by an act of his powerful will, called *the word of his power*, Heb. 1:3; or, by his substantial Word, his son, *by whom he made the worlds*, Heb. 1:2; Ps. 33:6, who is called *The Word*, partly, if not principally, for this reason, John 1:1-3, 10.[95]

---

90. Rijssen, *Summa theol.*, IV.ix, controversia I, argumenta 1-2 (O.T.); cf. Amyraut, *De mysterio trinitatis*, IV, p. 164 ; Downame, *Summe*, i (p. 32).

91. Rijssen, *Summa theol.*, IV.ix, controversia I, argumentum 3.

92. Rijssen, *Summa theol.*, IV.ix, controversia I, argumentum 3; similarly Zanchi, *De tribus Elohim*, pt. I, II.i.2 (col. 25); Bucanus, *Institutions*, i (pp. 8-9); Leigh, *Treatise*, II.xvi (pp. 130-131).

93. Cf. the discussion of *dicta probantia* in PRRD, II, 7.5 (B).

94. Poole, *Commentary*, Gen. 1:2 in loc. (I, p. 2).

95. Poole, *Commentary*, Gen, 1:2 in loc. (I, p. 2).

If Calvin hesitated to infer a trinitarian reading from the *Elohim* of Genesis 1:1, he readily affirmed the trinitarian implications of Genesis 1:26, "Let us make man in our own image." "Christians," he wrote,

> properly contend, from this testimony, that there exists a plurality of Persons in the Godhead. God summons no foreign counselor; hence we infer that he finds within himself something distinct; as, in truth, his eternal wisdom and power reside within him.[96]

As ought to be expected, the exegetical investigation of Genesis 1:26 also continued to yield up a trinitarian consideration in the era of Reformed orthodoxy, granting what the exegetes of the day felt to be the insuperable textual obstacles to alternative interpretations, such as a plural of respect or a heavenly council of other creative powers with God, as advanced by various antitrinitarians and, as the seventeenth century faded into the eighteenth, by the early proponents of a historical method. Thus, Poole:

> The plurals *us* and *our* afford an evident proof of a plurality of persons in the Godhead. It is plain from many other texts, as well as from the nature and reason of the thing, that God alone is man's Creator: the angels rejoiced at the work of creation, but only God wrought it, Job 38:4-7. And it is no less plain from this text, and from divers other places, that man had more creators than one person: see Job 35:10; John 1:2-3, etc.; Heb. 1:3. And as other texts assure us that there is but one God, so this shows that there are more persons in the Godhead; nor can the seeming contradiction of one and more being in the Godhead be otherwise reconciled, than by acknowledging a plurality of persons in the unity of essence.[97]

Poole also noted that the use of the plural verb ought not to be interpreted, as some of the antitrinitarians of the era alleged, as merely a grammatical form of deference — such usage is foreign to Scripture:

> It is pretended that God here speaks after the manner of princes, in the plural number, who used to say, *We will and require,* or, *it is our pleasure.* But this is only the invention and practice of latter times, and no way agreeable to the simplicity, either of the first ages of the world, or of the Hebrew style. The kings of Israel used to speak of themselves in the singular number, 2 Sam. 3:28; 1 Chron. 21:17; 29:14; 2 Chron. 2:6. And so did the eastern monarchs too, yea, even in their decrees and orders, which now run in the plural number, as Ezra 6:8 (Darius) *make a decree;* Ezra 7:21, *even Artaxerxes the king, do make a decree.* Nor do I remember one example in Scripture to the contrary.[98]

---

96. Calvin, *Commentary on Genesis,* 1:26 (CTS *Genesis,* I, pp. 92-93); cf. Belgic Confession, IX (in Schaff, *Creeds,* III, pp. 390-391).

97. Poole, *Commentary,* Gen. 1:26 in loc. (I, p. 4); similarly, Diodati, *Pious and Learned Annotations,* Gen. 1:26 in loc.; Trapp, *Commentary,* Gen. 1:27 in loc. (I, p. 10); Ainsworth, *Annotations upon Genesis,* Gen. 1:26 in loc.

98. Poole, *Commentary,* Gen. 1:26 in loc. (I, p. 4).

Similarly, the text from the narrative of the tower of Babel, "let us go down, and there confound their language" (Gen. 11:7), is also a traditional trinitarian text, although as Calvin indicates, was understood in rabbinic exegesis as God calling on the angelic host:

> The Jews think that he addresses himself to the angels. But since no mention is made of the angels, and God places those to whom he speaks in the same rank with himself, this exposition is harsh, and deservedly rejected. This passage rather answers to the former, which occurs in the account of man's creation, when the Lord said, "Let us make man after our image." For God aptly and wisely opposes his own eternal wisdom and power to this great multitude; as if he had said, that he had no need of foreign auxiliaries, but possessed within himself what would suffice for their destruction. Wherefore, this passage is not improperly adduced in proof that Three Persons subsist in One Essence of Deity.[99]

Ainsworth, in the early orthodox era, understood the text of Genesis 11:7 in precisely the same way, relating its plural "let us go down" to the plural in Genesis 1:26, "let us make man," commenting, "the holy Trinity here determineth ... against the former determination of vain men."[100]

Of the threefold blessing in Numbers 6:24-26 — "The Lord bless you and keep you; the Lord make his face to shine upon you, and be gracious unto you; the Lord lift up his countenance upon you and give you peace" — Turretin comments "this threefold repetition can be employed for no other purpose than to designate the three persons from whom, as from the sole true Jehovah, that blessing derives."[101] The argument remains a significant element of orthodox exegesis long into the eighteenth century, as evidenced by Klinkenberg's comment that the Jews themselves did not understand the "mystery" enclosed in the text, namely, the trinitarian reference to God the Father "as the first cause of all grace," the Son and Mediator "as the cause of reconciliation," and the Holy Spirit as "the Comforter."[102]

The first two verses of "the last words of David" in 2 Samuel 23:2-3 occupy a significant place in the trinitarian exegetical tradition inasmuch as in very short order they refer to "the Spirit of the Lord," "the God of Israel," and "the Rock of Israel" and include the juxtaposition "the Spirit of the Lord spake by me, and his word was in my tongue" — although not all of the orthodox theologians and exegetes of the post-Reformation era chose to develop the doctrine at this point. On the one hand, the entirety of Trapp's brief annotation is devoted to the trinitarian interpretation: "the Spirit of the Lord spake by me" he paraphrases as a statement of David that "Both

---

99. Calvin, *Commentary on Genesis*, 11:7 (CTS *Genesis*, I, p. 331).

100. Ainsworth, *Annotation on the Pentateuch*, Gen. 11:7 in loc.; similarly, Diodati, *Pious and Learned Annotation*, Gen. 48:16 in loc.; Poole, *Commentary*, Gen. 11:7 in loc. (I, p. 30).

101. Turretin, *Inst. theol. elencticae*, III.xxvi.1; cf. Ainsworth, *Pentateuch*, Num. 6:24 in loc., for a similar statement, exegetically argued, with rabbinic citation; also Trapp, *Commentary*, I, p. 260. Calvin makes no trinitarian reference at this point: see *Harmony of the Four Last Books*, Numb. 6:24-26 (CTS *Harmony*, II, pp. 246-247).

102. Klinkenberg, *Bijbel verklaerd*, III, Num. 6:24-26 in loc.

here and in other psalms composed by me; I had from the Holy Ghost both matter and words." He continues, "*The God of Israel.*] God the Father. *The Rock of Israel.*] God the Son, who is one with the Father and the Holy Spirit.[103] Some writers also understand the juxtaposition of the "Spirit" with the "word" as indicating both Spirit and Son.[104] On the other side of the argument, both the *Westminster Annotations* and Poole omitted explicit reference to the doctrine of the Trinity, but identified the "Spirit of the Lord" as the Holy Spirit, and emphasized the messianic implication of the phrase "Rock of Israel."[105] Klinkenberg, probably echoing the *Dutch Annotations*, similarly notes the "Spirit of the Lord" in verse 2 and comments at length on the messianic meaning of the third verse.[106] Henry points, without passing judgment, to the exegetical tradition: "some think," he writes, that this text "is an intimation of the Trinity of persons in the Godhead," while Diodati entirely omits trinitarian reference.[107]

3. Trinity in the Writings. A text often cited in the tradition as a trinitarian point of reference on the Old Testament is Psalm 33:6, "By the word of the Lord were the heavens made; and all the host of them by the breath [or spirit] of his mouth." This is a difficult text, offering a juxtaposition of word and Spirit similar to that encountered in 2 Sam 23:2 and subject to varied readings among the Reformers and the orthodox and virtually never used as a primary text in debate with the Socinians. Bullinger reads it in relation to Psalm 110:1, "the Lord said unto my Lord, Sit thou at my right hand...," as certain testimony to the trinitarian faith of the Old Testament and, therefore, to the antiquity of the Christian religion.[108] The problem of interpretation is seen immediately in Calvin's reading. Creation of the heavens by the word of God "magnifies" the power of God; but, Calvin continues, it is proper here "to infer ... that the world was made by God's eternal Word, his only begotten Son." The next clause, Calvin continues, was used "by the ancients" as a "proof of the eternal Deity of the Holy Spirit against the Sabellians"; but since "breath of his mouth" most probably indicates "effective speech," this text ought not to be pressed into easy service against heresy. It is sufficient to see here a testimony to "the eternal Deity of Christ."[109] Musculus accepts the text directly and without qualification.[110]

Among the seventeenth-century writers, Dickson finds no trinitarian reference in Psalm 33:6: creation by "the word of the Lord" indicates the "omnipotence and wisdom of God in creating the world," and the phrase "breath of his mouth" manifests

---

103. Trapp, *Commentary*, in loc. (I, p. 533). N.B., the single square bracket is a fairly typical seventeenth-century typographical practice, used to separate the cited biblical text from the comment on it.

104. Amyraut, *De mysterio trinitatis*, IV, p. 230.

105. *Westminster Annotations*, in loc.; Poole, *Commentary*, in loc.

106. Klinkenberg, *Bijbel verklaerd*, VI, 2 Sam. 23:1-2 in loc.; cf. *Dutch Annotations*, in loc.

107. Henry, *Exposition*, in loc.; Diodati, *Pious and Learned Annotations*, in loc.

108. Bullinger, *Old Faith*, pp. 53, 57.

109. Calvin, *Commentary upon the Psalms*, 33:6 (CTS *Psalms*, I, p. 543).

110. Musculus, *Commonplaces*, I (p. 16, col. 2).

the ease of creation and governance.[111] Poole rather nicely indicates all of the options: the "word of the Lord," he notes, can mean either "the hypostatical Word," which is identified in precisely this way in John 1:1 as the agent of creation — or, he adds, the phrase can simply mean "the will or command" of God, as would appear from the fourth and ninth verses of the Psalm. As for the phrase, "the breath of his mouth," it can be taken as indicating the Holy Spirit, as in Job 33:4 — or it may be a parallelism, indicating the creative word of God, as in Isaiah 11:4 and 2 Thessalonians 2:8.[112] Henry and Klinkenberg follow the full trinitarian reading of the text — as, among the dogmaticians, do Amyraut, Turretin, Witsius, Mastricht, and Venema, albeit without extensive comment.[113] Similar arguments are found in the orthodox discussions of Proverbs 8, in which Wisdom, hypostatized, speaks: this is the "Son of God ... the Fathers subsisting wisdom."[114]

4. Trinity in the prophetic books. The prophetic books, like the Psalter, provided the precritical exegete with a harvest of materials for arguing various aspects of trinitarian doctrine, given the parallelisms in their God language, the repetition of divine names and attributes in various formulae, their messianic content and, in particular, either their frequent identification of God as Redeemer or their attribution of holy names and divine attributes to the Messiah or Christ. The *triasagion*, "*Sanctus, Sanctus, Sanctus Jehova Exereituum*" of Isaiah 6:3, like the threefold benedictions of Numbers 6:24-26, also points toward the Trinity.[115] Calvin, echoed by many later Reformed exegetes, had indicated that this text has been used by "the ancients" in order to argue "three persons in one essence of the Godhead" — and that he himself had "no doubt that "the angels here describe one God in three persons" — but that better arguments ought to be used against the heretics, given that the number "three" often indicated perfection in Scripture.[116] The trinitarian conclusion, although admittedly the result of a traditionary explanation, was not argued absolutely by the later Reformed. Poole, for one, argued two possible meanings of the text — the repetition of "Holy" indicating "either" the "Trinity of persons united in the divine essence" or the eminence of the divine holiness, "such repetitions being very frequent in Scripture, for the greater assurance of the thing."[117]

Certain of the messianic passages in the Prophets demand for their interpretation a plurality of persons in the Godhead: this is particularly the case with Isaiah 61:1-2,

---

111. Dickson, *Explication of the Psalms*, 33:6 (I, p. 172).

112. Poole, *Commentary*, in loc.; so also Trapp, *Commentary*, in loc. (II, p. 504).

113. Henry, *Exposition*, Ps. 33:6 in loc.; Klinkenberg, *Bijbel verklaerd*, X, in loc.; Amyraut, *De mysterio trinitatis*, IV, pp. 231-232; Turretin, *Inst. theol. elencticae*, III.xxvi.6, 8; Witsius, *Exercitationes*, VI.vi; Mastricht, *Theoretico-practica theol.*, II.xxiv.12; Venema, *Inst. theol.*, IX (p. 211).

114. Cf. Diodati, *Pious and Learned Annotations*, Prov. 8:15 in loc.; Amyraut, *De mysterio trinitatis*, IV, pp. 184-186; and note Poole, *Commentary*, Prov. 8:1 in loc., who registers at length the debate among the orthodox themselves over whether wisdom here indicates the divine attribute or the second Person of the Trinity.

115. Rijssen, *Summa theol.*, IV.ix, argumentum 6 (O.T.).

116. Calvin, *Commentary on Isaiah*, 6:3 (CTS Isaiah, I, p. 205) Poole, *Commentary*, in loc.

117. Poole, *Commentary*, Isaiah 6:3 in loc. (II, p. 337).

"The Spirit of the Lord is upon me; because the Lord hath anointed me to the evangelization of the meek." When approaching Isaiah 61:1-2, Calvin both knows and adopts the Lyra-like reading of the text. In addition, as should be expected given his exegetical method, Calvin does not discuss the Trinity in a doctrinal form in his exegesis of this text. He begins his exposition by differing with those commentators who "limit" the application of the text to Christ, as if Christ alone is the speaker and the text cannot be understood with reference to the anointing of the Spirit that belongs to all of the prophets. Of course, in Luke 4:18, Christ does apply the passage to himself, as the one anointed by God to prophetic office — but the chapter, Calvin writes, ought to be understood as referring to Christ as "the Head of the prophets," occupying "first place," but also to Isaiah and the other prophets who also make known the benefits of Christ. Still, the text does refer to the Holy Spirit as the one by whom Christ and the prophets are anointed and identify the Spirit as the "Spirit of God," and provide Calvin with a reference to the relationship of the Spirit to the work of Christ.[118]

The double literal sense continues to be the model in later Reformed exegetes. Poole, for example, indicates that the phrase "the Spirit of the Lord is upon me" serves to identify the transition from the preceding chapter: "that which is foretold and promised in the foregoing chapter" is now being "accomplished." The "Spirit of the Lord" signifies, therefore, either the Holy Spirit or, specifically, the "spirit" or "gift of prophecy." This sense of the phrase and of its connection with the preceding passage yields a double conclusion: "though the prophet may speak this of himself in person, yet that it is principally understood of Christ is evident, because he applies this text unto himself, Luke 4:18."[119]

The trinitarian conclusion, as Turretin argues, rests on a series of interrelated points: first, Christ himself indicates, Luke 4:21, that Isaiah 61:1-2 refers to him. But the work identified as messianic by Isaiah is consistently described as a divine work and divine attributes are consistently ascribed to the Messiah. Thus, the Messiah must be understood as divine (as well as human), and his divinity, in such passages as this, is distinguished from the Lord and the Spirit of the Lord by whom he is anointed.[120]

Many sixteenth- and seventeenth-century theologians and exegetes argue that the three persons of the Trinity appear in the accomplishment of the work of salvation, in the liberation of Israel out of Egypt, particularly as it is clarified and interpreted in Isaiah, chapter 63. Calvin's exegesis of Isaiah 63:7-12, like so many of his readings of the biblical text, does not offer any gathered or inferred dogmatic conclusions, such as one would find in a formal *locus* drawn out of the text — but it clearly provides much of the basis for such a doctrinal gathering. With reference to the phrase in verse 9, "and the Angel of his presence saved them," Calvin comments "I have not doubt that the office of Saviour is ascribed to Christ, as we know that he was the angel of

118. Calvin, *Commentary on Isaiah*, 61:1 in loc. (CTS *Isaiah*, IV, p. 303).

119. Poole, *Commentary*, Isa. 61:1-2 in loc. (II, p. 472); cf. Klinkenberg, *Bijbel verklaerd*, XIII, in loc.

120. Turretin, *Inst. theol. elencticae*, III.xxvi.10; cf. Amyraut, *De mysterio trinitatis*, IV, pp. 235-237; Diodati, *Pious and Learned Annotations*, in loc.

the highest rank." Nor does Calvin have any doubt that the Holy Spirit referenced in verse 10 is the third person of the Trinity.[121]

Among the orthodox, the exegesis of the text offers an example of the collation of texts for the sake of drawing conclusions: Isaiah 63:7ff. collated with Exodus 3:2. That the *Angelus Jehovae* first mentioned in Exodus 3:2, "is the uncreated angel (*angelum increatum*) the Son of God himself (*ipsum Dei Filium*) is clearly shown from his description and from the various attributes that are given to him — which are such that they may only belong to God."[122] This conclusion follows necessarily when the verses in Exodus are conferred with Isaiah 63:7, 8, 9ff: "I will mention the loving-kindness of the Lord.... For he said, Surely they are my people ... he was their Savior ... the Angel of his presence saved them according to his love ... but they rebelled, and vexed his Holy Spirit." Given that Isaiah 63:11-12 refers to the miracle at the Red Sea, the hermeneutical "conference" of the passages in Isaiah and Exodus arises out of the very fabric of the older exegesis.[123] Rijssen concludes that in this text, three distinct persons are indicated, "Jehovah, the Angel of his presence, and the Holy Spirit," and that three distinct operations are attributed to them — to Jehovah, mercy or loving-kindness toward his people; to the angel of his presence, the work of redemption; and to the Holy Spirit, anger and contention against the people.[124]

Similarly, the text of Haggai 2:4-5 — "I am with you, saith the Lord of hosts; according to the Word that I have covenanted with you, so my Spirit remains among you" — virtually begs for a prophetic reading, looking toward the New Testament for the fulfillment of the covenant in the Word incarnate and for the gift of the Spirit as the Comforter who remains with the people of God. This is precisely the reading found in Calvin's commentary on Haggai. Calvin does not note specifically the doctrine of the Trinity — probably given his reluctance to develop *loci communes* in the course of his commentaries — but he does offer all of the trinitarian elements that later Reformed exegetes would draw out into their doctrinal systems. God promises his people that his Spirit would be among them and strengthen them, and he covenants with his people to be their redeemer, the fullness of which "was at length made known by the coming of Christ."[125]

The Reformed orthodox exhibit two patterns of interpretation of Haggai 2:4-5. Diodati, for one, maintains an approach very similar to Calvin, noting God, Christ, and the Spirit in his strongly covenantal reading of the text.[126] Others, however, draw

121. Calvin, *Commentary on Isaiah*, 63:9 (CTS *Isaiah*, I, pp. 348-349).

122. Rijssen, *Summa theol.*, IV.ix, controversia I, argumentum 4 (O.T.); cf. Klinkenberg, *Bijbel verklaerd*, XIII, Isa. 63:8 in loc.; Downame, *Summe*, i (p. 32).

123. Cf. Calvin, *Commentary on Isaiah*, 63:9-11 (CTS *Isaiah*, IV, pp. 348-351); Poole, *Commentary*, in loc. (II, p. 478); Trapp, *Commentary*, in loc. (III, p. 434); Henry, *Exposition*, in loc.; cf. Diodati, *Pious and Learned Annotations*, in loc.

124. Rijssen, *Summa theol.*, IV.ix; cf. Poole, *Commentary*, II, p. 478 and Henry, *Exposition*, II, pp. 864-865.

125. Calvin, *Commentaries on Haggai*, 2:1-5 (CTS *Haggai*, pp. 353-354).

126. Diodati, *Pious and Learned Annotations*, Hag. 2:4-5, in loc.

out the full dogmatic implication. According to several of the seventeenth-century exegetes and theologians, the doctrine of the Trinity necessarily results from the recognition that the text distinguishes the "Lord of Hosts," the covenanting "Word," and the "Spirit" in the work of salvation and, moreover, distinguishes them according to their respective work.[127] Trapp, following Tremellius, reads verse 5 as "With the Word, in and for whom I covenanted with you," and concludes "so it is a gracious promise that the whole Trinity will be with them.... Haggai, and other prophets and patriarchs of old, did well understand the mystery of the sacred Trinity."[128] Others, however, are cautious: Poole simply indicates that the "word" of verse 5 could mean *either* the "word of promise" or "the Word, the son of God, promised to them and us."[129]

C. Exegetical Issues and Trajectories: New Testament

1. Reformed exegesis of individual trinitarian texts in the Gospels. As in the preceding section, there is no attempt here to offer a full picture of sixteenth and seventeenth-century approaches to a trinitarian reading New Testament texts — although we can come closer here to a complete listing of the most important texts. The presence of clearer references to the Trinity in the New Testament impressed the Reformers as an evidence of the basic patterning of their biblical hermeneutics: "As God afforded a clearer manifestation of himself at the advent of Christ, the three persons also then became better known."[130] Again, the issue is patterns of interpretation and the transition from exegesis to doctrinal expression. As would be expected, the texts concerning Christ's baptism (Matthew 3:16-17; John 1:32), play a major role in the establishment of the doctrine of the Trinity and have a confessional status in the discussion, as does the Matthean baptismal formula (Matt. 28:19).[131] Such a reading of the text is typical among the Reformers,[132] and carries over into the exegesis of their successors. In the era of orthodoxy, Poole succinctly states, "This text (as is generally observed) is a clear proof of the Trinity of persons or subsistences in the one Divine Being: here was the Father speaking from heaven, the Son baptized and come out

---

127. Rijssen, *Summa theol.*, IV.ix, controversia I, argumentum 5 (O.T.); cf. Turretin, *Inst. theol. elencticae*, III.xxvi.10; Downame, *Summe*, i (p. 32).

128. Trapp, *Commentary*, Hag. 2:5 in loc. (IV, p. 377); cf. for Tremellius' reading, *Biblia sacra, sive libri canonici priscae Iudaeorum ecclesiae à Deo tradit, Latini recens ex Hebraeo facta ... ab Emanuele Tremmelio & Francisco Iunio, accesserunt libri qui vulgo dicuntur Apocryphi, Latine reddite ... à Francisco Iunio ... quibus etiam adjunximus Novi Testamenti libros ex sermone Syro ab Tremellio, et ex Graeco à Theodore Beza in Latinum versos*, secunda cura Francisci Iunii (London: G. B., 1593). Among the dogmaticians, note Venema, *Inst. theol.*, IX (p. 211).

129. Poole, *Commentary*, Hag. 2:5 in loc. (II, p. 986).

130. Calvin, *Institutes*, I.xiii.16 (Allen).

131. Cf. Belgic Confession, IX with Second Helvetic Confession, III.4 and Westminster Confession, II.iii (Schaff, *Creeds*, pp. 241, 391-392, 608).

132. Cf. Calvin, *Harmony of the Evangelists*, Matt. 3:16-17 in loc. (CTS *Harmony*, I, pp. 203-206); Augustin Marlorat, *A Catholike and Ecclesiasticall Exposition of the Holy Gospell after S. Matthew, gathered out of all the singular and approved divines* (London, 1570), in loc., citing from Calvin and Musculus.

of the water, the Holy Ghost descending in the form or shape of a dove."[133] In the seventeenth century, the issue of theophany as an indication of a distinct person became a matter of intense debate.[134]

Calvin takes the text of Matthew 28:19 as an opportunity to note the hermeneutical premise that, although the true nature of God was in fact known in the Old Testament, it was only "fully brought to light under the reign of Christ" — with the soteriological result that "God cannot be truly known" by Christians "unless our faith distinctly conceive of Three Persons in one essence; and the fruit and efficacy of baptism proceed from God the Father adopting us through his Son, and, after having cleansed us from the pollutions of the flesh through the Spirit, creating us anew to righteousness."[135]

In his comment on Matthew 28:19, Poole indicates that baptizing into the "name of the Father and of the Son and of the Holy Ghost" is a baptizing or a dedicating of the individual "into the profession of the trinity of persons in the one Divine Being" and therefore "obliging" the "persons baptized ... to worship and serve God the Father, Son, and Holy Ghost."[136] Against both the patristic reading of the text and the typical orthodox reading of the day, the Socinians indicate that the singular use of "name" with reference to Father, Son, and Spirit no more indicates the single "Name, Power, and Dignity" of the three than the text of Luke 9:26, where the Son of Man is spoken of as coming in "his own glory, and in his Father's, and of the holy angels," indicates a single glory of the Son, the Father, and the angels. The linking of Father, Son, and Spirit only indicates a common purpose.[137]

Owen, as would be expected, quite to the contrary, stresses the "name" as the "name of God" that is shared by the three persons:

> by the "name" of God either his being or his authority is signified; for other intention of it none have been able to invent. Take the "name" here in either sense, and it is sufficient to what we intend: for if it be used in the first way, then the being of the Spirit must be acknowledged to be the same with that of the Father; if in the latter, he hath the same divine authority with him. He who hath the nature and authority of God is God, — is a divine person.[138]

Not surprisingly, the Reformed orthodox writers mirror the Reformation-era exegesis of John 1:1-3 with precision, reflecting both the doctrinal reading of the text and also variant interpretations of the syntax. Diodati, like Calvin, understands the phrase "In

---

133. Poole, *Commentary*, Matt. 3:16-17 in loc. (III, p. 16) cf. Amyraut, *De mysterio trinitatis*, V, pp. 245-246; Bucanus, *Institutions*, i (p. 9); Downame, *Summe*, i (p. 32); Mastricht, *Theroetico-practica theol.* II.xiv.3.

134. See below 7.2 (B.4).

135. Calvin, *Harmony of the Evangelists*, in loc. (CTS *Harmony*, III, p. 387); cf. Belgic Confession, IX (Schaff, *Creeds*, III, p. 391).

136. Poole, *Commentary*, in loc. (III, p. 146); Downame, *Summe*, i (p. 32).

137. Biddle, *XII Arguments* (1691), p. 8; cf. the comments on Schlichting, *De trinitate*, in Owen, *ΠΝΕΥΜΑΤΟΛΟΓΙΑ*, I.iii, in *Works*, III, p. 73.

138. Owen, *ΠΝΕΥΜΑΤΟΛΟΓΙΑ*, I.iii, in *Works*, III, p. 73; cf. Amyraut, *De mysterio trinitatis*, V, pp. 248-249.

the beginning," as indicating that "before the creation of the world, when there was neither time nor temporall things, but only the eternity, the Son of God had then his beeing."[139] Poole, by way of contrast, reads "In the beginning" as intentionally parallel with the Genesis narrative and meaning "the beginning of all things, when the foundations of the world were laid." The eternity of the Word, for Poole, is to be inferred from the tense of the verb: "Nor is it said, that in the beginning was the Word created ... but *was* the Word: this proveth the eternal existence of the Second Person of the Trinity; for what *was* in the beginning did not then begin to be."[140]

The evangelist's language, moreover, referencing the Word "without the addition of God," like the subsequent statement that the Word was "with God," teaches that the Word is a distinct "subsistence" or "person," who is "equall with the Father in essence and in glory."[141] The second verse of the chapter confirms the teaching of the first verse and "effectually" confutes various ancient heretics: the Eunomians, "who distinguished betwixt the Word which in the beginning was with God, and that Word by which all things were made"; the Arians, "who made the Father to have existed before the Son"; and the Anomians, "who would make the Father and the Son diverse both in nature and in will."[142] The third verse, also, has particular significance for the doctrine of the Trinity:

> By him] Not only as by a joint and co-operating cause with the Father, but also according to his personall property, operating by the immediate and next application of his operations. *Without him*] this seems to be added, to shew, that the Son creating the world, hath made it in the unity of the essence, with the communion of the will, counsell, and virtue of the Father, who must alwaies be acknowledged to be as the well-spring, and beginning of every thing, operating in his Son, and by him.[143]

Even so, the Word "is not the undifferentiated (*simplex*) command of God" as is clear from the collation of Moses words with those of the Gospel of John (1:1ff): the text of the initial verses of the Gospel of John consciously reflects the first chapter of Genesis, where the creative word is uttered by God. "Nor is it possible to understand either an external ... or an internal word of God," since in the first place, the possible ministers of an external or spoken word, the angels, were not yet created; and in the second place, the text will not allow an internal word, as if God were simply speaking, granting that the text (of John 1:3) is in the third person, as if a person other than God were

139. Diodati, *Pious and Learned Annotations*, John 1:1 in loc.; similarly, George Hutcheson, *An Exposition of the Gospel of Jesus Christ, according to John* (London: Ralph Smith, 1657; reissued, Edinburgh, 1841), John 1:1, in loc. (p. 10).

140. Poole, *Commentary*, John 1:1 in loc. (III, p. 277); cf. Trapp, *Commentary*, John 1:1, in loc. (V, p. 344).

141. Diodati, *Pious and Learned Annotations*, John 1:1 in loc.; Poole, *Commentary*, John 1:1, in loc. (III, p. 277).

142. Poole, *Commentary*, John 1:1 in loc. (III, p. 278).

143. Diodati, *Pious and Learned Annotations*, John 1:1 in loc.; similarly, Hutcheson, *Exposition of the Gospel of John*, John 1:1, in loc. (p. 10).

the agent of creation. Thus the "Word" indicates the personal word *(sermo personalis)* or Son of God.[144]

That the oneness of the Father and the Son taught in John 10:30 (or, if 1 John 5:7 were added to the list of texts, of the Father, the Son, and the Spirit), referred to a "union" of some sort was not in dispute — but was it merely a "union in consent and agreement," as the Socinians claimed,[145] or a "union of essence"? The Reformed orthodox commentators tend to argue the traditional trinitarian sense of John 10:30 as given by Bullinger (unity of essence), rather than Calvin's non-trinitarian reading (unity of agreement, ironically in accord with the Socinians) — but they register the difficulty of the text, and some note both possible meanings: "I and my Father are one," according to Trapp speaks "both for nature or essence, and for one consent, both in willing and working," on the assumption that oneness of essence and oneness of will and work are implicates of one another.[146] Poole notes the two meanings, acknowledges that eminent exegetes have held for a unity of agreement or consent, but argues contextually that unity of essence is preferable: the Jews would not have identified a claim of agreement with God's will on Jesus' part as blasphemy.[147] Pictet, reflecting the contextual argument found in such exegetes as Piscator, Poole, and the *Dutch Annotations*, argues that

> this passage cannot be explained of a unity of consent or will, for Christ thus speaks, to prove that none can pluck his sheep out of his hand, seeing that he was one with the Father, whose power, he says, is so great that no one can pluck these sheep out of his hand. He means, therefore, to prove that his own power is not less than that of his Father, because he was one with him in essence; and in this sense the Jews understood him, for they attempted to stone him, because he made himself God.[148]

In this view, the text indicates that "As I am everlasting Son, I am of the same essence and power as my Father," a point which Diodati confirms from verse 33, where the Jews accuse Jesus of blasphemy, for declaring himself to be God — acknowledging that they understood the text as a declaration of full divinity. Verse 32, where Jesus states that he is from the Father, indicates that God the father "is the first author, by order of subsistency and operation" of what Christ, as Mediator, does by his "commission and power."[149] Henry juxtaposes the parallel phrases from verses 28 and 29 as a basis for reading the oneness of the Father and the Son in the following verse:

---

144. Rijssen, *Summa theol.*, IV.ix, controversia I, argumentum 3; cf. Leigh, *Treatise*, II.xvi (p. 130).

145. Cf. Biddle, *XII Arguments*, (1691), p. 9.

146. Trapp, *Commentary*, John 10:30 in loc. (V, p. 381); cf. Hutcheson, *Exposition of the Gospel of John*, John 10:30 in loc. (p. 213); Poole, *Commentary*, John 10:30, in loc. (III, p. 335).

147. Poole, *Commentary*, in loc (III, p. 335).

148. Pictet, *Theol. Chr.*, II.xvi.3; cf. Piscator, *Analysys logica Evangelii secundum Johannem*, in loc. (p. 115); Haak, *Dutch Annotations*, John 10:30 in loc.

149. Diodati, *Pious and Learned Annotations*, in loc.

He proves that none could pluck them out *of his hand*, because they could not pluck them out *of the Father's hand*; which had not been a conclusive argument, if the Son had not had the same almighty power as the Father, and, consequently, been one with him in essence and operation.[150]

2. Trinitarian readings in the Epistles. The Apostolic benediction, "The grace of the Lord Jesus Christ, the love of God, and the communion of the Holy Spirit, be with you all" (2 Corinthians 13:14), offers three blessings that, in Turretin's words, embrace "the whole plan of salvation." Here, the "Lord who confers grace," the "God who bestows love," and the Holy Spirit who provides communion with God are surely distinct persons, "distinguished by three names."[151] Calvin's commentary on the text does not raise the dogmatic issue of the Trinity, although it clearly presupposes the doctrine.[152] Later writers, like Poole, tend to offer some comment on the doctrine of the Trinity — Poole noting that "in this text is an eminent proof of the Trinity, all the Persons being distinctly named in it (as in the commission about baptism)": "the apostle calleth the Father, *God*; the Son, *Lord*: he attributeth *love* to the Father (moved by which he sent his only begotten Son into the world, John 3:16); *grace* to the Son, who loved us freely, and died for the fellowship of *communion of the Holy Ghost*, by whom the Father and the Son communicate their love and grace to the saints."[153]

1 Timothy 3:16 continued to be a point of contention between the Reformed orthodox and various antitrinitarians and textual critics during the high orthodox era and continued to cause difficulty on into the late orthodox era, given developments in the text-criticism of the passage.[154] The Socinians took a two-pronged approach to the text: they both called it into question textually and reinterpreted it theologically. On the textual side of the argument, they noted that "the Latin Vulgate, the Syriac, and Arabic versions" omitted the word "God," leaving the text as a testimony to the manifestation of "the mystery of godliness." On the theological side of the argument, the Socinians add, unsure of the ultimate result of the textual argument, that even with the word "God" in the text, "there is no reason why it might not be referred to God the Father; since these things might be truly affirmed of the Father,—that he was manifested in the flesh, that is, in Christ and the apostles, or by Christ and the apostles, who were flesh."[155] The divine manifestation, then, is God's revelation "of the hidden secrets of his will." The subsequent phrases in the text, indicating that God was "seen of angels, preached unto the Gentiles, believed on in the world, received up into glory," can also be understood as a reference to God the Father, meaning that "the same secrets of his will were at length perceived by the angels, and were preached

---

150. Henry, *Exposition*, John 10:22-28 in loc.

151. Turretin, *Inst. theol. elencticae*, III.xxv.11.

152. Calvin, *Commentary on 2 Corinthians*, (CTS II Cor., pp. 403-404); cf. Belgic Confession, IX (Schaff, *Creeds*, III, p. 392).

153. Poole, *Commentary*, 2 Cor. 13:14 in loc (III, p. 639); cf., less elaborately, Diodati, *Pious and Learned Annotations*, in loc.

154. Cf. *PRRD*, II, 6.2 (B.3).

155. Racovian Catechism, iv.1 (p. 121).

not to the Jews alone but also to the Gentiles; that the world believed in God, and received him in a most distinguished manner and with the highest glory."[156]

The textual difficulty was debated throughout the seventeenth century, to little conclusion. Grotius noted that the alteration of the text had been recognized in earlier times, adding that Hincmar of Rheims (who was, of course, following the Vulgate), had argued that the alteration derived initially from the Nestorians. Grotius concluded that the Θεὸς ἐφανερώθη ἐν σαρκὶ, "God manifested in the flesh," was an altered reading, replacing ὃ ἐφανερώθη ἐν σαρκὶ, "the one manifest in the flesh." The removal of Θεὸς, Grotius concluded, "makes good sense" of the text. His reading of the verse, lacking the Θεὸς, paralleled the Socinian reading, much to the irritation of the orthodox.[157]

The Reformed orthodox typically stand in continuity with the Reformers and uphold the traditional reading of the text, which, they note, has the support of many of the fathers of the first five centuries. Diodati, Poole, Trapp, and Henry accept the reading, "God was manifest in the flesh," without comment on the textual difficulties — and all four understand the text as a testimony to the identity of Christ as the eternal Son or Word of God.[158] The orthodox writers of the day were not ready to give up 1 Timothy 3:16 to the Socinians or the text critics — from their perspective the balance of evidence, whether textual from the extant codices or theological from the grammar of the text, favored their cause. Against the Racovian Catechism, Pearson commented that "when they tell us that God, that is, the will of God, *was manifested in the flesh*, that is, was revealed by frail and mortal men, *and received up in glory*, ... they teach us a language which the scriptures know not, and the Holy Ghost never used.[159] Referring directly to the texts of Liberatus Diaconus and Hincmar of Rheims, moreover, Pearson disputed the claim that the alteration could have come from the Nestorians, given the presence of Θεὸς in the writings of the Greek fathers prior to the Nestorian controversy and in the writings of Cyril of Alexandria, Nestorius' opponent. Given also the number of Greek codices that concurred with the orthodox fathers' reading, Pearson concluded that Θεὸς was a valid reading, as ancient as ὃ or ὃς.[160]

On the theological side of the debate, following out the older Reformed hermeneutic of interpreting Scripture by means of Scripture, Owen noted the several biblical parallels to the phrase "manifest in the flesh," and concluded that, as with John 1:14 and

156. Racovian Catechism, iv.1 (p. 122).

157. Grotius, *Annotationes in Novum Testamentum*, 1 Tim. 3:16 in loc.; cf. Owen, *Vindiciae evangelicae*, in *Works*, 12, pp. 297-299. The typical modern solution, namely, the assumption that the uncial ΟΣ or ΟϚ was mistakenly read as ΘΣ or ΘϚ and taken as an abbreviation for ΘΕΟΣ, probably derives from Wetstein: see the discussion in *PRRD*, II, 2.3 (C.3). This understanding of the variant was also known, in the patristic era, to Liberatus Diaconus (ca. 560 A.D.), from whose work it passed over into Hincmar: see the citation of Liberatus and discussion in *The Expositor's Greek New Testament*, ed. W. Robertson Nicoll, 5 vols. (Grand Rapids: Eerdmans, 1956), in loc. (IV, p. 118).

158. Diodati, *Pious and Learned Annotations*, 1 Tim. 3:16 in loc.; Poole, *Commentary*, in loc. (III, p. 781); Trapp, *Commentary*, in loc. (V, p. 642); Henry, *Exposition*, in loc..

159. Pearson, *Exposition of the Creed*, II.iii.31 (1887, p. 198).

160. Pearson, *Exposition of the Creed*, II.iii.31 (1887, pp. 199-200).

Romans 8:3, the one made manifest or visible in the flesh is Christ. Nor do the other phrases in the text indicate anyone but Christ: numerous texts state that he was known to, seen by, announced by, and will return with angels! Owen also cites texts referring to Jesus' ministry and his being received up into glory, concluding "that what is here spoken *may* refer to the Father, is a very sorry shift against all those considerations which show that it *ought* to be referred to the Son."[161] Even so, there is no "tolerable sense" in which the text can be referred to the Father as manifest in the flesh, seen by angels, justified in the Spirit, or taken up into glory — nor is there "one instance" in Scripture in which "God" is understood to mean "the will of God" or the phrase "manifest in the flesh" refers to the gospel message.[162]

In the late orthodox era, Venema (who rejected the "Johannine Comma" on text-critical grounds) quite pointedly defended the text, indicating that "the Socinians, indeed, have recourse to various readings and substitute ὅς or ὁ for Θεὸς, which is countenanced by some of the manuscripts and by the Latin Vulgate." On the contrary, Venema comments,

> The Greek Fathers are all in favor of Θεὸς. And the epithets employed require that a rational subject be meant to whom they apply. For it cannot be said of a mystery of godliness that it was manifest in the flesh. It is spoken peculiarly of the Son, as in another passage we read that the Word was made flesh, so here as God he was manifest.[163]

Venema's bibliographically exhaustive contemporary De Moor also defended the text as originally reading Θεὸς, citing, among other authorities of the era, John Mill, whose annotations had concluded in favor of the received text on this point.[164]

Hebrews 1:1-3, long used by trinitarian orthodoxy as a key text in the identification of the unity and distinction of the Father and the Son, became a point of controversy in the seventeenth century as Socinian exegetes and theologians offered an alternative,

---

161. Owen, *Vindiciae evangelicae*, in *Works*, 12, pp. 295-297, citing Heb. 1:6, Luke 2:9-14; Matt. 4:11; Luke 22:43; Matt. 26:53; Matt. 25:31; and 2 Thess. 1:7 (seen by angels); Acts 2:5; John 1:10-11 (preached to the Gentiles); Acts 1:2, 9-11; Mark 16:19 (taken up into glory).

162. Owen, *Vindiciae evangelicae*, in *Works*, XII, p. 297.

163. Venema, *Inst. theol.*, x (p. 226); note also Herman Venema, *Exercitationes de vera Christi Divinitate, ex locis Act. XX: 28, I Tim. III:16, I Joh. V: 20 et Col. I:16, 17: quibus de vera lectione et genuio sensu eorum accuratius disseritur* (Leovardiae: Gulielmus Coulon, 1755); also note Owen, *Vindiciae evangelicae*, in *Works*, 12, pp. 296-297.

164. De Moor, *Commentarius perpetuus*, I.xxi.1, citing John Mill: see Mill's *Novum testamentum graecum, cum lectionibus variantibus mss. exemplarium, versionum, editionum, ss. patrum et scriptorum ecclesiasticorum; et in easdem notis. Accedunt loca scripturae parallela, aliaque exegetica. Praemittitur dissertatio de libris N.T. canonis constitutione, et s. textus n. foederis ad nostra usque tempora historia,* studio et labore Joannis Millii S.T.P. Collectionem millianam recensuit, meliori ordine disposuit, novisque accessionibus locupletavit Ludolphus Kusterus, editio secunda. (Amstelodami: Apud Jacobum Westenium, 1746), 1 Tim. 3:16 in loc.

antitrinitarian reading.[165] The Racovian Catechism singles out the text of Hebrews 1:3 to ground its denial of Christ's divinity:

> It cannot be proved from Christ's being the Word of God that he possesses a divine nature: indeed the contrary is the rather to be inferred ; for since he is the Word of the one God, it is evident that he is not that one God. And the same may be replied to those testimonies wherein Christ is called 'the image of the invisible God' and 'the express image of his person.'[166]

The text — "Who being the brightness of his glory, and the express image of his person (*hypostasis*), upholding all things by the world of his power" — is important historically inasmuch as it is the one text in the New Testament that both uses one of the standard terms of the orthodox trinitarian vocabulary and also offers a sense that the terms indicates a distinction in the Godhead. The text is used consistently by the church fathers in this sense.[167] Following the tradition, Calvin comments that "when the Apostle calls the Son of God 'the express image of his person,' he undoubtedly does assign to the Father some subsistence in which he differs from the Son."[168] Calvin notes that "it would be strange to say that the essence of God is impressed on Christ, as the essence of both is simply the same." Thus, the fathers understand *hypostasis* to mean something other than *ousia*: Hilary, Calvin notes, renders *hypostasis* as person, and the orthodox fathers consistently identify God as three in *hypostasis* and as "simply one" in essence.[169]

The text retained the significance given it by the Reformers in the biblical interpretation of the Reformed orthodox.[170] In response to the Socinians, moreover, the orthodox develop fairly lengthy discussions of doctrine at this point in their commentaries on the Epistle to the Hebrews. Gouge, commenting on the Authorized Version, indicates that the word *hypostasis* is "fitly translated person" given that "according to the proper notation and derivation of the word, it signifieth a substance or subsistence, which are in a manner Latin words, and set out the being of a thing; even a particular or distinct being, which is most properly called a person."[171] This usage stands in contrast to "essence" or "nature," which indicate "a common being, as Deity or Godhead, which is common to the Father, Son, Holy Ghost. ... But subsistence or person implieth a different, distinct, individual, incommunicable property; such are these three, Father, Son, Holy Ghost."[172]

---

165. Cf. Biddle, *Confession of Faith Touching the Holy Trinity*, p. 12; Crellius, *Two Books*, pp. 139-140.

166. Racovian Catechism, p. 140.

167. Cf. Athanasius, etc.

168. Calvin, *Institutes*, I.xiii.2; cf. Calvin, *Commentary on Hebrews*, 1:3, (CTS Hebrews, p. 37).

169. Calvin, *Commentary on Hebrews*, 1:3, (CTS Hebrews, p. 37).

170. Thus, Diodati, *Pious and Learned Annotations*, in loc.; Poole, *Commentary*, Heb. 1:3 (III, pp. 809-810); Gomarus, *Disputationes*, VI.14; Turretin, *Inst. theol. elencticae*, III.xxiii.6.

171. Gouge, *Commentary on Hebrews*, I, §21; cf. Owen, *Exposition of the Epistle to the Hebrews*, 1:3, in loc. (I, p. 95); Diodati, *Pious and Learned Annotations*, in loc.

172. Gouge, *Commentary on Hebrews*, I, §21.

3. The Johannine Comma — trajectories of interpretation. The so-called Johannine Comma, 1 John 5:7, posed a textual problem for Protestant exegetes from the beginnings of the Reformation — from the time of Erasmus' Greek New Testament — and gradually came to be a significant point of contention between the orthodox trinitarians and the various antitrinitarian writers.[173] This gradual shift in the discussion from a largely textual to a highly charged theological debate with textual overtones demands some examination. Calvin's discussion of the text is of interest, given his tendency to accept the verse as legitimate on textual grounds, his unwillingness to rest great doctrinal questions on a disputed text, and his readiness to omit the text from theological discussion without any polemic, despite his own acceptance and his own positive exposition of the theological point. Clearly, Calvin did not regard 1 John 5:7 as crucial to the doctrine of the Trinity.

> The whole of this verse has been by some omitted. Jerome thinks that this has happened through design rather than through mistake, and that indeed only on the part of the Latins. But as even the Greek copies do not agree, I dare not assert any thing on the subject. Since, however, the passage flows better when this clause is added, and as I see that it is found in the best and most approved copies, I am inclined to receive it as the true reading. And the meaning would be, that God, in order to confirm most abundantly our faith in Christ, testifies in three ways that we ought to acquiesce in him. For as our faith acknowledges three persons in the one divine essence, so it is called in so many ways to Christ that it may rest on him.[174]

Musculus also accepted it as a basic proof.[175] Calvin also observes, with obvious interest in the texts and their variants,

> When he says, These three are one, he refers not to essence, but on the contrary to consent; as though he had said that the Father and his eternal Word and Spirit harmoniously testify the same thing respecting Christ. Hence some copies have εἰ ἔν, "for one." But though you read ἔν εἰσιν, as in other copies, yet there is no doubt but that the Father, the Word and the Spirit are said to be one, in the same sense in which afterwards the blood and the water and the Spirit are said to agree in one. But as the Spirit, who is one witness, is mentioned twice, it seems to be an unnecessary repetition. To this I reply, that since he testifies of Christ in various ways, a twofold testimony is fitly ascribed to him. For the Father, together with his eternal Wisdom and Spirit, declares Jesus to be the Christ as it were authoritatively, then, in this ease, the sole majesty of the deity is to be considered by us. But as the Spirit, dwelling in our hearts, is an earnest, a pledge, and a seal, to confirm that decree, so he thus again speaks on earth by his grace. But inasmuch as all do not receive this reading, I will

---

173. See the discussion in Franz Posset, "John Bugenhagen and the Comma Johanneum," in *Concordia Theological Quarterly*, 49 (1985), pp. 245-251.

174. Calvin, *Commentary on 1 John*, 5:7, in loc. (CTS 1 John, pp. 257-258).

175. Musculus, *Commonplaces*, I (p. 16, col. 2).

therefore so expound what follows, as though the Apostle referred to the witnesses only on the earth.[176]

The Belgic and Scots Confessions resonate Calvin's point by citing the Comma for confessional purposes.[177] Given the history of the text, the early sixteenth-century objections to the removal of the verse, and the place of the verse in antitrinitarian polemic, the confessional citation of the Comma is hardly surprising — and its confessional use is certainly one of the grounds for the later orthodox emphasis on the maintenance of the text in the canon as a trinitarian reference.

Among the framers of early orthodoxy, Zanchi made substantive use of the text as his initial citation (after noting the name Elohim) in arguing the Trinity, collating it interpretively with Matthew 3:17 and 17:5, references to the "beloved Son," and with Romans 12:6 and 1 Corinthians 11:8 — although, given the length of his exegesis of other texts, he in no way understood the doctrine of the Trinity as dependent on the Comma.[178] Zanchi, moreover, does not register the textual debate to any noticeable degree, but instead refutes those opponents who deny the applicability of the text to Christ and therefore the question of the unity of essence between Father and Son. On the contrary, the text refers to the Logos, who clearly is identified in other places in Scripture as the Son and, incarnate, as Christ — nor can the phrase "these three are one" be interpreted any other way than as indicating that "these three are one God."[179]

The Johannine Comma continued to be cited confessionally in the era of orthodoxy,[180] but critical pressure on the text, particularly in the late seventeenth century and the late orthodox era, left it less and less available to the Reformed orthodox as a definitive biblical proof of the Trinity. Thus, the Comma remained a point of fairly intense controversy through the seventeenth century — with theologians and exegetes arguing its legitimacy on the basis of patristic evidence and assigning denials of its presence in the genuine text of the New Testament as either Socinian claims or as over zealous text criticism deluded by the textual damage wrought by ancient heretics. In the seventeenth century, the tide turned, and even orthodox writers tended to omit the text from trinitarian proofs, often with grounds.[181]

Thus, many exegetes and theologians of the seventeenth century continued to accept the text of the Johannine comma without question,[182] with some, notably the *Dutch*

---

176. Calvin, *Commentary on 1 John*, 5:7, in loc. (CTS 1 John, p. 258); cf. the discussion in Vermigli, *Loci communes*, I.xii.10-11.

177. Belgic Confession, IX; Scots Confession, I (Schaff, *Creeds*, III, pp. 392, 439).

178. Zanchi, *De tribus Elohim*, pt. I, I.i.3 (col. 4).

179. Zanchi, *De tribus Elohim*, pt. II, V.iii.3 (col. 525); cf. pt. I, VII.vii.[9] (cols. 330-331); cf. Bucanus, *Institutions*, i (p. 9).

180. Westminster Confession, II.iii (1648 ed., p. 8); Larger Catechism, q. 9 (1648 ed., p. 3).

181. See the discussion of text criticism and the "Comma" in PRRD, II, 6.2 (B.3).

182. Cf. e.g., Cocceius, *Aphorismi prolixiores*, VI.4; Downame, *Summe*, i (p. 33); John Mayer, *A Commentarie upon the New Testament. Representing the divers expositions thereof, out of the workes of the most learned , both ancient Fathers, and moderne Writers*, 3 vols. (London, 1631), III, pp. 215-216;

Annotations, arguing its omission from some manuscripts through the machinations of heretics:

> *For* [This verse seeing it contains a very clear testimony of the holy Trinity, seems to have been left out of some copies by the Arrians, but is found in almost all Greek copies, and even by many ancient and worthy Teachers also, who lived before the times of the Arrians, brought out of them proof of the holy Trinity: and the opposition of the witness upon earth (verse 8) sheweth clearly that this verse must be there; as appears also by the ninth verse, where is spoken of this testimony of God] *there are three* [namely, persons, and distinct witnesses] *who witness in heaven,* [that is, give from heaven an heavenly and divine testimony hereof, which may never be doubted of. See Matt. 3:16, 17 and chap. 17:5, John 3:31, Acts 2:1 &c.] *the Father, the Word* [that is, the Son of God. See John 1:1] *and the Holy Ghost, and these three* [namely, persons. See Matt. 3:16, 17 and chap. 28:19] *are one.* [namely, of essence and nature: who testifie of this thing all three together of the same thing. A very clear proof of the Trinity of persons in the unity of the divine essence. See John 10:30.][183]

Even so, when Benjamin Needler approached the doctrine of the Trinity in 1659 as the subject of his contribution to the famous series of "morning exercises" known as the *Puritan Sermons*, he offered the title, "The Trinity Proved by Scripture," and although the sermon cited many collateral texts, its basic biblical proof and the subject of its extended exegesis remained 1 John 5:7. What is more, Needler offered no indication that the text's authenticity had been questioned.[184] A decade later, Ezekiel Hopkins could similarly cite the same text as the place where "the Scripture hath expressly declared to us" the mystery of the Trinity — also without any indication of the debate over the text.[185]

The unsettled nature of the case, even after the textual work of Simon, Bentley, and others, is evidenced by the varied treatment of the Comma in the theological systems of early eighteenth-century Reformed thinkers, ranging from use with little or no attempt to justify the validity of the verse to extended textual argumentation within the *locus* on the Trinity. By way of example, Rijssen, fairly representative of the arguments and conclusions of the high orthodox era, offers a note on the various extant codices and their inclusion or exclusion of 1 John 5:7: he notes that his own assessment yields the result that the best codices then accessible include the text. Thus, Jerome, in his preface to the canonical epistles, notes that the verse appears in the

---

Westminster Annotations, in loc.; Trapp, *Commentary on the New Testament*, in loc.; Diodati, *Pious and Learned Annotations*, in loc.

183. *Dutch Annotations*, 1 John 5:7 in loc.

184. Benjamin Needler, "The Trinity Proved by Scripture," in *Puritan Sermons, 1659-1689: Being the Morning Exercises at Cripplegate, St. Giles in the Fields, and Southwark by Seventy-five Ministers of the Gospel in or Near London*, 6 vols. (London, 1661-1675; republished, with notes and translations by James Nichols, London: Tegg, 1844-1845), VI, pp. 54-66.

185. Ezekiel Hopkins, *A Discourse on the State and Way of Salvation*, in *The Works of Ezekiel Hopkins, successively Bishop of Raphoe and Derry*, ed. Charles W. Quick, 3 vols. (1874; repr. Morgan, Pa.: Soli Deo Gloria Publications, 1995-1998), III, p. 453.

Greek codices; Erasmus reveals that the text is contained in the most ancient British codex. The most praiseworthy editions also contain it: the *Compultensis*, the *Antwerpiensis*, and the editions of Arius Montanus and Valtonus (i.e., Brian Walton, the "London Polyglott").[186] Pictet notes that, inasmuch as three persons in the one divine essence are explicitly testified by the disputed passage, 1 John 5:7, and given that the triunity of God is established fully elsewhere, there is far greater likelihood of heretics striking out such a passage than of orthodox inserting it.[187] Beyond this, the context seems to demand the verse:

> for unless this verse be admitted, there seems no reason why John should say, "There are three that bear witness *in earth*," not having before said anything about "three witnesses *in heaven*." Nor can it be objected that these words, *in earth*, were also added afterwards, for the contrary appears from verse 9, where mention is made both of the *divine* and the *human* testimony, "If we receive the witness of men, the witness of God is greater."[188]

Among the British divines, Boston takes the text as the basis of his presentation of the doctrine of the Trinity, making no comment on the debate.[189] Ridgley, by way of contrast, in recognition of the difficulties posed by the text, reserves his discussion of 1 John 5:7 until the conclusion of his analysis of the biblical basis for the doctrine of the Trinity and notes, "I would not wholly pass over that which some call a controverted text of Scripture ... lest it should be thought that I conclude that the arguments brought by the antitrinitarians sufficiently conclusive to prove it spurious."[190] The text, Ridgley notes, has surely been "corrupted," either by the addition or by the deletion of the verse. The problem remains, given the difficulty — Ridgley assumes virtual impossibility — of proving which manuscripts are older or, regardless of age, genuine. Thus, Richard Simon's discovery of a manuscript in which the Comma had been inserted by an editor or copyist as a marginal gloss does not prove that the Comma is in fact an addition, first offered as a gloss and later incorporated into the text: this marginal addition might just as easily be interpreted as a scribal attempt to correct a corrupted manuscript on the basis of an earlier text in which the verse was present! The likelihood of this being the case is increased, according to various of late orthodox exegetes, by the possible deletion of the phrase through the common error of "haplography" — the eye of the scribe skipping from a phrase to its repetition several lines below and leaving out the intervening text in his copy, in this case moving from

---

186. Rijssen, *Summa theol.*, IV.ix, cont. I, arg. 3 (N.T.). The state of scholarly opinion on this verse has, of course, been reversed with the discovery of more ancient codices; similar arguments appear in Amyraut, *De mysterio trinitatis*, V, pp. 289-291; Ridgley, *Body of Divinity*, p. 154, col. 1 - p. 156, col. 2; cf. also Gill, *Exposition of the New Testament*, 1 John 5:7 in loc.

187. Pictet, *Theol. chr.*, II.ix, p. 100; similarly, Rijssen, *Summa theol.*, IV.ix, controversia I, argumentum 3 (N.T.).

188. Pictet, *Theol. chr.*, II.ix, p. 100; similarly, Rijssen, *Summa theol.*, IV.ix, controversia I, argumentum 3 (N.T.).

189. Boston, *Commentary on the Shorter Catechism*, I, p. 142.

190. Ridgley, *Body of Divinity* (1855), I, p. 190.

the first "three that bear" (verse 7) to the second "three that bear" (verse 8) and omitting the intervening portion of the text, namely, "record in heaven, the Father, the Word, and the Holy Ghost: and these three are one. And there are...."[191]

More important to the case than inconclusive debate over the antiquity of manuscripts or the possible reasons for deletion or augmentation in the text, Ridgley continues, is the patristic testimony. From the fifth century onward, he notes, many writers cite the text in defense of the doctrine of the Trinity. The failure of fourth-century writers like Athanasius, Gregory of Nazianzen, Cyril, Chrysostom, and Augustine indicates, at most, that they did not possess the text — given the clear citation of the text by Cyprian in his *De unitate ecclesiae*, § 5, and his passing reference to it in his epistle to Jubianus (Ep. lxxiii). These sometimes disputed citations Ridgley finds satisfactory to his argument, although it is clear from his introductory comments that he does not view the text as necessary to the doctrine of the Trinity.[192]

The shift in understanding of the text among the late orthodox is seen in the differences among Ridgley, writing in the first half of the century, Gill writing toward the middle, and Venema, writing in the second half. Gill affirms the genuineness of the verse and argues through a wide variety of critical opinions, noting perhaps even more of the codices and versions related to the question than Ridgley. He also uses the text substantively in the chapter on the Trinity in his *Body of Divinity*. What is quite striking, however, is that in Gill's commentary the debate appears to be entirely textual or philological: he makes no mention of the role of Socinian or other antitrinitarians in the debate, and he accuses no one of perverting the text for the purposes of supporting heresy.[193] Nor, significantly, did Gill cite the text in his treatise on the Trinity — although it does appear, without comment, in the discussions of the love and goodness of God. In the *Body of Divinity*, the argumentation is much the same as in the commentary, albeit augmented with discussion of the possibility that ancient heretics — second-century followers of Artemon or, later, the Arians — altered

---

191. Ridgley, *Body of Divinity* (1855), I, p. 191. It is of minor interest that modern text-critical scholars regularly invoke haplography in order to explain omissions in other places: cf. Bruce Metzger, *The Text of the New Testament: Its Transmission, Corruption, and Restoration*, third edition, enlarged (New York: Oxford University Press, 1992), pp. 189-190.

192. Ridgley, *Body of Divinity* (1855), I, pp. 191-192, citing Cyprian, *De unitate ecclesiae*, § 5, and idem, Epistle to Jubianus (Ep. lxxiii) ; cf. also Gill, *Exposition of the New Testament*, 1 John 5:7, in loc., and note the negative comments of Ridgley's nineteenth-century editor, ibid., pp. 252-253, which express what is surely the modern consensus, that the text is indeed an interpolation and, after all, not necessary to the defense of the doctrine of the Trinity, particularly given the absence of reference to the comma in the writings of the great fourth and early fifth-century defenders of the doctrine of the Trinity. Cf. the summation of the negative argument in Samuel Clarke, *A Reply to the Objections of Robert Nelson, and of an anonymous author against Dr. Clarke's Scripture-Doctrine of the Trinity. To which is added, An answer to the remarks of the author of Some considerations concerning the Trinity* (London: James Knapton, 1714), in *Works*, IV, pp. 322-324, and idem, *Scripture Doctrine of the Trinity*, in *Works*, IV, p. 121.

193. Gill, *Exposition of the New Testament*, 1 John 5:7 in loc.

the text to their ends. Even here, however, Gill's emphasis is on textual issues and problems of the copyists.[194]

Venema works through an extended series of New Testament texts that demonstrate the Trinity and only after the conclusion of his exposition comments on 1 John 5:7 — specifically, to give his reasons for not using the text. First, Venema notes, the text cannot be definitively be shown to be genuine, and even exegetes of unquestioned orthodoxy have expressed their doubts: he mentions Luther and Bugenhagen and comments that Calvin offered "no opinion." Venema then offers a series of textual reasons for rejecting the Comma, including the unqualified remark that "All rules of criticism, which are applicable to the determination of the genuineness of readings are against it": there is no ancient attestation — no Greek text before the fifth century, no Latin text before the invention of printing, and no other ancient versions include the Comma — and (rejecting the allusions in Cyprian) there is no genuine patristic attestation before the sixth century.[195] Venema accepts Simon's argument that the Comma was introduced on the basis of a marginal gloss, and he specifically rejects as spurious the references usually claimed to have been made by Athanasius and Jerome, referring for his patristic judgments to the seventeenth-century Benedictine edition of Athanasius and to the early eighteenth-century critical work of Mill. What is more, Venema comments, the disputed verse makes no good sense in its context: the genuine sixth verse refers to "water and blood" and to the Spirit as bearing witness — with an echo in the eighth verse, where the Spirit, the water, and the blood are said to bear witness. The seventh verse offers what is apparently a "superfluous" reference to Father, Son, and Spirit. Nor was there any need for "three to bear record in heaven," as if "testimony were needed there! Those who doubt these arguments, he states, ought to consult Mill, Bengel, and Wetstein.[196] Of course, if one does consult Bengel, one finds there a lengthy analysis of the textual debate, followed by a detailed analysis of the argument of 1 John 5:1-13 in the context of the theology of 1 John, all to the justification of retaining the Comma. Mill also retained the Comma. Similarly, Vitringa cited the Comma as part of his trinitarian argument, offering a massive footnote summarizing the debate of some two centuries and noting briefly that the text could still be used.[197]

4. Trinity in the Revelation. Among the more significant pieces of trinitarian exegesis is the orthodox reading of Rev. 1:4-5, 8, 17-18, and collateral texts. The main phrases examined in the discussion are: "[4] Grace be unto you and peace, from him which is, and which was, and which is to come; and from the seven Spirits which are before his throne; [5] and from Jesus Christ, who is the faithful witness.... [8] I am

---

194. Gill, *Body of Divinity*, I, p. 113, 134, 184, 194.

195. Venema, *Inst. theol.*, ix (pp. 214-215).

196. Venema, *Inst. theol.*, ix (p. 214).

197. Johann Albert Bengel, *Gnomon Novi Testamenti, in quo ex nativa verborum vi simplicitas, profunditas, concinnitas, salubrita sensum coelestium indicatur* (Tübingen, 1742. 3rd ed., edited by Johann Steudel. London: Williams and Norgate, 1855), in loc.; Vitringa, *De doctrina christiana*, I.v.33 (pp. 216-218); similarly, Brown, *Compendious View*, II.ii (p. 133).

Alpha and Omega, the beginning and the ending, saith the Lord, which is, and which was, and which is to come, the Almighty. ... [17] And when I saw him, I fell at his feet as dead. And he laid his right hand upon me, saying unto me, Fear not; I am the first and the last: [18] I am he that liveth, and was dead; and, behold, I am alive for evermore...." The first chapter of the Apocalypse, particularly the juxtaposition of verses just noted, offered the tradition a fundamental testimony to the deity of Christ and his equality with the Father — given the identification of God as Alpha and Omega, the beginning and the end, or the first and the last, in verse 4 and Christ with the same language in verse 17.[198]

The Racovian Catechism understood the trinitarian arguments drawn from the book of Revelation as among the most significant supports of the traditional orthodoxy and accordingly listed Revelation 1:4, 5, 7, 8, and the parallel testimony in 4:8 as two out of the nine places to be exegeted in order to show that Jesus was not given titles unique to God anywhere in Scripture. The trinitarian reading of these texts depends — according to the Socinians — on the repeated phrase "which was, and is, and is to come" with reference to God or the Lord. In the orthodox view, the Socinians aver, such passages refer to Christ and identify him as God and Lord, given that Christ alone can be rightly identified as the one who "is to come." Socinian critique, at least in the catechism, rests on the translation of the word ἐρχόμενος, usually rendered "to come," but equally well rendered as "to be." By way of example, in "John 16:13, our Lord says of the spirit which he promised to the apostles, that 'he would show them things to come or to be.'" Similarly, in Acts 18:21, the catechism continues, "we read of a feast that was to come, or to be." Both of these references offer examples of ἐρχόμενος in which it means *venturus*, "to be hereafter."[199] The texts in the Revelation ought, therefore, to be rendered as "who was, who is, and who is to be," so that "the whole passage may be understood of existence; and not the first two [clauses] of existence, and the last of a future appearance": the subject of the passage is the divine eternity that "comprehends all past, present, and future time." When, therefore, one reads in Revelation 1:4-5, "Grace be unto you, and peace, from him who is, who was, and who is to come" or "who is to be" and "from Jesus Christ who is the faithful witness," it becomes quite clear that, according to the precise, literal reading of the text, "Jesus Christ is a being wholly distinct from him who is, and who was, and who is to be, or agreeably with the Greek idiom, 'who is to come.'"[200]

Arguably, the Reformed orthodox exegesis was consistently more sophisticated on this particular point than the Socinian attack, given that the doctrinal issue does not depend, in their exegesis, on so narrow a point of translation. A fairly standard orthodox reading of the text is found in Diodati, who begins his annotations on the Apocalypse by noting that the reference to "God" in verse one identified "the Father,"

---

198. Cf. Diodati, *Pious and Learned Annotations*, Rev. 1:8 in loc.; Trapp, *Commentary*, Rev. 1:4 in loc. (V, p. 740); Poole, *Commentary*, Rev. 1:4 in loc.; Henry, *Exposition*, Rev. 1:4-8 in loc.

199. Racovian Catechism, iv.1 (p. 82).

200. Racovian Catechism, iv.1 (p. 83).

citing John 3:33ff., 8:26-27, and 12:49 as evidence of similar Johannine references.[201] At verse 4, he also identifies God the Father, but also the Holy Spirit:

> From him] namely, from God the Father, whose eternity is described by these three times, according to the capacity of humane apprehension, and who in himself, and by himself, hath an everlasting an unchangeable subsistence. From the seven] that is, from the holy Ghost, whose power is most perfect, (the number seven in Scripture intimating perfection) and whose operations are also very divers.[202]

Indeed, the seven spirits should be understood as the one Spirit giving a sevenfold gift.[203] Brightman, who noted the trinitarian reading of verse 4 and its source, Aretius, rejected the reading on the ground earlier proposed by Junius that such language applies to the entire Godhead, particularly the language of Exodus 3:13-14 — thus, for Junius the text refers to "the immutable estate of God our Father as he is both in his own essence and throughout all," and for Brightman, who fastens on the economic aspect of Junius' double interpretation, "this threefold difference of time belonges to the unchangeable and steadfast truth of God concerning his promises."[204] This reading also allows Junius and Brightman to move from the Father (1:4a) to the Spirit, as understood by the "seven Spirits" (1:4b).[205]

Brakel adds to this exegesis the point that "who is, and who was, and who will come" (v. 4) reflects the name of God, Jehovah, and its implication of divine eternity. He also points to verse 5, with its reference to Christ, as a reference to "God the Son" in his mediatorial office, thus completing the full trinitarian revelation.[206] Poole, similarly, sees a double reference: the text is a "description of God, particularly of Jesus Christ in his eternity and immutability: he was from eternity; he is now; and he shall be forever." Or, Poole adds, the text may also refer to Christ as "he was in his promises before his incarnation; he is now God manifested in the flesh; and he is to come as Judge, to judge the quick and the dead."[207]

At verse 8, Diodati identifies the reference to Alpha and Omega as a clear indication of "the indeterminable eternity of the Son of God, equall with the Father in essence

---

201. Diodati, *Pious and Learned Annotations*, Rev. 1:1 in loc.; cf. *Dutch Annotations*, Rev. 1:1 in loc.

202. Diodati, *Pious and Learned Annotations*, Rev. 1:4 in loc.

203. *Dutch Annotations*, Rev. 1:4 in loc., citing James 1:17 and 2 Cor. 13:13 [14].

204. Junius, *Apocalyps*, 1:4 in loc (p. 8); Thomas Brightman, *A Revelation of the Apocalyps, that is the Apocalyps of S. Iohn, illustrated with an Analysis & Scolions* (Amsterdam: Hondius & Laurensz, 1611), 1:4 in loc (pp. 8-9).

205. Junius, *Apocalyps*, 1:4 in loc (pp. 10-11); Brightman, *Revelation of the Apocalyps*, 1:4, in loc (pp. 9-10).

206. Brakel, *Verklaring van de Openbaringen aan Johannes*: Part 3 of ΛΟΓΙΚΗ ΛΑΤΡΕΙΑ, *dat is Redelijke Godsdienst*, 3 parts (Dordrecht, 1700; 2nd printing, Leiden: D. Donner, 1893-94), in loc. (III, p. 144).

207. Poole, *Commentary*, Rev. 1:4 in loc. (III, p. 949).

and glory."[208] Brakel comments that, in the light of the identification of Christ as Alpha and Omega, this verse teaches the full divinity of Christ, "the majesty, veracity, immutability and omnipotence of [his] Person" — "he is JHWH, who is, who was, and who will come, the eternal, almighty God, who calls the things that are not as though they were, who speaks and it is so."[209] In nearly all the exegetes, the identification of the Son as God in the language of verse 8 rests on the identification of the subject of 1:4a as God in an unrestricted sense, and, on consideration of the parallel between the language of 1:4a and 1:8: over against the Socinian reading, the exegetical issue for the Reformed is that the phrase "who is, who was, and who will come," here clearly associated with Christ, reiterates the sense of verse 4, which was a clear reference to God. The Reformed trinitarian exegesis does not depend on the identification of Christ as the one "who is to come" exclusive of the possible reading of ἐρχόμενος as "to be," as assumed in the antitrinitarian exegesis found in the Racovian Catechism.

The same reading is found among other Reformed exegetes of the era,[210] although some, following Aretius, also raise the possibility that verse 8, by itself, with its reference to the one "which is, and which was, and which is to come, the Almighty," is itself a trinitarian reference: "the Father is called 'He that is,' Ex. 3:13. The Son, 'He that was,' John 1:1. The Holy Ghost, 'He that cometh,' John 16:8-13."[211] Trapp appears to look on this reading positively, at least as one of several possible alternatives, another being the "indeterminable eternity of the Son of God" — taking over directly the words of Diodati.[212] Gill registered three of the Reformed readings of the phrase "who is, who was, and who is to come," noting that some take it as a reference to Jesus Christ, some as a full trinitarian reference to Father, Son, and Spirit, respectively, and others to the eternity of God the Father: he argues the validity of the latter, based on the parallel with Exodus 3:15, "I am who I am" and the rabbinic exegesis of the passage, citing "Rabbi Isaac" to the effect that, "the holy blessed God said to Moses, Say unto them, I am he that was, and I am he that now is, and I am he that is to come, wherefore אהיה is written three times."[213]

In the second half of the seventeenth century, in part because of the Socinian attack, Durham made a point of elaborating on the doctrine of the Trinity at this place, to

---

208. Diodati, *Pious and Learned Annotations*, Rev. 1:8 in loc.; cf. Junius, *Apocalyps*, 1:4 in loc. (pp. 10-11); similarly, Poole, *Commentary*, Rev. 1:8 in loc. (III, p. 950).

209. Brakel, *Verklaring van de Openbaringen*, in loc. (III, p. 145), using the language of Romans 4:17.

210. Poole, *Commentary*, Rev. 1:2, 4, 8 in loc. (III, pp. 948-950); Trapp, *Commentary*, Rev. 1:2, 4, 8 in loc. (V, pp. 740-741); James Durham, *A Commentarie Upon the Book of Revelation. Wherein the Text is explained ... together with some practical Observations, and several Digressions necessary for vindicating, clearing, and confirming weighty and important Truths* (London: Company of Stationers, 1658; reissued, Willow Street, Pa.: Old Paths Publications, 2000), Rev. 1:8 in loc. (p. 32).

211. Trapp, *Commentary*, Rev. 1:8 in loc. (V, p. 741), citing Aretius.

212. Trapp, *Commentary*, Rev. 1:8 in loc. (V, p. 741).

213. John Gill, *Exposition of the New Testament*, Rev. 1:4 in loc., citing *Shemot Rabba*, sect. 3, fol. 73. 2.

the point of developing a *locus* on the "Holy Trinity and Object of Worship" immediately following his trinitarian reading of verses 1-4. "Observe," writes Durham,

> There are three distinct Persons of the blessed Trinity, the Father, the son, and the Spirit, who are the same one God: in the Name of these Three, is Baptism administrated; and from Them, Grace is wished and prayed for, 2 Cor. 13.14. For, 1. That there are Three, who are distinctly mentioned here, cannot be denied; that the first is the Father; and the third, Jesus Christ, really distinct from the Father, is clear: for the Son, and not the Father was incarnate: and therefore the like must be said of the seven Spirits, that they set forth the Holy Ghost personally, seeing it is He who in the like places useth to be joined with the Father and the Son, as 2 Cor. 13:13, 1 John 5:7,8, and therefore it's said in the seven Epistles, to be *what the Spirit saith*.[214]

Durham notes two other reasons for identifying this as a fully trinitarian reference and as a testimony to the unity of the three divine persons. His second reason is that the Son and Spirit are given equality with the Father, most notably in the subsequent attribution to the Son (v. 18) of what is here attributed to the Father, that the same petition is prayerfully addressed here to all three, and that the "Grace and Peace, which only God can give" come as a gift from all three. Such grace and peace, moreover, are "divine essential Attributes," so that the assumption of joint predication indicates also a common divinity.[215] Third, the Apocalypse testifies clearly (1:1; 22:18-19) that "this Revelation and Salvation [are] from one God," and yet, in 1:4 also indicates "that this Revelation and Salvation cometh from the Father, Son, and Spirit: therefore They are that One God."[216]

Against this Reformed reading, the Socinians object that in this passage, Christ is referred to as having been dead — and clearly, therefore, cannot be God. In response, Durham comments that it is "one thing to speak of Him who was dead, another to say that it speaks of Him as such": whereas the text does state that one who is God died, it does not state that he died "as God." All that the reference to Christ's death proves is that Jesus Christ is truly human — which is not something that the orthodox deny. Indeed, the reference to Christ's death and resurrection together with the identification of Christ, with the Father, as first and last, beginning and end, indicates clearly precisely what the Socinians wish to deny, that the person of Christ is both divine and human.[217] Nor is the objection that the text refers to "seven Spirits," meaning seven angels, of any weight — not only do the seven epsitles that follow consistently state that "the Spirit saith," but the rest of the Apocalypse does not confirm that this is a reference to seven angels: rather it speaks symbolically of sevens: seven churches, seven vials, seven trumpets, and seven seals. Moreover, in Revelation 5:6, we read of the seven eyes of the Lamb which are "seven Spirits of God sent forth into

---

214. Durham, *Commentarie upon the Book of Revelation*, Rev. 1:1-4, in loc. (p. 6), citing *ad fin.*, Rev. 2:7, 11, 17, 29, "what the Spirit saith unto the churches."

215. Durham, *Commentarie upon the Book of Revelation*, Rev. 1:1-4, in loc. (p. 6).

216. Durham, *Commentarie upon the Book of Revelation*, Rev. 1:1-4, in loc. (p. 6).

217. Durham, *Commentarie upon the Book of Revelation*, Rev. 1:1-4, in loc. (p. 6).

all the earth," a clear reference to the Holy Spirit, who alone can bestow the blessings here indicated by the Apocalypse.[218]

---

218. Venema, *Inst. theol.*, x (p. 214).

5

The Deity and Person of the Father

5.1 God the Father: Exegetical Foundations and Doctrinal Definitions

A. God as "Father" in Exegesis and Doctrine

1. The logic of the *locus*: individual discussion of the persons. Following the general arguments concerning the divinity of the three persons in the Godhead, the orthodox typically examine the three persons individually in order to identify both the grounds for the confession of the divinity of each person in detail and the meaning of the names, relational terms, and titles given to each person. Pictet clearly notes this point of transition in the argument of his *locus on the Trinity:* "Having stated that the divine nature is in Scripture attributed to three persons, the Father, the Son, and the Holy Spirit, we must now treat of these persons separately."[1] The Reformed orthodox doctrine of the full Godhead or divinity of Father, Son, and Spirit is typically argued under four general categories, all of which are primarily biblical and grounded either in the direct exegesis of texts or in the hermeneutical process of drawing conclusions from biblical texts. Thus, the persons of the Trinity are individually known to be divine:

> I. From those divine names which are given to them, that are peculiar to God alone.
> II. From their having the divine attributes ascribed to them, and consequently the divine nature.
> III. From their having manifested their divine glory, by those works that none but God can perform.
> IV. From their having a right to divine worship, which none but God is worthy to receive.[2]

---

1. Pictet, *Theol. chr.,* II.xiv.1.
2. Ridgley, *Body of Divinity,* p. 134, cols. 1-2.

These grounds of argument are stated by a large number of the Reformed orthodox and are repeated, in only slightly varied forms, in the discussions of each of the persons.

2. The exegesis of "Father": two implications of the biblical language. The deity of God the Father was, of course, never a matter of dispute, given the consistent biblical identification of God as Father — the issue that the Reformed would have to deal with was the distinct personhood of the Father. Given that God is so frequently identified as "Father" in Scripture, distinction must be made between the "essential" and the "personal" use of the terms — as applied either to the Godhead generally or to the Father personally.[3]

Thus, Scripture calls God "Father," without indication of any distinctions between the persons in such texts as Malachi 2:10, Hebrews 12:9, and (by implication) Acts 17:26-28.[4] In the first of these — "Have we not all one Father? hath not one God created us?" — the text merely speaks of God as the "common Father to all mankind."[5] There no reference here to "Father" in the sense of "the Father of Christ" but only to God as the creator and governor of the world — not to the exclusion of the Son and Spirit, who are elsewhere in Scripture identified as creating the world.[6] The point can also be argued from Hebrews 12:9, where God is identified as "the Father of [our] spirits," juxtaposed with the "fathers of our flesh": even Owen, whose massive commentary on Hebrews is consistently sensitive to the problems raised by the Socinians, fails to take up any trinitarian implication in this place.[7] In the text from Acts 17, the identification of human beings generally as the "offspring" of God also directs our attention to divine Fatherhood, a theme known, as Paul here shows, to the ancient pagan poets and philosophers.[8] Ursinus notes, further, that the essential use of the name "Father" can be applied to other persons of the Trinity: thus, "the Son is expressly called by Isaiah, 'the everlasting Father' (Is. 9:6),"[9] as opposed to the genuine trinitarian passages where the first person is identified as "Father" in distinction from the Son and the Spirit. Thus, "when the word Father is attributed to God *essentially*, though all creatures are excluded, yet all three Divine persons are included, because they are co-equal, they have one nature, will and worship; they are one and the same God."[10]

Some debate occurred among the Reformed over the reference to "Father" in the Lord's Prayer. According to quite a few of the British seventeenth-century writers, the initial address of the Lord's Prayer refers to the Godhead in its oneness by the name

---

3. Polanus, *Syntagma theol.*, III.iv; Ursinus, *Commentary*, p. 140; Cheynell, *Triunity*, p. 326; Witsius, *Exercitationes*, vii.1.

4. Witsius, *Exercitationes*, vii.1.

5. Henry, *Exposition*, Mal. 2:10 in loc.; cf. Ridgley, *Body of Divinity*, II, p. 603.

6. Zanchi, *De tribus Elohim*, pt. 2, V.v.3 (col. 539).

7. Owen, *Hebrews*, 12:9, VIII, pp. 269-271.

8. Henry, *Exposition*, Acts 17:26-28 in loc.

9. Ursinus, *Commentary*, p. 140; cf. Calvin, *Commentary on Isaiah*, 9:6 (CTS *Isaiah*, I, pp. 311-12); Poole, *Commentary*, Isa. 9:6 in loc. (II, pp. 347-7); Trapp, *Commentary*, Isa. 9:6 in loc. (III, p. 320).

10. Cheynell, *Triunity*, p. 326.

"Father,"[11] and therefore belongs to the group of texts — like Malachi 2:10, Hebrews 12:9, and Acts 17:26-28 — that use the term "Father" to indicate the Deity and not one of the persons in the Trinity. Others, however, typically continental Reformed writers, argue strongly that "Father" in the Lord's Prayer indicates the first person of the Trinity.[12] Calvin had certainly not used the text as a major trinitarian reference: in his commentary on the Lord's Prayer, he associated the phrase with the "fatherly love" of God toward humanity: "God is willing to receive us graciously, ... ready to listen to our prayers ... disposed to aid us." Calvin also tells his readers — in keeping with the theme of the *duplex cognitio Dei* — that "it would be the folly and madness of presumption, to call God our Father, except on the ground that, through our union to the body of Christ, we are acknowledged as his children."[13] The *Institutes* takes up this theme at greater length and does speak of Christ as the "beloved Son," the "true Son," and the "only-begotten Son"of God and also speaks of the instruction of the Spirit necessary to right prayer, implying that "Father" is a reference to the first person of the Trinity, but offering no explicit trinitarian argument.[14] Elsewhere, Calvin comments that in places where the divine persons are mentioned together in the New Testament, the name "God" is often specifically a reference to the Father,[15] and conversely, in places such as John 17:8, where Christ prays concerning the words he has received from the Father, that Christ speaks in the person of the Mediator and "Father" means "God" and not the first person of the Trinity.[16]

The same logic with perhaps an unexpected turn is found in Ursinus' lectures on the Heidelberg Catechism. Ursinus insists that we are able to call God "our Father" because of the work of the "only begotten and natural Son of God," through which "we are adopted children of God" and are privileged to call God Father. He is our Father because he gave his Son to die for us. As in the case of Calvin's argument, one might conclude that Ursinus understood the "Father" of the Lord's Prayer as a trinitarian title — but the opposite is the case. In answer to the objection that this prayer to the Father teaches us not to pray to the Son or the Spirit, Ursinus indicates that here Father is to be understood "essentially," in opposition not to the other persons of the Godhead but to creatures. The Lord's Prayer, thus, addresses the triune Godhead, not only the person of the Father: "Father," in the prayer, then, refers to God.[17]

Without laying down a hard and fast rule, the British Reformed writers in the tradition of Westminster tend toward the view that "Father" in the Lord's Prayer is

---

11. Cf., explicitly, Trapp, *Commentary*, Matt. 6:9 (V, p. 92); Watson, *Body of Divinity*, p. 401; and implied in Flavel, *Exposition of the Catechism*, in *Works*, VI, pp. 296-297; Poole, *Commentary*, Matt. 6:9 (III, p. 27); Henry, *Exposition*, Matt.6:9 in loc.; Ridgley, *Body of Divinity* (1855), II, pp. 602-607.

12. Witsius, *Dissertations on the Lord's Prayer*, VII (pp. 154-155); Van der Kemp, *Christian Entirely the Property of Christ*, II, p. 415.

13. Calvin, *Harmony of the Evangelists*, Matt.6:9 in loc. (CTS *Harmony*, I, p. 317).

14. Calvin, *Institutes*, III.xx.34, 36-38.

15. Calvin, *Institutes*, I.xiii.20.

16. Calvin, *Commentary on John*, 17:8 in loc. (CTS *John*, II, p. 171).

17. Ursinus, *Commentary*, pp. 626-627.

a reference to the One God, without trinitarian implication, whereas the continental Reformed, *in the seventeenth century*, tend toward the view that this is indeed a trinitarian reference. Oddly, the British writers are closer to Calvin and Ursinus than the seventeenth-century continental writers are on this particular point. One may even detect a slight pique in the words of the normally irenic Witsius, who acknowledges, on grounds of the doctrine of the Trinity, that the entire Godhead may be "denominated Father" and then goes on to say that he agrees with "those judicious interpreters who maintain that the Father of our Lord Jesus Christ is particularly addressed" in the Lord's Prayer.[18] Van der Kemp, who references the Heidelberg Catechism explicitly at this point — albeit without examining Ursinus' lectures — also infers that the reference is especially to the first person of the Trinity: "although the essence of God, and also the Son and the Holy Ghost may be called Father, and ought to be worshiped, nevertheless we must understand here, by the instructor, by the Father, the first person: for he says, in order to explain this, that God is become our Father through Christ."[19]

Debate with the Socinians became intense over the distinction between essential and personal usage of "Father" — particularly with reference to various biblical texts. Given the readings of Acts 17:29, and Galatians 1:4 as references to "Father" as an essential name, the Socinians, notably Crell, contended that other texts, such as 1 Corinthians 8:6, Ephesians 1:3 and 4:6, and 1 Thessalonians 1:3 and 3:11, were also references to the Godhead in general as "Father." With reference to the first of these texts, the Socinians note that immediately prior, in verse 4, the apostle indicates that "there is no God but one" and then states (verse 6), "there is but one God, the Father, of whom are all things, and we in him; and one Lord Jesus Christ, by whom are all things, and we by him." In the Socinian exegesis, the meaning of the reference to God the Father in verse 6 was determined by verse 4, yielding the argument the Father alone is God, in contrast to Jesus Christ. The point of the text, as in the Socinian interpretation of Colossians 1:16, is the subordination of Christ to God: all things are "of" the Father as the "first cause" but only "by" Jesus Christ as a "second cause" — from which one can only conclude that Christ cannot be God by nature.[20] The Reformed orthodox respond that the very phrasing of verse 6 argues the contrary, that Jesus Christ, as the one involved with the Father in creation, is also by implication God, indeed, the second person of the Trinity. What is more, the verse indicates the order of trinitarian operation as "of the Father" and "by the Son."[21] As for Ephesians 4:6, the statement that there is one God and Father over all things also has a trinitarian

---

18. Witsius, *Dissertations on the Lord's Prayer*, VII (p. 155).

19. Van der Kemp, *Christian Entirely the Property of Christ*, II, p. 414, citing Heidelberg Catechism, q. 120.

20. *Racovian Catechism*, iii.1 (p. 34); iv.1 (pp. 91, 97-98).

21. Owen, *Vindiciae evangelicae*, in *Works*, XII, pp 325-326); Venema, *Inst. theol.*, x (p. 219); cf. Diodati, *Pious and Learned Annotations*, 1 Cor. 8:6 in loc; Poole, *Commentary*, 1 Cor. 8:6 in loc. (III, p. 564)

implication — Father as indicating the entire Godhead — given that Scripture also speaks of Christ as over all things.[22]

Similarly, John 17:3 became important to the trinitarian exegesis of the seventeenth century because of its use in the Socinian argument against the deity of the Son. To the Socinians, the text offered clear testimony to the sole deity of the Father and to the identity of Jesus as a messenger sent by God, himself not divine. In response, differing with Calvin's reading of the text, but finding the same basic sense as Calvin did, Rijssen and various of the seventeenth-century Reformed exegetes argued that the word *monon*, "only," limits not the subject of the phrase, "thee," but the predicate "true God," indicating not "*te solum esse verum Deum*," but "*Te, qui es solus verus Deus*" — not "that you alone are the true God," but "you, who alone are the true God...." Thus, the statement that the Father is the one true God stands in opposition not to the divinity of the Son and the Spirit, but to the claims of the false gods of the Gentiles.[23] The second objection is logical: "*Qui sunt tres numero, non sunt unus Deus.*" Clearly three gods cannot be one God — but three persons thus enumerated which participate in the same divine essence may be one God.[24] Nor does this oneness together with threeness constitute a quaternity, since the three are not distinct *realiter* in essence.[25]

3. The personality of the Father. Apart from their disagreement over the interpretation of the salutation to the Lord's Prayer, all the Reformed orthodox agree that Scripture also calls the first person of the Trinity "Father," in distinction from the Son and the Spirit.[26] The point is most clearly made by recourse to a text like John 17:2-3, where Christ first prays "Father, the hour has come; glorify thy Son that the Son may glorify thee" and then continues (with the antecedent of "thee" being "Father"), "This is life eternal, that they might know thee the only true God, and Jesus Christ whom thou hast sent." The divinity of the Father and the priority of the person of the Father in the order of the Godhead were not a matter of direct controversy. Yet, the identity of the Father as one of the divine persons rather than as merely one of the names of the one God is an issue at the root of the debate with the Socinians. And it is an exegetical issue as well, given that such texts as John 17:2-3, in the words of Van der Kemp, are "a stone of stumbling, and a rock of offense to the Socinians,"

---

22. Zanchi, *De tribus Elohim*, pt. 2, V.v.3 (col. 539), citing John 3:31; Rom. 9:5; and Heb. 1:3.

23. Rijssen, *Summa theol.*, IV.ix, controversia I, objectiones: "Non opposite ad Filium & Spiritum S., sed opposite ad Deos fictitios Gentilium" (*responsio ad obj.* 1); cf. Poole, *Commentary*, in loc. (III, pp. 367-368); Diodati, *Pious and Learned Annotations*, in loc.

24. Rijssen, *Summa theol.*, IV.ix: "Tres numero Dii non possunt esse unus, sed tres numero personae, quae participant eandem essentiam divinam" (*resp. ad obj.* 2).

25. Rijssen, *Summa theol.*, IV.ix, obj. 3 & resp. "Ubi sunt unum & tria, ibi sunt quatuor. R. Si sunt realiter distincta ab essentia; sed hic non"; cf. the further discussion of this text below, 6.2 (C.2).

26. Witsius, *Exercitationes*, VII.1.

who use them as proof that the "Father alone [is] God, rather than the Son and the Holy Ghost.[27]

The orthodox are careful to indicate a series of ways in which the name "Father" is applied to the first person of the Trinity that teach his individual identity, his relation to the other persons, and his relation to the order of creation and redemption. Several of these applications of the name are identified, moreover, with specific documents — namely, the reference to God the Father in the Apostles' Creed and the reference to God as Father in the Lord's Prayer (as interpreted by the continental Reformed). In the creedal form, as in the basic formulation of the doctrine of the Trinity, the first person of the Trinity

> is ... called the *Father*, not in reference to *creation*, by which we are all "his offspring" (Acts 17:28), or to *adoption* in Christ, (Eph. 1:5), but in reference to that singular relation which he bears to his only Son (*Filium proprium*).[28]

Specifically, the credal phrase is not a reference to God "considered essentially," but to God "considered personally," specifically as the first Person of the Trinity, the Father. The creed intentionally here distinguishes God the Father, as person, from God the Son and God the Spirit.[29]

This is not to say that these other aspects of divine paternity are to be set aside, but only that the creedal form itself points toward the primary reason for the identification of the first person as "Father," namely, his relation to the divine Son. In Perkins' words:

> The Father, is a person without beginning, from all eternity begetting the Son.... In the generation of the Son, these properties must be noted: I. He that begetteth, and he that is begotten are together, and not one before another in time. II. He that begetteth, doth communicate with him that is begotten, not some one part, but his whole essence. III. The Father begot the Son, not out of himself but within himself. The incommunicable property of the Father is to be unbegotten, to be a Father, and to beget. He is the beginning of actions, because he beginneth every action of himself, effecting it by the Son and the holy Ghost.[30]

Given these relations to the other persons — as also the role of the first person of the Trinity in the various relations of the Godhead *ad extra*, the first person is rightly called "Father." In general, "a person is a father, in consequence of his having a child or children," and God is Father in this sense, on several grounds.[31]

---

27. Van der Kemp, *Christian Entirely the Property of Christ*, I, p. 193, citing also Rom. 3:25; 1 Cor. 13:13; and Gal. 4:6.

28. Pictet, *Theol. chr.*, II.xiv.2; cf. Junius, *Theses theol.*, XIII.2; Arminius, *Disputationes publicae* V.1.

29. Van der Kemp, *Christian Entirely the Property of Christ*, I, p. 193.

30. Perkins, *Golden Chaine*, V (p. 14, col. 2).

31. Van der Kemp, *Christian Entirely the Property of Christ*, I, p. 195, citing Ps. 2:7; John 5:26.

First, God the Father is Father to the second person of the Trinity "by an eternal and inconceivable generation, Psalm 2:7."[32] He is Father in relation to Jesus Christ, the "only-begotten Son."[33] There is, accordingly, a relationship between the divine Father and the divine Son unlike the entirely conceivable relationship between human fathers and human sons: as we read in the Gospel of John, "as the Father hath life in himself, so hath he also given to the Son to have life in himself" (John 5:26).

Second, God is "Father" to all believers, for the sake of Christ, his Son — as Christ himself declares, to his "brethren," he ascends to his Father, who is also their Father.[34] God, in this sense, is the adoptive father of the elect, who are accepted and adopted in his only-begotten son, Christ Jesus.[35] Thus, the God and Father of Jesus Christ is also the God and Father of believers (John 20:17), and is so on three grounds. In the first place, believers are participants in the new birth or regeneration, according to which they are fashioned anew according to the image of God, having been born again neither of blood nor of human will but of God (John 1:12-13), and are therefore capable of calling God Father. Next, in a conjugal sense, believers acknowledge God as Father in view of their "spiritual marriage" to his Son: Christ is the "husband" of believers (Isa. 54:5) and believers are "the bride and wife of the Lamb" (Rev. 21:9) — with the result that "God, the Father of the Son, is also the Father of his bride and wife, who is therefore called the 'daughter' of the Father,' Psalm 45:16."[36] (It is worth noting that this piety of spiritual marriage, with its central image of believers as the bride of Christ, was a major theme of the *Nadere Reformatie*, and that this particular argument for the fatherhood of God occupied a significant place in late seventeenth-century Reformed thought.)[37] Finally, in an adoptive sense, believers know God as Father because of their gracious adoption into the household of God, so that, "being children, they are also heirs of God, and joint heirs with Christ" (Rom. 8:17)."[38]

Third, God, the Father Almighty, is also identified as "Father" of all creatures, particularly of human beings, inasmuch as all "have received life from him by creation," as testified in Malachi 2:10, "Have we not all one Father? Hath not one God created us?"[39] In summary, "to believe in God the Father ... is to believe in that God who is the Father of our Lord Jesus Christ; and to believe that he is also my Father, and as such has a fatherly affection toward me, for and on account of Christ, in whom he has adopted me as his son."[40]

---

32. Van der Kemp, *Christian Entirely the Property of Christ*, I, p. 195.

33. Ursinus, *Commentary*, p. 140.

34. Van der Kemp, *Christian Entirely the Property of Christ*, I, p. 195, citing John 20:17.

35. Ursinus, *Commentary*, p. 140.

36. Van der Kemp, *Christian Entirely the Property of Christ*, I, p. 195.

37. See, e.g., Abraham Hellenbroeck, *Het Hooglied van Salomo verklaart en vergeestelyk* (Amsterdam: Hendrik Burgers, 1718).

38. Van der Kemp, *Christian Entirely the Property of Christ*, I, pp. 195-196.

39. Van der Kemp, *Christian Entirely the Property of Christ*, I, p. 196; cf. Ursinus, *Commentary*, p. 140.

40. Ursinus, *Commentary*, p. 140.

B. The Personal Properties of the Father

1. God the Father as personally distinct: general issues. The importance of the discussion of the personal properties rests on the fact that the persons are not distinct from one another as finite things having different essences are distinct: as the medieval scholastics had indicated, there can be no essential or substantive distinctions between the persons. This topic, albeit somewhat rarified, was not one ignored by the Reformers: Calvin comments that

> when the Son is joined with the Father, relation comes into view, and so we distinguish between the Persons. But as the Personal subsistences carry an order with them, the principle and origin being in the Father, whenever mention is made of the Father and Son, or of the Father and Spirit together, the name of God is specially given to the Father. In this way the unity of essence is retained, and respect is had to the order, which, however derogates in no respect from the divinity of the Son and Spirit.[41]

The person of the Father is distinct from the person of the Son "not according to being" (*non secundum esse*), but according to the manner of subsistence that is proper to him as a divine person.[42] Conversely, the manner or mode of his subsistence is identified by the personal — as distinct from essential — properties belonging to the Father. De Moor comments that, in the ancient church, the Father was consistently identified as *causa, principium, fons, origo*, and even *totius deitatis*.[43] These personal properties of the Father are variously enumerated: first, there is unbegottenness or aseity; second there is primacy; and third and fourth, some of the orthodox argue active generation and active spiration as properties of the Father,[44] while others discuss these terms as personal acts or operations, distinct to the Father or as properties to be discussed once the order of operation of the Godhead has been defined.[45] In what follows, unbegottenness, aseity, and primacy are discussed as personal properties; active generation and active spiration are noted under the discussion of the intra-trinitarian operations.

2. Unbegottenness and aseity. The initial *proprietas* distinctive of the Father is the negative property "unbegottenness" (*agennesia*) or as it is sometimes called "self-begottenness" (*autogennesia*), according to which his subsistence "*non est ab alia persona, sed Filius & Spiritus ab ipso*" — "is not from another person, but the Son and the Spirit are [both] from Him." Even so, Scripture generally places the Father first in references to the Trinity (cf. Matt. 28:19; 1 John 5:7) not because of temporal precedence or greater dignity — for all three are eternal and possess the same perfections — but rather because "he is represented as *begetting the Son* and as *sending the Holy Spirit*" and is

---

41. Calvin, *Institutes*, I.xiii.20.

42. Junius, *Theses theol.*, XIII.5.

43. De Moor, *Commentarius perpetuus*, I.v.7, citing Bull, *Defensio*, IV.i.1-6, without noting Bull's fairly radical subordination of the Son.

44. Mastricht, *Theoretico-practica theol.*, II.xv.6; Van Til, *Theol. rev. compendium*, II.iii (pp. 45-46); De Moor, *Commentarius perpetuus*, I.v.7.

45. E.g., Witsius, *Exercitationes*, VII.ix-xii; cf. Vii.vii.

not himself begotten or sent by any.[46] The Father, therefore, is traditionally identified as the *principium*, the "source" (sometimes the "cause"), and the "origin of all divinity" (*originem totius Deitatis*).[47]

Thus, the primary positive personal property of the Father is that he is *a se*, of or from himself. This *aseitas*, moreover, is not merely the essential *aseitas* common to all persons of the Trinity, it is also the personal property of the Father: the Father is utterly self-existent, not only as God but also as Father — nor does the Father ever work by the power of another. The Father, unlike the Son and the Spirit, has no *principium*: he is ἄναρχον, whether according to essence or according to person.[48] (The Son and the Spirit can be considered as existing *a se* only according to essence, given that their persons proceed from the Father as the *principium* of the Godhead.)

Wendelin can add a second ultimate property of the Father: the Father alone eternally generates the Son, *homoousios* with himself, so that begetting or generating is in a sense a property belonging solely to the Father.[49] The procession of the Spirit, of course, does not apply here, since it belongs both to the Father and to the Son: we have here a hint of the medieval notion of reflex relations — just as it belongs to the Son alone to be generated, so does it belong to the Father alone to generate.

The Father, as the Reformed orthodox argue, is *not* first in duration, nature or causality, dignity or excellence, but rather in subsistence and operation.[50] The absence of priority in duration argues that God the Father was always Father: the "fatherhood" of the first person of the Godhead is not an added property, brought about in God (as the Arians would have it) by the temporal act of begetting the Son; just as the first person of the Trinity is eternally God, so also is he eternally Father.[51]

The second of these points, that the Father is not first in order of nature or causality, raises a point of connection between the Reformed orthodox view of the Trinity and the formulations of the Latin fathers (particularly following Augustine) and a point of contrast, if not ultimately in meaning, certainly in terminology, between the Reformed orthodox view and that of the Greek fathers. Witsius indicates that a priority in nature or causality is "nowhere affirmed in Scripture" given that a "cause is ... that which gives existence to something else" — and such giving of existence does not and cannot take place in the Godhead, inasmuch as the essence of the divine persons is a single, ultimate essence. It is incorrect, Witsius adds, to argue "any priority or posteriority of nature" among the divine persons, given that the "nature is one."[52]

This consideration leads to the admission that just such a vocabulary of causality can be found among the orthodox Greek fathers, who distinguished between "the

46. Pictet, *Theol. chr.*, II.xiv.1.
47. Marckius, *Compendium*, V.vii.
48. Junius, *Theses theol.*, XIII.7; cf. Mastricht, *Theoretico-practica theol.*, II.xv.6
49. Wendelin, *Christianae theologiae libri duo*, I.ii.4 (3).
50. Witsius, *Exercitationes*, VII.iv-vii.
51. Beza et al., *Propositions and Principles*, III.ii.
52. Witsius, *Exercitationes*, VII.iv.

cause and what is caused" (τὸ αἴτιον καὶ τὸ αἰτιατὸν) in the Godhead.[53] This language, the Reformed conclude, was quite unfortunate, although since the same fathers denied that God the Father has "priority or inequality of nature" over the Son and the Spirit, their basic doctrinal intention was sound. Thus, John of Damascus denies "any precedence in time or superiority in nature of the Father over the Son," indeed any and all superiority of the Father except in "causation" — by which he means specifically that "the Son is begotten of the Father and not the Father of the Son, and that the Father is naturally the cause of the Son," equating the language of causality with that of begetting.[54] This use of language of causation, Witsius argues, is "inaccurate," not to mention "harsh, indistinct, and unscriptural." The sense, however, of the Damascene remains orthodox inasmuch as the causality indicates only the divine begetting. Still, adds Witsius, reflecting a more Augustinian reading of texts like John 14:28, this begetting is no ground for arguing the superiority of the Father, given that it indicates the essential equality of the persons and that the Son (Phil. 2:6) did not count it "robbery" to be "equal with God."[55] Similarly, the Father is not greater in either dignity or excellence, since "infinite and supreme excellence is an essential attribute of Deity: and if any person were possessed of greater excellency and dignity than the Son or Holy Spirit, neither of these persons could be the Most High God."[56]

3. Primacy. Although in no way that relates to essence or essential attributes, there is a primacy of the Father in the Godhead — a "personal primacy in operation, both *ad intra* ... and *ad extra*," according to which the Father is said to work "of himself (*a se*), by the Son and by the Spirit."[57] The Father is the origin or source and *principium* of the Son and the Spirit.[58] Even so, Scripture identifies the Father as God more frequently than it identifies either the Son or the Spirit specifically as God.[59] The Father is first, specifically, in subsistence or *hypostasis*, as is indicated in Hebrews 1:3; the Son is the "express image" or "character" of the person or "hypostasis" of the Father, or in Colossians 1:15, the Son is the "image of invisible God" — yielding the conclusion that "the Father is the *archetype*, the Son the *resemblance*.[60] Even so, in the mystery of revelation, "the Father, according to the distribution of the work of grace among the divine Persons, undertook to display in his Person the majesty of the Godhead, and to reveal it in its glory, as the Son undertook to make himself of no reputation, and the Holy Ghost to act as the ambassador of the Father and the Son."[61]

---

53. Thus, Gregory of Nazianzus, *Oratio*, XXVIII.15; John of Damascus, *De fidei orthodoxa*, I.8; cf. Forbes, *Institutiones*, I.xx; with Witsius, *Exercitationes*, VII.vi.

54. John of Damascus, *De fidei orthodoxa*, I.8.

55. Witsius, *Exercitationes*, VII.iv.

56. Witsius, *Exercitationes*, VII.v.

57. Mastricht, *Theoretico-practica theol.*, II.xv.6.

58. Beza et al., *Propositions and Principles*, III.i-ii.

59. Van der Kemp, *Christian Entirely the Property of Christ*, I, p. 193; cf. Beza et al., *Propositions and Principles*, III.i.

60. Witsius, *Exercitationes*, VII.vi.

61. Van der Kemp, *Christian Entirely the Property of Christ*, I, p. 193.

Thus, the Father's primacy in subsistence or mode of subsisting points directly toward the issue of the other personal properties of the Father, namely, aseity, the begetting of the Son, and the processing, together with the Son, of the Holy Spirit,[62] and as well to the issue of the order of operation of the Godhead. It is this primacy both in subsistence and in revelation, according to which the Father displays the majesty of the Godhead, that yields the identification of God as the cause of all things in such texts as 1 Corinthians 1:24, "We have but one God, the Father, of whom are all things."[63]

For Witsius, the primacy of the Father in the Godhead and in the order of operation of the persons also relates to the form of prayer: in the Lord's Prayer, "the Son enjoins us to call God Father," indicating "expressly the first person of the Godhead, who is the Father of Christ, and in Christ and on Christ's account is our Father." There is, however, the trinitarian assumption that we do not address God the Father without also addressing or invoking the Son and the Spirit, given that "they are one in nature and in honour" and that "what is in common to all three persons in the Godhead" is properly called "Father."[64] Witsius continues by noting his acceptance of the trinitarian reading and he offers the following rule of interpretation:

> In the economy of grace the Father is represented to us under that character in which we ought to address him in our prayers, as sustaining the power and majesty of the Godhead, and as originating and bestowing all saving benefits; the son, as opening up our way to the Father, and providing for us opportunities of approach by his merits and intercession; and the Spirit as forming within us our prayers and groans. And this is the reason why most frequently, and indeed almost always, in Scripture, we find worship addressed to the Father; rarely to the Son; very rarely to the Spirit.[65]

5.2   The Father as Origin and Source: "Works" of the Godhead *Ad intra* and *Ad extra*

A. Views of the Reformers

At the outset of the Christological section of Vermigli's *Commonplaces*, the editor set a series of significant meditations on the relationship of the Trinity and its mode of operation to the incarnation and work of Christ. Vermigli here acknowledges the the significance of the traditional question of "How ... is the Son alone said to be incarnate?" — given that the incarnation is an undivided work of the one God.[66]

---

62. Witsius, *Exercitationes*, VII.viii-xvi.

63. Van der Kemp, *Christian Entirely the Property of Christ*, I, p. 193.

64. Witsius, *Dissertations on the Lord's Prayer*, VII (p. 154).

65. Witsius, *Dissertations on the Lord's Prayer*, VII (p. 155).

66. *Loci communes*, II.xvii.1 (p. 411): "Vere quidem Deus ad nos venire dicitur, multis modis. Proprie tamen & singulariter venit filius Dei, qui ipse est vere Deus, in natura humana ad servandum humanum genus. Etsi enim Deus sit ubique, tamen eum venisse dicimus, quoniam induit naturam humanam: atque ita dicimus venisse ad nos, & sese nobis, repraesentasse & Patrem & Filium, & Spiritum sanctum. Etsi enim opera Trinitatis, quod ad interna attinet, sint singularia, qualia sunt generare, spirare, procedere, ista enim fiunt a vi divina, quae tribus personis est communis, tamen

Musculus similarly noted, "the three persons of the holy triad effect this work of incarnation, but only one truly puts on the flesh."[67]

Vermigli recognizes as a fundamental presupposition of his argument that the actions of the Father, Son, and Spirit are distinct only *ad intra* and that all acts *ad extra* have as their cause or author the One God: the entire Godhead acts as one in all works or relations that "go out" from the Godhead. Vermigli also holds as a presupposition that the order of operation of the persons manifested in the divine economy and the assignment of a work to a particular person corresponds to and indicates the order of existence or mode of relation of the persons *ad intra*. Thus Vermigli can state both that the entire Trinity, Father, Son, and Spirit, is presented to us in the incarnation even though "Christ alone took on himself human nature."[68]

Indeed, the problem faced by the doctrine of the incarnation is that it appears to divide the Godhead, given that in the incarnation the Son of God comes to us *proprie tamen & singulariter* as the Son:

> For if indeed God is everywhere, we nevertheless say he came, for he took human nature: and thus we say that he came to us and presented himself to us, the Father, the Son, and the Holy Spirit. For if indeed the works of the trinity which are inward are also singular — such as to generate, to spirate, and to proceed — these indeed are done by the divine power which is common to the three persons; however those (works) which pertain to externals, are indivisible.[69]

In order to resolve the problem, Vermigli distinguished the incarnation into two categories of divine operation, the divine *actio* and the resultant divine *opus*. The *actio*, or action, of God in the sending of the Son is clearly understood by Scripture as an action of the Father and the Spirit, and, indeed, of the Son himself as well: "efficiens enim causa & actio, ad tres personas pertinuit." Vermigli acknowledges the difficulty of identifying the Son both with cause and effect in incarnation, but he insists that this must be done — the Son is both sender and sent.[70]

Although Calvin does not state the principle clearly in his *Institutes*, one only need go to the commentaries to find the concept of the indivisible work of the Trinity *ad extra*: "We must therefore believe that there is such a unity between the Father and

---

ea, quod ad externa attinet, sunt indivisa. Cur ergo, inquies, solus Filius dicitur incarnatus?"

67. Musculus, *Loci communes*, cap.18 (p. 145): "Sic, inquiunt, tres sacrae Triadis personae operatae quidem sunt in opere incarnationis huius, verum una ex illis tantum carnem induit."

68. Vermigli, *Commonplaces*, II.xvii (p. 599, col. 2).

69. *Loci communes*, II.xvii.1 (p. 411): "Vere quidem Deus ad nos venire dicitur, multis modis. Proprie tamen & singulariter venit filius Dei, qui ipse est vere Deus, in natura humana ad servandum humanum genus. Etsi enim Deus sit ubique, tamen eum venisse dicimus, quoniam induit naturam humanam: atque ita dicimus venisse ad nos, & sese nobis, repraesentasse & Patrem & Filium, & Spiritum sanctum. Etsi enim opera Trinitatis, quod ad interna attinet, sint singularia, qualia sunt generare, spirare, procedere, ista enim fiunt a vi divina, quae tribus personis est communis, tamen ea, quod ad externa attinet, sunt indivisa. Cur ergo, inquies, solus Filius dicitur incarnatus?"

70. *Loci communes*, II.xvii.1 (p. 411): "Durum quidem illud videri potest, idem esse & efficientem causam, & effectum."

the Son as makes it impossible that they shall have anything separate from each other."[71] In order to make more clear the concurrence of the three persons in incarnation but the actual incarnation of the Son alone, Vermigli distinguishes between the *action* of God in incarnation and the *work* of the incarnate God. Christ alone took to himself our human nature, but the efficient cause of the action is the entire Godhead: as the Scriptures state, Christ is sent by the Father and by the Spirit; the Son, moreover, "was the cause of his own coming."[72] It is only the union of natures in the person of Christ and the work of salvation accomplished in the incarnate one that belong restrictively to the Son — and, of course, even these events are willed by the triune God.[73]

B. The Era of Orthodoxy: Traditionary Understandings

1. **Divided** *ad intra* — **undivided** *ad extra*: **the orthodox understanding of "works" of the Godhead in general.** In the era of orthodoxy, despite the intense pressure from the Socinian polemic to develop and clarify the doctrine of the Trinity, the Reformed orthodox virtually never attempted to enter speculatively into the sacred precincts of the divine work *ad intra*, but rather sought to lay down rules for the discussion of God and his works — rules that would reflect the numerical unity of the divine essence and the distinction of the persons both *ad intra* and in their work *ad extra*. Polanus offered the following two ways of dividing the subject:

> First, the works of God (*opera Dei*) are either personal (*personalia*) or essential (*essentialia*). The personal works of God are of two kinds (*duum generum*): either purely personal (*simpliciter personalia*) or [personal] in a certain manner (*certo modo*).
> Second, the works of God are either internal or external. The internal works of God in like manner are either personal or essential. The internal essential works of God are the eternal counsel and the decree of God (*aeternum consilium & Decretum Dei*).
> ... The external works of God are of two kinds: creation and providence.[74]

The seemingly missing category of "personal internal works of God" was, in fact, dealt with previously in Polanus' arrangement of topics and is found in the *Synopsis* of book III: "The distinction of persons according to operation is twofold: either according to the manner of working in essential operations, or according to the personal operations." The former member of this division, "the manner of working in essential operations," corresponds with the personal works "in a certain manner"; the latter member of the division, "personal operations" corresponds with the "purely personal" works.

Once this further pairing is recognized, there are four categories of *opera Dei*: the inward personal works or operations, the divine begetting and proceeding, which are

---

71. Calvin, *Commentary on John*, 17:10 (*CTS John*, II, p. 174).
72. Vermigli, *Commonplaces*, II.xvii (p. 600, col. 1).
73. Vermigli, *Commonplaces*, II.xvii (p. 600, col. 1).
74. Polanus, *Syntagma*, Synopsis libri IV, V.

"purely personal"; the inward essential works, the counsel and decree, which are common works of all three persons; the outward essential works, which are the undivided work of the three persons; and the outward works that are considered "personal in a certain manner," namely, the outward works, like incarnation and sanctification, that are performed by the entire Godhead but that terminate on one or another of the persons.

> The essential works of God are those performed by the divine essence, the Father, Son, and Holy Spirit in common, and completed in creatures; which is to say the common work of the Father, Son, and Holy Spirit, willed *communiter* by the Father, Son, and Holy Spirit according to the unity of divine essence and directed *communiter* toward creatures. The point of distinction between the essential and personal works of God is that the former have as their principle the divine essence absolutely considered, operating by the divine power possessed in common by the persons.[75]

There are several canons or rules for clarifying the notion of divine operations. First, the "immanent or internal works" of God are not "different from the divine essence."[76] There are, of course, distinctions that can be made within the Godhead, among the various immanent or internal works, but these distinctions, like the distinctions of persons and attributes, are not to be understood as parts of God, as alterations of the being of the Godhead, or as incidental properties belonging only to God for the duration of their outward effects. Second, of the Trinity, it may be laid down as a rule that the

> *opera Trinitatis ad extra sunt indivisa*, the outward works which concern the creature, belong to one person as well as the other, as to create, govern; but *opera ad intra sunt divisa*, the personal properties or internal works are distinguished, as the Father begets, the Son is begotten of the Father, and the Holy Ghost proceeds from the Father and the Son.[77]

"Distinct actions" may indeed be attributed to each of the divine persons — as they are in numerous places in Scripture — but, given the oneness of God, "this must not be understood to intimate that either the power or the operation of the Persons is divided, or that any one of them accomplished his work more *immediately* that another."[78] Inasmuch as God is one, the "power and operation of all the Persons are one and undivided; and each Person is the immediate and perfect cause of the whole work."[79] Or, as Perkins had defined the point,

> The workes of God are all those which he doth out of himselfe, that is, out of his divine essence. These are common to the Trinitie, the peculiar manner of working alwaies reserved to every person.[80]

---

75. Polanus, *Syntagma*, IV.iii (p. 237, col. 1).
76. Wollebius, *Compendium*, I.iv, canons B.ii.
77. Leigh, *Treatise*, II.xvi (p. 128); cf. the citations in Heppe, *Reformed Dogmatics*, pp. 116-117.
78. Witsius, *Exercitationes*, VI.ii.
79. Witsius, *Exercitationes*, VI.ii; cf. Amyraut et al., *Syntagma thesium theologicarum*, I.xvii.16.
80. Perkins, *Golden Chaine*, vi, in *Workes*, p. 15, col. 1.

Therefore, as a further rule of the discussion, it can be argued that "one and the same external work, in a different consideration, is both personal and essential.[81] Inasmuch as "the essence is common to all of the persons," the "essential operations" are also common operations that can be considered both essentially and personally.[82] Thus, by way of example, "the incarnation of Christ, in respect of inchoation or initiation, is the essential work of the whole Trinity, but in respect of bounds or termination, it is the personal work of the Son alone," given that Father, Son, and Spirit are equally the "cause" of the incarnation, but only the Son is incarnate. So also, the *ad extra* works of creation, redemption, and sanctification, are works of the entire Godhead, but they are nonetheless each attributed, in view of their *terminus*, to one of the persons, namely, to the Father, the Son, and the Spirit, respectively.[83] The underlying issues addressed by these distinctions are the unity of the Godhead and the distinction of the persons — specifically the issue that the revelation *ad extra* corresponds with the reality *ad intra*, and the issue, so prominent also in the Reformed orthodox discussion of the attributes, that the *ad extra* manifestations of God are fully grounded in the essential reality of God.

Owen makes the same point concerning the relation of the *opera ad extra* to the divine essence, relating it closely to issues of piety and Christian life:

> Although the formal object of divine worship be the nature of God, and the persons are not worshipped as distinct, but as they are each of them God; yet, as God, they are every one of them distinctly to be worshipped. ... Hence, the Scripture speaks not of anything *between God and us* but what is founded on this account. The Father worketh, the Son worketh, and the Holy Ghost worketh. The Father worketh not but by the Son and his Spirit; the Son and Spirit work not but from the Father. The Father glorifieth the Son, the Son glorifieth the Father, and the Holy Ghost glorifieth them both. Before the foundation of the world the Son was with the Father, and rejoiced in his peculiar work for the redemption of mankind. At the creation, the Father made all things, but by the Son and the power of the Spirit. In redemption, the Father sends the Son; the Son, by his own condescension, undertakes the work, and is incarnate by the Holy Ghost. The Father, as was said, communicates his love and all the fruits of it unto us by the Son, as the Holy Ghost doth the merits and fruits of the mediation of the Son.[84]

The language used here argues both unity and distinction in the divine works. The Godhead is never to be conceived as divided or separated — as the formula indicates, there is *alius* and *alius*, not *aliud* and *aliud*, namely, an other and another "person," not an other and another "thing" — and the distinction of works must be stated in such a way as to respect the doctrine of unity in trinity and trinity in unity. (The use of *aliud* here, moreover, the neuter noun ti indicate specifically not merely "another,"

---

81. Wollebius, *Compendium*, I.iv, canons A.i.

82. Wollebius, *Compendium*, I.iv, canons A.ii.

83. Wollebius, *Compendium*, I.iv, canons A.i.

84. Owen, *Divine Original*, in *Works*, XVI, p. 342.

but "another thing," reflects the traditional usage, ensconced in the decisions of the Fourth Lateran Council, that the personal threeness of the Godhead must be understood as coordinate with the identity of God as one *res*, one "reality" or "thing.")

These arguments yield three categories for the "acts" or operations of the Godhead: first, the essential works of the Godhead in which all of the persons work equally and undividedly — notably, the eternal decree and all of the works *ad extra*; second the internal, personal works of the Godhead and the "personal properties" related to them, which constitute the distinctions between the persons; and third, the so-called *appropriata* or *opera appropriata*, the external works of the Godhead that are attributed more to one person than to another, not so as to divide the *opera ad extra* among the persons but so as to indicate that the divine work terminates on one person rather than another or for the sake of glorifying the persons "distinctly according to their appropriated acts."[85]

2. The Father's active generation of the Son. In accord with the medieval tradition, some of the Reformed include among the personal properties of the Father terms that identify the Father's action as distinct from the Son's and the Spirit's in the *ad intra* operations of the Trinity. Thus, instead of merely identifying the generation or begetting of the Son, the act of the Father and the act of the Son can be distinguished — the former, an "active generation" (*generatio activa*), the latter a "passive generation" (*generatio passiva*). The point of the doctrine is simply to identify the Father as the source of the action, the begetter or one generating, the Son as the recipient of the action, the begotten or generated one.[86] The theses debated at Saumur make a point of noting that the Father generates the Son "voluntarily" — freely and without coercion — but that *voluntarius* in this sense is not distinguished from *naturalis*, as if it signified something contingent, that could be or not be. The inward divine emanations are free and without coercion, but they are also natural and occur by a necessity of nature. They are also eternal, denoting no change in God — in fact, indicating the eternity of the generated or emanated persons, who being eternally produced must have a duration identical with that of the Father.[87]

This dogmatic language typically referred for its exegetical foundation to Psalm 2:7, "Thou art my Son, this day have I begotten thee," on the ground that the verse is directly applied to Christ in Acts 13:33 and that the entire Psalm is given a messianic interpretation in Acts 4:25-26.[88] There was some debate, however, among the interpreters of the Reformation and orthodox eras over the meaning and application

---

85. Leigh, *Body of Divinity*, II.xvi (p. 253).

86. Mastricht, *Theoretico-practica theol.*, II.xv.6; Amyraut et al., *Syntagma thesium theologicarum*, I.xvii.15; Van Til, *Theol. rev. compendium*, II.iii (pp. 45-46).

87. Amyraut et al., *Syntagma thesium theologicarum*, I.xvii.17; cf. Gürtler, *Synopsis theol.*, vi.25-26, 31, 33.

88. De Moor, *Commentarius perpetuus*, I.v.8; cf. Mastricht, *Theoretico-practica theol.*, II.xv.6; Van Til, *Theol. rev. compendium*, II.iii (pp. 45-46). The perpetuation of this reading of the Psalm in conjunction with Acts long beyond the high orthodox era is seen in Bengel, *Gnomon*, Acts 4:27 in loc. — "agit Psalmus ille de *regno* Christi."

of the text. Calvin, following out the older pattern of identifying a double literal sense of the text, understands the text as fulfilled in David, who "was begotten by God when the choice of him to be king was clearly manifested," and as "more truly fulfilled in Christ," who is prefigured or "represented" by David in the Psalm. "This day," therefore, indicates "the time of this manifestation," whether of David or of Christ, not the moment of birth for either David or Jesus, nor the eternal begetting of the second person of the Trinity, but the moment of official manifestation as the one sent by the Father. Calvin therefore associates Psalm 2:7 with John 1:14, "We have seen his glory, as of the only begotten of the Father." This reading leads Calvin to argue that the ultimate reference of the test is to Christ as God's "only begotten Son," but in his mediatorial manifestation, and not in his "eternal generation." There is no ground in the text for reading "this day" as a reference to God's eternity "without any relation to time." The "begetting" indicated in the verse, therefore, "ought not to be understood of the mutual love that exists between the Father and the Son."[89]

In accord with Calvin, the later Reformed exegetes do understand the primary referent of the text to be Christ as the only-begotten Son of the Father, but they often differ over the implications of the reference: does it refer to Christ's temporal manifestation and to his assumption of the office of mediator in whole or in part, as both Ainsworth and Dickson argue, the former emphasizing the priestly, the latter the prophetic office; or as Diodati and Poole argue, does it refer to the eternal begetting, specifically to the active generation of the Son by the Father?[90] In the case of Poole's exegesis, moreover, all three understandings are noted: David as the primary referent, in the day of his establishment in his kingdom; Christ as the primary referent, either in his eternal generation or in his temporal manifestation. Reluctant to argue a double referent in the text, Poole refers to the Davidic interpretation as "far-fetched and doubtful" and identifies the two christological readings as suitable, with "this day" either referring to the divine eternity in which "there is no succession ... but it is all as one continued day or moment, without change or flux," or day or moment when Christ was "declared to be the son of God in power" as indicated in Romans 1:4 and by the reference to Psalm 2:7 in Acts 13:33.[91]

The exegetical debate among the Reformed rendered the text of Psalm 2:7 a less than adequate proof of a doctrine on which all were agreed and a point for difficult debate with the Socinians, who declared it a reference to David alone and irrelevant to the doctrine of the Trinity.[92] Significantly, the text is not argued at much length by Owen, despite his profound interest in the relation between the Father and the Son, his assumption that the text did speak of the eternal begetting, and his intense debate with the Socinians.[93] The argument is catalogued through a series of

---

89. Calvin, *Commentary upon the Psalms*, 2:7 in loc. (CTS *Psalms*, I, pp. 16-18).

90. Cf. Ainsworth, *Annotations upon the Psalms*, 2:7 in loc.; Dickson, *Exposition of the Psalms*, in loc.; Diodati, *Pious and Learned Annotations*, in loc.; Poole, *Commentary*, in loc. (II, p. 3).

91. Poole, *Commentary*, in loc. (II, p. 3).

92. Arnold, *Religio Sociniana seu Catechesis Racoviana ... refutata*, i.16, 19.

93. Cf. Owen's brief note on the text in *Vindiciae evangelicae*, in *Works*, XII, pp. 213-214.

commentators and dogmaticians by De Moor — is the text a reference to the eternal filiation or active generation of the Son by the Father, or is it a reference to the manifestation of the Messiah?[94] Ultimately, De Moor sees no difficulty in reading the text as testimony to the twofold birth or generation of the Son: the Psalm speaks of the begetting of the Son as declared in the decree of God, prior to which the Son is Son by nature and actively generated by the Father in eternity, subsequent to which the Son is to be "exhibited in time" as the Messiah.[95]

3. The Father's active spiration, with the Son, of the Holy Ghost. As in the preceding comments on the Father's active generation of the Son, so in the inward work of the Trinity is the Father said to spirate or process the Spirit in the active sense — *spiratio activa* — and, in view of the *filioque*, to do so with the Son, as indicated by John 15:26 and to a lesser extent by Galatians 4:6. Thus, active spiration is not a sole property or operation of the Father, but belongs also to the Son. Like the role of the Son in the begetting or generation of the second person, the Spirit's role in his own emanation or spiration is, by definition, passive: he does not spirate himself, but is spirated by the Father and the Son. The Reformed orthodox note this traditionary point but typically do not elaborate it either dogmatically or exegetically apart from their discussions of the *filioque*,[96] nor will they dwell on the question of a difference between the active generation of the Son and the spiration of the Spirit.[97] Since the inward divine actions or emanations have no analogy in the created order, they cannot be adequately conceived by human beings: all that can be inferred is that they neither divide the divine essence into parts or multiply it into different beings — rather these actions result in the multiplicity of persons in the undivided essence.[98]

4. Personal distinctions in the undivided work *ad extra*. The personal distinction of the works, therefore, assumes the undivided work of the Godhead but identifies both "the order of the Persons, which ought to be observed in their operation, as well as in their subsistence," and the termination of each divine act *ad extra* "upon some certain Person."[99] From the first point, the order of persons in operation as well as subsistence, arises the attribution of creation to the Father: just as the Father is the first and unbegotten person of the Trinity, the one in whom the other two persons find their beginning or foundation *ad intra*, so is creation the first work of the Godhead *ad extra* and the beginning or foundation of all of the other works of God *ad extra*. Still, in this attribution of creation to the Father, the agency of Son and Spirit is assumed.[100]

---

94. De Moor, *Commentarius perpetuus*, I.v.8.

95. De Moor, *Commentarius perpetuus*, I.v.8.

96. Mastricht, *Theoretico-practica theol.*, II.xv.6; Van Til, *Theol. rev. compendium*, II.iii (p. 46). On the *filioque*, see below 7.4 (A.2).

97. Ames *Medulla*, I.v.15; Voetius, *Syllabus problematum*, iv (fol. H4v); Venema, *Inst. theol.*, x (p. 220).

98. Beza et al., *Propositions and Principles*, III.v.

99. Witsius, *Exercitations*, VI.iii; Beza et al., *Propositions and Principles*, IV.iv.

100. Witsius, *Exercitations*, VI.iii.

The second point, the ascription of particular works to particular persons on grounds of the personal *terminus* of the work, respects the identification of the Son and the Spirit as Redeemer and Sanctifier. Thus, the work of redemption is attributed especially to the Son, inasmuch as the Son (and neither the Father nor the Spirit) is the divine person for union with whom Jesus' humanity was conceived and who is the incarnate Savior. Yet, the Father is also active in the work of redemption, inasmuch as Scripture testifies that he "reconciled the world to himself" in Christ and "made peace by the blood of the cross of Christ."[101] Perkins can comment of the Son that "His proper manner of working is to execute actions from the Father, by the Holy Ghost."[102]

Witsius also notes a third way in which the attribution of distinct works to the individual persons is sometimes argued: some have distinguished between remote and proximate or mediate and immediate principles of operation in the divine acts *ad extra*. In this view, the entire Godhead is the remote and mediate cause or principle of sanctification and the Holy Spirit the proximate and immediate cause or principle. This view, Witsius indicates, must be rejected: "for one divine person does not act by another, as an intermediate cause; and as the power of all the persons is one and the same, each of them accomplishes an effect by the same immediate operation."[103] When God is identified as the sanctifier of his people (Ezek. 20:12), it is God, "essentially considered," who performs the work — "the Father and the Son perform this work no less immediately that the Spirit; for the power and the operation of all three are the same" even though, in the order of operation, "the Father acts by the Son and through the Holy Spirit." Witsius concludes that "it is only where there is a diversity of essences and operations, that the distinction betwixt a mediate and an immediate cause can have any place."[104]

C. Reformed Approaches to Essential and Personal Works of the Trinity *Ad intra*

1. The Father and the works or operations of the Trinity: general considerations. Discussion of the Father's primacy in the Godhead leads directly toward and serves to define the work of the Father as distinct in order (albeit never separate) from the work of the Son and the Spirit. Although the entire divine work *ad extra* is consistently defined as the common work of all three persons, it is nonetheless not a work that disobliges the distinction of persons — indeed, it follows out the manner of the working of the persons *ad intra*, where there are distinct personal operations even, according to some of the Reformed, in the unified *opera essentialia*, namely, in the decrees of God. These considerations lead the Reformed orthodox to discuss the *opera essentialia* in their relation to the *opera personalia* in some detail, in close relation to the form of the divine work *ad extra*. There is, moreover, a fair amount of variety and difference

---

101. Witsius, *Exercitations*, VI.iii; citing 2 Cor. 5:19 and Col. 1:20.
102. Perkins, *Golden Chaine*, V (p. 15, col. 1).
103. Witsius, *Exercitations*, VI.iii.
104. Witsius, *Exercitations*, VI.iii; cf. Forbes, *Instructiones in hist. theol*, I.10.

among the Reformed on this point, with some holding close to the traditional definition of the *opera essentialia* as the common work of the persons and offering little by way of distinction of personal roles, others developing a highly complex discussion of the distinct *ad intra* roles of the persons in the essential work of God. Thus,

> The persons of the Trinity have among them a certain economy, according to which the works common and undivided as to operation are claimed as proper to certain persons in respect of mode of operation. The principle of operation is the same, common Deity, will, power: the operation is common to all the persons. As to inception and operation the work is common; as regards mode of operating it is peculiar and distinct, according to the resemblance to that which is truly proper to any person, and according to the dispensation of the mystery of godliness and of human salvation.[105]

Thus, although the essential works of the Godhead have as their *principium* the divine essence "absolutely considered" and operating or working as a common or conjoint work, there is still an order or economy of the persons belonging to it.[106]

> According then to the order of subsisting and acting, even as the Father is *a se*, subsists and operates through Son and Holy Spirit, the Son is and operates *a Patre* through the Holy Spirit, the Holy Spirit is and operates *a Patre et Filio*, so, suitably to this order of subsisting and acting *ad intra*, there is also assigned to the Father *ad extra* the inauguration of things, or creation; to the Son their continuation, or redemption; to the Holy Spirit their consummation, or sanctification and regeneration. Likewise, because of the terminus of the action and of the disposition peculiar to the particular person whose operation is specifically illuminated in the work, the incarnation, although the work of the entire Trinity, is referred singly to the Son.[107]

Thus, the inward trinitarian work of grounding or founding salvation moves toward completion *ad extra* in the Son and the Spirit, manifesting a triadic structure of the entire eternal and temporal work of salvation:

> There are three sorts of work by which our salvation is completed and accomplished.
> 1. *Immanent* in God toward us, as his eternal love set and passed *upon* us, out of which he chose us, and designed this and all blessings to us.
> 2. *Transient*, in Christ done *for* us; in all he did or suffered representing of us, and in our stead.
> 3. *Applicatory*, wrought *in* and upon us, in the endowing us with all those blessings by the Spirit; as calling, justification, sanctification, glorification.[108]

Venema similarly speaks of the priority of the Father in the order of working, according to which the Father "begins the work, the Son executes it, and the Holy Spirit perfects

---

105. Heidegger, *Corpus theol.*, iv.45; cf. Heppe, *Reformed Dogmatics*, p. 118.
106. Polanus, *Syntagma theol.*, IV.iii (p. 237, col. 1); cf. the discussion in Muller, *Christ and the Decree*, pp. 149-151.
107. Heidegger, *Corpus theol.*, iv.45; cf. Heppe, *Reformed Dogmatics*, p. 118.
108. Goodwin, *Work of the Holy Ghost*, IX.i (p. 405).

it" — or, in the case of the eternal decree, the Father in a sense decrees, the Son executes, and the Spirit consummates the work.[109]

It was quite typical of the early orthodox to develop this point and to insist on an understanding of the divine decree *ad intra* as a trinitarian work. Beyond this, several seventeenth-century theologians, particularly those with federal inclinations (whether Cocceian or Voetian), also argue an economy of operation both *ad intra* and *ad extra* of the Godhead in which the Father has a specific role, reflecting his primacy, without, of course, removing the essential oneness of the Godhead. The preeminent example of understanding the *ad intra* divine work in a trinitarian sense — specifically, the essential work that in its execution *ad extra* is the common work of the three persons — is the Reformed doctrine of the *pactum salutis*.

2. The eternal decree and the election of Christ. As Perkins indicates in his initial bifurcation of the category of the "work" of God, "The worke or action of God is either his decree, or the execution of his decree."[110] The decree itself, of course, is an *ad intra* work, the execution, an *ad extra* work of God. Yet the decree is not one of the *opera personalia* — rather it is an essential work of God, a work of the whole Godhead. Thus, as Polanus indicates,

> The Father indeed elects us, not as Father, since election is not the proper work of the person of the Father; but as God, for as much as election is the common work of the whole sacred Trinity, of which the principle is the Father.[111]

One of the emphases characteristic of the trinitarian conception of the decree found in early Reformed orthodox writers like Polanus, Perkins, Bucanus, Keckermann, and Ames was the detailed discussion of the relationship of Christ as both divine Son and divine-human Mediator to the eternal decree.

> Christ is, according to both natures, divine and human, one Son of God, not two: according to the divine, by natural generation from the Father, so that, thus, according to it he is Son of God, not elected, but generated; according to the human (he is Son of God) truly first by eternal election, in the second place by creation in the image of God, and in the third place by the grace of personal union with the divine nature.[112]

So also,

> though it be true that Christ is set apart to the worke of mediation, as he is Mediatour, or as he is man, yet as he is God he doth design & set himselfe apart to the same work. For to design the Mediator is a common action of the three persons, the Father, the Sonne, and the Holy Ghost; and yet considering the Father is first in order, and

---

109. Venema, *Inst. theol.*, x (p. 222).

110. Perkins, *Golden Chaine*, VI (p. 15, col. 1).

111. Polanus, *Syntagma*, IV.ix (p. 245, col. 1); cf. Scharpius, *Cursus theol.*, I, cols. 244-245.

112. Polanus, *Syntagma theol.*, IV.viii (p. 244, col. 2).

therefore hath the beginning of the action: for this cause he is said especially to designe, as when Saint John saith, *Him the Father hath sealed.*[113]

Thus, according to Perkins,

> The ordaining of a Mediatour is that, whereby the second person beeing the Sonne of God, is appointed from all eternitie to bee a Mediatour betweene God himselfe & men. And hence it is, that Peter saith, that "Christ was foreknowne before the foundation of the world." And well saith Augustine, that "Christ was predestinated to bee our head." For howsoever as hee is (*logos*) the substantiall word of the Father, or the Sonne, he doth predestinate with the Father, and the Holy Ghost; yet as hee is the Mediatour, he is predestinated himselfe.[114]

3. The love of the Father for the Son and the *pactum salutis*. There are, certainly, two historical antecedents for the notion of the *pactum salutis* in Reformed circles — first, the early orthodox trinitarian understanding of the essential work of God *ad intra* and, second, the more traditional discussion of the Son as the eternal object of the Father's love. It is also the case that, if the Reformed were less than universally enthusiastic over arguments for the Trinity based on such metaphors and similes, they were very much in favor of describing the relation between the Father and the Son in the Godhead in terms of a mutual love.

For Owen, the love of God as expressed in the interrelationship of the divine persons is the deepest mystery of the universe, "the principle part of the blessedness of God" and "the only fountain and prototype of all that is truly called love." The divine love is "eternal and necessary," inasmuch as it is one of the essential properties of the divine being. The divine love, according to Owen, is "natural and necessary unto the Divine Being" more specifically defined as the "ineffable mutual love of the Father and the Son, both in and by that Spirit which proceeds from them both."[115] Christ, as Son of God, is the "principle object" of this love inasmuch as "the Father loves, and cannot but love, his own nature and essential image in him." Thus,

> the person of Christ in his divine nature is the adequate object of that love of the Father which is 'ad intra' — a natural necessary act of the divine essence in its distinct personal existence; and the person of Christ as incarnate, as clothed with human nature, is the first and full object of the Father in those acts of it which are 'ad extra,' or are towards anything without himself.[116]

The Father, as first person of the Trinity, has a fundamental role in the *pactum salutis* or covenant of redemption: it is the particular dispensation or economy of the father that, "according to his eternal purpose ... he appointed his Son to be a surety, and

---

113. Perkins, *Exposition of the Creed*, p. 169, col. 1A-B; also, see Wollebius, *Compendium*, I.xvii, props. 3, 4, 6, 8; Ames, *Marrow*, I.xix.4-6 (where the *pactum salutis* enters the formulation); *Conf. West*, VIII.i and iii; and Watson, *Body of Practical Divinity*, IV.6 (p. 192).

114. Perkins, *Trestise of Predestination*, p. 608, cols. 1D-2A; cf. *Golden Chaine*, p. 105, col. 2A.

115. Owen, ΧΡΙΣΤΟΛΟΓΙΑ, in *Works*, I, p. 145.

116. Owen, ΧΡΙΣΤΟΛΟΓΙΑ, in *Works*, I, p. 145.

delivered the elect to him, that he might redeem them."[117] The doctrine of the *pactum salutis*, characteristic of the work of Cocceius and the federalist theologians of the mid-seventeenth century, had significant roots in earlier orthodox Reformed meditation on the eternal foundation in God of all divine works *ad extra*. Although the doctrine is, specifically, a part of the *locus de foedere*, and not typically discussed in the context of the doctrine of the Trinity, it deserves mention here, given its trinitarian implications and, indeed, given its relation to the earlier Reformed discussion of the relationship of the Son of God to the eternal decree and to its execution in time. Thus, prior to the development of the *pactum salutis*, Polanus writes of the trinitarian aspect of election with reference to the Son as *sponsus*:

> The Son, indeed, is incarnate because he wills voluntarily to be made our sponsor, voluntarily subjecting himself to the Father not according to nature, but according to the voluntary arrangement (*oeconomia*) or dispensation: a natural subjection is, surely, distinct from an economic or dispensatory subjection: he is made freely obedient to the Father, not according to the divine nature in itself (*in se*), but according to will: obedience, indeed, is not the natural act of a nature (*actus naturalis naturae*), but of the will or free accord of the person of Christ (*voluntarius personae Christi*).[118]

The federal theologians of the seventeenth century also elaborate on the trinitarian work in the incarnation by referring it to the covenant of redemption, or *pactum salutis*:

> This event took place according to an agreement between the Father and the Son, or, as it is expressed by Zechariah (6:12-13), according to "the counsel of peace," which was between "the Lord of Hosts," the Father, and "the man," the Son, who was to become man, "whose name is the Branch," being raised up by God (Is. 6:2; Mal. 1:11), and being the new root of a new family, or of the Sons of God according to the Spirit.[119]

Witsius further identifies three periods of the covenant of redemption — the "commencement" of the covenant in the eternal counsel of God; the "intercession" of Christ, which begins immediately after the fall of Adam and Eve; and the voluntary servitude of Christ in the work of incarnation.[120] The first of these is an eternal intra-trinitarian work that serves as the foundation of the entire work of salvation *ad extra*.

D. *Opera Appropriata*: Works *Ad extra* "in a Certain Manner" Personal

1. The works *ad extra*: undivided but trinitarian.[121] Although the work of the Godhead *ad extra* is, by definition, the work of the one God and, therefore, the conjoint

---

117. Van der Kemp, *Christian Entirely the Property of Christ*, I, p. 194, citing Jer. 30:21 and John 17:6; cf. Cocceius, *Summa theol.*, xxxiii.1-6; Witsius, *Oeconomia foederum*, II.ii.2, 10; iii.2.

118. Polanus, *Syntagma*, VI.xiii (p. 364, col. 2).

119. Witsius, *Exercitations*, XIV.xvii.

120. Witsius, *De oeconomia foederis*, II.ii.2-4.

121. N.B., given that the topics in the following sections belong to the broader body of doctrine, I have presented them only from the perspective of the trinitarian work *ad extra* and the concept of *opera appropriata* — there is no attempt to offer a full discussion of the various topics.

work of all three persons, there are still particular aspects of the divine work in the temporal economy that pertain particularly to one or another of the persons.[122] This consideration follows quite logically from the doctrine of the Trinity itself, according to which there is a single divine essence, distinguished into three modes of subsisting: just as there is a single divine essence, there is a single *ad extra* divine work — so also, just as there are three persons or modes of subsistence in the Godhead, each distinguished by personal properties and a specific operation, there are also three modes of working in the single *ad extra* divine work.[123] This is one of the points of more detailed, even speculative, elaboration of the doctrine of the Trinity that the Reformed orthodox share with the medieval scholastics.[124]

The basic doctrinal point is quite simple: the order of the persons *ad intra* in the *opera personalia* is mirrored *ad extra* in the *opera appropriata*. The *opera appropriata*, moreover, are distinct not in the sense of separated works but in the sense of modes of operation contributing to the ultimately undivided work of the Godhead *ad extra*. In this distinction of modes of operation, moreover, each of the persons not only performs what is appropriate to each, but also the works assigned to the Son and the Spirit are said to terminate on their persons. This usage of "terminate" or identification of one of the persons as a *terminus* carries with it an important implication that must not be overlooked. In the logical language of the older orthodoxy, *terminus* is paired with *fundamentum*. Taken together, the terms are used in descriptions of relations or of acts bringing about relations. The *fundamentum* is the foundation or source of the relationship, and in the statement or proposition that defined the relationship, it stands as the subject. The *terminus* is the conclusion of the action constituting the relationship that stands in the objective position in the descriptive proposition. Thus, in all actions or operations of the Godhead, the Father is the *fundamentum* or *fons* who works by the Son (as *terminus*) or with and through the Son by the Spirit (as *terminus*).

Thus, after dividing the external works of God into two kinds, works of nature and works of grace and then identifying the works of nature as creation, providence, and government, Venema comments that in the work of nature, "the three persons have their respective place, the Father being the originating — the Son the efficient — and the Holy Spirit the perfecting cause" and, by extension, the work of creation is typically assigned to the Father, redemption to the Son, and sanctification to the Spirit. This extension of the argument, however, is a highly "unsatisfactory" way of understanding the divine work *ad extra*, particularly given the biblical texts (John 1:3; Eph. 3:9; Col. 1:16; and Heb. 1:2) in which the Father is revealed as creating by the Son. It is more precise, therefore, to state that the Father is the "foundation" or source of the entire divine work, whether in eternally decreeing all things or in actually

---

122. Amyraut et al., *Syntagma thesium theologicarum*, I.xvii.16.

123. Cf. Owen, *Pneumatologia*, III.1, in *Works*, III, p. 209; Venema, *Inst. theol.*, xiv (p. 260); cf. Henry, "On Some Implications of the 'Ex Patre Filioque,'" pp. 22-23.

124. Thus, e.g., Bonaventure, *Breviloquium*, VI.1. See above 1.3 (A.2, 3).

creating them.[125] Owen, similarly, writes of the work of salvation as the work of "the whole blessed Trinity, and each person therein," in such a way that

> the spring or fountain of the whole lieth in the kindness and love of God, even the Father. ... The procuring cause of the application of the love and kindness of God unto us is Jesus Christ our Saviour, in the whole work of his mediation.... And the immediate efficient cause in the communication of this love and kindness of the Father, and through the mediation of the Son, unto us, is the Holy Spirit.[126]

This qualification of the Father's role in the economy of divine working reflects the identity of the Father as the "source of all that is divine and of all the persons (*fons omnis deitatis, & omnium personarum*)."[127]

2. The primacy of the Father in all *opera ad extra*. Given that the Father is the *fundamentum* or *fons* of the Godhead and of divine persons *ad intra* and remains the foundation and source in all works *ad extra*, the primacy of the Father can be identified in all of the works of God. Thus, first, the work of creation belongs to the Father in the specific sense that creation is the means by which the eternal counsel is executed. This execution of the eternal counsel, moreover, relates to the creative work of God in two ways: in the first place, since God has eternally determined to give his grace to the elect, he must bring the elect into existence. The Father, as the divine person from whom all flows and from whom arises the economy of the *pactum salutis*, is therefore also identified as Creator: creation is the means to the end of his elective will. In the second place, creation is the means by which God initially reveals the covenant of works, in which mankind is promised eternal fellowship in return for obedience. Here, too, God the Father, as promulgator of the covenant of works, is the one to whom creation belongs.[128]

Second, the establishment and "administration of the covenant of Grace under the Old Testament also belongs to the dispensation of the Father,"[129] insofar as the Son was not yet fully revealed and insofar as it is the Father who promises the Son as redeemer. Yet, on this point, there are differences of opinion among the Reformed: Ball, for one, was reluctant to use trinitarian language in relation to the Old Testament economy of the covenant of grace in view of the obscurity of the Old Testament references to the Trinity and of the fact that God is fully revealed as Father only in the redemptive work of the Son.[130]

Third, the Father performs particular works in relation to the redemptive activity of Son and Spirit. In Goodwin's words, "God the Father had but two grand gifts to bestow; and when once they should be given out of him, he had left them nothing that was great (comparatively) to give, for they contained all good in them; and these

---

125. Venema, *Inst. theol.*, xiv (p. 260).
126. Owen, *Pneumatologia*, III.1, in *Works*, III, p. 209.
127. Mastricht, *Theoretico-practica theol.*, II.xxv.3.
128. Van der Kemp, *Christian Entirely the Property of Christ*, I, p. 194
129. Van der Kemp, *Christian Entirely the Property of Christ*, I, p. 194.
130. Cf. Ball, *Treatise of the Covenant of Grace*, pp. 200-201.

two gifts were his Son, who was his promise in the Old Testament, and his Spirit, the promise of the New."[131] Thus, it is the Father who sends the Son in the temporal economy, to be made man, born of Mary, and placed under the law. It is also the work of the Father to demand of the Son the debt for sin and, following the Son's payment, to raise him from the dead. With reference to the Holy Spirit, it is the Father who bestows the Spirit on the Son and who sends the Spirit into the hearts of believers.[132]

Fourth, the Father has a "special dispensation with respect to the elect," namely, "that he bestows his Son and all his sovereign benefits upon them."[133] So too, fifth, although the office of judgment at the eschaton is of given to Christ, seated at the right hand of God, the person of the Father is, for a series reasons belonging to the economy of divine operations, identified as the Judge of the world:

> The Father in the work of salvation is considered as the supreme Judge, who directs all things, who requires satisfaction, who receives it from the one he sent to procure it, and who, to sum up all in a word, maintains the majesty of the Godhead, for which reason he is sometimes called God in contradistinction from the other persons.[134]

A right understanding of the work of the Father, argues Van der Kemp, sets aside the Socinian objections to the divinity of the Son and Spirit. The "offense" that they take at "the Godhead of the Father, the humiliation of the Son, and the sending of the Holy Spirit" that leads them to declare only the Father to be God is removed or set aside by right consideration of the manner of the working of the Godhead, specifically in these "the dispensations" or administrations of the Father — inasmuch as "we may thus clearly comprehend in what manner the Son and the Holy Spirit, who are consubstantial with the Father, can be sent, and in what manner the Son, who is himself God, is the servant of God and satisfied the justice of God."[135]

3. Creation: appropriate to the Father. The work of creation, the incarnation, and the redemption of humanity in regeneration and sanctification serve as significant illustrations of the basic principle that the *opera trinitatis ad extra sunt indivisa*, but also, in coordination with that basic principle, they also serve to illustrate the association of certain works of God with individual persons of the Trinity. Creation is a case in point. It would be as erroneous to assign creation purely to the Father as it would be to assign incarnation purely to the Son and the work of regeneration and sanctification purely to the Spirit.

The Father, as foundation and source, arranges "all things by his determinate purpose" and assigns "to them their order and arrangement." He is also specifically identified by Scripture as the creator of the "heavens and the earth," namely, of the material foundation of all finite things (Gen. 1:1). Yet, the Son, as the Word of God,

---

131. Goodwin, *Work of the Holy Ghost*, I.ii (p. 9).

132. Van der Kemp, *Christian Entirely the Property of Christ*, I, pp. 194-195.

133. Van der Kemp, *Christian Entirely the Property of Christ*, I, p. 195.

134. Pictet, *Theol. chr.*, II.xiv.1.

135. Van der Kemp, *Christian Entirely the Property of Christ*, I, p. 195; cf. Witsius, *Oeconomia foederum*, II.iii.5-7.

is identified as the one by whom all subsequent work of creation is accomplished. It is "the work of the Son," therefore, "to execute the will of the Father, by creating all things as to their form" — "thus the creation of each part belongs to him, as God in the beginning declares when he is said to have made all things 'by his word,' Psalm 33:6."[136] The Spirit also has a role in this work, specifically in "carrying all things in creation and providence to a consummation, and in his adapting them to their several ends." Accordingly, the "beauty, harmony, and motion" of all things in creation are understood as the work of the Spirit.[137]

This particular appropriation of the creation of the underlying matter of the universe to the Father follows from the traditional trinitarian reading of Genesis 1 — but is not universally argued among the Reformed, probably because, if pressed too far, it violates the underlying assumption that the Father works by the agency of the Son and the Spirit. The first verse of Genesis 1, "In the beginning God created the heavens and the earth," is subject to several possible interpretations. Since the name of God in this place is Elohim, the combination of the plural name with the singular verb lead some of the traditionary exegetes to argue the Trinity from the very beginning of the text, while others, notably Calvin,[138] argued against a trinitarian reading of the first verse and postponed discussion of persons of the Trinity until verses 2 and 3, where the Spirit and the divine speech in creation are introduced. Still others, following out the assumption that use of a general designation for God, when conjoined with references to Word and Spirit, ought to be taken as a reference to the Father, understand the first verse of Genesis 1 as a reference to God the Father rather than to the Trinity.

4. Incarnation — appropriate to and "terminating on" the Son. As for the incarnation, the underlying difficulty of the doctrine from the perspective of a trinitarian monotheism is to identify the work as genuinely the work of the one God but also as a work in which only one of the divine persons is incarnate. This difficulty was observed early on in the history of the doctrine, as indicated by one of Augustine's theological letters.[139] Augustine attempts to resolve the problem by drawing on a set of basic questions (*An sit, quid sit, quale sit?*) used in the rhetorical tradition, arguing that any thing must always have about it a certain threefoldness — namely, the existence or original cause of existence by which a thing "is," the identity, species or form by which it is "this" or "that," and quality or condition in which it remains. These are the modes of its existence: "whatever *is* must forthwith be *this* or *that*, and must *remain* so far as possible in its own generic form," and therefore, "these Three do nothing in which all do not have a part."[140] In God there is existence itself, the "is" of God, which is Father; there is also the identity or identifying form, the species, the "that" or "this"

---

136. Venema, *Inst. theol.*, xiv (p. 262).

137. Venema, *Inst. theol.*, xiv (p. 262).

138. Calvin, *Commentary on Genesis*, Gen. 1:1 in loc. (*CTS Genesis*, I, pp. 70-72); and see *PRRD*, III, 4.2 (B.6) for discussion of Elohim as a divine name.

139. Augustine, *Letter XI*, to Nebridus, in *NPNF*, 1ˢᵗ series, I, pp. 228-230.

140. Augustine, *Letter XI*, to Nebridus, 3 (p. 229).

of God, which is Son (here we see, probably a natural Neoplatonic association of Word, Logos, and form); and finally, there is the condition in which it remains, which is Spirit. What God is — the form, the Word, the Son — teaches both *that* God is and *that* God remains what he is: it is the function of the "that" to identify existence and condition. Even so, the Son reveals the Father and the Spirit. Thus, the incarnation of the Son refers not to a division of essence but to a distinction of operation. In one sense Augustine's answer merely turns the question back on itself: God as revealed in the flesh is the second person, because the second person is the revelatory modality of the Godhead. Thus incarnation is described as the unified work of the three persons which, in the interpenetration or circumincession of the persons, terminates upon the second person, the Word, the Godhead in its revelatory modality.[141]

Polanus poses the question: "since the incarnation of Christ is the common work of the whole sacred trinity, why is the entire sacred Trinity not incarnate?" This question points toward a distinction and toward a fundamentally Augustinian answer. Scripture teaches that "the Word was made flesh," indicating that, in Witsius' words, "the subject of the incarnation, or he who became man, is not the Father, nor the Holt Spirit, but the Son alone," given that "although the essence and operation of the three persons in the Godhead are the same, the flesh was not assumed by the divine *essence*, but by a certain *person*."[142] The incarnation, considered "inchoatively" or from the perspective of its inception, as one of the works of the Godhead *ad extra*, must be an undivided or common work (*opus commune*) of all persons in the Trinity. However, considered "terminatively" or from the perspective of its completion, it is a divine work that concludes in the person of the Son with the assumption of human nature and is, therefore, the *opus proprium* of the Son. Thus, "after a certain manner" (*certo modo*) the incarnation is a personal work belonging to the economy of the Godhead *ad extra*, not an essential or common work. Only the Son, not the Father or the Spirit, assumes human nature.[143] Thus, there is a sense that, although the entire undivided divine essence is incarnate, the divine essence in union with Christ's humanity is not to be understood *simpliciter*, but as the "natura divina determinata in Filio, id est, hypostasis sua persona Filii."[144] In brief,

> The principal efficient cause and author of the incarnation is the entire sacred trinity, Father, Son, and Holy Spirit, in such a way that the human nature is created and suited for the person of the Son by the Father, Son, and Spirit acting together.[145]

---

141. Augustine, *Letter XI*, to Nebridus, 5 (p. 230). N.B., "mode" or "modality" in this context is unrelated to the problem of "modalism" as exhibited in the patristic heresy known as Modalistic Monarchianism, inasmuch as the "modes" in Modalistic Monarchianism are "roles" that belong to God's revelation in the temporal economy, whereas the "modes" in Augustine's language are logical modalities representing the inward disposition of the divine essence.

142. Witsius, *Exercitations*, XIV.iv.

143. Polanus, *Syntagma*, VI.xiii (p. 364, col. 1).

144. Polanus, *Syntagma*, VI.xiii (p. 364, col. 1).

145. Polanus, *Syntagma*, VI.xiii (p. 364, col. 1).

Scripture itself teaches that all three persons of the Godhead "concur" in the work, and that the work is to be attributed to each of the divine persons. Hebrews 10:5 teaches that incarnation is the work of the Father, Philippians 2:7 that it is the work of the Son, and Luke 1:35 and Matthew 1:18, 20 that it is the work of the Spirit.[146]

5. Regeneration as the proper work of the Spirit. Although the Spirit is involved in all of the work of God *ad extra*, there are "especial works" that are considered as the operations of the Spirit — notably those works relating to "the calling, building, and carrying on the church unto perfection." Owen further divides the work of the Spirit into three parts, "1. Of sanctifying grace; 2. Of especial gifts; 3. Of peculiar evangelical privileges." Owen also declares that regeneration is "the proper and peculiar work of the Holy Spirit."[147] All of these works stand in the category of "applicatory" as distinct from "immanent" or "transient" works of the Godhead.[148] From the trinitarian perspective the question arises, as in the case of the incarnation of the Son, as to how the Spirit is considered the particular author of the gifts of calling, regeneration, faith, and sanctification when all of the *ad extra* works of God are the works of the one, entire Godhead.

For many of the commentators on the Heidelberg Catechism, the issue of the *opera appropriata* of the Spirit was raised directly by questions and answers 53 and 65:

> Q. 53. What dost thou believe concerning the Holy Ghost?
> A. First, that he is true and co-essential God with the Father and the Son; secondly, that he is also given unto me, to make me by a true faith, partaker of Christ, and all his benefits, that he may comfort me, and abide with me forever....
> Q. 65. Since then we are made partaker of Christ and all his benefits by faith only, whence comes this faith?
> A. The Holy Ghost works it in our hearts by the preaching of the holy gospel, and confirms it by the use of the holy sacraments.[149]

Under the former question, Ursinus argues that the effectual working of the Spirit in believers belongs to "the giving of the Holy Ghost by the Father and the Son" and, therefore, must be understood as a trinitarian work that respects the "order of working" of the three persons in the Godhead. This order is "the same as the order of their existence": "the will of the Father precedes, the will of the Son comes next, and that of the Holy Ghost follows the will of both the Father and the Son, yet not in time, but in order."[150] Accordingly, by way of example, Scripture teaches that faith is the gift of the Father (Eph. 2:8), but also that the apostles prayed to Christ that their faith might be increased (Luke 17:5), and that the Holy Spirit is "the Spirit of faith" (2 Cor.

---

146. Witsius, *Exercitations*, XIV.xv.

147. Owen, *Pneumatologia*, II.5-III.1, in *Works*, 3, pp. 206-207; cf. Witsius, *Exercitations*, XXXIII.xxxv-xxxvi.

148. Goodwin, *Work of the Holy Ghost*, IX.i (p. 405), cited, above, 5.2 (C.1).

149. Heidelberg Catechism, qq. 53, 65, in Schaff, *Creeds*, III, pp. 324, 328.

150. Ursinus, *Commentary*, p. 281.

4:13). The "outward" work of conferring faith, is, thus, "common to the three persons," but it is ascribed peculiarly to the Spirit — so that, "according to the distribution of the work of grace among the divine Persons ... the Father ordained grace for the elect, the Son purchased it, and the Holy Ghost applies and dispenses it to the favorites of God."[151]

---

151. Van der Kemp, *Christian Entirely the Property of Christ*, II, p. 5.

6

The Person and Deity of the Son

6.1 The Person and Generation of the Son

A. The Personality or Personhood of the Son: Issues and Debate

1. Jesus Christ as the only-begotten Son of God. Few objections had ever been raised in the history of the church to the personality of Son apart from his divinity — except for the antitrinitarian theory of Sabellius, Noetus, and their followers — but in the late seventeenth century the Arminian Le Clerc attempted to render *Logos* in John 1:1 as "reason" and to argue that the Son was no more than "the eternal reason of God" or "a quality in God." In addition, the Socinians, although they were quite willing to identify Christ as "Son of God," grounded the identification not in the essential divinity of Christ but in Jesus' appointment to the office of Mediator, in his miraculous birth from the virgin Mary, in his extraordinary spiritual gifts and his resurrection, and in the exceeding love of God for him. Calovius managed to list some thirteen reasons, gathered out of various Socinian works — other than essential divinity or divine Sonship — that the Socinians used to explain the biblical language of Christ as "Son of God."[1] The orthodox theologians consistently, therefore, offer arguments for the unique personality or personhood of the divine Son and his eternal generation from the Father — whether against the classical heresies and their more recent representatives or, in the high and late orthodox eras, specifically against Le Clerc, the Socinians, various other antitrinitarians, and those who followed their arguments.[2] Like the ongoing complaint against Epicureans and skeptics, orthodox-era complaint against classical trinitarian heresies should not be understood as pro forma attacks

---

1. Hoornbeeck, *Socinianismus confutatus*, II.i (pp. 6-8); cf. Abraham Calovius, *Socinianismus profligatus, hoc est, Errorum Socinianorum luculenta confutato* (Wittenberg: Joh. Borckard, 1668), ii.6 (p. 201).

2. Hoornbeeck, *Socinianismus confutatus*, II.i (pp. 8-9).

on ancient problems but as present worries over their contemporary versions, heresies revived in the wake either of a more historically oriented patristic scholarship or as the result of changing patterns of exegesis.[3]

As a preliminary point of argument, the orthodox acknowledge that the various grounds acknowledged by the Socinians for identifying Christ as the Son of God are genuine evidences of Christ's sonship, but not at all suitable grounds for the identification of him as Son. Were he not the Son of God, none of these evidences of Sonship would belong to him: he would not be the Mediator, he would not have been miraculously born or endowed with such a degree of spiritual gifts, and he would not have been raised from the dead.[4] Thus, specifically,

> that Christ is the Son of God's love, and that he, who is the begotten Son, is also the beloved Son of God, is certain; but God's love to him is not the foundation or cause of this relation. The reason why he is the Son of God, is not because God loves him; but the reason why he loves him, is because he is the Son of God.[5]

Rather Christ is called Son of God, in his divinity, because of his relation to God the Father in the order of the inward subsistence of the Godhead.

Hoornbeeck argues the point, beginning with an extended examination of Psalm 2:7, "thou art my Son, this day have I begotten thee," using the *analogia scripturae* to draw out the messianic understanding of the Psalm and the eternality of the begetting of the Son.[6] Ridgley notes that personal pronouns are used to distinguish the Father and the Son — as in Psalm 110. The name "Son of God," whatever else it entails, very clearly "denotes him a Person distinct from the Father" as do the frequent New Testament references to the sending of the Son by the Father. Moreover, references to the Son as Redeemer, Mediator, Surety, Creator, Prophet, Priest, King, also denote personality "and all those works which he performs, as sustaining these characters or relations, are properly personal."[7] Neither are the Father or the Spirit ever referred to by these names or said to do the work indicated by them.

As indicated above in the context of antitrinitarian objections, the title "Son of God" itself was a major point of debate. Certainly, all human beings can be called "sons" or "children" of God — but, contrary to the claims of the Socinians, this sonship does not merely refer to Christ's birth from the Virgin Mary.[8] The identification of Christ as "Son of God" carries with it a distinct "force and meaning," a "higher sense" than other applications of the phrase: he is called "the son of God with power" (Rom. 1:4), "the first-born of every creature" (Col. 1:15), "the only-begotten Son" (John 1:18),

---

3. Cf. the remarks on Epicureanism and skepticism in *PRRD*, I, 1.3 (A.4); 6.3 (B.3); III, 3.2 (B.1, 4; C.3); changing patterns of exegesis are discussed in *PRRD*, II, 2.3 (B-C).

4. Venema, *Inst. theol.*, xiii (p. 245).

5. Gill, *Doctrine of the Trinity*, pp. 145-146.

6. Hoornbeeck, *Socinianismus confutatus*, II.i (pp. 9-19).

7. Ridgley, *Body of Divinity*, p. 118, col. 1.

8. Gürtler, *Synopsis theol.*, vi.29; note the prior element in the Socinian argument, namely, the attribution of "God" to beings that are not divine: see *PRRD*, III, 4.2 (B.6).

and God's "own Son" (Rom. 8:32), all indicating that he is called Son of God in a manner peculiar to him, and on the ground of "something higher than his human nature."[9] The text in Colossians 1:15 indicates, for example, not that he was "created" but that he was *genitus*, prior to all creatures.[10] This conclusion follows from the fact that Scripture identifies him as the firstborn of every creature, speaks of his glory as the only-begotten Son and of his identity as the divine Word before his incarnation and the assumption of the flesh: he is called "Son of God" because of his divine essence — which is the foundation of the incarnation, his mediatorial office, and his work of redemption.[11]

The orthodox identify three exegetical arguments used by the Socinians against the traditional claim that the title "Son of God" is an indication of divinity. First, from the nativity as recounted in Luke 1:31-35, where the angel announces to Mary that Holy Spirit shall "come upon" her and the power of the "Highest" shall "overshadow" her and that, therefore, her child shall be "called the Son of God."[12] To the Socinian theologian or exegete, the text simply indicated that the divine title was accorded to the human Jesus because he was born by the agency of the Spirit.[13] Second, the divinity of Christ was questioned on the basis of the argument, drawn from John 10:36, "Say ye of him whom the Father hath sanctified and sent into the world, 'Thou blasphemest'; because I said, 'I am the Son of God'?" The inference here is that the title "Son of God" rests on the sanctification and sending of Jesus by the Father, namely, on the appointment of Jesus to the office of Mediator, not on his divinity.[14] The third argument against sonship implying divinity, based on the citation of Psalm 2:7 in Acts 13:32-33, was particularly dangerous to the seventeenth-century orthodox position. Given the citation of the Psalm in Acts 13:33, it had an assured christological reference and, in the view of a large number, perhaps the majority of precritical exegetes, a very specific reference to the eternal generation of the Son from the Father. In this particular facet of the debate, the literal meaning and limits of Acts 13:32-33 were turned against the traditional dogmatic understanding — yielding the dilemma that the very text used to argue the traditional doctrine had now been turned against it. The text in Acts reads, "we declare unto you glad tidings, how that the promise which was made unto the fathers, God hath fulfilled the same unto us their children, in that he hath raised up Jesus again; as it is also written in the second psalm, 'Thou art my Son, this day have I begotten thee.'" Where the tradition had used the citation to argue a christological reading of the Psalm as its primary meaning, the antitrinitarian criticism extended the argument to read the Psalm through the text of Acts 13:32-33, yielding

---

9. Venema, *Inst. theol.*, xiv (pp. 245-246).

10. Zanchi, *De tribus Elohim*, pt. 2, III.xii.4 (col. 494).

11. Venema, *Inst. theol.*, xiv (p. 246).

12. Venema, *Inst. theol.*, xiv (p. 257).

13. Racovian Catechism, iv.1 (pp. 53-54); Biddle, *Duae Catecheses*, iv (pp. 48-49).

14. Biddle, *Duae Catecheses*, iv (p. 49).

the argument that the begetting of the Son in the Psalm was not a reference to the inner life of the Trinity but rather to the resurrection.[15]

In response to each of these three arguments, the Reformed note that the biblical texts cited do not state causes or reasons for Christ to be called the Son of God but rather of the signs given to the world that he is indeed God's Son: the texts themselves indicate the priority of Christ's sonship over the event referred to in the text and identify the event as a manifestation of the sonship. In the case of Luke 1:35, "The Holy Ghost shall come upon thee, and the power of the Highest shall overshadow thee: therefore also that holy thing which shall be born of thee shall be called the Son of God," the phrase, "therefore also" (διὸ καὶ), "does not point to his miraculous birth as the only reason why he should be so designated"; rather, the phrase teaches his sonship and eternal generation and leads the reader "to the sure conclusion that he who was born of Mary was the Son of God."[16]

As for the claim, resting on John 10:36, that Christ is called Son of God because of his sanctification by the Father to the mediatorial office, the text itself indicates otherwise, given the preceding statement, "I and the Father are one" (v. 30), which "gave offense to the Jews," given its implication of divinity: the following text (vv. 35-36) is part of Jesus' response to the Jewish objectors. The reference to his sanctification by the Father is not a basis for his being named "Son of God," but an appeal "to his sanctification by the Father and to his mission into the world in evidence of the reality of his sonship."[17] The use of Acts 13:32-33 to disprove eternal divine sonship fails for similar reasons. Diodati specifically counters this antitrinitarian claim in his *Annotations*: "not that the eternal Son was engendered of the Father at his resurrection, or after it, but because by it all humane weaknesse which he had put on, being put off, he was gloriously, and undoubtedly declared to be the Son of God."[18] The Psalm itself, as cited in Acts 13, drives home the point: in Venema's reading, Psalm 2:7, "this day have I begotten thee," does not refer to the eternal begetting of the Son but to a "public sign" that Christ is the Son of God, capable of being paraphrased as "I have not only constituted thee my Son, but I have shown that thou art also," similar to the implication of Matthew 3:17, "This is my beloved Son in whom I am well pleased."[19]

2. Sonship and the problem of subordination. The orthodox examine also a series of objections drawn from Scripture: first, resting on Acts 2:36, some have asserted that *Christus factus est Dominus post resurrectionem*. This text refers not to his "essential lordship, which he had from the foundation of the world," argues Rijssen, "but to the fulness of the manifestation and inauguration of his personal and economical rule,

---

15. Biddle, *Duae Catecheses*, iv (p. 49); cf. Venema, *Inst. theol.*, xiv (p. 259). Note the discussion of the exegesis of the Psalm above, 5.2, B.2.

16. Venema, *Inst. theol.*, xiv (p. 257); cf. Amyraut, *De mysterio trinitatis*, V, p. 244.

17. Venema, *Inst. theol.*, xiv (p. 258).

18. Diodati, *Pious and Learned Annotations*, Acts 13:33 in loc., citing Rom. 14 as collateral argumentation.

19. Venema, *Inst. theol.*, xiv (p. 259); cf. Amyraut, *De mysterio trinitatis.*, V, p. 245.

which is given to him as he is the God-man."[20] Similarly, from Hebrews 1:2 it can be argued that in so far as Christ had to be "constituted" heir of God, he must not be essentially divine: yet his being heir is "not a gift of grace but a property of his nature" in other words, "he is not Son in so far as he is heir, but heir insofar as he is Son."[21]

At various points in his exegesis of John 14, Calvin indicates that various heretics have abused the text — most notably, perhaps, verse 28, "for the Father is greater than I," used by the Arians to claim that Christ "is some sort of inferior God." Still, Calvin does not accept the usual orthodox patristic reading of the text: the fathers, in order to refute the Arians, referred the passage to Christ's humanity, but, comments Calvin, the subordination of Christ to the Father does not refer here either to his humanity or to his divinity or, indeed, to the way in which Christ differs from the Father, but instead to the reason that "he descended to us," namely, "to unite us to God."[22]

Among the later exegetes, Diodati specifically reflects Calvin's reading of the text at the point that Christ speaks of the Father as greater than himself (v. 28), without, however, explicitly contradicting the patristic reading of the text:

> Is greater] not in respect of his nature or essentiall glory, for therein the Sonne is equall with the Father, John 5:18; Phil. 2:6, but in the order of redemption, in which the Father holds the degree of party principall, as representing the whole Deity in its glory and Majesty: and the Sonne as that of Mediatour of peace and Reconciliator. The meaning is: seeing that I am issued from the Father, and have been manifested in the flesh for this worke, my return to the Father in his glory, shall be a certain proof to you that all things are accomplished.[23]

Hutcheson reads the text similarly, making no reference at all to the use of this passage in arguments over the essential equality of the Son with the Father, but refers it to the greatness of the Father in contrast to Christ's humanity and mediatorial office in the state of humiliation: Christ here tells believers that, in "departing out of the world ... as God he layeth aside that veil under which he appeared in his state of humiliation," evidencing "not only his advancement" but also his accomplishment of "all things for which he came into the world." In the eschaton, on grounds of his accomplishment, the Mediator will be "advanced to be next in glory to the Father."[24]

Poole, by contrast, lines out both the patristic and the more distinctly Reformed reading. He notes, explicitly against the Arians and the Socinians, that the text does

---

20. Rijssen, *Summa theol.*, IV.ix, controversia II, obj. 1 & resp.; cf. Turretin, *Inst. theol. elencticae*, III.xxviii.30.

21. Rijssen, *Summa theol.*, IV.ix, controversia 2, obj. 2 & resp.; cf. Turretin, *Inst. theol. elencticae*, III.xxviii.31.

22. Calvin, *Commentary on John*, 14:28 in loc. (*CTS John*, II, p. 102).

23. Diodati, *Pious and Learned Annotations*, in loc.; so also Trapp. *Commentary*, John 14:28, in loc. (V, p. 397); cf. Zanchi, *De tribus Elohim*, pt. 2, V.vii.3 (col. 554).

24. Hutcheson, *Exposition of the Gospel of John*, 14:28 in loc. (p. 310).

not indicate the Father to be "greater in essence" than the Son, but can be understood to have three meanings:

> 1. Either as to the order amongst the Divine Persons; because the Father begat, the Son is begotten; the Father is he from whom the Son proceeded by eternal generation: in which sense, divers of the ancients, amongst whom Athanasius, Cyril, and Augustine, and some modern interpreters, understand it. Or, 2. As a Mediator sent from the Father, so he is greater than I. Or, 3. In respect of my present state, while I am here in the form of a servant; and in my state of humiliation.[25]

The last of these meanings, comments Poole, giving the nod to the Reformed reading of the text without criticizing the fathers, is the best of the three in view of the preceding text, "yea would rejoice, because I said, I go unto my Father" — indicating the passage from the state of humiliation into the state of exaltation.[26]

The divinity of the Son seems also to be denied by Colossians 1:15, which calls him "the firstborn of all creatures." Rijssen points out that the Greek of the text is *protokotos* and not *protoktistos*: it refers to the lordship that Christ has over all things made by him. He does not receive this title as a created thing set foremost among creatures, for if this were so, the text would not also say that he was in the beginning and that he formed all things.[27] Thus, the text allows two readings, namely, that the "first-born" is the one "begotten by the Father, of his own proper essence, and equall with him before anything was created ... that is to say, everlasting" or that "he is as Gods great Deputy and Viceregent in the world, as the first-born were in families."[28] Davenant specifically adds that the text must not be used to infer a begetting of the Son in time or, as the Arians claimed, that the Son is a creature.[29] A similar explanation obtains in the case of Rev. 3:14, where Christ is called the *principium creaturae Dei*. This text speaks of Christ "not passively, as if he were the first creature, but actively, as if all creatures take their origin from him — as explained in the citation from Paul,"[30] although many of the Reformed exegetes restrict the sense of this usage of "beginning" to mean the redemptive beginning of those "creatures of God" that have been "created in Christ Jesus unto good works" (cf. Eph. 2:10).[31] And, again, when it is said that

---

25. Poole, *Commentary*, John 14:28 in loc. (III, p. 357); cf. Zanchi, *De tribus Elohim*, pt. 2, I.ii.3 (cols. 384-385), strongly arguing the second.

26. Poole, *Commentary*, John 14:28 in loc. (III, p. 357).

27. Rijssen, *Summa theol.*, IV.ix,, controversia 2, obj. 3 & resp.; cf. Turretin, *Inst. theol. elencticae*, III.xxviii.37.

28. Diodati, *Pious and Learned Annotations*, in loc., citing Ps. 89:27 as an example of the latter point.

29. Davenant, *Exposition of Colossians*, 1:15 in loc (I, pp. 185-186).

30. Rijssen, *Summa theol.*, IV.ix, controversia 2, obj. 4, resp.; cf. Turretin, *Inst. theol. elencticae*, III.xxviii.37; also, Diodati, *Pious and Learned Annotations*, in loc.

31. Thus, Junius, *Exposition upon the Apocalyps*, p. 47; cf. Poole *Commentary*, Rev. 3:14 in loc., allowing either or both readings (III, p. 959).

Christ *habet principium*, it is said *communicationis*, by communication, not *inchoationis*, not by way of a beginning.[32]

Some would also use 1 Corinthians 8:4-6 against the divinity of the Son — for there Scripture states that the Father is the one God to the exclusion of other Gods. The context here, however, does not manifest a contrast being made between the divinity of the Father and the divinity of the Son or the Spirit, but rather — as is seen from verse 4 — a contrast between the divinity of the true God and the false claims to divinity of the idols.[33] Thus, the text of verses 4 and 5 indicates that "there is none other God but one" even though there are "many" beings and things identified as "gods" and "lords" both "in heaven and on earth": this is the common usage whether of Scripture or of human language in general, inasmuch as the term "god" is applied "to the true God, and to divers creatures, though not in an equal sense of truth, nor in equall reality, but either by errour, or by some resemblance, or analogy."[34] When the text goes on to declare "one God, the Father, of whom are all things, and we in him; and one Lord Jesus Christ, by whom are all things, and we by him" (v. 6), it in no way implies that Christ is not God — no more than it takes dominion away from the Father by calling Christ "Lord." The text does distinguish between God the Father in his eternal glory and God the Son in his mediatorial work, especially in the phrase "and we by him."[35] The language "of whom are all things" with reference to the Father and "by whom are all things" with reference to Christ refers specifically to the "order of working in the holy Trinity" — showing also that the order of working of the Godhead is the same in redemption as it is in creation.[36]

3. Divine begetting and incarnation: debate over eternity and immutability. From the earliest encounter with antitrinitarians, the Reformed were pressed to argue the divine begetting of the Word and the incarnation as the operations of an eternal and immutable being. Calvin noted the "outcry" of certain persons who feared to deny the divinity of Christ but who nonetheless denied his eternity, claiming that "the Word only began to be when God opened his sacred mouth in the creation of the world."[37] To claim this is to deny the immutability of God. Rather, the interpretation of the text ought to observe the rule that "the names of God, which have respect to external work, began to be ascribed to him from the existence of the work, as when he is called the Creator of heaven and earth." Even so "piety does not recognize or admit any name

---

32. Rijssen, *Summa theol.*, IV.ix,, controversia 2, obj. 6, resp.; cf. Turretin, *Inst. theol. elencticae*, III.xxviii.36.

33. Rijssen, *Summa theol.*, IV.ix, cont. II, obj. 5 & resp.; cf. Turretin, *Inst. theol. elencticae*, III.xxviii.38.

34. Diodati, *Pious and Learned Annotations*, 1 Cor. 8:5 in loc.

35. Diodati, *Pious and Learned Annotations*, 1 Cor. 8:5 in loc.

36. Poole, *Commentary*, 1 Cor. 8:6 in loc. (III, p. 564); Diodati, *Pious and Learned Annotations*, 1 Cor. 8:5 in loc.; and note the nearly identical exposition in Calvin, *Commentary on the First Epistle to the Corinthians*, 8:5-6 in loc. (CTS *Corinthians*, I, pp. 276-278).

37. Calvin, *Institutes*, I.xiii.8.

which might indicate that a change had taken place in God himself."[38] Calvin returned to the question from a different perspective when confronting Servetus' claim that Christ's sonship derived from the fact that "he was begotten in the womb of the Virgin by the Holy Spirit." On the contrary, Calvin insists that "the definition of the Church stands unmoved, that he is accounted the Son of God" in his humanity "because the Word begotten by the Father before all ages assumed human nature by hypostatic union, a term used by ancient writers to denote the union which of two natures constitutes one person," and the Word himself "is called a Son on account of his Godhead and eternal essence."[39]

In the course of the seventeenth-century debate with the Socinians, the Reformed orthodox continued to debate the problem of incarnation, divine sonship, and the doctrine of the full divinity of the Son. Socinian theologians continued to interpret the title "Son of God," as found in Luke 1:35, as no more than a reference to Jesus' miraculous birth — with the result that the incarnation was read as a "miraculous exercise of divine power" and "Son of God" a term indicating Jesus' origin by the work of the Spirit, not an indication that "as we believe, he proceeded from eternity from God"[40] The filiation of the Son is a most unique "communication of essence from the Father" by an eternal act of generation. This conclusion arises from the fact that Christ is not simply called "the Son" of God by way of eminence (Matt. 16:16; Heb. 1:5) but God's "own Son" (John 5:18; Rom. 8:2) and is identified as the "only begotten Son" (John 1:14, 18) and the "most beloved" Son (Matt. 3:17), all implying essential Sonship. "If he were called Son only on account of a gracious communication of existence and glory," Turretin argues, he would not have been called God's "own Son" or the "only begotten": sonship resting on the "communication of existence and glory" is attributed to angels, to Adam, to believers, and even to magistrates, none of whom are also identified as God's "only" Son or as the "only begotten."

> Therefore it is necessary that there be some other mode of filiation proper and singular to him, which can be no other than by generation, so that by nature he may obtain what is conferred on others by grace, as the apostle argues in Hebrews 1:5, where he teaches that Christ is so the Son that, with respect to him, not even angels are or can be called sons.[41]

This filiation, moreover, does not in any way contradict the divine attributes and cannot be used as an argument against the divine immutability. The logical objection is simple:

---

38. Calvin, *Institutes*, I.xiii.8.

39. Calvin, *Institutes*, II.xiv.5.

40. Venema, *Inst. theol.*, iv (p. 257); cf. Biddle, *Duae Catecheses*, iv (pp. 48-49), for a version of the Socinian argument; and see below 6.2 (B.1-2) on the debate over the title "Son of God."

41. Turretin, *Inst. theol. elencticae*, III.xxix.14.

The Son of God, true God, was made man in time, prior to which he was not man. God is not, therefore, utterly immutable.[42]

This problem was addressed by the fathers, who argue that the Son was incarnate without alteration of his divinity: in the incarnation, the divinity does not take on human attributes and the humanity is not absorbed into the divine — either of these things would indeed indicate change in God, but neither occurs in the incarnation. There is no mutation of the Logos in substance or nature. Beyond this, the mutation belongs to that which comes into existence, namely, the human nature of Christ, which did come to exist in time, before which it did not exist, and which was exalted by gifts conferred in the union. The divine nature, however, existed prior to the union and was not altered by it.[43]

B. The Eternal Generation of the Son

1. Orthodoxy in polemic against the Socinians. Underlying the Socinian attack on the traditional doctrine of the Trinity was their radical assumption of the oneness of God as underscored by their denial of the generability of divine substance. Thus, the Socinians argued that

> this generation out of the Father's essence involves a contradiction. For if Christ had been generated out of the essence of his Father, he must have taken either a part of it, or the whole. He could not have taken a part of it, because the divine essence is indivisible. Neither could he have taken the whole; for in this case the Father would have ceased to be the Father, and would have become the Son: and again, since the divine essence is numerically one, and therefore incommunicable, this could by no means have happened.[44]

From Owen's perspective, the Socinian claim is a product of rationalistic reductionism: "this is the fruit of measuring spiritual things by carnal, infinite by finite, God by ourselves, the object of faith by corrupted rules of corrupted reason."[45] The Socinians had, in other words, failed to relegate reason to an ancillary status — failing both to recognize its corruption and limitation or to acknowledge its proper use.[46] Owen begins with the premiss that the divine begetting is in fact indicated by Scripture. Given this revelation from God, the notion of a divine begetting cannot be declared impossible by human reason. What is more, once the distinction between infinite God and the finite creation is acknowledged, the theologian ought to be prepared to recognize that "what is impossible in finite, limited essences, may be possible and convenient to that

---

42. Zanchi, *De natura Dei*, II.iv, q. 2.2 (col. 79).

43. Zanchi, *De natura Dei*, II.iv, q. 2.2 (col. 79).

44. Racovian Catechism, iv.1 (p. 70); cf. the citation in Owen, *Vindiciae evangelicae*, in *Works*, XII, p. 237.

45. Owen, *Vindiciae evangelicae*, in *Works*, XII, p. 237.

46. Cf. discussion of the Reformed approach in *PRRD*, I, 8.3 (A-B).

which is infinite and unlimited, as is that whereof we speak."[47] Clearly, in a finite essence, generation implies some sort of division or separation — but in the infinite, simple divine essence, generation does not indicate a division or separation, much less a partitioning of the divine essence. Traditional orthodoxy has defined the generation as a communication of "personal existence" or subsistence without any "multiplication or division" of the divine essence. In the generation of the Son, the divine essence remains undivided. The claim that such a generation is impossible, Owen comments, rests on the error of arguing limitations of the divine on the basis of "properties and attendancies of that which is finite."[48]

Just as the general arguments of the Socinians are not to the point, so do their exegetical arguments miss the mark. The Racovian Catechism indicates that the eternal generation of the Son is argued primarily from four texts — in the order of the catechism's argumentation, Micah 5:2; Psalm 2:7; Psalm 110:3; and Proverbs 8:23. In the Socinian view, Micah 5:2 — "But thou, Bethlehem Ephratah, though thou be little among the thousands of Judah, yet out of thee shall he come forth unto me that is to be ruler in Israel; whose goings forth have been from of old, from everlasting" or, as in the Vulgate, "from the days of eternity" — has no reference at all to the generation of Christ from the Father nor reference to an eternal event, but rather to "beginnings and days, which in eternity have not place": the word *olam*, they note, ought to be rendered "the days of an age," not as "everlasting" or "days of eternity." As for the reference to a nativity here, the reference is to Christ only by way of his ancestor, David, who was from Bethlehem.[49]

In response, Owen comments that the Reformed use of this text has been misrepresented by the Socinians: it has been used, he indicates, to argue the eternity of Christ's generation, the generation of Christ from the Father having been argued from numerous other texts. Thus, the Socinian arguments that the text does not refer to the generation of Christ's essence from the Father are simply not to the point — that doctrine is proved elsewhere. As for the Socinian claim that the text refers to "beginnings and days" and cannot therefore refer to eternity, Owen notes that there is no reference in the text to "beginnings" (this is an incorrect rendering of the phrase "from of old") and that Scripture often uses references to "days" in precisely this sense, namely, as comparative references to God's eternity over against human duration, as in Job 10:5 and Daniel 7:9. The word *olam*, moreover, has, admittedly, "various significations," indicating a great extent of time, perpetuity, or eternity: it derives, Owen comments, "from a word signifying 'to hide,' and denotes an unknown, hidden duration." It can, therefore, indicate simply "a very long time" or have a sense of perpetuity, as in Genesis 9:12 and 16. With reference to God's sovereignty as in Genesis 17:13, or when "ascribed to God as a property" as in Genesis 21:33, *olam* does signify

---

47. Owen, *Vindiciae evangelicae*, in *Works*, XII, p. 237.

48. Owen, *Vindiciae evangelicae*, in *Works*, XII, p. 237.

49. Racovian Catechism (1652), [IV] Of the Knowledge of Christ, i (p. 33); cf. the citation in Owen, *Vindiciae evangelicae*, in *Works*, XII, p. 237-238; citing among the Socinian exegetes Smalcius, *Contra Smiglecius*, xxvi; Ostorodius, *Institutio*, vii.

"eternal" — as is the case throughout the Old Testament.[50] The usage and meaning of *olam*, as supported by the way the Septuagint translates it, is identical to ἀιών in the New Testament, which can also be understood as "from eternity," as in 2 Tim. 1:9 and Titus 1:2.[51]

In the case of Psalm 2:7, the Socinians denied that this refers to "an eternal and proper generation from the Father," characterizing the begetting as a temporal generation not directly or "properly" from the Godhead. "This day" or "today" signifies a particular time, in fact the time of David's being declared "son of God" — and David was "neither begotten from eternity, nor out of the essence of God." The Psalm is only applied to Christ in a secondary, messianic sense by the apostle Paul and the "Author to the Hebrews."[52] Hoornbeeck replies that the text of the Psalm ought not to be in a human and temporal manner given its divine subject, but *theoprepos*, as attributing a temporal moment to God, who is above time and who is utterly free of its vicissitudes." This attribution of a day to God belongs to the pattern of accommodation of the biblical text to human understanding — the "lisping" of God to his children.[53] Moreover, the Socinian claim of a primary reference to David and a secondary application to Christ is questionable: the text goes on, beyond verse 7, to call on the kings of the earth to worship the Son and are "pronounced blessed" if they "put their trust" in him. This cannot be referred to David, who was no more worthy of divine worship than any man — and Scripture, in any case, explicitly says that they are cursed who put their trust in man (Jer. 17:5-8).[54]

The next text cited by the Socinians as mistakenly used to argue eternal generation, Psalm 110:3, is simply rendered incorrectly in the Vulgate as "before the day star I begot thee" and is not to the point: the text cannot be pressed against the Protestant teaching on eternal generation, because the Protestant theologians and exegetes typically do not use it to that purpose. Owen sets it aside categorically, and with it the Socinian objection.[55] Poole notes several possible readings of the text, now rendered "from the womb of the morning: thou hast the dew of thy youth": it might be a reference to Christ's eternal generation, but equally so to "his human nature and birth," or, given the flow of the prophetic testimony in the Psalm, a reference to "Christ's

---

50. Owen, *Vindiciae evangelicae*, in *Works*, XII, p. 238; note the extended exegesis in Edward Pococke, *A Commentary on the Prophecy of Micah* (Oxford: Printed at the Theatre, 1692), 5:2 in loc. (p. 49), noting also Ps. 90:2, "necessarily rendered *from everlasting to everlasting*" and denoting eternity as an existence "not circumscribed by daies"; cf. Poole, *Commentary*, Gen. 17:13 in loc. (I, p. 40) and Micah 5:2 in loc. (II, p. 948); Diodati, *Pious and Learned Annotations*, Micah 5:2 in loc.

51. Owen, *Vindiciae evangelicae*, in *Works*, XII, p. 239; cf. Ainsworth, *Annotations upon Genesis*, Gen. 21:33 in loc., who also offers "God of eternity" and "God of the world" as possibilities, but also agrees with the Septuagint in the sense of "eternal God" and of *olam* as rightly rendered ἀιών.

52. Racovian Catechism (1652), [IV] Of the Knowledge of Christ, i (p. 34), citing Acts 13:33 and Heb. 5:5.

53. Hoornbeeck, *Socinianismus confutatus*, II.i (p. 17), not only echoing Calvin's concept of accommodation, but using the same metaphor.

54. Owen, *Vindiciae evangelicae*, in *Works*, XII, p. 241.

55. Owen, *Vindiciae evangelicae*, in *Works*, XII, p. 243.

subjects and people." In any case, Poole identifies this text as "the most difficult and obscure of any in this book" and subject to various readings — not exactly a primary ground for a doctrinal point.[56] In accord with Poole's third reading and strongly echoing Calvin, Diodati understood the text as a reference to the rising up of God's elect people "at the first manifestation of [the] Gospel."[57]

This leaves Proverbs 8:23, "I was set up from everlasting, from the beginning, or ever the earth was." The Racovian Catechism presents the orthodox conclusion as a standard example of the method of juxtaposing texts from Scripture and drawing conclusions: the Wisdom of God is begotten from eternity (Prov. 8:22-24); Christ is the wisdom of God (1 Cor. 1:24); therefore Christ is begotten from eternity. In response to this argument, while not disputing the syllogistic pattern of biblical interpretation, the Socinians attempt to undermine the traditional reading of the terms. First, the text in Proverbs speaks only of "wisdom," whereas 1 Corinthians 1:24 speaks of "the wisdom of God": the middle terms of the syllogism are not equivalent, and the argument is improper. Second, many exegetes, including some "whom the Adversaries themselves account to be orthodox," do not interpret Proverbs as referring to "wisdom" as a "person," whereas Paul does identify "wisdom as a "person." What is more, third, even if the text in Proverbs refers to wisdom as a person, the person of reference is the Holy Spirit, not Christ, as demonstrated from such passages in the Old Testament as Isaiah 4:4; 11:1-5; and Exodus 31:1-6. Fourth, the Hebrew words rendered "from everlasting" or "from eternity" ought not to be so translated, but rather as "from the age or from of old."[58]

Against this reading of the text, the orthodox respond that Proverbs 8:23 does indeed refer to the second person of the Trinity "under the name of Wisdom" and that the text does in fact indicate that the divine wisdom is "begotten from everlasting." Nor is the orthodox argument the simple syllogism proffered and refuted by the Socinians. In the first place, Solomon clearly intended to refer to the wisdom of God — although the text does not specify the phrase, the meaning ought to be obvious. This wisdom, moreover, was with God "in the beginning of his way, before his works of old" (Prov. 8:22), which is affirmed in much the same way of Christ as divine Word in John 1:1. What is said of Wisdom in Proverbs 8, moreover, cannot be said of anyone other than the second person of the Trinity — and Christ is called the wisdom of God "in Scripture, not only in the expression of ὁ Λόγος, but ῥητῶς [specifically], 1 Cor. 1:30," and is so called "absolutely and simply" in Matthew 11:19. The whole chapter in Proverbs, moreover, clearly speaks of wisdom as a "person."[59] As for the Hebrew word *olam*, the Reformed argument is precisely the same as presented with reference to Micah 5:2: the word can and should be rendered as "eternal" or "from everlasting" — particularly so in Proverbs 8:23, where "everlasting, from the beginning" is explained

---

56. Poole, *Commentary*, Ps. 110:3 in loc. (II, p. 173).

57. Diodati, *Pious and Learned Annotations*, Ps. 110:3 in loc.; cf. Calvin, *Commentary on the Psalms*, 110:3 in loc. (*CTS Psalms*, IV, pp. 302-303).

58. Racovian Catechism (1652), [IV] Of the Knowledge of Christ, i (pp. 35-36).

59. Owen, *Vindiciae evangelicae*, in *Works*, XII, pp. 243-244.

by the phrase in the preceding verse "the Lord possessed me in the beginning of his way, before his works of old" and by the entire remaining passage (vv. 24-29), where clearly this wisdom is said to exist before the creation itself.[60]

2. The positive doctrine of the Reformed orthodox. The Son is said to be by *generatio à Patre*: this generation of the Son is defined as an act of both the Father and the Son, of the one generating and the one generated, actively performed by the Father, passively accomplished in the Son. Scripture explicitly refers to the generation of the Son (Psalm 2:7) and to the fact that the Son is beloved (*dilectus*: Matt 3:17; 17:5), the proper (*proprius*) Son of God (John 5:18; Rom 8:32), and only begotten (*unigenitus*: John 1:14, 18; 3:16, 18; 1 John 4:9).[61] This generation is, moreover, eternal and perpetual, and unlike the generation of things in the physical world. Marckius argues, thus, that the generation of the Son is not a physical but a "hyperphysical" generation from which — as in the *via negativa* approach to the attributes — all "imperfection, dependence, succession, mutation, division, and multiplication" is absent. Nonetheless, he adds, this is a "proper," not a "metaphorical," generation, a genuine filiation flowing (*fluens*) from the Father according to which the Son is the true image of the invisible God, the representation of the glory and character of the Father's person (cf. Col. 1:15; Heb. 1:3). By this generation, the Son is "produced from the Father" in an "eternal and incomprehensible communication of the unitary divine essence."[62]

Scripture thus teaches, in addition to the divinity of the Son, that he is "begotten of the Father": in the second Psalm (v. 7) God declares he has begotten his Son and in Proverbs 8:24-25 "states that 'Wisdom was brought forth from him' ... And this is the true reason why the Son of God is called 'the only begotten' (John 1:14) ... [and] is distinguished from others, who in the scripture are called sons of God, either by creation, or by adoption."[63] The generation of the Son is beyond our comprehension, and the doctrine, as stated by theology, indicates only "that the Father from all eternity communicated his name, his perfections, and his glory, to the Son."[64] We understand the begetting of the Son as from eternity:

It is thus shown by all those passages [in which Christ is called eternal] that Christ is God, since God is eternal. Christ is not therefore called the Son, either on account of his conception by the Holy Ghost, or his appointment to the mediatorial office, or by his resurrection from the dead, or his exaltation to the Father's right hand. ... He is ... called the Son of God, because begotten of the Father, and because, "as the Father hath life in himself, so hath he given to the Son to have life in himself" (John 5:26). We must observe also that the mode of this generation is not to be estimated by the

---

60. Owen, *Vindiciae evangelicae*, in *Works*, XII, pp. 244.

61. Cf. the exegetical discussion of Ps. 2:7 in Calvin, *Commentary upon the Psalms*, 2:7 in loc. (*CTS Psalms*, I, pp. 16-18); Poole, *Commentary*, Psalm 2:7 in loc. (II, p. 3); Diodati, *Pious and Learned Annotations*, in loc.; Amyraut et al., *Syntagma thesium theologicarum*, I.xvii.15; also above 5.2 (B.2) on the Father's active generation of the Son.

62. Marckius, *Compendium*, V.viii; cf. Gürtler, *Synopsis theol.*, vi.24.

63. Pictet, *Theol. chr.*, II.xvii.1.

64. Pictet, *Theol. chr.*, II.xvii.2.

laws of human nativity, or any created thing, for the heaven is not as far from the earth as the generation of the Son is from other generations; for in this generation the begetter is not older than the begotten, nor the generated younger than the generator; both are eternal, and this generation took place without any mutation.[65]

Pictet refutes two possible objections to his interpretation of Scripture:

But if anything is said concerning the Father, which is not said concerning the Son, as when the Father is said to *beget* the Son, this only proves that there is a distinction between the Father and the Son.... Again, if the Son is said in any passage to be inferior to the Father, and to work by the Father, such passage only shows that there is something in Christ besides the divine nature, viz. the human nature, according to which he is inferior to the Father, and also that there is a certain order of operation between the Father, Son, and Holy Ghost, and a kind of economy; but it by no means proves that Christ, *as God*, is inferior to the Father.[66]

Not only does Pictet move from the logic of his scriptural argument to the enunciation of a doctrinal determination, he also states one of the central presuppositions of the Reformed soteriology, the aseity of Christ considered as God.

6.2   The Full Deity of the Son

A. Exegetical and Doctrinal Argument in the Era of the Reformation

1. Calvin on the deity of the Son: the shape of argument in the *Institutes*. The deity of the Son as second person of the Trinity became a major issue for Reformed theology early in its development, given the rise of antitrinitarianism, on the one hand, and, on the other, the Reformed assumption of that the Son is not only divine but also, as God, has all of the divine attributes, including the attribute of aseity. The argumentation of the Reformers is perhaps less complex and less neatly marshaled than that of the orthodox, but its substance and sometimes even its structure is remarkably similar, particularly in its assumptions that the deity of Christ can be argued biblically by the fact that Scripture regularly gives to Christ the names and attributes of God and regularly ascribed to him works that can only be divine works. In their basic outlines and content the arguments presented by the orthodox are little different from the discussion found in Calvin's *Institutes*. Immediately after his discussion of the basic issue of the oneness and threeness of the Godhead, Calvin devoted considerable space to a demonstration or proof, based on Scripture, of the deity of the Son and the Spirit before going on to argue the distinction in essence and function between these two divine persons. Calvin divides his discussion of the divinity of the Son into a series of responses to heretical objections — notably the denials of the Son's eternity and the claim, similar in effect, that the Word gained an independent subsistence only in the divine act of creation. (On the latter point, Calvin certainly has in mind the objections of Servetus and other sixteenth-century antitrinitarians,

---

65. Pictet, *Theol. chr.*, II.xvii.3; cf. Rijssen, *Summa theol.*, IV.xi.
66. Pictet, *Theol. Chr.*, II.xvi.9.

who had already begun to argue the differences between pre-Nicene and post-Nicene understandings of God — this historical debate would only intensify in the seventeenth century.)

The shape of his argument is of interest in itself, inasmuch as he offers first a general discussion of the deity of the Son based on the identity of the Son as the Logos of the eternal Father.[67] He next devotes two sections of the *Institutes* to the identification of Christ by means of divine names given to him in the Old Testament, notably, Elohim and Jehovah.[68] Calvin then addresses New Testament texts in which Christ is given other names and attributes assignable only to God,[69] and he concludes with a lengthy discussion of the divine work, particularly the work of salvation, performed by Christ. The pattern will be reproduced by the Reformed orthodox, who likewise insisted against various antitrinitarians that the Old as well as the New Testament was foundational to the doctrines of the Trinity and Christ.[70]

The divine "Word," Calvin argues, is nowhere in Scripture used as a name for a "fleeting and evanescent voice" but rather is the name of "the Wisdom, ever dwelling with God, and by which all oracles and prophecies were inspired." And, since this "Word" is indicated as belonging to God before the incarnation, it must be understood as "begotten of the Father before all ages."[71] The divinity of this Word, moreover, is evidenced in its irresistible power among the prophets and even more so by its presence in the very creation of the world. To those who claim that the speech of God in creation is simply a divine "order or command," Calvin responds with the apostolic interpretation of creation in Hebrews 1:2, where the agent of creation is clearly identified as the Son — with confirmation from Proverbs 8:22: clearly, the agent of creation is the "eternal and essential Word of the Father."[72]

The divinity of Christ is also clearly attested throughout the Old Testament by the divine names given to him and by the divine powers attributed to him. Calvin notes the messianic Psalm, "Thy throne, O God, is forever and ever" (Ps. 45:6) — and whereas "the Jews quibble that the name Elohim is applied to angels and sovereign powers," here to Solomon, the text itself points beyond the literal sense of Solomon and his coronation to Christ and his eternal kingdom. Calvin notes that "no passage is to be found in Scripture, where an eternal throne is set up for a creature": Christ is identified here as God and as "the eternal Ruler." So also in Isaiah 9:6, "Christ is introduced both as God, and as possessed of supreme power, one of the peculiar attributes of God," whereas in Ezekiel 48:35, Christ is identified as "the true Jehovah from whom righteousness flows."[73] Beyond this, there are the "numerous passages"

---

67. Calvin, *Institutes*, I.xiii.7-8.
68. Calvin, *Institutes*, I.xiii.9-10.
69. Calvin, *Institutes*, I.xiii.11.
70. Calvin, *Institutes*, I.xiii.12-13.
71. Calvin, *Institutes*, I.xiii.7.
72. Calvin, *Institutes*, I.xiii.7.
73. Calvin, *Institutes*, I.xiii.9; cf. Calvin, *Commentary upon the Book of Psalms*, 45:6 (CTS Psalms I, pp. 178-183), offering a Lyra-like movement from the literal-historical Solomon to the broader,

in which Jehovah appears in the form of an angel — Calvin comments, following patristic exegesis, "the orthodox doctors of the Church have correctly and wisely expounded, that the Word of God was the supreme angel, who then began, as it were by anticipation, to perform the office of Mediator."[74] In the New Testament, particularly by way of the fulfillment of Old Testament prophecies, various divine names and attributes are assigned to Christ. Thus, Isaiah 8:14 indicates that the "Lord of Hosts" will become "a stone of stumbling" and a "rock of offense" — and Paul (Rom. 9:33) applies the prophecy directly to Christ. Similarly, Paul cites the passage in Isaiah 45:23, "As I live, saith the Lord, every knee shall bow to me, and every tongue shall confess to God," and applies it to the coming "judgment seat of Christ" (Rom. 14:10-11).[75]

Finally, Calvin comes to the evidence provided by Christ's works. This testimony, in Calvin's view, is irrefutable:

> The divinity of Christ, if judged by the works which are ascribed to him in Scripture, becomes still more evident. When he said of himself, "My Father worketh hitherto, and I work," the Jews, though most dull in regard to his other sayings, perceived that he was laying claim to divine power. And, therefore, as John relates (John 5:17), they sought the more to kill him, because he not only broke the Sabbath, but also said that God was his Father, making himself equal with God. What, then, will be our stupidity if we do not perceive from the same passage that his divinity is plainly instructed? To govern the world by his power and providence, and regulate all things by an energy inherent in himself (this an Apostle ascribes to him, Heb. 1:3), surely belongs to none but the Creator. Nor does he merely share the government of the world with the Father, but also each of the other offices, which cannot be communicated to creatures. The Lord proclaims by his prophets "I, even I, am he that blotteth out thy transgressions for mine own sake" (Is. 43:25). When, in accordance with this declaration, the Jews thought that injustice was done to God when Christ forgave sins, he not only asserted, in distinct terms, that this power belonged to him, but also proved it by a miracle (Matt. 9:6). We thus see that he possessed in himself not the ministry of forgiving sins, but the inherent power which the Lord declares he will not give to another. What! Is it not the province of God alone to penetrate and interrogate the secret thoughts of the heart? But Christ also had this power, and therefore we infer that Christ is God.[76]

Exegetically, in his commentaries, Calvin offers his readers far more material concerning the eternal deity of the Son or Word than can be inferred from the *Institutes*. There, by way of example, Calvin offers a very brief comment on Micah 5:2 in justification of Christ's eternal sonship — in his commentary on the text, by way of

---

prophetic sense. Also note the discussion of these passages in Warfield, "Calvin's Doctrine of the Trinity," pp. 242-243.

74. Calvin, *Institutes*, I.xiii.10.

75. Calvin, *Institutes*, I.xiii.11; cf. the discussion of this interpretive issue in David L. Puckett, *John Calvin's Exegesis of the Old Testament* (Louisville: Westminster John Knox Press, 1995), pp. 88-100.

76. Calvin, *Institutes*, I.xiii.12.

contrast, he provides an extended analysis of the point.[77] In his commentary, Calvin not only identifies the text as messianic, he also contrasts the "going forth" of Christ in "the fulness of time" in the incarnation with the "going forth" from the beginning or "from the days of eternity" indicated in the text." The text, according to Calvin, refers to the eternal Word, the creator of all things, who was to become the "Head of the Church": "the going forth of Christ has been from the beginning or from all ages ... Christ who was manifested in the flesh that he might redeem the Church of God, was the eternal Word ... destined by the eternal counsel of God to be the first-born of every creature."[78] (Calvin's rendering of the final clauses of the text, "whose goings forth have been from the beginning, from the days of ages" [*et egressus ejus ab initio, a diebus seculi*] is reminiscent of the Vulgate in its reference to the "beginning" and, like other similar renderings, would play into the hands of the Socinians, who argued against a reference to eternity at this point in the text.)

2. The divinity of Christ in Calvin's commentaries: select texts. Calvin clearly echoes the traditional trinitarian exegesis in his reading of Genesis 48:15-16, just as he echoes the typical reading of the text by other Reformers and points toward the later Reformed exegetical and doctrinal tradition: "[15] ... God, before whom my fathers Abraham and Isaac did walk, the God which fed me all my life and unto this day, [16] the Angel which redeemed me from all evil, bless the lads ... and let them grow into a multitude in the midst of the earth." Calvin writes,

> He so joins the Angel to God as to make him his equal. Truly he offers him divine worship, and asks the same things from him as from God. If this be understood indifferently of any angel what ever, the sentence is absurd. ... Wherefore it is necessary that Christ should be here meant, who does not bear in vain the title of Angel, because he had become the perpetual Mediator. And Paul testifies that he was the Leader and Guide of the journey of his ancient people (1 Cor. 10:4). He had not yet indeed been sent by the Father, to approach more nearly to us by taking our flesh, but because he was always the bond of connection between God and man, and because God formally manifested himself in no other way than through him, he is properly called the Angel.[79]

Calvin's reading of the various passages concerning the Angel of the Lord in the account of the liberation of Israel from Egypt follows a similar pattern of interpretation. Calvin commented extensively on Exodus 3:2-6, in the spirit of his comment on Genesis 48:16 and with the same Pauline interpretive confirmation:

> *And the Angel of the Lord appeared unto him.* ... For thus we must believe that God, as often as he appeared of old to the holy patriarchs, descended in some way from his majesty, that he might reveal himself as far as was useful, and as far as their comprehension would admit. ... But let us inquire who this Angel was? since soon afterwards he not only calls himself Jehovah, but claims the glory of the eternal and

---

77. Cf. Calvin, *Institutes*, II.xiv.7, with Calvin, *Commentaries on Micah*, 5:2 in loc. (*CTS Minor Prophets*, III, pp. 295-303).

78. Calvin, *Commentaries on Micah*, 5:2 in loc. (*CTS Minor Prophets*, III, pp. 299-300).

79. Calvin, *Commentary on Genesis*, 48:16 (*CTS Genesis*, I, pp. 428-429).

only God. Now, although this is an allowable manner of speaking, because the angels transfer to themselves the person and titles of God ... the ancient teachers of the Church have rightly understood that the Eternal Son of God is so called in respect to his office as Mediator, which he figuratively bore from the beginning, although he really took it upon him only at his Incarnation. And Paul sufficiently expounds this mystery to us, when he plainly asserts that Christ was the leader of his people in the Desert (1 Corinthians 10:4).[80]

Calvin reads Exodus 14:19; 23:20, 23, and 33:14 in accord with his understanding of the first reference in Exodus to "the Angel of the Lord."[81] Here again, the later orthodox reading of the passages will follow quite specifically on the traditionary understanding and, in particular the teaching of the Reformers.

As a final example of exegetical patterns in Calvin's christological reading of the Old Testament, we note Malachi 3:1. "Behold, I will send my messenger, and he shall prepare the way before me: and the Lord, whom ye seek, shall suddenly come to his temple, even the messenger of the covenant, who ye delight in: behold, he shall come, saith the Lord of hosts." Calvin, like many other exegetes in the Christian tradition, distinguishes carefully between the initial "messenger" of the text, identified as John the Baptist, and the second messenger or "angel," who is named by the Prophet both "Lord" and the "messenger [or angel] of the covenant":

> He introduces here, not Jehovah, but the Lord, *Adun*; and hence he speaks distinctly of Christ, who is afterwards called the *Angel* or Messenger *of the covenant*. But the word *Adun*, commonly used for a Mediator, as in Psalm 110, and also in Daniel 9:17; where it is expressly said, "Hear, O Jehovah, for the sake of the Lord."[82]

If we turn to Calvin's exegesis of the New Testament, we find a significant understanding of the divinity of the Son at Luke 1:35, "The Holy Ghost shall come upon thee, and the power of the Highest shall overshadow thee: therefore also that holy thing which shall be born of thee shall be called the Son of God." As Calvin, notes, there are several significant trinitarian points to be drawn from the text: the clause concerning the "power of the Highest" appears to be a parallelism with the first clause, leading not only to the identification of the Holy Spirit as the power of the Highest but, as Calvin indicates, as "the essential power of God." Calvin also notes that heretics "seize on the particle *therefore*" as evidence that Jesus is merely called Son of God because of the "remarkable manner" of his conception. This, however, "is a false conclusion: for, though he was manifested to be the Son of God in the flesh, it does not follow that he was not the Word begotten of the Father before all ages."[83]

---

80. Calvin, *Harmony of the Four Last Books of Moses*, Exod. 3:2 in loc. (*CTS Harmony*, I, pp. 60-61).

81. Calvin, *Harmony of the Four Last Books of Moses*, Exod. 14:19 in loc., the same reading, as Ex. 3:2, confirmed by the same Pauline citation; similarly, ibid., Exod. 23:20, 23; 33:14 in loc. (*CTS Harmony*, I, pp. 248, 402-404; III, p. 375).

82. Calvin, *Commentaries on Malachi*, 3:1 in loc. (*CTS Malachi*, p. 568).

83. Calvin, *Harmony of the Evangelists*, in loc. (*CTS Harmony*, I, p. 43).

Calvin's commentary on the prologue to the Gospel of John stands as one of the few places in the commentaries where Calvin explicitly identifies his adversaries — in this case, Servetus on doctrinal matters and the "Sorbonne theologians" on matters of translation. Against the "haughty scoundrel" Servetus, Calvin argued the impropriety of understanding the juxtaposition of God and Logos as indicating the beginning of the divine Logos in time for the "creation of the world, as if he did not exist before his power was made known by external operation."[84] The text does not indicate "the beginning of time," but rather "the beginning" without modifier, meaning that the Logos was "before all ages." This is, moreover, precisely the meaning of the next clause, which states that the Logos was "with God": the passage expressly "excludes" the notion that Christ belongs to "the common order of the world" and makes it equally an insult to God the Father to claim the beginning of the Logos in time, inasmuch as such a reading would "deprive" God of this "Eternal Wisdom."[85]

In Calvin's view, the Gospel not only testifies undeniably to the divinity of Christ but also to the distinct divine subsistence of the Son:

> We have already said that the Son of God is thus placed above the world and above all the creatures, and is declared to have existed before all ages. But at the same time this mode of expression attributes to him a distinct personality from the Father; for it would have been absurd in the Evangelist to say that *the Discourse was* always *with God*, if he had not some kind of subsistence peculiar to himself in God. This passage serves, therefore, to refute the error of Sabellius; for it shows that the Son is distinct from the Father.[86]

Calvin also, here, as in the *Institutes*, argued the valid use of the patristic terminology, after indicating his reservations about the use of such descriptors in speaking of the mystery of the Trinity:

> I have already remarked that we ought to be sober in thinking, and modest in speaking, about such high mysteries. And yet the ancient writers of the Church were excusable, when, finding that they could not in any other way maintain sound and pure doctrine in opposition to the perplexed and ambiguous phraseology of the heretics, they were compelled to invent some words, which after all had no other meaning than what is taught in the Scriptures. They said that there are three Hypostases, or Subsistences, or Persons, in the one and simple essence of God. The word ὑπόστασις occurs in this sense in Hebrews 1:3, to which corresponds the Latin word *Substantia*, as it is employed by Hilary. The Persons (τὰ πρόσωπα) were called by them distinct properties in God, which present themselves to the view of our minds; as Gregory Nazianzen says,

---

84. Calvin, *Commentary on John*, 1:1 in loc. (CTS *John*, I, p. 26).

85. Calvin, *Commentary on John*, 1:1 in loc. (CTS *John*, I, p. 27).

86. Calvin, *Commentary on John*, 1:1 in loc. (CTS *John*, I, pp. 28). N.B., Calvin disputed the traditional translation of λόγος as *verbum*, indicating that *verbum* better rendered ῥῆμα. *Sermo* was his preferred translation of λόγος — in the above text, I have translated Calvin's *sermo* as "discourse" rather than, as frequently seen, "speech."

"I cannot think of the One (God) without having the Three (Persons) shining around me."[87]

On the third verse, "All things were made by him," Calvin comments, "Having affirmed that the Discourse is God, and having asserted his eternal essence, he now proves his Divinity from his works."[88] This reading not only confirms Calvin's distinctly trinitarian reading of the text, it also find the order of argument taken up both in the *Institutes* and in the later orthodox dogmatics rooted in the text of the Gospel: first, the proof of the essential divinity of Christ, then, the argument from his works.

From the beginnings of the Reformation, there were differences, even among the orthodox or magisterial Reformers over the interpretation of John 10:29-30. Calvin, for one, recognized the heavy use made of the text in patristic trinitarian theology but still did not regard the text as a proof of the *homoousios* of the Father and the Son:

> [Christ] therefore testifies that his affairs are so closely united to those of the Father, that the Father's assistance will never be withheld from himself and his sheep. The ancients made a wrong use of this passage to prove that Christ is of the same essence with the Father. For Christ does not argue about the unity of substance, but about the agreement which he has with the Father, so that whatever is done by Christ will be confirmed by the power of his Father.[89]

By way of contrast, Bullinger read the text in precise agreement with the post-Nicene orthodox fathers:

> When he saith "one," he overthrows those who separate or rend the divine substance or nature: and when he saith "*sunt*," and not "*sum*," therein he refutes those who confound the subsistences or persons in the Trinity. Therefore the apostolic and catholic doctrine teaches and confesses, that they are three, distinguished in properties; and that of those three there is but one and the same nature, or essence, the same omnipotence, majesty, goodness, and wisdom. For although there is an order in the Trinity, yet there can be no inequality in it at all. None of them is before other in time, or worthier than other in dignity: but of the three there is one Godhead, and they three are one and eternal God.[90]

John 14:16, 28 receives the most detailed attention of virtually all of the trinitarian passages in Scripture, inasmuch as it declares the identity and indicates the relationship of the persons — and, if read wrongly, can lead to enormous misconceptions concerning the Trinity. The importance of the passage is also indicated by its use in various Reformed confessions.[91] Calvin notes the seeming conflict between verse 16, "I will pray to the Father, and he will give you another Comforter" and the earlier statement

---

87. Calvin, *Commentary on John*, 1:1 in loc. (*CTS John*, I, pp. 28-29).
88. Calvin, *Commentary on John*, 1:1 in loc. (*CTS John*, I, p. 29).
89. Calvin, *Commentary on John*, 10:30 (*CTS John*, I, pp. 417).
90. Bullinger, *Decade*, IV.iii (p. 157).
91. *Belgic Confession*, IX, XI, citing Jn. 14:16; *Second Helvetic Confession*, III.4, citing Jn. 14:26 (Schaff, *Creeds.*, III, pp. 241, 392, 394).

(16:7), "If I depart, I will send him to you." This is not a contradiction, given that both of the texts are true: "in so far as Christ is our Mediator and Intercessor, he obtains from *the Father* the grace of the Spirit, but in so far as he is Son, he bestows that grace from himself."[92] Calvin also emphasized the fact that the text does not merely speak of the sending of the Comforter, but of the sending of "another Comforter," indicating that Christ himself is the Comforter and protector of the disciples as well as the Spirit — and from this, Calvin allows the conclusion to be drawn that there is "a distinction of persons" resting on a specific characteristic or property of the Spirit in which he differs from the Son.[93]

Calvin recognized that John 17:3 — "And this is life eternal, that they may know thee, the only true God, and him whom thou hast sent, Jesus Christ" — could be read as if "Christ disclaims for himself the right and title of divinity." The words "*true* and *only*," however, indicate here "that faith must distinguish God from the vain inventions of men" and that "there is nothing defective or imperfect" in God. As for the syntax of the text, Calvin prefers the reading that associated the "only" with "thee" rather than with "true God": not "That they may know thee, who alone art God," but "That they may know thee alone to be the true God." Still, the text is not, in its grammatical intention, antitrinitarian — the textual distinction between the Father as God and Jesus Christ as sent by God follows the "manner of speaking" typical of Christ's discourses in the Gospel of John:

> Christ, appearing in the form of a man, describes, under the person of the Father, the power, essence, and majesty of God. So then the Father of Christ is *the only* true *God;* that is, he is *the one God,* who formerly promised a Redeemer to the world; but in Christ the *oneness* and *truth* of Godhead will be found, because Christ was humbled, in order that he might raise us on high. When we have arrived at this point, then his Divine majesty displays itself; then we perceive that he is wholly in the Father, and that the Father is wholly in him. In short, he who separates Christ from the Divinity of the Father, does not yet acknowledge Him who is *the only true* God, but rather invents for himself a strange god. This is the reason why we are enjoined *to know God, and Jesus Christ whom he hath sent,* by whom, as it were, with outstretched hand, he invites us to himself.[94]

The text of John 17, therefore, does testify, albeit obliquely, to the divinity of Christ — what it does not do, however, is testify to the union between the Father and the Son in the Godhead. Calvin was convinced that, given the self-representation of Jesus in this text (and throughout the Gospel of John) as the Person of the Mediator, "Christ's design" here "was widely different from raising our minds to a mere speculation about his hidden Divinity." Rather the union between the Son and the Father, like that among believers and between believers and Christ their head is a unity in the Spirit,

---

92. Calvin, *Commentary on John,* 14:16 in loc. (*CTS John,* II, p. 92).
93. Calvin, *Commentary on John,* 14:16 in loc. (*CTS John,* II, p. 93).
94. Calvin, *Commentary on John,* 17:3 in loc. (*CTS John,* II, p. 167).

identified by the presence of the blessings of salvation.[95] This line of argument carries over into the later Reformed tradition.[96]

Calvin's comment on 1 Timothy 3:16 — "And without controversy great is the mystery of godliness: God was manifest in the flesh, justified in the Spirit, seen of angels, preached unto the Gentiles, believed on in the world, received up into glory" — is of considerable interest to the later Reformed orthodox reading inasmuch as it not only highlights the importance of the text to traditional doctrinal understanding and even focuses on the phrase "God manifested in the flesh" (*Deus manifestatus in carne*) as a primary christological reference but also adumbrates the textual problems of orthodoxy. Calvin begins his comment by noting that "the Vulgate's translator, by leaving out the name of God, refers what follows to "the mystery," but altogether unskillfully and inappropriately, as will clearly be seen on a bare perusal."[97] The Vulgate text reads, "and manifestly great is the mystery of piety which was manifest in the flesh," the phrase in question being *quod manifestatum est in carne* — which implies a reading of the Greek as ὅς ἐφανερώθη ἐν σαρκί. Calvin also indicates his knowledge of this reading in Erasmus' New Testament, commenting that this alteration of text is unworthy of refutation. "All the Greek copies," Calvin continues, "undoubtedly agree in this rendering, 'God manifested in the flesh.'" Despite his dismissal of Erasmus, Calvin nonetheless indicates his own underlying worry about the text, as well as his resolution to follow the tradition:

> But granting that Paul did not express the name of God, still any one who shall carefully examine the whole matter, will acknowledge that the name of Christ ought to be supplied. For my own part, I have no hesitation in following the reading which has been adopted in the Greek copies.[98]

Calvin then proceeds to work through the text, stressing how "appropriate" a designation of Christ is the phrase "God manifested in the flesh," perhaps by way of justifying his reliance on the uncial Greek copies against Erasmus.[99] From a theological perspective, once accepted in the form that Calvin argues, the text holds several significant points for christological and trinitarian formulation:

> First, we have here an express testimony of both natures; for he declares at the same time that Christ is true God and true man. Secondly, he points out the distinction between the two natures, when, on the one hand, he calls him God, and, on the other, expresses his "manifestation, in the flesh." Thirdly, he asserts the unity of the person, when he declares, that it is one and the same who was God, and who has been manifested in the flesh.

---

95. Calvin, *Commentary on John*, 17:21 in loc. (*CTS John*, II, p. 183).

96. Cf. Diodati, *Pious and Learned Annotations*, Jn. 17:21 in loc.; Poole, *Commentary*, in loc. (III, p. 370).

97. Calvin, *Commentary on 1 Timothy*, 3:16 in loc. (*CTS 1 Timothy*, p. 92).

98. Calvin, *Commentary on 1 Timothy*, 3:16 in loc. (*CTS 1 Timothy*, p. 92).

99. On the importance of the phrase to Calvin's own Christology, see Muller, *Christ and the Decree*, pp. 28, 37, 191, n. 92.

Thus, by this single passage, the true and orthodox faith is powerfully defended against Arius, Marcion, Nestorius, and Eutyches. There is also great emphasis in the contrast of the two words, *God in flesh.* How wide is the difference between God and man! And yet in Christ we behold the infinite glory of God united to our polluted flesh in such a manner that they become one.[100]

Calvin rather nicely summed up the historical problem of Titus 2:13 — "Looking for that blessed hope, and the appearing of the glory of the great God and our Savior Jesus Christ"[101] — for the larger part of the history of interpretation:

> It is uncertain whether these words should be read together thus, "the glory of our Lord Jesus Christ, the great God and our Savior," or separately, as of the Father and the Son, "the glory of the great God, and of our Savior, the Lord Jesus Christ." The Arians, seizing on this latter sense, have endeavored to prove from it, that the Son is less than the Father, because here Paul calls the Father "the great God" by way of distinction from the Son. The orthodox teachers of the Church, for the purpose of shutting out this slander, eagerly contended that both are affirmed of Christ. But the Arians may be refuted in a few words and by solid argument; for Paul, having spoken of the revelation of the glory of "the great God," immediately added "Christ," in order to inform us, that the revelation of glory will be in his person; as if he had said that, when Christ shall appear, the greatness of the divine glory shall then be revealed to us.[102]

For Calvin, 1 John 5:20 — "… and we are in him that is true, even in his Son Jesus Christ. This is the true God, and eternal life" — was an incontestible statement of the divinity of Christ. He offered a curt dismissal of heretical readings, both ancient and of the sixteenth-century: "Though the Arians have attempted to elude this passage, and some agree with them at this day, yet we have here a remarkable testimony of the divinity of Christ." The Arian exegesis identifies the last cited sentence as a reference to God the Father, "as though," Calvin comments, "the Apostle should again repeat that he is true God." Inasmuch as the text has already identified God the Father twice as the true God who sent Christ in to the world, Calvin finds the repetition of meaning unacceptable. The apostle John often refers to Christ as "eternal life," and what is more, "the relative οὗτος usually refers to the last person" indicated, which in "his Son Jesus Christ." Thus, both the precise grammar of the text and the Johannine usage testify "that when we have Christ, we enjoy the true and eternal God, for nowhere else is he to be sought."[103]

3. Christ's divinity according to Musculus and Vermigli. Musculus similarly addresses the problem of Christ's divinity, writing that "the Holy Scriptures report

---

100. Calvin, *Commentary on 1 Timothy,* 3:16 in loc. (CTS *1 Timothy,* pp. 92-93).

101. Following Calvin's reading of the verse; alternatively, the KJV reads "Looking for that blessed hope, and the glorious appearing of the great God and our Saviour Jesus Christ."

102. Calvin, *Commentary on Titus,* 2:13 (CTS *Titus,* pp. 320-321).

103. Calvin, *Commentaries on the First Epistle of John,* 1 John 5:20 in loc. (CTS *1 John,* p. 274).

of Christ that he is the everlasting Word of God, by whom all things were made."[104] John, in the first chapter of his Gospel, states also that the Word was God, while Paul in Colossians, chapter 1, calls him "the image of invisible God" who is before all things, all things being made in him and by him. "These things," argues Musculus, "cannot be attributed to any creature: there fore it is necessary to conclude that he is God."[105]

Scripture also consistently speaks of Christ as the Son of God — not, writes Musculus, in the sense of his being "an adopted son, as we all are, as many as are elect" but as "John the Evangelist" states, "the only begotten Son" who comes from the Father and who alone has seen the Father. Thus, as "only begotten," Christ is "distinguished from adoptive sons as one who is a natural son."[106] Scripture, furthermore, in many places calls Christ "God," as in Thomas' confession, "My Lord and my God" (John 20), or in Romans 9, where Christ is called "God blessed above all things." Christ, moreover, claims for himself attributes which can belong only to God, as in John 5 where he says that whatsoever the Father does, he does also, or in John 6 and 10, where he claims to bestow life everlasting. Even so, in John 8 he declares, "Before Abraham was, I am" and in the seventeenth chapter he speaks of the glory that he had with the Father before the world began.[107]

The Son's divinity is proved against all hints of Arianism by the baptismal formula of Matt 28:19, where Father, Son, and Holy Ghost are manifestly shown as "three persons coequal with one another." Nor could John call Christ "the first and principal good, or else eternal life, unless he were God" (citing John 14:6 and 17:3). Even so, when the high priest asked of Christ whether he were "the son of the living God" (Matt 26:63), he answered, "Thou hast said." The first chapter of John offers definitive proof in saying, first, that "God was the word" and, then, "the word was made flesh." Furthermore in the words of John 1:18, "No man hath seen the father at any time, but the Son ... he hath declared him." These words show that Christ as Son of God "is exempted from the common condition of men."[108]

The "subtle argument of the Arians" that Christ was called God but was less than divine, thus, cannot hold.

> It is said by the same John (1:3) *All things are made by him*. Upon which place *Augustine* doth very well infer, that the Son of God was not made: for if he had been made, then all things that were made, had not been created by him; at leastwise he had been created by another thing.[109]

Calvin similarly argues full equality of the Son in the context of the sending of the Comforter in John 14:16 —

---

104. Musculus, *Loci communes*, ii (*Commonplaces*, p. 14, col. 2).

105. Musculus, *Loci communes*, ii (*Commonplaces*, p. 15, col. 1).

106. Musculus, *Loci communes*, ii (*Commonplaces*, p. 15, col. 1).

107. Musculus, *Loci communes*, ii (*Commonplaces*, p. 15, col. 2-p. 16, col. 1).

108. Vermigli, *Commonplaces*, I.xii.4.

109. Vermigli, *Commonplaces*, I.xii.4.

Here he calls the Spirit the gift of the Father, but a gift which he will obtain by his prayers; in another passage he promises that he will give the Spirit. If I depart, says he, I will send Him to you (John 16:7). Both statements are true and correct; for in so far as Christ is our Mediator and Intercessor, he obtains from the Father the grace of the Spirit, but in so far as he is God, he bestows that grace from himself.[110]

Vermigli also employs Thomas' confession, "My Lord and my God" (John 20:28), as a proof of Christ's divinity and Christ's own words to his heavenly Father, "*glorify me, O Father, with the glory, which I had with thee, before the world was made*: which saying might not stand, unless that Christ had the divine nature; for his human nature was not before the world was made. Also the Lord said; *All things that my Father hath, are mine*: and that the father hath the divine nature, is by none called into question; and so of necessity the Son is not without the same. Besides, Christ testifieth and saith; *All things that my father doth, I also do*: but the action of them both, being all one, the natures of them must needs be one and the same."[111] Similarly John 8:58, "Before Abraham was I am," and John 11:25, "I am the resurrection and the life," must be referred to a divine nature. The equality of the Son with the Father is seen from John 5:26, "As the father hath life in himself, so he hath granted to the son to have life in himself."[112]

Christ's divinity is also proved by the conference of Deuteronomy 6:13, "Thou shalt worship the Lord thy God and him only shalt thou serve" with Philippians 2:10, "In the name of Jesus, let every knee bow, both of things in heaven, of things in earth, and things under the earth."[113] Vermigli continues to cite Scripture out of both Testaments which attribute divinity to Christ: one is struck by the minimum of patristic and scholastic terminology and the restriction of the argument to a conferring of one Scripture text with another. One is also struck by the continued reliance on Old Testament texts as well as texts from the New Testament and the insistence on the definite, albeit partial, revelation of the Trinity in the Old Testament as well as in the New.

B. Grounds of Doctrinal Argument in the Era of the Reformed Orthodoxy

1. The deity of the Son: general argumentation. The Reformed orthodox of the late sixteenth and seventeenth centuries codified and developed these categories of argument, but in no way altered the underlying exegetical patterns of the doctrinal discussion. As also in the case of the doctrine of the Holy Spirit, the Reformed orthodox typically present two sets of closely interrelated arguments, one concerning the full divinity or deity of the Son, the other concerning the personhood or individual subsistence of the Son. The order of these sets of arguments varies, as does the order of argument within each set. The reason for this exhaustive and potentially somewhat

---

110. Calvin, *Commentary on John*, 14:16 (*CTS John*, II, p. 92).
111. Vermigli, *Commonplaces*, I.xii.4; citing John 17:5, 16:15; 5:19, respectively.
112. Vermigli, *Commonplaces*, I.xii.4
113. Vermigli, *Commonplaces*, I.xii.5

cumbersome approach is certainly the nature of the various heresies — some of which acknowledge the divinity of the Son or Word but deny personhood, instead identifying the Word as a power of the Godhead, namely, adoptionism or dynamic monarchianism; some of which acknowledge the personhood of the Son or Word, but deny his full divinity, namely Arianism. In their own day, the Reformed orthodox encountered Arian or Arianizing and Socinian or Socinianizing thinkers who represented these particular problems, with the Arians tending toward an identification of the Son as a "person" but as less than divine and some of the Socinian or Socinianizing writers reducing the Word to a power of the Godhead. Thus, the orthodox argue that the Word is both fully divine and an individual subsistence in the Godhead, usually in that order.

In their polemic with the Socinians and, in the English context, with antitrinitarian deists as well, the orthodox were obliged to defend the eternal deity of the Son, "who in the fulness of time assumed human nature."[114] In other words, the name "Son" or "Son of God" itself was a focus of debate. The antitrinitarian arguments of the era indicate a variety of reasons for the title "Son of God" other than identification of the Son as an eternal divine subsistence: namely, that the name refers to Christ's miraculous conception by the Spirit of God and his birth from the Virgin Mary, as indicated in Luke 1:31-35; or that his sonship indicates his sanctification to mediatorial office and his endowment with special gifts by the Spirit (cf. John 10:35-36); or that he was identified as divine Son in his resurrection from the dead, as implied by the use of Psalm 2:7 in Acts 13:32-33.[115]

The orthodox had to combat, moreover, not only a variety of simple denials of Christ's divinity but also a more subtle adoptionist Christology: the point is to prove the Son's eternal and essential deity. The argument must show three things: "1) that Christ is God; 2) that he the most high God, equal to the Father; and 3) that he is begotten of the Father."[116] Or, as Rijssen states the question, "Whether our Saviour Jesus Christ is himself the most high God." Against the Socinian identification of Christ as Son of God in a "precarious and dependent" sense, on grounds only of his preeminence on earth, his authority, lordship, and office, as well as against the Arian and semi-Arian tendencies evident particularly in Britain, the Reformed insist that Christ is "properly" the son of God.[117] Contrary to all such adoptionistic or subordinationistic heretics — Ebion, Cerinthus, Arius, the Jews, Mohammedans, and the Socinians — who either deny the divinity of Christ or who confess him to be less than God or not absolute God, Christ must be confessed to be God

> not by office, nor by favor, nor by similitude, nor in a figure, as sometimes Angels and Magistrates are called gods, but by nature; he is equal and coessential with his Father:

114. Pictet, *Theol. chr.*, II.xv.1.
115. Venema, *Inst. theol.*, xiv (pp. 257-259).
116. Pictet, *Theol. chr.*, II.xv.1.
117. Rijssen, *Summa theol.*, IV.ix, controversia II.

there is one Godhead common to all three persons, the Father, the Son, and the Spirit.[118]

Thus the Reformed exclude interpretations of passages like John 1:1, "The Word was God," which would denominate him "a kind of subordinate and created God." Scripture does not employ the word "God" in such improper fashion.[119]

2. The divinity of the Son in the interpretation of Scripture: hermeneutical issues. There is very little pure rational argumentation in this division of the orthodox system: the divinity of Christ must stand upon Scripture. The orthodox arguments on this point explicitly follow their hermeneutical assumption that doctrine arises either from explicit statements of Scripture or by way of legitimate conclusions drawn from the text, just as the pattern of argument also obliges the instrumental function of reason, illustrating the orthodox theologians' use of the rules of argument set forth in their prolegomena. Thus, writes Leigh, the divinity of Christ may be argued in two ways —

> (1) By clear texts of Scripture affirming this truth in so many words. The Prophets foretelling of him, saith this is his name by which you shall call him, *Jehovah*, or *the Lord* our righteousness, Jerem. 23:6. and *the mighty* God, Is. 9:6. *Paul* saith, 1 Tim. 3:16. *Great is the mystery of Godliness*, God manifested in the flesh; and accordingly *Thomas* made his confession, John 20:28. *My Lord, and my God*, which title he accepteth and praiseth *Thomas* for believing, and that he could not have done without extreme impiety, had he not been God.[120]
>
> (2) By evident reasons drawn from the Scripture. ... Divine Names and Titles are given to Christ; He is *the only blessed Potentate*, 1 Tim. 6:15. *the King of Kings*, Rev. 1:5 and *Lord of Lords*, Rev. 17:14 and 19:16. He is called *the Image of the invisible God*, Col. 1:25; *the brightness of his glory*, Heb. 1:3; the word and wisdom of the Father, John 1:1, 2; Prov. 8:21 and 9:1.[121]

The interpretive model indicated here is the basic approach of the Reformation and of Reformed orthodoxy: a doctrinal point is considered established when it rests either on the explicit statements of Scripture or on conclusions capable of being drawn from explicit statements of Scripture, often by the collation and comparison of texts. The orthodox assumption, then, is that the doctrine of the divinity of Christ is established not from only a few texts of Scripture but also from an extended series of texts, some used as direct attestations to the doctrine, others used as grounds of argumentation.

Owen, for one, objected nearly as much to the Socinians' distorted or reductionistic approach to the traditional argumentation as he did to their doctrine: he found that both Biddle and the Racovian Catechism tended to divide up the traditional exegetical arguments, severing texts used in argumentation from collateral texts and often failing to acknowledge either the structure of the argumentation or the large number of texts

---

118. Leigh, *Treatise*, II.xvi (p. 135).
119. Pictet, *Theol. chr.*, II.xv.2.
120. Leigh, *Treatise*, II.xvi (p. 131).
121. Leigh, *Treatise*, II.xvi (pp. 131-132).

brought to bear by the tradition on each doctrinal issue. Thus, he faults the Socinians for citing only four texts (Ps. 2:7; 110:3; Prov. 7:23; Micah 5:2) as indicating the eternity of the Son and for severing the discussion of Christ's eternity from discussion of his generation from the Father, as if generation from the Father were not itself a form of testimony to eternity: "Let the gentleman take their own way and method," comments Owen sarcastically, "we shall meet them at the first stile, or rather brazen wall, which they endeavour to climb over."[122] Much of the debate was specifically over the method of interpretation of Scripture.

These hermeneutical considerations tended to yield a topical pattern of argument in the orthodox proofs of the divinity of the Son, much as they had done in other contexts as well. The underlying model of movement from exegesis to doctrine remains, therefore, the *locus* model introduced into Protestant theology by Melanchthon and followed in one form or another by a majority of the Reformers and their successors. In the present instance, the topical argumentation follows out the logic of the general hermeneutical model noted above: each of the topical divisions of the argument rests both on the clear testimonies of Scripture (as confirmed by the exegesis of the era) and on "evident reasons drawn from Scripture," usually by the collation of texts. Accordingly, the orthodox doctrine of Christ's divinity is demonstrated, against the arguments of the "antitrinitarians," on four scriptural grounds: "1) From the divine names... 2) From the divine attributes... 3) From the divine works... 4) And finally from the divine worship" accorded to the Son.[123] A major subcategory of the exegesis of the divine names, moreover, requiring separate discussion is the identification of Christ as the "Angel of the Lord" in the Old Testament.

C. The Divine Names and Attributes of the Son in the Reformed Orthodox Theology

The importance of this subtopic, and its exegetical nature arises from the fact that the antitrinitarians of the sixteenth and seventeenth centuries expended considerable exegetical effort in an attempt to show that the Father alone was God and that various divine names and titles did not properly apply to the Son. The former point could be argued directly from a series of biblical texts: Malachi 2:10; John 17:3; 1 Corinthians 8:6; and Ephesians 4:6.[124] The Reformed respond by arguing the applicability of the divine names, without qualification, to Christ.

1. The name of God: "Jehovah." "Jehovah," the personal name of God, which must be peculiar to God, is attributed to Christ. This attribution occurs when passages in the Old Testament that speak of Jehovah are applied to Christ by the writers of

---

122. Owen, *Vindiciae evangelicae*, in *Works*, XII, p. 236.

123. Marckius, *Compendium theologiae*, V.xxi; cf. the same pattern of argument in Owen, *Brief Vindication of the Trinity*, in *Works*, II, pp. 387-388; Turretin, *Inst. theol. elencticae*, III.xxviii.5; Mastricht, *Theoretico-practica theol.*, II.xxvi.8; Ridgley, *Body of Divinity*, p. 134, cols. 1-2; and note the similar logic of the proofs of the Spirit's divinity in Marckius, *Compendium theologiae*, V.xxvi.

124. Cf. Zanchi, *De tribus Elohim*, pt. 2, V.v.3 (col. 539).

the New Testament.[125] This particular argument is, moreover, the point at which a refutation of Socinian views first registered in the doctrine of the divine names bears its ultimate fruit: the Socinians had labored to show that Jehovah was not the proper name of God, belonging to God alone — and the orthodox exegetes had rather nicely shown that all of the exceptions noted by the Socinians were not in fact applications of the Holy Name to creatures or things.[126] Having succeeded in this prior argument, the Reformed orthodox could argue coherently that the attribution of the name of God to Jesus Christ was indeed a proper predication. Given, moreover, that the name "Jehovah" belongs to God *essentialiter*, *absolutè*, and *indistinctè* apart from any identification or determination of the persons of the Godhead, Scripture can also apply the name and the texts in which it occurs to individual persons, namely, to Christ. The threefold glory of Isaiah 6:3 is, thus, applied to Christ by the evangelist John.[127] A preeminent example of this predication is the New Testament's use of Isaiah 40:3, "The voice of him that crieth in the wilderness, prepare ye the way of the Lord (Jehovah), make straight in the desert a high-way for our God": this text is applied directly to Christ by Matthew 3:3, which identifies the "voice" as John, the forerunner of Jesus.[128]

Similarly in Numbers 21:5-7, the Lord, that is to say, Jehovah, sent fiery serpents against those who sinned against him — but in 1 Corinthians 10:9, Paul refers this text to Christ: "Neither let us tempt Christ, as some of them also tempted, and were destroyed by serpents." The Socinians suggested that the Pauline argument presented a parallel between Christ in Paul's time and someone else in the time of the Exodus, probably Moses or Aaron, "for what Christ is now to us, they were then, in some respects, to the Israelites, particularly Moses, who ... indeed is called Christ, their anointed, Habakkuk 3:13."[129] Few of the Reformed exegetes take up this gambit at Numbers 21:5, and only a few of the dogmaticians note it among their lists of texts identifying Christ as Jehovah — among the British, Ridgley refers to it positively; among the continental theologians, Turretin and Mastricht note it in passing.[130] On the other hand, the Reformed do address 1 Corinthians 10:9 as a clear reference to the preincarnate divinity of Christ. Calvin commented that "this is a remarkable passage in proof of the eternity of Christ." He also noted his disdain for Erasmus' exegesis: "the cavil of Erasmus has not force — 'Let us not tempt Christ, as some of them tempted God'; for to supply the word *God* is extremely forced."[131] Similarly, Poole argued,

---

125. Turretin, *Inst. theol. elencticae*, III.xxviii.6.

126. Cf. Racovian Catechism, iv.1 (pp. 76-77), with Turretin, *Inst. theol. elencticae*, III.ix.13-16; and see the longer discussion in *PRRD*, III, 4.2 (B.2-3).

127. Jasz-Berenyi, *Examen doctrinæ ariano-socinianæ*, p. 29, citing John 12:41.

128. Ridgley, *Body of Divinity*, p. 139, col. 1.

129. Racovian Catechism, iv.1 (p. 113).

130. Ridgley, *Body of Divinity*, p. 139, col. 2; Turretin, *Inst. theol. elencticae*, III.xxviii.6; Mastricht, *Theoretico-practica theol.*, II.xxvi.9.

131. Calvin, *Commentary on 1 Corinthians*, 1 Cor. 10:9, in loc. (CTS *Corinthains*, I, pp. 325-326).

The term *Christ* here is very remarkable to prove Christ's Divine nature and existence before he was incarnate; for the same person who is here called *Christ* is called *God*, Ps. 106:14 and Jehovah also, in the same Psalm; neither could they have been tempted by Christ at that time , if at that time he had not been existent. *Were destroyed by serpents*; by serpents he meaneth the fiery serpents; we have the history, Numb. 21:6-9.[132]

Further, Isaiah's vision of Jehovah (6:5) is applied to Christ in the Gospel of John (12:41), "These things said Isaiah, when he saw his glory, and spake of him." "From whence it is evident," argues Ridgley, echoing one trajectory in the exegetical tradition, "that the Person who appeared to him, sitting on a throne, whom he calls *Jehovah*, was our Saviour."[133] Conference of the verses indicates not only that Christ is called Jehovah but that he is "naturally and essentially God."[134]

The orthodox also adduce the truly remarkable passage in Isaiah 45 (vv. 21-25) as proof of the deity of Christ and the attribution to him, along with the Father, of the holy name of the One God. Isaiah's prophecy says first, "there is no God else besides me, a just God and a Saviour, there is none besides me. Look unto me, and be ye saved, all the ends of the earth; for I am God and there is none else," clearly manifesting God to be the Saviour and "the object of faith." Isaiah next prophesies that before this God every knee shall bow and every tongue shall swear — a text applied directly to Christ both in Romans 14:10-12 and Philippians 2:10-11. Finally Isaiah states (v. 25), "In the Lord (Jehovah) shall all the seed of Israel be justified, and shall glory": here, argue the orthodox, the same Jehovah is also clearly and undeniably applied to the Mediator in his work of justification. In the case of Philippians 2:9, the statement that Christ is given the "name above every other name" can only mean that he is to be called "Jehovah." Nor, as Arians claim, is this name applied only after the resurrection: he was humiliated and died as a man; he was exalted as a man — but it is not as a man that he is called Jehovah. The fallacy of the adversaries here is the fallacy *secundum quid*: they move from a relative statement to one that is made absolutely or *simpliciter*; the revelation is given post-resurrection, but it is not stated simply and absolutely of the resurrected Christ or of his humanity.[135]

Similarly, Jeremiah (23:6) says "he shall be called the Jehovah, our righteousness" in a direct reference to the Messiah. The identification of this reference to "Jehovah our Righteousness" as to the Messiah rather than simply to God as such rests on the full passage where the preceding verse speaks of the Lord or Jehovah raising up "unto

132. Poole, *Commentary*, 1 Cor. 10:9 in loc. (III, p. 572).

133. Ridgley, *Body of Divinity*, p. 139, col. 2; cf. Calvin, *Commentary on the Gospel of John*, 12:41: "the Evangelist takes for granted, that Isaiah saw the glory of Christ; and hence he infers, that Isaiah accommodates his instruction to the future state of Christ's kingdom" (*CTS John*, II, p. 44); Poole, *Commentary*, III, p. 347, on John 12:41: "The evangelist expounds this [i.e., Isa. 6:1] of Christ, which is an evident proof of the Deity of Christ, that he is Jehovah; for it was Jehovah whom the prophet saw"; and note Turretin, *Inst. theol. elencticae*, III.xxviii.5-6.

134. Pearson, *Exposition of the Creed*, II.iii (1887, p. 194).

135. Zanchi *De tribus Elohim*, pt. 2, III.xii.2-3 (cols. 493-494).

David a righteous Branch," namely, "a King" who will "reign and prosper, and shall execute judgement and justice in the earth" — this one, as the next verse testifies, "shall be called, Jehovah our Righteousness." The reference "must be understood of the Messiah."[136] Diodati also comments that, according to this passage in Jeremiah, Christ "shall be acknowledged to be the true everlasting God, who in his humane nature shall fulfill all manner of righteousness for his Church."[137]

2. Lord and God. Malachi 3:1, "... the Lord, whom ye seek, shall suddenly come to his temple, even the messenger of the covenant, who ye delight in: behold, he shall come, saith the Lord of hosts." The reading of this text found in Calvin's commentary is followed nearly exactly by later exegetes in the Reformed tradition: thus, Diodati comments,

> *Suddenly*] presently after that *John* shall begin to preach, Christ the true everlasting God shall appear, and publickly exercise his office. ... *The Messenger*] namely, Christ the Mediatour, and foundation of the covenant of grace, with the elect, see Ex. 23:20, 21; Isa. 63:9; Heb. 8:6; 9:15; 12:24.[138]

Other Reformed exegetes of the era offer much the same interpretation,[139] and the theologians incorporate the exegesis into their doctrinal discussions:

> In Mal. 3:1, he is called "the Lord" who shall come into his temple, which the evangelists indicate is to be spoken of the Messiah, Mk. 1:2; Lk. 1:76. Now, who is the Lord to whom the temple belongs by way of eminence, but God?[140]

Christ is also specifically identified as "God": in Isaiah 9:6 the future Messianic king is called "mighty God" and "everlasting Father," a designation of his divine "majesty and glory."[141] Here the Reformed have two distinct adversaries to refute — Grotius and the Socinians — who pose rather different readings of the passage against the traditional orthodox reading. Grotius, for his part, understood the text as a reference to an "infant recently born," probably Hezekiah.[142] The orthodox respond that the language of the verse is clearly messianic and is endowed with divine attributes,

---

136. Turretin, *Inst. theol. elencticae*, III.xxviii.5; cf. De Moor, *Commentarius perpetuus*, I.xxi.1; Ridgley, *Body of Divinity*, p. 139, col. 2-p. 140, col. 2; Calvin, *Commentaries on Jeremiah*, 23:6 in loc. (*CTS Jeremiah*, III, p. 138); and Poole, *Commentary*, II, p. 430.

137. Diodati, *Pious and Learned Annotations*, Jer. 23:6 in loc.

138. Diodati, *Pious and Learned Annotations*, Mal. 3:1 in loc.; cf. Calvin, *Commentaries on Malachi*, 3:1, in loc. (*CTS Malachi*, pp. 568-569).

139. Poole, *Commentary*, Mal. 3:1 in loc. (II, p. 1025); Trapp, *Commentary*, Mal. 3:1 in loc. (IV, p. 514); Henry, *Exposition*, Mal. 3:1 in loc..

140. Turretin, *Inst. theol. elencticae*, III.xxviii.5; cf. Mastricht, *Theoretico-practica theol*, II.xxvi.9.

141. Turretin, *Inst. theol. elencticae*, III.xxviii.5; Amyraut, *De mysterio trinitatis*, IV, pp. 199-201.

142. See Grotius, *Annotationes ad Vetus Testamentum*, Isa. 9:6-7 in loc.; and see Owen, *Vindiciae evangelicae*, in *Works*, 12, pp. 315-321, noting that Grotius' reading corresponds to that of some of the rabbinic commentators.

such as are inapplicable to a human ruler such as Hezekiah and, in fact, can only point to one who is both divine and human.[143]

In the case of the Socinians, there is a fair amount of difference between the edition of the Racovian Catechism cited by Owen and the edition of 1680, translated by Rees. The earlier edition follows out the same form of argument as found in the discussion of 1 Timothy 3:16 — first, denying the received text and, then, even if the received text is allowed, offering a variant reading. Owen singles out for his critique the earlier edition's contention that the passage does not refer to Christ, but rather to God the Father as "everlasting Father" or "Father of eternity," followed by its statement that, if the text is taken as referring to Christ, the phrase "Father of eternity" indicates that Christ is "the prince or author of eternal life, which is future." Owen comments that this approach is clearly self-contradictory:

> our catechists ... fix only on that expression, "The eternal Father," and then say that we cannot intend the Son here, because we say he is not the Father; and yet so do these gentlemen themselves! They say the Christ is the Son of God, and no way the same with the Father; and yet they say that upon a peculiar account he is here called "The eternal Father."[144]

Owen does not dispute the second part of the Socinian argument concerning the meaning of the phrase, but only the conclusion that the catechism draws from it: whether the text refers to Christ as "Father of eternity" because of his eternal deity or because of his authorship of our future salvation is quite irrelevant to the issue in dispute, given that however the clause is interpreted, it is placed in the text in relation to such other phrases as "the mighty God" and "Prince of Peace," which, taken together, must refer to one who is fully divine.[145] The later version of the catechism leaves out the claim that the title "Father of eternity" refers to God the Father and concentrates on the second line of argument only.[146]

Christ is also called both "Lord" and "God" in the New Testament. These references are, the Reformed writers argue, of a demonstrably different character than references to idols or to creatures or creaturely masters as lords and gods.[147] The references to him as "Lord" are of particular significance to the doctrinal point, but also the focus of considerable debate. Leigh notes with some emphasis that in the New Testament, Christ is also called "ho kyrios by which name the Septuagint expressed Jehovah the proper name of God alone, John 20:28, My Lord; Jude 4, the only Lord; Acts 10:36, the Lord of all; 1 Cor. 15:47, the Lord from Heaven; 1 Cor. 2:8, the Lord of glory."[148] Christ

---

143. Amyraut, De mysterio trinitatis, IV, p. 208.

144. Owen, Vindiciae evangelicae, in Works, XII, pp. 314-315.

145. Owen, Vindiciae evangelicae, in Works, XII, p. 314.

146. See Racovian Catechism, iv.1 (pp. 138-139).

147. Ridgley, Body of Divinity, pp. 142-143, citing Rev. 1:5; 17:14; 1 Cor. 2:8; Hebrews 1:8.

148. Leigh, Treatise, II.xvi (p. 132); N.B., κύριος is only in some of the codices of 1 Cor. 15:47 — see the collation in The Greek New Testament, ed. Aland et al., in loc. In addition, note that the word translated as "Lord" in the phrase cited from Jude 4 is not κύριος but δεσπότης, on which see

"is called *ho theos cum articulo*, John 1:1; Acts 20:28; 1 Tim 3:16; ... *the great God*, Titus 2:13; *the true God*, 1 John 5:20; *God over all*, or *blessed above all*, Rom 9:5; *the most high*, Luke 1:76."[149]

The names "Lord" and "God," particularly the former, are on occasion given to creatures, but the biblical text always provides "sufficient light, whereby we may plainly discern when they are applied to the one living and true God, and when not" — and if not conclusively from the text itself, then from the "context." The word "lord" when applied to a creature simply denotes a certain superiority as of a master over a servant — whereas in each of the biblical texts cited, the implication is clearly a divine title.[150] So also, when the word "god" is predicated of a creature, it invariably is reflected in the words of the text, which speaks of "strange gods" (Deut 32:16) or "molten gods" (Exod. 34:17) or "new gods" (Judg. 5:8) or some similar expression denoting the creaturely or idolatrous character of the "god."[151]

Each of these texts associates the word "God" with Christ and was the subject of considerable exegetical argument — particularly the syntactically difficult Titus 2:13. We see here the bearing of the orthodox hermeneutic upon the actual determination of doctrine: the systems included a great deal of exegesis, whether in the form of direct, positive exposition of text or in the form of refutation of alternative, frequently Socinian, readings. If, after the initial controversies, much of this exegesis appears as a kind of repetitive proof-texting, it was not so at the outset — and enough controversy arose throughout the seventeenth and even the early eighteenth century to prevent the orthodox exegetical enterprise from ever growing entirely stale. By the same token, the "new" rationalist or critical exegesis of the period should be judged fresh or stale to the extent that it is truly inventive or merely repeats old trinitarian and christological heresies.

In John 20:28, Thomas confesses Christ to be "my Lord and my God." In the typical reformed exegesis of the era, the text clearly indicated that Thomas identified Christ as God — indeed, it was the first place in the narrative scheme of the New Testament where this confession or revelation appears, given that it is in and through the resurrection that Christ is "declared to be the son of God in power."[152] As Turretin insists, only an act of exegetical "violence" can yield an alternative reading.[153] The "violence" of which Turretin speaks is certainly to be found, accepting seventeenth-century Reformed standards, in the Racovian Catechism, where the text of John 20:28 is dismissed rather obliquely following the examination of Acts 20:28: inasmuch as

---

Beza, *Annotationes in Novum Testamentum*, in loc.: also see the discussion of the text below, this section.

149. Leigh, *Treatise*, II.xvi (p. 132).

150. Ridgley, *Body of Divinity*, p. 141, col. 2-p. 142, col. 1.

151. Ridgley, *Body of Divinity*, pp. 142-143, citing Rev. 1:5; 17:14; 1 Cor. 2:8; Hebrews 1:8.

152. Poole, *Commentary*, John 20:28 in loc., citing collaterally Rom. 1:4; cf. Hutcheson, *Exposition of the Gospel of John*, in loc.; and note also Calvin, *Commentary on John*, in loc. (CTS John, II, pp. 275-278).

153. Turretin, *Inst. theol. elencticae*, III.xxviii.10.

some Greek texts emend the phrase, "the church of God," to read "the church of the Lord and God," the Socinians argue, a parallel can be identified in the words of Thomas, so that "Thomas, if he addressed those words to Christ, was not satisfied with addressing him Lord, but styled him also God, that he might acknowledge, not his ordinary, but his divine authority over him."[154] The problem that the Socinians fail to note is that, however one reads the final clause of Acts 20:28 concerning the purchase of salvation with "his blood," the phrase "Lord and God" found in some of the manuscripts remains a reference to God — and, if it is used as a key to the reading of John 20:28, the variant in Acts actually supports the orthodox reading of the Johannine text! Thus, the accusation of "violence." As Turretin points out, Thomas' exclamation, "my Lord and my God," is preceded in the text of the Gospel by the words "he said unto him," rendering the reference utterly certain.[155]

Nor does the antitrinitarian reading of John 17:3 argue the contrary: there Jesus prays to the Father "that they might know thee the only true God, and Jesus Christ whom thou hast sent." Socinians and other objectors declare that these words prove that the Father alone is God and that Christ is simply his messenger. The text states that the Father alone is the true God — not that only the Father is God. The point of the passage, specifically, is that there is no God beside the God who is the Father. It therefore is no denial of the deity of Son and Spirit: indeed, if the Father were not true God, the Son could not be genuinely divine. This reading of the text is confirmed by conference with 1 John 5:20.[156] The purpose of the text is to identify the "true God" — fully identified on the basis of other biblical passages as "the one only divine essence subsisting in three persons" — thereby excluding the false gods of the "heathen." The phrase "Jesus Christ whom thou hast sent" refers to Christ in his mediatorial office.[157]

Debate over the understanding of 1 John 5:20 was also quite intense, particularly because of its just noted use in confirming the orthodox reading of John 17:3: "And we know that the Son of God is come, and hath given us an understanding, that we may know him that is true, and we are in him that is true, even in his Son Jesus Christ. This is the true God, and eternal life." The antitrinitarians of the seventeenth century offered much the same argument concerning 1 John 5:20 as that attributed by Calvin to the "Arians," namely, that "this," as the subject of the final clause, referred to the "his" of the previous clause — that is, to the Father, and not to "his Son." In other words, "this" refers not to the person spoken of immediately before, not to the immediate antecedent and the proper subject of the verse. The orthodox dispute this

---

154. Racovian Catechism, iv.1 (p. 84). N.B., the catechism is correct concerning the variant readings: cf. *The Greek New Testament*, ed. Aland, et al., in loc.

155. Turretin, *Inst. theol. elencticae*, III.xxviii.10.

156. Wyttenbach, *Tentamen theol.*, I, iii, §338.2; cf. the argument in Johannes Piscator, *Analysis logica evangelii secundum Johannem: una cum scholiis & observationibus locorum doctrinae* (London: George Bishop, 1595), John 17:3 in loc. (p. 174); Jasz-Berenyi, *Examen doctrinæ ariano-socinianæ*, p. 22; also Poole, *Commentary*, in loc. (III, p. 367).

157. *Dutch Annotations*, in loc.; cf. Jasz-Berenyi, *Examen doctrinæ ariano-socinianæ*, p. 22; Poole, *Commentary*, in loc. (III, p. 367); also note Calvin's similar reading of the text, 6.2 (A.2).

reading on purely logical and grammatical grounds: the phrase "the true God and eternal life," prefaced by "this" must refer to Christ, concerning whom the text had spoken just before, as normal grammar would indicate. This reading is also substantiated by "the scope of the apostle, which is to teach us that Christ is come in order that we might be led to the knowledge and communion of the true God."[158]

Beyond this, "God" in the final clause of the text is set in apposition to "eternal life" and shares the same verb. Now God the Father is never called "eternal life" by Scripture, but only the giver of eternal life; whereas

> it is not only said concerning our Saviour, that *in him was life*, John 1:4 but he says, John 14:6. *I am the life*; and 'tis said in 1 John 1:2. *The life was manifested, and we have seen it*, or him, *and show you that eternal life, which was with the Father, pros ton patera*, which is an explanation of his own words, John 1:1. *pros ton theon, with God*; and then he explains what he said in ver. 14. of the same Chapter, when he says, *the word of Life*, or the Person who calls himself *the life* was *manifested unto us*; which seems to be a peculiar phrase used by this Apostle, where he sets forth our Saviour's glory under this character, whom he calls *Life*, or *eternal life*; and he that is so, is the same Person, who is called true God.[159]

This text yields, moreover, a second biblical text (in addition to John 17:3) in which there is a declaration of the "true God," here the Son, obviously not to the exclusion of the deity of the Father. The clear identification of the Father as "true God" in John 17:3 now serves the trinitarian cause — as the orthodox point out, the Son could not be divine if the Father were not.[160] This reading of the texts also corresponds with that of the fathers, notably Athanasius, Gregory of Nazianzus, Basil, and Chrysostom.[161] By orthodox standards this is the perfect application of accepted exegetical method: the explanation of a difficult text by collation with other texts — and by any standard, it was a close analysis of Johannine usage.

As Pictet comments, the identification of Christ as God, indeed, as fully equal in divinity to God the Father, is directly taught by the apostle Paul. He cites

> Phil. 2:6, where the holy apostle says of Christ, "who [namely, Christ] being in the form of God, he thought it not robbery to be equal with God." What could be said more directly — and is it likely that Paul would have broken forth into these expressions, if Christ had not been the true and supreme God?[162]

The Socinian rejoinder is that the equality indicated in the text derives from the fact that Christ did the Father's work, not from an equality in essence — "in the Greek

---

158. Turretin, *Inst. theol. elencticae*, III.xxviii.8; cf. Ridgley, *Body of Divinity*, p. 146, cols. 1-2.

159. Ridgley, *Body of Divinity*, p. 147, col. 2; similarly, Turretin, *Inst. theol. elencticae*, III.xxviii.8.

160. Piscator, *Analysis logica evangelii secundum Johannem*, John 17:3 in loc. (p. 174); cf. *Dutch Annotations*, 1 John 5:20, in loc.; Poole, *Commentary*, John 17:3 and 1 John 5:20 in loc. (III, pp. 367, 941); cf. Wyttenbach, *Tentamen theol.*, I, iii, §338.2.

161. Jasz-Berenyi, *Examen doctrinæ ariano-socinianæ*, p. 22.

162. Pictet, *Theol. chr.*, II.xvi.1.

it is not that he is equal to God, but... that he is equally God, is like God." Neither this statement nor the following statement, that Christ laid aside the form of God, "comport with him who is God by nature."[163] "The form of God cannot mean here the nature of God, since the apostle states that Christ emptied himself of this form: but God cannot in any respect empty himself of his nature."[164] Yet, Turretin replies, recognizing that form is not identical to nature, how could Christ have had the "form of God" if he were not "God by nature"? Nor can the phrase "form of God" be used to explain Christ's performance of divine work or his miracles — given that Scripture does not designate anyone else who performed miracles as having the "form of God." What is more, the Greek word, ἴσα, cannot mean merely similar here, "since such an ἰσότης is to be understood here as arises from the possession of the form of God, which indicates not only a similitude, but a genuine equality and identity."[165]

Against the Socinians, Reformed writers declare that Titus 2:13 must refer to Christ as "God," inasmuch as a single article governs the phrase "the glorious appearing of the great God and Savior, Jesus Christ."[166] Of the older Reformed writers, Calvin is not decided on the exegetical point, but clearly recognizes the problem:

> It is uncertain whether these words should be read together thus, "the glory of our Lord Jesus Christ, the great God and our Savior," or separately, as of the Father and the Son, "the glory of the great God, and of our Savior, the Lord Jesus Christ." The Arians, seizing on this latter sense, have endeavored to prove from it, that the Son is less than the Father, because here Paul calls the Father "the great God" by way of distinction from the Son. The orthodox teachers of the Church, for the purpose of shutting out this slander, eagerly contended that both are affirmed of Christ. But the Arians may be refuted in a few words and by solid argument; for Paul, having spoken of the revelation of the glory of "the great God," immediately added "Christ," in order to inform us, that that revelation of glory will be in his person; as if he had said that, when Christ shall appear, the greatness of the divine glory shall then be revealed to us.[167]

The Socinians' approach to the text of Titus 2:13, together with their exegesis of Jude 4 ("denying the only Lord God, and our Lord Jesus Christ" — καὶ τὸν μόνον δεσπότην καὶ κύριον ἡμων Ιησουν Χριστὸν ἀρονούμενοι), begins by examining the grammatical argumentation of the orthodox, namely, that "since in the Greek there is but one article prefixed to both titles, they ought, conformably to a rule of Greek composition, to be considered as designating one person only, that is Jesus Christ."[168] The Socinian response to this claim is that Greek composition does not always follow the rule, and that the "circumstances" of the individual text must

---

163. Racovian Catechism, iv.1 (pp. 133-134).

164. Racovian Catechism, iv.1 (pp. 119).

165. Turretin, *Inst. theol. elencticae*, III.xxviii.11.

166. Turretin, *Inst. theol. elencticae*, III.xxviii.9.

167. Calvin, *Commentary on Titus*, 2:16 (CTS *Titus*, p. 321).

168. Racovian Catechism, iv.1 (p. 80).

determine the meaning: thus, in Hebrews 9:19, the phrase "the blood of calves and goats" has one article, but does not identify calves and goats — and likewise, in Ephesians 2:20 and 3:5, the phrase "the apostles and prophets" does not identify prophets and apostles. Similarly, the language of Titus 2:13, "the great God and our Savior Jesus Christ," hardly demands an identification of God with Jesus.[169] Second, the Socinian exegesis takes on the more significant question of the meaning of the specific text, where, in the case of Titus 2:13, the Greek rule of composition seems to be supported by the fact that Christians expect the future appearance of the Son, not of the Father — and here, quite clearly, the one who appears is called "the great God." But there is no reason to claim, the Socinians argue, that the glory of the Father will not be revealed in Christ:

> Now that it may be truly said that the glory of God will appear when Christ shall come in judgment, is evident from the declaration of our Lord, that "he shall come in glory," that is, in the glory of God his Father. There is, however, no impropriety in saying that God the Father will come, or rather will appear, when the Son shall come to judge the world. For will not Christ, in judging the world, sustain and represent the person of God the Father, as the sovereign from whom he will have received his judicial office."[170]

There is little variation in the exegesis of Titus 2:13 in the era of orthodoxy. Diodati simply states, without noting any controversy, that in the phrase "the great God," the apostle "gives Christ Jesus this title, because he is despised of the world, and intimates that his glory and greatness shall then appear."[171] Poole does not mention controversy either, but his commentary clearly reflects debate over the text with the Socinians. "The same person," he writes, "is here meant by *the great God and our Saviour Jesus Christ*." Poole also offers two grounds for this conclusion beyond the grammar of the passage — first, it is Christ who has been "appointed to be the judge of the quick and the dead," and presumably, therefore, the text must point to one and only one who comes in glory; and second, "ἐπιφάνεια, by us translated *appearing*, is attributed only to the Second Person in the Blessed Trinity, 2 Thess. 2:8; 1 Tim. 6:14; 2 Tim. 4:1, 8." This point is not found in Calvin. It does add considerably to the argument, without what might be called the addition of a dogmatic grid: given the broad New Testament denial of the visibility of God the Father and the inability of human beings ever to see God and given the identification of Christ alone as the one who will return visibly, however one reads the conjunction, there is an insurmountable difficulty entailed on a reading that claims the future "appearing" of the Father (or, indeed, of the Spirit). Poole concludes, "From this text the Divine nature of Christ is irrefragably concluded; he is not only called *God*, but μέγας Θεὸς, *the great God*, which cannot be understood of a made God."[172]

---

169. Racovian Catechism, iv.1 (pp. 80-81).
170. Racovian Catechism, iv.1 (pp. 81-82).
171. Diodati, *Pious and Learned Annotations*, in loc.
172. Poole, *Commentary*, Titus 2:13, in loc. (III, p. 803).

There is, moreover, the statement in Acts (20:28) that God purchased the church with his own blood.[173] These arguments are placed beyond doubt by Matthew 1:23, which speaks of the Savior as "Emmanuel, ... God with us."[174] "These titles," comments Leigh, "are too high and excellent to be given to any mere man whatsoever; God therefore who will not have his glory given to another, would never have given these titles to another, if he were not God."[175]

Socinians (and various others not to be easily classed as antitrinitarians, such as, in England, Samuel Clarke)[176] protested against the traditional reading of Romans 9:5 and its use in substantiating the divinity of Christ: in place of "as concerning the flesh, Christ came, who is over all, God blessed forever," the Socinians would read, "as concerning the flesh, Christ. Let God (i.e. the Father), who is over all, be blessed forever," making a separate sentence of the two final clauses of the verse. The orthodox object that their reading agrees more precisely with the Greek and note that the ancient versions and the Fathers also confirm this reading. "The Apostle," reasoned Ridgley, "had been speaking of our Saviour, as descending from the father, according to the flesh, or considering him as to his human nature; therefore it is very reasonable to suppose he would speak of him as to his divine nature, especially since both these natures are spoken of together in John 1:14, and elsewhere."[177] Thus, the text of Romans 9:5 is not a "doxological apostrophe to the Father," but a clear reference to Christ, who is the only possible antecedent of the phrase.[178]

There are also several places in the New Testament where Old Testament references to God are applied directly to Christ. In John 12:39-41, the evangelist applies to Christ words of Isaiah by which the prophet intended "the supreme God"; similarly Paul in Romans 14:10 applies the words of Isaiah, "Look to me, and be ye saved, all the ends of the earth; for I am God, and there is none else" (Isaiah 45:22-23) to the judgment seat of Christ. In both cases logic requires that we understand the New Testament text as testimony to Christ's divinity.[179]

3. Word of God. The Johannine identification of Jesus as the *Logos* also figured strongly in the Reformed orthodox discussion. Leigh writes that "He is called the Word, because he is so often spoken of and promised in the Scripture, and is in a manner the whole subject of Scripture."[180] The Johannine language carries with it several

---

173. Leigh, *Treatise*, II.xvi (p. 131, margin).

174. Ridgley, *Body of Divinity*, p. 143, col. 2.

175. Leigh, *Treatise*, II.xvi (p. 132).

176. Cf. Clarke, *Scripture Doctrine of the Trinity*, in *Works*, IV, pp. 46-47. Exemplifying the difficulty of assigning a name to the problem, note Thomas Burnet, *The Scripture Trinity Intelligibly Explained: or, an Essay toward the Demonstration of a Trinity in Unity, from Reasons an Scripture. In a Chain of Consequences from Certain Principles. Which ... may serve as an answer to Dr. Waterland and Dr. Clarke and all Others ... whether Arians, Socinians, or whatever other Denomination.* (London: J. Roberts, 1720).

177. Ridgley, *Body of Divinity*, p. 146, col. 1; cf. Turretin, *Inst. theol. elencticae*, III.xxviii.9.

178. Turretin, *Inst. theol. elencticae*, III.xxviii.9.

179. Pictet, *Theol. chr.*, II.xvi.4-5.

180. Leigh, *Treatise*, II.xvi (p. 132).

implications: first, "For this cause also he is the WORD of the Father, not a vanishing but an essential word."[181] Second, the incommunicable property of the Word is "to be begotten": reflecting the medieval and specifically Thomist interpretation of the Son's procession as intellectual, Perkins explains, "because as a word is, as it were, begotten of the mind, so is the Son begotten of the Father." Third, the Son is also called Word "because he bringeth glad tidings from the bosom of the Father." Each of these three implications of "Word," moreover, carries with it the assumption of full divinity.[182]

The Socinian counter to the orthodox argumentation interprets "Word" and "Word of God" entirely differently. "It cannot be proved from Christ's being the Word of God," the Racovian Catechism contends, "that he possesses a divine nature." In fact, the correct inference is the opposite,

> for since he is the Word of the one God, it is evident that he is not that God. ... Jesus is called the Word or Speech of God because he is the immediate interpreter, and at the same time the executor, of the divine will: for this belongs properly to the Word of God. In the Greek, the article is prefixed to the term Word (ὁ λόγος) in order to designate this illustrious, or most excellent and divine interpreter and executor of the divine will; by whom, as we learn from what follows, God effected the new creation of the world and of all things. John himself, explaining this title a little further on, writes (John 1:18), "No man hath seen God at any time; the only begotten Son, who is in the bosom of the Father, he hath declared him."[183]

Given that "Word" is merely the title of the interpreter of God and that the creation of worlds by the Word indicates not the original creation but the redemptive re-creation of the world through the Gospel, it follows that the "beginning" of which the prologue to John's Gospel refers is the beginning of the Gospel: "there is no reference here to an antecedent eternity, without commencement; because mention is made here of a beginning, which is opposed to that eternity." The word "beginning," without article, "used absolutely, is to be understood of the subject matter under consideration," namely, the Gospel message. This reading is confirmed by the similar usage in 1 John 1:1, "That which was from the beginning, which we have heard ... and our hands have handled, of the Word of life" — the "evangelist," thus, "states himself to have been present" at this "beginning." Quite simply, the meaning of both passages is "that the Word was in the beginning of the Gospel."[184] As for John 1:14, "the Word was made flesh," the text clearly means that "the Word was made flesh in the days of the writer," and it indicates also "what it was made, when it was made, — namely, flesh" and therefore that "the Word, although endued with as much divinity as the language of John ascribes to it, was as to its substance a man."[185]

---

181. Perkins, *Golden Chaine*, V (p. 14, col. 2).
182. Perkins, *Golden Chaine*, V (p. 14, col. 2- p. 15, col. 1); cf. Venema, *Inst. theol.*, xi (p. 224).
183. Racovian Catechism, iv.1 (pp. 139-140).
184. Racovian Catechism, iv.1 (pp. 63-65).
185. Racovian Catechism, iv.1 (pp. 118-119).

When Turretin cites John 1:1 for the purpose of arguing that the divine attribute of eternity ought to be ascribed to Christ, he refers to the Socinian claim, commenting that "in the beginning" cannot be read as meaning "in the beginning of the gospel or of the new creation, as our adversaries would like, but in the beginning of time, for no other beginning can be understood here than that with which Moses was concerned, Genesis 1:1; to which John clearly alludes, as the scope of his gospel demonstrates." The Socinian reading, Turretin continues, is "absurd."[186] Reformed commentators, often without naming the Socinians, make the same point: the "beginning" referenced in John 1:1 can only be the beginning of the world, and not the beginning of the Gospel — as if also the case with the text of 1 John 1:1 and 2:13.[187] The impact of the Socinian exegesis is still evident in Gill's commentary on John 1:1, to the effect that "this is said not of the written word, but of the essential word of God, the Lord Jesus Christ, is clear, from all that is said from hence, to John 1:14, as that this word was in the beginning, was with God, and is God." Then, clearly reflecting the problem of the Socinian reading, Gill continues,

> This word, he says, was in the beginning ... nor is the beginning of the Gospel of Christ, by the preaching of John the Baptist, intended here ... but by the beginning is here meant, the beginning of the world, or the creation of all things; and which is expressive of the eternity of Christ, he was in the beginning, as the Maker of all creatures, and therefore must be before them all.[188]

4. The "Angel of the Lord" and the divinity of Christ. Virtually a separate class of texts are those containing references to angelic mediators. These texts, moreover, not only occupy a distinct place in the Reformed orthodox reading of the Old Testament, they also stand as a distinct portion of the argument in the thought of the Reformers, notably, Calvin.[189] The exegetical point and its doctrinal application are, in other words, still further indications of the nature of the continuity in Reformed theology from the era of the Reformation through the orthodox era.

Although, as in other places in the Old Testament, there are differences among the exegetes as to the reading of particular passages, the key to the trinitarian understanding of Exodus is its frequent and substantive reference to the "Angel of Jehovah," who stands next to God as divine. That the Angel is distinct from God is clear from the passages themselves, as is the divinity of the Angel, given his description in attributes that can only be predicated of God: the Angel is identified as the divine presence (Exod. 33:14) or as having "in him" the name of God (Exod. 23:21). The

---

186. Turretin, *Inst. theol. elencticae*, III.xxviii.14; cf. the virtually identical exegetical point in Pearson, *Exposition of the Creed*, II.iii (1887, p. 184).

187. Thus, Poole, *Commentary*, John 1:1 and 1 John 1:1; 2:13 in loc. (III, pp. 277, 929, 932).

188. Gill, *Exposition of the New Testament*, John 1:1 in loc.

189. Calvin, *Institutes*, I.xiii.10; cf. Pierre Allix, *A Dissertation concerning the Angel who is called the Redeemer*, Gen. XLVIII (London: R. Chiswell, 1699).

Angel also identifies himself to Moses as the "God of Abraham, Isaac, and Jacob" and sends Moses to deliver "his people" from Pharaoh (Exod. 3:2-6).[190]

The Reformed orthodox reading of these texts simply follows out the view of the Reformers and the older tradition. Allix notes that the "whole difficulty of the place may be reduced to three heads," namely, whether the God, *Elohim*, noted in verse 15, is indeed *Jehovah*; whether the angel identified in the following verse is to be identified syntactically as the *Elohim* of verse 15 or is to be distinguished "from him as a Creature ... from its Creator"; and whether the prayer is "made to God alone or to the Redeeming Angel together with him."[191] This angel, declares Poole, is surely not

> a created angel, but Christ Jesus, who is called an *Angel*, Ex. 23:20, and *the Angel of the covenant*, Mal. 3:1, who was the conductor of the Israelites in the wilderness, as plainly appears by comparing of Ex. 23:20-21, with 1 Cor. 10:4, 9. Add hereunto that this Angel is called Jacob's *Redeemer*, which is the title appropriate by God to himself, Is. 43:14; 47:4, and that *from all evil*, and therefore from sin, from which no created angel can deliver us, but Christ only, Matt. 1:21; and that Jacob worshippeth and prayeth to the Angel.[192]

There is a distinct continuity between the seventeenth century Reformed exegetes and the older tradition, including the Reformers, in the exegesis of these texts from Exodus — although contrary to what might be expected, the seventeenth-century writers do not read all of the "angel" text from Exodus in a uniformly trinitarian or christological manner. They reflect, perhaps, textual debate in the seventeenth-century, including the more literalistic readings argued by Grotius, and exercise more caution than Calvin. For Poole, as for a majority of the seventeenth-century orthodox exegetes, the determinative text is Exodus 3:2-6, and the others are read in terms of their relationship to it. At verse 2, Poole comments that "the Angel of the Lord" is clearly

> not a created angel, but the angel of the covenant, Christ Jesus, who then and ever was God, and was to be man, and to be sent into the world in our flesh, as a messenger from God. ... That this Angel was no creature, plainly appears by the whole context, and specially by his saying, *I am the Lord, &c.*[193]

He is less anxious to press the trinitarian interpretation and the parallel with the usage of Exodus 3:2, however, at Exodus 14:19 — the text refers to the "angel of God, which

---

190. Zanchi, *De tribus Elohim*, pt. I, II.ii.1 (col. 35); Amyraut, *De mysterio trinitatis*, IV, pp. 174-178; Downame, *Summe*, i (pp. 37-39); Turretin, *Inst. theol. elencticae*, III.xxvi.9.

191. Allix, *Dissertation Concerning the Angel*, p. 436.

192. Poole, *Commentary*, Gen. 48:15-16 in loc. (I, p. 107); cf. Diodati, *Pious and Learned Annotation*, Gen. 48:16 in loc.; Ainsworth, *Annotation on the Pentateuch*, Gen. 48:15-16 in loc.; Downame, *Summe*, i (pp. 37-39).

193. Poole, *Commentary*, Exod. 3:2 in loc. (I, p. 120); similarly, Diodati, *Pious and Learned Annotations*, Exo. 3:2 in loc.; cf. Trapp, *Commentary*, in loc. (I, p. 184); and note Ainsworth, *Annotations upon Exodus*, Ex. 3:2 in loc., citing rabbinic exegesis to the effect that the Angel of the Lord is the Redeemer.

went before the camp of Israel" and then to the pillars of cloud and fire, which Poole takes as a reference to God, without qualifier, and then notes that these assignments of place do not imply "change of place" for God and therefore do not compromise the divine omnipresence.[194] Diodati differs and declares the angel of Exodus 14:19 to be "the son of God Himself, the perfect intercessor and eternall Mediator between God and men."[195] The reading of Exodus 23:20, "Behold, I send an angel before thee, to keep thee in the way, and to bring thee into the place which I have prepared," however, is typically trinitarian: this, according to Poole, refers to "Christ, the Angel of the covenant," with Diodati adding that Moses here "represents the Father or the Holy Trinity as sending the Sonne, Is. 48:16."[196] Poole does not parallel Calvin by developing the identity of the "angel of [God's] presence" in Exodus 33:14 — rather he offers a collateral citation to the same phrase in Isaiah 63:9, noting that this is the same angel that guided Israel through the wilderness and is variously called "an angel," "his presence," and "Jehovah" in Exodus. This, he comments, "must be the Lord Jesus Christ, who appeared to Moses in the bush, as Stephen doth interpret it, Acts 7:35 &c." Diodati, however, draws out the point at Exodus 33:14, with a collateral reference to Isaiah 63:9 — while Trapp makes no comment and Ainsworth is only obliquely chirstological.[197]

Among the later exegetes, Henry reflects the result of critical debate in the late seventeenth century and notes the spectrum of readings of the texts: on Exodus 3:2, he writes that "an angel of the Lord appeared to [Moses]; some think, a created angel, who speaks in the language of him who sent him; others, the second person, the Angel of the covenant, who is himself Jehovah."[198] Nor does Henry add the christological reading at Exodus 14:19 — rather he postpones the point until Exodus 23:20. Here, the salvific implication is sufficient to demand the christological or trinitarian reading, although Henry still notes the two possible interpretations of the text, "a created angel" and "minister of God's providence" or "the son of God, the Angel of the covenant" and then concludes, somewhat weakly, "we may as well suppose him God's Messenger, and the Church's Redeemer, before his incarnation," given that it is Christ whose redemptive task it is to prepare "a place for his followers."[199] Henry also avoids christological readings at Exodus 33:14.

---

194. Poole, *Commentary*, Exod. 14:19 in loc. (I, p. 146).

195. Diodati, *Pious and Learned Annotations*, Exod. 14:19 in loc.; so also Ainsworth, *Annotations upon Exodus*, Ex. 14:19 in loc..; and Trapp, *Commentary*, Exod. 14:19 in loc. (I, p. 199).

196. Poole, *Commentary* Exod. 23:20 in loc. (I, p. 169); Diodati, *Pious and Learned Annotations*, Exod. 23:20 in loc.; so also Ainsworth, *Annotations upon Exodus*, Exod. 23:20 in loc.; and Trapp, *Commentary*, Exod. 23:20 in loc. (I, p. 216).

197. Poole, *Commentary* Isa. 63:9 in loc. (II, p. 478); Diodati, *Pious and Learned Annotations*, Exod. 33:14 in loc.; Trapp, *Commentary*, Exod. 33:14-15 in loc. (I, p. 225); Ainsworth, *Annotations upon Exodus*, Exod. 33:14-15 in loc.

198. Henry, *Exposition*, Exod. 3:2 in loc.

199. Henry, *Exposition*, Exod. 23:20 in loc.

5. Other names and titles. Christ is called the "Father of eternity" by Isaiah, a title only suitable for one who is divine, indeed, who is "Eternitie it selfe, and the Author of it."[200] So too, the identifications of Christ as a "rock of offense" and "stumbling-stone" (1 Pet. 2:5-8; cf. Matt. 21:42; Rom. 9:32-33) immediately raise the issue of the divinity of Christ and the problem of those monotheists — that is, the Jews, whether of the era of the New Testament or in seventeenth-century polemic and apologetic — who refuse to accept the divinity of Christ. Henry notes the parallel with Isa. 8:13-14, where the terms are applied to God himself, and concludes that this is *both* a significant trinitarian text and a warning to the high priests and "Jewish doctors."[201]

6. Arguments for the divinity of Christ from divine attributes accorded to him in Scripture. The divine attributes are predicated of Christ — and since these include predicates or attributes that can belong only to God, they offer clear proof of Christ's true divinity. "Not only is he called God," argues Pictet, "but all the attributes of deity belong to him."[202] Ridgley argues,

> We proceed to consider how our Saviour's deity appears, from those divine attributes, which are ascribed to him, which are proper to God alone; to which we will add those high and glorious titles, by which he is described in Scripture: the attributes of God, as has been before observed, are all essential to him, and therefore cannot, in a proper sense, be any of them applied to a creature, as they are to Christ.[203]

The reference to previous discussion of the essential character of the divine attributes is a reference to Ridgley's treatment of question 7 of the catechism, "What is God?" — the *locus* of the formal treatment of the divine essence and attributes. Thus we establish a formal relationship between the portions of the *locus de Deo* that deal with the divine essence and various attributes and the specific *locus de Trinitate*: instead of the separate treatment devoting an entirely philosophical treatment of essence and attributes, it now is seen to be merely a delineation of steps in the argument.

The Son must be understood as both immense and omnipresent, given the ways in which he is described in various biblical texts.[204] He is with his people wherever they are gathered together (Matt. 18:20) and promises to be so even to the end of the world (Matt. 28:20).[205] He also declares that "No man hath ascended up to heaven, but he that came down from heaven, even the Son of Man which is in heaven" (John 3:13) — a text that the Socinians attempt to distort by ignoring the present tense of the final clause as well as the location of the speaker. The one who is the Son of Man, while on earth, states that he came down from heaven and "is in heaven." To be both on earth and in heaven at the same time is an indication of omnipresence:

200. Downame, *Summe*, i (pp. 41, 44).
201. Henry, *Exposition*, Isa. 8:13-14 in loc.
202. Pictet, *Theol. chr.*, II.xv.3; cf. Leigh, *Treatise*, II.xvi (pp. 131-133).
203. Ridgley, *Body of Divinity*, p. 160, col. 2; cf. Turretin, *Inst. theol. elencticae*, III.xxviii.13.
204. Turretin, *Inst. theol. elencticae*, III.xxviii.14.
205. Rijssen, *Summa theol.*, IV.ix, cont. II, arg. 2.

Christ is rightly "said to have descended from heaven by incarnation" and at the same time to be in heaven "by immensity."[206]

The attribute of eternity, the Reformed declare in opposition both to the Socinians and to the Arians, belongs definitively to Christ. The former count the beginning of the Son's existence from his conception in the womb of the Virgin Mary. The latter "distinguish between Christ's being in the beginning of time and his being from eternity."[207] Even when the Arians state that "there was not a point of time in which Christ was not, or that he was before the world, they are far from asserting that he was without beginning, or properly from eternity."[208]

> In answer hereunto, let it be considered, that we cannot conceive of any medium between time and eternity; therefore what was before time, must be from eternity, in the same sense in which God is eternal. That this may appear, let us consider that time is the measure of finite beings, therefore it is very absurd, and little less than a contradiction, to say that there was any finite being produced before time; for that is, in effect, to assert that a limited duration is antecedent to that measure whereby it is determined, or limited. If we should allow that there might have been some things created before God began to create the heavens and the earth, though these things might be said to have had a being longer than time has had, yet they could not have existed before time, for time would have begun with them; therefore if Christ had been created a thousand millions of ages before the world, it would be inferred from hence, that time, which would have taken its beginning from his existence, had continued so many ages; therefore that which existed before time, must have existed before all finite beings, and consequently was not produced out of nothing, or did not begin to be, and is properly from eternity.[209]

In Pictet's view,

> Eternity is ascribed to him, for he is not merely said to have been "before Abraham was" (John 8:58), nor merely to "have been in the beginning" (John 1:1), but before all the works of God: for thus speaks eternal Wisdom, which is the same as the Son, "the Lord possessed me in the beginning of his ways, before his works of old...." (Prov. 8:22-24) ... For no one can doubt the eternity of God's wisdom, any more than the eternity of God himself. Nor would a being deserve the name of God, who could have been at any time without wisdom.[210]

---

206. Turretin, *Inst. theol. elencticae*, III.xxviii.16; so also Pictet, *Theol. chr.*, I.xv.4; cf. Calvin, *Commentary on John*, 3:13 in loc. (*CTS John*, I, p. 121); *Dutch Annotations*, in loc.; Poole, *Commentary*, in loc (III, p. 292), adding a comment against the Lutherans, who ascribe immensity to Christ's humanity — which, Poole notes, "is to ascribe a body unto Christ which is indeed no body, according to any notion we have of a body." Cf. the Lutheran definitions in Schmid, *Doctrinal Theology*, pp. 314-315, 327-334.

207. Ridgley, *Body of Divinity*, p. 161, col. 1.

208. Ridgley, *Body of Divinity*, p. 161, col. 1; cf. Turretin, *Inst. theol. elencticae*, III.xxviii.14.

209. Ridgley, *Body of Divinity*, p. 161, cols. 1-2.

210. Pictet, *Theol. chr.*, II.xv.3; cf. Downame, *Summe*, i (p. 41); Leigh, *Treatise*, II.xvi (pp. 131-133).

So also is he called "Father of eternity" in Isaiah 9:5 [6] and the "Alpha and Omega" in Revelation 1:8, 11.[211]

Christ, moreover, "is said to be unchangeable, which perfection not only belongs to God, but is that whereby he is considered as opposed to all created beings, which are dependent on him."[212] The immutability of Christ is easily seen from the words of Psalm 102:25-27, "they shall be changed; but thou art the same, and thy years shall have no end," which are applied specifically to Christ in Hebrews 1:10-12. The author of Hebrews also testifies to the eternity of Christ's kingdom (1:8) and states (13:8) that Christ "is the same yesterday, today, and forever." In this latter place the Scripture intends "to establish" the faith of Christians on "the consideration of Christ's immutability, whatever changes they are liable to from the death of their teachers, or the innovations of those who succeed them, and endeavor to carry them away by divers and strange doctrines."[213] Nor ought the incarnation to be taken as an objection to the essential immutability of the second person of the Trinity. In Witsius' words, "the incarnation of the Son was effected ... not by a change of the divinity into humanity, for it is altogether incapable of change" but "by the assumption of the human nature into the individual unity of the Divine person." Witsius comments that "most absurdly have some inconsiderate men restricted this perfection to the deity of the Father: for the divine nature is one only; immutability is clearly ascribed to God the Son (Ps. 102:27; cf. Heb. 1:12); and even after becoming man, he continued God (Rom. 9:5)."[214] Even so the phrase "the Word became flesh" (John 1:14) indicates not the "transmutation of Divinity into humanity," an utterly intimate "union" of humanity with divinity.[215]

Christ's omniscience is amply testified by John 21:17, where Peter says to Christ, "Lord, thou knowest all things, thou knowest that I love thee." And the point is confirmed by John 16:30, "Now we are sure that thou knowest all things," by the identification of Christ as the "searcher of hearts" (Rev. 2:23) and as the one who knows the thoughts of the heart (Luke 6:8; John 2:24-25).[216] This understanding is also confirmed by John 1:18, where the Son alone sees and reveals the Father.[217] "Besides, this," comments Ridgley,

> there is another expression that abundantly proves this matter, wherein he is denominated the searcher of hearts, which is a glory that God appropriates to himself, in Jer. 17:10 ... and ... 1 Chron. 28:9. ... and all creatures are excluded from having

---

211. Amyraut, *De mysterio trinitatis*, V, p. 305; cf. Downame, *Summe*, i (pp. 41, 43). N.B., Amyraut cites Isa. 9:5 — the versification of English Bibles differs, thus, 9:6.

212. Ridgley, *Body of Divinity*, p. 161, col. 2.

213. Ridgley, *Body of Divinity*, p. 162, col. 1; cf. Turretin, *Inst. theol. elencticae*, III.xxviii.19; Rijssen, *Summa theol.*, IV.ix, controversia II, arg. 2; Leigh, *Treatise*, II.xvi (p. 133).

214. Witsius, *Exercitationes*, XIV.vii-viii.

215. Witsius, *Exercitationes*, XIV.xi.

216. Turretin, *Inst. theol. elencticae*, III.xxviii.18.

217. Downame, *Summe*, i (p. 33).

any branch of this glory, when it is said, in 1 Kings 8:39. *thou only knowest the hearts of all the children of men*: now such a knowledge as this is ascribed to Christ; sometimes he is said to know the *inward thoughts and secret reasonings of men within themselves*, Mark 2:8.[218]

Nor ought 1 Kings 8:39 be used to argue that only the Father is omniscient — any more that Christ's statement that he knows not the day of the final judgment (Matt. 13:32) be taken in this way. In the latter text, Christ speaks as to his questioners as Son of Man, namely, with reference to the limitation of his human knowledge, not as Son of God, who knows all things. When Scripture states that God the Father knows something, this is not to be taken to the exclusion of the Son and the Spirit, but as reference to the knowledge of God in which God is referred to under the general use of the name "Father."[219] Furthermore, the statement that the Father alone knows no more excludes the knowledge of the Son and the Spirit than the statement that "No one can know the Father, save the Son" (Matt. 11:27) should be understood as a claim that the Father is "ignorant of himself"![220]

On this point, particularly with reference to Colossians 2:3, "In whom are hid all the treasures of wisdom and knowledge," the Reformed came into conflict with the Lutherans, who held that the divine omniscience, like the divine omnipotence, was communicated to the human nature of Jesus. This teaching, according to the Reformed, fails to distinguish rightly between the "uncreated wisdom" or knowledge belonging to the second person of the Trinity and the created wisdom that belongs to Jesus' humanity — the former is a knowledge of all possibility, literally, "of all that God can do" that comprehends the fullness of the Godhead. This the soul of Christ cannot know, even though it may know all that can be known concerning all creatures — as is necessary for the one who is the final Judge of the world. The medieval scholastics, notes Davenant, argued a blessed, an infused, and an acquired knowledge in Jesus, and some, like Alexander of Hales, argued a special knowledge through the grace of union. But the distinction remains between the infinite knowledge belonging to Christ's divinity and the exalted but finite knowledge belonging to the human mind or soul of Jesus.[221]

Christ is also given by Scripture the attribute of omnipotence.[222] The modern Arians deny this power to Christ and to the Spirit and argue that it belongs only to the Father, who has power over all creation and also over his Son and his Spirit.[223] Nevertheless, such power indeed seems to be attributed to Christ in Isaiah 9:6, where he is called

---

218. Ridgley, *Body of Divinity*, p. 165, col. 1, citing also John 2:25; 6:64 and Rev. 2:23; cf. Rijssen, *Summa theol.*, IV.ix, cont. II, arg. 2.

219. See above 5.1 (A.2).

220. Turretin, *Inst. theol. elencticae*, III.xxviii.18.

221. Davenant, *Exposition of Colossians*, 2:3 in loc. (I, pp. 361-363); and cf. the discussion in *PRRD*, I, 5.4 (A-B) and note Preus, *Theology of Post-Reformation Lutheranism*, I, pp. 168-173.

222. Rijssen, *Summa theol.*, IV.ix, cont. II, arg. 2; Leigh, *Treatise*, II.xvi (p. 133), cites Rev. 1:8 and Phil. 3:21.

223. Ridgley, *Body of Divinity*, p. 166, col. 2.

"the mighty God," and in Psalm 45:3, where he is called "mighty one" or "most mighty." Christ is also said (Phil. 3:21) to be able to change our corrupt body into a glorious body like his own "according to the working, whereby he is able to subdue all things to himself." John 5:27 states that he does all that the Father does, while 5:21 attributes the same power to raise the dead to the Son as its does to the Father. In Hebrews 1:3 we read that he upholds all things by his power. Revelation 1:8 and 11:17 distinctly refer to Christ both as "Alpha and Omega" and as "the Almighty," *ho pantokrator*, not to mention all the other divine titles given to Christ in that book.[224] Finally, Matthew 28:18 states that "all power" is given to him — and it is impossible to understand him as having "all power in heaven and on earth" unless he is omnipotent God. Here, as in John 5:19, where the Son is said to do nothing by himself, without the Father also willing it, the conferring or derivation of power (*diversitas ordinis*) implies no limitation or diminution but only an order in working: "diversity in order does not create a diversity in essence and power (*diversitatem essentiae et virtutis*).[225]

D. Other Grounds for the Divinity of Christ according to the Reformed Orthodox

1. Christ's divinity demonstrated *ex operis divinis*. The orthodox also argue that specifically divine works are consistently ascribed to Christ in Scripture.[226] From a purely doctrinal perspective this argument, although consistently placed after arguments based on direct predication of names and attributes, occupies a central place in the orthodox trinitarian and christological discussion — inasmuch as the identification of Christ as divine in his work is one of the underlying points of the satisfaction or substitution theory of atonement held by orthodoxy. Christ performs both *ad intra* and *ad extra* divine works. *Ad intra*, "He sendeth forth the Holy Ghost out of his owne substance, and therefore is indeed and truely God, if (as shall bee prooved anon) the Holy Ghost himself bee God."[227]

The proof of Christ's divinity from his divine works, specifically the work of creation, was posed in exegetical detail by the orthodox as a direct counter to the Socinian reading of John 1:3, Colossians 1:16, Hebrews 1:2 and various other texts, where the traditional argument that one who, with the Father, creates the world must be truly God was undermined by the claim that the text identifies the Son as a means or instrument rather than a coequal creator.[228]

> Divine works argue a divine efficient, or that he has infinite power, and consequently that he is an infinite person, or truly and properly God, who performs them. Now these works are of two sorts; either of nature and common providence, or of grace, to wit,

---

224. Ridgley, *Body of Divinity*, pp. 167-169; cf. Amyraut, *De mysterio trinitatis*, V, p. 306; Turretin, *Inst. theol. elencticae*, III.xxviii.17.

225. Turretin, *Inst. theol. elencticae*, III.xxviii.17; cf. Amyraut, *De mysterio trinitatis*, V, p. 306.

226. Rijssen, *Summa theol.*, IV.ix, cont. III, arg. 3.

227. Downame, *Summe*, i (p. 45).

228. Cf. Crell, *Expiation of a Sinner*, fol. B2v with Racovian Catechism, iv.1 (pp. 91-94).

such as immediately respect our salvation; in all which, he acts beyond the power of a creature, and therefore appears to be a divine person.[229]

Christ is clearly denominated creator of the world in John 1:3 and Colossians 1:16, and in Hebrews 1:2 and Ephesians 3:9 he is called cocreator with the Father. Thus, on Hebrews 1:2, the Westminster *Annotations* indicate that the Son works with the Father in creation "not as by an instrument or inferior cause, but by Him as by his eternall wisdome, and by way of a conjoyned cooperating and equal cause."[230] Hebrews 1:10, spoken by God the Father, also refers to the Son as creator, and Hebrews 1:3 refers to his providential work in preserving what he has created.[231] "He who upholds all things by his powerful word is God, so doth Christ, therefore he is God."[232]

Nor, indeed, does the Socinians' alternative reading of John 1:3, "all things were made by him," as the "second creation" or "beginning" of the Gospel or work of salvation offer a substantive reading of the text — any more that their similar claims function as a reading of "the beginning" in John 1:1.[233] The text of John indicates no limitation or restriction to the work of making "all things" such as appears in references to the "new creation": this verse refers to the "universal creation" as clearly indicated by the second clause, "and without him was not any thing made that was made," and by the tenth verse, in which the evangelist refers to the creation of whole world, specifically as the world, as it is ignorant of Christ apart from the Gospel. Such a reading of Christ as creator of the world also accords with Paul's words in Colossians 1:16-18.[234] As for divine works of grace,

No one will deny that the work of *redemption* is attributed to him (Acts xx.28), also *remission of sins, sanctification,* the *sending of the Holy Ghost,* the *giving of eternal life,* the *judgment of the world,* and the *raising of the dead. . . .* The *building* of the church is attributed to him, in Heb. iii.4, from which passage the deity of Christ is indisputably established.[235]

Similar arguments appear, at length, in Leigh and Turretin.[236] Neither do the arguments of the antitrinitarians that Christ only enacted the will of the Father or worked

---

229. Ridgley, *Body of Divinity*, p. 169, col. 2-p. 170, col. 1; cf. Witsius, *Exercitationes*, viii.50.

230. *Westminster Annotations*, in loc.; cf. Gouge, *Commentary on Hebrews*, p. 14; Poole, *Commentary*, in loc.; Amyraut, *De mysterio trinitatis*, V, pp. 307-308.

231. Ridgley, *Body of Divinity*, pp. 170-176; Pictet, *Theol. chr.*, I.xv.8.

232. Leigh, *Treatise*, II.xvi (p. 132).

233. Cf. above 6.2 (C.3).

234. Turretin, *Inst. theol. elencticae*, III.xxviii.22.

235. Pictet, *Theol. chr.*, I.xv.8.

236. Leigh, *Treatise*, II.xvi (p. 132), citing John 6:54; 5:21 as "divine miracles"; Luke 1:68; Matt. 20:28; Eph 1:7; Rev. 1:5 for the work of redemption; John 14:16 and 21:22 for his sending the Holy Spirit; his sending of angels, Matt. 13:41 and Rev. 1:1; and the forgiveness of sins, Mark 9:2, 5; John 10:28, the gift of eternal life. Cf. Turretin, *Inst. theol. elencticae*, III.xxviii.21.

according to the power of the Father avail, given that Christ himself states that he and the Father are one and that the Father is in him and he in the Father.[237]

2. Christ's divinity argued from worship and faith. The Reformed orthodox registered the debate over this point that had occurred among the Socinians themselves. Socinus had held that, in a limited sense, Christ could be understood as the object of worship, whereas others among the Polish Brethren and several of the Hungarian antitrinitarians had denied any sense in which Christ might be the object of worship and had specifically argued that no text in Scripture could be properly understood as implying wither that Christ could be worshiped or that his name could be invoked in worship.[238]

The Reformed orthodox argue, utterly to the contrary, that Scripture commands believers to worship Christ and have faith in him in a manner suitable only to God. Christ himself commands us to *believe* in him: "Ye believe in God, believe also in me"; also to place our *hope* and *trust* in him. Even the angels (Heb. 1:6) are commanded to worship him.[239]

> Every knee is commanded "to bow" to him (Phil. 2:10). The apostles seek "grace and peace" from him as well as from the Father (Rom. 1:7; 1 Cor. 1:3; Rev.1:4, 5). The faithful are described as those who call on the name of Christ (Acts 9:14; 1 Cor. 1:2) and "every creature" is introduced as ascribing "Honour, glory, and power unto the Lamb" (Rev. 5:13). From all that has been said, therefore, it is plain that Christ is God ... so much the less can this be denied, because, since God "giveth not his glory to another," as he declares by Isaiah (48:11), it is impossible that *he* should not be God to whom are ascribed the name, the attributes, and the works of God, in which his glory consists.[240]

A similar hermeneutical use of Isaiah 48:11, collated with biblical references to Christ forgiving sins, sustaining the world, hearing those who call on him, requiring belief, and being one in whom believers rejoice, is found as proof of divinity in various other Reformed orthodox writers.[241]

> All the arguments which prove Christ to be truly God, prove him to be the *supreme God*, and *equal with the Father*. For to suppose two Gods, one of whom is inferior to the other, is to be totally ignorant of what God is. For the idea of God is the idea of a Being than whom there is none greater, more powerful, more perfect.[242]

---

237. Zanchi, *De tribus Elohim*, pt. 2, V.vii.3 (col. 554).

238. See above 2.2 (B) on the Socinian debate; note the comments in Venema, *Inst. theol.*, xii (pp. 238-239); Ridgley, *Body of Divinity* (1855), I, p. 225

239. Pictet, *Theol. chr.*, II.xv.9; cf. Rijssen, *Summa theol.*, IV.ix, cont. II, argumentum 4, "Ex honore divin. In ipsum credendum. Joh. 3:16. In eius nomen baptizandum. Matth. 28:19. Ad eius nomen flectendum omnegenu. Phil. 2.10."

240. Pictet, *Theol. chr.*, II.xv.9.

241. Cf. Bastingius, *Exposition or Commentarie upon the Catechism*, q. 33 (p. 43, verso); Cheynell, *Trinuity*, p. 31.

242. Pictet, *Theol. Chr.*, II.xvi.1.

Again we encounter the adaptation of language from Anselm's ontological argument — in Pictet's case, probably by way of Cartesian philosophy — as a proof of the oneness of God and therefore the equality in unity of Father and Son.

6.3   The *Aseitas,* or Self-Existence, of the Son

A. Views of the Reformers

The Reformed doctrine of the Trinity (and, of course, also the doctrine of the Person of Christ) is characterized by a declaration of the aseity of Christ's divinity: considered as God, the Second Person of the Trinity is divine *a se ipso* — he is *autotheos.* This had been a point of controversy with both the antitrinitarians and with Rome since the time of Calvin, and in the course of the development of Reformed dogmatics in the late sixteenth and the seventeenth century, it became not only the distinctive feature of Reformed trinitarianism but also a crucial point, defended against any and all opponents.

Calvin consistently agreed with traditional orthodoxy that the person of the Son subsists in relation to the Father by generation, but he also insists that, considered according to his full divinity, the Son shares the divine attribute of self-existence, or *aseitas.* After all, the essence is undivided in the three persons, so that each of the persons contains in and of himself the full essence of the Godhead.[243] Calvin also argued the Son's aseity in answer to the attack on his views made by Chaponneau and Courtois, both pastors of Neufchâtel. They, like his earlier opponent Caroli, had accused Calvin of heresy for claiming the self-existence of the Son. Calvin insisted that the subordination of the Son and the Spirit was a matter of order, not of essence, and that the subordination referred only to the generation of the Son and the procession of the Spirit.[244] The aseity of the Son, moreover, was indicated by the text of Colossians 2:9, "in Him dwelleth the fulness of the Godhead":[245]

> Truly this is where these donkeys are deceived: since they do not consider that the name of the Son is spoken of the person, and therefore is included in the predicament of relation, which relation has no place where we are speaking simply (*simpliciter*) of the divinity of Christ.[246]

---

243. Calvin, *Institutes,* I.xiii.19, 25; cf. Warfield, "Calvin's Doctrine of the Trinity," pp. 233-243.

244. Calvin, *Institutes,* I.xiii.17-18; cf. Warfield, "Calvin's Doctrine of the Trinity," p. 237; and Niesel, *Theology of Calvin,* p. 59.

245. Calvin, Letter to the Ministers of Neufchâtel (May 1543), in CO, XI, col. 560: "Quantum ad locum illum ubi quasi ex tripode haereticos pronunciat qui dicunt Christum, in quantum Deus est, a se ipso esse, facilis est responsio. Primum mihi respondent annon verus et perfectus Deus sit Christus? Nisi Dei essentiam partiri velit, totem in Christo fateri cogetur. Et Pauli expressa sunt verba: quod in eo habet plenitudo divinitatis. Iterum rogo, a se ipsane an aliunde sit illa divinitatis plenitudo? At obiicet, filium esse a patre. Quis negat? Id ego quidem libenter non modo semper confessus sum sed etiam praedicavi. Verum hoc est...." Cf. Calvin, *Commentary on Colossians,* 1:19; 2:9-10 (CTS *Colossians,* pp. 154, 182-183).

246. Calvin, Letter to the Ministers of Neufchâtel, CO, XI, col. 560: "Verum hoc est in quo asini isti falluntur: quia non considerant nomen filii dici de persona ideoque in praedicamento relationis

Debate over the use of the terms *autotheos* and *a se ipso* or *aseitas* continued in Calvin's further troubles with Caroli in 1545,[247] and it reappeared in Calvin's response to the anti-trinitarian heresies of Blandrata and Gentile in 1558. Against Caroli, Calvin insisted that in discussion of "the divinity of Christ," understood in the strictest sense as the divine essence, "all that is proper to God" must be attributed to Christ — given that such discussion does not raise the issue of the distinction between Father and Son but addresses only the question of the divine essence itself as shared indivisibly by the three persons: "in this sense, it is correct to say that Christ is the one eternal God, existing of himself." Calvin continues his argument by denying explicitly that the Son is from the Father "with respect to his eternal essence."[248] Citing both Cyril of Alexandria and Augustine, Calvin comments that neither of these fathers would deny that Christ has life and immortality of himself or that, as God, he was self-existent: the names and attributes that refer to the divine essence or substance belong equally to each of the divine persons — so that Christ is "from another" only as concerns his person, not as concerns his essence, which is underived.[249]

Gentile's debate with Calvin had a different cast, given that Gentile held an antitrinitarian view and insisted on a radical monotheism of the Father, arguing that "the Father is a unique essence ... the Father is the only true God; it is he who gives his essence to the other persons of the Divinity." Gentile further insisted that a formulation such as Calvin's implied a quaternity — a divine essence, plus the three divine persons that share in it. Gentile's alternative was to argue three distinct divine persons, but the Father alone as fully and of himself God: Son and Spirit were subordinate to the Father.[250] In his response, as he had done against Caroli, Calvin specifically identified the Son as *autotheos* and as God *a se ipso* — the latter phrase underlying the term *aseitas* — over against the views, particularly of Gentile.[251] As Calvin pressed the point, the concept of the Son's aseity became a defining factor in his understanding of the Son's eternal generation: specifically, Calvin defines the generation of the Son from the Father as an origination of sonship, not of divinity. The generation of the Son, therefore, is neither an origin in time nor an origin of being:

---

contineri, quae relatio locum non habet ubi de Christi divinitate simpliciter agitur." Cf. Warfield, "Calvin's Doctrine of the Trinity," p. 238.

247. See John Calvin, *Pro G. Farello et collegis eius adversus Petri Caroli calumnias defensio*, in CO, VII, col. 289 et seq.

248. John Calvin, *Pro Farello et collegis eius*, CO, VII, col. 322; cf. the citation and analysis in Warfield, "Calvin's Doctrine of the Trinity, p. 240.

249. Calvin, *Pro Farello et collegis eius*, CO VII cols. 322-323.

250. Cited in Gaberel, *Histoire de l'Église de Génève*, II, p. 227. A survey of these controversies is available in Rotondo, *Calvin and the Italian Anti-trinitarians*.

251. Calvin, *Expositio impietatis Valentini Gentilis*, in CO, IX, col. 368.: "Atque haec una furendi causa quod Athanasius filium facit *autotheon*. Unde perspicuum fit hunc esse causae statum, quod contendit Valentinus Christum aliunde esse Deum, qui ab alio mutuatus sit id quod est. Valde enim logodaedalum, qui eius personam sumpsit, delectant iste voces: unum esse Deum patrem, qui et sit *autotheos*, et solus *autousian* in se habeat."

"as to his essence, the Son is *absque principio*, while considered as to his person, he finds his *principium* in the Father."[252] Calvin's view, like that of many of the later Reformed, follows out the line of the Western, Augustinian, trinitarian model, as defined by the Fourth Lateran Council, rather than the Greek model.[253]

B. The Reformed Orthodox Debate over Aseity

1. Early orthodox diversity and debate. The radical statement of the Son's aseity found in Calvin's trinitarian polemic is not echoed by all of the early orthodox Reformed theologians: as Amyraut noted, there was no debate among the orthodox over the distinct personal identify of the Son, but there was discussion over whether he stood in utterly equal majesty and dignity with the Father.[254] Ursinus, for one, offers a series of trinitarian definitions in which he consistently speaks of the "communication" of the divine essence from the Father to the Son in the eternal act of begetting.[255]

> The essence of man is communicable, and common to many men, generically, but not individually. But the essence of God is communicable individually, because the Deity or nature of God is the same and entire in all the three persons of the Godhead. ... The sum of this distinction between the terms Essence and Person, as applied to God, is this: essence is absolute and communicable — Person is relative and incommunicable.[256]

This argument leads Ursinus to the declaration that

> God the Father is that Being who is of himself, and not from another. The Son is that self-same Being, or essence, not of himself, but of the Father.[257]

The potential contrast among the Reformed themselves is clear from Polanus and Bucanus, who virtually duplicate Calvin's argument: "The Son of God is the second person of the Godhead, ever begotten (*semper generata*) of the Father, not however according to his essential existence, but according to his personal existence."[258]

Polanus goes on to argue that the Son of God, considered as a "person or subsistence of the Godhead" has "the entire divine essence by nature" and therefore is by nature "Jehovah, *autotheos*, God according to essence, existing of himself" — and "with respect to the divine essence, which singly is common to the three persons, not only the Father,

---

252. Calvin, *Expositio impietatis Valen. Gentilis*, in CO, IX, col. 368. Cf. Calvin, *Institutes*, I.xiii.17-18.

253. Contra Thomas F. Torrance, "Calvin's Doctrine of the Trinity," pp. 165-193; idem, "The Doctrine of the Holy Trinity: Gregory of Nazianzen and John Calvin," pp. 7-19; cf. above 1.2 (B.2) on the Fourth Lateran Council.

254. Amyraut, *De mysterio trinitatis*, V, p. 296.

255. Ursinus, *Commentary*, p. 135.

256. Ursinus, *Commentary*, p. 130.

257. Ursinus, *Commentary*, p. 130.

258. Polanus, *Syntagma theol.*, III.v (p. 204); cf. Bucanus, *Institutions*, i (p. 11).

but also the Son and the Holy Spirit, is God primarily and through himself."[259] This argument does not, of course, contravene the doctrine of the generation of the Son from the "essence and subsistence of the Father," but it does certainly qualify what can be meant by generation: the generation is not material and is not a "dilation of the Father's essence," not a propagation of the essence — but a "communication" of existence or subsistence, such that the Son is begotten, but the divine essence that he has is itself not begotten.[260] These formulations are, to say the least, quite distinct: where Ursinus speaks of a communication of Deity or Godhead by eternal generation, Polanus speaks more restrictively of a communication of Sonship or subsistence.

Still, definitions that speak of the communication of essence are not necessarily opposed to the notion of the Son's *aseitas*: Bucanus also speaks of the essence as communicated, but notes that it is not begotten — sonship alone is "begotten."[261] As Perkins defined the point,

> The other two persons have the Godhead, or the whole divine essence, of the Father by communication, namely the Son and the holy Ghost. The Son is the second person, begotten of the Father from all eternity. ... Although the Son be begotten of his Father, yet nevertheless he is of and by himself very God: for he must be considered either according to his essence, or according to his filiation or Sonship. In regard of his essence he is *autotheos* that is, of and by himself very God: for the Deity which is common to all the three persons, is not begotten. But as he is a person, and the Son of the Father, he is not of himself, but from another: for he is the eternal Son of the Father. And thus he is truly said to be *very God* of *very God*.[262]

Perkins, thus, makes a distinction between begetting or proceeding and the communication of essence that identifies the Father alone as *principium* of the Godhead but nonetheless argues the aseity of the essence and, therefore, according to essence, the aseity of all the persons.

When considered in terms of his sonship, the second person of the Trinity is begotten and second in order — when considered in terms of essence, however, he is God *a se ipso*: the divine essence as such is not begotten.

> Although the Sonne bee begotten of his Father, yet neverthelesse he is of and by himselfe very God: for hee must bee considered either according to his essence or according to his filiation or Sonneship. In regard of his essence he is *autotheos* that is, of and by himselfe very God: for the Deitie which is common to all the persons is not begotten. But as he is a person and the Sonne of the Father hee is not of himselfe, but from another: for hee is the eternal Sonne of his Father. And thus he is truely said to be *very God of very God*. For this cause he is said to be sent from the Father. Iohn

---

259. Polanus, *Syntagma theol.*, III.v (pp. 205-206); cf. Bucanus, *Institutions*, i (p. 11).

260. Polanus, *Syntagma theol.*, III.v (p. 215); Amyraut et al., *Syntagma thesium theologicarum*, I.xvii.13.

261. Bucanus, *Institutions*, i (p. 11).

262. Perkins, *Golden Chaine*, V (p. 14, col. 2); similarly, Zanchi, *De tribus Elohim*, col. 540; Beza et al., *Propositions and Principles*, III.viii; Ainsworth, *Orthodox Foundation*, p. 14.

8.42. ... This sending taketh not away the equality of essence and power, but declareth the order of persons. Iohn 5.18. ... His proper manner of working is to execute actions from the Father by the Holy Ghost. 1 Cor. 8.6 ... Ioh. 5.19.[263]

The Son is *"non autohuios* tamen *autotheos."*[264]

> For the thing itselfe, it is Christ; who must be considered two waies, as he is a Sonne, and as hee is God. As he is a sonne, he is not of himselfe, but the sonne of the father begotten of him: nevertheless as he is God, he is of himselfe, neither begotten, nor proceeding; for the essence or godhead of the Father is of itselfe without all beginning, but the godhead of the sonne is one and the same with the godhead of the Father: because by what godhead the Father is God, by the same and no other the sonne is God: therefore the sonne, as he is God, he is God of himselfe without beginning even as the Father. Whereupon it followes, that the Sonne is begotten of the Father as he is a sonne, but not as he is God.[265]

As for Christ's work as the Mediator, he said to be "sent" from the Father in such a way as does not detract from the equality of his "essence and power" but as "declareth the order of the persons."[266] The distinction, to say the least, is difficult to define and, therefore, difficult to maintain in this form, creating a problem for the Reformed orthodox formulation.

Toward the end of the sixteenth century, Roman Catholic polemicists, notably the theologian and exegete Gilbertus Genebrardus, accused Calvin of heresy on the specific point of the identification of the Son as *autotheos*. Much to the discomfiture of the Roman church of the day, Bellarmine examined Calvin's work with some care and pronounced his christology orthodox.[267] Still, the formulation of the doctrinal point was a issue over which theologians differed, even in the Reformed context. One early orthodox debate in particular can be singled out as a significant index to the doctrinal problem: beginning in 1606 with a student's query, Arminius and his colleague at Leiden, Lucas Trelcatius II, debated the suitability of identifying the Son as *autotheos*. Arminius had taught that the term could be used in definitions of the divinity of the Son if it were understood as "truly God" — but it ought not be understood as "God from himself," which was not only the typical usage and the etymological sense of the term but also the sense in which Trelcatius used the term in his theology.[268] Whereas Trelcatius, quite in line with the definitions that we have already extracted from

---

263. Perkins, *Golden Chaine*, V, p. 14, col. 2-p. 15, col. 1 (my italics).

264. Perkins, *Exposition of the Creed*, p. 171, cols. 1-2, and margin; cf. Bucanus, *Institutions*, i (p. 11).

265. Perkins, *Exposition of the Creed*, p. 171, cols. 1-2; cf. Zanchi, *De tribus Elohim*, col. 540.

266. Perkins, *Golden Chaine*, V (p. 14, col. 2).

267. Bellarmine, *De Christo*, II.xix.

268. Arminius, *Apologia adversus articulos XXXI. in vulgus sparsos*, in *Opera*, pp. 134-183: art. *xxi*, *"Duptici* autem *sensu* accipi posse iuxta *Eymon*, ut vel significet, qui *vere & seipso Deus est*, vel qui *a se Deus est: ilto sensu* dixi vocem *tolerari posse*, hoc sensu contravenire Scripturis & orthodoxae vetustati, (Arminius' italics). Cf. *Dec. sent.*, pp. 124-125.

Polanus and Perkins, held that only the sonship or begottenness — and not the essence — of the second person was generated, Arminius insisted that Christ, as God, has both his sonship and his essence by generation.[269] Arminius, in short, rejected the distinction, then generally accepted among the Reformed, between the second person of the Trinity considered personally and the second person of the Trinity considered essentially.[270] In Arminius' view, the Reformed doctrine of the Son's aseity or self-existence, departed from the patristic norm — specifically by identifying each of the persons as having the essence *a se ipso* and, as a consequence, losing the unity of the Godhead, in effect, lapsing into tritheism.[271] The fathers, Arminius argued, intended "by the word 'Son' a certain mode of having [the divine essence], which is through communication from the Father, that is, through generation." Thus, "to have deity from no one" can be characteristic of the Father only who, in the teaching of the fathers is the sole *principium* of the Godhead.[272]

2. **Formulation of the doctrine in high and late orthodoxy.** Reformed insistence on the essential aseity of the Son in contrast to the personal begottenness continued to be a matter of both positive doctrine and polemic in the period of high orthodoxy and was noted as a significant doctrinal issue on into the late orthodox era. It is certainly arguable in this particular case that the relative diversity of early orthodox statement failed to carry over easily into the later theology because of the association of denials of the Son's aseity with Arminius and the subsequent connections between Remonstrant theology and the heterodoxies bred by Vorstius and the Socinians. Not only was the denial of aseity a characteristic of Arminius' theology, it became in the course of the seventeenth century a subordinationistic problem associated with the antitrinitarianism of the age. Indications of the importance of the issue as an index of Reformed orthodoxy are found throughout the high orthodox era and on into late orthodoxy, as evidenced by the extended discussion of the point in diverse works ranging chronologically from Leigh's *Treatise of Divinity* (1646) and Amyraut's *De mysterio trinitatis* (1661) to De Moor's *Commentarius* (1761-71). Amyraut draws out in detail the argument that, considered according to the divine nature and essence that he has, Christ is *a se*, while considered according to the communication of that essence in the generation of his sonship, Christ is *a Patre*. This distinction, he observes is respected by neither Petavius nor Arminius — but it was quite clearly identified by Calvin, Polanus, and Danaeus.[273] In the case of De Moor, in the latter half of the

---

269. Arminius, *Epistola ad Hippolytum*, pp. 938-940.

270. Arminius, *Epistola ad Hippolytum*, pp 938-940; cf. Arminius, *Apologia*, art. xxi with the discussion in Heppe, *Reformed Dogmatics*, pp. 121-123.

271. Arminius, *Epistola ad Hippolytum*, pp. 938-940, and *Dec. Sent.*, pp. 124-125, with Gentile, as cited in Muller, *Christ and the Decree*, pp. 30-31.

272. Arminius, *Dec. Sent.*, pp. 124-125; cf. idem, *Epistola ad Hippolytum*, p. 939: "Voce Dei significatur generatim, id quod essentiam Divinam habet citra certum subsistendi modum: at voce Filii significatur certus modus habendi, nempe per communicationem à Patre, id est, per generationem."

273. Amyraut, *De mysterio trinitatis*, VII (pp. 525-526).

eighteenth century, the issue is not only engaged at length, but its history, beginning in Calvin's polemics and running through the Arminian controversy, is documented as part of the movement toward positive formulation of doctrine.[274]

The New Testament, Marckius argues, teaches the "true deity" (1 John 5:20), the divine "eminence" (Rom. 9:5), and the essential "independence" (John 5:26; Rev. 1:8, 11, etc.) of the Son. "Nor could he be true God, even as the Father, and eternal, unless he was *Deus à se*."[275] Leigh presents the issue as a fundamental trinitarian distinction in almost propositional form:

> Christ as God is from himself, but if the Deity of Christ be considered as in the person of the Son, so it is from the Father.
> The Son in respect of his essence is from none; in respect of the manner of subsistence he is from the Father.[276]

This doctrine must be defended against "Origen, Valentin Gentile, Arminius, various Lutherans, and above all the Papists, who call our teaching the Autotheanistic heresy" on the pretext of such New Testament verses as Matt. 11:27, John 5:26; 7:29; and 17:8. These texts, Marckius notes, point either to the Christ's mission and his coming in the flesh in time or to Christ as distinct from the Father by generation — and are therefore not to the point, for the Reformed never claimed that the Son or second person was Son of himself (*Filius à se*) and are fully in accord with the Nicene confession of Christ as *Deum de Deo et Lumen de Lumine*.[277]

Thus, "the Son is said to be from the Father, but is no less also called *autotheos*, not by reason of person, but by reason of essence, not in relation as the Son (for in this sense he is of the Father) but in an absolute sense as God: thus the Son is God *à seipso*, but he is not *à seipso* Son."[278] Various "Papists," like Genebrardus, and heretics like Valentin Gentile identified the divine essence so with the Father as to deny the attribute of aseity to the Son and the Spirit — but the scrupulous Bellarmine himself had exonerated Calvin of heresy on this point and had thus undercut the arguments of earlier Roman polemicists.[279]

Even so, all subordinationist passages in the New Testament — such as John 14:28, "My Father is greater than I" — are to be referred either to the human nature of Christ or, preferably, to his person in his official status as Mediator.[280] Forbes makes this Reformed orthodox point with reference to what is arguably the primary Western or Latin trinitarian answer to the problem of subordinationistic passages in the New Testament, forcefully present in the writings of Hilary and Augustine: "according to the form of God the son is equal to the Father ... according to the form of a servant

---

274. De Moor, *Commentarius perpetuus*, I.v.10.

275. Marckius, *Compendium*, V.x.

276. Leigh, *Treatise*, II.xvi (p. 133).

277. Marckius, *Compendium*, V.x.

278. Rijssen, *Summa theol.*, IV.x.

279. Rijssen, *Summa theol.*, IV.x, citing Bellarmine, *De Christo*, II.xix.

280. Cf. Witsius, *De oeconomia foederum*, II.iii.20; Leigh, *Treatise*, II.xvi (p. 134).

he is less than the Father ... for he emptied himself, not setting aside the divinity but assuming the humanity." Forbes also points to a similar solution in the Greek fathers: as Athanasius had argued, "the Son has the same nature as the Father and is subject not according to the divine nature, but according to the economy of [his] humanity."[281] Thus also, God is not the Father of Christ and our Father in the same way: he is the Father of Christ in view of a natural relation and our Father "not according to nature but by the grace of adoption."[282] The "natural relation," moreover, given that it is the relationship of the Father as God to the Son as God, cannot imply an essential subordination.

In the era of late orthodoxy, particularly among the English writers, extended controversy over Socinianism and Arianism yielded further worries over the suitability of trinitarian terminology. As evidenced by Ridgley's extended analysis, various terms and arguments, such as the identification of the Father as the "cause" of the Son, discussion of differences between generation and procession, the definition of generation in relation to the role of the Father and the role of the Son, and arguments concerning the communication of essence from the Father to the Son, could be viewed as at best unwarranted and in the worst case fundamentally destructive of the doctrine of the Trinity. Ridgley's solution was to excise some of the more speculative vocabulary, particularly when the vocabulary itself defies definition: thus, the expression "eternal generation" or "eternal production" of the Son, given its presupposition that this generation or production is different from any other generation or production, ought in Ridgley's view, to be set aside.[283]

The generation of the Son is understood, Ridgley notes, as a "communication" — so that, in the act of generation, "the Father communicated the divine essence, or, at least, personality to him, which is [the Father's] act alone."[284] Here, in a late orthodox form, the difficulty identified in Perkins' definition and in Arminius' critique is registered in a refusal to acknowledge the intelligibility and therefore usefulness of all of the traditional language: discussions of the communication of essence, Ridgley continues, often "enter too far into the explication of this unsearchable mystery."[285]

His own view of the communication of essence, Ridgley hopes, will not trouble any orthodox trinitarians — he assumes that the term "communicate" must be construed in such a way as never to imply that the Father imparts or conveys the divine essence to the Son or the Spirit. Rather the communication of essence, like the christological language of *communicatio idiomatum in concreto*, ought to be taken to mean "that all the perfections of the divine nature are communicated, that is, equally attributed to, or predicated of, the Father, Son and Spirit."[286]

281. Forbes, *Instructiones hist.*, I.xxv.1-2; cf. Hilary, *De trin.*, X.22: "Evacuatio formae non est abolitio naturae."

282. Forbes, *Instructiones hist.*, I.xxx.1.

283. Ridgley, *Body of Divinity* (1855), I, p. 157.

284. Ridgley, *Body of Divinity* (1855), I, p. 158.

285. Ridgley, *Body of Divinity* (1855), I, p. 158.

286. Ridgley, *Body of Divinity* (1855), I, p. 158.

As to the specific question of the ground of the Son's aseity in the underived or ingenerate divine essence, Ridgley comments,

> I cannot but take note of another nicety of inquiry, — namely, whether, in the eternal generation, the Son is considered as co-existent with the Father, or as having the divine essence, and hereby deriving only the sonship from him, from all eternity; or whether he derives both his sonship and his essence. The former of these is the more generally received opinion. But I am not desirous to enter into this inquiry.[287]

Still, despite his confessed unwillingness to enter into the discussion, Ridgley goes on to argue that the full divinity of the Son (and of the Spirit as well) demands that one recognize that the Son's Essence is not derived — and, in addition, that neither the Son nor the Spirit has "a communicated personality." Many theologians assert this, Ridgley notes, "but, I think, without sufficient proof; for I cannot but conclude that the divine personality, not only of the Father, but of the Son and the Spirit, is as much independent and underived, as the divine essence."[288] Underlying the point is Ridgley's assumption that neither divinity or divine essence nor individuality or personhood can be imparted from one individual to another: his teaching presses on the boundaries of orthodoxy and leans toward Sabellianism, largely because of his desire to avoid the subordinationistic pitfalls of his day.

---

287. Ridgley, *Body of Divinity* (1855), I, p. 159.
288. Ridgley, *Body of Divinity* (1855), I, p. 159.

7

The Deity and Person of the Holy Spirit

7.1 "Spirit" and Deity in the Reformed Doctrine of God

A. Initial Definitions: The Positive Doctrine and the Issues Argued

1. The Reformers on the Spirit: definitions, issues, and adversaries. The Reformers' approach to the definition of the Holy Spirit as one of the three persons of the Godhead is fairly uniform. There was also little attempt on the part of the various Reformers to present an independent *locus* on the Holy Spirit — rather, their doctrine of the Spirit stands as a subset of the doctrine of the Trinity supplemented by polemical and exegetical comments. Calvin's early statement of the doctrine, in the 1536 *Institutes*, is instructive in its brevity, its close adherence to the traditional language of the doctrine of the Trinity, and its echo of Melanchthon with reference to the proper approach to such deep mysteries of the faith:

> we confess that we believe the Holy Spirit to be true God with the Father and the Son, the third person of the holy trinity, consubstantial and coeternal with the father and the Son, omnipotent, and the creator of all things. As has been stated, there are three distinct persons, one essence. Which, since they are exalted and profound mysteries, ought better to be adored than investigated — for they neither ought nor can be ascertained either by the small measures of our imaginations or by the reckonings of our tongues.[1]

---

1. Calvin, *Institutio* (1536), ii (p. 135); cf. Melanchthon, *Loci communes* (1521), p. 21. On Calvin's doctrine of the Spirit, see Niesel, *Theology of Calvin*, pp. 58-60, 120-124; Wendel, *Calvin*, pp. 165-169, 233, 238-242; Parker, *Calvin: An Introduction*, pp. 31-34, 78-84; Butin, *Revelation, Redemption, and Response*, pp. 52-53, 65-67, 76-94 et passim; Torrance, "Calvin's Doctrine of the Trinity," pp. 174-175. The most extensive study of Calvin's doctrine of the Holy Spirit remains Werner Krusche, *Das Wirken des Hl. Geistes nach Calvin* (Göttingen: Vandenhoeck & Ruprecht, 1957).

Bullinger, more simply, refers to the Holy Spirit as "the third Person in the reverend Trinity," to be believe in as "one God with the Father and the Son." Our faith in the Spirit, therefore, Bullinger continues, is "rightly ... joined to faith in the Father and the Son."[2]

Although the chief trinitarian debates noted by the Reformers were debate concerning the divinity of Christ, several of their cautions relate also to the doctrine of the Holy Spirit. Thus, Calvin warns that partial denials of Arianism and Sabellianism, characterized by lack of the language of orthodoxy, can yield accusations of either heresy: one must speak of the consubstantiality of the persons and of their genuine distinction in order to avoid the heresies entirely. His discussion of the Holy Spirit, therefore, will argue both that the Spirit is truly God and that the Spirit is a distinct subsistence in God.[3] Calvin also commented on the problem of "Libertines" who held the apparently pantheistic doctrine that there was a single divine Spirit that is the sole substance of all things.[4] In addition to his refutation of ancient heresies, such as the patripassian or Sabellian, and his arguments against Servetus, Hutchinson recognized the importance of showing the Spirit to be "a substance, not an inspiration coming from God," given the mistaken notions of various contemporary "English Sadduccees and outlandish Libertines."[5]

2. The Reformed orthodox doctrine of the Spirit — definition and points of debate. The issues and doctrines addressed by the orthodox writers of the seventeenth century are little different from those addressed by the Reformers, although here again, the hermeneutical strains and stresses are far more difficult for theological system to bear than they were at the beginning of the sixteenth century. First, by way of definition:

> The Holy Ghost is the third person of the true and only Godhead, proceeding from the Father and the Son, being co-eternal, co-equal, and consubstantial with the Father and the Son, and is sent by both into the hearts of the faithful, that he may sanctify and fit them for eternal life. That this description or definition may be established against the heretics, the same things must be proven from the Scriptures concerning the divinity of the Holy Ghost which we have already demonstrated in regard to the divinity of the Son; viz., that the Holy Ghost is a person — that he is distinct from the Father and the Son — that he is equal with both, and that he is consubstantial with the Father and the Son.[6]

Pictet begins his doctrine of the Spirit at much the same place and with much the same issues to hand as did the Reformers:

---

2. Bullinger, *Decades*, I.vii (I, p. 155).

3. Calvin, *Institutes*, I.xiii.5, 14.

4. Calvin, *Against the Libertines*, xi, xiii (pp. 230-233, 238-241).

5. Hutchinson, *Image of God*, p. 135. N.B., these are probably different "Libertines" than those of Calvin's treatise. For a summary of the scholarship on the identity and teachings of Calvin's Libertine adversaries, see Farley's introduction in Calvin, *Against the Libertines*, pp. 162-173.

6. Ursinus, *Commentary*, p. 271.

Concerning the Holy Ghost we have to inquire, 1) what he is, whether a mere *power* of God, or really a *person* distinct from the Father and the Son; 2) whether he is *God*; 3) from whom he *proceeds*; 4) why he is called the *Spirit*; 5) why the *Holy Spirit?*[7]

The patterns of argument developed in the era of the Reformation by thinkers like Vermigli and Calvin are virtually identical with those found among the later Reformed orthodox and — as noted in the discussion of the divinity and personality of the Son — indicates the need to argue both deity and person, on the grounds that a heresy might potentially hold one point or the other of the orthodox view, namely, that the Spirit is a divine power but not a distinct person or that the Spirit is a distinct person and, therefore, not divine. The former is the view of Adoptionists and some Arians, while the latter was taught by other Arians, notably Aetius and Eunomius, and the Macedonians or Pneumatomachians.[8] The larger number of Socinians denied the personality of the Spirit, whereas the English Socinian John Biddle argued that the Spirit was a lesser or intermediary being — the patristic parallels did not go unnoticed by the orthodox.[9]

The Reformed orthodox typically mount their arguments for deity and distinct person of the Spirit in a manner similar to that used in their discussions of the Son's divinity and personhood — by collation of texts, following out their hermeneutic of citing the direct declarations of Scripture and of drawing conclusions from juxtaposed texts.

B. The Reformers' Views on "Spirit"

The doctrine of the Holy Spirit proved a significant point of contention for orthodox Protestantism throughout the eras of the Reformation and orthodoxy. Although denial of the deity of Christ was the focal point of their argument, the earliest antitrinitarians tended to doubt the distinct subsistence or personhood of the Spirit. All of the Reformers noted draw on and explain the traditional language of the Trinity in relation to their discussion of the doctrine of Spirit, with Vermigli's discussion drawing most consistently on the Athanasian and Nicene discussions of the Trinity for its definition of the divinity of the Spirit.[10] Among the great Reformed codifiers of the mid-sixteenth century, Calvin, Bullinger, and Vermigli each devoted considerable space to arguments for the divinity of the Holy Spirit, almost certainly in response to the beginnings of antitrinitarianism in the writings of Servetus, Blandrata, and Gentile. By comparison

---

7. Pictet, *Theol. chr.*, II.xviii.1; cf. Rijssen, *Summa theol.*, IV.xii: "De Spiritu S. quinque credi debent. 1. Quod sit persona. 2. Divina. 3. Distincta a Patre & Filio. 4. Ab iisdem procedens. 5. Tertia ordine."

8. See Kelly, *Early Christian Doctrine*, pp. 115-116, 118, 120 (Adoptionists, Paul of Samosata, patripassians); 256, 259 (Arians); 259-260 (Macedonians, Pneumatomachians); Seeberg, *History of Doctrines*, I, pp. 164 (Adoptionists); 231-232 (Arians); 227 (Macedonians).

9. Cf. Mastricht, *Theoretico-practica theol.*, II.xxvii.17-19; Ridgley, *Body of Divinity* (1855), I, pp. 153-154, 230.

10. Vermigli, *Commonplaces*, I.xii.9-19.

with Vermigli, Bullinger, and Calvin, Musculus' *Loci communes* engage in little discussion of the divinity of the Spirit: it should be enough to prove the divinity of the Spirit, Musculus comments, to show that Christ joined together in the baptismal formula the names of Father, Son and Spirit or to cite Psalm 33, where Spirit is conjoined with God and God's word, showing that the Spirit is of the same divine nature as the Father and the Son.[11]

Even allowing for differences in exposition caused by the editorial compilation of Vermigli's *Loci communes* by another hand in contrast to Calvin's own editorial hand in the *Institutes*, the difference between the expositions is remarkable: Calvin plunges into a largely exegetical or biblical discussion of the divinity of the Spirit, whereas Vermigli begins at what is the logically prior point, the meaning of the word "spirit" in its various uses, moving from the most general to the most specific, only arriving at the individual divinity of the Holy Spirit after having discussed all of the other applications of the term. Still, the Vermigli-Massonius *Loci communes* is also rooted in exegesis, inasmuch as it takes up the question "Whether the Holy Ghost is God" in a lengthy section drawn from Vermigli's commentary on 1 Corinthians 12.[12] Bullinger, similarly, takes up the definition of "spirit" in general first and, like Vermigli, makes the larger number of his points exegetically. Hutchinson's discussion of the Spirit is noteworthy, along similar lines, for its point, made against "English Sadduccees and Libertines," that the Holy Spirit is a "substance," not merely an inspiration, affection, or quality.[13]

Bullinger indicates that the discussion of the word "spirit" and its implications is an important topic for Christian meditation, given that Scripture itself uses the word "diversely," and interpreters who are ignorant of this textual problem will often mistake the meaning of Scripture. By spirit "properly" so called, Bullinger continues, Scripture means "an element, signifying air, wind, breath."[14] Vermigli offers an extended definition:

> This word spirit, sometimes signifies a certain motion, or a nature moveable; sometimes it is taken for life, or mind, or the force of the mind, whereby we are moved to do anything; it is also transferred to the signifying of things, which be separate from matter, as be the angels, which the philosophers call Intelligences: yea, and it is so far drawn, as it represents our souls. Which metaphor seems to have respect thereunto, because we sometimes signify by this name, the thin exhalations, which breath either from the earth, from the water, from the blood, or from the humors of living creatures: which exhalations, although they be not easily perceived by the senses, yet they are effectual, and of exceeding great force; as it appeareth by winds, earthquakes, and such like things.[15]

---

11. Musculus, *Loci communes*, i (*Commonplaces*, p. 16, cols. 1-2).

12. Vermigli, *Commonplaces*, I.xii.6-18.

13. Hutchinson, *Image of God*, xxiv (pp. 134-139).

14. Bullinger, *Decades*, IV.viii (III, p. 298).

15. Vermigli, *Commonplaces*, I.xii.6.

Bullinger notes that the apostle Paul uses the word "spirit" to mean the "breath or voice" — and in this context links the word "spirit" to the tongue in contrast to the "mind." This contrast, moreover, yields a broader usage: "by metaphor [spirit] is translated to every bodiless substance, and is set against the body."[16] Or as Vermigli comments, the various breathlike "exhalations" that we experience become the basis for identifying various beings as "spirits":

> And so it cometh to pass hereby, that the name of these most subtile bodies, whose force is exceeding great, hath been translated to the expressing of substances without bodies. Wherefore it is taken for a word general, both unto God, unto angels, and unto our souls. And that it is attributed unto God, Christ shows, when he says, *God is a spirit* (John 4:24), and thereupon concludes, that he must be worshipped in Spirit and truth.[17]

Thus, the word can mean "an angel, either good or bad" — as in the case of the psalmist's and the apostle Paul's references to angels as "ministering spirits." So also does Scripture speak of lesser spiritual beings, evil spirits, or unclean spirits, just as it is common to speak of ghosts "which have taken some shape that cannot be well discerned" as spirits. In addition, "spirit" is also used to identify "the reasonable soul of man."[18]

Finally, "spirit" can also refer to God, and do so in two ways: "it is attributed unto God, Christ shows, when he says, *God is a spirit* (John 4:24), and thereupon concludes, that he must be worshipped in Spirit and truth," and it also, more restrictedly, indicates the Holy Spirit, the third person of the Trinity.[19] Bullinger comments, after a review of this and other New Testament texts, that "the word [spirit] is common to all the persons of the reverend Trinity; howbeit it is peculiarly applied to the third person in the Trinity."[20] Although Calvin does not press the point in the *Insitutes* that "Spirit" is predicated of God in two distinct ways, he definitely concurs with Bullinger's and Vermigli's exegesis, even to the point of faulting the church fathers: "This passage [John 4:24] is frequently quoted by the Fathers against the Arians, to prove the Divinity of the Holy Spirit, but it is improper to strain it for such a purpose; for Christ simply declares here that his Father is of a spiritual nature, and, therefore, is not moved by frivolous matters, as men, through the lightness and unsteadiness of their character, are wont to be."[21]

---

16. Bullinger, *Decades*, IV.viii (III, p. 298), citing Ps. 104:4, Heb. 1:14.

17. Vermigli, *Commonplaces*, I.xii.6.

18. Bullinger, *Decades*, IV.viii (III, p. 298).

19. Vermigli, *Commonplaces*, I.xii.6.

20. Bullinger, *Decades*, IV.viii (III, p. 299).

21. Calvin, *Commentary on John*, 4:24 (CTS John, I, p. 164).

C. The Meaning of "Spirit" according to the Reformed Orthodox

1. "Spirit": the range of biblical meanings. When compared to the views of the Reformers, the teachings of the Reformed orthodox evidence an equal awareness of the difficulties of biblical language concerning the Holy Spirit, and they recognized, as clearly as Calvin, Bullinger, and Vermigli and, indeed, in much the same way, that some discussion of the varied biblical usage of "spirit" — *ruach* or *pneuma* — was a necessary prologue to the doctrine of the deity and personality of the Holy Spirit. The necessity, moreover, was a twofold one: on the one hand, the Reformed orthodox present the basic exegetical task of studying and defining the biblical usages, given that the term "spirit," like the term "word," is used is several ways in Scripture, not always as the designation of a divine person, and the usages must be clarified for the sake of formulating Christian doctrine; on the other hand, the Reformed orthodox note that, particularly in their own times, the ambiguity or equivocity of the biblical usage has been used as a pretext for heterodox teachings and such problems must be dealt with for the preservation of true doctrine in the church.[22] In the course of the seventeenth century, other issues and problems also plagued the orthodox doctrine of the Spirit, perhaps the most significant problem being raised by Cartesian philosophy, which did not recognize "spirit" as a distinct substantial entity and proposed "thought" and "extension" as the basic kinds of substance, or by Hobbes, who denied the existence of immaterial spirit entirely. These philosophical developments rendered all the more important the analysis of possible meanings of the word "spirit" in the orthodox Reformed theology — pointing to a significant new use of an exegetical argument that they held in continuity with the Reformers.

The doctrinal clarification of the biblical language, moreover, fits well into the structure and assumptions of the older hermeneutics. Owen declares at the outset of his discussion of "the names and titles of the Holy Spirit" that although "some make their advantage of the ambiguous use" of the term "spirit" in the Bible, "the Scripture is able of itself to manifest its own intention and meaning unto humble and diligent inquirers into it."[23] The method for clarifying and developing correct doctrine, in other words, assumes the clarity or perspicuity of Scripture as a whole and proceeds by the comparison of text with text.[24] In addition, from the perspective of the orthodox, the exegetical problem caused by Socinians and other adversaries for the biblical language of "spirit" is quite similar to the way in which the Socinians treated the problem of other usages, notably, the use of Jehovah: ambiguities found in particular places are drawn into argument for the sake of confusing the meaning of even the clearest texts. The biblical range of meaning is of the highest significance to the orthodox, inasmuch as no one sense of the word can be used as the exclusive index to the meaning of all biblical occurrences, and each occurrence must be established in its own sense within

---

22. Cf. Witsius, *Exercitationes*, XXIII.ii-v; Mastricht, *Theoretico-practica theol.*, II.xxvii.1-4; Owen, *ΠΝΕΥΜΑΤΟΛΟΓΙΑ*, I.ii, in *Works*, III, pp. 47-64; Ridgley, *Body of Divinity* (1855), I, pp. 230-241.

23. Owen, *ΠΝΕΥΜΑΤΟΛΟΓΙΑ*, I.ii, in *Works*, III, p. 47.

24. See the discussion in *PRRD*, II, 5.4 (B.4); 7.4 (C).

the probable range of meaning — and also because of shifting senses of the term "spirit" in the seventeenth century and the need for theology to be certain of its own meaning as specified by the text of Scripture.

The words *ruach* and *pneuma*, taken in their most basic sense, indicate a "wind" or "spirit," in the sense of "any thing which moves and is not seen."[25] Scripture also evidences a highly generalized use of the words *ruach* and *pneuma*, indicating "any thing that cannot be seen or touched, but is itself *material* and *corporeal*, or absolutely *spiritual* and *immaterial*."[26] More specifically, the term "spirit" can refer either to a cause or to an effect — and "when taken for the cause it means the being or force that puts anything in motion, and is either uncreated or created."[27] The varied usage of Scripture, together with this pattern of understanding something unseen that moves, whether as uncreated or created, cause or effect, yields some six possibilities of meaning — without, however, yielding any lack of clarity in the text, given as Owen remarks, that "every place where it is used gives [the word a] determinate sense."[28]

There are various references in Scripture to created spirits, which are either immaterial or material. First, the former category — immaterial spirits — includes angels, whether good or evil, and human souls. The Psalmist says that God "maketh his angels spirits" (Psalm 104:4). Evil angels or devils are also identified as "spirits" — as in the text, "and there came forth a spirit, and stood before the Lord, and said I will persuade him [Ahab] ... and I will be a lying spirit in the mouth of all his prophets" (1 Kings 22:21-22).[29] The human soul as well is identified as "spirit" in Scripture, in such texts as Hebrews 12:23, "the spirits of just men made perfect," a reference, Gouge's words, to "the excellency of men's souls, as they are spiritual substances." Gouge emphasizes the point that a right reading of the text and of the biblical notion of the soul demands the conclusion that it is a distinct "spiritual substance": souls, after all, come from God, who is called "the God of the spirits of all flesh" (Num. 16:22; 27:16) and "the Father of spirits" (Heb. 12:9) — and the human being is said to be created in the image of God, "which a mere body without a spirit could not be."[30] Note that this point became a matter of contention in the seventeenth century, when not only a materialist philosopher like Hobbes but also various Socinians will argue that the divine substance and angelic substance, like all other substances, are both corporeal and dimensive.

Second, the latter category — material spirits — includes the wind and "vapors." Scripture refers to the wind as "spirit," blowing "where it listeth" (John 3:8), indicating the air that has been moved by the word "spirit" or "breath," or indicating the effect of the air, namely, the "motion" or movement of the air as experienced, or indicating

---

25. Owen, *ΠΝΕΥΜΑΤΟΛΟΓΙΑ*, I.ii, in *Works*, III, p. 48.

26. Owen, *ΠΝΕΥΜΑΤΟΛΟΓΙΑ*, I.ii, in *Works*, III, p. 52.

27. Ursinus, *Commentary*, p. 270.

28. Owen, *ΠΝΕΥΜΑΤΟΛΟΓΙΑ*, I.ii, in *Works*, III, p. 52.

29. Diodati, *Pious and Learned Annotations*, in loc.; Trapp, *Commentary*, in loc. (I, p. 590).

30. Gouge, *Commentary on Hebrewes*, XII, §110 (p. 347).

the variations of the wind or vapors.[31] Here also belongs what Owen calls the "vital breath which we and other living creatures breathe ... by which our lives are maintained in respiration," mentioned in Genesis 7:22, as "the breath of the spirit of life." This, too, is a material vapor or air.[32]

Third, by metonymy, Scripture also uses the term "spirit" or "wind" to indicate a place from which the wind blows, notably the "four corners of the earth." Thus, Ezekiel states, "I will scatter a third part into all the winds" (Ezek. 5:12) — and we read of "the four winds" in Matthew 24:31, indicating all parts of the earth.[33]

Fourth, the "unaccountable variation, inconstancy, and changes" of the wind yields a series of metaphorical uses in Scripture that indicate vanity, falsehood, and uncertainty. Given that wind is uncertain and untrustworthy, the wise man who "observeth the wind shall not sow" (Eccl. 11:4) — or, conversely, one may ask "what profit heth he who hath laboured for the wind?" (Eccl. 5:16). Job questions, rhetorically, "Should a wise man utter knowledge of wind?" (Job 15:2) — and refers to intellectual vanity and "pretense of knowledge and wisdom" as "words of wind" (Job. 16:3).[34]

Fifth, in Scripture, "spirit" can refer by metonymy "to the affections of the mind or soul of man ... whether they be good or evil."[35] In other words, "spiritual affections, and exercises whether good or bad," like "the spirit of fear," belong to this extended meaning. Even so, we identify as "spirit" or "spiritual" the gifts of the Holy Spirit. In the latter sense, referring to gifts, Paul says, "Quench not the Spirit" (1 Thess. 5:19).[36] So also, "because evil spirits are wont to torment the minds and bodies of men, therefore evil thoughts, disorders of mind, wicked purposes ... are called ... sometimes 'an evil spirit.'"[37]

Sixth, Scripture does use the term "spirit" to indicate the uncreated creator or mover of all things: God is referred to as spirit inasmuch as he is the uncreated cause of all things who puts them, as it were, in motion. As such, God is both "essentially and personally a Spirit, that is, incorporeal, indivisible, having a spiritual essence, but no bodily dimensions."[38] This is what Scripture intends when it states that "God is a spirit" (John 4:24). This final sense of the term "spirit," as a reference to God, must also be qualified. In the most general sense of its application to God, therefore, the term "spirit" indicates not a particular characteristic of the third person of the Trinity, but "that nature whereof each person is a partaker."[39] But there are also the biblical references to "the spirit of God," where a more specific identification of "spirit" is required —

---

31. Ursinus, *Commentary*, p. 271.

32. Owen, *ΠΝΕΥΜΑΤΟΛΟΓΙΑ*, I.ii, in *Works*, III, p. 52.

33. Owen, *ΠΝΕΥΜΑΤΟΛΟΓΙΑ*, I.ii, in *Works*, III, p. 51; cf. Calvin, *Harmony of the Evangelists*, in loc. (CTS *Harmony*, III, p 148).

34. Owen, *ΠΝΕΥΜΑΤΟΛΟΓΙΑ*, I.ii, in *Works*, III, p. 51.

35. Owen, *ΠΝΕΥΜΑΤΟΛΟΓΙΑ*, I.ii, in *Works*, III, p. 52.

36. Ursinus, *Commentary*, p. 271; Downame, *Summe*, i (p. 30).

37. Owen, *ΠΝΕΥΜΑΤΟΛΟΓΙΑ*, I.ii, in *Works*, III, p. 53.

38. Ursinus, *Commentary*, pp. 270-271.

39. Owen, *ΠΝΕΥΜΑΤΟΛΟΓΙΑ*, I.ii, in *Works*, III, p. 55.

given that, among other things, these phrases parallel the biblical usage "Son of God," in which another divine person is indicated.[40] The orthodox, therefore, offer an extended discussion of the biblical references to the divine "spirit."

2. The divine "Spirit" in the language of the Bible and orthodoxy. With reference to those texts in Scripture in which "spirit" refers to God or the works of God, three basic usages can be distinguished:

> the term *Spirit*, when used with respect to God, is taken either *essentially*, or *personally*, or *metonymically*. It is taken *essentially*, when it is ascribed to God in reference to the essence common to all the persons (John 4:24); *personally*, when it is attributed to some one person, whether the second (Mk. 2:8; 1 Cor. 15:45; Rom. 1:4; 1 Tim. 3:16; 1 Pet. 3:18, 19), or the third (Matt. 28:19; 1 John 5:7); *metonymically*, when it denotes certain effects or gifts, as in John 7:39, where "the spirit" signifies those gifts, the effusion of which had been predicted by Joel and other Prophets.[41]

Thus, 1) the Holy Spirit is "Spirit" essentially, "because he is a spiritual essence, immaterial and invisible" and, as such, "is God, equal and the same with the Father and the Son; and God is a Spirit."[42] But the Holy Spirit is also identified personally as Spirit: therefore, 2) when the third person of the trinity is specifically identified as the Spirit, the point of the text is frequently not to refer to what he has in common with the Father and the Son, namely, that he is "a most simple essence, intelligent, and exempt from all corporeal imperfection" (which, of course, is the case, inasmuch as the Spirit is fully God), but rather to refer to his "mode of procession" or to his personal "operations."[43] The Holy Spirit is not, therefore, called "spirit" simply because of the essential attribute of spirituality (which is shared by the three persons) and which the Holy Spirit has *in actu primo* as a fundamental attribute of essence like life, understanding, will, and power, but because of his distinct mode and operation — so that as person, the Spirit is spirit *in actu secundo* as well.[44] From this perspective, namely, the identity of the third person as Spirit *in actu secundo*, the "third person is called the Holy Ghost" or Holy Spirit "because he is *spired* or *breathed* from the Father and from the Son, in that he proceeds from them both."[45]

There is also 3) the identification of the Holy Spirit as "Spirit" on the basis of his special operation *ad extra*. Just as he is "inspired" or "breathed" forth from the Father and the Son, so also is the Spirit the "immediate agent of divine works," the person "through whom the Father and Son immediately influence the hearts of the elect," an activity for which he is called "the power of the Highest."[46] This point, moreover,

---

40. Owen, *ΠΝΕΥΜΑΤΟΛΟΓΙΑ*, I.ii, in *Works*, III, pp. 59-60; Downame, *Summe*, i (p. 32).

41. Witsius, *Exercitationes*, XXIII.iii; cf. Alsted, *Theologia didactica*, I.xxxiv.

42. Ursinus, *Commentary*, p. 271.

43. Witsius, *Exercitationes*, XXIII.iv.

44. Alsted, *Theologia didactica*, I.xxxiv.

45. Perkins, *Exposition of the Creed*, p. 274, col. 2B; cf. Ursinus, *Commentary*, p. 271; Beza et al., *Propositions and Principles*, IV.i-ii.

46. Ursinus, *Commentary*, p. 271.

returns to the initial definition of spirit as either cause or effect, created or uncreated, immaterial or material: the Holy Spirit is the uncreated "cause which influences or moves [and] works effectively in the minds of men."[47]

By the end of the era of orthodoxy, this view of the relationship between uncreated Spirit and the problem of causality — including what must have seemed fairly obvious in Ursinus' time, that spirit, whether infinite or finite, uncreated or created, is a fundamental cause of motion from potency to act in other things — has so altered that the argument seemed difficult to justify. The difficulty was particularly intense in the context of Cartesian and post-Cartesian metaphysics, which saw no connection between spiritual or intellective substance in general and corporeal or extended substance in general, to the point of undoing the traditional connection between soul and body and undermining the concept of secondary causality or intermediate movers.[48] Perhaps, comments Pictet, he is called the Spirit because he is "that power by which the Father performs everything which he has decreed in his wisdom: for it is almost always the custom, in every class of things, to attribute the power of self-motion and the power of moving things to some spirit." This question, according to Pictet, cannot be decided definitively.[49]

The Spirit, further, is called "Holy" because, on the one hand, of "his unsullied purity and glorious majesty" — not, however, as if he were holier than the Father and the Son, for all are holy and "the divine holiness, being infinite, does not admit of degrees."[50] Holiness, after all, is expressly attributed both to the Father (John 17:11) and to the Son (Luke 1:35; Acts 4:27), and is a divine attribute that belongs indivisibly to the Godhead: the Father, Son, and Spirit, considered as God are "holy by one and the same holiness."[51] Holiness, as an essential attribute of the Godhead, is equally attributed to each of the divine persons — and, inasmuch as the divine holiness is infinite, it does not admit of "degrees of comparison" — so that the Holy Spirit is not called "holy" "by way of eminence" in the Godhead itself.[52]

Rather, the specific attribution of holiness to the Spirit arises because it is his special operation to make us holy: "in the order of the divine operations, the sanctification of believers is usually attributed to him, as election is to the Father, and redemption to the Son."[53] Still, as in the case of all divine operations or works *ad extra*, sanctification is the work of the entire Godhead: it is not as if the sanctification of believers were a separate work of the Spirit, apart from the will and the work of the Father and the

---

47. Ursinus, *Commentary*, p. 271.

48. See J. A. van Ruler, *The Crisis of Causality Causality: Voetius and Descartes on God, Nature, and Change* (Leiden: E.J. Brill, 1995), pp. 177-187, 95-198, 201-205, 255-259, et passim; and cf. Richard A. Watson, *The Downfall of Cartesianism, 1673-1712: A Study of Epistemological Issues in Late 17th Century Catresianism* (Den Haag: Nijhoff, 1966), pp. 31-39.

49. Pictet, *Theol. chr.*, II.xx.5.

50. Pictet, *Theol. chr.*, II.xx.6.

51. Perkins, *Exposition of the Creed*, p. 274, col. 2A; cf. Witsius, *Exercitations*, XXIII.v.

52. Witsius, *Exercitations*, XXIII.v.

53. Pictet, *Theol. chr.*, II.xx.6.

Son — "but such is the order of the operations of God, that although they are effected by the common counsel of the same will, and by the same energy of the same power, yet some of them are appropriated to each person respectively."[54] Thus, the Holy Spirit is the person of the Godhead "who immediately sanctifies and makes holy the people of God," while the Father and the Son participate in this work "through the Holy Ghost," acting "mediately."[55]

7.2 The Personality or Individuality of the Spirit

The twofold pattern of argument concerning the Spirit — arguing his divinity and arguing also his distinct personality — although a rather traditionary procedure grounded in the patristic heresies, took on particular significance in the era of the Reformation and orthodoxy, with the revival of diverse forms of antitrinitarianism. On the one hand, some of the antitrinitarians, notably a majority of the Socinians, acknowledged the divinity of the Spirit, but identified that divinity as merely the power of God exerted in a particular way, thus denying the individual subsistence or personality of the Spirit. The Arians of the seventeenth century, on the other hand, were willing to identify the Spirit as an individual subsistence, but as a necessary consequence of his individuality, as a being less than God the Father. Thus, there are three points to be argued concerning the Holy Spirit: first, "that he is a Person"; second, that he is divine, namely, a "divine person"; and third, that as a "divine person" he is also "distinct from the Father and the Son."[56]

A. Arguments of the Reformers.

Vermigli's exposition evidences perhaps the clearest argumentative structure, developing two bifurcations in argument: first, he distinguishes between different biblical attributions of "spirit" to God, some of which indicate the Godhead itself, while others indicate the specifically Holy Spirit:

> When [Spirit] is so taken, this name comprehends under it, the Father, the Son, and the Holy Ghost. But sometimes it is taken particularly; for the third person of the Trinity, which is distinct from the Father and the Son.[57]

A second bifurcation serves to define the parts of the doctrine of the Spirit:

> And of this person we speak at this time, wherein two things must be showed: first, that he is a person distinct as well from the Father as the Son: secondly, we will show that by this means the Holy Ghost is described to be God.[58]

---

54. Witsius, *Exercitations*, XXIII.v; similarly, Perkins, *Exposition of the Creed*, in *Workes*, I, p. 274, col. 2A-B.
55. Ursinus, *Commentary*, p. 271.
56. Witsius, *Exercitationes*, XXIII.vi.
57. Vermigli, *Commonplaces*, I.xii.6.
58. Vermigli, *Commonplaces*, I.xii.6.

Vermigli continues:

> As touching the first, the apostles are commanded in the Gospel, that they should baptize in the name of the Father, of the Son, and of the Holy Ghost. Which place doth most plainly express the distinction of the three persons, and doth signify nothing else, but that we may be delivered from our sins, by the name, power, and authority of the Father, of the Son, and of the Holy Ghost.[59]

Similarly, at the baptism of Christ, Luke teaches that the voice of the Father identified Jesus as his "beloved son" and the Holy Spirit appeared in the form of a dove: clearly the Spirit is identified as a distinct person.[60]

The Gospel of John in particular offered the Reformers (as it had offered the older tradition of the church) its most telling arguments for the distinct subsistence of the Holy Spirit. Thus, Vermigli indicates,

> In *John* it is said; *I will ask my Father, and he shall give you another Comforter*. Here also the Son prays, the Father hears, and the Comforter is sent.[61]

Although he does not elaborate on the passage in the *Institutes*, Calvin cites it to argue the distinction of the Spirit, and in his commentary on John, after having emphasized the soteriological focus of the passage, he adds (with greater clarity than in the *Institutes*), "yet there would be no impropriety in inferring from this passage a distinction of Persons; for there must be some peculiarity in which the Spirit differs from the Son so as to be another than the Son."[62]

So also the text of John 16:13-14 — the phrase "He will take of what is mine, and will declare it to you" signifies "that the Holy Ghost doth so differ from the Father and the Son, as he is derived from both."[63] It also indicates that "every thing which the Holy Spirit shall bring proceeds from God himself."[64] Nonetheless, over against misrepresentations of meaning of the text, "these words take nothing away from the majesty of the Spirit, as if he were not God, or as if he were inferior to the Father, but are accommodated to the capacity of our understanding."[65] Again, the Gospel points toward the distinct personality of the Spirit, without indicating any subordination.

> And least that any man should think, that when Christ promised that the holy Ghost should come upon the believers (as in the day of Pentecost it came to pass) only a divine inspiration and motion of mind was signified, the words of Christ are against it, wherein he said; *He shall teach you all things, and bring all things to your remembrance which I have told you*. But inspiration and motion of mind, do not teach nor prompt any thing; but are only instruments, whereby something is taught and prompted. And the action of

---

59. Vermigli, *Commonplaces*, I.xii.7, citing Matt. 28:19.
60. Vermigli, *Commonplaces*, I.xii.7, citing Luke 3:21 and Matt. 3:16.
61. Vermigli, *Commonplaces*, I.xii.7, citing John 14:16.
62. Calvin, *Commentary on John*, 14:16 (CTS John, II, p. 93); cf. *Institutes*, I.xiii.17.
63. Vermigli, *Commonplaces*, I.xii.7, citing John 16:14.
64. Calvin, *Commentary on John*, 16:13 (CTS John, II, p. 144).
65. Calvin, *Commentary on John*, 16:13 (CTS John, II, p. 144).

teaching and prompting, cannot be attributed but unto one that is a person indeed. Which is proved by other words of Christ, when he said of the Holy Ghost; *He shall speak whatsoever he shall hear.*[66]

Even so, the work of inspiration also testifies to the distinct personality of the Spirit: when Peter teaches that "Holy men of God spake by the inspiration of the Holy Ghost," he "putteth a plain difference between him and an inspiration: for he is not an inspiration, but the worker thereof, the sender of it," for "as the workman is not his work ... as Apelles is not Venus, the carpenter is not the house; nomore is the Holy Spirit an inspiration."[67]

B. The Reformed Orthodox Approach to the Person of the Spirit

1. The problem of the personality of the "Spirit": objections to the doctrine and Reformed responses. Given the recognition on the part of both Reformers and Reformed orthodox that "spirit" could (and often does) refer to motions of air, vapors of various sorts, nonphysical being in general, and God in particular, without any added implication of distinct personhood, the identification of the Holy Spirit as a distinct divine person was not only an important but also hotly debated point of doctrine during the era of orthodoxy. Whereas there was never any debate over the distinct subsistence of God the Father, but only over whether the Father was one of three fully divine subsistences — and virtually no debate over the independent subsistence of the Son, but only over the full divinity of his subsistence — there was intense debate over the personal subsistence or personality of the Spirit.[68] In brief, the Reformed defended the doctrine in four sets of arguments — from the personal properties attributed to the Spirit, from personal appearances or theophanies of the Spirit, from personal "operations" of the Spirit, and from biblical references to the Spirit in conjunction with but also distinct from the Father and the Son.[69]

Objections ranged from the ancient Macedonian or Pneumatomachian objection, typical of the Socinians, that the Spirit was merely a power of God to the materialist denial of spiritual being as such, found in or extrapolated from the new rational philosophies of the seventeenth century, notably that of Hobbes and the Cartesians. Accordingly, the orthodox indicate that proof of the distinct personality of the Spirit is particularly needed since it is so strenuously denied:

The distinct personality of the Spirit ... is denied, not only by the *Sabellians*, but by some of the *Socinians*; yea, even by *Socinus* himself; who describes the Holy Ghost as the power of God, intending hereby ... the energy of the divine nature; or that whereby the Father, who is the only one, to whom, according to him, the divine nature is

---

66. Vermigli, *Commonplaces*, I.xii.7, citing John 14:26; 16:13; 15:26.
67. Hutchinson, *Image of God*, pp. 136-137, citing 2 Peter 1:21.
68. Cf. Turretin, *Inst. theol. elencticae*, III.xxx.1-2.
69. Witsius, *Exercitationes*, XXIII.vii-x.

attributed, produces those effects which require infinite power; so that they call the Spirit, the power of God essentially considered.[70]

The texts cited by Socinians to prove the point are Luke 1:35 and 24:49, collated with Acts 1:4-5, 8; 10:38, the former texts speaking in conjunction with the Spirit or power from "on high," the latter texts speaking of anointing by the Spirit and power. But the texts, even if they do identify the Spirit as the "power of God," given the forms of expression found in Scripture, do not constitute a denial of personality: after all, the followers of Simon Magus identified him as "the great power of God" (Acts 8:10) without denying his individual personality, and the apostle Paul speaks of Christ as "the power of God" (1 Cor. 1:24) without implying that Christ is not a person.[71] Witsius also notes that such phraseology is also found among the Rabbis, who use the word גבורה [gᵉburah], "power," with the article, to indicate God — a locution which may in fact be found in the New Testament verse, "Ye shall see the Son of Man sitting in the right hand of power" (Mark 14:62). The possible identification of the Spirit as "the power of God," therefore, provides "no solid objection" to his personality or personal subsistence, although, notes Witsius, the texts do not actually make the identification in the way the Socinians claim.[72]

Others, notably Crellius, in order to give further support to Socinus' claims, that "all that is affirmed of the Spirit as a person must be understood figuratively as a prosopopoeia, just as Paul speaks of charity as suffering long, kind, and seeking not her own, 1 Cor. 13:4, &c., and of sin as reigning, having dominion, and working death in him, Rom. 6:12, 14; 7:13," or, indeed, of Scripture "foreseeing" the justification of the Gentiles through faith (Gal. 3:8).[73] Against this latter denial of personhood, the Reformed orthodox point out that the claim of figurative language, specifically prosopopoeia or personification, cannot stand scrutiny. Scripture stands, when viewed as a whole, as a clear and accurate revelation. The difficult passages may consistently be illuminated by comparison with clear passages, and no point concerned with the salvation of humanity (which is the primary divine intention in the revelation) will ultimately be opaque to the community of belief. This assumption belongs to the center of the orthodox Protestant exegetical enterprise.[74] Specifically to the point of the claim that all references to the Spirit that appear to be personal are merely figurative personifications, the orthodox respond that the clarity or perspicuity of Scripture is such that "there is no instance of its continually employing the prosopopoeia": surely, the figure of prosopopoeia does appear in Scripture and both sin and charity are personified, but it is also quite clear from other places in the scriptural account that sin and charity are not regarded by Scripture as persons. Typically, Scripture employs the figure to personify things that lack "life and sense," as in the texts which speak

---

70. Ridgley, *Body of Divinity*, p. 118, col. 1; cf. Turretin, *Inst. theol. elencticae*, III.xxx.3.
71. Witsius, *Exercitationes*, XXIII.xxii.
72. Witsius, *Exercitationes*, XXIII.xxii, citing the talmudic lexica of Levita and Buxtorf.
73. Venema, *Inst. theol.*, xiv (p. 255); Witsius, *Exercitationes*, XXIII.xiii.
74. Cf. *PRRD*, II, 5.4 (B.4); 7.4 (C).

of the heavens hearing or the rivers clapping their hands.[75] There is no case in the entire text of Scripture in which a thing or effect that is not a person is uniformly referred to as such — which would have to be the case if the personal references to the Spirit were merely figures. Nor can the personal references to the Spirit be the only biblical exceptions to this rule, inasmuch as prosopopoeia "is never employed except about objects in regard to which no one doubts that they are not persons," a rule of rhetorical usage that is quite evident in the counterexamples of heavens, rivers, sin, and charity.[76]

It is abundantly clear, the orthodox insist, that the divine names and attributes given to the Spirit, the distinction made between him and the Father and the Son, and the various theophanies or "personal actions" and operations of the Spirit mentioned in Scripture evidence a personal sense of the word "spirit" that is impossible to reduce to a figure of speech. Such passages as Matthew 28:19, where believers are enjoined to baptize in the name of the Father, the Son, and the Spirit, understand "Spirit" as no more a figure than "Father" and "Son." The same is true of 1 Corinthians 12:11, where the "communion of the Holy Spirit" is juxtaposed with the grace of Christ and the love of God — the passage makes no sense if the word "Spirit" is read figuratively while "Christ" and "God" are read personally.[77] So also is the Spirit said to be "grieved" (Isa. 63:10), to have anointed Christ and sent him to preach to the poor (Isa. 61:1), and to have led Israel through the wilderness (Isa. 63:11-14).[78]

Even so, Crell's attempt to read the crying of the Spirit, "Abba, Father," in the heart of believers as a personification (Gal. 4:6), by paralleling it with the apostle's earlier statement that Scripture foresaw the redemption of the Gentiles (Gal. 3:8), falls short of valid interpretation of either passage. (The debate here is interesting particularly because both the Socinians and the orthodox use the technique of comparing texts for the sake of drawing conclusions.) The one passage states that the Spirit is sent into the hearts of believers and, by operating in the heart, cries out — in other words, the Spirit, present in the heart "so causeth us to cry, that our crying is his voice." This is not personification, but a direct reference to an operation of the Spirit. In the other passage, "the Scripture is said to foresee, because the Spirit who dictates the Scripture, foresees." Neither is this a personification rather it is a metonymy. In short, the passages are not parallel, and the reference to the Spirit is so clearly a reference to a subsistent individual that Crell is forced to label it an instance of prosopopoeia in order to dismiss it as evidence.[79]

Nor can the Socinian reading of a series of references to the Spirit, Romans 8:9, 1 Corinthians 12:3, 2 Corinthians 3:6, and James 4:12, as personifications of the "doctrine of the Gospel" be sustained. The Socinian claim was that the contrast

75. Turretin, *Inst. theol. elencticae*, III.xxx.5.
76. Venema, *Inst. theol.*, xiv (pp. 255-256), and cf. *PRRD*, II, 7.3 (B.1-3) and 7.4 (B.2) on the interpretation of figurative language in Scripture.
77. Venema, *Inst. theol.*, xiv (p. 256).
78. Downame, *Summe*, i (p. 30).
79. Witsius, *Exercitationes*, XXIII.xiii.

between being "in the flesh" and being "in the Spirit" or between the "letter" that kills and the "Spirit" that give life, and the statement that no one can say that "Jesus is Lord, but by the Holy Ghost," are merely references to the gospel, specifically, to the contrast between law and gospel, with the gospel personified as the Spirit. On the contrary, the passages do not identify "law" and "letter" implying a similar identification of "gospel" and "Spirit" — rather the text "teaches that the letter is in the law, and the Spirit in the gospel, so that they who minister to the law, minister to the letter; they who minister to the gospel, to the Spirit."[80] The "Spirit" in such texts indicates both the divine person and his grace, which are both "disclosed, and rendered efficacious, by means of the Gospel." This contrast between Spirit and gospel, moreover, is confirmed textually by the apostle — he speaks of the Corinthian believers as an "epistle written in our hearts," and then states that this epistle was "written not with ink, but with the Spirit of the living God": the Spirit, in this passage, is clearly distinguished from the doctrine.[81]

2. The names, attributes, and operations of the Spirit. The personality of the Spirit, like that of the Son, also appears from the names and activities predicated of him — Sanctifier, Reprover, Witness, Comforter — and from the works attributed to him — teaching, comforting, witnessing.[82] In other words, the Spirit is understood to be a subsistence or person, given that "the properties of a person are continually attributed to him."[83] The Holy Ghost is also said "to constitute or appoint" believers to an office (Acts 20:28).[84] So also is the Spirit said to have understanding, will, and power or to act powerfully (1 Cor 2:10-11; 12:11; Luke 1:35; 24:49; Acts 10:38; 15:28) — which are characteristics of persons only.[85]

When Scripture states that the Spirit "searches the deep things of God" and that no human being knows the "things of God," but only the Spirit, it clearly identifies the Spirit as having understanding. Nor do these passages refer to a human being endowed with the Spirit, for the Spirit is consistently distinguished from the human beings to whom his gifts are given. The personal distinction of the Spirit and the distinction of the Spirit from human beings is also implied in the statement that God has revealed things to us by his Spirit (1 Cor. 2:10). Even so, the Spirit is a giver of gifts who works "as he wills" (1 Cor. 12:11).[86] For Owen, this attribution of understanding or wisdom to the Spirit underlines the Spirit's personal identity inasmuch as this attribute "is the first inseparable property of an intelligent subsistence."[87]

Witsius notes that in the passages that refer to the Spirit and power, there is a clear distinction made by Scripture between the Spirit and the power that he has. Thus,

---

80. Witsius, *Exercitationes*, XXIII.xiv.

81. Witsius, *Exercitationes*, XXIII.xiv.

82. Ridgley, *Body of Divinity*, p. 118, col. 2.

83. Ursinus, *Commentary*, p. 272.

84. Ursinus, *Commentary*, p. 272.

85. Witsius, *Exercitationes*, XXIII.vii, xii; Ridgley, *Body of Divinity*, p. 119, col. 1.

86. Witsius, *Exercitationes*, XXIII.vii.

87. Owen, *ΠΝΕΥΜΑΤΟΛΟΓΙΑ*, I.iii, in *Works*, III, p. 78.

Luke 24:49 indicates that the "power from on high" is given to the Apostles, meaning the power with which they were filled — which is not the Spirit himself, but a gift of which the Spirit is the author. This is not only the implication of the text in Luke; it is the necessary conclusion drawn when this particular text in Luke is compared to other places, such as Acts 1:8, where the Apostles are told, "ye shall receive power, after that the Holy Ghost is come upon you." Similarly, in Acts 10:38, God is said to have anointed Jesus "with the Holy Ghost and with power."[88]

The Spirit comforts (John 14:16, 18), teaches and testifies (John 14:26; 15:26), prophesies the future (Luke 2:26, the death of Simeon; Acts 10:19, to Peter concerning Simeon), guides believers into all truth (John 16:13), prevents Paul and Silas from entering Bithynia (Acts 16:7), makes intercession for believers with unutterable groanings (Romans 8:26), is tempted or tested by individuals who lie to him (Acts 5:9), and bears witness in heaven with the Father and the Son (1 John 5:7). Clearly, argues Pictet, the Holy Spirit is a "*person subsisting* distinct from the Father and the Son" as is demonstrated particularly in the Johannine references to the Spirit as Comforter, as one who abides, as guide into truth, and as one who speaks not of himself but of Christ.[89]

> Again, dwelling is a personal character ... but the Holy Ghost is said to dwell in believers, John 14:17. and alluding hereto, as also connoting his divine personality 'tis said, 1 Cor. 6:19. *Your body is the temple of the Holy Ghost*; as a house is the dwelling place of a person, so a temple is the dwelling place of a divine Person.[90]

Similarly the frequently mentioned sins against the Spirit — as in Isaiah 63:10, where Israel is said to "vex" the Holy Spirit, or Matt. 12:31-32, where we read of "blasphemy against the Holy Spirit," or Acts 5:3 where Ananias and Sapphira are accused of "lying" to the Spirit — manifest the Spirit as a person: "Is autem, adversus quem peccamus, non potest non esse persona divina." This is particularly the case since the sin against the Spirit is thus expressly distinguished from sin against the Father and the Son.[91]

Socinian objectors argue that personal characteristics are attributed metaphorically only to the Spirit even as conscience is said to witness (Romans 9:1). Biddle, who assumes that the Spirit is not God but an intermediary being, notes that all sins are against God, so that mention of a specific sin against the Holy Spirit, far from proving the Spirit's divinity, actually disproves it![92] In answer, the orthodox note that most metaphorical attributions occur in poetical passages — whereas the Spirit is referred to personally throughout Scripture.[93] Furthermore, the Socinian argument is weak, since it rests on the supposition that some metaphorical characterizations of impersonal things in a personal way show other personal references to be merely metaphorical

---

88. Witsius, *Exercitationes*, XXIII.xii.

89. Pictet, *Theol. chr.*, II.xxiii.1

90. Ridgley, *Body of Divinity*, p. 118, col. 2.

91. Rijssen, *Summa theol.*, IV.xii, cont. I, arg. 5; cf. Turretin, *Inst. theol. elencticae*, III.xxx.9.

92. Biddle, *XII Arguments* (1691), p. 11.

93. Ridgley, *Body of Divinity*, p. 120, col. 1.

— but similar modes of speaking do not necessarily indicate the same meaning. No one claims that the use of personal language in referring to God the Father is purely metaphorical. Nor is it usual to stretch the use of metaphors to include not only personal characteristics but also personal works and personal relations — as Scripture continually does of the Son and the Spirit. In particular, the personal properties of begetting, begottenness, and proceeding attributed to the Father, the Son, and the Spirit, respectively, manifest them as distinct persons.[94]

3. The distinction of the Spirit from the Father and the Son. Not only is the Spirit personal as God, but he is clearly a person distinct from the Father and the Son: there are passages in Scripture, like Matthew 28:19, in which the Spirit is "joined in the same place and order with persons, without any mark of difference": we are enjoined to baptize in the name of the Holy Spirit "no less than of the Father and the Son."[95] Given that when a deed is performed in the name of someone it is done by his authority, and that the authority of the Spirit here appears to be equal to that of the other persons, the Spirit must be understood as a person and as the equal of the Father and the Son in "the ordinance of baptism."[96]

Witsius recognizes that there are objections to this reading of Matthew 28:19 — some have argued that there are passages in Scripture that link persons with "things that are not persons," like Acts 20:32, where "Paul commends the Church 'to God, and to the word of his grace.'" The objection fails on two counts: in the first place, nowhere in Scripture is there an instance where something is said "to be done in the name of that which is not person," so that the comparison of Acts 20:32 (where nothing is done in the name of a person) with Matthew 28:19 (where baptism is commanded to be performed in the name of persons) is not germane. Second, there is the distinct possibility that in Acts 20:32, the phrase "word of his grace" is not a reference to the gospel, but a reference to Christ. Witsius takes the argument from Gomarus: given that Christ is called "the Word" in the Gospel of John and even "the Word of life," the phrase "word of his grace" may in this context refer to the person of Christ.[97]

The Spirit is consistently called the "Spirit of the Father" and the "Spirit of Christ" or the Son, "but no one is his own spirit, no more than he is his own father or his own son."[98] Even so, Scripture specifically indicates that the Spirit is distinct from the Father and the Son: Christ prays to the Father that he would send a Comforter (John 14:16). It is clear that one who is sent by another is distinct: a person does not send himself — yet Scripture consistently speaks in this way of the Spirit. Christ sends the Spirit from the Father (John 15:26), and the Father sends the Spirit in Christ's name (John 14:26). The Spirit "bears witness *with* the Father and the Son in heaven (1 John 5:7).[99]

---

94. Ridgley, *Body of Divinity*, pp. 120-121.
95. Witsius, *Exercitationes*, XXIII.x; cf. Amyraut, *De mysterio trinitatis*, V, p. 309.
96. Witsius, *Exercitationes*, XXIII.x.
97. Witsius, *Exercitationes*, XXIII.x.
98. Ursinus, *Commentary*, pp. 272-273.
99. Turretin, *Inst. theol. elencticae*, III.xxx.6.

As various Johannine passages (14:16; 15:26; 16:27) show, the Spirit is sent by both the Father and the Son. Diodati explicitly reflects elements of Calvin's reading of John 14. Christ, he notes, states that he sends "another" (v. 16) inasmuch as the Holy Spirit "is distinct from the Sonne in his personall subsistence, and in the manner of working in beleevers."[100] The name "Paraclete" or "Comforter," moreover, is an indication of a personal work (*officium personale*), and the word *pneuma*, a negative noun, is joined with a masculine pronoun in John 16:13.[101]

Objections to the distinct personality of the Spirit are also raised on the ground that the Spirit is identified by Scripture not as a person but as "the power of God," an argument based on Luke 1:35; 24:49 compared with such texts as Acts 1:4-5, 8; 10:38. Since Christ is also called "the power of God" (1 Cor. 1:24), and since "power" is one of the titles of God Himself, it would not be a credible objection to the personality of the Spirit that he is sometimes called "the power of God." But, Witsius argues, even this contention cannot be proven, given that in all of the texts brought forward to indicate that the Spirit is called the power of God, there is a distinction made between the Spirit and divine power.[102]

4. Theophanies and "personal actions" of the Spirit. There are places in Scripture that teach of appearances of the Spirit in visible forms: in Matthew 3:16 and Luke 3:22, the Spirit descends in the bodily form of a dove and Acts 2:3, the Spirit appears on the heads of the disciples in the form of "tongues of fire." Such appearances indicate individual subsistence inasmuch as "it is not possible for any quality or exercise of mind or heart to assume and wear a bodily form; for an accident does not only not assume any particular form, but it even requires something else to which it may attach itself, and in which it may exist."[103] The point is well taken in the context of a traditional Christian Aristotelianism, in which incidental properties such as qualities and functions of beings cannot have an independent status apart from the being of which they are the properties: attributes and properties are not and cannot be freestanding realities. They cannot, therefore, act independently, and they cannot become the subjects of other properties. Thus, if it was the Spirit that took on the forms of a dove and of fire, the Spirit is not merely a property but an independent subsistence — if the Spirit is not an independent subsistence, then some other subsistence took on the appearances of a dove and fire, but Scripture clearly identifies the Spirit as the subject of these forms. Owen takes particularly angry exception to Crell's argument that, inasmuch as a dove is not a person, having no understanding, the text cannot be taken to indicate that

---

100. Diodati, *Pious and Learned Anotations*, in loc.; similarly, Poole, *Commentary*, John 14:16 in loc. (III, p. 355); Hutcheson, *Exposition of the Gospel of John*, 14:16 in loc. (p. 303); cf. Amyraut, *De mysterio trinitatis*, V, p. 247.

101. Rijssen, *Summa theol.*, IV.xii, cont. I, arg. 2.

102. Witsius, *Exercitationes*, XXIII.xii.

103. Ursinus, *Commentary*, pp. 271-272; cf. Witsius, *Exercitationes*, XXIII.viii; Turretin, *Inst. theol. elencticae*, III.xxx.8.

the Spirit is a person: the point is that only an individual subsistent would appear as an individual subsistent.[104]

If, moreover, it is objected that "things which are not persons are sometimes figuratively said to come down from heaven, and that such things may be adumbrated by some external appearance," as at Pentecost, when the gift of "speaking in various languages" was manifest in the form of tongues of fire on the heads of the apostles, the objection does not in fact undermine the basic argument: "we do not deny that the gifts of God, which are not always persons, descend from heaven: we only urge that nothing which is not a person, ever came from above clothes with a bodily shape." In matter of fact, the tongues of fire on the apostles' heads did not directly indicate the gift of tongues — rather they denoted "the person of the Holy Spirit, the Author of that gift, 'who gave them utterance,' as it is explained in the fourth verse."[105]

7.3   The Full Deity of the Spirit

A. The Divinity of the Spirit in the Teaching of the Reformers

1. Reformation-era approaches to the divinity of the Spirit. Although the nature of the polemic in the era of the Reformation was such that the emphasis of trinitarian discussion was placed on the divinity of the Son, there was nonetheless some concerted discussion of the divinity of the Spirit. The Vermigli-Massonius *Loci communes*, Calvin's *Institutes*, and Musculus' *Loci communes* all provided later orthodoxy with examples of carefully structured discussions of the doctrine of the Holy Spirit. Despite Massonius' use of Calvin's *Institutes* as a basic model for his Vermigli *Loci communes*, the pattern of argument in the *Loci communes* is quite different from the pattern of the *Institutes*. We have already seen Vermigli bifurcate his discussion of divine Spirit into the general reference of Spirit to God and the specific reference to the Holy Spirit, with an initial accent on the identification of the Spirit as "person." Once he has shown that the Spirit is a person and is distinct from the Father and the Son, Vermigli again bifurcates his discussion and presents arguments showing that the person of the Spirit is divine.[106]

Calvin begins his examination of the Holy Spirit with the comment that "in asserting the divinity of the Spirit, the proof must be derived from the same sources," namely, the same sources used to argue the divinity of the Son. The shape of the argument is, thus, quite different from the Vermigli *Loci*: Calvin has first presented the doctrine of the trinity and then moved to discuss the divinity of the Son and the Spirit, reserving discussion of the unity and distinction in the Godhead as a final point in his positive argument. The "sources" of his argument are those biblical passages that, like the passages used in the preceding sections of the *Institutes*, demonstrate that the Spirit is (in the words of the sixteenth-century editors of the apparatus to the *Institutes*) "the Creator and Preserver of the world," the one who "sent the Prophets," and who "quickens all things," who is "everywhere present," who "renews the saints, and fits

---

104. Owen, *ΠΝΕΥΜΑΤΟΛΟΓΙΑ*, I.iii, in *Works*, III, pp. 77-78.

105. Witsius, *Exercitationes*, XXIII.viii.

106. Vermigli, *Commonplaces*, I.xii.8.

them for eternal life," and to whom "all the offices of Deity belong."[107] The following sections offer a composite view of the thoughts of Calvin and various of his contemporaries on these biblical foundations of the doctrine of the divinity of the Spirit.

Musculus' *Loci communes* offers a very straightforward approach to the doctrine of God, presenting a first chapter on God, a second on the divinity of Christ, and a third on the divinity of the Spirit.[108] The third is quite brief and appeals to the baptismal formula as more than enough to demonstrate the full divinity and personhood of the Spirit: it would hardly be suitable to take the formula of baptism in the name of the Father, the Son, and the Holy Spirit as indicating three Gods — nor is it possible that the one God could have more than a single nature or essence, as would be the case "if the holy spirite were not of the same essence and of the same nature of godhead with the father and the sonne."[109]

2. Divine names, titles, and attributes given to the Spirit. In this category of argument as well, the theology and exegesis of the Reformers offers a precedent for the teaching of the later orthodox, if only in the form of a mediated tradition of exegetical result. Calvin argues the divinity of the Spirit from the simple fact that "Scripture ... in speaking of him," uses "the name of God." Specifically, when Scripture speaks of believers as temples of God, it explains this designation on the ground that the Spirit dwells in them. So also when Peter confronts Ananias in Acts 5:3-4 for lying to the Holy Spirit, he states that Ananias has lied to God. Calvin also cites Augustine on the point: Augustine had indicated that it "would be clear proof of the Spirit's divinity" if Scripture enjoined us to build temples for the Spirit — and, just so, Scripture has called believers the temple of God.[110] In his commentary on the text, Calvin writes,

> we must note, that he saith that he lieth to God who doth lie to the Holy Ghost. For the divinity of the Holy Ghost is manifestly proved by this form of speech. In like sort Paul saith, "Ye are the temples of God, because his Spirit dwelleth in you," (1 Cor. 3:16-17; 6:19).[111]

Much the same argument is offered by Bullinger and Vermigli.[112]

Calvin also offers arguments for the omnipresence of the Spirit that fall largely into the category of conclusions drawn from the statements of Scripture. Thus, the Spirit who is "diffused over all space, sustaining, invigorating, and quickening all things, both in heaven and on the earth," cannot be a mere creature. So too do the Scriptures indicate that the Spirit is "not ... circumscribed by any limits."[113] Nor does the language

---

107. Calvin, *Institutes*, I.xiii.14.

108. Musculus, *Loci communes* (1573), I, II, III: note that the *Commonplaces* (1578) merges these chapters into one and thereby conceals the trinitarian beginning of the *Loci communes*.

109. Musculus, *Commonplaces*, I (p. 16, cols. 1-2).

110. Calvin, *Institutes*, I.xiii.15, citing Augustine, Letter clxx.2 (*PL* 33, col. 749); cf. Musculus, *Commonplaces*, I (p. 16, col. 2).

111. Calvin, *Commentary on Acts*, 5:4 in loc. (*CTS Acts*, I, p. 198).

112. Bullinger, *Decades*, IV.viii (III, p. 302); Vermigli, *Loci communes*, I.xii.8.

113. Calvin, *Institutes*, I.xiii.14.

of Matthew 3:16, indicating that the Spirit "descended" in the form of a dove, imply either a physical nature of the Spirit or a local presence (as if *descending* implied that the Spirit does not fill all things), or an essential visibility of the Spirit.[114] Bullinger and Vermigli find a variant of this particular argument so attractive that they cite it out of Jerome's version of Didymus the Blind's treatise on the Spirit, in Bullinger's case, at length. Since the Holy Spirit "is in many places," Bullinger declares, he cannot be said to have "a limitable substance." Specifically, Scripture tells us that the Spirit dwelt in the apostles as they spread the gospel abroad throughout the earth — "severed one from another with a very great distance of place, and yet [they] had present with them the Holy Ghost dwelling with them." Clearly the Spirit is without limit of place.[115]

There is also a textual argument that can be made on the basis of 1 Corinthians 2:10, "The things which be of man, no man knoweth, but the spirit of man which is in him; even so the things that be of God, none knoweth but the spirit of God." Vermigli comments that "even as the spirit of man is unto man; so the spirit of God is towards God" — and, given that "the spirit of man belongeth unto the nature of man," it is clear that, according to the text, "the spirit of God is of his divine nature." Similar conclusions must be drawn, Vermigli notes, from the several texts that identify the Holy Spirit as the Spirit of the Father and of the Son: since the Spirit is from them, he must be "wholly partaker of their nature," and therefore, as Basil argued against Eunomius, truly God.[116] Similarly, as Basil also argued, if we are adopted as children of God by the Holy Spirit and the Spirit is consistently identified as "the Spirit of adoption," his divinity should be clear, as by a direct attribution: "none that is not God can adopt any to be the children of God."[117]

3. Divine works attributed to the Spirit. No less important to the understanding of the divinity of the Spirit than the explicit biblical attribution of divine names and attributes to him are the numerous places in Scripture where the Spirit is identified as performing a divine work. "By operations," writes Bullinger, "we manifestly acknowledge, that the Holy Ghost is God, of the same essence and power with the Father and the Son."[118]

First, the Spirit is identified by Scripture as creator and preserver of the world. Since this power to create belongs only to God, the Spirit is "undoubtedly" God.[119] The divinity of the Spirit is first attested in Genesis 1:2, "when [Moses] says that the Spirit of God was expanded over the abyss or shapeless matter; for it shows not only that the beauty which the world displays is maintained by the invigorating power of the Spirit, but that even before this beauty existed the Spirit was at work cherishing the

---

114. Calvin, *Harmony of the Evangelists*, Matt. 3:16 in loc. (*CTS Harmony*, I, p. 205).

115. Bullinger, *Decades*, IV.viii (III, pp. 303-304); cf. Vermigli, *Loci communes*, I.xii.9.

116. Vermigli, *Commonplaces*, I.xii.8.

117. Vermigli, *Commonplaces*, I.xii.9.

118. Bullinger, *Decades*, IV.viii (III, p. 301).

119. Vermigli, *Loci communes*, I.xii.8, 9.

confused mass."[120] Bullinger appeals to two texts from Job as proof that "the Holy ghost from the beginning before all creatures, visible and invisible, is a Creator and not a creature," namely, "His Spirit hath garnished the heavens" (Job 26:13), and "the spirit of God hath made me, and the breath of the Almighty hath given me life" (Job 33:4).[121] The Spirit, moreover, breathes "into all things ... being, life, and motion."[122]

Second, the Spirit is also identified by Isaiah as governing and guiding the Israelites in their journey out of Egypt, just as the Spirit "governeth now the present congregation: for Christ promiseth that 'he would pray the Father to send us another Comforter, to abide with us forever.'"[123]

Third, the Spirit was sent to and spoke through the prophets. Drawing on this point, Calvin and Bullinger both juxtapose combinations of texts to press the conclusion that the Holy Spirit is indeed the Lord of Hosts. Thus, the prophets consistently indicate that they speak the words of the Lord and we read in the Gospel of Luke that "the Lord God of Israel ... spake by the mouth of his holy prophets, which have been since the world began" (1:68, 70). From the New Testament, however, we also learn that it is the Holy Spirit who speaks through the prophets (Acts 6:10; 2 Pet. 1:21). Isaiah refers to the Lord of Hosts as speaking (Isa. 6:9) and Paul cites the text with reference to the Holy Spirit (Acts 28:25-26).[124] The point is significant from a hermeneutical as well as a doctrinal perspective, inasmuch as Calvin and Bullinger avail themselves of the technique of drawing conclusions from juxtaposed biblical texts as a basis for doctrinal formulation — the technique stands in continuity with the earlier practices of the church and with the later Reformed orthodox.

Fourth, the Spirit graciously regenerates the elect and preserves them to life eternal. Citing 1 Corinthians 6:11, "now ye are cleansed, and sanctified, and lastly justified, through the name of the Lord Jesus Christ, and by the Spirit of our God," Bullinger argues that the text yields the conclusion that "it is, as it were, the property of the Holy Ghost to sanctify." We ought to recognize "the power in working" that Scripture attributes consistently to the Spirit — specifically, "that all the faithful are cleansed, washed, regenerated, sanctified, enlightened, and enriched of God ... through the Holy Ghost." This, indicates Bullinger, is the primary ground for our belief in the Holy Ghost.[125] "The Holy Ghost doth sanctify, renew, regenerate, give life and save," and these, states Bullinger, "are operations agreeable to God only."[126] So also does the Spirit teach us "all things" (John 14: 26) — which is the proper work of God alone.[127]

---

120. Calvin, *Institutes*, I.xiii.14; cf. Calvin, *Commentary on Genesis*, 1:2 (*CTS Genesis*, I, pp. 73-74).

121. Bullinger, *Decades*, IV.viii (III, p. 301).

122. Calvin, *Institutes*, I.xiii.14.

123. Hutchinson, *Image of God*, p. 135, citing Isaiah 63:14 and John 14:16.

124. Calvin, *Institutes*, I.xiii.15; Bullinger, *Decades*, IV.viii (III, p. 302).

125. Bullinger, *Decades*, I.viii (I, pp. 155-156).

126. Bullinger, *Decades*, IV.viii (III, p. 301).

127. Musculus, *Commonplaces*, I (p. 16, col. 2)

Thus, the work of the Spirit, which he does by his own personal power, testifies to his divinity:

> if regeneration to incorruptible life is higher, and much more excellent than any present quickening, what must be thought of him by whose energy it is produced? Now, many passages of Scripture show that he is the author of regeneration, not by a borrowed, but by an intrinsic energy; and not only so, but that he is also the author of future immortality.[128]

For Calvin, Bullinger, and Vermigli, the divinity of the Holy Spirit is demonstrated not only by the nature and character of the gifts of the Spirit but also by the syntax of the biblical references to the gifts of the Spirit.

> This doth *Paul* show ... when it is said; *There be diversity of gifts, but one Spirit; diversity of operations, but one and the same God.* But to give gifts and spiritual faculties, is no whit less, than to distribute operations: wherefore, seeing the Holy Ghost is said to distribute gifts, and God to impart actions unto men, it is manifest that the Holy Ghost is God.[129]

Since, moreover, the apostle Paul not only states that the Spirit is the source of God's gifts but also that the Spirit distributes the gifts "even as he will" (1 Cor. 3:16), the Spirit has in himself "the sovereign choice ... to impart gifts," which is certainly the power of God alone. Vermigli also draws the conclusion that "if the Spirit be the author of graces, and the Father of operations; it is meet that the Holy Ghost should be equal to God the Father."[130] Calvin offers a similar argument from the same text:

> Particular attention is due to Paul's expression, that though there are diversities of gifts, "all these worketh that one and the self-same Spirit" (1 Cor. 12:11), he being not only the beginning or origin, but also the author; as is even more clearly expressed immediately after in these words "dividing to every man severally as he will." For were he not something subsisting in God, will and arbitrary disposal would never be ascribed to him. Most clearly, therefore does Paul ascribe divine power to the Spirit, and demonstrate that he dwells hypostatically in God.[131]

B. The Reformed Orthodox Approach to the Deity of the Spirit

1. The framework of argument. In arguments similar to those found in the works of Calvin, Vermigli, Bullinger, and other Reformers, the Reformed orthodox argue the divinity of the Spirit under five basic categories, reflecting closely the arguments for the divinity of Christ. Some writers present arguments for the *aseity* of the Spirit, paralleling those noted in the discussion of the deity of Christ.[132] More broadly, the Spirit is known to be a divine person 1) from the divine names given to him; 2) from

128. Calvin, *Institutes*, I.xiii.14.
129. Vermigli, *Commonplaces*, I.xii.8, citing 1 Cor. 12:4, 6.
130. Vermigli, *Commonplaces*, I.xii.8.
131. Calvin, *Institutes*, I.xiii.14.
132. E.g., Ainsworth, *Orthodox Foundation*, p. 14.

the divine attributes acknowledged to belong to him; 3) from the divine works he performs; 4) from the divine worship accorded to him; and 5) from his placement, at the same divine "rank and order," with the Father and the Son in statements concerning the Godhead.[133] Granting that the Spirit could be clearly distinguished as a "person" or subsistence distinct from the Father and the Son, the argument for the divinity of the Spirit as a divine person was of considerable importance to the theology of the orthodox inasmuch as various antitrinitarians, dissenting from Socinus, define the Spirit as a Person less than God himself — as "the chief of created Spirits, or the Head of the Angels." Owen and Ridgley cite the English Unitarian Biddle as an example of this doctrine.[134]

2. The divine names given to the Spirit. Although, as Witsius indicates, Scripture nowhere states simply and explicitly that "the Holy Spirit is the Most High God," it certainly offers clear attestation of the divinity of the Spirit when the hermeneutical step of comparing various passages is taken — for things are affirmed of the Holy Spirit in some passages that are predicated of God alone in other texts.[135] Specifically, there are passages in which the Spirit is clearly identified that parallel other passages in which the person spoken of is Jehovah himself, and there are other passages in which things are affirmed of the Spirit that either are elsewhere affirmed of Jehovah or can only be affirmed of Jehovah. In both instances, the necessary conclusion is that the person of the Spirit is fully divine.[136] (Given, moreover, that, in the order of argument, the Spirit has already been shown to be a person, these latter arguments cannot be directed toward the conclusion that the Spirit is merely a power of God.)

There are major arguments for the divinity of the Spirit by way of collation or comparison that are of interest hermeneutically, given that they illustrate the orthodox sense of the larger scope of Scripture and the mutually interpretive relationship of texts: Lev. 16:1-34 collated with Heb. 9:7-10; Lev. 26:11-13 collated with 1 Cor. 3:16; 6:19, and 2 Cor. 6:16; Ps. 95:7-11 collated with Isa. 63:10-11, 14; Deut. 9:24-25; 32:12; and Heb. 3:7; and Isa. 6:3, 9 collated with Acts 28:25-26.[137] The arguments, for the most part are quite simple: the passage cited from Leviticus 16 recounts the direct words of Jehovah to Moses and Aaron concerning the annual offering of sacrifices for sin before the altar of the Lord, specifically sacrifices for the atonement of sin made

---

133. Marckius, *Compendium theologiae*, V.xxvi; cf. Owen, *Brief Vindication of the Trinity*, in *Works*, vol. 2, pp. 401-3; Turretin, *Inst. theol. elencticae*, III.xxx.12-15; Pictet, *Theol. chr.*, II.xix.1; Witsius, *Exercitationes*, XXIII.xv; Wollebius, *Compendium*, I.ii (also cited in Heppe, *Reformed Dogmatics*, pp. 129-30). Marckius, Turretin, Pictet, Witsius, and Wollebius give the first four arguments; the fifth is added from Owen and from Witsius brief note at *Exercitationes*, XXIII.xxxiv. Also note Ursinus, *Commentary*, pp. 274-277.

134. Cf. Biddle, *Confession of Faith*, article VI with Owen, *Vindiciae Evangelicae*, in *Works*, vol. 12, particularly p. 334 and Ridgley, *Body of Divinity*, p. 118, col. 1-2.

135. Witsius, *Exercitationes*, XXIII.xvi.

136. Witsius, *Exercitationes*, XXIII.xvi.

137. Ursinus, *Commentary*, p. 277; Brakel, *Redelijke Godsdienst*, I.iv.28; Van der Kemp, *Christian Entirely the Property of Christ*, I, p. 405; Witsius, *Exercitationes*, XXIII.xvii-xviii; Turretin, *Inst. theol. elencticae*, III.xxx.12; Pictet, *Theol. chr.*, II.xix.2.

by the sprinkling of blood. There is no question that the speaker throughout the passage is God, quite specifically, Jehovah. Hebrews 9:7-10 refers directly to the passage in Leviticus, identifying the discourse concerning yearly blood sacrifice as a "figure" of the sacrifice of Christ, and stating that "the Holy Ghost thus signifying that the way into the holiest of all was not yet made manifest." Reformed exegetes concluded that the Holy Ghost, as "author of all the Mosaicall institutions," was also the speaker in the passage in Leviticus.[138] The Holy Ghost is, thus, Jehovah, and the text demonstrates that as "the institutor of all these worships," the Holy Ghost is "one true eternal God, with the Father and the Son, and yet a distinct person."[139]

The words of 2 Corinthians 6:16, "...ye are the temple of the living God; as God hath said, I will dwell in them, and walk in them: and I will be their God, and they shall be my people," are drawn in part from Leviticus 26:11-13 and in part from Ezekiel 37:27. The text from Leviticus is important to the argument because it yields the Holy Name of God: the divine speaker states, "I am Jehovah, your God"(v. 13) — and, therefore, the "living God" of 2 Cor. 6:16 who dwells in and walks with his people, making them his "temple" is Jehovah. But 1 Cor. 3:16, which also identifies believers as "the temple of God," states that it is the "Spirit of God" that dwells in them, while 1 Cor. 6:19 identifies the believer's body as "the temple of the Holy Ghost." Again, the conclusion, based on collation, is that Scripture identified the Holy Spirit as Jehovah.[140]

Psalm 95:1, 8-9, "O come, let us sing unto the Lord ... for the Lord is a great God," continues with the intercessory prayer, "harden not your heart ... as in the day of temptation in the wilderness: when your fathers tempted me." Witsius comments that "none will deny that he is the Supreme God" who utters these and the following words concerning himself.[141] This temptation, in turn, is identified in Isaiah 63:10 as a time in which Israel "rebelled, and vexed his Holy Spirit." Moreover, by way of citation in Hebrews 3:7-9, the apostle indicates to us that these words refer to the Holy Spirit, indeed, are his own words: "wherefore as the Holy Spirit saith ... harden not your hearts ... as in the day of temptation in the wilderness: when your fathers tempted me." Thus, the "God," identified as the "Lord" or "Jehovah" in Psalm 95 is shown to be the Holy Spirit.[142]

Similarly, in Isaiah 6:3, God is called the "Lord of Hosts," "Jehovah Sabaoth," and subsequently, in verses 8-9, the "voice of the Lord" tells Isaiah, "Go, and tell this people, Hear ye indeed, but understand not," while in Acts 28:25-26, the apostle Paul states, "Well spake the Holy Ghost by Esajas the prophet unto our fathers, Saying, Go unto this people, and say, Hearing ye shall hear, and shall not understand." The conclusion follows ineluctably:

---

138. Poole, *Commentary*, Heb. 9:8, in loc. (III, p. 847).
139. *Dutch Annotations*, Heb. 9:8, in loc.
140. Cf. Ursinus, *Commentary*, p. 277, with Turretin, *Inst. theol. elencticae*, III.xxx.12.
141. Witsius, *Exercitationes*, XXIII.xvii.
142. Witsius, *Exercitationes*, XXIII.xviii.

for in the Acts, Paul shows that Isaiah is speaking of the Holy Ghost, "Well spake the Holy Ghost by Esaias the prophet unto our fathers." But ... Isaiah is speaking of the supreme God.[143]

The Old Testament reference to Jehovah, collated with its citation in the New Testament, identifies the Holy Spirit as fully divine.[144] As in the case of all the arguments by collation of Old with New Testament texts, the fact that the Old Testament speaks of Jehovah and does not clearly identify the Holy Spirit, while the New Testament citation of the Old Testament identifies Jehovah in the person of the Holy Spirit, fits the general model of the Reformed hermeneutic of the Old and New Testaments — there is a single covenant of grace, a single promise of salvation, but a diversity of administrations and, in or through those administrations, a movement from promise to fulfillment. What is offered in types and shadows under the Old Testament is revealed with clarity under the New Testament.

The Socinian exegetes, who used the method of collation of texts and drawing conclusions when it suited them, branded this particular collation as "frivolous" and called into question this "kind of arguing" on the part of their "adversaries." Biddle comments that, by the same method, he might collate Exodus 32:11, where "the Lord" is said to have "brought forth" his people out of the land of Egypt, with verse 7 of the same chapter, where Moses is described by the Lord as the one who brought forth Israel out of Egypt, and conclude that Moses is the Lord! Or, again, in Isaiah 65:1, "the Lord" says "I am found of them that sought me not," while in Romans 10:20, the apostle Paul states that Isaiah was "very bold" to say "I was found of them that sought me not." From this collation, Biddle remarks, one would conclude that Isaiah was the Lord.[145]

The Reformed orthodox respond, in part, by showing that the collation of texts from the Old and New Testaments is not necessary to their argument, given that the New Testament, taken by itself, offers a clear testimony to the divinity of the Holy Spirit. The baptismal formula of Matthew 28:19 is the best example, but there are numerous other testimonies. Apart from the collation with texts from Leviticus, the Spirit is identified indirectly as "God" when believers are identified as the "temple of God" because the "Spirit of God" is said to dwell in them (1 Cor. 3:16). So too are believers called "the temple of the Holy Spirit" — and "a temple is the residence of God alone."[146] In Ridgley's view, the text indicates not only that the Spirit is fully divine but also that he is a distinct divine person.[147]

---

143. Pictet, Theol. chr., II.xix.2; cf. Brakel, Redelijke Godsdienst, I.iv.28; Van der Kemp, Christian Entirely the Property of Christ, I, p. 405; Turretin, Inst. theol. elencticae, III.xxx.12.

144. Brakel, Redelijke Godsdienst, I.iv.28; cf. Turretin, Inst. theol. elencticae, III.xxx.12.

145. Biddle, XII Arguments, p. 12.

146. Pictet, Theol. chr., II.xix.4; cf. Ridgley, Body of Divinity, p. 119, col. 1; Turretin, Inst. theol. elencticae, III.xxx.12.

147. Ridgley, Body of Divinity (1855), I, p. 232.

Similarly, the divinity of the Spirit (as well as the personality) can be shown from Acts 5:3-4: there, Witsius points out, "Ananias, whom Peter declares to have 'lied to the Holy Ghost' is said also to have 'lied unto God.'" The point of the text is to identify a sin against the Holy Ghost as a "most heinous sin" by indicating that a sin against the Holy Ghost is a sin against God. The Holy Spirit is, therefore, God — as Witsius points out, the argument of the apostle would not hold if the Spirit were not fully divine.[148] The continuity of exegetical argument is here at its clearest: the orthodox reproduce nearly verbatim the views of the Reformers.[149] In the orthodox discussions, however, there are a pair of objections to be dealt with, based on exegetical and philological considerations of the text raised by various Socinian adversaries.[150] In Biddle's view, the passage "neither expressly ... nor by good Consequence" can be read as identifying the Holy Spirit as God: the text contains a "metonymy of the adjunct" — "the Holy Spirit being put for Men endued with the Holy Spirit." This reading of the text, Biddle adds, is found even in an orthodox Reformed writer like Piscator. It therefore does not follow that "Ananias by lying to Men endued with the Holy Spirit ... lied not to Men, but to God," and, therefore, one cannot conclude that the Holy Spirit is God. A person may lie to God by lying to God's messengers, whether the apostles or the Spirit — but this is not ground for identifying the messengers as God. The text is in fact analogous to 1 Thessalonians 4:8, "he therefore that despiseth, despiseth not man, but God, who hath also given unto us his Holy Spirit" where neither the Holy Spirit nor the Apostles are identified with God, and the despising of God is inferred from the despising of his messengers.[151] As Nye put the argument,

'tis manifest, that those who despised the Apostles, are said to despise God, because God was in them by his Spirit: What hinders then, but for that same reason, those that lied to the Apostles, should be said and understood to lie to God?[152]

(Piscator would probably not have appreciated this use of his commentary — or, indeed, of the metonymy of the adjunct — given that his point was not Biddle's, namely, that by metonymy the Apostles, who were filled with the Spirit were to be understood by the reference to the Spirit, with the result that the text indicated only that Ananias had lied to the apostles. Rather, Piscator's point was that, by lying to the apostles, Ananias had in fact lied to the Spirit and that the author of the Acts used a metonymy of the adjunct to state that point directly.)[153]

Biddle and other Socinians offer a more pointed philological argument on the text of Acts 5:3-4: the phrases "to lie to the Spirit" and "to lie to God" are not equivalent

---

148. Witsius, *Exercitationes*, XXIII.xxi; cf. Pictet, *Theol. chr.*, II.xix.3; Ursinus, *Commentary*, p. 277; Ridgley, *Body of Divinity*, p. 119, col. 1; Brakel, *Redelijke Godsdienst*, I.iv.28; Van der Kemp, *Christian Entirely the Property of Christ*, I, p. 405.

149. Cf. Calvin, *Commentary on Acts*, 5:3 in loc. (CTS *Acts*, I, pp. 196-197).

150. Biddle, *XII Arguments*, pp. 9-10.

151. Biddle, *XII Arguments*, p. 9.

152. Nye, *Brief History*, p. 107.

153. Piscator, *Analysis Acta Apostolorum*, 5:3, scholia, in loc. (p. 56).

— in verse 3, the aorist infinitive ψεύσασθαί is followed by "Spirit" in the accusative
— whereas in verse 4, the aorist middle, second person singular ἐψεύσω is followed
by "God" in the dative. They argue that the first instance of the verb ought not to
be translated as "to lie to" but rather "to belie, pretend, or counterfeit," yielding the
sense that Ananias (v. 3) pretended to be moved by the Spirit and, in so doing, (v.
4) lied to the Apostles, the messengers of God, by implication, lying to God. This
reading, Biddle notes, was allowed by Erasmus, Calvin, and Aretius — he does not
note that Calvin preferred the traditional reading, "lied to the Holy Spirit."[154]

From Witsius' perspective, neither of these Socinian arguments is successful. It
is certainly true that the passage in 1 Thessalonians does not indicate that the Apostles
are God, but the point, much like that of the text in Acts 5, is that "contempt of the
discourses which the Apostles preached by the inspiration of the Spirit of God, recoils
upon God himself." Even so, in Acts 5:3-4, "the lie of Ananias, which he endeavored
to impose upon the Apostles, ultimately redounded against the Holy Spirit," who, "by
consequence" of the argument in the text, is known to be God.[155] Had Peter intended
to claim that the Holy Spirit, like the Apostles, was a messenger of God and that
Ananias lied to God by way of lying to the Apostles and by way of lying to their source
of inspiration, the Spirit, as if the Spirit were a "medium, or middle person, between
God and the Apostles," the text would have read "Thou hast not lied unto men, nor
unto the Holy Ghost, but unto God."[156] As for the philological argument of the
Socinians, Witsius indicates that this, too, is specious, given that ψεύσασθαι is used
"indiscriminately" in classical Greek with either the dative or the accusative and can
mean "to lie to" with its object in either case. He cites a series of examples.[157]

3. The divine attributes acknowledged to belong to the Spirit. Beyond these
texts, there is also the fact that Scripture consistently applies or attributes to the Spirit
a variety of things that can only be spoken of God: the Spirit is eternal, immense or
omnipresent, omnipotent, omniscient, immensely good and holy, immutable, and true.
The apostle teaches, for example, that "Christ through the eternal Spirit offered himself
up without spot unto God" (Heb. 9:14), a verse which is best explained as a reference
to the Spirit as distinct from Christ and, therefore, as the attribution of eternity to
the Holy Spirit.[158] Admittedly, the text could be taken as a reference to "Christ's eternal

---

154. Biddle, *XII Arguments*, p. 10; cf. Calvin, *Commentary on the Acts*, 5:3 (*CTS Acts*, I, pp. 196-
197); cf. similarly, Rudolph Gualther, *An Hundred, Threescore and Fiftene Homelyes or Sermons uppon
the Actes of the Apostles, written by Saint Luke* (London: Henrie Denham, 1572), 5:3-4 in loc. (pp.
231-232), noting two possible meanings for verse 3, namely, that Ananias "falsely fayned [that] he
was ledde by the holye ghost" or that he in fact lied to or "went about to beguyle the Church," both
of which demonstrate his evil and are to be considered lies to God, who searches all hearts.

155. Witsius, *Exercitationes*, XXIII.xxi.

156. Witsius, *Exercitationes*, XXIII.xxi; similarly, at length, Ridgley, *Body of Divinity* (1855), I, pp.
231-232.

157. Witsius, *Exercitationes*, XXIII.xxi; cf. Turretin, *Inst. theol. elencticae*, III.xxx.10.

158. Witsius, *Exercitationes*, XXIII.xxii; cf. Mastricht, *Theoretico-practica theol.*, II.xxvii.8; Van der
Kemp, *Christian Entirely the Property of Christ*, I, p. 405.

Godhead," as some exegetes had argued,[159] but in the view of many of the Reformed writers of the era of orthodoxy, the best construction of the passage identified the "eternal Spirit" as the Holy Spirit in his work of anointing Christ to the task of Mediator, in order that his "oblation" might be "without blemish."[160] Owen wrote at length on the passage, noting the variations in ancient texts and versions — with the Vulgate and some Greek codices reading "the Holy Spirit," but the Syriac and a majority of the best Greek codices reading "eternal Spirit." Still, he argued the coherence of both readings, given that "the Holy Spirit is no less an eternal Spirit than is the Deity of Christ Himself" and that "both these concurred in, and were absolutely necessary unto the offering of Christ."[161] Both readings, moreover, Owen writes, are "equally destructive" of Socinian theology, given that one established the deity of Christ, the other the deity of the Spirit.[162] (It is also worth noting here that the text-critical and exegetical detail of the commentaries together with the varied readings found in the theological systems of the era illustrates both the complex interrelation of biblical interpretation and theology in the seventeenth century and the fact that the writers of the day were not involved in a haphazard process of proof-texting.)

The eternity of the Spirit can also be inferred from his presence in the beginning of creation and from the fact that "God never has been without his Spirit."[163] In Genesis we read that the "Spirit of God moved upon the face of the waters" (1:2), while Job testified that God has "garnished the heavens" and has made human beings by his Spirit (Job 26:13; 33:4). In the case of the passage in Genesis, "spirit" cannot mean a wind, given that the air was not created "til the second day, when God made the firmament."[164] The eternity of the Spirit is demonstrated by these texts, inasmuch as "he who made the world and all finite things, wherewith time began, must have been before them, and consequently everlasting."[165]

The attribute of immensity or omnipresence attributed to the Spirit in the traditional exegesis of such texts as Psalm 139:7, "Wither shall I go from thy Spirit? or wither shall I flee from thy presence?" was also a matter of controversy.[166] Witsius adds to his argument the exegetical proposal of an anonymous Greek catena on the Psalter that the two parallel questions of the text indicated the Spirit and the Son, the Son being identified with the divine "presence." This reading, comments Witsius, is supported by the frequent reference to the Son as the "presence" of God in the Old

159. E.g., Poole, *Commentary*, Heb. 9:14 in loc.; *Dutch Annotations*, Heb. 9:14 in loc.

160. Ridgley, *Body of Divinity* (1855), I, p. 233.

161. Owen, *Exposition of Hebrews*, 9:13-14 in loc. (VI, pp. 303-304).

162. Owen, *Exposition of Hebrews*, 9:13-14 in loc. (VI, pp. 306).

163. Ursinus, *Commentary*, p. 274; Brakel, *Redelijke Godsdienst*, I.iv.28; Rijssen, *Summa theol.*, IV.xii, cont. II, arg. 2; also cf. Ridgley, *Body of Divinity*, pp. 192-201; Turretin, *Inst. theol. elencticae*, III.xxx.13.

164. Ridgley, *Body of Divinity* (1855), I, p. 234.

165. Ridgley, *Body of Divinity* (1855), I, p. 233.

166. Pictet, *Theol. chr.*, II.xix.6; Turretin, *Inst. theol. elencticae*, III.xxx.13; Mastricht, *Theoretico-practica theol.*, II.xxvii.8; Van der Kemp, *Christian Entirely the Property of Christ*, I, p. 405.

Testament: in Malachi the Lord says, "Behold I will send my messenger, and he shall prepare the way for my presence" (Mal. 3:1) — where the messenger is clearly John the Baptist, and John prepared the way for the revelation of the Son. So also, in Exodus, God promises to send his Angel before the Israelites to prepare their way to the Promised Land and he also says that his presence will go before them: in both cases, these are references to the work of the Son.[167] Given the reference to the Son and the identify of the Son as a person, it follows that "Spirit ought surely to be understood in a similar manner" — and that, therefore, the Psalm teaches "the immensity of the whole adorable Trinity, with regard to essence, knowledge, power, and effectual operation."[168]

Biddle in particular took umbrage at this doctrine and endeavored at length to argue against the traditional exegesis. From Biddle's perspective, the argument for omnipresence was a case of an unbiblical appeal to reason or philosophy from those who tended to decry reason as used by the Socinians and to demand unreasoned acceptance of the words of Scripture and of divine mysteries.[169] Scripture speaks of the Spirit being "sent down from heaven" (1 Pet. 1:12) and as "descending" in the form of a dove (Matt. 3:16): in both places, Biddle insists, the clear meaning of the text is that the Spirit moves from place to place and does not remain in heaven when sent to earth — a clear denial of omnipresence. As for the text in Matthew, Biddle insists, it does not say that the form or shape of the dove descended, "but the Spirit in the Shape."[170] From Biddle's perspective (as distinct from the more typical Socinian exegesis of the Spirit as a power of God) the biblical references to theophanies of the Spirit, used by the orthodox to identify the Spirit as personal, served also to identify the Spirit as a finite intermediary.[171]

In the orthodox view, Scripture teaches that the Spirit extends his influence everywhere and also that the Spirit dwells in all the children of God, something that would be impossible were the Spirit not capable of being everywhere; if, Brakel argues, "the Holy Spirit is everywhere in his Being, as the psalmist says, so must he be the true God" — precisely the logic attacked by Biddle as unbecoming those who consistently resort to claims of mystery.[172] In Biddle's view, the ability of the Spirit to "be in so many persons" is no different than the ability of Satan to threaten the salvation of so many Christians — and no one would claim that Satan, a finite spiritual being, was omnipresent. Such abilities refer not to essential omnipresence but to the exertion of power, in the case of the Spirit, to the bestowing of gifts and effects on

---

167. Witsius, *Exercitationes*, XXIII.xxiii; and see above 6.2 (C.4) on the exegesis of the "Angel of the Lord" passages.

168. Witsius, *Exercitationes*, XXIII.xxiii.

169. Biddle, *XII Arguments*, pp. 14-16.

170. Biddle, *XII Arguments*, pp. 14-15.

171. Biddle, *Confession of Faith*, VI, pp. 44, 56-58; cf. Biddle, *Letter written to Sir H. V.*, in *Faith of One God*, pp. 12-13.

172. Brakel, *Redelijke Godsdienst*, I.iv.29; cf. Ursinus, *Commentary*, p. 274, citing 1 Cor. 3:16; and note Biddle, *XII Arguments*, p. 14.

believers. For, Biddle comments, the Spirit is not omnipresent "in his Person or Substance, for then his Person or Substance would fill the World, and dwell in all Men a-like, whereas the indwelling of the Holy Spirit is by the Scripture made a peculiar Priviledg of the Saints."[173]

Turretin explicitly states the contrary point against the Socinians, namely, that such passages refer to "the presence of his essence and not only of his power, as was proved, above, in the question concerning the immensity of God."[174] The point is important on several counts — Turretin here offers an indication of the interrelationship of the discussions of the divine attributes and the Trinity, he confirms the significance of the discussion of the attributes as not merely a speculative exercise, and he indicates the extent to which fundamental soteriological questions, such as those raised by the Socinians, belong to the formulation of the doctrine of God.

The divine omnipotence belongs to the Spirit inasmuch as he "created and preserved all things in connection with the Father and the Son."[175] So also does the apostle attribute "the most sovereign will and omnipotent power" to the Spirit, inasmuch as the Spirit "works divine effects, and divides divine gifts, as he will, by his own power, and according to his own pleasure," as testified in 1 Cor. 12:11.[176] "It is now surely evident that [the Spirit] is the true God; for he who is not God cannot be eternal, omnipresent, all-knowing, ... and sovereignly mighty."[177] The Spirit is also directly identified in Scripture as "the power of the highest" (Luke. 1:35). One of the points to be noted is that this attribute is to be understood as not merely essential, but personal: the Spirit is not merely the essential power of God exercised, but is a divine person exercising his power.[178]

Omniscience can be inferred from 1 Corinthians 2:10-11, "the Spirit searcheth all things, yea, the deep things of God ... even so the things of God no man knoweth, but the Spirit of God." The text offers evidence that the Spirit has "a knowledge entirely divine" given that the text indicates 1) that "the Spirit of God knows 'all things' absolutely"; 2) that the Spirit knows "'the deep things of God,' the most hidden mysteries of [God's] essence and perfections, and the secrets of the divine counsels"; 3) "that he knows them exactly as if he had searched them with great care"; 4) "that he knows the most secret counsels of God as *his own counsels*, just as the mind of a man knows the things of a man"; and 5) "that all these are evidence of a knowledge

---

173. Biddle, *XII Arguments*, p. 16.

174. Turretin, *Inst. theol. elencticae*, III.xxx.13.

175. Ursinus, *Commentary*, p. 274.

176. Witsius, *Exercitationes*, XXIII.xxv, citing 1 Cor. 12:11; cf. Van der Kemp, *Christian Entirely the Property of Christ*, I, p. 406; Wollebius, *Compendium*, I.ii (in Heppe, *Reformed Dogmatics*, p. 129) and Henry, *Exposition*, 1 Cor. 12:11 in loc.

177. Van der Kemp, *Christian Entirely the Property of Christ*, I, p. 406; cf. Mastricht, *Theoretico-practica theol.*, II.xxvii.8.

178. Turretin, *Inst. theol. elencticae*, III.xxx.13.

entirely divine."[179] There is also a collateral argument based on 1 Corinthians 2:11. The text reads, "The things which be of man, no man knoweth, but the spirit of man which is in him; even so the things that be of God, none knoweth but the spirit of God." The parallel of the human spirit with the divine Spirit presses the argument that "just as the spirit which is in man is of the essence of man, so the Spirit which is in God is of the essence of God."[180] Similarly,

> This allusion seems to imply that the Holy Spirit is as much in God as a man's mind is in himself. Now the mind of the man is plainly essential to him. He cannot be without his mind. Nor can God be without his Spirit.[181]

Or, as the *Dutch Annotations* indicate, collating the text with other Scriptures, "for the Son knoweth the Father, and the Father the Son, Matt. 11:27; and here also the Holy Ghost, as one only God with the Father and the Son, Rom. 8:27, *knoweth that which is of God.*"[182]

Scripture teaches the immutability of the Holy Spirit in his counsel and promises: what the Spirit speaks will be fulfilled.[183] The Spirit is also immeasurably good, holy, and true, leading, as Ursinus remarks, to the "production of the same in creatures." Thus, the psalmist tells us that "the Spirit is good" and prays that the Spirit will "lead" him "into the land of uprightness" (Ps.143:10), and Paul indicates that the Spirit has the power by which we are justified (1 Cor. 6:11). As for the attribute of truth, the Spirit is identified as "the Spirit of truth" (John 15:26) and called "truth" itself (1 John 5:6).[184] The Spirit also has divine life, inasmuch as he is the one who vivifies our mortal bodies (1 Cor. 15:45; Rom. 8:11).[185]

So also, does the Spirit have "economic attributes" or relative attributes belonging specifically to his office: he is "holy," as his name itself indicates; "good" as taught in Psalm 143:10; a Spirit of "grace" (Heb. 10:29; Zech 12:10); powerful (Luke 1:35); and a Spirit of "glory," inasmuch as he is the one who leads the faithful to their eternal glory (1 Pet. 4:14).[186] In each case, these are attributes and/or powers that belong only to God.

4. The divine works performed by the Spirit. The Spirit performs specific works that can only be attributed to God, namely, creation, providence, regeneration, sanctification, and various miracles. Thus, Scripture ascribes to the Spirit the works

---

179. Witsius, *Exercitationes*, XXIII.xxiv; cf. Pictet, *Theol. chr.*, II.xix.6; Brakel, *Redelijke Godsdienst*, I.iv.29; Turretin, *Inst. theol. elencticae*, III.xxx.13; Mastricht, *Theoretico-practica theol.*, II.xxvii.8; Venema, *Inst. theol.*, xii (p. 241); Diodati, *Pious and Learned Annotations*, 1 Cor. 2:10 in loc.; Poole, *Commentary*, 1 Cor. 2:10 in loc.; Henry, *Exposition*, 1 Cor. 2:10 in loc.

180. Ursinus, *Commentary*, p. 273; cf. Poole, *Commentary*, 1 Cor. 2:11 in loc.

181. Henry, *Exposition*, 1 Cor. 2:11 in loc.

182. *Dutch Annotations*, 1 Cor. 2:11 in loc.

183. Ursinus, *Commentary*, p. 274, citing Acts 1:16.

184. Ursinus, *Commentary*, p. 274.

185. Turretin, *Inst. theol. elencticae*, III.xxx.13.

186. Mastricht, *Theoretico-practica theol.*, II.xxvii.15.

of God: creation (Job 26:13; Psalm 33:6), the preservation and sustenance of the created order (Gen. 1:2; Zech. 4:6).[187] The "brooding" or "hovering" over the deep attributed to the Spirit in Genesis 1:2 is variously explained by the Reformed orthodox. Witsius argues that this is the creative power being exercised on unformed matter, whereas Wollebius holds that this is the providential preservation of the world as initially created out of nothing — yielding a providential aspect to the creative work of the Spirit.[188]

Following the *Statenvertaling* annotations, Witsius argues that the metaphor in Genesis 1:2 of the Spirit moving or hovering over the face of the waters

> is taken from birds, which brood upon their nests, and hatch their young by the genial heat they communicate. The Spirit of God thus brooded on the shapeless mass, and by his influence rendered it productive of so vast a multitude of beautiful creatures.[189]

Witsius points out that this interpretation is not only justified by a collation with Deuteronomy 32:11, where similar language described the nesting mother eagle, but also by various Jewish exegetes. He adds, echoing the arguments of various philosophers and historians of the era, that all ancient wisdom was rooted in the contact of ancient peoples with Israel, that "the symbolical theology of the Egyptians, which represents the world as coming from God, like an egg, perhaps took its rise from this metaphor.[190] The basic exegetical point is replicated in numerous exegetical works of the era which interpret the Spirit's "brooding" as a metaphorical expression drawn from the image of birds hatching eggs — thus, the Spirit "quickens and disposes" the unfinished matter of the world "to the production" of the manifold things of the world order.[191] Wollebius had the strong precedent of Calvin's exegesis for his interpretation,[192] nor were the two readings mutually exclusive:

> He became to that rude dead mass, a quickening, comforting Spirit. He kept it together which else would have shattered. And so he doth still, or else all would soon fall asunder (Heb. 1:3; Ps. 104:29), were not his conserving mercy still over, or upon, all his works (Ps. 145:9).[193]

---

187. Leigh, *Treatise*, II.xvi (p. 136); Brakel, *Redelijke Godsdienst*, I.iv.30; cf. Turretin, *Inst. theol. elencticae*, III.xxx.14.

188. Cf. Witsius, *Exercitationes*, XXIII.xxv, with Wollebius, *Compendium*, I.ii (in Heppe, *Reformed Dogmatics*, p. 129).

189. Witsius, *Exercitationes*, XXIII.xxv; cf. *Dutch Annotations*, Gen. 1:2 in loc.; Mastricht, *Theoretico-practica theol.*, II.xxvii.9, 11.

190. Witsius, *Exercitationes*, XXIII.xxv; cf. Gale, *Court of the Gentiles*, I, III.ii.7, for various classical parallels to Gen. 1:2.

191. Poole, *Commentary*, Gen. 1:2 in loc.; cf. Ainsworth, *Pentateuch*, Gen. 1:2 in loc.; Henry, *Exposition*, Gen. 1:2 in loc.

192. Calvin, *Commentary on Genesis*, Gen. 1:2 (*CTS Genesis*, I, p. 73-4).

193. Trapp, *Commentary*, Gen. 1:2 in loc. (I, p. 3).

Other texts, such as Psalm 104:29-30, also indicate the office of the Spirit in the conservation and government of the world.[194]

Similarly, Scripture attributes other "divine works" to the Spirit, such as "the *conception of Christ* (Luke 1:35), the *working of miracles* (Matt. 12:28; 1 Cor. 12:4-5), the *governing of the church*, and *the sending of ministers* (Acts 13:2; 20:28)." The working of miracles is of particular importance, given the orthodox assumption, based on Psalm 72:18 ("Praised be the Lord God, the God of Israel, which alone doth wonders"), that only God can perform miracles. The apostle writes of "mighty signs, and wonders," performed "by the power of the Spirit of God" (Rom. 15:19; cf. 1 Cor. 12:9, 10) and Christ himself testified that he performed miracles by the power of the Spirit (Matt. 12:28). Thus, the Holy Spirit must truly be God.[195] The Spirit, moreover, is the one who anoints Christ to his work as Mediator, which is clearly a divine work.[196]

The Spirit is the one who accomplishes the redemption, illumination, and sanctification of believers, and the resurrection of the flesh (1 Cor. 2:10 and Rom. 8:11).[197] The Spirit also distributes graces "according to his pleasure" (1 Cor. 12:4, 11), instructed the prophets (2 Pet. 1:21), and called or made apostles (Acts 13:2; 20:28).[198] The Spirit is termed "the Spirit of truth" (John 14:26), "the Spirit of Adoption" (Rom. 8:15), "the Spirit of sanctification" (Rom. 1:4), and "the Spirit of renewing" (Titus 3:5).[199] In such passages, the Spirit is identified as the active effector of regeneration, adoption, and sanctification, not merely as the instrument by which these blessings are accomplished. Indeed, sanctification is attributed both to the Spirit and to the Word, but in different respects, inasmuch as "the moral efficacy of the word depends entirely on the supernatural and efficacious operation of the Spirit" — "the Spirit is joined with the Word, and yet distinguished from the word."[200]

5. The divine honor and worship accorded to the Spirit. Both Scripture and the church's tradition indicate that the Spirit is to be honored and worshiped as divine. We are enjoined by Scripture to "worship the Holy Ghost, as the source of all blessings" and taught also that we must worship only the Lord God.[201] Brakel makes the point a matter of logical argument: the one

> in whose name we ought to be baptized, from whom we ought to beseech all gifts, whom we must obey, he is the true God. But we must needs be baptized in the name of the

---

194. Turretin, *Inst. theol. elencticae*, III.xxx.14.

195. Witsius, *Exercitationes*, XXIII.xxviii; cf. Amyraut, *De mysterio trinitatis*, V, pp. 310-311 Mastricht, *Theoretico-practica theol.*, II.xxvii.9.

196. Mastricht, *Theoretico-practica theol.*, II.xxvii.9, citing Isa. 61:1 and Luke 4:18.

197. Pictet, *Theol. chr.*, II.xix.6; Rijssen, *Summa theol.*, IV.xii, cont. II, arg. 2 & 3; Witsius, *Exercitationes*, XXIII.xxvi-xxviii; Brakel, *Redelijke Godsdienst*, I.iv.30; Leigh, *Treatise*, II.xvi (p. 136).

198. Leigh, *Treatise*, II.xvi (p. 136).

199. Leigh, *Treatise*, II.xvi (p. 136).

200. Witsius, *Exercitationes*, XXIII.xxvii.

201. Van der Kemp, *Christian Entirely the Property of Christ*, I, p. 406; cf. Pictet, *Theol. chr.*, II.xix.7; Rijssen, *Summa theol.*, IV.xii, cont. II, arg. 2 & 3.

Holy Spirit, and from him must all gifts be sought: therefore the Holy Spirit is the true God.[202]

He then lines out each part of the argument biblically. That we must be baptized in the name of the Spirit is clear from the baptismal formula itself, that we baptize "in the name of the Father, and of the Son, and of the Holy Spirit." Baptism expresses our covenant with the three persons of the Trinity and explicitly refers to all three persons because "the Father works through the Son and the Holy Spirit in the faithful" and indicates that "the Holy Spirit is granted the same dignity as the Father and the Son: thus the Holy Spirit is the same God with the Father and the Son."[203] Even so, the spirit is the source of God's gifts to us and ought to be petitioned — and that the Spirit should be served is clear from the biblical warnings that we ought not to sin against the Spirit or vex the Spirit as the Israelites did.[204] Turretin adds that the Apostle's Creed accords equality in reverence to the Father, the Son, and the Spirit and that "the early church always invoked him" in its hymns, notably, the *Gloria* and the *Veni, Creator Spiritus*.[205]

"Add to this that we are consecrated as a *Temple* to the Holy Spirit ... 'Know ye not that your body is the temple of the Holy Spirit, which is in you.'"[206] Scripture here also identifies the Spirit as an object of worship — one to whom a temple may be rightly consecrated — and, therefore, as divine. There is, moreover, no force in the objection, leveled by Socinians and others, that the believer is only called a "temple" metaphorically for, as Witsius comments, "the analogy must be preserved" even in the metaphor.[207] As Augustine commented, if it is sacrilege to build a temple to a creature, how much more sacrilegious would it be to identify ourselves as temples of one who is not God![208]

Witsius offers another argument, based on the collation of texts: the Gospel of Matthew enjoins believers, "Pray ye therefore the Lord of the harvest, that he will send forth laborers into his harvest" (Matt. 9:38). Acts 13:2 offers an "instance of the precept," the sending forth of laborers into the divine harvest: "As they ministered to the Lord and fasted, the Holy Ghost said, Separate me Barnabas and Saul for the work whereunto I have called them." The conclusion is that the Spirit is the Lord of the harvest and the divine object of "religious adoration."[209] A similar reverencing

---

202. Brakel, *Redelijke Godsdienst*, I.iv.31.

203. Brakel, *Redelijke Godsdienst*, I.iv.31; cf. Turretin, *Inst. theol. elencticae*, III.xxx.15; Witsius, *Exercitationes*, XXIII.xxxi.

204. Brakel, *Redelijke Godsdienst*, I.iv.31.

205. Turretin, *Inst. theol. elencticae*, III.xxx.15.

206. Witsius, *Exercitationes*, XXIII.xxxii, citing 1 Cor. 3:16; 6:19; cf. Poole, *Commentary*, 1 Cor. 3:16, in loc., "from this text may be fetched an evident proof of the Divine nature of the Third Person in the blessed Trinity."

207. Witsius, *Exercitationes*, XXIII.xxxii.

208. Augustine, *Collatio cum Maximo*, as cited in Turretin, *Inst. theol. elencticae*. III.xxx.12 (cf. *PL* 42, col. 722).

209. Witsius, *Exercitationes*, XXIII.xxix; cf. Pictet, *Theol. chr.*, II.xix.6.

of the Spirit with the Father and the Son is found in the Pauline benediction of 2 Corinthians 13:14, where divine communication or communion is promised from the Spirit.[210]

Witsius also argues the divinity of the Spirit from the salutation to the seven churches of Asia found in the Apocalypse, a point that we have already noted in passing in the discussion of trinitarian exegesis of Revelation 1:4.[211] The text reads, "John to the seven churches which are in Asia: Grace be unto you, and peace, from him which is, and which was, and which is to come; and from the seven Spirits which are before his throne." Testimony to the divinity of the Holy Spirit arises from the passage once it is shown "what the seven Spirits denote" and "in what manner John calls upon them."[212] The "seven Spirits" are not created spirits, but the Holy Spirit, the "third person of the Godhead," as is evident both from the symbolic language of the text and from other usages throughout the Apocalypse. "The number seven is a symbol of multitude and of perfection" just as the grace of the Holy Spirit is "most abundant and most perfect."[213] This interpretation coheres with the imagery in the Apocalypse of "the golden candlestick with its seven lamps in the tabernacle of Moses" as implied in the reference to "seven lamps of fire burning before the throne, which are the seven Spirits of God" (Rev. 4:5) — the tabernacle, Witsius continues, was a symbol of the church and the golden candlestick a symbol of the Holy Spirit, who illuminates the church. The candlestick "though one in itself, had seven distinct lamps" which belong to the candlestick and proceed from it, symbolizing the multitude of graces that belong essentially to the Spirit and that proceed from him in his work.[214] This reading of the symbolic language is born out by the text itself: the seven Spirits are called "the Spirit of God" (Rev. 4:5), and they are placed (Rev. 1:4-5) between the Father and the Son "as of the same dignity." So also is the Holy Spirit identified as the seven horns and seven eyes of the Lamb (Rev. 5:6). Nor does the Apocalypse speak of these seven Spirits as worshiping God, although it does say this of the "living creatures" and the "elders" before the throne. Rather, these Spirits are invoked by John in the same breath that he invokes the Father and the Son.[215]

Finally, there is the issue of the obedience that is due to the Holy Spirit. Witsius returns to the text of Hebrews 3:7-12 —

Wherefore (as the Holy Ghost saith, To day if ye will hear his voice, Harden not your hearts, as in the provocation, in the day of temptation in the wilderness: When your fathers tempted me, proved me, and saw my works forty years. Wherefore I was grieved

---

210. Witsius, *Exercitationes*, XXIII.xxx.

211. See above, 4.2 (C.4).

212. Witsius, *Exercitationes*, XXIII.xxx; cf. Turretin, *Inst. theol. elencticae*, III.xxx.15.

213. Witsius, *Exercitationes*, XXIII.xxx; cf. Junius, *Exposition of the Apocalyps*, 1:4 in loc.; Gill, *Exposition of Revelation*, 1:4, in loc.

214. Witsius, *Exercitationes*, XXIII.xxx.

215. Witsius, *Exercitationes*, XXIII.xxx; cf. Junius, *Exposition of the Apocalyps*, 1:4 in loc. on the reading of the seven horns and seven eyes of Rev. 5:6; also note Turretin, *Inst. theol. elencticae*, III.xxx.15.

with that generation, and said, They do always err in their heart; and they have not known my ways. So I swear in my wrath, They shall not enter into my rest.) Take heed, brethren, lest there be in any of you an evil heart of unbelief, in departing from the living God.

The text, which had been referenced earlier, in conjunction with Isaiah 63:10 and Psalm 95:1, 8-9, as showing by necessary conclusions that the Holy Spirit is God, can also be used as an independent basis for arguing the divinity of the Spirit: here, "the Spirit of God was justly offended, because that sacred obedience which was an honor due to his Majesty, had not been rendered to him."[216] Similarly, Scripture speaks of the "sin against the Holy Spirit" as a sin "so heinous in the sight of God" that it is unpardonable: if the Spirit were not God, Witsius argues, how could a sin against him be of such magnitude? Indeed, once this proof is noted, one might ask whether the Spirit ranks higher as God than either the Father or the Son, given that sins against them can be forgiven! The resolution of the problem, however, lies not in a difference in rank or status, given that the "infinity of the Godhead excludes all disparity" among the persons, but in the fact that the Spirit is the one who works redemption and who bestows the grace without which there can be no salvation: the rejection of the Spirit places a person outside of his work.[217] Turretin adds that blasphemy is, quite specifically and restrictively, a sin against God — and Scripture specifies that there is a blasphemy against the Holy Spirit, distinct from blasphemies against the Father or the Son. Thus, the Spirit must be a distinct divine person.[218]

6. The placement of the Spirit at the same divine "rank and order," with the Father and the Son. The Spirit is identified as equal in divine rank and essential (as distinct from personal) order with the Father and the Son in such places as the baptismal formula of Matthew 28:19 and the apostolic benediction of 2 Corinthians 13:14. Scripture would not place "the name of a mere power or virtue" on an equal level with the Father and the Son.[219] Nor could we "grieve the Spirit" (Eph. 4:30) or sin against the Holy Ghost (Matt. 12:31-32) if he were not a person, indeed, a divine person.[220] 1 Cor. 12:4ff. distinguishes between the Spirit and the gifts or operations of the Spirit just as it distinguishes between God and his operations or the Lord and his ministrations (vv. 5 and 6);

> to which we may add those passages, in which the Spirit is represented as descending in the shape of a dove, or of divided tongues. For only persons, and not virtues or accidents, can assume visible appearances or forms of this kind. We conclude, therefore, that the Holy Spirit is a person subsisting distinctly from the Father and the Son.[221]

---

216. Witsius, *Exercitationes*, XXIII.xxxiii.
217. Witsius, *Exercitationes*, XXIII.xxxiii.
218. Turretin, *Inst. theol. elencticae*, III.xxx.9.
219. Pictet, *Theol. chr.*, II.xviii.1; cf. Rijssen, *Summa theol.*, IV.xii, cont. I, arg. 1; Turretin, *Inst. theol. elencticae*, III.xxx.7.
220. Pictet, *Theol. chr.*, II.xviii.1; cf. Rijssen, *Summa theol.*, IV.xii, cont. I, arg. 1.
221. Pictet, *Theol. chr.*, II.xviii.1; Rijssen, *Summa theol.*, IV.xii, controversia 1, arg. 4.

As a fourth argument Pictet returned to the baptismal formula of Matthew 28:19 —

> for not only does this passage prove the Spirit to be a person, but also a divine person. For he, in whose name we are baptized, is considered as the author of the covenant of grace, who has authority to institute sacraments for the sealing of that covenant; who can promise and give grace; and whom those that are admitted into the covenant are bound to worship and serve; none of which can be said of any created thing.[222]

The baptismal formula also demonstrates the equality in power and authority of Father, Son, and Spirit — particularly inasmuch as it indicates that the ratification of the "ceremony" is referred to the persons as distinct, accomplished by "each one by the special property of its operation."[223]

Nor do the various objections to the deity of the Spirit hold. For example, some object that the Spirit cannot be truly God because he is called "the Spirit of God" — but surely this is said of the Spirit just as it is said of the Son that he is the Son of God: that is, it is spoken of God *personaliter* as Father. The similar objection that the Spirit is called the "finger of God" (Luke 11:20) is solved by recognizing that "the finger of God" denotes not the Spirit but "the finger of the Spirit," which is to say, the power of the Spirit.[224] From John 7:39 it is argued that the Spirit was not in existence prior to the glorification of Christ: but the text is not stated absolutely, of the existence of the Spirit, but only of the gift of the Spirit.[225]

7.4 Operations of the Spirit *Ad intra* and *Ad extra*

A. The *Ad intra* Operation or "Procession" of the Spirit

1. *Processio* or ἐκπόρευσις defined. Once the full divinity and independent subsistence of the Spirit have been acknowledged, the procession of the Spirit becomes the crucial point of differentiation between the Spirit and the other persons of the Trinity. Vermigli writes, "And that this third person proceedeth from the Father and the Son, it is evident enough in the same Gospel of *John*, where it is written; *When the Comforter shall come, whom I will send unto you: even the Spirit of truth, which proceedeth from the Father.*"[226]

The incommunicable property of the Holy Ghost is his "proceeding," which neither the Scriptures nor the church can precisely distinguish from "begetting." Still, the term "procession" is to be accepted and to be understood as specific to the Spirit: just as "generation" or "begetting" is argued of the Son, so is "procession" argued of the Spirit — nor is the meaning of the term "procession" to be taken in the broadest sense, of having "origin from some one" or as coming forth from some one, given that in this

---

222. Pictet, *Theol. chr.*, II.xix.5.
223. Cf. Diodati, *Pious and Learned Annotations*, Matt. 28:19 in loc., with Rijssen, *Summa. theol.*, IV.xii, cont. I, arg. 3; cont. II, arg. 6, citing also 2 Cor. 13:13 and 1 John 5:7.
224. Rijssen, *Summa theol.*, IV.xii, cont. II, obj. 1 & 2 & resp.
225. Rijssen, *Summa theol.*, IV.xii, cont. II, obj. 3.
226. Vermigli, *Commonplaces*, I.xii.7, citing John 14:26; 16:13; 15:26.

sense the term might as well be applied to the Son (cf. John 16:28; Mic. 5:2). Rather it is to be understood strictly as denoting "an emanation from the Father and the Son, distinct from the generation of the Son."[227] This distinct emanation of the Holy Ghost corresponds, moreover, to his "proper manner of working [which] is, to finish an action, effecting it, as from the Father and the Son."[228] As far as this "manner of working" is a description of the divine economy, it must be further clarified by the dictum that all works of God *ad extra* are performed "out of his divine essence" and "are common to the Trinity, the peculiar manner of working always reserved to every person."[229]

Turretin notes that the debate of his time does not concern the latter point, the "temporal and external procession," but only the "eternal and internal procession" — not the *ad extra* activity according to which the divine work, appropriated to the Spirit, terminates on God's creatures, but the *ad intra* activity that is "terminated inwardly," namely, the "mode of communication of the divine essence ... by which the third person of the Trinity has from the Father and the Son the same numerical essence which the Father and the Son have."[230]

Given the fact that the Spirit is a different person from the Son, it is clear that his procession must differ from the generation of the Son: were the emanations identical, the persons would be also, but the Spirit and the Son are "different persons who stand related to each other in origin" from the Father.[231] The Reformed orthodox, however, typically take the path of the later fathers as opposed to that of the medieval scholastics: they recognize that there is a difference but refrain from speculation concerning the nature of the difference between the procession of the Spirit and the generation of the Son. They also cite both Augustine and John of Damascus to this effect.[232]

The sending of the Spirit is not a sign of his inferiority to the Father and the Son: his being sent is not a matter of being ordered, but by his consent and, even so, it indicates a "diversity of work, but not of essence." Similarly, the statement that "the Spirit searcheth ... the deep things of God" (1 Cor. 2:10) does not imply a subordination of the Spirit, as is seen when the text is conferred with Romans 8:27, "he that searcheth the hearts knoweth what is the mind of the Spirit": as Rijssen points out, searching does not mean "investigation," implying lack of knowledge and discursive thinking, but an "intimate penetration."[233] Nor does Romans 8:26, where the Spirit is said to pray for us, make the Spirit subordinate as a mediator between men and God, for the Spirit does "not pray for us as Christ, the mediator, did, presenting to the heavenly Father his merits, but the Spirit prays in our place and in us, raising up our infirmities when we are unable to pray."[234]

---

227. Turretin, *Inst. theol. elencticae*, III.xxxi.1.
228. Perkins, *Golden Chaine*, V (p. 15, col. 1).
229. Perkins, *Golden Chaine*, VI (p. 15, col. 1).
230. Turretin, *Inst. theol. elencticae*, III.xxxi.2.
231. Turretin, *Inst. theol. elencticae*, III.xxxi.3.
232. Turretin, *Inst. theol. elencticae*, III.xxxi.3; see further below 7.4 (A.3).
233. Rijssen, *Summa theol.*, IV.xii, cont. II, obj. 4 & 5 & resp.
234. Rijssen, *Summa theol.*, IV.xii, cont. II, obj. 6 & resp.

2. The demonstration of the *filioque*: "double procession." The traditionally Western trinitarian concept of the double procession of the Holy Spirit was consistently upheld by the Reformers and argued with some vigor against the Greek Orthodox view. The Reformed exegetes, moreover, understood the issue to be one of exegesis, not merely an issue of the form of the Niceno-Constantinopolitan Creed, and found the biblical text to be entirely of one accord in favor of double procession. Vermigli writes, with reference to John 15:26,

> Seeing the Son saith, that he will send the Spirit, and (as we said before) affirmeth him to receive of his; no man doubteth, but that he proceedeth from the Son. And now he expressly addeth; *Who proceedeth from the Father.*[235]

Calvin took the point with equal seriousness, noting in his commentary on the same text,

> When he says that he will send him from the Father, and, again, that *he proceedeth from the Father*, he does so in order to increase the weight of his authority; for the testimony of *the Spirit* would not be sufficient against attacks so powerful, and against efforts so numerous and fierce, if we were not convinced that he *proceedeth from God*. So then it is Christ who sends the Spirit, but it is from the heavenly glory, that we may know that it is not a gift of men, but a sure pledge of Divine grace. Hence it appears how idle was the subtlety of the Greeks, when they argued, on the ground of these words, that the Spirit does not *proceed* from the Son; for here Christ, according to his custom, mentions the Father in order to raise our eyes to the contemplation of his Divinity.[236]

As in Vermigli's comment, Calvin's analysis of the text assumes the sending of the Spirit by Christ and therefore the procession of the Spirit from the Son and views the further statement of the Gospel that the Spirit proceeds from the Father not restrictively but as an expansion of the meaning to include the Father.

Calvin rather emphatically takes the words "he proceeds from the Father" as an indication of the authority of the Spirit, not of the sole origin of his eternal procession: Christ here sends the Spirit, but manifests the Spirit as a "sure pledge of divine grace." It is, he concludes, an "idle subtlety of the Greeks" to claim this text as warrant for their denial of double procession.[237] Calvin points out in his comment on Romans 8:9,

> But let readers observe here, that the Spirit is, without any distinction, called sometimes the Spirit of God the Father, and sometimes the Spirit of Christ; and thus called, not only because his whole fulness was poured on Christ as our Mediator and head, so that from him a portion might descend on each of us, but also because he is equally the

---

235. Vermigli, *Commonplaces*, I.xii.7, citing John 14:26; 16:13; 15:26.

236. Calvin, *Commentary on John*, 15:26 (CTS *John*, II, p. 131).

237. Calvin, *Commentary on John*, 15:26 (CTS *John*, II, p. 131); cf. Second Helvetic Confession, III.4 (Schaff, *Creeds*, III, p. 241).

Spirit of the Father and of the Son, who have one essence, and the same eternal divinity.[238]

The orthodox follow the Reformers in upholding the Western doctrine of the *filioque*. The orthodox Reformed writers not only argue the Augustinian doctrine of double procession they insist on it as a biblical point held over against the teachings of the Greek Orthodox:

> The property of the Son in respect of the Holy Ghost is to send him out, John 15:26. Hence arose the Schism between the Western and the Eastern Churches, they affirming the procession from the Father and the Son, these from the Father alone.[239]

Among the Reformed orthodox theologians, Pictet notes the clear distinction of persons in John 15:26:

> Here the Comforter, or Spirit, is plainly distinct from the Father and the Son. Again, they are so distinguished, that some things are said of the Father which cannot be said of the Son, and some things of the Son which are no where said of the Spirit. The Father is said *to have begotten* the Son ... the Spirit is said to *proceed* from the Father, and to be *sent* by the Son; but nowhere is the Father said to proceed from nor the Son to be sent by the Spirit. Yet are these persons distinct in such a manner, that they are not three Gods but one God; for the scripture everywhere proves and reason confirms, the unity of the Godhead.[240]

Similar statements are found among the Reformed exegetes of the era. Poole notes that the text has been read variously: some exegetes understand the Spirit's procession from the Father merely as his coming forth or being poured out at Pentecost, whereas others — "the generality of the best interpreters" — understand the text as a reference to "the Holy Spirit's eternal proceeding."[241] Owen, by way of contrast, argues the primary meaning of the text to be that the Spirit "goeth forth or proceedeth" in order to "put into execution" the salvific counsel of God in the application of grace and views the immanent procession of the Spirit as a secondary meaning, a conclusion to be drawn from the text.[242]

As Pictet notes, the Reformed orthodox uniformly follow the Western doctrine:

> That the Spirit proceeds *from the Son*, is proved by those passages in which he is represented as being sent no less by the Son than by the Father; nor is he any less the Spirit of the Son than of the Father: Rom. 8:9, "any one who does not have the Spirit of Christ..."; Gal. 4:6, "God has sent the Spirit of his Son into our hearts"; John 16:7,

---

238. Calvin, *Commentary on Romans*, 8:9 (*CTS Romans*, p. 290).

239. Leigh, *Treatise*, II.xvi (p. 138); Downame, *Summe*, i (p. 35).

240. Pictet, *Theol. chr.*, II.ix (p. 99); cf. Rijssen, *Summa*, IV.ix, cont. 1, arg. 4 (N.T.); and note Westminster Confession, II.iii.

241. Poole, *Commentary*, John 15:26 in loc. (III, p. 362): among those who can be included here are Grotius, *Annotationes in Novum Testamentum*, in loc.

242. Owen, *ΠΝΕΥΜΑΤΟΛΟΓΙΑ*, I.v, in *Works*, III, p. 117.

"If I do not go away, Comforter will not come to you, but if I go, I will send him to you."[243]

Nor is this a minor point in theology that can be dismissed:

> To deny the procession of the Holy Ghost from the Son, is a grievous error of Divinity, and would have grated the foundation, if the Greek Church had so denied the procession of the Holy Ghost from the Son, as that they had made an inequality between the Persons. But since their form of speech is, *that the Holy Ghost proceedeth from the Father by the Son, and is the Spirit of the Son*, without making any difference in the consubstantiality of the Persons it is a true though erroneous Church in this particular; divers learned men think that *à Filio & per Filium* in the sense of the Greek Church, was but a question *in modo loquendi*, in manner of speech, and not fundamental.[244]

The problem of the *filioque* was, therefore, not something that the Reformed orthodox could ignore: they refused to go so far as to claim that the Greek church was a false church, but they still insisted that it ensconced an error in its doctrinal explanations of the creed.

From the Reformed perspective, moreover, the Greek critique of the *filioque*, that it implied two ultimate *principia* or *archai* in the Godhead, did not hold — for there could only be two *archai* if the Father and the Son separately and equally were the sources of the Spirit's procession. The orthodox conception of the *filioque*, however, insisted on the unity of the act of the Father and the Son, so that the Holy Spirit proceeds from Father and Son by "one and the same breathing" and does so from both equally, the Father and the Son acting in communion with one another. Thus, the Holy Ghost, the third person, proceeds from the Father and the Son: "and albeit the Father and the Son are distinct persons, yet they are both but one beginning of the holy Ghost."[245] At the same time, following the Western pattern, the Reformed orthodox insisted on the begetting of the Son as placing the Son second in order, thus maintaining the Father as ultimate source of the personal distinctions and the Father and the Son together as the source of the Spirit.[246]

Thus, when addressing the question of the procession of the Spirit, Owen indicates that the "fountain" or "source" of the Spirit's procession is the Father, as indicated by John 15:26. There is, moreover, he adds, a "twofold *ekporeusis* or 'procession' of the Spirit: 1. *physike* or *hypostatike*, in respect substance and personality; 2. *oikonomike* or dispensatory, in respect of the work of grace."[247] The hypostatic procession, furthermore, must be understood in terms of the *filioque*: "he is the Spirit of the Father and the Son, proceeding from both eternally, so receiving his substance and personality." Once stated, however, the point cannot, indeed, may not be elaborated,

---

243. Pictet, *Theol. chr.*, II.xx.3.
244. Leigh, *Treatise*, II.xvi (p. 138).
245. Perkins, *Golden Chaine*, V (p. 15, col. 1); cf. Amyraut, *De mysteria trin.*, VII (p. 533).
246. Rijssen, *Summa theol.*, IV.xiii.
247. Owen, *Communion with the Holy Ghost*, in *Works*, II, p. 226.

but rather accepted as "the bare acquiescence of faith in the mystery revealed."[248] It is only of the economic procession of the Spirit *ad extra* in the work of grace that Owen feels capable of speaking.

3. Procession and the scholastic tradition: Reformed reservations. The distinction between procession and begetting is also clear, albeit indefinable by finite creatures:

> That procession may be distinguished from generation can be demonstrated from the fact that the Holy Spirit is always said to proceed from, and never to have been begotten by, the Father; nor is he ever called *the image* of God — but we must not curiously inquire into the nature of the difference. Let us guard against the unbridled and unsuccessful boldness of the schoolmen, who attempt to explain it: *I certainly do not grasp the distinction between generation and procession, I am not desirous of this, nor am I able.*[249]

The usual unwillingness of the Protestant scholastics to enter into a lengthy discussion of the way in which the emanations of the second and third persons of the Trinity differ represents a rather significant example of the difference between medieval and Protestant scholasticism: the Protestants revert to the caveat of Gregory of Nazianzen against excessive inquiry into the mystery and emulate the Reformers in their somewhat reserved acceptance of the tradition without further explanation. The extensive and frequently cogent speculation of the medieval doctors concerning the relation of the emanations to the divine nature, intellect, and will (itself an extension of the Augustinian metaphors) is simply ignored by most of the Reformed orthodox. Keckermann's early orthodox discussion of the procession of the Spirit as a volitional act of love in the Godhead, framed as part of a logical argument for the Trinity as three modes of existing in the one God, is quite unique in the era of orthodoxy.[250]

A few writers note the problem and reflect on the medieval solutions, some with a high degree of distaste for the Augustinian metaphors and for speculative elaboration of the doctrine.[251] Thus, Turretin, Heidegger, Pictet, and Rijssen indicate that the procession of the Spirit denotes a relation to the other persons of the Godhead different from the relation of the Son to the Father by generation. Both comment that what this difference is remains a mystery — we cannot explain it nor ought we to inquire into it as did the medieval scholastics. Turretin and Rijssen note, without any angry polemic, that the scholastics compared the operations of intellect and will to generation and procession, as if the Son, the Wisdom of God, were generated in an intellective manner (*per modum intellectus*) and the Spirit, identified with the divine love, proceeded in a volitional manner (*per modum voluntatis*). These arguments were posed, however, he continues, without the express corroboration of Scripture — and they serve to

---

248. Owen, *Communion with the Holy Ghost*, in *Works*, II, p. 227.
249. Pictet, *Theol. chr.*, II.xx.4; cf. Rijssen, *Summa theol.*, IV.xiii.
250. Keckermann, *Systema theologiae*, I.iii (pp. 28-33); see further, above, 3.1 (C.3).
251. Heidegger, *Corpus theol.*, IV.4; cf. the partial citation in Heppe, *Reformed Dogmatics*, p. 130.

confuse even as they attempt to explain.[252] Heidegger similarly rejects these distinctions as *alogon*, having no basis in Scripture or reason: after all, he notes, the correct doctrine of the divine attributes understands them as equally belonging to each of the persons, so that the *intellectus Dei* cannot pertain differently to the Father and the Son or the *voluntas Dei* differently by the Father and the Spirit.[253] The relative gentleness of the criticism derives, perhaps, from Rijssen's, Heidegger's, and Turretin's recognition that some of their Reformed predecessors had adopted the medieval solutions on this point.

Still, it is clear that the Spirit is different from the Son, related to the Son in origin, but a distinct person. It is also permissible to note three grounds of this distinction: first, *in principio* or foundation, for the Son emanates from the Father alone, the Spirit from both the Father and the Son. Thus, the Father alone is the *principium* of the Son, whereas the Father and the Son together are the *principium* of the Spirit. Second, *in modo*, since "the way of generation" terminates not only in the *personalitas* of the Son but also in a "similitude," according to which the Son is called "the image of the Father" and according to which "the Son receives the property of communicating the same essence to another person." In contrast, the Spirit "does not receive the property of communicating that essence to another person," inasmuch as "the way of spiration" terminates "only in the *personalitas*" of the Spirit and not in a similitude of the Father.[254] Third, there is a difference *in ordine* according to "our mode of perception," insofar as the generation of the Son is somehow prior to the operation or procession of the Spirit, although, of course, the persons are coeternal — the spiration or procession of the Spirit presumes the generation of the Son, given the procession of the Spirit from the Son as well as from the Father.[255]

Whereas most of the orthodox follow this line of argument and define the procession of the Spirit as a "spiration," which is to say analogically, a "breathing forth," some of the later writers, perhaps because of the confusion of "spirit" and "thought" in debates over Cartesianism, find the usage less than satisfactory, despite the patristic and medieval precedent: "Some think he is so called, because he proceeds from God in a way of *breathing*, but this is to explain what is obscure by what is still more obscure,"[256] or, in the words of another later orthodox writer, if "spiration" is a "mere metaphorical expression," it is unsuitable to the identification of distinct subsistence or personhood. "Since we are much in the dark about this mode of speaking, it would be better to lay it aside, as many modern writers have done."[257]

Ridgley notes that "some" have "pretended" to define the difference between the generation of the Son and the procession of the Spirit as identified by the power to communicate essence — a power communicated by the Father to the Son, but not

---

252. Rijssen, *Summa theol.*, IV.xiv; identically, Turretin, *Inst. theol. elencticae*, III.xxxi.3; cf. Marckius, *Compendium*, V.xii.

253. Heidegger, *Corpus theol.*, IV.4.

254. Rijssen, *Summa theol.*, IV.xiv; Turretin, *Inst. theol. elencticae*, III.xxxi.3.

255. Rijssen, *Summa theol.*, IV.xiv; Turretin, *Inst. theol. elencticae*, III.xxxi.3.

256. Pictet, *Theol. chr.*, II.xx.5.

257. Ridgley, *Body of Divinity* (1855), I, p. 157.

communicated by the Father and the Son to the Spirit. The Spirit, therefore, does not have a power "to communicate the divine essence to any other as a fourth Person in the Godhead." For Ridgley, this is an excessive speculation into an "unsearchable mystery."[258] All that can be said is that the various biblical texts that refer to the relationship of the Spirit to the Father and the Son "evince the truth" of the "communication of his divine essence or, at least, his personality, and that his being 'sent by the Son,' implies that this communication is from him as well as from the Father" — and, in Ridgley's view, the question remains as to whether the biblical texts refer to an *ad intra* procession or merely to an *ad extra* sending.[259]

B. The *Ad extra* "Sending" and the Office of the Spirit

1. The "sending" of the Spirit. The *ad intra* procession of the Spirit is mirrored and followed by the *ad extra* procession or "mission" of the Spirit. Indeed, the *ad intra* procession, or, in Greek, ἐκπόρευσις, of the Spirit takes its name from the identification of the Spirit as "sent" or "sent forth" (John 15:26). The commentators often indicate, moreover, that the Johannine text can be subject to two interpretations.

> What proceeding from the Father is here meant, is questioned among the divines: some understand it only of his coming out from the Father, and being poured out upon the disciples in the days of Pentecost: others understand it of the Holy Spirit's eternal proceeding.[260]

In any case, the term "procession" or sending is drawn from this text as descriptive both of the eternal, *ad intra* life and of the temporal, *ad extra* activity of the Spirit. Of course, whatever the interpretation of this particular text, the *ad extra* sending or procession of the Spirit was never in question: it is clearly taught in John 14:26, "the Comforter, which is the Holy Ghost, whom the Father will send in my name"; Joel 2:28-29, as cited in Acts 2:16-17, "It shall come to pass in the last days, saith God, I will pour out my Spirit upon all flesh"; Luke 24:49, "behold I send the promise of my Father upon you" (usually interpreted as referring to the Spirit at Pentecost, given Acts 1:4 and 2:33); and Galatians 4:6, "God hath sent forth the Spirit of his Son into your hearts."[261]

This outward sending of the Spirit, moreover, observes the pattern described in general in the discussion of works of the Godhead *ad extra*: there is an undivided work of the Godhead in which the persons have "appropriate" tasks, manifesting not only the unity of God's work but the distinction of persons and the exercise of their personal

---

258. Ridgley, *Body of Divinity* (1855), I, p. 158.

259. Ridgley, *Body of Divinity* (1855), I, pp. 166-167, citing Owen, *Vindiciae evangelicae*, in *Works*, XII, p. 342.

260. Poole, *Commentary*, John 15:26 in loc. (III, p. 362); cf. Calvin, *Commentary on John*, 15:26 (CTS *John*, II, p. 131) who here understands the eternal procession.

261. Cf. Goodwin, *Work of the Holy Ghost*, I.ii (pp. 8-9); Owen, *ΠΝΕΥΜΑΤΟΛΟΓΙΑ*, I.v (pp. 110-111).

properties.[262] In the case of the Spirit, as in the earthly work of Christ, these tasks can be distinguished into the "ordinary" and the "extraordinary," namely, the work that the Spirit performs broadly and generally, according to the general biblical revelation of his proper work, and discrete works, particularly miracles, that are performed but once for a very specific purpose. In no case ought the Spirit to be regarded as a mere instrument of God, as an "instrumental cause" or a "servant," but rather as one working together with the Father and the Son, without any inferiority of station.[263]

In the controversies of the seventeenth century, argument over the sending of the Spirit proceeded in several directions. Among the Socinians, Biddle understood John 15:26 and related texts not only as an *ad extra* description of the divine mandate to the Spirit; he also argued that they disproved the omnipresence of the Spirit, given that "sending" refers to a movement from place to place.[264] Nye, who held the more usual Socinian doctrine of the Spirit, focused his reading of the text on the Spirit as testifying or witnessing, and, as he had argued of John 16:13, where the "Spirit of Truth" is promised as the apostles' guide "into all truth," he claimed that John 15:26 identifies the Spirit not as a divine person but as the power or inspiration of God.[265]

Against the more typical Socinian argument, the Reformed emphasize the "sending" of the Spirit: the language applies to a person, not to a power or an inspiration. As noted above of the person of the Spirit, in such biblical passages as Matthew 3:16, Luke 3:22, and John 1:32, the descent of the Spirit in the form of a dove indicates his independent subsistence, as do the powers attributed to him: one who *has* subsistence, understanding, will, and power is not a mere power or inspiration, but a person.[266] Against arguments like those of Biddle, Reformed orthodox writers insisted that care should be taken so as not to use the language of procession or sending *ad extra* in such a way as to imply either a local motion of the Spirit or a change in the Godhead. When the Spirit is identified as "sent," this ought to be understood as God's "eternal will and decree to accomplish something by the ... Holy Ghost, and of the execution and manifestation of his will through the working of the ... Holy Ghost."[267] Thus the sending of the Spirit on Pentecost does not indicate the absence of the omnipresent Spirit before Pentecost: the Spirit is understood as "sent into the world, not because [he] began to exist where [he] did not exist before; but because [he] accomplished in the world what was the will of the Father, and showed [himself] present and efficacious according to the will of the Father."[268]

2. The "office" of the Spirit. This sending of the Spirit points directly toward what can be called the *officium oeconomicum*, the office or work of the Spirit in the economy

---

262. Beza et al., *Propositions and Principles*, IV.iv.
263. Beza et al., *Propositions and Principles*, IV.v-vi.
264. Biddle, *XII Arguments*, p. 31.
265. Nye, *Brief History of the Unitarians*, p. 101.
266. Owen, *ΠΝΕΥΜΑΤΟΛΟΓΙΑ*, I.iii (pp. 74-75, 77-78, 80-81).
267. Ursinus, *Commentary*, p. 137.
268. Ursinus, *Commentary*, p. 137.

or administration of the world order and, especially, of salvation.[269] As indicated previously in discussion the identification of the third person of the Trinity as "Spirit," he is, as Spirit in the personal sense, the "immediate agent of divine works," the person "through whom the Father and Son immediately influence the hearts of the elect."[270] The Spirit is both the *emissarius Trinitatis* and the *advocatus Trinitatis* in the fulfillment of the decree, the former in the work of creation, the latter in the work of salvation: for the Father "delineates" or "designates" the work; the Son, in his office, "obtains" or "accomplishes" the objective result; the Spirit "completes" or "finishes" the work.[271]

The "office" or "work" of the Holy Spirit, then, follows from this definition of the Spirit's relation to the Father and the Son and from the nature of the work performed through him: in creation, the Spirit is said to brood or hover over the waters (Gen. 1:2) in the same terms that a hen is said to gather and protect her chicks (Deut. 32:11) — as, in the same sense, the Spirit is called the "finger of God" (Luke 11:20) and the "power of God" (Luke 1:35; Rom. 15:13) or the one who works miracles (Matt. 12:28), all of which identify him as the "emissary of the Trinity," perfecting and completing the work that he shares with the Father and the Son.[272]

The Spirit is also called the "paraclete" — manifesting him as *advocatus Trinitatis* in the work of perfecting the salvation of human beings, again, completing what the Father designs and the Son accomplishes objectively.[273] In the work of salvation,

> the office of the Holy Ghost is to produce sanctification in the people of God. This he performs immediately from the Father and the Son. It is for this reason that he is called the Spirit of holiness. The office of the Holy Ghost may be said to embrace the following things: to instruct, to regenerate, to unite to Christ and God, to rule, to comfort and strengthen us.[274]

To this definition, it may be objected that all of the works performed belong to the Father and the Son and, therefore, do not constitute a distinct office in any way specific to the Spirit. The office of the Spirit appears, however, in the distinction of the manner of working — for in all of these activities, although they are included in the willing and effecting of the work or gift, the Father and the Son do not work immediately, but through the Spirit, while the Spirit works immediately in believers. Thus, there is a distinct office that belongs to the immediate agent of the work.[275] In the words of Goodwin,

> whereas both God and Christ, those other two persons, are also in Scripture said to be in us, and to dwell in us, yet this indwelling is more special, and *immediationi suppositi*, attributed to the Holy ghost; which, as it serves to give an honor peculiar to him, so

---

269. Mastricht, *Theoretico-practica theol.*, II.xxvii.11.
270. Ursinus, *Commentary*, p. 271.
271. Mastricht, *Theoretico-practica theol.*, II.xxvii.11.
272. Mastricht, *Theoretico-practica theol.*, II.xxvii.11.
273. Mastricht, *Theoretico-practica theol.*, II.xxvii.11.
274. Ursinus, *Commentary*, p. 277; cf. Beza et al., *Propositions and Principles*, IV.vii.
275. Ursinus, *Commentary*, p. 279.

when set in such a comparison, even with them, must be meant and understood of this person immediately, and not by his graces only. Yes, the other two persons are said to dwell in us, and the Godhead itself, because the Holy Ghost dwells in us, he being the person that makes entry, and takes possession first, in the name and for the use of the other two, and bringeth them in.[276]

The Spirit specifically performs the work of God among human beings, leading them toward faith in Christ the Mediator, thereby confirming with sanctification what the Father decrees and the Son has accomplished. In this context, the Spirit is said to teach (John 14:26), to send forth the teachers of the church (Acts 13:2), to give them the requisite gifts (Acts 2:4), to inspire the authors of Scripture (2 Pet. 1:21), and in all this, to be the "Spirit of truth" (John 14:17).[277]

---

276. Goodwin, *Work of the Holy Ghost*, in *Works*, VI, p. 64.
277. Mastricht, *Theoretico-practica theol.*, II.xxvii.12.

8

Conclusion: The Character of Reformed Orthodoxy

8.1 The Problem of Continuity in the Protestant Theological Tradition

A. The Historical Assessment of Reformed Orthodoxy

1. Patterns and paradigms of analysis. At the outset of the first volume of this study, some attention was given to the various paradigms that have been used to understand the development of post-Reformation Reformed theology.[1] Both in the course of this study and in the work of other historians written during the course of the last several decades, the problems inherent in those paradigms have become clearer — and, arguably, the burden of proof as to the nature and character of the developing Protestant tradition has shifted from the shoulders of reappraisal to the back of the older theories.[2] In other words, it is the hypothesis of a radical discontinuity between Reformation and orthodoxy, of a christocentric Calvin against a "Bezan" predestinarian metaphysic, of a "biblical humanism" against "Aristotelian scholasticism," or of a "dynamic" preaching of reform against a "cold rationalism" that has little scholarly support and even less documentary evidence behind it.

---

1. See *PRRD*, I, 2.5-2.6; cf. the somewhat differently focused discussion in Muller, *Christ and the Decree*, pp. 1-13.

2. Martin I. Klauber, "Continuity and Discontinuity in Post-Reformation Reformed Theology: An Evaluation of the Muller Thesis," in *Journal of the Evangelical Theological Society*, 33 (1990), pp. 467-475; Willem J. van Asselt, "Protestantse scholastiek: Methodologische kwesties bij de bestudering van haar ontwikkeling," in *Tijdschrift voor Nederlandse Kerkgeschiedenis*, 4/3 (Sept. 2001), pp. 64-69; Willem J. Van Asselt, P. L. Rouwendal, et al., *Inleiding in de Gereformeerde Scholastiek* (Zoetermeer: Boekencentrum, 1998), pp. 18-28; *Protestant Scholasticism*, ed. Trueman and Clark, pp. 11-19; and *Reformation and Scholasticism*, ed. Van Asselt and Dekker, pp. 11-43.

Given both the variety within the older paradigms and the shifts in emphasis that have occurred during the course of the current reappraisal of the materials, some review is in order. First, from the perspective of the concentrated interest of the older scholarship on the Reformed doctrine of predestination, at least two readings of the material can be identified. An earlier model, associated with the work of Alexander Schweizer, Heinrich Heppe, Paul Althaus, Hans Emil Weber, and Ernst Bizer, saw predestination (whether for good or for ill) as the central pivot of Reformed thought from the Reformation onward and that, accordingly, argued the development of a largely deductive, synthetic theology among the Reformed, based on the central predestinarian focus of Calvin. A more recent approach has taken the predestinarian central-dogma model of Schweizer and the others as a correct reading of the later Reformed, but as incorrect for Calvin, and has argued that the development of a predestinarian model, now seen as characteristic of the later Reformed, arose because of the rise of an Aristotelian scholasticism within the Reformed faith, as engineered by Theodore Beza. In this understanding, the later theology represents a "distortion" of Calvin's thought, grounded in a recrudescence of things medieval (notably, scholasticism, Aristotelianism, and dogmatism) and a loss of Calvin's more humanistic and exegetical approach.

Characteristic of both these approaches is their fundamentally dogmatic interest and their concentration on particular dogmatic readings of the thought of Calvin as a legitimate beginning point for the Reformed tradition. Neither approach typically looks to Calvin as a second-generation codifier of a reform movement — and neither approach typically sets Calvin into the historical context of his predecessors and contemporaries in order to analyze his theology. Perhaps even more importantly, neither approach has paid particular attention to the medieval and Renaissance background of the Reformation as a broader historical context for understanding the thought both of the Reformers and of their "orthodox" or "scholastic" successors. There is, of course, in some of the versions of this older approach, an appeal to Calvin as biblical or even christocentric "humanist" over against his successors as dogmatic, predestinarian, and "scholastic,"[3] but this is much less an appeal to historical trajectories of logic, rhetoric, method, doctrine, and doctrinal emphases that carry through the era of the Reformation into the era of orthodoxy than it is an appeal to purportedly mutually exclusive camps or categories of thought that enables proponents of the older approach to pose neat oppositions between persons — for example, Calvin the humanist, Beza the scholastic.

At the heart of the older paradigms is the assumption that the development of Reformed thought was largely the logical or organic development of doctrinal or what might be called (in the case of the "humanist" motif) ideological foci. Such approaches are often characterized by stark dichotomies — humanist versus scholastic; Calvin versus the Calvinists — and by overly simplistic and often value-laden accounts of historical development. By way of illustration of the latter problem, Calvin's thought,

---

3. See the critique of this view in David C. Steinmetz, "The Scholastic Calvin," in *Protestant Scholasticism*, ed. Trueman and Clark, pp. 16-30.

read out of its historical context, becomes the index for assessing the theological value of the thought of a later Reformed writer: the later thinker is praised for identity of expression or for the fuller realization of something implicit in Calvin or, alternatively, condemned as a deviant for not mimicking the Reformer.

Both versions of these dogmatic-development theories, moreover, have had highly presentized dogmatic motivations and results. In the approach that argued the organic development of a predestinarian focus of Calvin's thought toward the full realization of a theology focused on the central motif of God's determination of all things, the end product of the development is a Schleiermacherian theology. In the approach that offered a humanistic, christocentric Calvin clearly set apart from an increasingly scholastic, rationalistic, and predestinarian orthodoxy, the proposed end product of a doctrinal return to Calvin's Reformation has often been neoorthodoxy. Of course, a neoorthodox Calvin stands in discontinuity with later sixteenth-century and with seventeenth-century Reformed thought: but the neoorthodox Calvin also stands in discontinuity with the historical Calvin. Calvin's thought differed from that of the seventeenth-century Reformed — as it did from the thought of his Reformed contemporaries — but the large dogmatic categories used by the older scholarship do not offer an adequate analysis of those differences (or, indeed, of the continuities that also exist). A proper analysis of the relationship of Reformation and orthodoxy entails reading the thought of Calvin and other Reformers in its sixteenth-century context and then tracing out the ongoing dialogue that accompanied the entry of Reformed thought into various later sixteenth- and seventeenth-century contexts. In short, such an analysis entails setting aside the agendas of neoorthodox and other dogmatically laden historiographies as intellectually bankrupt.[4]

In an era such as ours, at the beginning of the twenty-first century, when the discipline of intellectual history has been roundly critiqued by social historians for its tendency to trace out ideas apart from a clear grasp of the historical context out of which those ideas have arisen, the methodological problems inherent in the older approaches ought to be self-evident. Hopefully, the scholastic maxim still holds: *abusus non tollit usum*. Scholars of intellectual history have in fact critiqued their own discipline and provided methodological foundations for moving it forward, often with recognition of the advances made by social historians.[5] Conversely, many social historians have recognized that the documents, contextually understood, do not permit an easy distinction between popular religion and a doctrinal theology of the elite,[6] and that the documents, whether popular or technical, demand a religious reading and not a sociological or ideological reinterpretation.[7] And to the present point, without a

---

4. Cf. the discussion in Muller, *Unaccommodated Calvin*, pp. 3-14, 188.

5. E.g., Quentin Skinner, "Meaning and Understanding in the History of Ideas," in *History and Theory*, 8 (1969), pp. 3-53.

6. Cf. Thomas Lambert, "Daily Religion in Early Reformed Geneva," in *Institut d'Histoire de la Réformation: Bulletin Annuel*, 21 (1999-2000), pp. 33-54.

7. Thus, e.g., Brad S. Gregory, *Salvation at Stake: Christian Martyrdom in Early Modern Europe* (Cambridge, Mass.: Harvard University Press, 1999), note particularly pp. 99-105.

reasonably rigorous reconstruction of the intellectual history of the Reformation and Protestant orthodoxy, a reconstruction conscious of the need to set the doctrines into their proper historical context, the dogmatic reading of the Reformation for the sake of modern theological projects is freed of critique and bidden *bon voyage* on its deconstructionist tour of the past. Some distinction must be made between the historically contexualized discussion of theological ideas and the dogmatic reading of the Reformation.[8]

An intellectual history of Protestantism must, among other things, contextualize Calvin — not only socially, politically, and culturally, but also intellectually. Calvin's thought (and, similarly, the thought of a myriad of Reformation-era and later Protestant writers) must be read in the context of his contemporaries, not in the context of a later era, whether seventeenth, nineteenth, twentieth, or twenty-first century. The history of Reformed thought, then, needs to be read forward, not backward, and read as the history of a tradition that is represented by a wide variety of writers in a series of diverse historical contexts. The context of ideas ought to be addressed from at least two perspectives — first, the perspective of the broad similarities of expression shared by diverse thinkers at various times and in various historical contexts; second, that of the peculiarities of the forms of expression found in the writings of specific individuals. In the first instance, the context is traditionary, belonging to trajectories of theology, philosophy, exegesis, rhetoric, academic, or what might be called parish culture. In the second instance, the context is the immediate intellectual, social, political, or cultural circumstance of the writer. From the former, the study of Reformed thought draws much of its sense of the continuities between Reformation and orthodoxy as well as a sense of broadly cultural developmental changes, including large-scale discontinuities that become visible over the course, not of years, but of decades. From the latter, the study gains both a sense of particularized discontinuities and a sense of the more inclusive character of the tradition, given the coexistence of the various forms of expression within ecclesial or confessional boundaries.

Given this more contextualized approach, study of the course and varieties of Reformed thought from the Reformation into the era of orthodoxy recognizes, among other things, that the dogmatic questions of nineteenth- and twentieth-century theologians are rarely answered in the materials of the sixteenth and seventeenth centuries and are certainly never answered in nineteenth- and twentieth-century terms. It has taken several decades of work in reappraisal first to discern and then to jettison those questions — and then to refocus inquiry with the assumption that the theological issues raised in those materials are rooted in trajectories of debate that run through the later Middle Ages and Renaissance into the eras of the Reformation and of orthodoxy and that were modified and reread in particularized sixteenth- and seventeenth-century contexts.

The arguments found in various essays in reappraisal to the effect that "continuities and discontinuities" must be examined, whether between the Middle Ages or

---

8. Cf. Muller, *Unaccommodated Calvin*, pp. 3-17, 185-188.

Renaissance and the Reformation, or between the Reformation and post-Reformation eras are usually efforts to deal with both the trajectories of thought and the particularities of specific contexts. Reference to continuity and discontinuity as an issue, therefore, indicates the understanding of the reappraisal that examination of the historical materials must not continue to oblige the dogmatic standard, that continuity is demonstrated by mimicry and discontinuity by any change: just as the Reformation produced theological definitions and arguments that differed from those of the later Middle Ages, so did the rise of Protestant orthodoxy produce theological formulae and methods that differed from those of the Reformers. Let it be said (as if the foregoing volumes did not demonstrate it!), that Reformed orthodoxy was, in many ways, different from the Reformation. But let it also be said (again, as demonstrated in the foregoing volumes) that difference does not necessarily indicate discontinuity. It may only indicate development and adaptation in a new context, whether chronologically, geographically, or socioculturally defined.

2. Reforming and the Reformed: trajectories from the later Middle Ages to the close of the era of orthodoxy. Students of the Reformation have learned, from several generations of scholars in the second half of the twentieth century, that the Reformation cannot be understood apart from an examination of its intellectual and spiritual roots in the later Middle Ages and Renaissance. These roots, moreover, have been shown to be positive as well as negative, with the result that the Reformation of the sixteenth century is now recognized as standing on major trajectories of theological, exegetical, linguistic, and pedagogical development that run with remarkable continuity from the medieval through the early modern era.[9] This scholarly revision has resulted in a far more nuanced understanding of the continuities and discontinuities between the Reformation and the preceding eras, as well as a

---

9. Cf. e.g., Heiko A. Oberman, *The Harvest of Medieval Theology: Gabriel Biel and Late Medieval Nominalism*, rev. ed. (Grand Rapids: Eerdmans, 1967); idem, *Masters of the Reformation: Emergence of a New Intellectual Climate in Europe*, trans. Dennis Martin (Cambridge: Cambridge University Press, 1981); idem, *The Dawn of the Reformation: Essays in Late Medieval and Early Reformation Thought* (Edinburgh: T. & T. Clark, 1986); idem, *The Reformation: Roots and Ramifications*, trans. Andrew C. Gow (Grand Rapids: Eerdmans, 1994); Stephen Ozment, ed., *The Reformation in Medieval Perspective* (Chicago: University of Chicago Press, 1971); Stephen Ozment, *The Age of Reform, 1250-1550: An Intellectual and Religious History of Late Medieval and Reformation Europe* (New Haven and London: Yale University Press, 1980); idem, "Luther and the Late Middle Ages: The Formation of Reformation Thought," in *Transition and Revolution: Problems and Issues of European Renaissance and Reformation History*, ed. Robert M. Kingdon (Minneapolis: Burgess, 1974), pp. 109-129; Lewis W. Spitz, *The Religious Renaissance of the German Humanists* (Cambridge, Mass.: Harvard University Press, 1963); idem, *The Renaissance and Reformation Movements*, rev. ed., 2 vols. (St. Louis: Concordia, 1987); idem, *Luther and German Humanism* (Brookfield, Vt.: Ashgate-Variorum, 1996); idem, *The Reformation: Education and History* (Brookfield, Vt.: Ashgate-Variorum, 1997); David C. Steinmetz, *Luther and Staupitz: An Essay in the Intellectual Origins of the Protestant Reformation* (Durham: Duke University Press, 1980); idem, *Calvin in Context* (Oxford and New York: Oxford University Press, 1995). Also note E. M. W. Tillyard, *The Elizabethan World Picture* (New York: Vintage, 1942), pp. 3-8.

fundamentally altered perspective on the so-called medieval "forerunners" of the Reformation. In Heiko Oberman's words,

> Forerunners of the Reformation are ... not primarily to be regarded as individual thinkers who express particular ideas which "point beyond" themselves to a century to come, but participants in an ongoing dialogue — not necessarily friendly — that is continued in the sixteenth century. It is then not the identity of the answers but the similarity of the questions which makes the categorizing of Forerunners valid and necessary. ... the idea of a limited number of theologians foreshadowing Luther's theological ideas is abandoned in favor of the concept of a history of the confrontation of a series of central ideas as the common point of reference....[10]

Oberman's understanding of this crucial issue does not necessarily remove such famous names as Wyclif, Hus, and Savonarola from the list of forerunners — rather it removes the traditional reasons for their inclusion, and it adds a host of other thinkers, such as Thomas Bradwardine, Gregory of Rimini, Wessel Gansfort, Rudolf Agricola, who were not notable for their attempts to reform ecclesiastical abuses or for their condemnations, whether of or by, the medieval papacy.[11]

If acknowledgment of the medieval roots of the Reformation yields a clearer picture of the fundamental continuity of the Reformers with the earlier tradition — their fundamental catholicity! — and of their unique or individual contributions to the history of Christianity, so also does the application of a similar method and perspective to the development of Protestantism yield a clearer picture of the fundamental continuity of the late Reformation, the so-called Second Reformation and the era of Protestant orthodoxy, with the preceding eras, both later Middle Ages and Reformation, and of the differences between Protestant thought in the era of orthodoxy and the time of the Reformers. The methodological point, drawn from Oberman's comment is simple: in moving from the Reformation into the era of orthodoxy and Protestant scholasticism the historians task is not to determine continuity on the basis of an exact "identity of the answers" given by theologians, but on the basis of "the similarity of the questions" within a developing tradition. Identification of "participants in an ongoing dialogue — not necessarily friendly" — becomes the primary feature of the analysis rather than an attempt to find "a limited number of theologians" whose teachings are precisely foreshadowed by a Luther or a Calvin or, indeed, by a Thomas Aquinas or a Duns Scotus.

3. Reformed orthodoxy in its confessional breadth and theological diversity: restating issues of continuity and discontinuity. The Reformed orthodox prolegomena and *principia*, the theological *loci* in which the definition of theology, together with such topics as natural and supernatural revelation, the relation of theology to

---

10. Heiko A. Oberman, *Forerunners of the Reformation* (New York: Holt, Rinehart & Winston, 1966), pp. 42-43.

11. For the older approach, see, e.g., Herbert B. Workman, *The Dawn of the Reformation*, 2 vols. (London: Charles Kelley, 1901-2); Philip Schaff, *History of the Christian Church*, 3rd ed., revised, 8 vols. (New York: Scribners, 1910; reprint, Grand Rapids: Eerdmans, 1976), VI, pp. 314-399.

philosophy, and the concept of fundamental doctrines, and the doctrines of Scripture and God as the fundamental or foundational topics in Christian theology, provide, of course, only a partial index to the character of Reformed orthodoxy. As indicated, moreover, in the introductory chapters to each of these subjects, the trajectories of different arguments and different topics as they move from the late medieval period into the era of the Reformation and of Protestant orthodoxy witness rather different aspects of the problem of intellectual continuity and discontinuity.

The basic point made in the introduction to volume 1, concerning the international and the relative confessional breadth of the Reformed development has been documented at some length throughout the study, albeit not noted repeatedly.[12] Suffice it to say by way of conclusion that the apparatus of all four volumes has consistently cited British, Dutch, Swiss, German, and French Reformed, federalist and non-federalist, Salmurian and anti-Salmurian, and so forth. Connections between the British divines and their continental counterparts have been identified as has, by way of cross-citation of sources, the general agreement of the British divines with their orthodox continental counterparts. Perhaps more interestingly, the perspectives shared by the various trajectories within orthodoxy, including the federalist and the Salmurian, on the definition and meaning of theology, the authority and interpretation of Scripture, and the divine essence, attributes, and Trinity have been noted. Thus, neither confessionally nor on the particulars of prolegomenal and principial matters can a rigid contrast of "Salmurian" and "orthodox" or "federalist" and "orthodox" theology be maintained — and, by extension, the claim of a "rigid orthodoxy," made (ironically) by modern theological students of hypothetical universalism and federalism at the expense of the identification of the Salmurian and federalist theologians as "orthodox," must also be jettisoned.

One of the lessons learned in the examination of these trajectories is certainly that there is often as much difference between contemporary formulators on a particular point as there is between earlier and later formulators of the same point. In the concrete, this observation undercuts the entire methodology of the "Calvin against the Calvinists" approach to the development and history of Reformed orthodoxy. The "Calvin against the Calvinists" model, like the older identification of rebellious and persecuted teachers of the Middle Ages as forerunners of the Reformation, rests on untenable premises and asks an ill-framed and unsuitable question. Marking out Calvin as the norm for the Reformed theology of the Reformation era (to the exclusion of Bucer, Bullinger, Musculus, or Vermigli) and identifying Beza, Gomarus, or Turretin as the norm for understanding the later Reformed thought (to the exclusion of Junius, Walaeus, Davenant, Cocceius, Voetius, Burman, or even Amyraut) biases the discussion and mistakes the nature, breadth, and boundaries of confessional orthodoxy. Flat, one-for-one comparisons of documents like Calvin's *Institutio christianae religionis* and Turretin's *Institutio theologiae elencticae* ignore not only significant differences in historical context but also significant differences in literary genre (despite the similarity

---

12. See the discussion in *PRRD*, I, 1.3 (A.3, B.2-3).

of title) — not to mention the problem of claiming a hypothetical developmental trajectory that leads from Calvin, abstracted from his context and viewed as sole arbiter, to Turretin, equally alone and abstracted from the theological currents of his time.

A significant example of the problem is found in Rohls' study of the theology of the Reformed confessions, where the section on the history of the Reformed confessions in the sixteenth and seventeenth centuries appears, on closer examination, not to be a history of confessional development but a history of dogmatic controversies. Rohls' focus on such issues as the Bolsec Controversy, Beza's predestinarianism, Ramism, Aristotelianism, Cocceius, and the federal theology takes him into narrowly defined issues of doctrinal formulation not addressed in the confessions and not at issue in confessional debates. Indeed, the work is so entrenched in an out-dated dogmatic analysis of the history of Reformed doctrine that it lacks reliability as a historical analysis: thus we read of Beza and the central dogma theory, of "formal" and "material" principles" of the Reformation, of the predestinarian "particularism" of Dort over against the "christocentric universalism" of the Arminians, of the salvation-historical and a posteriori tendencies of Ramism over against a priori predestinarianism, and of the Cocceian covenant theology that "made an essential contribution to dissolving the doctrine of predestination."[13] Among other points that could be made here, "christocentric universalism" is hardly a useful characterization of the Arminian position, and it is fundamentally inaccurate to understand Cocceian federalism as running counter to the predestinarian definitions of the Synod of Dort! In addition, several of these issues (notably, Ramism and the Cocceian controversy) are not part of the confessional history, strictly defined: properly to understand the history, whether of the confessions or of orthodoxy in general, distinction needs to be made between the debates concerning confessional boundaries and doctrinal polemics either beyond or within the confessional boundaries.

In addition, greater variety of formulation and, therefore, a greater sense of difference or, indeed, discontinuity, between particular theologians of the Reformation era and particular theologians of the era of orthodoxy would certainly appear in the examination of other theological *loci*: there is certainly as much diversity of formulation among the Reformed orthodox on such topics as predestination and the Lord's Supper as there is in the prolegomena, doctrine of Scripture, and doctrine of God — and certainly far more diversity in the eschatological formulation of the seventeenth-century writers. This kind of discontinuity must, of course, be understood in a rather different way than large-scale discontinuities between the thought of one branch of a confessional family and another or, indeed, between one era and another.[14] Thus, a discussion of covenant would reveal a greater spectrum of opinion than a discussion of the doctrine of the divine attributes: after all, already in the Reformation, some theologians — notably Zwingli, Bullinger, and Musculus — manifested a topical interest in the concept

13. Jan Rohls, *Reformed Confessions: Theology from Zurich to Barmen*, trans. John Hoffmeyer, intro. by Jack Stotts (Louisville: Westminster John Knox Press, 1998), pp. 23-25, 293.

14. See further in Muller, "Calvin and the Calvinists: Assessing Continuities and Discontinuities Between Reformation and Orthodoxy," in *After Calvin*, pp. 63-102.

of covenant greater than that manifested in the thought of Calvin or Vermigli and, indeed, presented dimensions of the doctrine not as easily identified in Calvin's or Vermigli's teaching. The contrast is, perhaps, clearest between Bullinger and Calvin, although it is certainly not so great as to indicate two distinct Reformed traditions.[15] Similar differences appear in later Reformed thought, particularly in view of the development of the so-called covenant theology — which itself was subject to considerable variety of formulation within the Reformed tradition.[16]

So too, there was a variety of sacramental theology within the Reformed tradition itself from its beginnings. The debates between Calvin and Bullinger that led to the *Consensus Tigurinus* in 1551 were clearly enough presaged in the rather different eucharistic theologies of Bucer and Zwingli — and it is clear also that the *Consensus Tigurinus*, albeit intentionally a bridge-document, did not succeed in obliterating the differences, particularly in conceptions of sacramental presence and in the language of instrumentality, that obtained between Calvin and Bullinger.[17] (Arguably, the obliteration of differences was never the intention of the document.) There were also differences in ecclesiology and eschatology, particularly in later Reformed thought — with the result that, in the seventeenth century, neither the "presbyterian" church structure nor the so-called Augustinian "amillennial" view of the last things were universally held. These variations in doctrine within the Reformed tradition point to patterns of continuity and discontinuity not only between the Reformation and the era of orthodoxy but also between individual Reformers and between Protestantism and various trajectories of thought throughout the history of Christianity.

These variations within the Reformed tradition also point toward a significant element in the identification of Reformed orthodoxy that has often been overlooked by those who have examined it. The "orthodoxy" of the Reformed was not defined either by one or another of the methodological variants of scholasticism present in the Reformed tradition or by any one of the various strands of Reformed thought on such topics as predestination (infralapsarian, supralapsarian, or hypothetical

---

15. Cf. the scholarly discussion represented in such essays as Leonard Trinterud, "The Origins of Puritanism," in *Church History*, 20 (1951), pp. 37-57; Jens Moeller,"The Beginnings of Puritan Covenant Theology," in *Journal of Ecclesiastical History*, 14 (1963), pp. 46-67; Richard Greaves, "The Origins and Early Development of English Covenant Thought," in *The Historian*, 21 (1968), pp. 21-35; J. Wayne Baker, *Heinrich Bullinger and the Covenant: The Other Reformed Tradition* (Athens, Ohio: University of Ohio Press, 1980); Lyle D. Bierma, "The Covenant Theology of Caspar Olevian." (Ph.D. diss., Duke University, 1980); idem, "Federal Theology in the Sixteenth Century: Two Traditions?" in *Westminster Theological Journal*, 45 (1983), pp. 304-321; idem, "Covenant or Covenants in the Theology of Olevianus," in *Calvin Theological Journal*, 22 (1987), pp. 228-250; and idem, "The Role of Covenant Theology in Early Reformed Orthodoxy," in *Sixteenth Century Journal*, 21/3 (1990), pp. 453-462; John Von Rohr, *The Covenant of Grace in Puritan Thought* (Atlanta: Scholars Press, 1986).

16. Cf. Van Asselt, "Doctrine of the Abrogations," pp. 101-116 with Muller, *After Calvin*, chap. 11, on "The Covenant of Works and the Stability of Divine Law in Seventeenth-Century Reformed Orthodoxy."

17. See Paul Rorem, "Calvin and Bullinger on the Lord's Supper," in *Lutheran Quarterly*, NS 2 (1988), pp. 155-184, 357-389.

universalist), covenant (unilateral and bilateral definition, two- or three-covenant schemas, etc.), the Lord's supper (Bucerian, Zwinglian, or Calvinian), but by the broad lines of the Reformed confessions. As noted in the beginning of the analysis of Reformed prolegomena and in the discussion of fundamental doctrines, we misunderstand the phenomenon of Reformed orthodoxy if we make no distinction between extra-confessional and intra-confessional controversies. The Arminian or Remonstrant theology after the Synod of Dort and the Socinian theology of the seventeenth century were considered by the Reformed as heterodox, indeed, heretical — whereas the Amyraldian theory of hypothetical universalism was considered by a large number of Reformed writers as useful and by others, perhaps the majority, as unacceptable, but *not* as heretical. A similar generalization needs to be made concerning the federal theology: its contours were heatedly debated by the Reformed of the seventeenth century, but it was never understood as a heresy or as outside of the boundaries of the confessions. So also can similar variety be found in the Reformed understanding of issues in the prolegomena and the *principia* of theology.

Once these qualifications have been made, however, we can also point to the fact that the discontinuities or, more precisely, the varieties of formulation, appear within the Reformed confessional tradition on those issues and topics that do not belong either to the category of broad ecumenical standards or the somewhat less broad category of the confessions. Reformed theologians do not differ on the issue of the identity of the Godhead as one indivisible or simple essence distinguished into three persons or hypostases: they did differ on precisely how that doctrine ought to be elaborated exegetically and with what metaphors and patterns of explanation. Again, they did not differ on the point that human beings are saved by grace alone and that this understanding of grace assumed a divine predestination of some to salvation: they did differ over the shape of the definition — whether a single or double decree and, if double, whether infra- or supralapsarian. In the explicit cases of the prolegomena, the doctrine of Scripture, and the doctrine of God, there are a host of nuances that belie any attempt to argue precise continuity or large-scale discontinuity between Reformation and orthodoxy, and the development of thought does not follow in neat, straight lines of succession from one generation to the next.

B. Aristotelianism, Scholasticism, and the Trajectories of Late Renaissance Philosophy, Logic, and Rhetoric

1. Central dogmas, scholasticism, Aristotelianism, and rationalism: toward closure on an old debate. From the perspective of a detailed analysis of the Reformation and post-Reformation prolegomena and doctrines of Scripture and God, we are also in a position to state quite categorically that the older theories of the rise of Reformed orthodoxy, either as the development of a predestinarian system based on a single "central dogma" or as the result of rationalism, are not only wrong but also reductionistic and simplistic in the extreme. At what remains a very superficial level, we are in a position to declare that the historical evidence does not indicate any interest on the part of the Reformed orthodox in creating a deductive theological system based on a single doctrine. The Reformed orthodox theologians were not philosophical determinists interested in creating a deterministic system of Christian doctrine. At the same level, we can also declare categorically that philosophical rationalism, which understands human reason as the fundamental principle of knowledge (evident in the seventeenth century in the writings of Descartes, Spinoza, Leibniz, and their followers), was not determinative of the formulation of the norms and *principia* of Reformed orthodox theology, even among those Reformed who were open to Cartesian philosophy. The definitions of theology and the theological task that we have encountered in the Reformed prolegomena, the hermeneutical criteria found in the doctrine of Scripture, and the actual working-out of formulation in the doctrine of God, all evidence an attempt to balance revelation and reason, exegetical foundations and philosophical usages, leaving philosophy in an ancillary role.

The Protestant orthodox theological enterprise was both fundamentally exegetical and profoundly traditional. The intention of the orthodox dogmaticians was to produce, not a modern, logically cohesive, system of theology on the pattern of Schleiermacher or Tillich, but a body of doctrine in which the topics of biblical teaching were gathered into a coherent and defensible whole for the sake of the life and salvation of the church. The movement of theological argumentation was from Scripture and exegesis to traditional theological topic, by way of the examination of the teachings of the fathers and the great theologians of the history of the church and by way of the refutation of heresies: each and every text examined had both a history of interpretation and a traditional relationship to one or more doctrinal *loci*. To claim that the Reformed orthodox took a single doctrine (i.e., predestination) or a particular philosophical perspective (i.e., rationalism or even Aristotelianism) as the key to understanding all biblical passages and their relationships to the larger body of Christian doctrine is to ignore the very way in which they understood the theological task — in other words, to ignore the way in which they defined theology and its *principia* in their theological prolegomena, to ignore the implications of the *locus* method, both in terms of the relationship of dogmatics to exegesis and in terms of the way in which the series or order of topics was conceived and organized.

Underlying this misunderstanding is a misreading of scholasticism as well as a dogmatic misreading of historical materials. Against those modern readers of scholastic Protestant materials who conclude that Beza, Polanus, Voetius, Turretin, Pictet, Rijssen, and the other orthodox have simply ignored or set aside without notice their declared scriptural foundation and, on the grounds of philosophical reason, interspersed with a few biblical quotations wrenched out of context, have argued such doctrines as the simplicity, eternity, and immutability of God, the sixteenth- and seventeenth-century sources argue a different conclusion. The claim of a shift from biblical to philosophical thinking (like the parallel and equally mistaken notion of a movement from "Hebrew" to "Greek" thinking) does not do justice to the complexity of the materials and arguments that it pretends to critique. We do not find a pure Aristotelianism even in the thought of Albert the Great or Thomas Aquinas: there was, already, at this initial stage of the appropriation of Aristotelian metaphysics a sense of the usefulness of Aristotelian concepts to Christianity linked to a sense of the difference and of the inapplicability of some elements of Aristotle's thought. And, in addition to Aristotle, the medieval doctors also incorporated elements of Platonic and Neoplatonic philosophy as appropriated and adapted by the church fathers. So, too, was Aristotle capable of being filtered through the thought of Avicenna, Averroes, and Maimonides, who had given a "biblical" turn to Aristotelian theism even before Albert and Thomas. By the time of the Reformation and post-Reformation eras, the tradition of a Christian Aristotelianism or, more precisely, the tradition of a Christian philosophy that had incorporated elements of Aristotelianism and had consistently modified those elements, turning them to a Christian use, was so rich and variegated that it followed its own patterns rather than a neatly Aristotelian pattern of argument. Its definitions, when understood through the glass of pure Aristotelianism, are typically misunderstood.[18]

So, too, must the term "scholasticism" and the other "isms" of the medieval schools — Thomism, Scotism, nominalism — be applied with care and caution to the Protestant theologies of the seventeenth century. This caution is particularly necessary given the diverse patterns of the mediation of scholastic method and medieval theological approaches to Reformation and post-Reformation Protestantism. First, we must distinguish between the forms of medieval theology mediated to the Protestant orthodox by the Reformers themselves and the forms of medieval thought appropriated by the Protestant orthodox either through their direct reading of medieval materials or through their encounter with the Roman Catholic scholasticism of the late Renaissance. Second, equally importantly, we must recognize the presence of Thomistic, Scotistic, nominalistic, and other patterns in Reformed orthodoxy based on the streams of intellectual inheritance — whether via the Reformers or via the direct reappropriation of medieval tradition or via encounter with late Renaissance Roman Catholicism.

In other words, there are a series of paths by which scholastic models came into later Protestant thought — and, equally so, there was a very diverse reappropriation of those models. Here, too, the context of the appropriation can be identified, in some cases, with relative precision. Given the training of the first several generations of Protestant teachers in the forms of late medieval and Renaissance thought, specific elements of the medieval and Renaissance background can be identified in the thought of individual Reformers. Similarly, we are able to identify academic contexts, whether of the training or of the eventual work of a large number of later Reformed thinkers — and, fortunately, the late sixteenth- and seventeenth-century writers offer clearer references to their medieval sources than did the Reformers.

Similar strictures can be placed on the all-too-neat association of Reformed orthodoxy and scholasticism with the rise and development of rationalism.[19] The evidence gathered throughout this study has shown that there are certain common

---

18. See the discussion in *PRRD*, I, 8.1.

19. Cf. the preliminary statement of the historiographical problem in *PRRD*, I, 2.5 (A.1), 2.6 (A-C).

antecedents of Protestant thought in the eras of the Reformation and orthodoxy and the rationalist philosophy that rose and developed in the same centuries; namely, alterations in the teaching of logic and rhetoric in the later Middle Ages and Renaissance, the accompanying interest in method, the revival of interest in ancient learning, both linguistic and philosophical. Both Reformed orthodoxy and the rationalist philosophies opposed the philosophical skepticism of the late sixteenth century and argued that there were self-evident and irrefutable *principia* on which knowledge could be based. But the evidence has also demonstrated a series of profound differences over the reception and use of those antecedents, to the point of showing rather different histories for scholastic Protestantism and the various forms of rationalist philosophy characteristic of the seventeenth century. Understandings of method differed widely, rationalist philosophies did not understand *principia* in the same way as the Reformed orthodox, and, certainly in the case of the French rationalists, pagan Stoicism and Epicureanism figured as largely positive antecedents — the Reformed orthodox debated against both. The eighteenth-century result of these developments, moreover, was not a theological orthodoxy that merged into the stream of rationalist thought: with the partial exception of the Wolffian theologians, the remaining orthodox of the eighteenth century did not imbibe any of the newer philosophies with equanimity. Rather than evidence an ongoing alliance with philosophy, the late orthodox tended not to enter the philosophical mainstream and, given the demise of the traditional Christian Aristotelianism, tended to assert the older assumptions concerning the necessity of a special revelation and personal regeneration for the development of Christian theology without also providing a model for the coordination of theology and philosophy such as had been characteristic of the seventeenth-century orthodox.

2. Patterns and trajectories in the Reformed reception of scholastic models. Once these cautions have been acknowledged, some tentative conclusions can be drawn concerning the Reformed orthodox appropriation of scholastic models. First and foremost, that appropriation was eclectic. Among the second-generation Reformers, Musculus cited various medievals positively, notably Scotus and Ockham. Calvin, of course, has been argued to evidence Scotist inclinations, but the problem of documenting their source and extent is notorious. Vermigli, by contrast, leaned more clearly on Thomist models, typically with a strong Augustinian accent. Among the early orthodox, Polanus cited both Aquinas and Scotus. In the case of Lambert Daneau's use of Durandus of Sancto Porciano or of Richard Baxter's citations of Gregory of Rimini, initial interest may have arisen because of such a mundane reason as the availability of the medieval author's work in a sixteenth-century printing. As we move into the seventeenth century, a broader pattern of citation appears, notably a recognition of the medieval writers as a source of paradigms, especially the paradigm for identifying theology as a speculative or practical discipline, where, typically, Henry of Ghent, Durandus, Johannes Rada, Scotus, Bonaventure, Albert the Great, Giles of Rome, Thomas Aquinas, and Thomas of Strasbourg are cited as illustrative of the various possible definitions. The exact relationship of Reformed orthodoxy to these older sources is difficult to map, given that there was no motive for most Protestant thinkers of the late sixteenth and the seventeenth century to follow out the theology of a particular thinker or, certainly, a particular order — as there presumably was for their Dominican, Augustinian, or Jesuit contemporaries. Some necessarily preliminary conclusions can, nonetheless, be drawn from the Reformed usage found in the prolegomena and the doctrines of Scripture and God.

The various categories of definition offered by the Reformed orthodox in their prolegomena, beginning with Junius' *De vera theologia*, point toward an eclectic use of the medievals based on a set of rather particular concerns, themselves traceable in large part to the Reformation or to the roots of the Reformation in the concerns of late medieval theology. The typical identifications of theology by the Reformed as either a mixed theoretical-practical but primarily practical or as a purely practical discipline point toward the Augustinian and the Scotist definitions, respectively, and away from both the Thomist (theoretical-practical but primarily theoretical) and the Durandist (purely speculative) forms of definition. A minority opinion, represented by Du Moulin, followed the Thomist definition. This practical emphasis of the majority, moreover, coincided with the fundamentally voluntarist set of assumptions held by the Reformed, both concerning the divine will and the problem of human salvation — pointing again in the doctrine of God to an Augustinian or Scotist background and in the doctrine of salvation to an Augustinian background. Similarly, the identification of the object of theology as God revealed and the basic division of that topic into revelation as Creator and revelation as Redeemer, echo the definitions presented by medieval Augustinians like Giles of Rome and Gregory of Rimini.

On other topics, however, the Reformed do not typically follow out the Scotist line — rather they may, in these issues, look to Aquinas or to various Augustinians like Thomas of Strasbourg and Giles of Rome for a *via antiqua* model or Gregory of Rimini for a *via moderna* model. Specifically, on the question of the distinction of attributes in the Godhead, the greater number of Reformed avoid a strictly Scotist view of formally distinct attributes and gravitate either toward a Thomistic or *via antiqua* definition of the attributes as conceptually or rationally distinct in God or toward a nominalist or *via moderna* view that denies distinction of attributes in the Godhead and regards them as distinct only in their *ad extra* manifestation. In the case of the former option, Keckermann offers the clue that it was derived (at least by him) from the chronologically proximate Thomism of Cajetan. In either case, the options chosen by the Reformed stand in the way of an easy conclusion (on the basis of the identification of theology as practical and the voluntaristic conception of God) for a largely Scotist influence. The Reformed response to Molina's notion of *scientia media*, moreover, allies the Reformed with a later Thomist model as well, in particular the views of such late sixteenth-century Thomists as Baius and Bañez, who followed out the more Augustinian reading of Aquinas found in a late medieval follower like Capreolus rather than the reading of Cajetan or, indeed, of the Jesuits Molina and Suárez.

Although an enormous amount of study needs still to be done before the shape, the specific sources, or the rationale for this eclecticism can be fully identified, several observations can be made. If there is an internal logic to the majority of choices made, it points in the direction of a model that is epistemologically critical, but not skeptical, and a view of God and world, particularly of soteriological issues, that is highly Augustinian. The ontology of the Reformed, which often can identify the created order as having being "by participation," has *via antiqua*, probably Thomistic origin — albeit in those thinkers who argue the univocity of being, a decidedly Suárezian accent. The rhetorical restructuring of the proofs of the existence of God and the correlation between the self-evident and indemonstrable nature of *principia* with the identification of God as *principium essendi*, taken together with the assumption of a rational distinction of attributes in God, is neither nominalist nor Scotist in perspective. Nor, given its denial of demonstrability of the *principium essendi*, is it strictly a Thomistic model. As already noted, the voluntarism of the theology also points away from a purely Thomistic model.

At the same time, the Scotist resemblances can be accounted for as Augustinian tendencies — namely, the sense of theology as largely or wholly practical and the voluntaristic understanding of God and salvation. When the voluntarism is coupled with a very specific construction of the radical contingency of the world order, identified by Vos as "synchronic contingency," this may be a Scotist accent in Reformed theology, or it may be the result of the transmission of a teaching found in Scotus through a series of other thinkers, including such diverse figures as Thomas Bradwardine, Gregory of Rimini, and (contemporary with the Reformed orthodox) Diego Alvarez and Dominic Bañez. The trajectory of the transmission is unclear: there is more to the issue than the decision on the part of various seventeenth-century thinkers to rest an aspect of their thought on a distinction derivable from Scotus — nor given the strict soteriological monergism of the Reformed is it probable that this synchronic contingency works itself out in the Reformed model in precisely the same way in which it would operate in Scotus' thought. The parallel with Gregory of Rimini is significant inasmuch as it points toward an Augustinian, *via moderna* background; the potential connection with Alvarez and Bañez is also of interest, given the kinship of the Dominican and the Reformed oppositions to Molinism; and the linkage of the synchronic contingency construction with a notion of ultimate possibility, rooted by the Reformed of the era in the divine *potentia* rather than the divine intellect (as Scotus had argued), points perhaps toward an Ockhamist line of argument.[20] The question of background remains complex.

If, then, the Reformed patterns of reception and usage of scholastic models could be identified clearly as Thomist or Scotist, one would still need to use a qualifier — such as "modified Thomism" or "modified Scotism" — to describe them. Such usage, however, fails to represent the variety of the appropriation and also tends to depict one or another of the appropriated elements as a center around which the eclecticism coalesces and from which it gains a coherence not afforded by elements drawn from other sources. The quest for a single point of origin, a neat trajectory leading back

---

20. See further *PRRD*, III, 5.3 (F.1); 5.4 (C.2-3).

to one thinker or even to a medieval "school" of thought, or to a center, either theological or philosophical, will fail here, just as it did in the case of the central dogma theory. The late sixteenth- and seventeenth-century reception of medieval materials and methods, whether of individual themes that have Thomist, Scotist, Augustinian, or nominalist accents or of the broader patterns of scholastic method, was after all a *late sixteenth-* and *seventeenth-century* reception: these accents are not a throwback to an earlier era but elements of an ongoing discourse. Both the general scholastic method of the Reformed orthodox and the specific appropriations of medieval materials had a specified late sixteenth- and seventeenth-century context, having been filtered through the lenses of the Reformation and the late Renaissance. The Reformed reception of these elements of older tradition was not a return to the Middle Ages, but a historical development of academic or scholastic style and of theological and philosophical content in the wake of the Reformation and Renaissance. Here especially the continuities and discontinuities of the Protestant orthodox methods and teachings must be measured against both the medieval and the Renaissance-Reformation background and, as we have seen throughout this study, the impact of new contexts reckoned with: thus, the scholasticism of the seventeenth century, including the appropriations of Thomistic, Scotistic, Augustinian, and nominalist patterns, evidences elements of continuity (and discontinuity), not only with the Middle Ages but also with the Renaissance and Reformation, just as it evidences the immediate academic, cultural, and polemical context of Protestant orthodoxy.

8.2 The Character of Protestant Scholasticism: Prolegomena and *Principia* as Indices of Post-Reformation Orthodoxy

A. Theological Prolegomena

1. The rise of theological prolegomena and the question of continuity, discontinuity, and development. The Reformers did not typically write theological prolegomena. Just as they did not base their theological systems directly on the model of scholastic summas and sentence commentaries, but tended to follow catechetical and creedal models, so also did they not see the need to preface their theologies with the preliminary exercises that became typical of later medieval theological systems. It was only in the wake of the solidification of the Protestant theological system and the success of the Reformation in establishing itself as an institutional church, with its own universities and faculties, that the academic experience itself generated essays on the nature of theological system like Junius' *De vera theologia*. Here is, certainly, a point of difference between the forms of Reformation theology and the forms of post-Reformation orthodoxy. It is, moreover, a difference rooted quite identifiably in the altered context of post-Reformation theology, namely, the context of a movement in the process of institutionalization or confessionalization, in the case of the prolegomena, specifically with reference to the institutionalization of a Protestant academic culture.

Nonetheless, even here, we can trace the gradual development of Protestant thinking on the nature and character of theology, the manner and method of teaching theology, and the method for constructing theological system from its beginnings in the work of Melanchthon, to the essays on theological study by Bullinger and Hyperius, to the consideration of problems of knowledge of God and of systematic organization by Calvin and Musculus, and to the extended essay on theological method, also by Hyperius.[21] The choices made in the definition of such issues by Melanchthon, Calvin, Musculus, and Hyperius reflect both their own churchly and institutional contexts and the manner in which, in those contexts, they appropriated and transmitted elements of earlier theological conceptuality. If the identification of specific prolegomena and their placement as a prior *locus* in scholastic system came rather late in the sixteenth century (ca. 1580), the issues addressed by those prolegomena were already addressed in various writings of the Reformers extending back toward the beginnings of the Reformation, and those early Reformation writings themselves reflect choices made not merely over against but also, consistently, with reference to late medieval and Renaissance academic or educational culture.

Nowhere is this transmission and its various contexts clearer than in the discussion of "method" found in rhetorical, philosophical, and theological materials of the entire history running from the later Middle Ages through the seventeenth century. The issue of "method," literally the *meta / hodos* or "way through" a topic or topics, was raised for the earliest Reformers, most notably, Melanchthon, in their work of appropriating the topical or place-logic of the fifteenth century to the use of Reformation theological education. The impact of the method and of variations on it is seen in Melanchthon's own biblical commentaries and in his more or less systematic essay, the *Loci communes theologici*, in Calvin's commentaries and *Institutes*, and in the efforts of contemporary writers like Musculus and Vermigli. This *locus* method, in what can be called a Renaissance modification of scholastic approaches, carried over, with modification, into the thought of the early orthodox writers. Specific modification came to the method by way of Ramist logic and the methodological theories of Zabarella, both of which belong to the late Renaissance recovery and modification of classical and late medieval logical and rhetorical tools. These models in turn carry over into the "scholastic" methods of the seventeenth-century Protestants.[22] This transmission of method or approach underlines the academic or educational location of much of the codifying effort of the Reformers and their successors, and it also evidences the character of the continuity as well as of the difference between the work of the Reformers and that of their successors: it becomes impossible, for one thing, to label the former "humanist" and the latter "scholastic," as if the one drew on Renaissance methods and the other returned to medieval ways of thinking.

---

21. Cf. the discussion in PRRD, I, 2.3 (B.3) and 4.1 (A.2) with the analysis of Hyperius in Preus, *Theology of Post-Reformation Lutheranism*, I, pp. 82-88 and Willem van 't Spijker, *Principe, methode en functie van de theologie bij Andreas Hyperius*, Apeldoornse Studies, 26 (Kampen: J. H. Kok, 1990).
    22. See PRRD, I, 4.1.

The idea of *principia theologiae* itself offers evidence of the continuities of theology in its development from the medieval to the post-Reformation era, together with the impact of the Reformation on Protestant theological system, as, also, it manifests certain elements of discontinuity or, at least, difference between the various theologians and between the patterns of exposition in the various eras examined. The medieval doctors offered a carefully conceived analysis of the concept of *principia* in theology in relation to their discussion of the genus theology — given that the three primary forms of knowing, *intelligentia*, *scientia*, and *sapientia*, all represent a knowledge of principles. *Intelligentia* is a pure knowledge of first principles, *scientia* a knowledge of first principles and the conclusions that can be drawn from them, and *sapientia* a knowledge of first principles and the goals or end toward which they point. Once theology was identified as either a *scientia* or a *sapientia*, but in a subalternate sense, its *principia* could be identified as the revealed truths given in Scripture, on the basis of which theology could draw conclusions and indicate goals or ends.

This understanding of *principia* carried over into Protestantism, particularly in its assumption that Scripture provides the church with revealed truths from which conclusions can be drawn: from Luther's demand at Worms that he be convinced by Scripture and right reason to the Westminster Confession's claim that "the whole counsel of God, concerning all things necessary for his own glory, man's salvation, faith, and life, is either expressly set down in Scripture, or by good and necessary consequence may be deduced from Scripture,"[23] Protestant theology held to the traditional view of *principia*. Indeed, at the beginnings of the development of theological prolegomena, Lubbertus and Chandieu both discussed the use of *principia* or *axiomata* in precisely this manner.[24]

Lubbertus, however, in debate with Bellarmine over the identity of the normative canon of Scripture, moves on to identify the prophetic and apostolic books of Scripture as the *principium* in theology.[25] Here, the emphasis in the identification of *principia* passes over from the issue of the basic axioms of a science or wisdom from which conclusions may be drawn to the issue of the foundation or knowing that serves as the source of all authoritative axioms or *principia*. This line of argument led, in the decade following Lubbertus' *De principiis Christianorum dogmatum*, to the enunciation of two ultimate *principia* in Reformed theology by writers like Polanus and Trelcatius — the Scripture, or Word of God, as the *principium cognoscendi*, or cognitive foundation, of theology and God Himself as the *principium essendi*, or essential foundation, of theology. Biblical texts remain understood, however, as *principia* in the sense of *axiomata*

---

23. Westminster Confession, I.6, in Schaff, *Creeds of Christendom*, III, p. 603.

24. Cf. Sibrandus Lubbertus, *De principiis Christianorum dogmatum libri VII* (Franecker, 1591), I.i, with Antoine de la Roche Chandieu, *De verbo Dei scripto* in *Opera theologica* (Geneva, 1593), pp. 7-10, and with Donald W. Sinnema, "Antoine De Chandieu's Call for a Scholastic Reformed Theology (1580)," in *Later Calvinism: International Perspectives*, ed. W. Fred Graham (Kirksville, MO: Sixteenth Century Journal Publishers, 1994), pp. 176-179, and PRRD, I, 9.3 (A.1; B.1).

25. Lubbertus, *De principiis Christianorum dogmatum*, I.iii.

or as sources of *axiomata* for the drawing of theological conclusions.[26] At this point, arguably, the traditionary language of *principia theologiae* has been modified, albeit in scholastic terms, by the Reformation *sola Scriptura* — the Protestant orthodox formulation evidences a continuity both with medieval scholastic theology and with the fundamental emphasis of the Reformers on the biblical norm of doctrine.

In sum, the rise of prolegomena containing a discussion of the definitions of theology and of its *principia* marks a shift in the patterns of theologizing between the eras of the Reformation and orthodoxy. Although we have seen elements of prolegomena in the thought of the Reformers, including significant discussions of true and false religion, none of the Reformers either of the first or second generations offered a full theological prolegomenon analogous to the development after Junius' *De theologia vera*. Large-scale definition of the architectonics of theology was new to Protestantism. Arguably it drew together elements of medieval definitions of theology with elements of the thought of the Reformers to produce a perspective on the detailed work of academic theology, a perspective that stood in positive relationship with the Reformers' assumptions concerning the limitation of human knowledge, the necessity of revelation, the historical series and/or Pauline order of theological topics, and the relationship of exegesis to theology. But the exercise itself and a large portion of its terminology were different from the forms of argument present during the Reformation. In fact, like the issues we have already noted concerning scholasticism and the reception of the tradition by the Reformed orthodox, the development of prolegomena presses the analysis of Reformed orthodoxy past the simple registration of continuities and discontinuities to the more subtle issue of the development of increasingly variegated patterns of expression within a confessional and exegetical tradition. By way of example, the archetypal-ectypal distinction and the resulting identification of "our theology," *theologia nostra* as an ectypal theology of revelation, construed after the Fall in a fallible individual subject, does not appear, formally, like anything argued by the Reformers — yet, in substance one would be hard put to argue (to borrow words from the older scholarship) that these definitions either stood in "tension" with the theology of the Reformation or represented either "antitheses" or "antinomies" to the original thought patterns of the Reformers.

2. The example of Ramism. The primary issues addressed in the discussion of Ramism,[27] concerned its identity and impact over against many of the claims of the older scholarship. In brief, Ramism, as utilized by several generations of Reformed orthodox writers, was neither a thoroughly anti-Aristotelian development nor a humanistic, salvation-historical, a posteriori pattern of thought posed against a scholastic, predestinarian, a priori pattern: it served as a method of exposition and organization in nearly all of the academic disciplines; it had little impact on the content of those disciplines; and it served the development of a late Renaissance modification of scholastic method. Ramism, therefore, exemplifies the historiographical issues at

---

26. Polanus, *Syntagma theol.*, I.xiv; Trelcatius, *Schol. meth.*, I.i; cf. *PRRD*, I, 9.3; II, 7.4 (C.5).
27. See *PRRD*, I, 4.1 (B.1).

stake in the attempt to examine continuities and discontinuities as aspects of broader patterns of development and change within certain traditionary and confessional boundaries. In the first place, its origins in the late Renaissance modification of logic and rhetoric identify it as an academic, in the broadest sense, scholastic, tool, the use of which belonged to the process of institutionalization undergone by Protestantism in the late sixteenth century. That it belonged to this process and that it was a logical tool not available to the Reformers marks a point of discontinuity with the Reformation — that it had roots in the earlier Agricolan logic and served the *locus* method of exposition marks a point of continuity as well as change, a continuity in the context of development.

3. The prolegomena and the problem of rationalism. We are also in a position to draw some conclusions concerning the question of "rationalism" and the use of reason in theology. It was certainly the express rule of the Reformed orthodox theology that reason could never have principial status and was consistently to be used as an instrument in the formulation of theological conclusions. Still, some differences can be identified among the Reformed orthodox or scholastic theologians, particularly during the course of the seventeenth century. Thus, the theological argumentation in Pictet's discussion of the divine attributes evidences a more rationalistic approach than Polanus' argumentation a century earlier, and, as often noted in the discussion of the divine attributes, Polanus' argumentation, together with that of a large number of his contemporaries, marks a point of differentiation between the early orthodox theology and that of some writings of the codifiers of the Reformation, namely, a point of differentiation from Calvin's *Institutes*, but not from Musculus' *Loci communes* or Hyperius' *Methodus theologiae*, and certainly not from the broader exegetical tradition, including the exegesis of Calvin, or from the broad background of philosophical language used to exposit and explain the doctrine. Given the traditionary and exegetical root of so much of the discussion of the attributes, the development of discussion on this issue cannot be explained simplistically as a product of rationalism.

The problem of rationalism, then, does not coincide (contrary to the claims of much of the older scholarship on Reformed orthodoxy) either with the scholastic character of the dogmatics of the seventeenth century or with the tradition of Christian Aristotelianism that provided the orthodox theologians with a philosophical viewpoint for most of the era of orthodoxy. The specific points that we have noted as rationalist alterations of theology in the late seventeenth century are due not to the older Aristotelianism but to the newer rationalism, principally of the Cartesian variety. It is the Cartesian model that, in its more extreme forms, elevated reason over revelation, that produced (in the case of Poiret) the one truly deductive and "decretal" theology of the age, and that introduced untenable substance language (in the case of Sherlock) into the late orthodox trinitarian theology. It was the Cartesian model that, in some cases, led to a departure from the balance of revelation and reason characteristic of the theology allied to the traditional Christian Aristotelianism.

Of course, the Cartesian model, sometimes echoed and sometimes modified and adopted by various of the Reformed orthodox — notably Burman, Heidanus, Tronchin, and Pictet — did not necessarily lead to these problematic conclusions any more than did the older Christian Aristotelianism. Even more important historically is the fact that modified Cartesianism, like modified Aristotelianism in the Christian tradition, could be brought to the service of a Reformed orthodox theology and adapted to operate largely within the bounds assigned to philosophy in the orthodox prolegomena. This adaptation stands as fair proof that so-called scholastic orthodoxy in the post-Reformation era was not intrinsically "Aristotelian." What is more, the often restricted appropriation of elements of Cartesianism by various of the Reformed orthodox also serves to illustrate that, even in this instance, the orthodox theology of the seventeenth century was not driven by rationalism.

The distinction between Reformed orthodox theology and philosophical rationalism, as well as elements of continuity and discontinuity between Reformation and orthodoxy, can be illustrated by the Reformed approach to natural theology and metaphysics. There was no discussion of natural theology per se among the Reformers, although there were definite views expressed by them concerning the character and usefulness of natural revelation. From cne perspective, therefore, the increased interest in the content of natural revelation and the appearance of works on the subject of natural theology in the late sixteenth and early seventeenth centuries marks an element of discontinuity between the thought of the Reformers and that of their orthodox successors. It is equally clear, however, that the development of natural theology by a writer like Alsted did not mark the intrusion of a category of rational theology or philosophy into the system or body of Reformed doctrine, but rather the elaboration of the body of teaching concerning God and world in addition to the theology grounded primarily on the salvific or distinctly "supernatural" revelation in Scripture. One may identify the discontinuity between Alsted's eclectic philosophy and rather optimistic natural theology and the discussion of the limits of natural revelation at the beginning of Calvin's *Institutes* — or one may, with equal warrant, consider the continuity between the philosophically eclectic Calvin's highly positive and expansive presentation of natural revelation in his commentary on the Psalter and Alsted's development of a *theologia naturalis*.

Various writers of the era, like Ames, viewed natural theology and rational metaphysics with some suspicion — while others, like Keckermann and Maccovius, drew a rather sharp line between rational metaphysics and theology, to the point of refusing to discuss the divine essence and attributes under the topic of metaphysics. The Reformed orthodox discussions of proofs of God's existence and of the divine essence and attributes, therefore, ought not to be viewed simplistically as evidence of either large-scale natural theology or rationalist philosophy nor, indeed, as evidence of an assumption that supernatural theology must be grounded in natural theology. More important, perhaps, than the specific points just made is the general impression — that the Reformed orthodox were not products of a recrudescent philosophical and theological movement, but that their philosophical language was in direct dialogue with the current of the day. The continuities that we note are not static reproductions but developments within a fairly broad intellectual and confessional tradition. Where we can, finally, point to a clear discontinuity between the Reformers' views on natural revelation and altered approaches in the Reformed tradition is in the waning of orthodoxy in the eighteenth century, when natural theology does indeed become, in thinkers like Wyttenbach and Stapfer, a prologue to supernatural theology, preceding any consideration of scriptural revelation. This is, indeed, a shift — but, on purely historiographical grounds, it would be a mistake to claim that Alsted's version of natural theology stands on a path leading directly toward the Wolffian model or even that it contains the seed or germ of the later development.

B. The Doctrine of Scripture and the Continuity of the Interpretive Tradition in Orthodox Protestantism

1. Continuity, discontinuity, and the problem of perspective. Our study of the Reformed orthodox doctrine of Scripture has shown a clear continuity in the development of both doctrine and practice from the Reformation into the era of orthodoxy — although it is certainly a variegated development in which continuities and discontinuities have to be indexed to changing contexts in philosophy, historical understanding, textual criticism, and so forth. The historical trajectory of the Reformed doctrine of Scripture, moreover, evidences one version of the pattern of continuities and discontinuities that we have noted in the movement from the later Middle Ages and Renaissance, through the Reformation, into the era of orthodoxy. Identification of Scripture as the prior norm and sole ultimate authority in Christian doctrine, with tradition not absent but clearly subordinate, unites the Protestant orthodoxy not only with the Reformation but with the clear testimony of the major medieval scholastic teachers, including Aquinas and Scotus. Given that this "Tradition I" understanding of the structure of authority has medieval scholastic roots and that its debate with "Tradition II" (the coequal balance of Scripture and tradition) was also a late medieval development, we can identify a continuous development of the model from the Middle Ages to the era of orthodoxy — with the Reformers, the Protestant confessions, and the Protestant orthodoxy occupying the ground of Tradition I, and the Counter-Reformation and the Council of Trent occupying the ground of Tradition II.

There is also an element of discontinuity: the medieval founders of Tradition I did not envision the crisis of church and traditionary authority the confronted the Reformers — with the result that the Reformation and post-Reformation descendants of Tradition I recognized a separation between Scripture and tradition that the major medieval teachers did not and, without jettisoning tradition entirely, identified its subordination to Scripture in terms of the disagreements and errors of the fathers (and medievals) in contrast to the harmony and truth of Scripture. The tradition remains strong in Protestant circles, not as an easily wielded churchly authority, but as a variegated dialogue partner in the exegesis of the text of Scripture. On this point of discontinuity with the Middle Ages, there is continuity between the Reformation and the Protestant orthodoxy — a continuity in development, measured by the late sixteenth- and seventeenth-century reception of the fathers and of the diverse exegetical tradition, including the use of Judaica.

The demonstration of continuity between Reformation and orthodoxy has shown that much of what once passed for scholarship on this subject was little better than undocumented allegation. Specifically, J. K. S. Reid's claim that the Protestant orthodox ignored the concept of revelation falls before abundant evidence to the contrary: what we can say is that, unlike Reid and unlike Reid's caricature of the Reformation and the seventeenth century, neither the Reformers nor the Reformed orthodox had a restrictive concept of revelation that identified it as taking place only in the person of Jesus Christ or that identified it as an event or an encounter in our present.[28] Both the Reformers and the Reformed orthodox recognized revelation (natural and supernatural) as the only mode of the knowledge of God in this life and recognized the necessity of the biblical revelation for salvation: that teaching is patently evident both in their prolegomena to theology and in their doctrine of Scripture.

So, too, have we set aside the claim made by Rogers and others that the Reformed orthodox doctrine of Scripture can be reduced to a rigid notion of verbal inspiration coupled to an empirical concept of inerrancy and then set in contrast with the rich, dynamic, view of Scripture taught by the Reformers.[29] The Reformers' doctrine was not nearly as "dynamic" as claimed, nor the orthodox teaching as "rigid." There is a general continuity of definition running from the later Middle Ages through the Reformation into the era of orthodoxy: the divine origin of Scripture is described on the analogy of dictation, God is identified as the primary author and the human writers of the text as secondary authors or amanuenses. At the same time, both the Reformers and the Reformed orthodox insist on the individual character of the biblical books, the unique stylistic characteristics of individual authors, and the authors' use of their own vocabulary and historical or cultural knowledge. The process of inspiration is never likened to an oracular trance — and nowhere is an empirical standard of inerrancy used as the basis for establishing the authority of the text. Like Calvin and other Reformers, the orthodox writers of the seventeenth century continue to affirm — contrary to Rogers' unsubstantiated assertions — the accommodated nature of the biblical text and to argue the necessity of the internal testimony of the Spirit for the reception of the text as authoritative by individual Christians. If anything, the orthodox are clearer than the Reformers concerning the necessity of the work of the Spirit in biblical interpretation and the identity of the exegete as a faithful member of the church.

In addition, we have been able to recognize clear relationships and doctrinal continuities between the British and the continental divines during the era of orthodoxy. Rogers' theory of a pre-scholastic form of Reformed theology, embodied in the Westminster Confession and quite dramatically opposed to the scholastic theology of either the Dutch Reformed after Dort or of the Swiss Reformed in the

---

28. See J. K. S. Reid, *The Authority of Scripture: A Study of Reformation and Post-Reformation Understanding of the Bible* (London: Methuen, 1962), and the discussion in PRRD, II, 2.2 (A.1-2).

29. Most notably in Jack B. Rogers and Donald K. McKim, *The Authority and Interpretation of the Bible: An Historical Approach* (San Francisco: Harper & Row, 1979).

mid- and late seventeenth century, simply does not stand up before the evidence.[30] The development of scholastic orthodox forms of Protestantism, as evidenced by British thinkers like Perkins, Ames, Scharpius, Rollock, and Cameron, coincided in time with the continental developments found in such writers as Junius, Polanus, Bucanus, Keckermann, Paraeus, the elder and younger Trelcatius, Gomarus, and Maccovius — in the late sixteenth and the early seventeenth century. There was, in other words, a form of scholastic orthodoxy in place in English Puritan thought long before the convocation of the Westminster Assembly. Beyond that, the confluence and interrelationship of the British and continental forms was apparent from the beginning. All of the British thinkers just noted were well known, respected, and read widely on the continent, while all of the continental writers just noted, Trelcatius the Elder excepted, were published in England. This mutual interrelationship continued into the time of the Westminster Assembly, perhaps most notably in the cases of Twisse and Rutherford, many of whose major works were first published in the Netherlands.[31]

2. Exegetical continuities and developments. In the most general sense of exegetical or interpretive continuities, the post-Reformation orthodox era remained within the historical boundaries of what has come to be called "pre-critical" exegesis. Despite the significant differences between medieval exegesis and the biblical interpretation of the sixteenth and seventeenth centuries, the exegetical efforts of the Reformers and later orthodox writers continued to operate on the assumption that the historical sense of the text was the literal, grammatical sense and not something to be reconstructed underneath the text. In addition, the Reformation and post-Reformation exegetes assumed a fundamental unity of the entire text of Scripture, discernible through various patterns of promise and fulfillment, messianic typology, and figurative meaning.[32]

Beyond this broader developmental continuity that unites the exegetical patterns of the Middle Ages and the Reformation and post-Reformation eras, there are the continuities in more specific exegetical intent and in linguistic and philological methods that identify a more finely grained interpretive continuity between the Reformation and post-Reformation Protestantism. Orthodox Protestantism retained the Reformation-era stress on the literal sense of the text, on the scope of individual passages and the scope of the whole, and on the ability of the exegete to derive doctrinal

---

30. Jack B. Rogers, *Scripture in the Westminster Confession: A Problem of Historical Interpretation for American Presbyterianism* (Grand Rapids: Eerdmans, 1967).

31. See also Richard A. Muller, "'The Only Way of Man's Salvation': Scripture in the Westminster Confession," in *Calvin Studies VIII* (Proceedings of the Eighth Colloquium on Calvin Studies, Davidson College, Davidson, NC, January 26, 1996), pp. 14-34.

32. Cf. my comments in "Biblical Interpretation in the Era of the Reformation: The View From the Middle Ages," in *Biblical Interpretation in the Era of the Reformation*, ed. Richard A. Muller and John L. Thompson (Grand Rapids: Eerdmans, 1996), pp. 3-22 with the argument in David C. Steinmetz, "The Superiority of Pre-Critical Exegesis," in *Theology Today*, 37 (1980), pp. 27-38, and Brevard S. Childs, "The *Sensus Literalis* of Scripture: An Ancient and Modern Problem," in *Beiträge zur alttestamentlichen Theologie*, ed. Donner, Hanhart and Smend (Göttingen: Vandenhoeck & Ruprecht, 1977), pp. 80-93.

loci from the text. In addition, the humanistic methods of textual analysis, involving linguistic mastery and philological analysis, remained a constant in Protestant biblical study in the sixteenth and seventeenth centuries.

In the discussion of *dicta probantia*[33] and throughout the discussions of the various subtopics in the Reformed doctrine of the divine essence, attributes, and Trinity, we have consistently found an intimate, positive relationship between the Reformed orthodox dogmatics and the Protestant exegetical tradition. This generalization holds not only for the commentaries written during the period of orthodoxy but also for Reformation-era commentaries as well. Indeed, one of the great theological continuities between the Reformation and orthodoxy lies in the interpretation of biblical texts containing or implying theological issues and problems. A text like Genesis 22:12, where God says to Abraham, after Abraham's willingness to sacrifice Isaac, "now I know that you fear God," raised consistently, from the time of the Reformation to the era of high orthodoxy, the problem of divine eternity and omniscience. Similarly, Exodus 3:14, "And God said to Moses, I AM that I AM," consistently raised the issue of the divine eternity, changelessness, and essential necessity. In many instances, the exegetical tradition had carried over from the patristic and medieval commentators into the work of the Reformers and their successors.

These continuities indicate not only that the Protestant orthodox ought not to be faulted for a tendency to "proof-text" their theology without reference to exegesis, but also that the exegesis of the Reformers stood in considerable continuity not only with the exegesis but also with the dogmatics of the Protestant scholastics. The orthodox-era theologians, therefore, did not substitute a purely dogmatic exegesis for an earlier, humanistic, philological model used by the Reformers: the evidences do not point to a simplistic answer such as this. Both the Reformers and their orthodox successors followed out trajectories of literal, grammatical, philological study of the text — both, in short, drew on the results of Renaissance humanism. Both the Reformers and their orthodox successors also followed out established trajectories of doctrinal interpretation of text, resting on typological exegesis and on a method of drawing theological conclusions from the juxtaposition of texts.

The existence of these trajectories of interpretation of specific biblical texts, moreover, consistently points the discussion of the rise of orthodoxy away from an over-simplified continuity-discontinuity model. Differences in exegetical result obtain not only between individual Reformers and individual seventeenth-century thinkers, they also obtain among the Reformers themselves, and among the orthodox writers of any given epoch. The point can be illustrated in the mixed reception of Calvin's limitation of christological readings in the Old Testament: not all of his Reformed contemporaries followed this pattern, nor did all of the Reformed orthodox.[34]

Of course, if it becomes impossible to drive a wedge between the Reformers and the orthodox on such exegetical issues, it remains possible to claim that the entire

---

33. PRRD, II, 7.5.
34. See the discussion in Muller, *After Calvin*, pp. 164-169.

older exegetical tradition — including the Reformers and the orthodox — was guilty of a dogmatizing exegesis. This conclusion acknowledges the continuities in the theology and exegesis between Reformation and orthodoxy, but it leaves the modern critic of orthodoxy without a tractable Reformation.[35] There is, of course, an element of truth here: identification of the exegesis of the Reformers as well as that of the later orthodox writers as belonging to the tradition of pre-critical exegesis and as having, in common with the whole of that tradition, the assumption that doctrine can and must be drawn out of Scripture as an exegetical result, separates both the Reformers and the Reformed orthodox from modern, critical exegesis and, by extension, also from the theology that rests (or find itself incapable of resting) on so-called critical exegesis.

Even this claim of a dogmatizing exegesis, however, can be shown to miss the point: the Reformers and the orthodox shared, with the fathers and the medieval doctors, the assumption that the text of Scripture ought to be interpreted in and by the believing community and that the Word of God in Scripture spoke as a living Word to the ongoing people of God. The identification, by commentator after commentator, in Genesis 22:12 of a theological problem concerning divine knowledge and eternity, or in Exodus 3:14 of a doctrinal indication of the essential nature of God, arose out of the faithful encounter with the text in terms of the larger *scopus* of Scripture and the *analogia fidei*. This is not a matter of reading a text apart from its context — instead it is a matter of identifying the large context of belief to which the text speaks. Typically, the sixteenth- and seventeenth-century commentators do identify textual and linguistic problems, and they do, with some consistency, recognize the root meaning of the text in its textual and grammatical context; but they also recognize the larger context of theological significance within which the text resides and within which it is found to contribute to a larger biblical and churchly framework of meaning.

These reflections also point us toward the profound hermeneutical discussion and debate that can be fairly easily seen in the interpretive essays, the commentaries, and the text-critical efforts of the late Renaissance and the seventeenth century, but which also underlie many of the doctrinal debates of the era. The roots of this hermeneutical discussion take us back before the Renaissance and Reformation into the heart of medieval exegesis and its increasing concern to ground all meanings in the literal sense of the text. Given that the text at issue was Scripture, this insight tended to draw the doctrinal, moral, and eschatological (i.e., allegorical, tropological, and anagogical) meanings into the syntax of the biblical text and press exegetes away from a relatively loosely employed fourfold sense to various expanded forms of the literal sense. If this shift can be documented as in progress in the exegesis of Nicolas of Lyra and Denys the Carthusian, it can also be documented as largely accomplished in the exegesis of second-generation Reformers like Calvin.[36] In the historical progress of Reformed

---

35. Cf. Muller, *Unaccommodated Calvin*, pp. 10-11, 188.

36. Cf. Richard A. Muller, "The Hermeneutic of Promise and Fulfillment in Calvin's Exegesis of the Old Testament Prophecies of the Kingdom," in *The Bible in the Sixteenth Century*, ed., with an intro. by David C. Steinmetz (Durham, N.C.: Duke University Press, 1990), pp. 68-82.

orthodoxy, the difficulties of maintaining the patterns of churchly exegesis that had, in the patristic and medieval eras, so successfully generated orthodox Christian doctrine, became evident in the face of Socinian exegesis and in the face of the beginnings of historical criticism, both of which tended to isolate the meaning of the text in its dead past, or at least to remove the text from dialogue with the church's theology.

In its root form, this hermeneutical problem is nothing more or less than the question of the nature of the movement from the sacred text to the church's doctrine. In the patristic period this movement was achieved through the use of an interpretive method that included a fair amount of allegorical interpretation — and in the larger part of the Middle Ages, this approach was carried forward and then codified into what came to be called the *quadriga*. In the later Middle Ages, the Renaissance, and the Reformation era, this interpretive movement was increasingly grounded in the literal sense of the text, although the allegorizing of the Old Testament (in the strict sense of identifying *credenda*) hardly disappeared. With the codification of Reformation doctrine toward the mid-sixteenth century, this use of the literal sense was supported by the rhetorical practice of gathering *loci* out of the text and out of a variety of traditionary sources. In a very real sense, the use of the *locus* method relieved the potential hermeneutical strain of moving from text to church doctrine without the aid of a broader spectrum of meanings than the literal. At the same time, late sixteenth-century Protestant writers on interpretive method (like Whitaker) found that many of the results of the *quadriga* were in fact available by the identification of a *sensus compositivus*, a broader range of meaning within the letter, given the nature of the biblical language itself. The burden of high and late orthodoxy was the continuance of this approach under the increased pressure of philological, text-critical, and eventually historical-critical examinations of the Bible.[37]

A final point can be made concerning the relationship between the interpretive tradition and orthodoxy, one that functions also as a transition to the consideration of the Reformed orthodox treatment of the doctrine of God and, by extension, of other doctrinal topics. Not only does the interpretive tradition illustrate the major continuities between the Reformation and orthodoxy as well as the varieties and differences of approach and result within the Reformed tradition itself, it also illustrates, by way of the variety of literary genres that fall under the general rubric of "commentary," the relationship of theory to practice, academic theology to religion, that prevailed during the eras of the Reformation and orthodoxy. Here too, there is found a broad continuity of assumption coupled to differences in practical application, whether among the Reformers or among the orthodox. Specifically, given the fact that many of the more expanded commentaries, from those of Bullinger and Gualther in the mid-sixteenth century to those of writers like Durham and Jenkyn in the seventeenth, were initially delivered as sermons, they mark out the transition from a more academic or scholastic

---

37. I owe this paragraph, with its synoptic view of the argument of *PRRD* II, to discussions with my colleague, Willem van Asselt, in Utrecht.

expression of doctrine, suited to the university, and a more popular form of expression intended for consumption by the laity.

The lesson that is learned from these homiletical commentaries is that the scholastic orthodoxy of the era did indeed connect with the broader religious context. The sermons of the Reformed orthodox communicated a less-complex, vernacular version of the orthodox theology, a version quite overtly grounded in the exegesis and dogmatics of the era. Homiletical commentaries, moreover, evidence the movement from text to doctrine, the impact of the *locus* method, and a sense of the usefulness of Christian doctrine that mirrors the insistence of the more academic theological systems of the era that doctrine is either entirely or partially practical in implication and that all of the doctrinal topics spring from Scripture and have a "use" in the church and in Christian life.

C. The Doctrine of God in Its Protestant Development

1. The Reformed orthodox doctrine of God: rethinking the question. Very much as we saw in the discussion of the Reformed orthodox doctrine of Scripture, but in considerably more variety, we have identified a series of continuities and discontinuities between medieval scholastic theology, the Reformation, and the era of orthodoxy. In general, the scholasticism of the seventeenth-century Protestants was not the scholasticism of the Middle Ages. The differences between this later Protestant scholasticism and its medieval predecessor can be accounted for, moreover, only in part by the changes that took place in scholastic method itself as it moved through the later Middle Ages and the sixteenth century. Nor can the differences be wholly accounted for if alterations in philosophical perspective, notably the revival and reappraisal of Aristotle in the Renaissance, are added to the picture. Significantly, the Protestant scholastics of the seventeenth century are not as ready to engage in philosophical or theological speculation about the divine essence and attributes or about the internal workings of the Trinity as were their medieval forbears: here the clear influence of the Reformation is felt. More subtle continuities in developing lines of argument are also evident — as in the case of the grounding of Reformed theology in Scripture and God, understood as *principia*: the usage itself marks a development and change, but the pattern of argument, under both topics, where the principial understanding is posed against skepticism, reflects the ongoing debate over certainty and the rising concern over deism and forms of atheism. And the historiographical issue remains the charting of the debate and its impact on the development of the older theology: of course there are differences between the thought of the Reformers and that of the orthodox — and these differences relate to the ways in which the orthodox both appropriated and rejected elements of the medieval tradition and aspects of seventeenth-century thought in their attempts to carry the Reformed perspective forward into the uncharted waters of debate with skeptical philosophy, developing rationalism, Socinianism, and a host of other adversaries, at the same time that they attempted to produce an institutional theology for all levels in the church, from the academy or university course in theology to the tasks of preaching and catechizing.

Acceptance of scholastic method by Protestants also did not lead to an acceptance of such speculative discussions as were characteristic the late medieval dialectic of the *potentia absoluta* and *potentia ordinata*: these distinctions were recognized and used, but with very little speculative interest in the possible extent and application of God's absolute power. Similarly, the Protestant scholastics, particularly the Reformed, generally refrained from drawing on the medieval discussion of intra-trinitarian activity, specifically from discussion of the nature and character of the personal relations of begetting and proceeding. Indeed, the Reformed often note that even Augustine's more speculative psychological analogies were excessive. With specific reference to the doctrine of the divine attributes and the various distinctions made by the Reformed orthodox, the claim of excessive "speculation" also falls rather flat — the scholastic theology of the late sixteenth and seventeenth centuries did bring with it significant elaboration of doctrinal points, including the doctrine of the divine attributes. This elaboration did not, however, alter the basic meaning of the doctrine in general or of the particular attributes from the meaning held by the Reformers, notably the second-generation codifiers. What is more, this elaboration did not take the discussion out of the doctrinal framework in which the Reformers had been trained, namely, that of the latter Middle Ages — nor did this elaboration follow out those late medieval patterns of argument to which the Reformers had objected. Indeed, it can be argued that if late medieval discussions of the divine will and permission that led to various forms of soteriological synergism were at the center of the Reformation polemic against excessive speculation, then the development of the doctrine by the post-Reformation orthodox, albeit elaborated against various refined forms of synergism (such as represented by the Molinist *scientia media*), remained in continuity with the doctrinal intention of the Reformers.

2. Exegetical continuities and the issue of *dicta probantia*. Continuity with the Reformers and, particularly, with the codifiers and exegetes of the second generation of the Reformation is evidenced both in the restraint of the Protestant orthodox doctrine and in its highly biblical and exegetical content. Reformed scholastic discussion of the divine attributes, for example, although not paralleled precisely in the systematic essays of the Reformers and their immediate successors, does find firm rootage in the Reformation-era exegesis of passages in Scripture that deal with the attributes. It is quite common for points raised exegetically by the Reformers in the context of passages like Exodus 3:14 to carry over directly into the more systematic efforts of the scholastics.

With these exegetical continuities in mind, we return briefly to the issue of the *dicta probantia*, or "proof-texts," raised in the discussion of the Reformed orthodox doctrine of Scripture. Both in our analysis of the Reformed prolegomena and in our discussion of the divine essence, attributes, and Trinity, we have seen a consistent recourse to the text of Scripture even in the most dogmatic of sixteenth and seventeenth-century theological works and, in that context, a consistent reflection of the Protestant exegetical tradition. In other words, the so-called proof-texts in the older dogmatics do not stand as isolated texts wrenched out of their biblical and exegetical context, as is often alleged — rather they function as pointers from the dogmatic statement toward its exegetical roots as clearly identifiable in the commentaries of the day and in the older exegetical tradition generally. We have been able to trace, moreover, continuities of interpretation extending from the Reformers to the orthodox Reformed exegetes of the seventeenth century, often from the patristic period to the end of the seventeenth century. In addition, examination of the Reformed exegetical models also demonstrates continuity between the British and the continental thinkers.

The patterns of continuity were evident in the Reformed orthodox grounding of the doctrine of God in the biblical names of God: the dogmatic systems were constructed with consistent reference to biblical texts and to the meaning of the divine names in the original languages of the Bible, often with attention to etymology. What appears in relative brevity, moreover, in the theological systems, can be found at great length in the commentaries and the exegetical treatises of the era. These conclusions are also particularly apparent in the examination of specific texts related to the doctrine of the Trinity.[38] The brief citations found in the dogmatic systems of the era lead the reader back to the commentators, who, at great length, and often with considerable examination of the grammar and syntax of the passages in their original languages, consistently provide an exegetical foundation for the theological conclusions found in the more systematic works.

Of course, one response to this finding is the simple reiteration of Farrar's well-known condemnation (whether in its original form or in one of its more recent reiterations) of the era of orthodoxy as an era of dogmatizing eisegesis rather than exegesis. Given the continuity of the seventeenth-century orthodox reading of the text with the exegesis of the Reformers, including Calvin, the modern proponent of Farrar's view must also reject the Reformation as an era of dogmatic exegesis as well — and then, by extension, the exegesis of the church in all ages.

The evidence from the time, however, points away from eisegesis. The fundamental assumption of the so-called precritical exegesis was that the text of Scripture is the Word of God for the church in all time and therefore the vehicle of the highest and most perfect form both of God's revelation to his people and of holy teaching, *sacra doctrina*. The *locus* method of sixteenth- and seventeenth-century exegesis and the interpreters' insistence on identifying the "scope" of texts and books were designed to draw on the interpretation of the text in its original languages, including careful philological and text-critical work, in order to elicit the basic issues or topics addressed in each book of the Bible and in Scripture as a whole. We are not dealing with a dogmatic theological form imposed on the Bible, but with the result of centuries of meditation on the text in the context of a living Christian tradition. These are not, of course, the results of a modern, historical-critical method; but that method tends to cut against not only the dogmatic conclusions of the era of orthodoxy but also against the work of the Reformers themselves — not to mention the medieval tradition and the ancient fathers of the church. Comparison of the text of Scripture and its

---

38. Cf. *PRRD* IV, 4.2.

exegetically elicited meaning with the doctrinal claims of the Reformation and orthodoxy does not so much document the claim of proof-texting as it reveals the great divide in the history of exegesis between the precritical method shared by the Reformers and the Protestant orthodox and the historical-critical models of post-Enlightenment exegesis and theology. Let it be said simply: the precritical exegesis of the church both yields and supports traditional orthodoxy; the historical-critical method typically does not.

A case in point of the historical divide and of the exegetical and theological problem can be seen in contemporary reactions to the doctrine of divine immutability. The doctrine, it is said, has no basis in Scripture, inasmuch as it rationalizes away texts that indicate divine change and repentance as merely figurative and inasmuch as its identifies texts that deny divine change as having an ontological significance. The modern proponent of this argument rests his or her case on the assumption that the human biblical authors could never have understood God as ultimately changeless given that divine immutability is a Greek philosophical concept that cannot be found in the historically reconstructed ancient Israelite *Sitz im Leben*. This somewhat circular argument then permits the modern interpreter not merely to set aside a traditional (purportedly "Greek") ontology but also to substitute for it an alternative ontology: the texts referring to divine changelessness are now understood as figurative, while those referring to divine change and repentance are the supports of an alternative ontology. What separates the modern writer from the older orthodoxy is, among other things, the modern refusal of traditional assumptions about the authorship of the Bible and the ways in which its meaning is governed. The divide is not a matter of an unsupportable dogmatism on the side of divine immutability and a proper exegetical method on the side of divine change — rather the divide is a matter of two exegetical methods, the one churchly and at the foundation of the tradition of Christian doctrine and the other fundamentally non-churchly and purportedly "scientific."

3. The issue of natural theology and metaphysics in relation to the doctrine of God. In surveying the Reformed orthodox approach to the doctrine of God, we have seen a strong association of traditional metaphysics and various forms of natural theology with the discussion of divine essence and attributes. That certainly is a given. However, the point, frequently made by the older scholarship, that this association was a result of the reintroduction of scholasticism and, therefore, a sign of fairly radical discontinuity with the Reformation must be reformulated and nuanced: certainly, the theologians of the era of orthodoxy differed from the Reformers in the mere fact of having written natural theologies and treatises on metaphysics. None of the Reformers did so. Still, we have seen that the views of Calvin, Viret, Vermigli, Musculus, and others of their generation did not exclude, but instead pointed toward the possibility of a natural theology of the regenerate — and it is precisely such a natural theology that we find written by the likes of Alsted in the early seventeenth century. Alsted's model not only respects the concept of *duplex cognitio Dei* found in Calvin's *Institutes*, it also assumes the two-part understanding of the knowledge of God the

Creator — revealed both in nature and Scripture — as the starting point of a Christian natural theology.

Beyond this, the contrast between Calvin's lack of a developed view and the orthodox development of natural theology must also consider Calvin's intellectual context, which includes Viret's fairly extensive recourse to natural theology as a apologetic tool against irreligion and deism. Here we have the case of a close colleague of Calvin, against whose work Calvin uttered no protest, whose thought stands in strong continuity with the use of natural theology not only in Alsted but also in the apologist Mornay. In addition, the Reformed orthodox were clear about the limits of natural theology and metaphysics: they did not insert entire natural theologies or metaphysics into their systems of theology but, instead, used the results of these disciplines under the rubric of the ancillary use of reason. Thus, even in the doctrine of divine essence and attributes, the theological system does not reduce to metaphysics or natural theology: rather there is a movement in the locus from biblical exposition to rational argumentation, with the biblical exposition occupying the initial place and the rational argumentation following in support and elaboration. The *locus de Deo* does not, in other words, move from natural theology to supernatural theology or from metaphysics to biblical doctrine; rather, it moves from a biblical and rational/metaphysical presentation of the divine essence and attributes to a biblical and rational/metaphysical discussion of the Trinity, with the rational function and the metaphysical content operating from an ancillary position. In short, the doctrine of God observes the guidelines set forth in the prolegomena and understands the natural revelation as standing within the framework of a "true" and "ectypal theology," namely, within the framework of Christian meditation, given not only the fact of natural revelation but the biblical testimony to it.

In addition, just as there is a movement from the Reformers' indication of the possibility of a Christian natural theology to the Reformed orthodox writing of the natural theology, there is also a movement from the Reformers' often briefer discussion of particular divine attributes to the Reformed orthodox extended discussion. Even in the case of a Reformer like Calvin, whose *Institutes* does not contain lengthy statement of the divine attributes, the attributes are mentioned; they rest on an exegetical foundation that is virtually identical to the exegetical foundation offered by the orthodox, and their meaning is no different. The discontinuity on such issues as divine eternity, immutability, simplicity, and the divine affections is not one of content but one of elaboration and emphasis. What is shared by the Reformers and their orthodox successors is a common set of theological and philosophical assumptions, indeed, a common ontology.

In addition, the Reformed writers of the late sixteenth and seventeenth centuries were not unwary metaphysicians who simply reintroduced the categories and issues of medieval scholastic philosophy and theology. Rather, their understanding of metaphysics in general and, in particular, of the metaphysical issues related to the formulation of the doctrine of God evidence a critical appropriation of various elements of medieval scholastic thought and of late Renaissance philosophy with a view to the maintenance of the basic assumptions of their Reformation predecessors and with a view, equally, to the crafting of a suitable philosophical model for use in their own times. By way of example, the lengthy discussions of divine simplicity and of the divine intellect and will found in the Reformed orthodox theologies evidence a doctrinal continuity with the thought of the Reformers on those topics and, arguably, a use of elements of the medieval trajectories that lay behind the Reformers' understanding of those topics, plus an ongoing dialogue and debate with related late Renaissance or early modern developments.

4. Essence, attributes, and Trinity — issues of development, discontinuity, and continuity. When we raise the issue of continuity and discontinuity in the development of the Reformed understanding of God from the era of the Reformation into the era of orthodoxy, the stage is set for a discussion of a highly variegated and complex historical development, framed by a set of fairly stable basic exegetical and doctrinal assumptions on the one hand and a series of shifts in emphasis, alterations in approach to detail, changes in method, and differences in historical context on the other. Thus, on the side of change and what might be counted toward discontinuity, the expositions of the earlier Reformers, with several notable exceptions (viz., Musculus, Hyperius, and Hutchinson), tended toward rather brief expositions of the doctrine of God in which the language of essence and attributes was stated and a lengthy discussion avoided, whereas the expositions of the Reformed orthodox, beginning with the generation of Ursinus and Zanchi became increasingly lengthy and began, rather quickly, to draw overtly on the definitions and distinctions employed by the medieval scholastics. The methodological discontinuities are relativized to a certain extent by the presence of scholastic elements in the thought of the Reformers themselves and by the development of method throughout the later Middle Ages and late Renaissance, with the result that, if the methods of the Reformed scholastics were not identical with those of the Reformers, neither were they identical with those of the medieval scholastics.

On the side of continuity, there are the trajectories of biblical interpretation that pass through the Reformation into the era of orthodoxy, the notable respect for the results of the Reformers' work of biblical interpretation, and the issue already alluded to at the beginning of this paragraph, namely, the stable doctrinal assumptions held by Reformers and orthodox alike, in accord with the churchly theological tradition. If, moreover, the orthodox theologians tended to develop concepts like simplicity and immutability or, in the case of the Trinity, personal properties and relations, in more detail than the Reformers had done, there remains, nonetheless, the continuity of the concept itself — a continuity running through the Middle Ages, into the Reformation, and into the era of orthodoxy. In the doctrine of the Trinity, there is a striking continuity of an Augustinian or Western line of argument, mediated through the medieval scholastics, codified at the Fourth Lateran Council and the Council of Florence, respected by the Reformers, and developed as well by the Reformed orthodox. Nor, indeed, on this point, is Calvin and exception: his trinitarianism does not read out as following a "Greek" rather than Western, Latin model.[39] Despite, therefore, the changes in method of presentation and in density of argument brought on by the institutionalization of Protestant theology and by the debates of the late sixteenth and seventeenth centuries, basic assumptions concerning the simplicity of God, the meanings of various attributes, and the patterns of definition of the Trinity remained constant.

Given this fairly constant set of basic assumptions, we conclude, therefore, that those scholars who have argued that the doctrine of the attributes provides, together with the doctrine of the eternal decree, the initial point of departure for a purely deductive system of theology have thoroughly misunderstood the Protestant orthodox system. Neither the doctrine of God nor any other *locus* in Reformed orthodox theology was logically deduced — rather all the *loci* were elicited from Scripture in the context of a long tradition of biblical interpretation that had, for centuries, worked in alliance with theological formulation. One is struck, not by a newness of logic in the Reformed systems, but by a massively traditionary pattern and substance that stands in the line of patristic orthodoxy, with the Augustinian tradition of the Middle Ages nuanced in various Thomistic, Scotistic, and sometimes nominalistic ways, and with the teachings of the Reformers. One is also struck by contextualization of these patterns in the seventeenth century, where the background for use of the traditionary materials is the shifting ground of early modern philosophy and the problems of deism, skepticism, and the new rationalism.

An example of this contextualization is found in the proofs of God's existence, where elements of the Thomistic "five ways" are used in rhetorical rather than in formally demonstrative arguments. Given, moreover, that God has been identified as the *principium essendi* of theology, the nominally Thomist a posteriori arguments no longer assume that God is not *per se nota*, not self-evident: rather, in a structure of argument that is profoundly anti-Thomistic, the arguments assume that God, as *principium*, is both self-evident and indemonstrable. In the Protestant orthodox model, the "five ways" (or remnants of them) serve, along with purely rhetorical arguments like the argument from universal consent, to confute the deist and the "practical atheist." Similarly, the modified forms of the ontological argument — which can be understood against a distantly Scotist background — have been mediated to a few of the Reformed by Descartes and belong to the quest for indubitable *principia* as well.

In the doctrine of God itself, we have seen an emphatic biblicism in the foundational use of divine names and a pronounced a posteriori element in the doctrine of the divine attributes. Thus, the orthodox Protestant emphasis on the will of God derives as much from the importance of the will of God in the temporal economy as from any abstract consideration of the being of God. What is more, the character of God's will as just toward all mankind but merciful toward those elect in Christ represents as much a reflection founded on the scriptural revelation of an *ordo salutis* — and then applied to the discussion of how God must be granting his revelation — as it does a preliminary

---

39. See above 2.1 (A.3).

speculation concerning the divine essence. As such, the doctrine of the divine attributes, as governed by the discussion of the distinction between the attributes, is concerned primarily to show that the nature of God is consistent with the pattern of divine revelation without ever being restrictively confined within it. There is also little or no evidence in the subsequent *loci* of the orthodox system that their place in the system or their doctrinal content rests on a process of deduction: like the doctrine of the essence and attributes itself, the primary reason for the presence of these other doctrines in the orthodox system is that they were received from the tradition as elicited from the text of Scripture.

Similarly, Gründler's assertion that the "christocentric orientation of Calvin's thinking" gave way to a "metaphysics of causality" and, consequently, Reformed theology "ceased to be a theology of revelation," simply does not fit the evidence.[40] Had he presented Zanchi's doctrine of God in full, Gründler would have found far more exegesis than his study indicates and, more to the point, far more interest in the Trinity and far less in metaphysics and causality per se — and had he offered a genuinely representative discussion of Zanchi's *De natura Dei*, he would have found far more interest in Trinity and Christology within Zanchi's doctrine of the divine essence and attributes than his conclusion admits. And, of course, Zanchi did write extensive treatises on the Trinity and the Incarnation.

As for the simple contrast between, for example, Calvin's *Institutes of the Christian Religion* and Zanchi's *De natura Dei* or Turretin's *Institutio theologiae elencticae*, the former having no extended discussion of divine attributes, the latter offering a lengthy and detailed discussion, we note that there is a contrast but that it can be (and has been) much overdrawn. It is not the case that Calvin's omission of the attributes was utterly characteristic of the Reformed theology of his day: his contemporaries Musculus and Hyperius offered extended discussion of the topic. There is also no correlation between what might be called a purely metaphysical interest and the expansion of discussion of various attributes: thus, the Reformers confessed but did not elaborate greatly on the concept of divine simplicity, and the Reformed orthodox did elaborate on the concept at length — but it is also the case that the divine holiness received little attention from the Reformers and a good deal from the orthodox. If discussion of simplicity is viewed as primarily metaphysical or speculative (a debatable point), it is clear that the discussion of holiness is primarily exegetical. In addition, as we have seen, the Reformed orthodox discussion of the attributes stands in broad exegetical continuity with the exegesis of the Reformation. Nor is it the case that the Reformed scholastic presentation of the attributes marks the only point at which the scholastics offered more extensive discussions than Calvin: they also discussed the covenant of grace and Christology more extensively. The orthodox discussions are more detailed; they are clarified and developed through use of scholastic method — but the doctrinal content of such topics as divine simplicity, eternity, omnipotence, and the divine affections in fact changed little. Indeed, the diversity of the later orthodox formulations

---

40. Gründler, "Thomism and Calvinism," p. 159.

reflects the diversity of the medieval background and, insofar as the Reformers themselves offer clarity on these issues, the diversity of the Reformation-era teaching as well.

The Reformed doctrine of the divine will offers an instructive example of continuity and development, a highly significant one given the emphasis placed on the orthodox doctrine of the divine will in the attempts of an older scholarship to argue discontinuity with the Reformers and a highly "speculative" or "metaphysical" interest among the orthodox.[41] We have seen, in general, that the use of term "speculative" in this manner is not at all supported by the view of some of the Reformed that theology is a partially speculative discipline, given that the traditional usage *theologia speculativa* did not indicate speculation in the sense implied by the modern scholarship.[42] We have also noted the major a posteriori component of the Reformed doctrine of the divine essence and attributes. Even so, with specific reference to the divine will, examination of the teaching of the Reformers and of the Reformed orthodox reveals significant continuities. Both the Reformation and the post-Reformation writers taught a doctrine of the absolute, inalterable, and utterly free will of God apart from which nothing can exist. In addition, they also argued a series of distinctions such as those between the ultimate *voluntas beneplaciti* and the *voluntas signi*, the effective and permissive willing of God, the antecedent and the consequent will. It is not as if the Reformers did not use such distinctions and the orthodox retrieved them from the medieval scholastics in discontinuity with the thought of the Reformation: rather, we have been able to indicate a continuous tradition of recourse to such distinctions extending from the Middle Ages, through the Reformation, into the era of orthodoxy. That tradition, moreover, contained various trajectories of understanding — such as one according to which God antecedently wills one thing and consequently, given his foreknowledge of human choice, wills another; and another according to which God does not alter his will but rather antecedently wills the grounds and conditions of salvation and consequent on his own determination wills to save some people only. Both the Reformers and their orthodox successors allowed the latter form of the distinction, not the former.[43]

There is a similar trajectory of development in the doctrine of the Trinity: except for the very early Reformation tendency to refrain from the use of traditionary terminology, there is a consistency of terminological use in the movement from Reformation to orthodoxy, a continuity of doctrinal interest, and a constant recourse to traditionary exegesis on the part of both Reformers and later orthodox. When, moreover, one examines the second-generation codifiers as a group, the potential

---

41. Cf., for example, the often cited definition of Brian Armstrong, which notes among other things that Protestant scholasticism "will comprehend a pronounced interest in metaphysical matters, in abstract, speculative thought, particularly with reference to the doctrine of God. This distinctive Protestant scholastic position is made to rest on a speculative formulation of the will of God," in *Calvinism and the Amyraut Heresy*, p. 32.

42. See *PRRD*, I, 7.3 (B).

43. See *PRRD*, III, 5.4 (E.5-6).

contrast between an emblematically employed Calvin and various later writers like Keckermann and Burman on such issues as trinitarian metaphors disappears and a rather different picture emerges: rather than a movement from an antimetaphorical, antispeculative beginning to a metaphorical and speculative development of the doctrine, we can document the use of the metaphors by a minority of the writers, whether among the Reformers (notably Viret) or among the orthodox (Keckermann, Ainsworth, Burman). We also note that differences over this issue within the trajectory of Reformed orthodoxy were not a matter of great controversy.

There is also the issue of the relative uniformity of the doctrine of God in the Reformed orthodox systems: we have examined a large series of minor variations within the Reformed tradition, stemming from different trajectories of argumentation mediated through the eras of the Renaissance and the Reformation, but we have also registered a confessional consensus on such issues as middle knowledge and the relationship of the divine will to the contingent order. This relative uniformity must be measured against the diversity of the other *loci* in the system, whether the variety of covenant formulations found among the seventeenth-century divines or the great diversity of Reformed eschatology in the era of orthodoxy. Quite simply, there was no neat deductive process by which the Reformed determined the shape or content of the remainder of their theological systems.

Finally, it is to be hoped that the detail and extent of the analysis of the whole Reformed doctrine of God — essence, attributes, and Trinity — has not obscured the initial and fundamental point that this is a single doctrinal *locus*, not a series of *loci* in which priority is given to reason, natural theology, and metaphysical speculation at the expense of an emphasis on the "personal" God who is the Trinity. That is a typical modern caricature of the older theology. We have seen that the Reformed orthodox were highly attentive to trinitarian issues in their discussions of the divine essence and attributes, just as they were highly attentive to the issues raised by discussion of essence and attributes in their analyses of the doctrine of the Trinity. The progress of the *locus* was determined both by the movement of discussion from the truth of the existence of the subject of discussion (*An sit?*), to the question of what the subject of discussion is (*Quid sit?*), to the question of what sort of being is under discussion (*Qualis sit?*). Nor does this order of discussion avoid what moderns have called the issue of personal identity, "Who," as opposed to "What." The issue of personal identity was, in fact, raised immediately with the initial discussion of essence, so typically introduced by a lengthy analysis of the biblical names of God. In addition, it is not only arguable that the older order of system does justice to the way in which the doctrine God connects with the remainder of the theological topics — namely by way of the discussion of the Trinity — it is also arguable that the oneness, soleness, and numerical singularity of the God who creates, sustains, and redeems the world is the fundamental datum of the biblical narrative and that the Trinity of this Godhead is the deeper truth that the church labored to construct out of the christological witness of the New Testament. The order of discussion in the older dogmatics, therefore, has a cogency that is lacking in the modern critique.

D. Reformation and Orthodoxy: Final Assessments and Directions

This study of the prolegomena and *principia* of Reformed theology from the Reformation to the end of the era of orthodoxy (ca. 1520 to ca. 1725) has argued a variegated continuity in a context of development and change between the thought of Calvin and his contemporaries and the thought of their orthodox and scholastic successors. In its shortest form, the thesis describes a fundamental continuity of doctrinal interest, accompanied by an alteration both of method and of contexts. The detailed and methodologically scholastic works of various later Reformed writers remained in substantive continuity with the teaching of the Reformers — while at the same time adapting and expanding the models of Reformed teaching to accommodate new academic, cultural, philosophical, and polemical issues. This adaptation, expansion, and development certainly did produce theologies that did not, in the most externalized and formal sense, look like the theologies of the Reformers and that often dealt with issues that were not discussed in the era of the Reformation (for example, the larger part of the prolegomena and the problem of a divine middle knowledge), that had been discussed in shorter form (viz., divine simplicity, infinity, omniscience, the relation of the persons in the Trinity, and so forth), or that intensified and altered over the course of the sixteenth century (e.g., the rise of skeptical philosophy and the problem of certainty). The development also brought an interest in the larger tradition, both patristic and medieval, with the Reformed orthodox demonstrating the catholicity of their own tradition by a critical reappropriation of the past.

Given the detail of the subject; the variety and complexity of patterns of discussion and debate both among the Reformers themselves and among the Reformed orthodox; the often subtle ways in which elements of the medieval tradition, whether methodological, philosophical, doctrinal, or exegetical, were mediated through the Reformation and modified by the Renaissance; and the altered contexts of later Reformed thought, the relation between Reformation and orthodoxy is complex — too complex for the old "Calvin against the Calvinists" model and its associated theories and too complex also for a simple claim of either continuity or discontinuity. The model adopted here describes a developing tradition having continuity within a confessional perspective, defined in its breadth through different contexts rather than by emblematic documents or purportedly dominant thinkers. The patterns of continuity and development shown on the subjects of prolegomena, Scripture, and God, albeit sufficient to refute the claims of nineteenth- and twentieth-century proponents of the "Calvin against the Calvinists" and "central dogma" models, do not yet offer a complete portrait of the development from Reformation to orthodoxy. We can certainly say, in brief, that scholastic orthodoxy represented a development and institutionaliza-tion of the Reformation that brought about certain discontinuities in method, expression, and detail of statement, discontinuities related to the altered contexts of formulation, but that, in the cases of the doctrines examined here, also stood in fundamental continuity of meaning and intention with both the theology of the Reformers and its confessional definition.

Just as the trajectory of the topics included in prolegomena moved in a different way from the trajectories of the doctrine of Scripture and the doctrine of God — not to mention the variety of subthemes and developments within these larger topics — so do other topics and issues follow rather different paths between Reformation and orthodoxy. Historiographical models akin to the one developed have been applied to the development of covenant theology by such authors as Bierma, Woolsey, and Van Asselt, with a very similar result. Similar approaches need still to be applied to such major doctrinal topics as predestination, the order of salvation, Christology, the church, and eschatology before a fuller picture of the development of Reformed orthodoxy can appear out of the shambles left of the older dogmatic approaches. In each case, the trajectories of thought will develop differently and the relationship of later orthodoxy to the work of particular Reformers will vary. Just as Calvin did not provide the primary model for the later development of covenant thought, so also will it be seen that he was not at all the primary model for Reformed eschatology — which, perhaps of all of the doctrinal *loci*, was the most varied both in formulation and in trajectories of interpretation in the seventeenth century.

Study has shown and further study will illuminate the identification of the Protestant orthodoxy and scholasticism that followed the Reformation, not as "dry," or "rigid" recrudescences of medieval thought and method, but as aspects of a living and variegated movement situated and contextualized, culturally and intellectually, in the late sixteenth and seventeenth centuries. The confessional and exegetical continuities of this later Protestant theology with the thought of the Reformers are clear, as is the variety of the movement, the diversity of its roots in the diverse traditions of the later Middle Ages, Renaissance, and Reformation, and the multiplicity of its own intellectual trajectories. By setting aside an older, itself rather dry and rigid dogmatic model for addressing (I hesitate to say, for understanding!) this era and its relationship to the Reformation, I hope that the vast reservoir of its materials will be increasingly opened to detailed and duly contextualized study.

Bibliography

I. Primary Sources[1]

1. Ancient, and Medieval Sources

Alanus ab Insulis. *Regulae de sacra theologia*, in *Patrologia Latina Cursus Completus* [PL], ed. J. P. Migne, 221 vols. (Paris: Vives, 1844-55), vol. 210, cols. 621-84.

Albert the Great. *Opera omnia*. Edited by Borgnet. 38 vols. Paris, 1890-99.

_____. *Super IV sententiarum*, in *Opera*, vols. 25-30.

_____. *Summa theologiae*, in *Opera*, vols. 31-33.

Alexander of Hales. *Summa theologica*. 4 vols. Quaracchi: Collegium S. Bonaventurae, 1924-48.

Anselm of Canterbury. *Saint Anselm: Basic Writings*. Translated by S. N. Deane. LaSalle, Illinois: Open Court, 1962.

The Ante-Nicene Fathers: Translations of the Writings of the Fathers down to A.D. 325. Edited by Roberts and Donaldson. 10 vols. Grand Rapids: Eerdmans, 1950-51.

Aristotle. *The Basic Works of Aristotle*. Edited by Richard McKeon. New York: Random House, 1941.

Augustine. *De civitate Dei*, in PL, 41.

_____. *De doctrina christiana*, in PL, 34.

_____. *The Literal Meaning of Genesis*. Translated by John Hammond Taylor. 2 vols. New York: Newman Press, 1982.

Bernard of Clairvaux, *Libellus contra capitulum Gilberti*, in PL, 185.

Biel, Gabriel. *Collectorium circa quattuor libros sententiarum*. Tübingen, 1501.

Bonaventure. *Breviloquium* in *Opera omnia*, vol. 5.

_____. *Commentarius in IV libros sententiarum*, in *Opera omnia*, vols. 1-4.

_____. *Opera omnia*. 11 vols. Quaracchi: Collegium S. Bonaventurae, 1882-1902.

---

1. N. B. several conventions have been observed in the following bibliographies. Alphabetization of titles ignores initial articles, definite and indefinite, in all languages, but uses prepositions. Latin works beginning with the preposition "De" have been alphabetized under "D," Dutch titles begir.ning with the article "De" have been alphabetized according to the initial letter of the following word. Alphabetization of Dutch names follows the European practice of citing the actual last name as the primary reference rather than listing all names with "van" or "van den" under "V": e.g., Willem J. van Asselt is found under "Asselt." Anonymous works and Bibles have been gathered into the primary source bibliography under the alphabetically placed headings "Anonymous Works" and "Bibles" rather than alphabetizing them separately by title. In references to works in which no place and/or publisher have been ascertained, I have used the abbreviations "S.l." and "s.n." — *Sine locus* indicating lack of place and *sine nomine* indicating lack of a publisher's or printer's name.

_____. *Saint Bonaventure's Disputed Questions on the Mystery of the Trinity*. Introduction and translation by Zachary Hayes. St Bonaventure, New York: Franciscan Institute, 1979.

_____. *The Works of Bonaventure*. Translated by José de Vinck. 5 vols. Paterson, N.J.: St. Antony Guild, 1960-70.

Capreolus, Johannes. *Defensiones theologiae Thomae Aquinatis in libros Sententiarum*. 4 vols. in 3. Venice, 1483-84.

D'Ailly, Pierre. *Quaestiones super libros sententiarum cum quibusdam in fine adjunctis*. Strasbourg, 1490; repr. Frankfurt: Minerva, 1968.

Duns Scotus, Johannes. *Contingency and Freedom. Lectura I 39*. Translated, with introduction and commentary by Antonie Vos, et al. Dordrecht, Boston, and London: Kluwer, 1994.

_____. *God and Creatures: the Quodlibetal Questions*. Translated, with an introduction, notes and glossary by Felix Alluntis and Alan B. Wolter. Washington, D. C.: Catholic University of America Press, 1981.

_____. *Opera omnia*. Edito nova iuxta editonem Waddingi. 26 vols. Paris: Vives, 1891-95.

_____. *Opera omnia, jussu et auctoritate ... totius Ordinis Fratrum Minorum ministri generalis studio et cura Commissionis Scotisticae ad fidem codicum edita*. Civitas Vaticana: Typis Polyglottis Vaticanis, 1950-.

_____. *Ordinatio* (Scotus' Oxford commentary on Lombard's Sentences), in *Opera* (Wadding), vols. VIII-XXI; *Opera* (Vatican), vols. I-XV.

Durandus of Sancto Porciano. *In Petri Lombardi sententias theologicas commentariorum libri IV*. Venice, 1571.

Eusebius Pamphilius. *The Theophaneia or Divine Manifestation of Our Lord and Saviour Jesus Christ*. Translated by Samuel Lee. Cambridge: Cambridge University Press, 1843.

Gerard of Bologna. *Summa, qq. i-xii: Quaestiones de ipsa sacra doctrina*. Edited by Paul de Vooght. Paris: Desclée de Brouwer, 1954. [Printed as an appendix in Paul De Vooght, *Les Sources de la doctrine Chrétienne d'aprés les théologiens du XIVe siécle et du début du XVe siécle*.]

Giles of Rome. *Errores philosophorum*. Critical text with notes and introduction by Josef Koch, translated by John O. Riedl. Milwaukee: Marquette University Press, 1944.

_____. *Primum sententiarum*. Venice, 1521.

_____. *Theorems on Existence and Essence (Theoremata de esse et essentia)*. Translated,, with an introduction by Michael V. Murray. Milwaukee: Marquette University Press, 1952.

Gregory of Rimini. *Lectura super primum et secundum sententiarum*. Edited by A. Damasus Trapp and Venicio Marcolino. 6 vols. Berlin and New York: Walter de Gruyter, 1979-81.

_____. *Super Primum et secundum sententiarum*. Venice, 1521. Reprint, St. Bonaventure, New York: Franciscan Institute, 1955.

Henry of Ghent. *Summa quaestionum ordinariarum theologi recepto praeconio solennis Henrici a Gandavo, cum duplici repertorio, tomos prior-posterior*. Paris, 1520. Reprint, 2 vols. St. Bonaventure, N. Y.: Franciscan Institute, 1953.

Hermes Trismegistus. *Hermes Mercurius Trismegistus, his Divine Pymander, in Seventeen Books*. Translated by Everard. London: J. S. for Thomas Brewster, 1657.

Hugh of St. Victor. *De sacramentis christianae fidei*, in *PL* 176, cols. 173-618.

_____. *The Didascalion of Hugh of St. Victor: A Medieval Guide to the Arts*. Translated,, with an introduction by Jerome Taylor. New York: Columbia University Press, 1961.

_____. *Eruditionis didascalicae libri vii*, in *PL* 176, cols. 739-838.

_____. *Summa sententiarum septem tractatibus distincta*, in *PL* 176, cols. 41-174.

Hus, John. *Super iv sententiarum*. Nach Handschriften zum Erstenmal herausgegeben von Wenzel Flajshans & Dr. Marie Kominkova. Prague, 1905. Reprint, Osnabrück: Biblio-Verlag, 1966.

John of Paris (Quidort). *Commentaire sur les Sentences. Reportation*. Édition critique par Jean-Pierre Muller. 2 vols. Rome: Pontifical Institute of S. Anselm, 1961-64.

John Pecham. *Questions concerning the Eternity of the World*. Translated by Vincent G. Potter. New York: Fordham University Press, 1993.

Lactantius. *Divinae institutiones*, in PL, 6.

Marsilius of Inghien. *Questiones Marsilii super quattour libros sententiarum*. Strasbourg, 1501.

Migne, J. P., ed. *Patrologia Graeca Cursus Completus*. 161 vols. Paris: Vives, 1857-66.

Migne, J. P., ed. *Patrologia Latina Cursus Completus*. 221 vols. Paris: Vives, 1844-55.

Moses Maimonides. *The Guide for the Perplexed*. Translated by M. Friedlaender. London: George Routledge, 1956.

Nicolaus of Lyra. *Biblia sacra cum Glossa interlineari, ordinaria, et Nicolai Lyrani Postilla*. 7 vols. Venice, 1588.

Origen. *On First Principles*. Translated by G. W. Butterworth. New York: Harper & Row, 1966.

Peter Abelard, *Theologia christiana*, in PL, vol. 187.

Peter Aureole. *Scriptum super primum sententiarum*. Rome, 1596.

_____. *Scriptum super primum sententiarum*. Edited by Eligius M. Buytaert. 2 vols. St. Bonaventure, New York: Franciscan Institute, 1952.

Peter Lombard. *Sententiae in IV libris distinctae*. Editio tertia. 2 vols. Quaracchi: Collegium S. Bonaventurae, 1971-81.

Richard of Middleton. *In IV libros sententiarum*. Venice, 1507-9.

Richard of St. Victor. *La Trinité*. Texte latin, introduction, traduction et notes de Gaston Salet. Paris: Editions du Cerf, 1959.

Robert Kilwardby, *De natura theologiae*. Edited by F. Stegmüller. Münster, Aschendorff, 1935.

A Select Library of the Nicene and Post-Nicene Fathers of the Christian Church. Edited by Philip Schaff and Henry Wace. 2 series in 28 vols. Grand Rapids: Eerdmans, 1956.

Thomas Aquinas. *Compendium of Theology*. Translated by Cyril Vollert. St. Louis and London: B. Herder, 1947.

_____. *In IV libri sententiarum*, in *Opera omnia*, vol. 1.

_____. *On the Truth of the Catholic Faith: Summa Contra Gentiles*. Translated by Anton C. Pegis, et al. 4 vols. Garden City, N. Y.: Doubleday Image Books, 1955.

_____. *Quaestiones disputatae de veritate*, in *Opera omnia*, vol. 3.

_____. *S. Thomae Aquinatis Opera omnia, ut sunt in indice thomistico: additis 61 scriptis ex aliis medii aevi auctoribus, curante Roberto Busa*. [I. *In quattuor libros sententiarum*. II. *Summa contra gentiles. Autographi deleta. Summa theologiae*. III. *Quaestiones disputatae. Quaestiones quodlibetales. Opuscula*. IV. *Commentaria in Aristotelem et alios*. V. *Commentaria in scripturas*. VI. *Reportationes. Opuscula dubiae authenticitatis*. VII. *Aliorum Medii Aevi auctorum scripta*.] Stuttgart-Bad Canstatt: Frommann-Holzboog, 1980.

_____. *St. Thomas Aquinas, Theological Texts*. Selected and translated, with notes by Thomas Gilby. Durham, N.C.: Labyrinth Press, 1982.

_____. *Summa theologica*. Translated by the Fathers of the English Dominican Province. 5 vols. 1911; repr. Westminster, MD: Christian Classics, 1981.

_____. *Summa theologiae cura fratrum in eiusdem ordinis*. 5 vols. Madrid: Biblioteca de Autores Cristianos, 1962-65. [Also in *Opera omnia*, vol. 2.]

Thomas of Strasbourg. *Commentaria in IIII libros Sententiarum Petri Lombardi, cura Fr. Simonis Brazzolati edita una cum auctoris vita ex variis scriptoribus collecta per Sebastianum Fanensem*. Venetiis, ex officina J. Ziletti, 1564. Reprint, Ridgewood, N.J., Gregg Press, 1965.

Thomas of Sutton. *Contra Quodlibet Iohannis Duns Scoti*. Edited by Johannes Schneider. Munich: Bayerischen Akademie der Wissenschaften, 1978.

Totting, Henry, of Oyta. *Quaestio de sacra scriptura et de veritatibus catholicis*. Edited by Albert Lang. Münster: Aschendorff, 1953.

Vollert, Cyril (ed.). *St. Thomas Aquinas, Siger of Brabant, St. Bonaventure: On the Eternity of the World*. Translated, with an introduction by Cyril Vollert, Lottie Kendierski and Paul Byrne. Milwaukee: Marquette University Press, 1964.

William of Auvergne. *De trinitate*. Edited, with an introduction by Bruno Switalski. Toronto: Pontifical Institute of Medieval Studies, 1976.

_____. *The Trinity, or the First Principle*. Translated by Roland J. Teske and Francis C. Wade. Milwaukee: Marquette University Press, 1989.

William of Auxerre. *Summa aurea*. Paris, 1500.

William of Ockham. *Centiloquium*, edited by P. Boehner, in *Franciscan Studies*, 1 (1941), pt. 1, p. 58ff; pt. 2, p. 35ff; pt. 3, p.62ff; 2(1942), pp. 49ff, 146ff, 251ff. [Traditionally attributed to Ockham, no longer viewed as his work.]

_____. *Opera philosophica et theologica*. St. Bonaventure, New York: The Franciscan Institute, 1967-86.

_____. *Predestination, God's Foreknowledge, and Future Contingents*. Second edition. Translated,, with introduction, notes and appendices by Marylin McCord Adams and Norman Kretzman. Indianapolis: Hackett, 1983.

_____. *Scriptum in librum primum sententiarum*, in *Opera*, vol. 1-4.

2. Protestant and Other Sixteenth and Seventeenth-Century Sources

Adams, Thomas. *A Commentary on the Second Epistle General of St. Peter*. London, 1633; reissued, Edinburgh: James Nichol, 1839. Reprint, Ligonier, PA: Soli Deo Gloria Publications, 1990.

Ainsworth, Henry. *Annotations upon the Fifth Book of Moses, called Deuteronomie....* [Amsterdam: Giles Thorp], 1619.

_____. *Annotations upon the First Book of Moses, called Genesis. Wherein the Hebrew words and sentences, are compared with, & explayned by the ancient Greek and Chaldee versions: but chiefly by conference with the holy Scriptures*. [Amsterdam: Giles Thorp], 1616.

_____. *Annotations upon the Five Books of Moses, the Book of Psalms, and the Song of Songs*. 7 vols. London: Miles Flesher, 1626-27; 2 vols. Edinburgh: Blackie & Sons, 1843. Reprint, Ligonier, PA: Soli Deo Gloria Publications, 1991.

_____. *Annotations upon the Fourth Book of Moses, called Numbers....* [Amsterdam: Giles Thorp], 1619.

_____. *Annotations upon the Second Book of Moses, called Exodus....* [Amsterdam: Giles Thorp], 1617.

_____. *Annotations upon the Third Book of Moses, called Leviticus....* [Amsterdam: Giles Thorp], 1618.

_____. *The Book of Psalmes: Englished both in Prose and Metre. With Annotations, opening the Words and Sentences, by Conference with Other Scriptures*. Amsterdam: Giles Thorp, 1612; 2nd ed., 1617.

_____. *A Defense of the Holy Scriptures, Worship and Ministrie*. Amsterdam: Giles Thorp, 1609.

_____. *The Orthodox Foundation of Religion, long since collected by that judicious and elegant man Mr. Henry Ainsworth, for the benefit of his private company: and now divulged for the publike good of all that desire to know that Cornerstone Christ Jesus Crucified*. [Edited] by Samuel White. London: R. C. for M. Sparke, 1641.

_____. *Solomons Song of Songs. In English Metre: with Annotations and References to other Scriptures, for the easiaer understanding of it*. [Amsterdam: Giles Thorp], 1623.

_____. *The Trying Out of the Truth: Begunn and Prosequuted in Certayn Letters or Passages between Iohn Aynsworth and Henry Aynsworth; the one pleading for, the other against the present religion of the Church of Rome*. [London]: E.P., 1615.

Allix, Pierre. *A Dissertation concerning the Angel who is called the Redeemer, Gen. XLVIII*. London: R. Chiswell, 1699. [Printed as an appendix to *The Judgment of the Ancient Jewish Church*.]

_____. *The judgement of the ancient Jewish church, against the Unitarians: in the controversy upon the holy Trinity, and the divinity of our Blessed Saviour*. London: R. Chiswell, 1699.

Alsted, Johann Heinrich. *Definitiones theologicae secundum ordinem locorum communium tradita*. Hanau, 1631.

_____. *Diatribe de mille annis apocalypticis*. Frankfurt: Conrad Eifrid, 1627.

_____. *Distinctiones per universam theologiam; sumtae ex canone sacrarum literarum, et classicic theologis*. Frankfurt, 1626.

_____. *Metaphysica [Methodus metaphysicae], tribus libris tractata: per praecepta methodica: theoremata selecta: & commentariola dilucida*. Herborn, 1613.

_____. *Methodus sacrosanctae theologiae octo libri tradita*. Hanau, 1614.

_____. *Praecognita theologiae*, I-II, in *Methodus*, as books I and II.

_____. *Scientiarum omnium encyclopaediae*. 4 vols. Leiden, 1649.

_____. *Theologia catechetica, exhibens sacratiaaimam novitiolorum christianorum scholam, in qua summa fidei et operum ... exponitur*. Hanau, 1622.

_____. *Theologia didactica, exhibens locos communes theologicos methodo scholastica*. Hanau, 1618; 2nd ed., 1627. [Heppe #23]

_____. *Theologia naturalis, exhibens augustissimam naturae scholam, in qua creaturi Dei communi sermone ad omnes pariter docendos utuntur: adversus Atheos, Epicureos et Sophistas huius temporis*. Hanau, 1623.

_____. *Theologia polemica, exhibens praecipuas huius aevi in religione negotio controversias*. Hanau, 1627.

Altenstaig, Johannes. *Lexicon theologicum quo tanquam clave theologiae fores aperiuntur, et omnium fere terminorum, et obscuriorum vocum, quae s. theologicae studios facile remorantur*. Köln, 1619.

Alting, Jacob. *Analysis exegetica catecheseos Palatinae*, in *Opera*, vol. 5.

_____. *Dissertationes de sacrae scripturae perfectione*, in *Opera*, vol. 5.

_____. *Methodus theologiae didacticae*, in *Opera*, vol. 5. [Heppe #41]

_____. *Opera omnia theologica: analytica exegetica, practica, problematica: & philogogica*. 5 vols. Amsterdam, 1687.

Ames, William. *An Analytical Exposition of both the Epistles of the Apostle Peter, illustrated by doctrines out of every text*. London: John Rothwell, 1641. [Also in *Workes*, vol. III.]

_____. *Bellarminus enervatus, sive disputationes anti-Bellarminianae*. 3rd ed. Oxford: William Turner, 1629.

_____. *Disputatio theologica de perfectione ss. Scripturae*. Cambridge: Roger Daniels, 1646.

_____. *The Marrow of Theology*. Translated, with introduction by John Dykstra Eusden. Boston: Pilgrim, 1966. Reprint, Durham, N.C.: Labyrinth Press, 1984.

_____. *Medulla ss. theologiae*. Amsterdam, 1623; London, 1630. [Heppe #31]

_____. *The Workes of the Reverend and Faithfull Minister of Christ William Ames, Doctor and Professor in that Famous University of Franecker in Friesland*. 3 vols. London: Iohn Rothwell, 1643.

Amyraut, Moyse. *Brief traitté de la predestination et de ses principales dependances*. Saumur: Lesnier & Desbordes, 1634.

_____. *De mysterio trinitatis, deque vocibus ac Phrasibus quibus tam Scriptura quam apud Patres explicatur, Dissertatio, septem partibus absoluta*. Saumur: Isaac Desbordes, 1661.

_____. *The Evidence of Things not Seen, or, Diverse Scriptural, and Philosophical Discourses*. London: Thomas Cockerill, n.d.

_____. *A Treatise Concerning Religions, in Refutation of the Opinion which accounts all Indifferent. Wherein is also evinc'd the Necessity of a particular Revelation and the Verity and preeminence of the Christian Religion*. London: M. Simons, 1660.

Amyraut, Moyse, Louis Cappel, and Josue La Place. *Syntagma thesium theologicarum in Academia Salmuriensi variis temporibus disputatarum*. 2nd ed. 4 parts. Saumur: Joannes Lesner, 1664; 2nd printing, 1665.

Annotations upon all the Books of the Old and New Testament, wherein the Text is Explained, Doubts Resolved, Scriptures Parallelled, and Various Readings observed. By the Joynt-Labour of certain Learned Divines. London, 1645 [Also known as the *Westminster Annotations*].

Anonymous Works:

ΧΡΙΣΤΟΣ ΑΥΤΟ ΘΕΟΣ or an Historical Account of the Heresie Denying the Godhead of Christ. London: Thomas Hodgkin, 1696.

A Defence of the Brief History of The Unitarians, Against Dr. Sherlock's Answer in his Vindication of the Holy Trinity. London: s.n., 1691. [Sometimes attributed to Pierre Allix.]

The faith of one God, who is only the Father; and of one mediator between God and men, who is only the man Christ Jesus; and of one Holy Spirit, the gift (and sent) of God; asserted and defended, in several tracts contained in this volume; the titles whereof the reader will find in the following leaf. And after that a preface to the whole, or an exhortation to an impartial and free enquiry into doctrines of religion. London: s.n., 1691. [Edited and published by Thomas Firmin.]

Gods glory vindicated and blasphemy confuted: being a brief and plain answer to that blasphemous book intituled, Twelve arguments against the deity of the Holy Ghost, written by Tho. Bidle, Master of Arts ...: wherein the arguments of the said book are set down together with proper answers thereto, and twelve anti-arguments proving the deity of the Holy Ghost. London: William Ley, 1647.

The judgment of the fathers concerning the doctrine of the Trinity opposed to Dr. G. Bull's Defence of the Nicene faith: Part I. The doctrine of the Catholick Church, during the first 150 years of Christianity, and the explication of the unity of God (in a Trinity of Divine Persons) by some of the following fathers, considered. London: s.n., 1695. [Attributed to Thomas Smalbroke. Also found in Thomas Firmin, ed., *A Third Collection of Tracts.*]

The Scriptures and the Athanasians compared in their accounts of God the Father and of our Lord Jesus Christ. London: S. Billingsley, 1722.

A Second Collection of tracts proving the God and father of our Lord Jesus Christ the only true God, and Jesus Christ the son of God, him whom the father sanctified and sent, raised from the dead and exalted, and disproving the doctrine of three almighty and equal persons, spirits, modes, subsistences, or somewhats in God, and of the incarnation. London?: s.n., 1693?. [Edited and published by Thomas Firmin.]

A Third Collection of tracts: proving the God and father of our Lord Jesus Christ the only true God, and Jesus Christ the Son of God, him whom the Father sanctified and sent, raised from the dead and exalted, and disproving the doctrine of three almighty, real, subsisting persons, minds, or spirits: giving also an account of the nominal Trinity, that is, three modes, subsistences, or somewhats in God, called by schoolmen Persons, and of the judgment of the Fathers and Catholick Church for the first 150 years. London?: s.n., 1695. [Edited and published by Thomas Firmin.]

Two letters on the subject of the divinity of the Son of God: one to the Right Honourable the Earl of Nottingham, and one to the Reverend Mr. William Whiston: shewing that in the present method of that controversy, they are both mistaken: with a preface and a postscript, wherein somthing farther is offer'd from the Scriptures on that important question. London: Tho. Edlin, 1721.

Aretius, Benedictus. *Examen theologicum, brevi et perspicua methodo conscriptum.* Lausanne, 1579.

_____. *A Short History of Valentinus Gentilis the Tritheist.* London, 1696. [Original Latin edition, Bern, 1567.]

_____. *S. S. theologiae problemata, seu loci communes, et miscellaneae quaestiones.* Editio quarta. Geneva, 1589. [Heppe #7]

Arminius, Jacobus. *Amica cum Francisco Iunio de praedestinatione per literas habita collatio: ciusque ad theses Iunii de praedestinatione notae,* in *Opera,* pp. 445-619.

_____. *Apologia adversus articulos XXXI, in vulgas sparsos,* in *Opera,* pp. 134-183.

_____. *Articuli nonnulli diligenti examine perpendendi, de praecipuis doctrinae Christianae capitibus sententiam plenius declarantes,* in *Opera* pp. 948-966.

_____. *The Auction Catalogue of the Library of J. Arminius.* A facsimile edition with an introduction by C. O. Bangs. Utrecht: HES Publishers, 1985.

_____. *Catalogus librorum viri D.D. Jocobi Arminii quondam in Academia Lugudensi theolog. professoris.* Leiden, 1610.

_____. *Declaratio sententie I. Arminii de praedestinatione, providentia Dei, libero arbitrio, gratia Dei, divinitate Filii Dei, & de iustificatione hominis coram Deo,* in *Opera,* pp. 91-133.

_____. *De vero et genuino sensu cap. VII. epistolae ad Romanos dissertatio,* in *Opera,* pp. 809-934.

_____. *Disputationes privatae,* in *Opera,* pp. 339-444.

_____. *Disputationes publicae,* in *Opera,* pp. 197-338.

_____. *Epistola ad Hippolytum à Collibus,* in *Opera,* pp. 935-947.

_____. *Examen modestum praedestinationis Perkinsianae,* in *Opera,* pp. 621-777.

_____. *Examen thesium D. Francisci Gomari de praedestinatione.* Amsterdam, 1645.

_____. *Opera theologica.* Leiden, 1629.

_____. *Oratio de componendo religionis inter Christianos dissidio,* in *Opera,* pp. 71-91.

_____. *Orationes tres: I. De obiecto theologiae. II. De auctore & fine theologiae. III. De certitudine ss. theologiae,* in *Opera,* pp. 26-41; 41-55; 56-71.

_____. *The Works of James Arminius.* London Edition. Translated by James Nichols and William Nichols, with an introduction by Carl Bangs. 3 vols. London, 1825, 1828, 1875. Reprint, Grand Rapids: Baker Book House, 1986.

Arnauld, Antoine. *Logic, or, The art of thinking: in which, besides the common, are contain'd many excellent new rules, very profitable for directing of reason and acquiring of judgment in things....* London: T.B. for H. Sawbridge, 1685.

Arnold, Nicolaus. *Atheismus Socinianvs â Johanne Bidello Anglo, nuper sub specioso Scripturæ titulo orbi obtrusus. Jam assertâ ubique Scripturarum Sacrarum veritate detectus atque refutatus.* Franeker: Johannes Wellens, 1659.

_____. *Religio Sociniana seu Catechesis Racoviana maior publicis disputationibus (inserto ubique formali ipsius catecheseos contextu) refutata.* Franequeræ: Idzardus Albertus & Joannes Jansonus, 1654.

Arrowsmith, John. *Armilla Catechetica; A Chain of Principles: Or, an Orderly Concatenation of Theological Aphorisms and Exercitations.* Cambridge, 1659.

_____. *Theanthropos, or, God-Man: being an Exposition upon the First Eighteen Verses of the First Chapter of the Gospel according to St. John, wherein is most accurately and divinely handled, the divinity and humanity of Jesus Christ, proving him to be God and Man, coequall and coeternall with the Father.* London: Humphrey Moseley and William Wilson, 1660.

Artopoeus, Petrus. *The Divisyon of the Places of the Law and of the Gospell.* London, 1548.

Ascham, Roger. *The Scholemaster, or Plaine and Perfite Way of Teaching Children.* London: Iohn Day, 1570.

Ashwell, George. *De Socino et socinianismo dissertatio.* Oxford: H. Hall, 1680.

Attersoll, William. *A commentarie upon the fourth booke of Moses, called Numbers; containing the foundation of the church and common-wealth of the Israelites, while they walked and wandered in the wildernesse ... Wherein the whole body of divinity is handled touching matters dogmatical ... ceremoniall ...[and] polemicall ... Heerein also the reader shall finde more then five hundred theological questions decided and determined.* London: William Jaggard, 1618.

Austin, Benjamin. *Scripture Manifestation of the Equality of the Father, Sonne, and Holy Ghost. Wherein .. this truth is clearely confirmed, namely that the Scriptures manifest the Sonne, and the Holy Ghost to be equall with the Father, by ascribing to them such Names, Attributes, Works, and Worship, as are proper to God alone.* London: P. W. and John Wright, 1650.

Bagshaw, Henry. *Diatribae; or, Discourses upon select texts: wherein several weighty truths are handled and applyed against the Papist and the Socinian.* London: R. Chiswell, 1680.

Baier, Johann Wilhelm. *Compendium theologiae positivae, adjectis notis amplioribus . . .* denuo edendum curavit C. F. G. Walther. 3 vols. in 4. St. Louis, 1879.

Ball, John. *A Treatise of the Covenant of Grace.* London, 1645.

Barlow, Thomas. *Exercitationes aliquot metaphysicale, de Deo: quod sit objectum metaphysicae.* London, 1637.

Baron, Robert. *Metaphysica generalis.* Cambridge: John Hayes, 1685.

_____. *Philosophia theologiae ancillans.* Oxford: Leonard Lichfield, 1641.

Basset, William. *An answer to the Brief history of the Unitarians, called also Socinians.* London: Randal Taylor, 1693.

Bastingius, Jeremias. *An Exposition or Commentarie upon the Catechism taught in the Lowe Countryes*. Cambridge, 1589.

_____. *In catechesin religionis christianae*. Heidelberg, 1590.

Bates, William. *Considerations of the existence of God and of the immortality of the soul, with the recompences of the future state: for the cure of infidelity, the hectick evil of the times*. London: Brabazon Aylmer, 1676.

_____. *The harmony of the divine attributes in the contrivance and accomplishment of man's redemption by the Lord Jesus Christ, or, Discourses: wherein is shewed how the wisdom, mercy, justice, holiness, power, and truth of God are glorified in that great and blessed work*. London: J. Darby, 1674.

Baumgarten, Sigmund Jacob. *Theses dogmaticae*. Halle, 1767.

Baxter, Richard. *Catholike Theologie: Plain, Pure, Peaceable; for Pacification of the Dogmatical Word-Warriours*. London: Robert White, 1675.

_____. *The Divine Life in Three Treatises: first, The Knowledge of God, and the Impression it Must make upon the Heart ... second, The Description, Reasons, and Reward of the Believer's Walking with God ... third, The Christian's Converse with God*. London, 1664.

_____. *Methodus theologiae christianae*. London, 1681.

_____. *The Reasons of the Christian Religion*. London, 1667.

_____. *The Saints' Everlasting Rest*. London, 1660.

Beck, Johann Christoph. *Fundamenta theologiae naturalis et revelatae*. Basel, 1757.

Bellarmine, Robert. *Disputationes de controversis christianae fidei adversus sui temporis haereticos*. 4 vols. Rome, 1581-93.

Bengel, Johann Albert. *Gnomon Novi Testamenti, in quo ex nativa verborum vi simplicitas, profunditas, concinnitas, salubrita sensum coelestium indicatur*. Tübingen, 1742. 3rd ed., edited by Johann Steudel. London: Williams and Norgate, 1855.

Bennet, Thomas. *A Discourse of the Everblessed Trinity in Unity, with an Examination of Dr. Clarke's Scripture Doctrine of the Trinity*. London, 1718.

Bentley, Richard. *Remarks on a late Discourse of Free-Thinking*. London, 1713.

Bergius, Johannes, *Apostolische Regell: Wie man in Religionssachen recht righten solle*. Elbing, 1641.

Bernsau, Henricus Gulielmus. *Compendium theologiae dogmaticae*. Franecker, 1755. [Heppe #51]

Berriman, William. *An Historical Account of the Controversies that have been in the Church, concerning the Doctrine of the Holy and Everblessed Trinity. In Eight Sermons preached at the Cathedral Church of St. Paul, London, in the years 1723 and 1724*. London: T. Ward and C. Rivington, 1725.

Beverley, Thomas. *The grand apocalyptical vision of the witnesses slain, dated to its periods of prophesie and history*. London: John Salusbury, 1689.

_____. *The Thousand Years Kingdom of Christ in its full Scripture-state, answering Mr. Baxters new treatise*. London: s.n., 1691.

Beza, Theodore. *A Booke of Christian Questions and Answers*. London, 1572.

_____. *Confessio christianae fidei, et eiusdem collatio cum Papisticis Haeresibus ... adjecta est altera brevis eiusdem Bezae fidei Confessio*. Geneva, 1560; London, 1575.

_____. *Confession de la foy chrestienne*. Geneva, 1558.

_____. *Epistolarum theologicarum Theodori Bezae Vezelii, liber unus*. 2nd ed. Geneva, 1575.

_____. *Iob Expounded....* Cambridge, 1589(?).

_____. *Jesu Christi Nostri Novum Testamentum, sine Novum Foedus, cuius Graeco contextui respondent interpretationes duae . . . . Eiusdem Theod. Bezae Annotationes.* Cambridge, 1642.

_____. *The Other Parte of Christian Questions and answeres, which is Concerning the Sacraments.* London, 1580.

_____. *Propositions and Principles of Divinitie Propounded and Disputed in the University of Geneva.under M. Theod. Beza and M. Anthonie Faius.* Translated by John Penry. Edinburgh, 1595.

_____. *The Psalmes of David, truly Opened and Explained by Paraphrasis....* London, 1590.

_____. *Quaestionum et responsionum christianarum libellus, in quo praecipua christianae religionis capita kat epitome proponunter.* Geneva, 1570; second part, Geneva, 1576.

_____. *Response de M. Th. de Bèze aux Actes de la conférence de Montbéliard imprimées a Tubingue.* Geneva, 1587.

_____. *Tractationes theologicae.* 3 vols. Geneva, 1570-82. [Heppe #8]

Bible:

Das Alt Testament dütsch der ursprünglichen Ebreischen waarheytnach uff das aller trüwlichest verdütschet. Zürich: Froschauer, 1524-29.

The Bible and Holy Scriptures conteyned in the Olde and Newe Testament. Translated according to the Ebrue and Greke, and conferred with the best translations in diuers languages. With moste profitable annotations upon all the hard places. Geneva, 1560; 1561. Facsimile edition, Madison, Milwaukee, and London: University of Wisconsin Press, 1969.

The Bible of John Calvin: Reconstructed from the Text of his Commentaries. Compiled by Richard F. Wevers. Grand Rapids: Digamma Publications, 1994.

Biblia Rabbinica. Edited by Johannes Buxtorf. 4 vols. Basel: L. König, 1618-19.

Biblia sacra polyglotta, complectentia textus originales Hebraicum, cum Pentateucho Samaritano, Chaldaicum, Graecum. 6 vols. London, 1653-57.

Biblia sacra, sive libri canonici priscae Iudaeorum ecclesiae à Deo tradit, Latini recens ex Hebraeo facta ... ab Emanuele Tremmelio & Francisco Iunio, accesserunt libri qui vulgo dicuntur Apocryphi, Latine reddite ... à Francisco Iunio ... quibus etiam adjunximus Novi Testamenti libros ex sermone Syro ab Tremellio, et ex Graeco à Theodore Beza in Latinum versos. Secunda cura Francisci Iunii. London: G. B., 1593.

The Geneva Bible (The Annotated New Testament, 1602 Edition). Edited by Gerald T. Sheppard, with introductory essays by Gerald T. Sheppard, Marvin W. Anderson, John H. Augustine, Nicholas W. S. Cranfield. New York: Pilgrim Press, 1989.

The Greek New Testament. Edited by Kurt Aland, Matthew Black, Carlo Martini, Bruce Metzger, and Allen Wikgren. 2nd ed. New York, London, Amsterdam, Stuttgart: United Bible Societies, 1968.

The Holy Bible, conteyning the Olde Testament and the Newe. Authorized and appointed to be read in churches. London, 1591. [Also known as the "Bishops' Bible]

The Holy Scriptures of the Olde and Newe Testamente; with the Apocrypha: faithfully Translated from the Hebrue and Greke by Miles Coverdale, sometime Lord Bishop of Exeter. Zürich, 1535. Reprint, London: Samuel Bagster, 1838.

The Nevv Testament of Iesus Christ, translated faithfully into English, out of the authentical Latin ... in the English College of Rhemes.... Rheims, 1582.

The New Testament of our Lord Jesus Christ, translated out of Greeke by Theod. Beza: With briefe summaries and expositions upon the hard places by the said Author, Ioac. Camer. and

P. Loseler. Villerius. Englished by L. Tomson. Together with the Annotations of Fr. Junius upon the Revelation by S. John. Imprinted at London by the Deputies of Christopher Barker, Printer to the Queens most Excellent Majestie, 1599.

Novum testamentum graecum, cum lectionibus variantibus mss. exemplarium, versionum, editionum, ss. patrum et scriptorum ecclesiasticorum; et in easdem notis. Accedunt loca scripturae parallela, aliaque exegetica. Praemittitur dissertatio de libris N.T. canonis constitutione, et s. textus n. foederis ad nostra usque tempora historia. Studio et labore Joannis Millii S.T.P. Collectionem millianam recensuit, meliori ordine disposuit, novisque accessionibus locupletavit Ludolphus Kusterus. Editio secunda. Amstelodami: Apud Jacobum Westenium, 1746.

Testamentis Veteris Biblia Sacra sive libri canonici priscae Iudaeorum Ecclesiae a Deo traditi, Latini recens ex Hebraeo facti ... ab Immanuele Tremellio & Francisco Iunio. London, 1585.

Bibliotheca fratrum polonorum quos Unitarios vocant. 6 vols. Eleutheropolis [Amsterdam]: s.n., 1656.

Biddle, John. *The apostolical and true opinion concerning the Holy Trinity revived and asserted: partly by twelve arguments levied against the traditional and false opinion about the Godhead of the Holy Spirit: partly by a confession of faith touching the three Persons: both which having been formerly set forth, in those yeers which the respective titles bear, are now so altered, so augumented, what with explications of the Scripture, what with reasons, what finally with testimonies of the Fathers and of others, together with observations thereupon, that they may justly seem new.* London: s.n., 1653.

_____. *The apostolical and true opinion concerning the Holy Trinity, revived and asserted: partly by twelve arguments levied against the traditional and false opinion about the Godhead of the Holy Spirit, partly by a confession of faith touching the three persons ...: with testimonies of the fathers, and of others all reprinted, anno 1653 by John Bidle ... and now again with the life of the author prefixed.* London: s.n., 1691.

_____. *A Confession of Faith Touching the Holy Trinity, According to the Scriptures.* London: s.n., 1648.

_____. *Duae catecheses: quarum prior simpliciter vocari potest catechesis scripturalis posterior, brevis catechesis scripturalis pro parvulis ... primum quidem a Johanne Biddello; in Latinam linguam translatæ per Nathanaelem Stuckey.* London: s.n., 1664.

_____. *In sacra Biblia Græca ex versione LXX. interpretum scholia: simul et interpretum cæterorum lectiones variantes.* London: Joannes Martin & Jacobus Allestrye, 1653.

_____. *A Twofold Catechism: the one simply called A Scripture-catechism; the other, A brief Scripture-catechism for children ... Composed for their sakes that would fain be meer Christians, and not of this or that sect.* London: J. Cottrel, for R. Moone, 1654.

_____. *XII arguments drawn out of the Scripture: wherein the commonly-received opinion touching deity of the Holy Spirit is clearly and fully refuted: to which is prefixed a letter tending to the same purpose, written to a member of the Parliament.* London: s.n., 1647. [Also found in Thomas Firmin, *The faith of one God.* London: s.n., 1691.]

Biggs, Noah. *Mataeotechnica medicinae praxeos. The Vanity of the Craft of Physick. Or, a New Dispensatory. Wherein is dissected the Errors, Ignorance, Impostures and Supinities of the Schools.* London, 1651.

Bingham, Joseph. *Origines Ecclesiasticae, or the Antiquities of the Christian Church.* 8 vols. London, 1708-22.

_____. *Origines Ecclesiasticae, or the Antiquities of the Christian Church, and other Works.* 9 vols. London: William Straker, 1840. [Cited as *Works*.]

_____. *A Sermon on the Trinity*, in *Works*, vol. 9, pp. 326-48.

_____. *Sermon II. On the Divinity of Christ*, in *Works*, vol. 9, pp. 359-82.

_____. *To the Reverend Clergy of the Deaneries of Winchester and Somborn Regis*, in *Works*, vol. 9, pp. 349-38.

Binning, Hugh. *The Works of the Rev. Hugh Binning, M. A.* Collected and edited by M. Leishman. Edinburgh, 1858. Reprint, Ligonier, Pa.: Soli Deo Gloria, 1992.

Blundeville, Thomas. *The art of logike: Plainely taught in the English tongue ... as well according to the doctrine of Aristotle, as of all other moderne and best accounted authors thereof. A very necessarie booke for all young students in any profession to find out thereby the truth in any doubtfull speech, but specially for such zealous ministers as haue not beene brought vp in any Vniuersity, and yet are desirous to know how to defend by sound argumentes the true Christian doctrine, against all subtill sophisters, and cauelling schismatikes, how to confute their false sillogismes, [and] captious arguments.* London: Iohn Windet, 1599.

Bodin, Jean. *Colloque entre sept scavans qui sont de differens sentimens des secrets cachez des choses relevees.* Texte presente et etabli par Francois Berriot avec la collaboration de Katharine Davies, Jean Larmat, et Jacques Roger. Travaux d'humanisme et Renaissance, 204. Geneve: Librairie Droz, 1984.

_____. *Colloquium of the seven about secrets of the sublime [Colloquium heptaplomeres de rerum sublimium arcanis abditis].* Translated, with introduction, annotations, and critical readings, by Marion Leathers Daniels Kuntz. Princeton, N.J.: Princeton University Press, 1975.

_____. *Vniversae naturae theatrum: in quo rerum omnium effectrices causae & fines quinque libris discutiuntur.* Lugduni: Apud Iacobum Roussin, 1596.

Boderherus, Nicolaus. *Sociniano-Remonstratismus: Hoc est, Evidens demonstratio qua Remonstrantes cum Socinianis siue reipsa, siue verbis, sive etiam methodo, in pluribus confessionis suae partibus consentire ostenditur.* Leiden: Iacobus Marcus, 1624.

Bogerman, Johannes. *Spieghel der Jesuiten, ofte catech. Van der Jesuyten secte ende leere.* Amsterdam: J. Cloppenburch, 1608.

Boquinus, Petrus. *Exegesis divinae atque humanae koinonias.* Heidelberg, 1561. [Heppe #14]

Bold, Samuel. *A brief account of the first rise of the name Protestant and what Protestantism is ... by a professed enemy to persecution.* London: s.n., 1688.

_____. *A reply to Mr. Edwards's brief reflections on A short discourse of the true knowledge of Christ Jesus, &c. to which is prefixed a preface wherein something is said concerning reason and antiquity in the chief controversies with the Socinians.* London: A. and J. Churchill, 1697.

_____. *A short discourse of the true knowledge of Christ Jesus to which are added some passages in the reasonableness of Christianity &c. and its vindication: with some animadversions on Mr. Edward's reflections on the reasonableness of Christianity and on his book entituled Socinianism unmask'd.* London: A. and J. Churchil, 1697.

_____. *Some passages in the Reasonableness of Christianity, &c. and its vindication, with some animadversions on Mr. Edwards's reflections on the Reasonableness of Christianity, and on his book, entitled, Socinianism unmask'd.* London: A. and J. Churchil, 1697.

Boston, Thomas. *An illustration of the doctrines of the Christian religion, with respect to faith and practice, upon the plan of the assembly's shorter catechism. Comprehending a complete body of divinity. Now first published from the manuscripts of ... Thomas Boston.* 2 vols. Edinburgh: John Reid, 1773; reissued, 1853.

Boyle, Robert. *A Discourse of Things Above Reason, Inquiring whether a Philosopher should admit that there are any such.* London: F. T. & R. H., 1681.

_____. *Of the High Veneration Man's Intellect Owes to God; Peculiarly His Wisdeom and Power.* London: M.F., 1685.

Brakel, Wilhelmus à. *De Bedeeling des Verbonds en de Handelingen Gods met zijne Kerk in het O. T. onder de Schaduwen, en in het N. T. onder de Vervulling.* [In *ΛΟΓΙΚΗ ΛΑΤΡΕΙΑ, dat is Redelijke Godsdienst*, as part 3/1.]

_____. *The Christian's Reasonable Service in which Divine Truths concerning the Covenant of Grace are Expounded, Defended against Opposing Parties, and their Practice Advocated.* 4 vols. Translated by Bartel Elshout, with a biographical sketch by W. Fieret and an essay on the "Dutch Second Reformation" by Joel Beeke. Ligonier, PA: Soli Deo Gloria Publications, 1992-95.

_____. *ΛΟΓΙΚΗ ΛΑΤΡΕΙΑ, dat is Redelijke Godsdienst in welken de goddelijke Waarheden van het Genade-Verbond worden verklaard ... alsmede de Bedeeling des Verbonds in het O. en N.T. en de Ontmoeting der Kerk in het N. T. vertoond in eene Verklaring van de Openbaringen aan Johannes.* 3 parts. Dordrecht, 1700; second printing, Leiden: D. Donner, 1893-94.

_____. *Verklaring van de Openbaringen aan Johannes.* [In *ΛΟΓΙΚΗ ΛΑΤΡΕΙΑ, dat is Redelijke Godsdienst*, as part 3/2].

Braunius, Johannes. *Doctrina foederum sive systema theologiae didacticae et elencticae.* Amsterdam, 1688. [Heppe #40]

_____. *Leere der verbonden: ofte kort begryp der onderwysige en wederleggige godgeleerdheid.* 3rd ed. Amsterdam: Isaac Stokmans, 1723.

Brès, Guido de. *Confession de foy ... Auec vne Remonstrance aux Magistrats, de Flandres, Braban, Hainault, Artois, Chastelenie de l'Isle, & autres regions circonuoisines.* Lyon: S. Barbier pour J. Frellon, 1561.

_____. *Confession de foy. Faicte d'vn commun accord par les fideles qui côuersent és pays bas, lesquels desirent viure selon la pureté de l'Euangile de nostre Seigneur Iesus Christ.* Rouen: Abel Clémence, 1561.

Brightman, Thomas. *The Revelation of St. John, illustrated with analysis and scholions: wherein the fence is opened by the scripture, and the events of things foretold, shewed by histories.* Amsterdam: Thomas Stafford, 1644.

_____. *A Revelation of the Apocalyps, that is the Apocalyps of S. Iohn, illustrated with an Analysis & Scolions.* Amsterdam: Hondius & Laurensz, 1611.

Broughton, Hugh. *The Works of the Great Albionian Divine, renown'd in many nations for rare skill in Salems and Athens Tongues, and familiar Acquaintance with all Rabbinical Learning, Mr. Hugh Broughton.* Collected into one Volume and Digested into Four Tomes. London: Nathan Ekins, 1662.

Brown, John, of Haddington. *A Compendious View of Natural and Revealed Religion. In seven books.* Glasgow: John Bryce for J. Matthews, 1782. 2nd ed. revised, Edinburgh: Murray and Cochrane, 1796. Reissued, Philadelphia: David Hogan, Griggs & Co., 1819. Reprint, Grand Rapids, Reformation Heritage Books, 2002.

Bucanus, Gulielmus. *Institutiones theologicae seu locorum communium christianae religionis.* Geneva, 1602. [Heppe #9]

_____. *Institutions of the Christian Religion, framed out of God's Word.* Translated by R. Hill. London: G. Snowdon, 1606. London: Daniel Pakeman, 1659.

Bucer, Martin. *Defensio adversus axioma catholicum id est criminationem R. P. Roberti episcopi Abrincensis* (1534). Edited by William Ian P. Hazlitt. Leiden: E. J. Brill, 2000. [*Opera Latina*, V]

_____. *Deutsche Schriften.* Gütersloh: Gerd Mohn, 1960-.

_____. *Enarratio in Evangelion Iohannis (1528, 1530, 1536).* Edited by Irena Backus. Leiden: E. J. Brill, 1988. [*Opera Latina*, II]

_____. *Opera Omnia. Series II, Opera Latina.* Leiden: E. J. Brill, 1986-.

_____. *Quomodo S. Literae pro Concionibus tractandae sint Instructio.* Text, with introduction and translation by François Wendel and Pierre Scherding, in *Revue d'histoire et de philosophie religieuses*, 26 (1946), pp. 32-75.

_____. *Summarischer Vergriff der Christlichen Lehre und Religion.* Strasbourg, 1548. Published under the title, *Résumé sommaire de la doctrine chrétienne*. With an introduction, text and translation by François Wendel, in *Revue d'histoire et de philosophie religieuses*, 31 (1951), pp. 1-101.

Buchius, Paulus. *The Divine Being and its Attributes Philosophically Demonstrated from the Holy Scriptures and the Original Nature of Things. According to the Philosophical Principles of F. M. B. of Helmont.* London: Randal Taylor, 1693.

Buddeus, Johannes Franciscus. *Isagoge historico-theologica ad theologiam universam.* Jena, 1727.

Bull, George. *The Consubstantiality and Coeternity of the Son of God with God the Father, Asserted; or, some few Animadversions on a treatise of Mr. Gilbert Clerke, entitled, AnteNicenismus*, in *English Theological Works*, pp. 409-44.

_____. *Defensio fidei nicaenae. Defence of the Nicene Creed, out of the Extant Writings of the Catholick Doctors, who Flourished during the First Three Centuries of the Christian Church* [1685]. A new translation. 2 vols. Oxford: Parker, 1851.

_____. *The Doctrine of the Catholic Church for the First Three Ages of Christianity, concerning the Blessed Trinity, considered, in opposition to Sabellianism and Tritheism* [1697], in *English Theological Works*, pp. 371-82.

_____. *The English Theological Works of George Bull, D.D., sometime Bishop of St. David's.* Oxford: J. H. Parker, 1844.

_____. *Judicium Ecclesiæ Catholicæ trium primorum seculorum, de necessitate credendi quod Dominus noster Jesus Christus sit verus Deus, assertum contra M. Simonem Episcopium aliosque.* Oxford: George West, 1694.

_____. *The Works of George Bull, D. D., lord bishop of St. David's collected and rev. by Edward Burton.* To which is prefixed the life of Bishop Bull, by Robert Nelson. 7 vols. in 8. Oxford: Oxford, University Press, 1846.

Bullinger, Heinrich. *Compendium christianae religionis.* Zürich, 1556. [Heppe #2]

_____. *Confessio et expositio simplex orthodoxae fidei....* Zurich, 1566; text in Schaff, *The Creeds of Christendom*, III, pp. 233-306.

_____. *The Decades of Henry Bullinger.* Translated by H.I., edited by Thomas Harding. 4 vols. Cambridge University Press, 1849-52.

_____. *De scripturae sanctae authoritate.* Zürich, 1538.

_____. *The Old Faith, an Evident Probacion out of the Holy Scripture, that the Christen Fayth ... hath Endured sens the Beginning of the Worlde* (1547). Translated by Myles Coverdale. Cambridge: Cambridge University Press, 1844.

_____. *Sermonum decades quinque*. Zürich, 1552.

Bunyan, John. *The Whole Works of John Bunyan, Accurately Reprinted from the Author's Own Editions*. With editorial prefaces, notes, and life of Bunyan by George Offor, esq. 3 vols. 1875. Reprint, Grand Rapids: Baker Book House, 1977.

Burgersdijk, Franco. *Idea philosophiæ, tum moralis, tum natvralis, sive, Epitome compendiosa utriusque ex Aristotele excerpta & methodicè disposita*. Leiden, 1622. Oxford: Henricus Curteyne, 1641. Oxford: R. Blagrave, 1654. Oxford: R. Davis, 1667, 1675.

_____. *Institutionum logicarum, libri duo*. Leiden, 1626.

_____. *Institvtionvm metaphysicarum, lib. II*. Leiden: 1640. London: J. Crook & J. Baker, 1653; also Oxford: R. Davis, 1675.

Burman, Franz. *Consilium de studio theologico feliciter instituendo*, in *Synopsis theologiae* (Geneva, 1678), pt. II, pp. 653-690.

_____. *De Kooningen Israels*. Amsterdam: J. van Someren, 1682. [exposition of I Kings-Esther]

_____. *Orationes. I. De collegiis theologicis et philosophicis; II. De doctrina Christiana; III. De Belgica afflicta; IV. De causis Belgicae afflictae*. 4 parts. Utrecht, 1700.

_____. *De Rigteren Israels*. Urecht: C. Noenaart, 1675. [exposition of Joshua, Judges, Ruth]

_____. *Samuel*. Utrecht: C. Noenaart, 1678. [exposition of I-II Samuel]

_____. *Synopsis theologiae et speciatim oeconomiae foederum Dei*. 2 parts. Geneva, 1678; Den Haag, 1687. [Heppe #38]

_____. See also: Descartes, René.

Burnet, Gilbert. *An Exposition of the Thirty-Nine Articles of the Church of England*. London, 1699. Revised and corrected, with notes by James R. Page. New York: Appleton, 1852.

_____. *A Modest Survey of the most considerable things in a Discourse lately published entitled the Naked Truth*. London: Moses Pitt, 1676.

Burnet, Thomas. *The Scripture Trinity Intelligibly Explained: or, an Essay toward the Demonstration of a Trinity in Unity, from Reasons an Scripture. In a Chain of Consequences from Certain Principles. Which ... may serve as an answer to Dr. Waterland and Dr. Clarke and all Others ... whether Arians, Socinians, or whatever other Denomination....* London: J. Roberts, 1720.

Burroughs, Jeremiah. *An Exposition of the Prophecy of Hosea*. 4 vols. London, 1643-51. Reissued in 1 vol. Edinburgh: James Nichol, 1865.

_____. *Irenicum to the Lovers of Truth and Peace. Heart-divisions opened in the causes and evils of them*. London, 1653.

Bury, Arthur. *A defence of the doctrines of the Holy Trinity and incarnation placed in their due light in answer to a letter, written to the clergy of both universities*. London?: s.n., 1694.

_____ [attrib.]. *The Doctrine of the Holy Trinity placed in its due light by an answer to a late book, entituled, Animadversions upon Dr. Sherlock's book, &c. [by Dr. Robert South]: also the doctrine of the incarnation of our Lord asserted and explain'd*. London: s.n., 1694. [Also attributed to William Sherlock.]

_____. *The judgment of a disinterested person concerning the controversy about the B. Trinity, depending between Dr. S--th and Dr. Sherlock*. London: E. Whitlock, 1696.

_____. *Latitudinarius orthodoxus accesserunt vindiciae, libertatis Christianae, Ecclesiae Anglicanae, & Arthur Bury, contra ineptias & calumnias P. Jurieu ... [I. In genere, de fide in religione naturali, Mosaica & Christiana, II. In particulari, de Christianae religionis mysteriis, Sancra Trinitate, Christi incarnatione, corporis resurrectione, coena Dominica]*. Londini: Sam. Buckley, 1697.

_____. *The naked gospel discovering I. What was the gospel which our Lord and his apostles preached, II. What additions and alterations latter ages have made in it, III. What advantages and damages have thereupon ensued: Part I. Of Faith, and therein, of the Holy Trinity, the incarnation of our Blessed Saviour, and the resurrection of the body*. London?: s.n., 1690; London: Nathanael Ranew, 1691.

Buxtorf, Johannes I. *Tiberias sive commentarius Masorethicus triplex: historicus, didacticus, criticus. Recognitus ... à Johanne Buxtorfio Fil*. Basel, 1665.

Buxtorf, Johannes II. *Anticritica seu vindiciae veritatis hebraica adversus Ludovici Cappelli criticam quam vocat sacram eiusque defensionem*. Basel, 1653.

_____. *Dissertationes philologico-theologicae. I. De linguae hebraeae origine, antiquitate et sanctitate. II. De linguae hebraeae confusione et plurium linguarum originae. III. De linguae hebraeae conservatione, propagatione et duratione. IV. De litterarum hebraicarum genuina antiquitate. V. De nominibus Dei hebraicis. VI. De Decalogo. VII. De primae coena Dominicae ritibus et forma*. Basel, 1645.

_____. *Tractatus de punctorum vocalium, et accentum, in libris Veteris Testamenti hebraicis, origine, antiquitate, et authoritate: oppositus arcano punctationis revelato Ludovici Cappelli*. Basel, 1648.

Cajetan, Thomas de Vio, Cardinal. *Commentary on Being and Essence (In De ente et Essentia d. Thomas Aquinatis)*. Translated, with and introduction by Lottie H. Kendzierski and Francis C. Wade. Milwaukee, Marquette University Press, 1964.

Calov, Abraham. *Socinismus profligatus, hoc est, Errorum Socinianorum luculenta confutatio: è S. literis, propriisq[ue] ipsorum testimoniis, per universam theologiam, trecentis quaestionibus methodo concinna, brevitate nervosa, ita instituta ... operâ & studio Abraham Calovii*. Wittenberg: Joh. Borckard, 1668.

Calvin, John. *Canons and Decrees of the Council of Trent: with the Antidote*, in *Selected Works*, vol. 3.

_____. *Calvin's Calvinism: Treatises on the Eternal Predestination of God and the Secret Providence of God*. Translated by Henry Cole. London, 1856. Reprint, Grand Rapids: Reformed Free Publishing Association, n.d.

_____. *Commentaries of John Calvin*. 46 vols. Edinburgh: Calvin Translation Society, 1844-55. Reprint, Grand Rapids: Baker Book House, 1979.

_____. *Concerning the Eternal Predestination of God*. Translated, with an introduction by J.K.S. Reid. London: James Clarke, 1961.

_____. "Four Letters from the Socinus-Calvin Correspondence (1549)," in *Italian Reformation Studies in Honor of Laelius Socinus*, edited by John Tedeschi (Florence, 1965), pp. 215-230.

_____. *Institutes of the Christian Religion* [1536]. Translated and annotated by Ford Lewis Battles. Rev. ed. Grand Rapids: Eerdmans, 1986.

_____. *Institutes of the Christian Religion*. 2 vols. Translated by Henry Beveridge. Edinburgh, 1845. Reprint, Grand Rapids: Eerdmans, 1994.

_____. *Institutes of Christian Religion*. Edited by John T. McNeill, translated by F. L. Battles. 2 vols. Philadelphia: Westminster, 1950.

_____. *Institutio christianae religionis, in libris quatuor nunc primum digesta, certisque distincta capitibus, ad aptissimam methodum: aucta etiam tam magna accessione ut propemodum opus novum haberi possit* Geneva: Robertus Stephanus, 1559. [Heppe #1]

_____. *Institution de la Religion chrestienne* [1541]. Edited by J. Pannier. Paris, 1936-39.

_____. *Ioannis Calvini opera quae supersunt omnia.* Edited by G. Baum, E. Cunitz, and E. Reuss. Brunswick: Schwetschke, 1863-1900.

_____. *Selected Works of John Calvin: Tracts and Letters.* Edited by Henry Beveridge and Jules Bonnet. 7 vols. Grand Rapids: Baker Book House, 1983.

_____. *Sermons of Maister Iohn Calvin, upon the Book of Iob.* Translated by Arthur Golding. London: George Bishop, 1574. Reprint, Edinburgh: Banner of Truth, 1993.

_____. *Sermons of M. John Calvin, on the Epistles of S. Paule to Timothie and Titus.* Translated by L. T. London: G. Bishop, 1579. Reprint, Edinburgh: Banner of Truth, 1983.

_____. *The Sermons of M. Iohn Calvin upon the Fifth Booke of Moses called Deuteronomie.* London: Henry Middleton, 1583. Reprint, Edinburgh: Banner of Truth, 1987.

_____. *Treatises Against the Anabaptists and Against the Libertines.* Translated and edited by Benjamin Wirt Farley. Grand Rapids: Baker Book House, 1982.

Camerarius, Joachim. *Commentarius in Novum Foedus: in quo figurae sermonis, et verborum significatio, et orationis sententia, ad illius Foederis intelligentiam certiorem, tractentur.* Cambridge, 1642.

Cameron, John. *An Examination of those Plausible Appearances which seeme most to commend the Romish Church, and to prejudice the Reformed.* Oxford: John Lichfield and William Turner, 1626.

_____. *A Tract of the Soveraigne Iudge of Controversies in Matters of Religion.* Translated by John Verneuil. Oxford: William Turner, 1648.

Campanella, Tommaso. *Universalis philosophiae, seu metaphysicarum rerum, iuxta propria dogmata, patres tres.* Paris, 1638. Reprint with an introduction by Luigi Firpo. Turin: Bottega d'Erasmo, 1961.

Cano, Melchior. *De locis theologicis* (1564), in J.-P. Migne, ed., *Theologiae cursus completus,* 10 vols. (Paris: Vives, 1837), vol. 1.

Cappel, Louis. *Arcanum punctationis revelatum, sive de punctorum vocalium et accentum apud Hebraeos vera et germanae antiquitate, libri duo.* Leiden: J. Maire, 1624.

_____. *Commentarii et notae criticae in Vetus Testamentum.* Amsterdam: P. & J. Blaeu, 1689.

_____. *Critica sacra, sive de variis quae in sacris veteri Testamenti libris occurunt lectionibus, libri sex.* Paris, 1650.

_____. *The Hinge of Faith and Religion; or, A Proof of the Deity against Atheists and Profane Persons, by Reason, and the Testimony of Scripture: the Divinity of which is Demonstrated.* Translated by Philip Marinel. London: Thomas Dring, 1660.

Caroli, Petrus. *Brevis explicatio orthodoxae fidei de uno Deo et Spiritu Sancto adversos blasphemos G. Blandratae et F. Davidis errores.* Wittenberg, 1571.

Cartwright, Christopher. *Electa thargumico-rabbinica; sive Annotationes in Exodum.* London, 1658.

_____. *Electa thargumico-rabbinica; sive Annotationes in Genesin.* London, 1648.

Cartwright, Thomas. *An Answere to the Preface of the Rhemish Testament.* London, 1602.

_____. *Christian Religion: substantially, methodicallie, plainlie, and profitablie treated.* London, 1611.

_____. *A Confutation of the Rhemists Translation, Glosses, and Annotations on the New Testament, so farre as they containe Manifest Impieties, Heresies, Idolatries....* Leiden, 1618.

_____. *A Dilucidation, or Exposition of the Epistle of St. Paul to the Colossians, Deliuered in Sundry Sermons.* Edited by A. B. Grosart. Edinburgh, 1864.

_____. *A Treatise of the Christian Religion, or the Whole Bodie and Substance of Divinitie.* London: Felix Kyngston, 1616.

Caryl, Joseph. *An Exposition with Practicall Observations upon .... the Booke of Iob.* 12 vols. London: G. Miller and M. Simmons, 1644-66.

Cave, William. *Scriptorum ecclesiasticorum historia literaria a Christo [nato] usque ad saec. XIV facili methodo digesto ..., authore Guilielo Cave, accedunt scriptores gentiles ... et cujusvis saeculi breviarium.* London: Richardi Chiswell, 1688.

_____. *Scriptorum ecclesiasticorum historia literaria, a Christo Nato usque ad saeculum XIV, facili methodo digesta, qua, de vita illorum ac rebus gestis, de secta, dogmatibus, elogio, stylo; de scriptis genuinis, dubiis, supposititiis, ineditis, deperditis, fragmentis; deque variis operum editionibus perspicue agitur, accedunt scriptores gentiles, christianae religionis oppugnatores; et cujusvis saeculi Breviarium; additur ad finem cujusque saeculi Conciliorum omnium, tum generalium tum particularium, historica notitia; ... accedunt ab aliis manibus appendices duae, ab ineunte saeculo XIV. ad annum usque MDXVII. nunc in unam congestae; ad calcem vero operis ejusdem Cavei dissertationes tres, I. De Scriptoribus Eccl. incertae Aetatis, II. De Libris et Officiis Eccl. Graecorum, III. De Eusebii Caesariensis Arianismo; adversus Johannem Clericum, una cum Epistola Apologetica adversus iniquas ejusdem Clerici criminationes.* Basel: Johann Rudolph Im-Hoff, 1741-45.

Chandieu, Antoine de la Roche. *De vera methodo theologice simul et scholastice disputandi,* preface to *De verbo Dei scripto,* in *Opera theologica.*

_____. *Disputationes accurate theologice et scholastice tractate.* Cambridge: Thomas Thomas, 1584.

_____. *Opera theologica.* Geneva, 1593.

_____. *A Treatise Touching the Word of God Written, against the Traditions of Men. Handled both Schoolelike and Divinelike.* London: John Harison, 1583.

Charnock, Stephen. *The Works of the late learned Divine Stephen Charnock, B.D.* 2 vols. London: Printed for Ben Griffin, and Tho. Cockeril, 1684.

_____. *Discourses upon the Existence and Attributes of God.* With his life and character, by William Symington, D.D. 2 vols. New York: Robert Carter, 1853.

Chemnitz, Martin. *Examination of the Council of Trent.* 4 vols. Translated by Fred Kramer. St. Louis: Concordia, 1971-86.

_____. *Loci theologici.* 3 vols. Frankfurt and Wittenberg, 1653.

_____. *Loci theologici.* 2 vols. Translated by J. A. O. Preus. St. Louis: Concordia, 1989.

Cheynell, Francis. *The Divine Triunity of the Father, Son, and Holy Spirit, and Holy Spirit: or, the blessed Doctrine of three Coessential Subsistents in the Eternall Godhead.* London: T. R. & E. M., 1650.

_____. *The Rise, Growth, and Danger of Socinianisme together with a plaine discovery of a desperate designe of corrupting the Protestant religion, whereby it appeares that the religion which hath been so violently contended for (by the Archbishop of Canterbury and his adherents) is not the true pure Protestant religion, but an hotchpotch of Arminianisme, Socinianisme and popery.* London: Samuel Gellibrand, 1643.

Chillingworth, William. *The Religion of Protestants, a safe way to salvation, or, An answer to a booke entitles Mercy and truth, or, Charity maintain'd by Catholiques, which pretends to prove the contrary.* Oxford: Leonard Lichfield, 1638.

Clarke, Samuel. *A Demonstration of the Being and Attributes of God. More Particularly in answer to Mr. Hobbes, Spinoza, and their followers. Being the substance of eight sermons preached in the year 1704 at the lecture founded by the honourable Robert Boyle, Esquire.* Edited by Ezio Vailati. Cambridge: Cambridge University Press, 1998.

_____. *A Discourse Concerning the Being and Attributes of God, the Obligations of Natural Religion, and the Truth and Certainty of Christian Revelation. In Answer to Mr Hobbes, Spinoza, the Author of the Oracles of Religion, and Other Deniers of Natural and Revealed Religion,* in *Works,* vol. II.

_____. *Observations on Dr. Waterland's Second Defense of Some Queries,* in *Works,* IV, pp. 483-530.

_____. *A Reply to the Objections of Robert Nelson, and of an anonymous author against Dr. Clarke's Scripture-Doctrine of the Trinity. To which is added, An answer to the remarks of the author of Some considerations concerning the Trinity.* London: James Knapton, 1714.

_____. *The Scripture Doctrine of the Trinity,* in *Works,* vol. IV.

_____. *Several Letters to the Reverend Dr. Clarke from a Gentleman in Gloucestershire, relating to the Discourse Concerning the Being and Attributes of God; with the Doctor's Answers Thereunto,* in *Works,* vol. II.

_____. *The Works of Samuel Clarke.* 4 vols. London, 1738. Reprint, New York: Garland, 1978.

Clerke, Gilbert. *Tractatus tres: quorum qui prior ante-Nicenismus dicitur, is exhibet testimonia patrum ante-Nicenorum, in quibus eluct sensus ecclesiæ primævo-catholicæ, quoad articulum de Trinitate: in secondo, Brevis responsio ordinatur ad D. G. Bulli defensionem synodi Nicenæ / authore Gilberto Clerke ... ; Argumentum postremi, vera & antiqua fides de divinitate Christi, explicata & asserta, contra D. Bulli, judicium ecclesiæ catholicæ &c. per anonymum.* London?: s.n., 1695.

Cloppenburg, Johannes. *Anti-Smalcius, de divinitate Jesu Christi: Pars prior, De munere Christi prophetico. Pars posterior, De munere Christi regio.* Franeker: Idzardus Balck, 1652.

_____. *Aphorismi theologiae christianae, ex scriptura prophetica et apostolica demonsrtati,* in *Opera,* vol. I.

_____. *Compendiolum Socinianismi.* Franekeræ: Idzardus Balck, 1651.

_____. *Disputationes XV. de canone theologiae et iudicio controversiarum secundum canonem,* in *Opera,* vol. II.

_____. *Exercitationes super locos communes theologicos,* in *Opera,* vol. I.

_____. *Gangrena theologiae Anabaptisticae, Dat is, Cancker v. d. Leere der Weder-dooperen.* Amsterdam: Hans Walschaert, 1625.

_____. *Kort begrijp van de opkomste ende leere der Socinianen, kortelick vervat in 11 capittelen, by een gebracht ende grontelick wederleyt in de Nederlantsche tale.* Dordrecht, Vincent Caimax, 1652.

_____. *Opera theologica.* 2 vols. Amsterdam, 1684.

_____. *Protheoria theologiae christianae; quo agitur de theologiae & religionis definitione, partitione & distributione,* in *Opera,* I.

_____. *Vindiciae pro deitate Spiritus Sancti adversus Pneumatomachum Johannem Biddellum Anglum.* Franecker, 1652. [also in *Opera,* II.]

Cocceius, Johannes. *Aphorismi per universam theologiam breviores,* in *Opera,* vol. 7, pp. 3-16.

_____. *Aphorismi per universam theologiam prolixiores,* in *Opera,* vol. 7, pp. 17-38.

_____. *Disputationes selectae,* in *Opera,* vol. 7, second pagination, pp. 73-202.

_____. *Explicatio catecheseos Heidelbergensis,* in *Opera,* vol. 7, second pagination, pp. 1-72.

_____. *De Heydelbergse Catechismus der Chr. Religie*. Translated by Abraham van Poot. Amsterdam: J. van Someren, 1679.

_____. *Ondersoek van der aert ende natuyre des Sabbaths en der Ruste des Nieuwen Testaments*. Leiden: J. Elsevier, 1659.

_____. *Ondersoek van der aert ende natuyre van der Kerk en Babylon*. Translated by Abraham van Poot. Amsterdam: J. van Someren, 1691.

_____. *Opera omnia theologica, exegetica, didactica, polemica, philologica*. 12 vols. Amsterdam, 1701-1706.

_____. *De prophetie van Exechiël met de uitleggingen van Johannes Coccejus*. Amsterdam, 1691.

_____. *Summa theologiae ex Scriptura repetita*. Geneva, 1665. Amsterdam, 1669. Also, in *Opera*, vol. 7, pp. 131-403. [Heppe #37a]

_____. *Summa doctrinae de foedere et testamento Dei*. Amsterdam, 1648. Also, in *Opera*, vol. 7, pp. 39-130. [Heppe #37b]

_____. *Van den Antichrist*. Translated by Abraham van Poot. Amsterdam: J. van Someren, 1679.

Concordia Triglotta ... *Triglot Concordia: The Symbolical Books of the Ev. Lutheran Church, German-Latin-English*. St. Louis: Concordia, 1921.

Cotgrave, Randle. *A Dictionarie of the French and English Tongues*. London: Adam Islip, 1611.

Coton, Pierre. *Geneue plagiaire ou verification des deprauations de la Parole de Dieu qui trouuent és Bibles de Geneue*. Paris, 1618.

Crell, Johann. *The Expiation of a Sinner in a Commentary upon the Epistle to the Hebrewes*. London, 1646.

_____. *The Two Books of John Crellius Francus, touching one God the Father wherein many things also concerning the nature of the Son of God and the Holy Spirit are discoursed of*. Kosmoburg [London]: s.n., 1665.

_____. *The Unity of God Asserted and Defended, &c*. London, 1691. [A reissuing of the preceding work.]

Crocius, Ludovicus. *Dyodecas dissertationum exegeticarum et apologeticarum syntagmatis sacrae theologiae*. Bremen: Berthold Villier, 1642.

_____. *Paraeneticus de theologia cryptica*. Bremen, 1615.

_____. *Syntagma sacrae theologiae quatuor libris adornatum*. Bremen: Berthold Villier, 1635. [Heppe #25]

Croft, Herbert [Bishop of Hereford]. *The Naked Truth*. London?: s.n., 1675.

Cudworth, Ralph. *The True Intellectual System of the Universe: the first part; wherein, all the reason and philosophy of atheism is confuted; and its impossibility demonstrated*. London: Printed for Richard Royston, 1678

_____. *The True Intellectual System of the Universe*. 2 vols. Andover, Mass., 1837-38.

Curcellaeus, Stephanus [Etienne de Courcelles]. *Opera theologica, quorum pars praecipua Institutio religionis Christianae*. Amsterdam: Daniel Elsevir, 1675.

_____. *Quaternio dissertationm theologicarum adversus Samuelem Maresium ... opus posthumum*. Amsterdam: Ioannes Henricus, 1659.

Daillé, Jean. *Apologia pro ecclesiis reformatis: in qua demonstratur eas falso & inique schismatis idcirco accusari, quod a PapaeRomani communione secesserint, cum appendice. Item De fidei ex scripturis demonstratione, adversus novam methodum*. 2 vols. Geneva: Samuel de Tournes, 1677.

_____. *Apologia pro duabus ecclesiarum in Gallia protestantium synodis nationalibus; altera alensone, anno [MD]CXXXVII: altera vero Carentone, anno [MD]CXLV habitis: adversus Friderici Spanhemii Exercitationes de gratia universali.* Amsterdam: Joannes Ravesteyn, 1655.

_____. *An Apologie for the Reformed Chruches, wherein is shew'd the necessitie of their separation from the Church of Rome: against those who accuse them of making a schisme in Christendome.* Cambridge: Thomas Buck, 1653.

_____. *Exposition de Jean Daillé sur la divine épître de l'apôtre S. Paul aux Filippiens en vingt-neuf sermons.* 2 pts. Geneva: J. Antoine & S. de Tournes, 1659-1660.

_____. *An Exposition of the Epistle of Saint Paul to the Colossians.* Translated by James Sherman. Edinburgh: James Nichol, 1863.

_____. *An Exposition of the Epistle of Saint Paul to the Philippians.* Translated by James Sherman. Edinburgh: James Nichol, 1863.

_____. *Faith Grounded upon the Holy Scriptures; against the New Methodists.* Translated by M. M. London: Benjamin Tooke, 1675.

_____. *Sermons sur le Catéchisme.* 3 vols. Geneva, 1701.

_____. *A Treatise of the Right Use of the Fathers, in the Decision of the Controversies Existing at this Day in Religion.* Translated by T. Smith. London: John Martin, 1651. 2nd ed., with a preface by G. Jekyll. London: Henry Bohn, 1843.

Daneau, Lambert. *Christianae isagoges ad christianorum theologorum locos communes, libri II.* Geneva, 1583. [Heppe #5]

_____. *Compendium sacrae theologiae seu eroternata theologica, in quibus totius verae theologiae christianae summa breviter comprehense est.* Montpellier, 1595.

_____. *A Fruitfull Commentarie upon the Twelve Small Prophets.* Cambridge, 1594.

_____. *In Petri Lombardi Episcopi Parisiensis (qui Magister Sentiarum appellatur) librum primum Sententiarum, qui est de vero Deo, essentia quidem uno, personis autem trino, Lamberti Danaei commentarius triplex.* Geneva, 1580.

_____. *Isagoges christianae. Pars altera, seu secunda.* Geneva, 1584.

_____. *Isagoges christianae. Pars quarta.* Geneva, 1586.

_____. *Isagoges christianae. Pars quinta.* Geneva, 1588.

_____. *Methodus sacrae scripturae in publicis tum praelectionibus, tum concionibus utiliter atque intelligenter tractandae.* Geneva, 1570.

_____. *Opuscula omnia theologica.* Geneva: E. Vignon, 1583.

Davenant, John. *Animadversions written by the Right Reverend Father in God, John, Lord Bishop of Sarisbury, upon a treatise intitled, Gods love to mankind.* Cambridge: R. Daniel, 1641.

_____. *The Determinationes; or Resolutions of Certain Theological Questions, publicly discussed in the University of Cambridge.* Translated from the corrected and enlarged edition of 1639 by Josiah Allport. London: Hamilton, Adams, 1846. [In A Treatise on Justification, vol. 2.]

_____. *A Dissertation on the Death of Christ, as to the Extent of its Benefits.* Translated by, Josiah Allport as volume 2 of the Exposition of the Epistle of St. Paul to the Colossians. London: Hamilton, Adams and Co., 1832.

_____. *Expositio epistolae ad Colossenses.* Cambridge, 1627.

_____. *An Exposition of the Epistle of St. Paul to the Colossians ... to which is added a translation of Dissertatio de morte Christi, by the same prelate.* Translated, with a life of the author and notes illustrative of the writers and authorities referred to in the work, by Josiah Allport. 2 vols. London: Hamilton, Adams and Co., 1831-32.

_____. On the Controversy among the French Divines of the Reformed Church, concerning the Gracious and Saving Will of God toward Men. Translated by Josiah Allport, in Exposition of the Epistle of St. Paul to the Colossians, vol. 2, pp. 561-569.

_____. A Treatise on Justification or the Disputatio de justitia habituali et actuali, of the right Rev. John Davenant ... together with translations of the "Determinationes" of the same prelate. Translated by Josiah Allport. 2 vols. London: Hamilton, Adams, 1844-46.

Dávid, Francis. Defensio Francisci Davidis; and, De dualitate tractatus Francisci Davidis, Cracoviae, 1582. Introduction by Mihály Balázs. Bibliotheca Unitariorum, vol. 1. Budapest: Akadémiai Kiadó, 1983.

Dávid, Francis, et al. De falsa et vera unius Dei Patris, Filii et Spiritus Sancti cognitione libri duo (1568). Introduced by Antal Pirnát, edited by Robert Dán. Bibliotheca Unitariorum, vol. 2. Utrecht: Foundation Bibilotheca Unitariorum/Budapest: Akadémiai Kiadó, 1988.

Day, William. An Exposition of the Book of the Prophet Isaiah. London: G.D. and S.G. for Ioshua Kirton, 1654.

Deacon, J. The fathers vindicated, or, Animadversions on a late Socinian book entitul'd The judgment of the Fathers touching the Trinity, against Doctor Bull's Defence of the Nicene faith by a presbyter of the Church of England. London: R. Chiswell, 1697.

De Dieu, Ludovicus. Critica sacra sive animadversiones in loca quaedam difficiliora Veteris et Novi Testamenti. Amsterdam, 1693.

De Laune, Thomas. Tropologia, or, A key to open Scripture metaphors: the first book containing sacred philology, or the tropes in Scripture, reduc'd under their proper heads, with a brief explication of each partly translated and partly compil'd from the works of the learned by T.D. The second and third books containing a practical improvement (parallel-wise) of several of the most frequent and useful metaphors, allegories, and express similitudes of the Old and New Testament by B[enjamin]. K[each]. London: John Richardson and John Darby, 1681.

De Luzancy, H. C. [Hippolyte du Chastelet]. Remarks on several late writings publish'd in English by the Socinians wherein is show'd the insufficiency and weakness of their answers to the texts brought against them by the orthodox: in four letters, written at the request of a Socinian gentleman. London: Tho. Warren, 1696.

De Moor, Bernhardus. Commentarius perpetuus in Joh. Marckii compendium theologiae christianae didactico-elencticum. 7 vols. in 6. Leiden, 1761-1771.

Descartes, René. Descartes' Conversation with Burman. Translated, with an introduction and commentary by John Cottingham. Oxford: Clarendon Press, 1976.

_____. Philosophical Letters. Translated by Anthony Kenny. Minneapolis: University of Minnesota Press, 1981.

_____. The Philosophical Works of Descartes, Translated by Elizabeth S. Haldane and G. R. T. Ross. 2 vols. London: Cambridge University Press, 1931.

_____. The Philosophical Writings of Descartes. Translated by John Cottingham, Robert Stoothoff, Dugald Murdoch, and Anthony Kenny. 3 vols. Cambridge: Cambridge University Press, 1985-91.

Dickson, David. A Brief Exposition of the Evangel of Jesus Christ according to Matthew. London: Ralph Smith, 1647.

_____. A Brief Exposition of the Psalms. 3 vols. London, 1653-55. Reissued as A Commentary on the Psalms. 2 vols. London: Banner of Truth, 1965.

_____. An Exposition of all St. Pauls Epistles together with ... St. James, Peter, John, and Jude. London: R. I. for Francis Eglesfield, 1659.

_____. *A Short Explanation of the Epistle of Paul to the Hebrews*. Dublin: Society of Stationers, 1637.

_____. *The Summe of Saving Knowledge, with the Practical Use Thereof*. Edinburgh: George Swintoun, 1671.

_____. *Truths Victory over Error. Or, an Abridgement of the Chief Controversies in Religion ... between those of the Orthodox Faith, and all Adversaries whatsoever*. Edinburgh: John Reid, 1684.

Diodati, Jean. *Pious and Learned Annotations upon the Holy Bible, plainly Expounding the Most Difficult Places Thereof*. Third edition. London: James Flesher, 1651.

Doederlein, Johann Christoph. *Institutio theologi christiani*. 2 vols. Altdorf, 1780. Nürnberg, 1787.

Downame, John [alias Downham]. *The Christian Warfare*. 4th edition. London, 1634.

_____. *Lectures upon the Foure First Chapters of Hosea*. London, 1608.

_____. *The Summe of Sacred Divinitie briefly and methodically propounded: and then more largely and cleerly handled and explaned*. London: W. Stansby, 1625, 1628.

Du Moulin, Pierre. *The Anatomy of Arminianisme: or the Opening of the Controversies lately handled in the Low Countries, concerning the Doctrine of Predestination, of the Death of Christ, of the Nature of Grace*. London: T. S. for Nathaniel Newbery, 1620.

_____. *The Buckler of the Faith, or, A Defence of the Confession of Faith of the Reformed churches in France: against the obiections of M. Arnoux the Iesuite*. Third edition. London: Iohn Beale, 1631.

_____. *De cognitione Dei tractatus*. London: John Bill, 1626.

_____. *A Defense of the Catholike Faith: Contained in the Booke of the Most Mightie, and Most Gracious King James the first ... against the Answere of N. Cosseteau*. London: W. Stansby, 1610.

_____. *A Learned Treatise of Traditions*. London: August Mathewes, 1631.

_____. *Opera philosophica, logica, physica, ethica*. Amsterdam, 1645.

_____. *Oration in the Praise of Divinitie. Spoken at Sedanum in an Auditory of Divines, VIII of the Ides of December, 1628*. Translated by J. M. London: Henry Shephard, 1649.

_____. *A Treatise of the Knowledge of God*. Translated by Robert Codrington. London: A. M., 1634.

Du Plessis-Mornay, Philippe. *A Worke concerning the Trunesse of the Christian Religion ... Against Atheists, Epicures, Paynims, Iewes, Mahumetists, and other Infidels*. Translated by Philip Sidney and Arthur Golding. London: George Potter, 1604.

Durham, James. *Clavis Cantici. A Key, Useful for Opening up the Song*, in *An Exposition of the Song of Solomon*, by J. Durham, pp. 23-61.

_____. *A Commentarie Upon the Book of Revelation. Wherein the Text is explained ... together with some practical Observations, and several Digressions necessary for vindicating, clearing, and confirming weighty and important Truths*. London: Company of Stationers, 1658. Reissued, Willow Street, Pa.: Old Paths Publications, 2000.

_____. *An Exposition of the Song of Solomon*. 1669. Reissued, 1840. Reprint, Edinburgh: Banner of Truth, 1982.

Dury, John. *A Seasonable Discourse ... briefly shewing these Particulars. 1. What the Grounds and Method of our Reformation ought to be in Religion and Learning. 2. How even in these times of distraction, the Worke may be advanced*. London, 1649.

Eck, Johann. *In primum librum sententiarum annotatiuculae D. Johanne Eckio praelectore*. Edited by Walter L. Moore. Leiden: E. J. Brill, 1976.

Edwards, John. *Brief remarks upon Mr. Whiston's New theory of the earth and upon an other gentleman's objections against some passages in a discourse of the existence and providence of God, relating to the Copernican hypothesis*. London: J. Robinson and J. Wyat, 1697.

_____ . *A brief vindication of the fundamental articles of the Christian faith as also of the clergy, universities and publick schools, from Mr. Lock's reflections upon them in his Book of education, &c.: with some animadversions on two other late pamphlets, viz., of Mr. Bold and a nameless Socinian writer*. London: J.Robinson and J. Wyat, 1697.

_____ . *A demonstration of the existence and providence of God, from the contemplation of the visible structure of the greater and the lesser world in two parts, the first shewing the excellent contrivance of the heavens, earth, sea, &c., the second the wonderful formation of the body of man*. London: Jonathan Robinson and John Wyat, 1696.

_____ . *A discourse concerning the authority, stile, and perfection of the books of the Old and New-Testament with a continued illustration of several difficult texts of scripture throughout the whole work*. London: Richard Wilkin, 1693. 2nd ed. J. D. for Jonathan Robinson, 1696.

_____ . *ΠΟΔΥΠΟΙΚΙΛΟΣ ΣΟΦΙΑ: A Compleat History or Survey of all the Dispensations or Methods of Religion, from the Beginning of the World to the Consummation of all Things*, 2 vols. London: Daniel Brown et al., 1699.

_____ . *A preservative against Socinianism shewing the direct and plain opposition between it, and the religion revealed by God in the Holy Scriptures*. Oxford: Henry Clements, 1693.

_____ . *The Socinian creed, or, A brief account of the professed tenents and doctrines of the foreign and English Socinians wherein is shew'd the tendency of them to irreligion and atheism, with proper antidotes against them*. London: J. Robinson and J. Wyat, 1697.

_____ . *Socinianism unmask'd: a discourse shewing the unreasonableness of a late writer's opinion concerning the necessity of only one article of Christian faith, and of his other assertions in his late book, entituled, The reasonableness of Christianity as deliver'd in the Scriptures, and in his vindication of it: with a brief reply to another (professed) Socinian writer*. London: J. Robinson and J. Wyat, 1696.

_____ . *Some thoughts concerning the several causes and occasions of atheism, especially in the present age: with some brief reflections on Socinianism, and on a late book entitled The reasonableness of Christianity as delivered in the Scriptures*. London: J. Robinson and J. Wyat, 1695.

_____ . *Theologia Reformata: or, the Body and Substance of the Christian Religion, comprised in distinct discourses or treatises upon the Apostles Creed, the Lord's Prayer, and the Ten Commandments*. 2 vols. London: John Lawrence et al., 1713.

_____ . *Theologia reformata, or, Discourses on those graces and duties which are purely evangelical : and not contained in the moral law, and on the helps, motives, and advantages of performing them, being an entire treatise in four parts, and if added to the two former volumes, makes a compleat body of divinity*. London: T. Cox, 1726.

Edwards, Thomas. *The First and Second Part of Gangraena: or A Catalogue and Discovery of many of the Errors, Heresies, Blasphemies and pernicious Practices of the Sectaries of this time, vented and acted in England in these four last yeers. Also a particular narration of divers stories ... an extract of many letters, all concerning the present sects; together with some observations*. London: Ralph Smith, 1646; 3rd ed., much enlarged, 1646.

_____. _The Third Part of Gangraena or, A new and higher Discovery of the Errors, Heresies, Blasphemies, and indolent Proceedings of the Sectaries of these times; with some Animadversions by way of Confutation upon many of the Errors and Heresies named._ London: Ralph Smith, 1646.

Eglinus, Raphael. _Tractatus theologicus de coena domini et foedere gratiae quinis disputationibus interstinctus._ Marburg, 1614. [Heppe #26]

Eilsheimus, Daniel Bernhard. _Oestfriesslaendisch Kleinod des wahren Glaubens._ Emden, 1612. [Heppe #22]

Elys, Edmund. _Dominus est Deus, Gloria æterna Domini nostri Jesu Christi vindicata, contra egregiam errorum farraginem quæ inferibitur catechesis Ecclesiarum Polonicarum._ Oxford: s.n., 1690.

Emlyn, Thomas. _A collection of tracts, relating to the deity, worship, and satisfaction of the Lord Jesus Christ, &c.: in two volumes._ London: J. Darby and T. Browne, 1731.

_____. _An examination of Mr. Leslie's last dialogue, relating to the satisfaction of Jesus Christ. Together with some remarks on Dr. Stillingfleet's true reasons of Christ's sufferings._ London: s.n., 1708.

_____. _Extracts from An humble inquiry into the Scripture account of Jesus Christ._ Boston: Samuel Hall, 1790.

_____. _An humble enquiry into the Scripture account of Jesus Christ, or, A short argument concerning his deity and glory, according to the gospel._ London, 1702.

Endemann, Samuel. _Institutiones theologiae dogmaticae._ 2 vols. Hanau, 1777-1778. [Heppe #55]

Episcopius, Simon. _Institutiones theologicae_, in _Opera_, vol. I.

_____. _Opera theologica._ 2 vols. Amsterdam, 1650.

Erasmus, Desiderius. _Inquisitio de fide: a Colloquy (1524)._ Edited with Introduction and Commentary by Craig R. Thompson. New Haven: Yale University Press, 1950.

Espine, J. de l'. _Opuscules théologiques._ 2 vols. Geneva, 1598.

_____. _Traité de la providence de Dieu (1590)_, in _Opuscules_, vol. 2.

Essenius, Andreas. _Christelike en een-voudige onderwyzing tegens de Sociniaensche en zommige daer aen grenzende dwalingen, gesteld._ Amsterdam: Johannes van Waesberge, 1663.

_____. _Compendium theologiae dogmaticum._ Utrecht: Meinardus à Dreunen, 1669.

_____. _Synopsis controversiarum theologicarum, et index locorum totius s. scripturae, quibus adversarii ad errores suos confirmandos, et veritatem impugnandum vel declinandum, praecipue abuti solent: ubi tum adversarii, qui iis abutuntur, tum singulae eorum collectiones brevi methodo proponuntur._ Utrecht: Meinardus a Dreunen, 1677.

_____. _Systematis theologici pars prior -tomus tertius: I. De natura theologiae, de fide, de S. Scriptura, de Deo, de personis divinis, dedecreto Dei, de creatione, de providentia, de foedere legali, & de peccato. II. De foedere evangelico, de Christo mediatore, de salutis impetratione, de vocatione & regeneratione, de justificatione, reconciliatione, & adoptione. III. De sanctificatione, de conservatione & corroboratione, de obsignatione, de glorificatione, & de Ecclesia._ 3 vols. Amsterdam: Johannes Ansonius, 1659-65.

Estwick, Nicolas. _Pneumatologia: or, A Treatise of the Holy Ghost, in which the Godhead of the third Person of the Trinitie is ... defended against the sophisticall subtleties of John Bidle._ London, 1648.

Fenner, Dudley. _The Arts of Logic and Rhetoric ... for ... the Resolution or Opening of certain Parts of Scripture._ Middelburg, 1584.

_____. *Certaine Godly and Learned Treatises*. Edinburgh, 1592.

_____. *The Groundes of Religion set Downe in Questions and Answers*. Middelburg, 1587.

_____. *Sacra theologia sive veritas qua est secundum pietatem ad unicae et verae methodi leges descripta*. London, 1585. Geneva 1589.

_____. *The Sacred Doctrine of Divinitie*. Middelburg, 1599. Revised ed., London, 1613. [Published anonymously and variously ascribed to Dudley Fenner, John Gordon, and Sir Henry Finch.]

Fiddes, Richard. *Theologia Practica: or, The Second Part of a Body of Divinity ... wherein are Explain'd the Duties of Natural and Revealed Religion*. London, 1720.

_____. *Theologia Speculativa: or, The First Part of a Body of Divinity ... wherein are Explain'd the Principles of Natural and Revealed Religion*. London, 1718.

Fisher, Edward. *The Marrow of Modern Divinity*. London, 1645.

_____. *The Scriptures Harmony*. London, 1643.

Flacius Illyricus, Matthias. *Clavis scripturae seu de sermone sacrorum literarum, plurimas generales regulas continentis*. Wittenberg, 1567.

Flavel, John. *An Exposition of the Assembly's Catechism, with Practical Inferences from Each Question*, in Works, vol. 6.

_____. *The Method of Grace in the Gospel of Redemption*, in Works, vol. 2.

_____. *The Reasonableness of Personal Reformation, and the Necessity of Conversion*, in Works, vol. 6.

_____. *The Works of John Flavel*. 6 vols. London: Baynes and Son, 1820. Reprint, Edinburgh: Banner of Truth, 1968.

Forbes of Corse, John. *Instructiones historico-theologicae de doctrina christiana*. Amsterdam, 1645.

Fotherby, Martin. *Atheomastix: Clearing foure Truthes, Against Atheists and Infidels: 1. That, There is a God. 2. That, There is but one God. 3. That, Jehovah, our God, is that One God. 4. That, The Holy Scripture is the Word of that God*. London: Nicholas Okes, 1622.

Francken, Aegidius. *Kern der Christelijke leer: dat is de waarheden van de Hervormde godsdienst, eenvoudig ter nedergesteld, en met de oefening der ware Godzaligheid aangedrongen*. Dordrecht: J. van Braam, 1713. Groningen: O.L. Schildkamp, 1862.

_____. *Stellige god-geleertheyd: dat is, De waarheden van de hervormde leer: eenvoudig ter nedergestelt, en met de oeffening der waare Godsaligheyd aangedrongen*. 3 vols. Dordrecht: J. van Braam, 1712.

Freylinghausen, Johannes Anastasius. *Fundamenta theologiae christianae, in doctrinis fidei ex verbo Dei perspicue traditis*. Magdeburg, 1734.

Fulke, William. *A Defense of the Sincere and True Translations of the Holy scriptures in the English Tongue, against the Cavils of Gregory Martin*. London, 1583. Reissued by the Parker Society, Cambridge, 1843.

Fuller, Nicholas. *Miscellaneorum theologicorum ... libri tres*. Oxford: Joseph Barnes, 1616. London: John Bill, 1617.

Gailhard, John. *The Blasphemous Socinian heresie disproved and confuted wherein the doctrinal and controversial parts of those points are handled, and the adversaries scripture and school-arguments answered: with animadversions upon a late book called, Christianity not mysterious, humbly dedicated to both houses of parliament*. London: R. Wellington and J. Hartley, 1697.

_____. *Serious advice to a preservative against the blasphemous heresie of Socinianism*. London: Geo. Grafton, 1695.

Gale, Theophilus. *The Court of the Gentiles, or, A discourse touching the original of human literature, both philologie and philosophie, from the Scriptures and Jewish church.* Oxford: W. Hall for Tho. Gilbert, 1670. 2nd ed., enlarged, 1672.

_____. *The Court of Gentiles. Part II. Of Barbaric and Grecianic Philosophy.* Oxford: W. Hall for Tho. Gilbert, 1671. 2nd ed., enlarged, London: J. Macock for Thomas Gilbert, 1676.

_____. *The Court of Gentiles. Part III. The Vanity of Pagan Philosophy: demonstrated from its causes, parts, proprieties, and effects, namely pagan idolatrie, Judaic apostasie, gnostic infusions, errors among the Greek fathers, specially Origen, Arianisme, Pelagianisme, and the whole systeme of papisme or antichristianisme: distributed into three parts, mystic, scholastic, and canonic theologie.* London: A. Maxwell and R. Roberts for T. Cockeril, 1677.

_____. *The Court of the Gentiles. Part IV. Of Reformed Philosophie. Wherein Plato's Moral and Metaphysic or Prime Philosophie is reduced to an useful Forme and Method.* London: J. Macock for Thomas Cockeril, 1677.

_____. *The Court of the Gentiles. Part IV. Of Reformed Philosophie. Book III. Of Divine Predetermination. Wherein the Nature of Divine Predetermination is fully Explicated and Demonstrated, both in the General and also more Particularly, as to the Substrate Matter or Entitative Act of Sin: with a Vindication of Calvinists and others from that Blasphemous Imputation of Making God the Author of Sin.* London: John Hill and Samuel Tidmarsh, 1678.

_____. *Idea theologiae, tam contemplative quam activae. Ad formam S. Scripturae delineata.* London: J. Robinson, 1673.

_____. *Philosophia generalis: in duas partes disterminata.* Londini: J.M. pro J. Robinson & J. Hancock, 1676.

Gassendi, Pierre. *Disquisitio metaphysica; seu, Dubitationes et instantiae adversus Renati Cartesii Metaphysicam et responsa.* Texte établi, traduit et annoté par Bernard Rochot. Paris: J. Vrin, 1962.

_____. *Institutio Logica (1658).* Critical edition with translation and introduction by Howard Jones. Assen: Van Gorcum, 1981.

_____. *Opera omnia in sex tomos divisa ... Hactenus edita auctor ante obitum recensuit, auxit, illustrauit. Posthuma vero totius naturae explicationem complectentia, in lucem nunc primum prodeunt, ex bibliotheca illustris virHenrici Lvdovici Haberti Mon-Morii.* 6 vols. Lvgdvni: sumptibus Lavrentii Anisson & Ioan. Bapt. Devenet, 1658-75.

Gataker, Thomas. *Antithesis, partim Gulielmi Amesii, partim Gisberti Voetii, de sorte thesibus reposita.* London, 1638.

_____. *De nomine tetragrammato dissertatio.* London: R. Cotes, 1645.

_____. *De novi instrumenti stylo dissertatio. Qua viri doctissimi Sebastiani Pfochenii, de linguae Gracae Novi Testamenti puritate; in qua Hebraismus, quae vulgo finguntur, quam plurimis larva detrahi dicitur.* London: T. Harper, 1648.

_____. *Dissertatio de tetragrammato suae vindicatio adversus Capellum.* London: Roger Daniel, 1652.

_____. *Shadowes without Substance, or Pretended New Lights: Together with the Impieties and Blasphemies that Lurk Under Them, further Discovered in a Reply to I. Saltmarsh.* London, 1646.

_____. *A Short Catechism.* London, 1624.

Gerhard, Johann. *Loci theologici.* 9 vols. Edited by Preuss. Berlin, 1863-75.

Geulincx, Arnold. *Metaphysics*. Translated, with a preface and notes by Martin Wilson. Wisbech, Cambridgeshire, U.K.: Christoffel Press, 1999.

_____. *Opera philosophica*. Recognovit J. P. N. Land. 3 vols. Den Haag: Martinus Nijhoff, 1891-93.

Gibbens, Nicholas. *Questions and Disputations Concerning the Holy Scripture*. London, 1601.

Gill, John. *The Cause of God and Truth. In four parts, with a Vindication of Part IV from the cavils, calumnies, and defamations, of Mr. Henry Heywood*. London, 1735-38. Reissued, London: W. Collinridge, 1855.

_____. *Complete Body of Doctrinal and Practical Divinity: or A System of Evangelical Truths Deduced from the Sacred Scriptures, with A Dissertation Concerning the Baptism of Jewish Proselytes*. 2 vols. London, 1769-70. Reissued, London: Tegg & Company, 1839. Reprint, Grand Rapids: Baker Book House, 1978.

_____. *A Dissertation Concerning the Antiquity of the Hebrew-language, Letters, Vowel-points, and Accents*. London: G. Keith, 1767.

_____. *An Exposition of the New Testament*. 3 vols. London, 1746-8.

_____. *An Exposition of the Old Testament*. 6 vols. London, 1748-63.

_____. *Sermons and Tracts*. New edition. 3 vols. London: T. Smith, 1814.

_____. *A Treatise on the Doctrine of the Trinity*. London, 1731. 2nd ed. London: G. Keith, 1752.

Gillespie, George. *A Treatise of Miscellany Questions*, in *Works*, vol. 2.

_____. *The Works of Mr. George Gillespie*. 2 vols. Edinburgh: Ogle, Oliver, and Boyd, 1846.

Gillespie, Patrick. *The Ark of the Testament Opened: or, the Secret of the Lords Covenant Unsealed in a Treatise of the Covenant of Grace*. London: R.C., 1661.

Glassius, Salomon. *Philologiae sacrae, qua totius sacrosanctae Veteris et Novi Testamenti scripturae ... stylus et literatura ... expenditur, libri duo*. Jena, 1626.

_____. *Philologiae sacrae, liber tertius et quartus, quibus grammatica sacra comprehensa*. Jena, 1634.

_____. *Philologiae sacrae, liber quintus, quo rhetorica sacra comprehensa*. Jena, 1636.

Gomarus, Franciscus. *Disputations theologicae*, in *Opera theologica*, vol. 2.

_____. *Opera theologica omnia*. 3 vols. Amsterdam, 1644.

Goodwin, Thomas. *A Discourse of Christ the Mediator*, in *Works*, vol. V.

_____. *The Work of the Holy Ghost in our Salvation*, in *Works*, vol. VI.

_____. *The Works of Thomas Goodwin, D.D., sometime President of Magdalen College, Oxford*. Preface by John C. Miller, memoir by Robert Halley. 12 vols. Edinburgh: James Nichol, 1861-66.

Gouge, William. *A Learned and very Useful Commentary on the Whole Epistle to the Hebrews*. London: A.M., T.W. and S.G., 1655.

Granger, Thomas. *Syntagma logicum, or the Divine Logike*. London, 1620.

Greenhill, William. *An Exposition of Ezekiel*. 5 vols. London, 1665-67. Reissued in one volume, Edinburgh: James Nichol, 1863. Reprint, Carlisle, PA: Banner of Truth, 1994.

Groenewegen, Henricus. *Oefeningen den Heidelbergschen Catechismus*. Gorinchem: Cornelis Lever, 1679.

Grotius, Hugo. *Annotationes ad Vetus Testamentum*, in *Opera*, vol. 1.

_____. *Annotationes in epistolas Apostolicas & Apocalypsin*, in *Opera*, vol. 2, part 2, pp. 669-1238.

_____. *Annotationes in quatuor Evangelia & Acta Apostolorum*, in *Opera*, vol. 2, part 1, pp. 1-668.

_____. *Opera omnia theologica*. 3 vols. Amsterdam, 1679. London: Moses Pitt, 1679.

_____. *The Truth of the Christian Religion, in Six Books*. Translated by John Clarke. Cambridge: J. Hall, 1860.

Guild, William. *Moses Unveiled: or, those Figures which served unto the Pattern and Shadow of Heavenly Things, pointing out the Messiah Christ Jesus*. London, 1626. Reprint, Edinburgh, 1755.

Gualther, Rudolph. *An Hundred, Threescore and Fiftene Homelyes or Sermons uppon the Actes of the Apostles, written by Saint Luke*. London: Henrie Denham, 1572.

Gürtler, Nicholaus. *Institutiones theologicae ordine maxime naturali dispositae ac variis accessionibus auctae*. Marburg: Müller, 1732. [Heppe #52]

_____. *Synopsis theologiae reformatae*. Marburg: Müller, 1731.

Haak, Theodore, trans. *The Dutch Annotations upon the Whole Bible: Or, All the holy canonical Scriptures of the Old and New Testament ... as ... appointed by the Synod of Dort, 1618, and published by authority, 1637*. 2 vols. London, 1657.

Hall, John. *A Humble Motion to the Parliament of England Concerning the Advancement of Learning: and the Reformation of the Universities*. London, 1649.

Hall, Joseph. *The Works of Joseph Hall, D.D. ... with some account of his life and sufferings, written by himself*. 12 vols. Oxford: Talboys, 1837-39.

_____. *Solomon's Divine Arts*. Edited by Gerald T. Sheppard. Pilgrim Classic Commentaries, vol. IV. Cleveland, Ohio: Pilgrim Press, 1991.

Hammond, Henry. *A Paraphrase and Annotations upon all of the Books of the New Testament*. 5th ed., corrected. London: J. Macock and M. Flesher, 1681.

An Harmony of the Confessions of the Faith of the Christian and Reformed Churches. Cambridge, 1586.

Harris, John. *The Atheistical Objections, against the Being of a God, and His Attributes, Fairly Considered and Fully Refuted in Eight Sermons*. London: J. L., 1698.

Harvey, Gideon. *Archeologia Philosophica Nova, or, New Principles of Philosophy. Containing Philosophy in General. Metaphysicks or Ontology. Dynamilogy, or a Discourse of Power. Religio Philosophi, or Natural Theology. Physicks, or Natural Philosophy*. London: J. H. for Samuel Thomson, 1663.

Hearne, Thomas, *An Account of all the Considerable Books and Pamphlets, that have been wrote on either side, in the Controversy concerning the Trinity, since the year 1712*. London, 1720.

Heereboord, Adriaan. *Meletemata philosophica in quibus pleraeque res Metaphysicae ventilantur, tota Ethica καταοκευαστικως καὶ ἀναοκευαστικως explicatur, universa Physica per theoremata & commentarios exponitur, summa rerum Logicarum per Disputationes traditur*. Editio nova. Amsterdam: Henricus Wetstenius, 1680.

_____. *Philosophia naturalis, cum Commentariis Peripateticis anthaec edita*. London: Wilmot & Crosley, 1684.

Heidanus, Abraham. *Corpus theologiae christianae in quindecim locos digestum*. 2 vols. Leiden, 1687. [Heppe #44]

_____. *De origine erroris libri octo*. Amsterdam, 1678.

_____. *Disputationes theologicae ordinariae repetitiae*. 2 parts. Leiden, 1654-59.

_____. *Fasciculus disputationum theologicarum de Socianismo*. Leiden, 1659.

Heidegger, Johann Heinrich. *Corpus theologiae christianae ... adeoque sit plenissimum theologiae didacticae, elenchticae, moralis et historicae systema.* 2 vols. Zurich: David Gessner, 1700. [Heppe #46]

_____. *De ratione studiorum theologiae.* Zurich, 1690.

_____. *Medulla theologiae christianae.* Zurich, 1696. [Heppe #46]

Hellenbroeck, Abraham. *De Evangelische Jesaya, ofte deszelfs voorname Evangelische prophetiën.* 4 vols. Amsterdam: Hendrik Burgers,1702.

_____. *Het Hooglied van Salomo verklaart en vergeestelyk.* 2 vols. Amsterdam: Hendrik Burgers, 1718.

_____. *A Specimen of Divine Truths, for the Instruction of Youth.* New York: Board of Publication of the Reformed Church in America, n.d.

_____. *Vorbeeld der Goddelijke Waarheden voor eenvoudigen: die zig bereiden tot de belijdenisse des geloofs; meest tot particulier gebruik opgesteld.* 1706. Amsterdam: Jacobus van Egmont, 1765.

Henry, Matthew. *An Exposition of the Old and New Testament: wherein each chapter is summed up in its contents: the sacred text inserted at large, in distinct paragraphs; each paragraph reduced to its proper heads: the sense given, and largely illustrated; with practical remarks and observations.* New edition, revised and corrected. 6 vols. London: James Nisbet, n.d.

Herbert, Edward, Baron of Cherbury. *De causis errorum. Pars prima.* London: Philemon Stephan, 1645.

_____. *De veritate.* Translated by Meyrick H. Carré. Bristol: Arrowsmith, 1937.

_____. *De veritate, prout distinguitur a revelatione, a verisimili, a possibili, et a falso.* 2nd ed. London: Augustine Matthew, 1633.

_____. *Lord Herbert of Cherbury's De religione laici.* Edited and translated by Harold R. Hutcheson. New Haven and London: Yale University Press, 1944.

Hibbert, Henry. *Exercitationes theologicae: or, Divine Discourses, carefully extracted and orderly digested into XII sections.* London: John Clark, 1662.

_____. *Syntagma theologicum: or, a Treatise, wherein is concisely comprehended the Body of Divinity, and the Fundamentals of Religion, orderly discussed.* London: John Clark, 1662.

Hobbes, Thomas. *The English Works of Thomas Hobbes of Malmesbury.* Edited by Sir William Molesworth, bart. 11 vols. Darmstadt: Scientia Verlag Aalen, 1962.

_____. *The Metaphysical system of Hobbes in Twelve Chapters from Elements of Philosophy concerning Body, together with breifer extracts from Human Nature and Leviathan.* Selected by Mary Whiton Calkins. Chicago: Open Court, 1913.

_____. *Opera philosophica quae latine scripsit omnia in unum corpus nunc primum collecta studio et labore Gulielmi Molesworth.* 5 vols. Darmstadt: Scientia Verlag Aalen, 1961.

Holdsworth, Richard. *Praelectiones theologicae.* London: Jacob Flesher, 1661.

Holdsworth, Thomas. *Impar Conatui: or, Mr. J. B. the Author of an Answer to the Animadversions on the Dean of St. Paul's Vindication of the Trinity, Rebuk'd.* London: William Keblewhite, 1695.

Hommius, Festus. *Disputationes theologicae adversus pontificios.* Leiden, 1614.

_____. *LXX disputationes theologicae.* 2nd ed. Oxford, 1630.

Hoornbeeck, Johannes. *Disputationes theologicae anti-Socinianae, de Christo; ejus natura, officiis, beneficiis.* Leiden: Johannes Elsevier, 1656.

_____. *Institutiones theologicos.* Utrecht, 1653.

_____. *Orationes habitae in Academia Ultrajectina.* Utrecht, 1658.

_____. *Socinianismus confutatus*. 3 vols. Utrecht, 1650-64.

_____. *Summa controversiarum religionis, cum infidelibus, haereticis, schismaticis*. Utrecht, 1653.

_____. *Theologia practica*. 2 vols. Utrecht, 1663-66.

Hopkins, Ezekiel. *A Discourse on the Omnipresence of God*, in *Works*, edited by C. Quick, vol. 3, pp. 389-404.

_____. *A Discourse on the State and Way of Salvation*, in *Works*, edited by C. Quick, vol. 3, pp. 445-475.

_____. *The Excellence of Heavenly Treasures*, in *Works*, edited by C. Quick, vol. 2, pp. 411-55.

_____. *An Exposition upon the Ten Commandments*, in *Works*, edited by C. Quick, vol. 1, pp. 236-535.

_____. *On Glorifying God in His Attributes*, in *Works*, edited by C. Quick, vol. 2, pp. 590-708.

_____. *A Practical Exposition on the Lord's Prayer*, in *Works*, edited by C. Quick, vol. 1, pp. 51-235.

_____. *The Works of Ezekiel Hopkins, successively Bishop of Raphoe and Derry*. Edited by Charles W. Quick. 3 vols. 1874. Reprint, Morgan, Pa.: Soli Deo Gloria Publications, 1995-1998.

_____. *The works of the Right Reverend and learned, Ezekiel Hopkins: late Lord Bishop of London-Derry in Ireland, collected into one volume containing: I. The vanity of the world. II. A practical exposition on the Ten commandments. III. An exposition on the Lord's prayer. IV. Several sermons and discourses on divers important subjects*. London: Printed for Jonathan Robinson, 1701.

Hottinger, Johann Heinrich. *Cursus theologicus methodo Altingiana expositus*. Duisburg: Adrian Wyngaerden, 1660. [Heppe #42]

Howe, John. *A Calm and Sober Inquiry concerning the Possibility of a Trinity in the Godhead, ... together with Certain Letters formerly written to Dr. Wallis on the same subject*, in *Works*, vol. II, pp. 527-73.

_____. *A Letter to a Friend, concerning a Postscript to the Defense of Dr. Sherlock's Notion of the Trinity in Unity*, in *Works*, vol. II, pp. 577-95.

_____. *The Living Temple, or, A Designed Improvement of that Notion, that a Good Man is the Temple of God. Part I. Concerning God's Existence and His Conversableness with Man against Atheism, or the Epicurean Deism* (1676). *Part II. Containing Animadversions on Spinoza, and a French Writer Pretending to Refute Him* (1702), in *Works*, vol. I, pp. 1-344.

_____. *A Postscript to the Letter of the Reconcilableness of God's Prescience, &c.*, in *Works*, vol. II, pp. 514-26.

_____. *The Reconcilableness of God's Prescience with the Sins of Men*, in *Works*, vol. II, pp. 474-513.

_____. *The Right Use of that Argument in Prayer, from the Name of God*, in *Works*, vol. III, pp. 207-79.

_____. *Summary Propositions Collected out of the Foregoing Discourses*, in *Works*, vol. II, pp. 574-76.

_____. *A Treatise of Delighting in God*, in *Works*, vol. I, pp. 474-664.

_____. *A View of that Part of the Late Considerations addressed to H. H. about the Trinity*, in *Works*, vol. II, pp. 596-626.

_____. *The Works of the Rev. John Howe, M.A.* 3 vols. London: William Tegg, 1848. Reprint, Ligonier, Pa.: Soli Deo Gloria Publications, 1990.

Hulsius, Antonius. *Non-ens prae-adamiticum, sive Confutatio vani & sicinizantis cujusdam somnii, quo S. Scripturae praetextu incuatioribus nuper imponere conatus est quidam anonymus, fingens ante Adamum primum homines fuisse in mundo.* Leiden, 1656.

Hutcheson, George. *An Exposition of the Gospel of Jesus Christ, according to John.* London: Ralph Smith, 1657. Reissued, Edinburgh, 1841. Reprint, Edinburgh: Banner of Truth, 1972.

Hutchinson, Roger. *The Image of God, or Laie Mans Book, in whych the Right Knowledge of God is Disclosed.* London: John Day, 1550. Also in *Works*, pp. 1-208.

_____. *The Works of Roger Hutchinson.* Cambridge: Cambridge University Press, 1842.

Hyperius, Andreas Gerardus. *De theologo, seu de ratione studii theologici, libri III.* Basel, 1556.

_____. *Elementa christianae religionis.* Marburg, 1563; new edition, Erlangen, 1901.

_____. *Methodus theologiae, sive praecipuorum christianae religionis locorum communium, libri tres.* Basel, 1568. [Heppe #13]

_____. *The Practis of Preaching, otherwise called the Pathway to the Pulpit.* Translated by I. Ludham. London, 1577.

Jackson, John. *A Collection of Queries. Wherein the most material Objections from Scripture, Reasons, and Antiquity, which have been alleged against Dr. Clarke's Scripture-Doctrine of the Trinity, and the defenses of it, are proposed and answered ... by a Clergyman in the Country.* London, 1716.

_____. *Remarks on Dr. Waterland's Second Defense of Some Queries. Being a brief consideration of his notion of the Trinity, as stated by himself in Three Questions ... by Philalethes Cantabridgiensis.* London, 1723.

_____. *A Reply to Dr. Waterland's Defense of his Queries; wherein is contained a full state of the whole controversy; and every particular alleged by that learned writer is distinctly considered by a Clergyman in the Country.* London: J. Knapton, 1722.

_____. *Three Letters to Dr. Clarke from a Clergyman, concerning his Scripture-Doctrine of the Trinity, with the Doctor's Replies.* London: John Barker, 1714.

Jackson, Richard. *A suddain essay with a sincere desire to vindicate Christianity, or the common faith, from the superlative heresies or phantasticall novelties of all selfe-particular Sciolists endeavouring the subversion of the same by seven arguments used in opposition to Mr. John Biddle.* London: Thomas Harper, 1655.

Jackson, Thomas. *A collection of the works of that holy man and profound divine, Thomas Iackson ... containing his comments upon the Apostles Creed, &c.: with the life of the author and an index annexed.* London: R. Norton, 1653.

_____. *An exact collection of the works of Doctor Jackson ... such as were not published before: Christ exercising his everlasting priesthood ... or, a treatise of that knowledge of Christ which consists in the true estimate or experimental valuation of his death, resurrection, and exercise of his everlasting sacerdotal function ...: this estimate cannot rightly be made without a right understanding of the primeval state of Adam.* London: R. Norton, 1654.

_____. *A Treatise of the Divine Essence and Attributes, in Two Parts.* London, 1627.

_____. *The works of the reverend and learned divine, Thomas Jackson, sometime president of Corpus Christi College in Oxon such as were, and such as never before were printed: in three volumes: with the authors life, and a large and useful table to the whole.* 3 vols. London: Andrew Clark, 1673.

Jasz-Berenyi, Paul P. *Examen doctrinæ ariano-socinianæ à quodam anonymo sub hoc titulo evulgate, Doctrina de Deo, & Christo, & Spiritu Sancto, ipsis scripturae verbis, ante paucos annos, à quodam divinæ veritatis confessore, in sermone Germanico concinnata, nunc vero, in gratiam exterorum, Latine edita.* London: Samuel Brown, 1662.

Jenkyn, William. *An Exposition upon the Epistle of Jude.* Revised and corrected by James Sherman. Edinburgh: James Nichol, 1863.

Jewel, John. *A View of a Seditious Bull sent into England from Pius Quintus Bishop of Rome ... whereunto is added A Short Treatise of the Holy Scriptures,* in *Works,* vol. 4.

_____. *The Works of John Jewel, Bishop of Salisbury.* 4 vols. Cambridge, 1845-50.

Jones, Meredith. *The doctrine of the Trinity as it stands deduced by the light of reason from the data laid down in the Scriptures, to which is added some remarks on the Arian controversy, also a Postscript, containing some observations of the writings of Justin Martyr and Irenaeus.* London: B. White, 1768.

Junius, Franciscus. *The Apocalyps, or Revelation of S. John with a Brief Exposition.* Cambridge: John Legat, 1596.

_____. *De vera theologia,* in *Opuscula,* edited by A. Kuyper, pp. 39-101.

_____. *Opuscula theologica selecta,* edited by Abraham Kuyper. Amsterdam: F. Muller, 1882.

_____. *Sacrorum parallelorum libri tres: id est comparatio locorum Scripturae sacrae, qui ex testamento vetere in Novo adducuntur.* Second edition. London: G. Bishop, n.d.

_____. *Theses theologicae quae in inclyta academia Ludgunobatava ad exercitia publicarum disputationum* [*Theses Leydenses*], in *Opuscula,* edited by A. Kuyper, pp. 103-289.

_____. *Theses aliquot theologicae in Heidelbergensi academia disputatae* [*Theses Heidelbergenses*], in *Opuscula,* edited by A. Kuyper, pp. 289-327.

Junius, Isaacus. *Anatapologia, sive Animadversiones in XVI. priora capita Apologiae Remonstrantium.* Delphi [Leiden]: Andreas Clouting, 1640.

Jurieu, Pierre. *La Religion du Latitudinaire, acev apologie pour la Sainte Trinité, appelle l'heresie des trois Dieux.* Rotterdam, 1696.

_____. *Le Vray systeme de 'église & la veritable analyse de la foy.* Dordrecht, 1686.

Keach, Benjamin. *Tropologia; A Key to Open Scripture Metaphors, in Four Books. To which are prefixed, Arguments to Prove the Divine Authority of the Holy Bible. Together with Types of the Old Testament.* London: City Press, 1856. [Contains Keach's *Troposchemalogia* and *Tropologia.*]

_____. *Tropologia, or, A key to open Scripture metaphors: the first book containing sacred philology, or the tropes in Scripture, reduc'd under their proper heads, with a brief explication of each partly translated and partly compil'd from the works of the learned by T[homas] D[eLaune]. The second and third books containing a practical improvement (parallel-wise) of several of the most frequent and useful metaphors, allegories, and express similitudes of the Old and New Testament by B.K.* London: John Richardson and John Darby, 1681.

_____. *Troposchemalogia, tropes and figures, or, A treatise of the metaphors, allegories, and express similitudes, &c., contained in the Bible of the Old and New Testament: to which is prefixed, divers arguments to prove the divine authority of the Holy Scriptures: wherein also 'tis largely evinced, that by the great whore, (mystery Babylon) is meant the Papal hierarchy, or present state and church of Rome: Philologia sacra, the second part: wherein the schemes, or figures in scripture, are reduced under their proper heads, with a brief explication of each: together with a treatise of types, parables, &c, with an improvement of them parallel-wise*. London: John Darby, 1682.

Keckermann, Bartholomaeus. *Brevis et simplex consideratio controversiae hoc tempore ... de pugna Philosophiae & Theologiae*, in *Opera*, I, col. 69ff.

_____. *Opera omnia quae extant*. 2 vols. Geneva, 1614.

_____. *Praecognita philosophica libri duo: naturam philosophiae explicantes, et rationem eius tum docendae, tum discendae monstrantes*, in *Opera*, I, col. 1ff.

_____. *Scientiae metaphysicae brevissima synopsis et compendium*, in *Opera*, I, col. 2013ff.

_____. *Systema logicae minus: succincto praeceptorum compendium*, in *Opera*, I, col. 161ff.

_____. *Systema logicae tribus libris adornatum*, in *Opera*, I, col. 542ff.

_____. *Systema sacrosanctae theologiae, tribus libris adornatum*. Heidelberg, 1602; Geneva, 1611. Also in *Opera omnia quae extant*, appended to vol. II, separate pagination. [Heppe #21]

Kellet, Edward. *Miscellanies of divinitie divided into three books, wherein is explained at large the estate of the soul in her origination, separation, particular judgement, and conduct to eternall blisse or torment*. Cambridge, 1635.

Kemp, Johannes van der. *De Christen geheel en al het Eigendom van Christus*. Rotterdam: R. van Doesburg, 1717.

_____. *The Christian Entirely the Property of Christ, in Life and Death, Exhibited in Fifty-three Sermons on the Heidelberg Catechism*. Translated by John M. Harlingen. 2 vols. New Brunswick: Abraham Blauvelt, 1810. Reprint, Grand Rapids: Reformation Heritage Books, 1997.

_____. *De Heid. Catechismus kortelyk geopened en verklaard by wyze van Vragen en Antwoorden*. Edited by D. van der Kemp. Rotterdam: P. Losel & J. Bosch, 1746.

Klinkenberg, Jacob van Nuys. *Onderwys in den godsdienst*. 11 vols. Amsterdam: J. Allart, 1780-94.

Klinkenberg, Jacob van Nuys, and Ger. Joh. Nahyus. *De Bijbel, door beknopte Uitbreidingen, en ophelderende Aenmerkingen, verklaerd*. 27 vols. Amsterdam: Johannes Allart, 1780-90.

Knapp, Georg Christian. *Lectures on Christian Theology*. Translated by Leonard Woods. New York: Tibbals, 1859.

Lampe, Friedrich Adolf. *Compendium theologiae naturalis*. Utrecht, 1734.

_____. *Einleitung zu dem Geheimnis des Gnadenbundes*. Marburg and Frankfurt, 1785. [Heppe #54]

_____. *Het gouden kleinoot van de leere der waarheid die naar de godsaligheid is, vervattet in den Heidelbergschen Catechismus*. Amsterdam, 1724.

_____. *Melk der waarheit volgens aanleydinge van den Heidelbergschen Catechismus: ten nutte van de leer-begeerige jeugdt opgesteld ... door Frederik Adolf Lampe*. 2nd ed. Amsterdam: Antony Schoonenburg, 1725.

_____. *De verborgentheit van het genade-verbondt: in de huyshoudingen der zaligheit, en voornamentlyk in de huyshouding der belofte, ter eeren van den verbondts-godt*. 4 vols. Amsterdam: Antony Schoonenburg, 1726-39.

La Peyrère, Isaac. *Men Before Adam, or, a discourse upon the twelfth, thirteenth, and fourteenth verses of the Epistle of Paul to the Romans*. London, 1656.

_____. *Prae-Adamitae. sive exercitaio super versibus duodecimus, decimotertio, & decimoquarto, capitis quniti epistolae Pauli ad Romanos. Quibus inducuntur primi homines ante Adamum conditi*. Amsterdam, 1655.

_____. *Systema theologicum, ex Praeadamitarum hypothesi, Pars prima.* Amsterdam, 1655.

_____. *A Theological System upon that presupposition that men were before Adam, Part I.* London, 1656.

Lapide, Cornelius à. *Commentaria in Scripturam Sacram R. P. Cornelii a Lapide, e Societate Jesu ... accurate recognovit.* Editio nova. 27 vols. Paris: Vives, 1866.

Lasco, Johannes à. *Opera tam edita quam inedita.* Edited by Abraham Kuyper. 2 vols. Amsterdam: F. Muller, 1866.

Lathom, Paul. *Christ crucified, or, The doctrine of the Gospel asserted against Pelagian and Socinian errours revived under the notion of new lights: wherein also the original, occasion and progress of errours are set down: and admonitions directed both to them that stand fast in the faith and to those that are fallen from it: unto which are added three sermons.* London: Tho. Milbourn, 1666.

Law, Edmund. *An enquiry into the ideas of space, time, immensity, and eternity: as also the self-existence, necessary existence, and unity of the divine nature: in answer to a book lately publish'd by Mr. Jackson, entitled, The existence and unity of God proved from His nature and attributes ... to which is added, A dissertation upon the argument a priori for proving the existence of a first cause by a learned hand.* Cambridge: W. Fenner and R. Beresford, 1734.

Lawson, George. *An exposition of the Epistle to the Hebrewes wherein the text is cleared, Theopolitica improved, the Socinian comment examined.* London: George Sawbridge, 1662.

Le Blanc, Ludovicus. *Theses theologicae, variis temporibus in Academia Sedanensi editae et ad disputandum propositae.* London: Moses Pitt, 1675.

Leibniz, Gottfried Wilhelm. *Discourse on Metaphysics, Correspondence with Arnauld, Monadology.* Introduction by Paul Janet, translated by George R. Montgomery. Lasalle, Ill.: Open Court, 1902, 1980.

_____. *Monadology and Other Philosophical Essays.* Translated by Paul Schrecker and Anne Martin Schrecker. Indianapolis: Bobbs-Merril, 1965.

_____. *Opera philosophiae quae extant.* Edited by J. E. Erdmann. 2 vols. Berlin, 1840.

_____. *Philosophical Papers and Letters.* A selection translated and edited, with an introduction by Leroy E. Loemker. 2 vols. Chicago, University of Chicago Press, 1956.

_____. *The Philosophical Works of Leibniz.* Translated by George Martin Duncan. Second edition. New Haven: Tuttle, Morehouse & Taylor, 1908.

_____. *Theodicy: Essays on the Goodness of God, the Freedom of Man, and the Origin of Evil.* Introduction by Austin Farrer, translated by E. M. Huggard. London: Routledge & Kegan Paul, 1951. Reprint, Chicago: Open Court, 1985.

Leigh, Edward. *Critica sacra: or Philologicall Observations upon all the Greek Words of the New Testament.* London, 1639.

_____. *A Systeme or Body of Divinity.* London, 1662.

_____. *A Treatise of Divinity.* London, 1646.

_____. *A Treatise of Religion and Learning.* London, 1656.

Leslie, Charles. *The charge of Socinianism against Dr. Tillotson considered in examination of some sermons he has lately published on purpose to clear himself from that imputation, by way of a dialogue betwixt F. a friend of Dr. T's and C. a Catholick Christian: to which is added some reflections upon the second of Dr. Burnet's four discourses, concerning the divinity and death of Christ, printed 1694: to which is likewise annexed, A supplement upon occasion of A history of religion, lately published....* Edinburgh?: s.n., 1695.

_____. *Five discourses by the author of The snake in the grass viz. On water baptism, episcopacy, primitive heresie of the Quakers, reflections on the Quakers, a brief account of the Socinian trinity; to which is added a preface to the whole.* London: C. Boone, W. Keblewhite, and G. Strahan, 1700.

Leydekker, Jacobus. *Dr. Bekkers Philosophische Duyvel.* Dordrecht: D. Goris, 1692.

_____. *De blyde Spinosist en de bedroefde Christenleeraar, over de wysgeerige verhandelinge van de Natuure Gods.* Rotterdam: R. van Doesburg, 1719.

Leydekker, Melchior. *Commentarius in Catecheseos Heidelberg. sive de veritate et sanctitate fidei Reformatae.* Utrecht, 1694.

_____. *De historia Jansenismi libri VI, quibus de Cornelii Jansennii vita et morte, nec non de ipsius et sequacium dogmatibus differitur* Utrecht: Halma, 1695.

_____. *Demonstratio evangelica, Dat is, de Evangelische Waerheyd van der Gereformeerde Godsdienst.* Utrecht: W. Clerck, 1684.

_____. *De oeconomia trium personarum in negotio salutis humanae.* Utrecht, 1682.

_____. *De veritate religionis reformatae seu evangelicae, libri VII.* Utrecht, 1688. [Heppe #35]

_____. *Disputatio historico-theologica de Arianismo, octava et ultima, quam ... sub praesidio Melchioris Leydeckeri publice defendet Antonius Arleboutius.* Utrecht: Meinardus a Dreunen, 1679.

_____. *Exercitationes selectae historico-theologicae.* 2 vols. Amsterdam, 1712.

_____. *Exercitationes theologicae qua praecipua quaedam dogmata Neopelagiana ex independentia et infinita perfectione divina refutantur, pars secunda, quam ... sub praesidio Melchioris Leydeckeri publice defendet Jacoe[b]us Hoog.* Utrecht: Meinardus a Dreunen, 1682.

_____. *Filius Dei Sponsor. Of de Loff en Eere Jesu Christi, onse Vredevorst en Borge.* Amsterdam: J. van Hardenberg, 1708.

_____. *De Goddelykheid en Waarheid der H. Schriften ... verdeedigt tegen de Betooverde Wereld van Balth. Bekker.* Utrecht: O. de Vries, 1692.

_____. *Synopsis controversiarum de Foedere et Testamento Dei.* Utrecht, 1690.

Lightfoot, John. *A Commentary on the New Testament from the Talmud and Hebraica: Matthew — I Corinthians.* 4 vols. Oxford: Oxford University Press, 1859. Reprint,, Grand Rapids: Baker Book House, 1979.

_____. *Horae hebraicae et talmudicae, or, Hebrew and Talmudical Exercitations, in Works* (1684), vol. II.

_____. *Some Genuine Remains of the Late Pious and Learned John Lightfoot, D. D., consisting of Three Tracts.* London: R. J. for J. Robinson, 1700.

_____. *The Temple Service as it Stood in the Days of Our Saviour.* London, 1649.

_____. *The Whole Works of the Rev. John Lightfoot, D. D. Master of Catharine Halle, Cambridge.* Edited by John Rogers Pitman. 13 vols. London: J. F. Dove, 1825.

_____. *The Works of the Reverend and Learned D. John Lightfoot, D. D.* 2 vols. London: W. R. for Robert Scott et al., 1684.

Limborch, Phillip van. *Theologia christiana ad praxin pietatis ac promotionem pacis christiana unice directa.* Amsterdam, 1735. [In its first edition, 1686, the work was entitled *Institutiones theologiae christianae.*]

Locke, John. *An Essay Concerning Human Understanding.* Collated and annotated by Alexander Campbell Fraser. 2 vols. New York: Dover, 1959.

Long, Thomas. *An answer to a Socinian treatise, call'd The naked Gospel, which was decreed by the University of Oxford, in convocation, August 19, Anno Dom. 1690 to be publickly burnt, as containing divers heretical propositions with a postscript, in answer to what is added by Dr. Bury, in the edition just published.* London: Freeman Collins, 1691.

Lubbertus, Sibrandus. *Commentarius in Catechesin Paltino-Belgicam.* Franecker, 1618.

_____. *De principiis Christianorum dogmatum libri VII.* Franecker, 1591.

Lukin, Henry. *An Introduction to the Holy Scripture, containing the several Tropes, Fighres, Properties of Speech used therein: with other Observations, necessary for the right Understanding thereof.* London, 1669.

Luther, Martin. *D. Martin Luthers Werke. Kritische Gesamtausgabe.* 66 vols. Weimar: Hermann Böhlaus Nachfolger, 1883-1987.

_____. *Loci communes D. Martini Lutheri, viri Dei & Prophetae Germanici, ex Scriptis ipsius Latinis forma gnomologica & aphoristica collecti, & in qinque classis distributi, a M. Theodosio Fabrico, ecclesiae Gorringensis pastore.* London: R. H. & W. E., 1651.

_____. *Luther's Works.* 56 vols. Edited by Jaroslav Pelikan and Helmut Lehmann. St. Louis: Concordia; Philadelphia: Fortress, 1955-86.

Maccovius, Johannes. *Collegia theologica quae extant omnia.* Franecker, 1641.

_____. *Distinctiones et regulae theologicae et philosophicae.* Amsterdam, 1656.

_____. *Loci communes theologici.* Amsterdam, 1658.

_____. *Metaphysica, ad usum quaestionum in philosophia ac theologia adornata & applicata.* Leiden, 1658.

_____. *Opuscula philosophica omnia.* Amsterdam, 1660.

Maimbourg, Louis. *Histoire de l'Arianisme depuis sa naissance jusqu'à sa sin: avec l'origine & le progrés de l'heresie des Sociniens.* Paris: Sebastien Mabre-Cramoisy, 1683.

_____. *The History of Arianism, by M. Maimbourg; shewing its influence upon civil affairs: and the causes of the dissolution of the Roman empire. To which are added, two introductory discourses.* With an appendix containing an account of the English writers in the Socinian and Arian controversies by William Webster. London: W. Roberts, 1728-1729.

Malebranche, Nicholas. *Dialogues on Metaphysics and Religion.* Edited by Nicholas Jolley, translated by David Scott. Cambridge: Cambridge University Press, 1997.

_____. *Elucidations of The Search after Truth.* Translated and edited by Thomas M. Lennon Cambridge: Cambridge University Press, 1997. [In Malebranche, *The Search,* pp. 531-753.]

_____. *Oeuvres completes.* 22 vols. in 11. Paris: J. Vrin, 1958- .

_____. *The Search after Truth.* Translated and edited by Thomas M. Lennon and Paul J. Olscamp. Cambridge: Cambridge University Press, 1997.

_____. *Treatise on Nature and Grace.* Translated, with an introduction and notes by Patrick Riley. Oxford: Clarendon Press, 1992.

Manton, Thomas. *The Complete Works of Thomas Manton.* 22 vols. London: J. Nisbet, 1870-75.

Marckius, Johannes. *Analysis exegetica capitis LIII. Jesaiae in qua alia complura vaticina de Messia illustrantur; accedit Mantissa observationum textualium.* Groningen, 1687.

_____. *Christianae theologiae medulla didactico elenctica.* Amsterdam, 1690.

_____. *Compendium theologiae christianae didactico-elencticum.* Groningen, 1686. [Heppe #50]

_____. *In apocalypsin Johannis commentarius seu analysis exegetica* Amsterdam, 1689.

_____. *In canticum Salomonis commentarius, seu analysis exegetica ... annexa est etiam analysis exegetica Psalmi XLV.* Amsterdam, 1703.

_____. *In Haggaeum, Zecharjam, & Malachiam commentarius seu analysis exegetica*. 2 vols. Amsterdam, 1701.

_____. *Scripturariae exercitationes ad quinque & viginti selecta loca Novi Testamenti*. Amsterdam, 1742.

_____. *Sylloge dissertationum philologico-theologicarum, ad selectos quosdam textus Veteris Testamenti*. Leiden, 1717.

Maresius, Samuel. *Collegium theologicum sive systema breve universae theologiae comprehensum octodecim disputationibus*. Groningen, 1645; 1659. [Heppe #34]

_____. *De abusu philosophiae Cartesianae in rebus theologicis et fidei*. Groningen: T. Everts, 1670.

_____. *Refutatio fabulae prae-adamiticae, absoluta septem primariis quaestionibus, cum praefatione apologetica pro authentia Scripturarum*. Groningen, 1656.

_____. *Theses theologicae de judice controversiarum*. Paris, 1625.

Marlorat, Augustin. *A Catholike and ecclesiasticall exposition of the Holy Gospell after S. Iohn*. London, 1575.

_____. *A Catholike and ecclesiasticall exposition of St. Marke and Luke*. 2 parts. London, 1583.

_____. *A Catholike and ecclesiasticall exposition of the Holy Gospell after S. Matthew, gathered out of all the singular and approved divines*. London, 1570.

_____. *A Catholike exposition upon the Revelation of Sainct Iohn*. London, 1574.

_____. *A Catholike exposition uppon the last two Epistles of Iohn*. London, 1578?

_____. *Propheticae, et apostolicae, id est, totius divinae ac canonicae Scripturae, thesaurus, in locos communes rerum, dogmatum suis exemplis illustratum*. London, 1574.

Martin, Gregory. *A Discouerie of the Manifold Corruptions of the Holy Scriptures by the Heretickes of our Daies: especially the English Sectaries, and of their foule dealing herein, by partial & false translations to the aduantage of their heresies*. Rheims: Iohn Fogny, 1582.

Martinius, Matthaeus. *Christianae doctrinae summa capita*. Herborn, 1603. [Heppe #28]

_____. *Christiana et catholics fides, quam symbolum apostolicum vocamus*. Bremen: Thomas Viller, 1618.

_____. *De Deo, summo illo bono & cause omnis boni, libelli duo*. Bremen: Johannes Wessel, 1616.

_____. *Disputationes theologicae ad summulam s. theologiae enarrandum publice habitarum decas prima*. Bremen: Johannes Wessel, 1611.

_____. *Sylloge quaestionum theologicarum ad summulam theologiae accomodatarum*. Bremen: Johannes Wessel, 1610.

Mastricht, Petrus van. *Methodus concionandi*. Frankfurt-on-Oder: M. Hübner, n.d.

_____. *Theologiae didactico-elenctico-practicae Prodromus tribus speciminibus*. Amsterdam: Johann van Sommern, 1666.

_____. *Theoretico-practica theologia, qua, per capita theologica, pars dogmatica, elenchtica et practica, perpetua successione conjugantur, praecedunt in usum operis, paraleipomena, seu sceleton de optima concionandi methodo*. 2 vols. Amsterdam: Henricus & Theodorus Boom, 1682-87.

_____. *Theoretico-practica theologia*. Utrecht: van de Water, Poolsum, Wagens & Paddenburg, 1714. Editio nova, 1724. [Heppe #43]

Mather, Samuel. *The Figures or Types of the Old Testament, by which Christ and the Heavenly Things of the Gospel were Preached and Shadowed unto the People of God of Old.* Dublin, 1683. Reprint, New York: Johnson Reprints, 1969.

Mayer, John. *A Commentarie upon the New Testament. Representing the divers expositions thereof, out of the workes of the most learned , both ancient Fathers, and moderne Writers.* 3 vols. London, 1631.

_____. *A Commentary upon all the Prophets both Great and Small: wherein the divers Translations and Expositions both Literal and Mystical of all the most famous Commentators both Ancient and Modern are propounded.* London, 1652.

Mede, Joseph. *Clavis apocalyptica: ex innatis & insitis visionum characteribus eruta & demonstrata: una cum commentario in Apocalypsin: quibus accessit hac tertia editione conjectura de Gogo & Magogo, ab eodem autore.* Cambridge: Thomas Buck, 1632.

_____. *The Key of the Revelation, searched and demonstrated out of the naturall and proper characters of the visions.* Translated by Richard More, with a preface by Dr. Twisse. London: Philip Stephens, 1643.

Meijer, Lodewijk. *Philosophiae S. Scripturae interpres.* Eleutheropolis: s.n., 1666.

_____. *La philosophie interprète de l'Écriture Sainte.* Translated,, with notes, by Jacqueline Lagrée and Pierre François Moreau. Paris: Intertextes 1988.

Melanchthon, Philip. *Brevis discendae theologiae ratio,* in *Opera,* vol. 2, cols. 455-462.

_____. *Loci communes,* in *Opera,* vol. 21.

_____. *Loci praeciupi theologici,* in *Opera,* vol. 21.

_____. *Opera quae supersunt omnia.* 28 vols. Edited by C. G. Bretschneider and H. E. Bindseil. Brunswick: Schwetschke, 1834-1860.

Mestrezat, Jean. *Traité de l'Escriture Saincte.* Geneva, 1633.

Milton, John. *Artis logicae plenior institutio, ad Petri Rami methodum concinnata: adjecta est Praxis annalytica & Petri Rami vita: libris duobus.* London: Spencer Hickman, 1672; also London: R. Boulter, 1673.

_____. *Complete Prose Works.* Edited by Don M. Wolfe. 7 vols. in 10, to date. New Haven and London: Yale University Press, 1953-.

Minutes of the Sessions of the Westminster Assembly of Divines. Edited by Alexander Mitchell and John Struthers. Edinburgh: Blackwood, 1874.

Molina, Luis de. *Concordia liberi arbitrii cum gratiae donis, divina praescientia, providentia, praedestinatione et reprobatione* (1588). Edited by Johann Rabeneck. Onia and Madrid: Collegium Maximum Societatis Jesu, 1953.

_____. *On Divine Foreknowledge.* Translated, with an introduction and notes by Alfred J. Freddoso. Ithaca: Cornell University Press, 1988.

More, Henry. *Divine Dialogues, containing sundry Disquisitions & Instructions concerning the Attributes of God and His Providence in the World.* 2 vols. London: James Flesher, 1668.

_____. *An Antidote against Atheisme.* 2nd ed. London: J. Flesher, 1655.

Musculus, Wolfgang. *Commonplaces of Christian Religion.* London: R. Wolfe, 1563. London: H. Bynneman, 1578.

_____. *Loci communes sacrae theologiae.* Basel: Johann Herwagen, 1560. 3rd ed. Basel: Johann Herwagen, 1573. [Heppe #6]

Newton, Isaac. *Theological Manuscripts.* Edited, with an introduction by H. McLachlan. Liverpool: Liverpool University Press, 1980.

Nicholls, William. *An answer to an heretical book called The naked Gospel which was condemned and ordered to be publickly burnt by the convocation of the University of Oxford, Aug. 19, 1690: with some reflections on Dr. Bury's new edition of that book: to which is added a short history of Socinianism.* London: Walter Kettilby, 1691.

Nichols, Thomas. *An Abridgement of the Whole Body of Divinity, extracted from the Learned Works of that ever-famous and reverend Divine, Mr. William Perkins.* London: W. B., for Will Hope, 1654.

Norton, John. *The growth of error being an exercitation concerning the rise and progress of Arminianism and more especially Socinianism, both abroad and now of late, in England.* London: John Salusbury, 1697.

Nye, Stephen. *An account of Mr. Firmin's religion, and of the present state of the Unitarian controversy.* London: s.n., 1698.

_____. *The agreement of the Unitarians with the Catholick Church: being also a full answer to the infamations of Mr. Edwards and the needless exceptions of my Lords the Bishops of Chichester, Worcester and Sarum, and of Monsieur De Luzancy.* London: s.n., 1697.

_____. *An answer to Dr. Wallis's three letters concerning the Doctrine of the Trinity.* S.l.: s.n., 1691.

_____. *A Brief History of the Unitarians, called also Socinians.* London: s.n., 1687.

_____. *Considerations on the explications of the doctrine of the Trinity by Dr. Wallis, Dr. Sherlock, Dr. S-th, Dr. Cudworth, and Mr. Hooker: as also on the account given by those that say the Trinity is an unconceivable and inexplicable mystery written to a person of quality.* London: s.n., 1693.

_____. *Considerations on the explications of the doctrine of the Trinity: occasioned by four sermons preached by His Grace the Lord Arch-Bishop of Canterbury: a sermon preached by the Lord-Bishop of Worcester: a discourse by the Lord-Bishop of Salisbury: a sheet by a very learned hand containing twenty eight propositions: a treatise by an eminent dissenting minister, being a calm discourse concerning the possibility of a Trinity and by a book in answer to the animadversions on Dr. Sherlock's vindication of the Trinity: in a letter to H.H.* London: s.n., 1694.

_____. *A discourse concerning natural and revealed religion: evidencing the truth and certainty of both, by considerations (for the most part) not yet touched by any: recommended to the consideration of atheists, deists and scepticks, and useful to confirm and nourish the faith and piety of others.* London: T.W. for Jonathan Robinson, 1696.

_____. *Doctor Wallis's letter touching the doctrine of the blessed Trinity: answer'd by his friend.* Published in *The faith of one God*, edited by Thomas Firmin. London: s.n., 1691.

_____. *The exceptions of Mr. Edwards in his Causes of atheism against the Reasonableness of Christianity, as deliver'd in the Scriptures, examin'd and found unreasonable, unscriptural, and injurious: also it's clearly proved by many testimonies of Holy Scripture, that the God and Father of our Lord Jesus Christ is the only God and Father of Christians.* London: s.n., 1695.

_____. *The Explication of the Articles of the Divine Unity, the Trinity and Incarnation, commonly received in the Catholick Church, Asserted and Vindicated. By Occasion of the late Books of the Reverend Dr. Samuel Clarke, and his Opposers; and of another Book, by a learned Socinian.* London: s.n., 1715.

_____ [attrib.]. *The grounds and occasions of the controversy concerning the unity of God &c.: the methods by which it has been managed, and the means to compose it, by a Divine of the Church of England.* London: E. Whitlock, 1698.

_____. *Observations on the four letters of Dr. John Wallis concerning the Trinity and the Creed of Athanasius*. London: s.n., 1691.

_____. *A reply to The second defence of the XXVIII propositions, said to be wrote in answer to a Socinian manuscript by the author of that ms. no Socinian, but a Christian and Unitarian*. London: s.n., 1695.

_____. *Some thoughts upon Dr. Sherlock's Vindication of the doctrine of the Holy Trinity: in a letter*. London: s.n., 1691.

Olevianus, Caspar. *De substantia foederis gratiuti inter Deum et electos itemque de mediis, quibus ea ipsa substantia nobis communicatur, libri duo*. Geneva, 1585. [Heppe #15]

_____. *Expositio symboli apostolici sive articulorum fidei: in qua summa gratiuti foederis aeterni inter Deum et fideles breviter & perspicué tractatur*. Frankfurt, 1584.

_____. *An Exposition of the Symbole of the Apostles*. London, 1581.

_____. *A Firm Foundation: An Aid to Interpreting the Heidelberg Catechism*. Translated and edited by Lyle D. Bierma. Grand Rapids: Baker Book House, 1995.

_____. *Vester Grundt, das ist, die artikel des alten, waren, ungezweifelten, christlichen Glaubens*. Heidelberg: Michel Schirat, 1567.

Oomius, Simon. *Dissertatie van de Onderwijsingen in de Practycke der Godgeleerdheid*. Bolsward: van Haringhouk, 1672. Reprint, Geldermalsen: De Schatkamer, 1997.

Owen, John. *A Brief Declaration and Vindication of the Doctrine of the Trinity: as also of the Person and Satisfaction of Christ* (1669), in *Works*, vol. 2, pp. 365-439.

_____. *The Causes, Ways, and Means of Understanding the Mind of God, as Revealed in His Word, with Assurance Therein. And a Declaraton of the Perspicuity of the Scriptures, with the External Means of the Interpretation of Them*, in *Works*, vol. 4.

_____. *ΧΡΙΣΤΟΛΟΓΙΑ: or, a Declaration of the Glorious Mystery of the Person of Christ* (1679), in *Works*, vol. 1, pp. 2-272.

_____. *A Display of Arminianism: Being a Discovery of the Old Pelagian Idol Free-Will* (1642), in *Works*, vol. 10, pp. 2-137.

_____. *A Dissertation on Divine Justice* (1653), in *Works*, vol. 10, pp. 481-642.

_____. *An Exposition of the Epistle to the Hebrews*. Edited by William H. Goold. 7 vols. London and Edinburgh: Johnstone and Hunter, 1855. [Originally 5 vols. London, 1668-84.]

_____. *Meditations and Discourses on the Glory of Christ* (1684-1691), in *Works*, vol. 1, pp. 274-461.

_____. *Of the Divine Original, Authority, Self-evidencing Light, and Power of the Scriptures*, in *Works*, vol. 16.

_____. *ΠΝΕΥΜΑΤΟΛΟΓΙΑ or, a Discourse concerning the Holy Spirit* (1674-1693) in *Works*, vols. 3-4.

_____. *Pro sacris scripturis exercitationes adversus fanaticos*, in *Works*, vol. 16.

_____. *The Reason of Faith*, in *Works*, vol. 4.

_____. *Review of the Annotations of Grotius*, in *Works*, vol. 12.

_____. *The Testimony of the Church is not the only nor the chief Reason for our Believing the Scripture to be the Word of God*, in *Works*, vol. 8.

_____. *Theologoumena pantodapa sive, De natura, ortu, progressu, et studio, verae theologiae, libri sex* (1661), in *Works*, vol 17.

_____. *Two Short Catechisms* (1645), in *Works*, vol. 1, pp. 463-494.

_____. *To the Christian Reader*, in James Durham, *Exposition of the Song of Solomon*, pp. 19-22.

_____. A Vindication of the Purity and Integrity of the Hebrew and Greek Texts of the Old and New Testament, in Works, vol. 16.

_____. Vindiciae evangelicae; or, the Mystery of the Gospel Vindicated and Socinianism Examined ... in confutation of a Scripture Catechism written by J. Biddle ... with the Vindication of the Testimonies of Scripture concerning the Deity and Satisfaction of Jesus Christ from the perverse Expositions and Interpretations of them by Hugo Grotius (1655), in Works, vol. 12, pp. 2-590.

_____. The Works of John Owen. Edited by William H. Goold. 17 vols. London and Edinburgh: Johnstone and Hunter, 1850-53. Reprint (lacking vol. 17), Edinburgh: Banner of Truth Trust, 1967.

Quick, John. Synodicon in Gallia Reformata: or, the Acts, Decisions, Decrees, and Canons of those famous National Councils of the Reformed Churches in France. 2 vols. London: T. Parkhurst and J. Robinson, 1692.

Parker, Samuel. A Free and Impartial Censure of the Platonick Philosophie. Oxford: W. Hall, 1666.

Pearson, John. An Exposition of the Creed by John, Lord Bishop of Chester. London, 1659; third edition, with additions, 1669; tenth edition, revised and corrected, 1715.

_____. An Exposition of the Creed. With an analysis by Edward Walford, M.A. [Bohn's Theological Library] London: Bell and Sons, 1887.

_____. Lectiones de Deo et attributis (ca. 1661), in Minor Works, vol. I.

_____. The Minor Theological Works of John Pearson, D.D. Now first collected, with a memoir of the author ... by Edward Churton. 2 vols. Oxford: Oxford University Press, 1844.

Pearson, John, et al. Critici Sacri: sive doctissimorum virorum in SS. Biblia annotationes, & tractatus. 9 vols. London, 1660.

Pemble, William. The Workes of William Pemble. 3rd ed. London, 1631.

_____. Tractatus de providentia Dei. London, 1631.

Perkins, William. The Art of Prophecying, in Workes, vol. II.

_____. A Clowd of Faithfull Witnesses ... a Commentarie Upon the Eleventh Chapter to the Hebrews [and] A Commentarie Upon Part of the Twelfth Chapter to the Hebrews, in Workes, vol. III.

_____. A Commentary on Galatians. Edited by Gerald T. Sheppard. Introductory essays by Brevard S. Childs, Gerald T. Sheppard, and John H. Augustine. Pilgrim Classic Commentaries, vol. 2. New York: Pilgrim Press, 1989.

_____. A Commentary on Hebrews 11 (1609 Edition). Edited by John H. Augustine. Introductory essays by John H. Augustine, Donald K. McKim, Gerald T. Sheppard, and Richard A. Muller. Pilgrim Classic Commentaries, vol. 3. New York: Pilgrim Press, 1991.

_____. De praedestinationis modo et ordine. Cantabrigiae: Iohannis Legat, 1598.

_____. An Exposition of the Five first Chapters of the Epistle to the Galatians: With the Continuation of the Commentary Upon the Sixth Chapter, in Workes, vol. II.

_____. An Exposition of the Symbole or Creed of the Apostles, in Workes, vol. I.

_____. A Golden Chaine, in Workes, vol. I.

_____. A Reformed Catholike in Works, vol. I.

_____. A Treatise of the Manner and Order of Predestination, in Workes, vol. II.

_____. The Workes of ... Mr. William Perkins. 3 vols. Cambridge: John Legatt, 1612-1619.

Pezelius, Christophorus. *Argumentorum et objectionum de praecipuis articulis doctrinae christianae cum responsionibus, quae passim extant in scriptis reverendi viri domini Philippi Melanchthonis.* Pars. I-VII. Neustadt, 1582-88. [Heppe #17a]

Pictet, Benedict. *Christian Theology.* Translated by Frederick Reyroux. Philadelphia: Presbyterian Board of Publication, n.d.

_____. *Dissertationis de consensu et dissensu inter Reformatos et Augustanae Confessionis fratres vindiciae adversus Animadversiones, quas edidit Lutheranus.* Geneva, 1700. [Heppe #47]

_____. *Theologia christiana ex puris ss. literarum fontibus hausta.* Geneva, 1696. [Heppe #47]

Piscator, Johannes. *Analysis logica evangelii secundum Johannem: una cum scholiis & observationibus locorum doctrinae.* London: George Bishop, 1595.

_____. *Analysis logica evangelii secundum Lucam.* London, 1596.

_____. *Analysis logica evangelii secundum Marcum.* London, 1595.

_____. *Analysis logica evangelii secundum Mattheum.* London, 1594.

_____. *Analysis logica libri S. Lucae qui inscribitur Acta Apostolorum.* London, 1597.

_____. *Analysis logica omnium epistolarum Pauli ... una cum scholiis & observationibus locorum doctrinae.* London: George Bishop, 1608.

_____. *Analysis logica septem epistolarum apostolicarum.* London, 1593.

_____. *Aphorismi doctrinae Christianae, maximam partem ex Institutione Calvini exerpti, seu Loci communes theologici, brevibus sententiis expositi.* Herborn, 1589. [Heppe #20]

_____. *Commentarii in omnes libros Novi Testamenti.* Herborn, 1613, 1658.

_____. *In P. Rami dialecticam animadversione.* London, 1581.

Pococke, Edward. *A Commentary on the Prophecy of Hosea.* Oxford: Printed at the Theater, 1685.

_____. *A Commentary on the Prophecy of Joel.* Oxford: Printed at the Theatre, 1691.

_____. *A Commentary on the Prophecy of Malachi.* Oxford: Printed at the Theatre, 1692.

_____. *A Commentary on the Prophecy of Micah.* Oxford: Printed at the Theatre, 1692.

_____. *The Theological Works of the Learned Dr. Pocock, sometime professor of the Hebrew and Arabick tongues, in the University of Oxford, and canon of Christ-Church: containing his Porta Mosis, and English commentaries on Hosea, Joel, Micah, and Malachi.* To which is prefixed, an account of his life and writings [by Leonard Twells]. 2 vols. London: Printed for the editor, and sold by R. Gosling, 1740.

Poiret, Pierre. *Cogitationum rationalium de Deo, anima et Malo, libri quatuor. In quibus quid de hisce Cartesius, eiusque sequaces, senserint, continentur.* Amsterdam, 1677.

_____. *L'oeconomie divine, ou système universel et démontré des Oeuvres et des Desseins de Dieu envers les hommes.* 7 vols. Amsterdam, 1687.

_____. *Fides et ratio collatae, ac suo utraque loco redditae, adversus principia Joannis Lockii.* Amsterdam, 1707.

Polanus von Polansdorf, Amandus. *Analysis libelli Prophetae Malachiae.* Basel, 1597.

_____. *Analysis libri Hoseae Prophetae.* Basel, 1601.

_____. *In Danielem Prophetam visionum amplitudine difficillimum ... commentarius.* Basel, 1599.

_____. *In librum prophetiarum Ezechielis commentarii.* Basel, 1608.

_____. *Partitiones theologiae christianae.* Pars I-II. Basel, 1590-96.

_____. *The Substance of the Christian Religion.* London, 1595. [A translation of part I of the *Partitiones.*]

_____. *Syntagma theologiae christianae*. Quarto ed., 2 parts. Hanau, 1609. Folio ed., Geneva, 1617. [Heppe #11]

Polyander à Kerckhoven, Johannes. *Ancker der ghelovige siele*. Leiden: van Ilpendam, 1628.

Poole, Matthew. *Annotations on the Holy Bible*. 2 vols. London, 1683-85. Reissued as *A Commentary on the Whole Bible*. 3 vols. London: Banner of Truth, 1962.

_____. *Blasphemoktonia: The Blasphemer Slain; or, a Plea for the Godhood of the Holy Ghost, vindicated from the Cavils of J. Bidle*. London, 1648. 2nd ed. London, 1654.

_____. *Synopsis criticorum aliorumque sacrae scripturae interpretum et commentatorum, summo studio et fide adornata*. 5 vols. London, 1669-76.

Preston, John. *Life Eternall, or, A Treatise of the Knowledge of the Divine Essence and Attributes*. London, 1631.

Prideaux, John. *Fasciculus controversiarum ad juniorum aut occupatorum captum sic colligatus*. 3rd ed. Oxford, 1664.

_____. *Hypomnemata: logica, rhetorica, physica, metaphysica, pneumatica, ethica, politica, œconomica*. Oxford: Leonard Lichfield, 1650.

_____. *Lectiones novem de totidem religionis capitibus praecipue hoc tempore controversis prout publice hebebantum Oxoniae*. Oxford, 1625.

_____. *Manductio ad theologiam polemicam*. Oxford: 1657.

_____. *Orationes novem inaugurales de totidem theologiae capitibus*. Oxford, 1626.

_____. *Scholasticae theologiae syntagma mnemonicum*. Oxford: Leonard Litchfield, 1651.

Puritan Sermons, 1659-1689: Being the Morning Exercises at Cripplegate, St. Giles in the Fields, and Southwark by Seventy-five Ministers of the Gospel in or Near London. 6 vols. London, 1661-75. Republished, with notes and translations by James Nichols, London: Tegg, 1844-45. Reprint, Wheaton, Ill.: Richard Owen Roberts, 1981.

The Racovian catechisme: wherein you have the substance of the confession of those churches, which in the kingdom of Poland and Great Dukedome of Lithuania, and other provinces appertaining to that kingdom, do affirm, that no other save the Father of our Lord Jesus Christ, is that one God of Israel, and that the man Jesus of Nazareth, who was born of the Virgin, and no other besides, or before him, is the onely begotten Sonne of God. Amsterdam: For Brooer Janz, 1652.

The Racovian Catechism. With notes and illustrations. Translated by Thomas Rees. London, 1609. Reprint, London: Longman, Hurst, 1818.

Rainolds, John. *Sex theses de sacra scriptura et ecclesia, publicis in Acad. Oxoniensi disputationibus explicatae*. London, 1580.

_____. *Six conclusions Touching the Holy Scripture and the Church*. London, 1598. [Appended to *The Summe of the Conference*, as pp. 593-675.]

_____. *The Summe of the Conference between Iohn Rainolds and Iohn Hart: Touching the Head and Faith of the Church. Wherein are handled sundry points, of the sufficiency and right expounding of the Scriptures, the ministrie of the church*. London, 1598.

Rambach, Johann Jacob. *Dogmatische Theologie der Christliche Glaubens-Lehre*. 2 vols. Frankfurt and Leipzig, 1744.

_____. *Schrifftmässige Erläuterung der Grundlegung der Theologie Herrn Johann Anastasii Freylingshausens*. Frankfurt, 1738.

Ramus, Petrus. *The art of logick. Gathered out of Aristotle, and set in due forme, according to his instructions, by Peter Ramus ... With a short exposition of the praecepts, by which any one of indifferent capacitie, may with a little paines, attaine to some competent knowledge and vse of that noble and necessary science.* Pub. for the instruction of the vnlearned, by Antony Wotton. London: I.D. for N. Bourne, 1626.

————. *Commentariorum de religione christiana libri quatuor.* Frankfurt: Andreas Wechel, 1576. Reprint, Frankfurt, Minerva, 1969.

————. *Dialectica in two bookes not only translated into English, but also digested into questions and answers ...* by R. F[age]. London: W. J[ones], 1632.

————. *Dialecticae institutiones: Aristotelicae animadversiones.* Faksimile-Neudruck der Ausgaben Paris 1543, mit einer Einleitung von Wilhelm Risse. Stuttgart: Friedrich Frommann, 1964.

————. *Dialecticae, libri duo.* London, 1576.

————. *Dialecticae libri duo: quibus loco commentarii perpetui post certa capita subjicitur, Guilielmi Amesii, demonstratio logicae verae, simul cum synopsi ejusdem, qua uno intuiti exhibetur tota ars bene differendi.* Cambridge: G. Morden, 1672.

————. *The logike of the most excellent philosopher P. Ramus martyr.* Newly translated, and in diuers places corrected after the mynde of the author. London: Thomas Vautroullier, 1574.

————. *The logike of the moste excellent philosopher P. Ramus, martyr.* Translated by Roland MacIlmaine (1574). Edited, with an introduction by Catherine M. Dunn. Northridge, Ca., San Fernando Valley State College, 1969.

R., C. [Richard Smith?]. *Of the Distinction of Fundamental and Not Fundamental Points of Faith.* N.p.: s.n., 1645.

Ravensperger, Hermann. *Wegweiser, d. i. schlecte und rechte Erklärung aller notwendigen Lehrpunkte christlicher Religion.* Groningen, 1615. [Heppe #27]

Reinbeck, Johann. *Betrachtungen über die in der Augspurgischen Confession.* 4 pts. Berlin, 1731-41.

Rennecherus, Hermann. *The Golden Chaine of Salvation.* London: Valentine Simmes, 1604.

Rhegius, Urbanus. *An Instruccyon of Christen Fayth howe to be Bolde upon the Promyse of God.* Translated by J. Foxe. London: Hugh Syngleton, n.d.

————. *A Necessary Instruction of Christian Faith and Hope.* Translated by J. Foxe. London: Hugh Singleton, 1579.

Ridgley, Thomas. *A Body of Divinity: Wherein the Doctrines of the Christian Religion are Explained and Defended, being the Substance of Several Lectures on the Assembly's Larger Catechism.* 2 vols. London, 1731-33.

————. *Commentary on the Larger Catechism; Previously Entitled A Body of Divinity....* Revised, with notes by John M. Wilson. 1855. Reprint, Edmonton: Still Waters Revival Books, 1993.

Rijssenius, Leonardus. *Dootstuypen der Cartesianen en Coccejanen, Vertoont in twee Boecken.* Utrecht: W. Clerck, 1676.

————. *De Oude Rechtsinnige Waerheyt verdonkert, en bedeckt door DesCartes, Cocceijus, Wittich, Burman, Wolzogen, Perizon, Groenewegen, Allinga, &c. En nu weder Op-geheldert, en ondeckt....* Middelburgh: Benedictus Smidt, 1674.

————. *Summa theologiae didactico-elencticae.* Amsterdam, 1695; Edinburgh, 1698; Frankfurt and Leipzig, 1731. [Heppe #49]

Rivetus, Andreas. *Isagoge, seu introductio generalis ad Scripturam Sacram Veteris et Novi Testamenti, in qua, eius natura, existentia, necessitas, puritas, versionem et interpretationem rationes et modi indagnatur, in Opera, vol. II.*

_____. *Opera theologia*. 3 vols. Rotterdam, 1651-60.

Roberts, Francis. *Clavis Bibliorum. The Key of the Bible, Unlocking the Richest Treasury of the Holy Scriptures, whereby the Order, Names, Times, Penmen, Occasion, Scope, and Principal Parts, containing the Subject-Matter of the Books of the Old and New Testament, are Familiarly and Briefly Opened*. London: T. R. & E. M. for George Calvert, 1649.

_____. *A Communicant Instructed; Or, Practicall Directions for Worthy Receiving of the Lords-Supper*. 3rd ed. London, 1656.

_____. *Mysterium & medulla Bibliorum: the mysterie and marrow of the Bible, viz. God's covenants with man in the first Adam before the fall, and in the last Adam, Iesvs Christ, after the fall, from the beginning to the end of the world: unfolded & illustrated in positive aphorisms & their explanation*. London: Printed by R.W. for George Calvert, 1657.

Röell, Herman Alexander. *Dissertatio de religione rationali ... cui adjuncta ext Oratio de theologia, et theologiae supernaturali prae naturali praestantia*. Franekcer: J. & F. Horreus, 1718.

Rollock, Robert. *Select Works of Robert Rollock*. Edited by William M. Gunn. 2 vols. Edinburgh, 1844-49.

_____. *A Treatise of Effectual Calling*. Translated by Henry Holland. London, 1603; also in *Select Works.*, vol. I.

Russell, William. *Blasphemoktonia: the Holy Ghost Vindicated*. London, 1648.

Rutherford, Samuel. *The covenant of life opened, or, A treatise of the covenant of grace: containing something of the nature of the covenant of works, the soveraignty of God, the extent of the death of Christ ... the covenant of grace ... of surety or redemption between the Lord and the Son Jesus Christ, infants right to Jesus Christ and the seal of baptisme: with some practicall questions and observations*. Edinburgh: Andro Anderson, 1655.

_____. *Disputatio scholastica de divina providentia, variis praelectionibus, quod attinet ad summa rerum capita ... Adjectae sunt disquisitiones metaphysicae de ente, possibili, dominio Dei in entia & non entia, & variae quaestiones*. Edinburgh: George Anderson, 1649.

_____. *Exercitationes apologeticae pro divina gratia, in quibus vindicatur doctrina orthodoxa de divinis decretis, & Dei tum aeterni decreti, tum gratiae efficacis operationis, cum hominis libertate consociatione & subordinatione amica*. Franecker: Johannes Dhüiringh, 1651.

Sanderson, Robert. *Logicæ artis compendium: In quo vniversiæ artis synopsis, methodo ac forma ad scholarum vsum, quàm fieri potuit, accommodatissimâ breviter proponitur*. Oxford: Ioseph Barnes, 1615.

Sandius, Christophorus. *Bibliotheca anti-trinitariorum, sive catalogus scriptorum, et succincta narratio de vita eorum auctorum..., opus posthumum Christophori Chr. Sandii; accedunt alia quaedam scripta, quorum seriem pagina post praefationem dabit, quae omnia simul juncta compendium historiae ecclesiasticae Unitariorum, qui Sociniani vulgo audiunt, exhibent*. Freistad: Johannam Aconium, 1684.

_____. *Nucleus historiae ecclesiasticae, exhibitus in historia Arianorum, tribus libris comprehensa*. Cologne, 1668. 2nd ed., 1676.

Sarcerius, Erasmus. *Common Places of Scripture orderly & after a Compendious Forme of Teaching*. Translated by Richard Taverner. London: Thomas East, 1577.

Scharpius, Johannes. *Cursus theologicus in quo controversia omnes de fide dogmatibus hoc seculo exagitate*. 2 vols. Geneva, 1620.

Schegk, Jacob. *Hyperaspistes responsi, ad quatuor epistolas Petri Rami contra se editas*. Tübingen: n.p., 1570. Reprint, Frankfurt: Minerva, 1976.

Servetus, Michael. *Christianismi restitutio. Totius eccelsiae apostolicae est ad sua limina vocatio, in integrum restituta cognitione Dei, fidei Christi...* Vienne: n.p., 1553.

_____. *The Two Treatises of Servetus on the Trinity.* Translated by E. M. Wilbur. Cambridge, Mass.: Harvard University Press, 1932.

Sherlock, William. *An answer to a late Dialogue between a new Catholick convert and a Protestant: to prove the mystery of the Trinity to be as absurd a doctrine as transubstantiation: by way of short notes on the said dialogue.* London: Thomas Bassett, 1687.

_____. *An apology for writing against Socinians, in defence of the doctrines of the Holy Trinity and incarnation: in answer to a late earnest and compassionate suit for forbearance to the learned writers of some controversies at present.* London: William Rogers, 1693.

_____. *A defence of Dr. Sherlock's notion of a Trinity in unity: in answer to the animadversions upon his vindication of the doctrine of the holy and ever Blessed Trinity: with a post-script relating to the calm discourse of a Trinity in the Godhead: in a letter to a friend.* London: William Rogers, 1694.

_____. *A defence of the Dean of St. Paul's Apology for writing against the Socinians: in answer to the antapologist.* London: William Rogers, 1694.

_____. *A discourse concerning the divine providence.* London: William Rogers, 1694.

_____. *The distinction between real and nominal trinitarians examined: and the doctrine of a real Trinity vindicated from the charge of Tritheism: in answer to a late Socinian pamphlet, entituled, The judgment of a disinterested person, concerning the controversie about the Blessed Trinity, depending between Dr. S--th, and Dr. Sherlock.* London: William Rogers, 1696.

_____. *A Modest examination of the authority and reason of the late decree of the Vice-Chancellor of Oxford and some heads of colleges concerning the heresy of three distinct and infinite persons in the Holy and Ever-Blessed Trinity.* London: William Rogers, 1695.

_____. *The present state of the Socinian controversy, and the doctrine of the Catholick fathers concerning a trinity in unity.* London: William Rogers, 1698.

_____. *The protestant resolution of faith: being an answer to three questions: I. How far we must depend on the authority of the church for the true sense of Scripture? II. Whether a visible succession from Christ to this day makes a church, which has this succession an infallible interpreter of Scripture, and whether no church, which has not this succession, can teach the true sense of Scripture? III. Whether the Church of England can make out such a visible succession?* London: F. Gardiner, 1683.

_____. *A vindication of the doctrine of the holy and ever blessed Trinity and the incarnation of the son of God: occasioned by the brief notes on the creed of St. Athanasius, and the brief history of the Vnitarians, or Socinians, and containing an answer to both.* London: William Rogers, 1690.

Simmler, Josias. *De aeterno dei filio domino et seruatore nostro Iesu Christo, & de Spiritu Sancto: aduersus veteres & nouos Antitrinitarios, id est, Arianos, Tritheitas, Samosatenianos, & Pneumatomachos, libri quatuor.* Zurich: Froschauer, 1582.

Simon, Richard. *Histoire critique du Vieux Testament.* 1678.

Skelton, Bernard. *Christus Deus The divinity of our Saviour: asserted and vindicated from the exceptions of the Socinians and others: in a sermon preached at St. Peter's Hungate, in Norwich, upon the festival of St. Philip and St. James, in the year 1673.* London: Jonathan Robinson and Samuel Oliver, 1692.

Smalbroke, Richard. *The pretended authority of the Clementine constitutions confuted: by their inconsistency with the inspired writings of the Old and New Testament, in answer to Whiston.* London: Printed for Timothy Childe, 1714.

Smith, John. *The designed end to the Socinian controversy, or, A rational and plain discourse to prove, that no other person but the Father of Christ is God most high.* London: s.n., 1695.

Snecanus, Gellius. *Methodica descriptio sive fundamentum praecipuorum locorum aut dogmatum S. Scripturae de cognitione Dei & hominis.* Harlem: Theopjilus, 1591.

Sohnius, Georg. *Opera.* Tom. I-IV. Herborn, 1591, 1609.[Heppe #18]

South, Robert. *Animadversions upon Dr. Sherlock's book, entituled A vindication of the holy and ever-blessed Trinity, &c,: together with a more necessary vindication of that sacred and prime article of the Christian faith from his new notions, and false explications of it humbly offered to his admirers, and to himself the chief of them, by a divine of the Church of England.* London: Randal Taylor, 1693.

_____. *Sermons Preached upon Several Occasions.* 5 vols. New York: Hurd & Houghton, 1866-1871.

_____. *Tritheism charged upon Dr. Sherlock's new notion of the Trinity and the charge made good: in an answer to the defense of the said notion against the Animadversions upon Dr. Sherlock's book, entituled, A vindication of the holy and ever-blessed Trinity, &c. by a divine of the Church of England.* London: John Whitlock, 1695.

Spangenberg, Johann. *Margarita theologica continens praecipuos locos doctrinae christianae.* London: G. Dawes, 1566. London: H. Bynneman, 1569; 1573.

_____. *The Sum of Divinitie.* London, 1548; 1560; 1561; 1570.

Spanheim, Friedrich, Sr. *Disputatio de gratia universali.* 3 vols. Leiden, 1644-48.

_____. *Disputationum theologicarum syntagma. Pars prima: Disputationum theologicarum miscellanearum; Pars secunda: Anti-Anabaptistica controversia.* Geneva, 1652.

_____. *Vindici exercitationum de gratia universali adversus Amyraldum.* Amsterdam: Elzevier, 1649.

Spencer, Thomas. *The Art of Logick delivered in the precepts of Aristotle and Ramus.* London: John Dawson, 1628.

Spinoza, Baruch. *The Chief Works of Benedict de Spinoza.* Translated, with an introduction by R. H. M. Elwes. 2 vols. London: George Bell & Sons, 1883. Reprint, New York: Dover, 1955.

_____. *Earlier Philosophical Writings: The Cartesian Principles and Thoughts on Metaphysics.* Translated by Frank A. Hayes, introduction by David Bidney. Indianapolis: Bobbs-Merrill, 1963.

_____. *Spinoza's short Treatise on God, Man, and Human Welfare.* Translated by Lydia Robinson. Chicago: Open Court, 1909.

Stackhouse, Thomas. *A Complete Body of Speculative and Practical Divinity.* 3 vols. Dumfries: Robert Jackson and William Boyd, 1776.

Stapfer, Johann Friedrich. *Auszug aus der Grundlegung zur Wahren Relgion.* 2 vols. Zürich, 1754.

_____. *Grundlegung zur wahren Religion.* 12 vols. Zürich, 1746-53.

_____. *Institutiones theologiae polemicae universae, ordine scientifico dispositae.* 4th ed. 5 vols. Zürich: Heidegger, 1756-57.

Stillingfleet, Edward. *The Bishop of Worcester's answer to Mr. Locke's letter, concerning some passages relating to his Essay of humane understanding, mention'd in the late Discourse in vindication of the Trinity with a postscript in answer to some reflections made on that treatise in a late Socinian pamphlet.* London: Henry Mortlock, 1697.

_____. *The Bishop of Worcester's answer to Mr. Locke's second letter wherein his notion of ideas is prov'd to be inconsistent with itself, and with the articles of the Christian faith.* London: Henry Mortlock, 1698.

_____. *A discourse concerning the doctrine of Christ's satisfaction, or, The true reasons of His sufferings with an answer to the Socinian objections: to which is added, a sermon concerning the mysteries of the Christian faith, preached, April 7, 1671: with a preface concerning the true state of the controversie about Christ's satisfaction.* London: Henry Mortlock, 1696.

_____. *A discourse concerning the doctrine of Christ's satisfaction. wherein the Antinomian and Socianian controversies about it are truly stated and explained: in answer to Mr. Lobb's Appeal and to several letters from the dissenting parties in London.* London: Henry Mortlock, 1700.

_____. *A discourse in vindication of the doctrine of the Trinity with an answer to the late Socinian objections against it from Scripture, antiquity and reason, and a preface concerning the different explications of the Trinity, and the tendency of the present Socinian controversie.* London: Henry Mortlock, 1697.

_____. *The doctrine of the Trinity and transubstantiation compared as to Scripture, reason, and tradition in a new dialogue between a protestant and a papist.* London: W. Rogers, 1687.

_____. *Irenicum, a Weapon Salve for the Churches Wounds.* London: Henry Mortlock, 1662.

_____. *Origines sacræ, or, A rational account of the grounds of Christian faith, as to the truth and divine authority of the Scriptures and the matters therein contained.* London: Henry Mortlock, 1662.

_____. *A Rational Account of the Ground of the Protestant Religion.* London: Henry Mortlock, 1665.

_____. *Six sermons with a discourse annexed, concerning the true reason of the suffering of Christ, wherein Crellius his answer to Grotius is considered.* London: Henry Mortlock, 1669.

Stoughton, John. *A Forme of Wholesome Words; or an Introduction to the Body of Divinity: in three sermons preached on 2 Timothy 1:13.* London: J. R. for J. Bellamy, 1640.

_____. *A Learned Treatise in Three Parts: 1. The Definition; 2. The Distribution of Divinity; 3. The Happinesse of Man: As it was Scholastically Handled.* London: Richard Hodgkinson, 1640.

Strigellus, Victorinus. *Loci theologici Strigelli, quibus loci communes Melanchthonis illustrantur.* Neustadt, 1582-83. [Heppe #17b]

Suárez, Franciscus. *De scientia Dei futurorum contingentia,* in *Opera omnia,* vol. 11.

_____. *Disputationes metaphysicae.* Salamanca, 1597. [Also in *Opera omnia,* vols. 25-26.]

_____. *On the Essence of Finite Being As Such, On the Existence of that Essence and Their Distinction.* Translated, with an introduction by Norman J. Wells. Milwaukee: Marquette University Press, 1983.

_____. *On the Various Kinds of Distinctions.* Translated, with an introduction by Cyril Vollert. Milwaukee: Marquette University Press, 1947.

_____. *Opera omnia.* 26 vols. Paris: Vives, 1856-77.

Synopsis purioris theologiae, disputationibus quinquaginta duabus comprehensa ac conscripta per Johannem Polyandrum, Andream Rivetum, Antonium Walaeum, Antonium Thysium. Leiden, 1625. Editio sexta, curavit et praefatus est Dr. H. Bavinck. Leiden: Donner, 1881. [Heppe #33]

Szegedinus, Stephanus. *Confessio verae fidei de uno vero Deo Patre, Filio, et Spiritu Sancto, libris duobus comprehensa, & perpetuis tabulis illustrata.* Basel, 1588. [In Szegedinus, *Theologiae sincerae,* pp. 507-665.]

_____. *Doctrinae papisticae summa, ex variis doctoribus scholasticis excerpts, ac in tabulis per certum ordinem digesta.* Basel, 1588. [In Szegedinus, *Theologiae sincerae,* pp. 468-506.]

_____. *Theologiae sincerae loci communes de Deo et Homine perpetuis Tabulis explicati et scholasticorum dogmatis illustrati* Basel, 1588. [Heppe #10]

Taylor, Thomas. *Christ Revealed: or, The Old Testament Explained. A Treatise of the Types and shadows of our Saviour contained throughout the whole Scripture: all Opened and Made Usefull for the benefit of Gods Church.* London, 1635. Reprint, Delmar: Scholar's Facsimiles and Reprints, 1979.

Temple, William. *A Logicall Analysis of Twentie Select Psalms.* London, 1605. Latin edition, 1611.

Theologorum Saxonicorum Consensus repetitus fidei verae Lutheranae (1655/64). Edited by Ernst Ludwig Henke. Marburg: Elwert, 1846.

Til, Salomon van. *Theologiae utriusque compendium cum naturalis tum revelatae.* Leiden, 1704. 3rd ed. Leiden: Samuel Luchtmans, 1719. [Heppe #45]

Tilenus, Daniel. *A Defense of the Sufficiency of the Holy Scripture.* London: L. S. for N. Butter, 1606.

_____. *Positions lately held by the L. du Perron against the Scriptures verie learnedly answered.* London: L. S. for N. Butter, 1606.

Tillotson, John. *A seasonable vindication of the B. Trinity being an answer to this question, why do you believe the doctrine of the Trinity? Collected from the works of the most Reverend, Dr. John Tillotson, late Lord Archbishop of Canterbury, and the right Reverend Dr. Edward Stillingfleet, now Lord Bishop of Worcester.* London: B. Aylmer, 1697.

Trapp, John. *Annotations upon the Old and New Testaments in Five Distinct Volumes.* London: Robert White, 1662

_____. *A Commentary on the Old and New Testaments.* 5 vols. London: Richard Dickinson, 1856-1868. Reprint, Eureka, Ca.: Tanski Publications, 1997.

Trelcatius, Lucas, Jr. *A Briefe Institution of the Commonplaces of Sacred Divinitie.* London: T. Purfoot, 1610.

_____. *Scholastica et methodica locorum communium institutio.* London: J. Bill, 1604. Hanau, 1610. [Heppe #29]

Trelcatius, Lucas, Sr. *Opuscula theologia omnia.* Leiden, 1614.

Trent, Council of. *Canones et decreta dogmatica Concilii Tridentini.* Rome, 1564. [In Schaff, *Creeds,* vol. 2, pp. 77-206.]

_____. *Catechism of the Council of Trent for Parish Priests.* Translated by John A. McHugh and Charles J. Callan. New York, 1923. Reprint, South Bend, Indiana: Marian Publications, 1976.

_____. *Catechismus ex decreto Concilii Tridentini Pii V jussu editus.* Rome, 1566.

_____. *Professio fidei Tridentinae.* Rome, 1564. [In Schaff, *Creeds,* vol. 2, pp. 207-212.]

Tossanus, Daniel. *A Synopsis or Compendium of the Fathers, or of the most Famous and Ancient Doctors of the Church, as also of the Schoolmen.* London: Daniel Frere, 1635.

Tossanus, Paulus. *Biblia, das ist die gantze Heilige Schrifft durch D. Martin Luther verteutscht: mit D. Pauli Tossani hiebevor ausgegangenen Glossen und Auslegungen.* 4 vols. Frankfurt, 1668.

Turnbull, Richard. *An Exposition Upon the Canonicall Epistle of Saint James.* London, 1591.

Turretin, Benedict. *Defense de la fidelité des traductions de la s. Bible faites à Geneve: opposee au livre de P. Coton.* Geneva, 1619.

Turretin, Francis. *Disputatio theologica de Scripturae Sacrae auctoritate, adversus pontificos,* in *Opera,* vol. 4, pp. 233-268.

_____. *Institutio theologiae elencticae.* 3 vols. Geneva, 1679-85; a new edition, Edinburgh, 1847. [Heppe #48]

_____. *Opera.* 4 vols. Edinburgh: Lowe, 1847.

Turretin, Jean-Alphonse. *Cogitationes et dissertationes theologicae. Quibus principia religionis, cum naturalis, tum revelatae, adstruuntur & defenditur; animique ad veritatis, pietatis, & pacis studium excitantur.* 2 vols. Geneva, 1737.

_____. *Cogitationes de variis theologiae capitibus,* in *Cogitationes et dissertationes,* vol. I.

_____. *De theologia naturali,* in *Cogitationes et dissertationes,* vol. I.

_____. *De Veritate religionis judaicae et christianae,* in *Cogitationes et dissertationes,* vol. II.

_____. *Orationes academicae.* Geneva, 1637.

Twisse, William. *Ad Jacobi Arminii Collationem cum Francisco Junio; & Johan. Arnoldi Corvini Defensionem sententiae Arminianae, de praedestinatione, gratia, & libero arbitrio, &c. Quam adversus Danielis Tileni Considerationem edidit, Animadversiones.* Amsterdam: Johannes Janssonius, 1649.

_____. *A Brief Catecheticall Exposition of Christian Doctrine.* London: G> M> for Robert Bird, 1632.

_____. *A Discovery of D. Jacksons Vanitie. Or, a Perspective glasse, whereby admirers of D. Jacksons profound discourses, may see the vanitie and weaknesse of them....* London, 1631.

_____. *Dissertatio de scientia media tribus libris absoluta.* Arnhem: Jacobus à Biesius, 1639.

_____. *The Doctrine of the Synod of Dort and Arles.* London, 1650/1.

_____. *The Scriptures Sufficiency to Determine all Matters of Faith, made good against the Papist.* London: Matthew Keynton, 1656.

_____. *Vindiciae gratiae, potestatis, ac providentiae Dei hoc est, ad examen libelli Perkinsiani de praedestinatione modo et ordine, institutum a J. Arminio, responsio scholastica.* Amsterdam, 1632.

Tyndale, William. *An Answer to Sir Thomas More's Dialogue.* Cambridge: Cambridge University Press, 1850.

_____. *Doctrinal Treatises and Introductions to Different Portions of the Holy Scriptures.* Cambridge: Cambridge University Press. 1848.

_____. *A Pathway Into the Holy Scripture* (1525/32), in *Doctrinal Treatises,* pp. 1-28.

Ursinus, Zacharias. *A Collection of Certaine Learned Discourses.* Oxford: J. Barnes, 1600.

_____. *The Commentary of Dr. Zacharias Ursinus on the Heidelberg Catechism.* Translated by G. W. Williard, introduction by John W. Nevin. Columbus, Ohio, 1852. Reprint, Phillipsburg, New Jersey: Presbyterian and Reformed Publishing Co., 1985.

_____. *Doctrinae christianae compendium.* Leiden: Iohannes Paetsius, 1584. Cambridge: Thomas Thomasius, 1585. [The earliest, unedited editions of the *Explicationes catecheseos*].

_____. *Explicationes catecheseos,* in *Opera,* vol. 1. [Heppe #16.2-3]

_____. *Loci theologici,* in *Opera,* vol. 1. [Heppe #16.1]

_____. *Opera theologica quibus orthodoxae religionis capita perspicue & breviter explicantur.* Edited by Quirinius Reuter. 3 vols. Heidelberg, 1612.

_____. *Schat-Boeck der Verklarigen over den Nederlandtschen Catechismus, uyt de Latijnshe Lessen van Dr. Zacharias Ursinus, op-gemaecht van Dr. David Paraeus, vertaelt, ende met Tafelen, &c. Verlicht, door Dr. Festus Hommius, nu van nieuws oversien ... door Johannes Spiljardus*. 2 parts. Amsterdam: Johannes van Revensteyn, 1664.

_____. *Scholastica materiis theologicis exercitationes, libri II*. Neustadt: Matthaeus Harnisch, 1589-90.

Ussher, James. *A Body of Divinity, or the Sum and Substance of Christian Religion*. 6th ed., enlarged. London, 1670.

Venema, Herman. *Commentarius ad librum prophetiarum Jeremiae quo conciones rite distinguuntur, scopus, nexus et series, sermonis accurate investigatur, perpetua paraphrasi exponitur, et selectis observatis voces et phrases illustrantur, ac inplementi demonstratione, ubi opus fuerit, confirmantur*. Leeuwarden: H.A. de Chalmot, 1765.

_____. *Exercitationes de vera Christi Divinitate, ex locis Act. XX: 28, I Tim. III:16, I Joh. V: 20 et Col. I:16, 17: quibus de vera lectione et genuio sensu eorum accuratius disseritur*. Leeuwarden: Gulielmus Coulon, 1755.

_____. *Institutes of Theology*, part I. Translated by Alexander Brown. Edinburgh: T. & T. Clark, 1850.

Vermigli, Peter Martyr. *The Common Places of Peter Martyr*. Translated by Anthony Marten. London: H. Denham, et al., 1583.

_____. *Loci communes D. Petri Martyris Vermilii ... ex variis ipsis autoris scriptis, in unum librum collecti & in quatuor Classes distributi*. London: Kyngston, 1576. Editio secunda, London: Thomas Vautrollerius, 1583. [Heppe #3]

_____. *Most fruitfull and learned commentaries ... with a very profitable tract of the matter and places*. [Internal title: *The Commentarie of Master Peter Martyr upon the Booke of Iudges*]. London: J. Daye, 1564.

_____. *Most learned and fruitfull commentaries ... upon the Epistle of S. Paul to the Romanes*. London: J. Daye, 1568.

_____. *The Peter Martyr Reader*. Edited by John Patrick Donnelly, Frank A. James III, and Joseph C. McLelland. Kirksville, Mo.: Trumen State University Press, 1999.

Vincent, Thomas. *An Explanation of the Assembly's Shorter Catechism*. Philadelphia: Presbyterian Board of Publication, n.d.

_____. *An explicatory catechism, or, An explanation of the Assemblies Shorter catechism: wherein all the answers in the Assemblies catechism are taken abroad in under questions and answers, the truths explained, and proved by reason and scripture, several cases of conscience resolved, some chief controversies in religion stated: with arguments against divers errors, itself, for the more and clear and through understanding of what is therein learned*. London: George Calvert et al., 1673.

_____. *The foundation of God standeth sure, or, A defence of those fundamental and so generally believed doctrines: of the Trinity of persons in the unity of the divine essence, of the satisfaction of Christ, the second person of the real and glorious Trinity, of the justification of the ungodly by the imputed righteousness of Christ, against the cavils of W. P. J. a Quaker in his pamphlet entituled The sandy foundation shaken &c.: wherein his and the Quakers hideous blasphemies, Socinian and damnably-heretical opinions are discovered and refuted*. London: s.n., 1668.

Virel, Matthew. *Dialogue de la réligion Chrestienne, distingué en X chapitres. ensemble un bref sommaire et conference d'icelle avec toutes les autres religions*. Geneva, 1582.

_____. *A Learned and Excellent Treatise Containing all the Principall Grounds of Christian Religion.* London, 1594.

_____. *Religionis christianae compendium.* Geneva, 1582. [Heppe #4]

Viret, Pierre. *Exposition de la doctrine de la foy chrestienne, touchant la vraye cognoissance & le vraye service de Dieu.* Geneva, 1564.

_____. *Exposition familière de l'oraison de nostre Seigneur Jésus Christ.* Geneva, 1548.

_____. *Exposition familière sur le Symbole des Apostres.* Geneva, 1560.

_____. *Disputationes chrestiennes.* Geneva: J. Gérard, 1552.

_____. *Instruction chrestienne en la doctrine de la Loy et de l'Évangile.* 2 parts. Geneva, 1564.

_____. *Le Monde à l'empire et le monde démoniacle, fait par dialogues.* Geneva: J. Berthet, 1561.

_____. *Pierre Viret d' après lui-même.* Pages extraites des oeuvres du Réformateur ... par Charles Schnetzler, Henri Vuilleumier, et Alfred Schroeder, avec la collaboration d' Eugène Choisy et de Philippe Godet. Lausanne: Georges Bridel, 1911.

_____. *A Verie familiare Exposition of the Apostles Crede.* London, n.d.

_____. *The Worlde Possessed with Devils.* London: T. Dawson, 1583.

Vitringa, Campegius. *Doctrina christianae religionis, per aphorismos summatim descripta.* 8 vols. Arnheim: Johannes Möeleman, 1761-86.

_____. *Korte stellingen: in welke vervat worden de grondstukken van de christelyke leere.* Amsterdam: Balthazar Lakeman, 1730.

Voetius, Gisbertus. *Een Aenhangsel der Leere vande Voorsienigheyd Godes, Praedestinatie, vrijen Wille....* Utrecht: E. Snellaert, 1641.

_____. *Catechesatie over den Heidelbergschen Catechismus.* Edited by Abraham Kuyper, from the 1662 edition of Poudroyen. 2 vols. Rotterdam: Huge, 1891.

_____. *Catechizatie over dem catechismus der Remonstranten, met de Formulieren van den H. Doop en het H. Avonmal.* Utrecht: E. Snellaert, 1641.

_____. *Exercitia et bibliotheca studiosi theologiae.* Utrecht, 1651.

_____. *Disputatio philosophico-theologica, continens quaestiones duas de distinctione attributorum divinorum, & libertate voluntatis.* Utrecht: Joannes à Waesberge, 1652.

_____. *Selectae disputationes theologicae.* 5 vols. Utrecht, 1648-1669. [Heppe #36]

_____. *Syllabus problematum theologicorum, quae pro re natâ proponi aut perstringi solent in privatis publicisque disputationum, examinum, collationum, consultationum exercitiis.* Utrecht: Aegidius Romanus, 1643.

_____. *Ta asketika sive Exercitia pietatis in usum juventutis academicae nunc edita. Addita est, ob materiam affinitatem, Oratio de pietate cum scientia conjungenda habita anno 1634.* Gorinchem, 1664.

_____. *Vraegen over den Catechismus ...; Op-gheteeckent ende vergadert uyt de Catechisatien van Gisb. Voetius ... uytgegeven door C. Poudroyen.* Utrecht: E. Snellaert, 1640.

Vossius, Gerardus Johannes. *Theses theologicae et historicae de variis doctrinae christianae capitibus, quas olim disputandas proposuit in Academia Leidensi.* 3rd ed. Den Haag, 1658.

Vossius, Isaac. *De Sibillinis aliisque quae Christi natalem praecessere Oraculis.* Oxford, 1679; Leiden, 1680.

Vorstius, Conrad. *Tractatus theologicus de Deo, sive, de natura et attributis Dei.* Steinfurt, 1610.

Walaeus, Antonius. *Enchiridion religionis reformatae, in Opera omnia.*

_____. *Loci communes s. theologiae.* Leiden, 1640. [Also in *Opera omnia.*] [Heppe #30]

_____. *Opera omnia.* Leiden, 1643.

Walker, George. *Socinianisme in the fundamentall point of justification discovered, and confuted, or, An answer to a written pamphlet maintaining that faith is in a proper sense without a trope imputed to beleevers in justification wherein the Socinian fallacies are discovered and confuted, and the true Christian doctrine maintained, viz. that the righteousnesse by which true beleevers are justified before God is the perfect righteousnesse and obedience which the Lord Iesus Christ God and man did perform to the Law of God.* London: Iohn Bartlet, 1641.

Walker, John. *No contradiction in the received doctrine of the Blessed Trinity: but that imputation plainly chargeable on the Arian heresie. A sermon [on I Cor.i.20] preach'd at the assizes held for the county of Devon, Aug. 14. 1723. in the cathedral church of St. Peter in Exeter.* London: R. Wilkin, 1723.

Wallis, John. *A brief and easie explanation of the Shorter catechism: presented by the Assembly of Divines at Westminster to both Houses of Parliament, and by them approved: wherein the meanest capacities may in a speedy and easie way be brought to understand the principles of religion: in imitation of a catechism.* London: Jane Underhill, 1662.

_____. *The doctrine of the blessed Trinity, briefly explained in a letter to a friend.* London: Tho. Parkhurst, 1690.

_____. *An eighth letter concerning the sacred Trinity: occasioned by some letters to him on that subject.* London: Tho. Parkhurst, 1692.

_____. *An explication and vindication of the Athanasian Creed: in a third letter, pursuant of two former, concerning the Sacred Trinity: together with a postscript, in answer to another letter.* London: Tho. Parkhurst, 1691.

_____. *A fifth letter, concerning the sacred Trinity: in answer to what is entituled, the Arians vindication of himself against Dr. Wallis's fourth letter on the Trinity.* London: Tho. Parkhurst, 1691.

_____. *A fourth letter concerning the sacred Trinity: in reply to what is entituled An answer to Dr. Wallis's three letters.* London: Tho. Parkhurst, 1691.

_____. *A second letter concerning the Holy Trinity: pursuant to the former from the same hand: occasioned by a letter there inserted from one unknown.* London: Tho. Parkhurst, 1691.

_____. *A seventh letter, concerning the sacred Trinity: occasioned by a second letter from W.J.* London: Tho. Parkhurst, 1691.

_____. *A sixth letter, concerning the sacred Trinity: in answer to a book entituled, Observations on the four letters, &c. [by Stephen Nye].* London: Tho. Parkhurst, 1691.

_____. *Theological discourses and sermons on several occasions. Part II.* London: Tho. Parkhurst, 1692.

_____. *Theological discourses: containing VIII letters and III sermons concerning the blessed Trinity.* London: Tho. Parkhurst, 1692.

_____. *Theological discourses, in two parts: the first containing VIII letters and III sermons concerning the blessed Trinity: the second, discourses & sermons on several occasions.* London: Tho. Parkhurst, 1695.

_____. *Three sermons concerning the sacred Trinity.* London: Tho. Parkhurst, 1691.

Walton, Brian. *The Considerator Considered : or, a Brief View of Certain Considerations upon the Biblia Polyglotta, the Prolegomena, and the Appendix Thereof.* London: Thomas Roycroft, 1659. [Also as volume II of Henry John Todd, *Memoirs of the Life and Writings of the Right Rev. Brian Walton, D.D.* 2 vols. London: Rivington, 1821.]

Walton, Brian, ed. *Biblia Sacra Polyglotta.* 6 vols. London, 1657.

_____ (ed.) *Biblicus apparatus, chronologico-topographico-philologicus: prout ille tomo praeliminari operis eximii polyglotti.* London, 1658. [Also found in *Biblia Sacra Polyglotta,* vol. 6 separately paginated.]

Ward, Richard. *Theological questions, dogmatical observations, and euangelical essays, upon the gospel of Iesus Christ according to St. Matthew.* London: Peter Cole, 1646.

Ward, Seth. *A Philosophicall Essay towards an Eviction of the Being and Attributes of God, the Immortality of the Souls of Men [and] the Truth and Authority of Scripture.* Oxford: Leonard Lichfield, 1652.

Waterland, Daniel. *Dissertation upon the argument a priori for proving the existence of a first cause.* Cambridge, 1734. [Published in Edmund Law, *An enquiry into the ideas of space, time, immensity, and eternity.*]

_____. *A Further Vindication of Christ's Divinity.* London, 1724.

_____. *The Scriptures and the Arians compar'd in their accounts of God the Father and God the Son: by way of rejoinder to a pamphlet intitul'd The Scripture and the Athanasians compar'd, &c.: in two parts.* London: John Clark, 1722.

_____. *A Second Vindication of Christ's Divinity, or a Second Defense of some Queries relating to Dr. Clarke's Scheme of the Holy Trinity.* London, 1723.

_____. *A Vindication of Christ's Divinity, being a Defense of some Queries relating to Dr. Clarke's Scheme of the Holy Trinity.* London, 1719.

Watson, Thomas. *A Body of Practical Divinity.* London, 1692.

_____. *Discourses on Important and Interesting Subjects: Being the Select Works of the Rev. Thomas Watson.* 2 vols. Glasgow, 1829. Reprint, Ligonier, Pa.: Soli Deo Gloria, 1990.

_____. *God's Anatomy upon Man's Heart,* in *Discourses,* vol. 2, pp. 147-170.

Weemse, John. *The Christian Synagogue, wherein is contained the diverse reading, the right poynting, translation and collation of Scripture with Scripture.* London, 1623. 2nd ed., 1633. [The second edition was published as *Workes,* vol. 1.]

_____. *Exercitations Divine. Containing diverse Questions and Solutions for the right understanding of the Scriptures. Proving the necessitie, majestie, integritie, perspicuitie, and sense thereof.* London, 1632.

_____. *The Workes of Mr. J. Weemes.* 3 vols. London, 1633; 1636.

Weismann, Christian Eberhard. *Institutiones theologiae exegetico- dogmaticae, quibus praemissa plerorumque dictorum piobantium justa exegesi: dogmatibus inde confirmatis: additisque porismatibus practicis....* Tubingen, 1739.

Welchman, Edward. *Dr. Clarke's Scripture-Doctrine of the Trinity Examined. To which are added some remarks on his sentiments, and a brief explanation of his doctrine by way of question and answer.* Oxford, 1714.

_____. *A Second Conference with an Arian, occasion'd by Mr. Whiston's reply to the ... Earl of Nottingham.* Oxford: L. Lichfield, 1723.

Wendelin, Marcus Friedrich. *Christianae theologiae libri duo.* Amsterdam, 1657.

_____. *Christianae theologiae systema majus duobus libris comprehensum.* Cassel, 1656. [Heppe #24a]

_____. *Collatio doctrinae christianae Reformatorum et Lutheranorum.* Cassel, 1660. [Heppe #24b]

_____. *Exercitationes theologicae vindices, pro theologia christiana Marci Friderici Wendelini ... oppositae Johannis Gerhardi ... collegio antiwendeliniano.* 2nd ed. Cassel, 1669.

Whiston, William. *Athanasius convicted of forgery: in a letter to Mr. Thirlby of Jesus-College in Cambridge*. London: A. Baldwin, 1712.

_____. *An essay upon the Epistles of Ignatius*. London: Benjamin Tooke, 1710.

_____. *Mr. Whiston's letter to the right honourable the Earl of Nottingham, concerning the eternity of the Son of God and of the Holy Spirit*. London: J. Senex and W. Taylor, 1719.

_____. *Mr. Whiston's Reply, to the Right Honourable the Earl of Nottingham's answer to his letter to him, concerning the eternity of the Son of God, and of the Holy Spirit*. Dublin: T. Hume, 1721.

_____. *Primitive Christianity reviv'd....* 5 vols. London: Printed for the author, 1711-12.

_____. *St. Clement's and St. Irenaeus's vindication of the apostolical constitutions, from several objections made against them. As also an account of the two antient rules thereunto belonging, for the celebration of Easter. With a postscript on occasion of Mr. Turner's Discourse of the apostolical constitutions*. London: J. Roberts, 1715.

_____. *Three essays, I. The council of Nice vindicated from the Athanasian heresy. II. A collection of ancient monuments relating to the Trinity and incarnation and to the history of the fourth century of the church. III. The liturgy of the Church of England reduc'd nearer to the primitive standard*. London: Printed for the author, 1713.

_____. *A vindication of the Sibylline oracles: To which are added the genuine oracles themselves; with the ancient citations from them; in their originals, and in English: and a few brief notes*. London: J. Roberts, 1715.

Whitaker, William. *A Disputation on Holy Scripture, against the Papists, especially Bellarmine and Stapleton*. Translated and edited by William Fitzgerald. Cambridge: Cambridge University Press, 1849.

Whitehead, George. *The Divinity of Christ, and the Unity of the Three that Bear Record in Heaven*. London, 1669.

Willet, Andrew. *Hexapla in Danielem*. Cambridge, 1610.

_____. *Hexapla in Exodum*. London, 1608.

_____. *Hexapla in Genesin*. Cambridge, 1605. 2nd ed., enlarged, Cambridge, 1608.

_____. *Hexapla in Leviticum*. London, 1631.

_____. *Hexapla: That is, a Six Fold Commentarie upon the Epistle to the Romans*. Cambridge, 1620.

Wilson, John. *The Scriptures Genuine Interpreter Asserted: Or, a Discourse concerning the Right Interpretation of Scripture, wherein a late Exercitation entituled, Philosophia S. Scripturae Interpres, is Examined, and the Protestant Point in that Doctrine Vindicated*. London: T. N. for R. Boulter, 1678.

Wilson, Thomas. *The Rule of Reason, Conteinyng the Arte of Logique*. Newely corrected. London: R. Grafton 1552.

Witsius, Herman. *De oeconomia foederum Dei cum hominibus libri quattuor*. Leeuwarden, 1685. Utrecht, 1694. [Heppe #39]

_____. *Exercitationes sacrae in symbolum quod Apostolorum dicitur. Et in Orationem dominicam*. Amsterdam, 1697.

_____. *Miscellanea sacrorum libri IV*. Utrecht, 1692.

_____. *Miscellanea sacrorum tomus alter continens XXII exercitationes*. Utrecht and Amsterdam, 1700.

_____. *The Oeconomy of the Covenants between God and Man. Comprehending a Complete Body of Divinity.* 3 vols. London: Edward and Charles Dilly, 1763. 2nd ed., revised and corrected, 1775.

_____. *On the Character of the True Divine: An Inaugural Oration, Delivered at Franecker, April 16, 1675.* Translated by John Donaldson, preface by William Cunningham. Edinburgh: James Wood, 1855.

_____. *Sacred Dissertations on the Lord's Prayer.* Translated, with notes, by William Pringle. Edinburgh: Thomas Clarke, 1839.

_____. *Sacred Dissertations on what is commonly called the Apostles' Creed.* Translated by D. Fraser. 2 vols. Edinburgh: A. Fullarton; Glasgow: Kull, Blackie & Co., 1823.

_____. *Theologus modestus.* Leiden, 1698.

Witte, Petrus de. *Catechizatie over den Heidelberghschen Catechismus der gereformeerde christelicke religie.* Amsterdam: Michiel de Groot, 1675.

_____. *Catechizing upon the Heidelbergh Catechisme of the Reformed Christian religion.* Amsterdam, 1664.

Wittichius, C. *Exercitationes theologicae.* Leiden, 1682.

_____. *Theologia pacifica.* Leiden, 1671.

Wolff, Christian. *Philosophia prima, sive ontologica, methodo scientifica pertractata, qua omnis cognitionis humanae principia continentur.* Editio nova. Frankfurt and Leipzig, 1736. Reprint, Hildesheim and New York: George Olms, 1977.

_____. *Theologia naturalis methodo scientifica pertractata.* 2 parts in 3. Frankfurt and Leipzig, 1739-41. Reprint,, with introductions by Jean École, Hildesheim and New York: George Olms, 1978-81.

Wollebius, Johannes. *The Abridgement of Christian Divinitie.* Translated, with annotations by Alexander Ross. London: T. Mab and A. Coles, 1650.

_____. *Compendium theologiae christianae.* Basel, 1626; Oxford, 1657. [Heppe #12]

_____. *Compendium theologiae christianae.* Edited by Ernst Bizer. Neukirchen: Neukirchner Verlag, 1935.

Wolzogen, Ludwig . *De Scripturarum interprete.* Utrecht, 1668.

Wren, Matthew. *Increpatio Barjesu, sive, Polemicæ adsertiones locorum aliquot S. Scripturæ, ab imposturis perversionum in catechesi Racoviana.* London: Jacob Flesher, 1660.

Wyttenbach, Daniel. *Praelectio inauguralis de iis, quae observanda sunt circa theologiam et dogmaticam et elenchticam docendam. Habita 17. Novemb. 1746.* Frankfurt: Joh. Benj. Andreae et Henr. Hort, 1749.

_____. *Tentamen theologiae dogmaticae methodo scientifico pertractatae.* 3 vols. Frankfurt: Joh. Benj. Andreae et Henr. Hort, 1747-49. [Heppe #53]

_____. *Theses theologicae praecipua christianae doctrinae capita ex primis principiis deducta continentes ... publicé defenderunt Isaacus Sigfrid ... & Daniel Wyttenbach ... MDCCXLVII.* Frankfurt: Joh. Benj. Andreae et Henr. Hort, 1749.

Yates, John. *A Modell of Divinitie, Catechetically Composed. Wherein is delivered the matter and methode of religion, according to the Creed, tenne Commandements, Lords Prayer, and the Sacraments.* 2nd. Edition, enlarged. London: John Legatt, 1623.

_____. *A Short Summe of Saving Knowledge; consisting of the Creed, ten Commandements, Lords Prayer, and the Sacraments. And is made as a profitable Intyroduction to the larger Art of Divinitie, composed by the methodicall tables of A[lexander] R[ichardson] and published by I[ohn] Y[ates].* London: I. D., 1621.

Zanchi, Jerome. *Commentarius in epistolam sancti Pauli ad Ephesios*. Edited by A. H. de Hartog. Amsterdam: Wormser, 1888-1889.

_____. *De natura Dei seu de divinis attributis*. Heidelberg: Jacob Mylius, 1577. [Also in *Operum theologicorum* (1605; 1617-19), vol. II.]

_____. *De religione christiana fides*. Neustadt: Matthaeus Harnisch, 1585; 1594. [Heppe #19; also in *Operum theologicorum* (1605; 1617-19), vol. VIII.]

_____. *De scriptura sacra*. Heidelberg: J. Harnisch, 1593. [Also in *Operum theologicorum* (1605; 1617-19), vol. VIII, with the internal title, *Praefatiuncula in locos communes: cum priore loco de sacris Scripturis agendum sit: & quae methodus servanda*.]

_____. *De tribus Elohim, aeterno Patre, Filio. Et Spiritu Sancto*. Frankfurt am Main: Georgius Corvinus, 1573. [Also in *Operum theologicorum* (1605; 1617-19), vol. I.]

_____. *Hieronymi Zanchii theologi celeberrimi Miscellaneorum*. Pars altera. Neustadt: Nischolas Schramm; London: John Bill, 1608.

_____. *Hier. Zanchii Miscellaneorum libri tres*. London: Jacobus Rimeus, 1605.

_____. *H. Zanchius, his Confession of Christian Religion*. London, 1559.

_____. *In Mosen et universa Biblia, Prolegomena*, in *Operum theologicorum* (1617-19), vol. VII/2.

_____. *Operum theologicorum D. Hieronymi Zanchii*. 8 vols. Heidelberg: Stephanus Gamonetus (v. 1-4, 7-8); Matthaeus Berjon (v. 5-6), 1605. [Vol. VII contains only the three books of *Miscellaneorum*, lacking the *pars altera*.]

_____. *Operum theologicorum D. Hieronymi Zanchii*. 10 vols. in 9. Geneva: Samuel Crispin, 1617-19. [Volume VII, Zanchi's *Miscellanea*, is in two separate "tomes," having added the *pars altera* as a separate pagination; volume IX, new to the Geneva edition, is largely letters.]

Zwicker, Daniel. *Irenicum irenicorum, seu, Reconciliatorus Christianorum hodiernorum norma triplex: sanaomnium homnium ratio, scriptura sacra & traditiones*. London: s.n., 1658.

_____. *Irenicomastix iterato victus & constrictus, imo obmutescens, seu Novum & memorabile exemplum infelicissimae pugnae J.A. Comenii contra Irenici irenicorum auctorem. Id ostendente Irenici irenicorum auctore*. Amsterodami: s.n., 1662.

Zwingli, Ulrich. *Commentary on True and False Religion*. Edited by Samuel Macauley Jackson and Clarence Nevin Heller. Philadelphia, 1929. Reprint, Durham, N.C.: Labyrinth Press, 1981.

_____. *De vera et falsa religione commentarius*, in *Opera*, vol. 3.

_____. *In catabaptistarum strophas elenchus*, in *Corpus Reformatorum*, vol. 93.

_____. *On the Clarity and Certainty of the Word*, in *Zwingli and Bullinger*, translated and edited by Geoffrey W. Bromiley (Philadelphia: Westminster, 1953), pp. 49-95.

_____. *On Providence and other Essays*. Translated by William John Hinke. Durham, N.C.: Labyrinth Press, 1983.

_____. *Opera completa editio prima*. Edited by Melchior Schuler and Johann Schulthess. 8 vols. in 6. Zürich: Schulthess and Höhr, 1828-42.

_____. *Sämtliche Werke*. Edited by Emil Egli and Georg Finsler, et al. 14 vols. Zürich: Theologischer Verlag, 1905-83 [Vols. 88ff. of the *Corpus Reformatorum*].

_____. *Sermon on the Providence of God*, in *On Providence and other Essays*, pp. 128-234.

II. Secondary Sources

Ackeren, G. F. van. *Sacra Doctrina: The Subject of the First Question of the Summa Theologiae*. Rome: Gregorian University, 1952.

Adams, Marylin McCord. "Ockham on Identity and Distinction," in *Franciscan Studies*, 36 (1976), pp. 5-74.

_____. *William Ockham*. 2 vols. Notre Dame: University of Notre Dame Press, 1987.

Adams, Robert Merrihew. "Middle Knowledge and the Problem of Evil," in *The Virtue of Faith and Other Essays in Philosophical Theology* by Robert Merrihew Adams (New York: Oxford University Press, 1987), pp. 77-93.

Adamson, J. H. "Milton's Arianism," in *Harvard Theological Review*, 53 (1960), pp. 269-276.

Adler, Jacob. "Divine Attributes in Spinoza: Intrinsic and Relational," in *Philosophy and Theology*, 4 (1989), pp. 33-52.

Adrianyi, Gabriel. "Pelbart von Temesvar (ca. 1435-1504) und seine trinitarischen Predigtvorlagen," in *Im Gespräch mit dem dreieinen Gott*, edited by M. Boehnke and H. Heinz (Düsseldorf: Patmos Verlag, 1985), pp. 276-284.

Albert, Karl. "Exodusmetaphysik und Metaphysische Erfahrung," in *Thomas von Aquino: Interpretation und Rezeption*, edited by Willehad Eckert (Mainz: Matthias-Grünewald-Verlag, 1974), pp. 80-95.

Aldridge, John William. *The Hermeneutic of Erasmus*. Richmond: John Knox, 1966.

Allen, Don Cameron. *Doubt's Boundless Sea: Skepticism and Faith in the Renaissance*. Baltimore: Johns Hopkins, 1964.

Allen, Joseph Henry. *An Historical Sketch of the Unitarian Movement*. New York: Christian Literature Company, 1894.

Alluntis, Felix. "Demonstrability and Demonstration of the Existence of God," in *John Duns Scotus, 1265-1965*, edited by John Ryan and Bernardine Bonansea (Washington: CUA Press, 1965), pp. 133-170.

Alluntis, Felix, and Allan B. Wolter. "Duns Scotus on the Omnipotence of God," in *Studies in Philosophy and the History of Philosophy*, 5 (1970), pp. 178-222.

Althaus, Paul. *Die Prinzipien der deutschen reformierten Dogmatik im Zeitalter er aristotelischen Scholastik*. Leipzig: Deichert, 1914.

_____. *The Theology of Martin Luther*. Translated by Robert C. Schultz. Philadelphia: Fortress, 1966.

Amann, É., and Paul Vignaux. "Occam, Guillaume d'," in *Dictionnaire de théologie catholique*, vol. II/1, col. 864-904.

Anderson, Marvin. *The Battle for the Gospel: the Bible and the Reformation, 1444-1589*. Grand Rapids: Baker, 1978.

_____. "Biblical Humanism and Catholic Reform (1510-1541): Contarini, Pole and Giberti," in *Concordia Theological Monthly*, 34 (1968), pp. 686-707.

_____. "The Geneva (Tomson/Junius) New Testament among Other English Bibles of the Period," in *The Geneva Bible: The Annotated New Testament, 1602 Edition*, edited by Gerald T. Sheppard, (New York: The Pilgrim Press, 1989), pp. 5-17.

_____. *Peter Martyr: A Reformer in Exile (1542-1562): A Chronology of Biblical Writings in England and Europe*. Nieuwkoop: De Graaf, 1975.

_____. "Peter Martyr, Reformed Theologian (1542-1562)," in *The Sixteenth Century Journal*, 4 (1973), pp. 41-64.

_____. "Peter Martyr Vermigli: Protestant Humanist," in *Peter Martyr Vermigli and Italian Reform*, edited by Joseph C. McLelland (Waterloo: Wilfrid Laurier University Press, 1980), pp. 65-151.

Anonymous. "Richard Baxter's 'End of Controversy,'" in *Bibliotheca Sacra and American Biblical Repository*, 12 (1855), pp. 348-385.

Antognazza, Maria Rosa. "Leibniz *de Deo Trino*: Philosophical Aspects of Leibniz's Conception of the Trinity," in *Religious Studies*, 37 (2001), pp. 1-13.

_____. *Trinità e Incarnazione: Il rapporto tra filosofia e teologia rivelata nel pensiero di Leibniz*. Milan: Vita e Pensiero, 1999.

Antognazza, Maria Rosa, and Howard Hotson, *Alsted and Leibniz on God, the Magistrate and the Millennium*. Texts edited with introduction and commentary. Wiesbaden: Harrassowitz, 1999.

Arias Reyero, Maximino. *Thomas Aquinas als Exeget: Die Prinzipien seiner Schriftdeutung und seine Lehre von den Schriftsinnen*. Münster: Johannes Verlag, 1971.

Ariew, Roger. *Descartes and the Last Scholastics*. Ithaca and London: Cornell University Press, 1999.

_____. "Descartes and Scholasticism: the Intellectual Background to Descartes' Thought," in *Cambridge Companion to Descartes*, edited by John Cottingham, pp. 58-90.

Ariew, Roger, and Marjorie Grene, *Descartes and His Contemporaries: Meditations, Objections, and Replies*. Chicago: University of Chicago Press, 1995.

Armogathe, Jean-Robert. "Proofs for the Existence of God," in *Cambridge History of Seventeenth-Century Philosophy*, edited by Daniel Garber and Michael Ayers, vol. I, pp. 305-330.

Armogathe, Jean-Robert, ed. *Le Grand Siècle de la Bible*. Vol. 6 of *Bible de tous les temps*. Paris: Beauchesne, 1989.

Armstrong, Brian G. *Calvinism and the Amyraut Heresy: Protestant Scholasticism and Humanism in Seventeenth-Century France*. Madison: University of Wisconsin Press, 1969.

Armstrong, Robert L. "Cambridge Platonists and Locke on Innate Ideas," in *Journal of the History of Ideas*, 30 (1969), pp. 187-202.

Asch, E. Dorothy. "Samuel Clarke's *Scripture-Doctrine of the Trinity* and the Controversy it Aroused." Ph.D. diss., University of Edinburgh, 1951.

Ashley, Clinton M. "John Calvin's Utilization of the Principle of Accommodation and its Continuing Significance for an Understanding of Biblical Language," Ph.D. diss., Southwestern Baptist Theological Seminary, 1972.

Ashley, Kathleen. "Divine Power in the Chester Cycle and Late Medieval Thought," in *Journal of the History of Ideas*, 39 (1978), pp. 387-404.

Asselt, Willem J. van. "*Amicitia Dei* as Ultimate Reality: An Outline of the Covenant Theology of Johannes Cocceius (1603-1669)," in *Ultimate Reality and Meaning: Interdisciplinary Studies in the Philosophy of Understanding*, 21/1 (1988), pp. 37-47.

_____. "Chiliasm and Reformed Eschatology in the Seventeenth and Eighteenth Centuries, in *Christian Hope in Context*, edited by A. van Egmond and D. van Keulen, 2 vols. (Zoetermeer: Meinema, 2001), I, pp. 11-29.

_____. "The Doctrine of the Abrogations in the Federal Theology of Johannes Cocceius," in *Calvin Theological Journal*, 29/1 (1994), pp. 101-116.

_____. *The Federal Theology of Johannes Cocceius (1603-1669)*. Translated by Raymond A. Blacketer. Leiden: E. J. Brill, 2001.

_____. "Johannes Cocceius Anti-Scholasticus?" in *Reformation and Scholasticism*, edited by W. van Asselt and E. Dekker, pp. 227-251.

_____. *Johannes Coccejus: Portret van een zeventiende-eeuws theoloog op oude en niewe wegen*. Heerenveen: Groen en Zoon, 1997.

_____. "Protestantse scholastiek. Methodologische kwesties bij de bestudering van haar ontwikkeling," in *Tijdschrift voor Nederlandse Kerkgeschiedenis*, 4/3 (Sept. 2001), pp. 64-69.

Asselt, Willem J. van, and Eef Dekker. *Reformation and Scholasticism: An Ecumenical Enterprise*. Grand Rapids: Baker Book House, 2001.

Asselt, Willem J. van, P. L. Rouwendal, et. al. *Inleiding in de Gereformeerde Scholastiek*. Zoetermeer: Boekencentrum, 1998.

Augustine, John. "Authority and Interpretation in Perkins' *Commentary on Galatians*," in *A Commentary on Galatians* by William Perkins, edited by G. Sheppard, pp. 11-41.

Auvray, Paul. *Richard Simon (1638-1712)*. Paris: Presses Universitaires de France, 1974.

Ayres, Lewis, and Michel R. Barnes. "God," s.v., in *Augustine Though the Ages*, edited by Allan D. Fitzgerald, pp. 384-390.

Bach, Josef. *Die Dogmengeschichte des Mittelalters vom christologischen Standpunkte*. 2 vols. Vienna, 1873. Reprint, Frankfurt: Minerva, 1966.

Backus, Irena. "'Aristotelianism' in Some of Calvin's and Beza's Expository and Exegetical Writings on the Doctrine of the Trinity, with Particular Reference to the Terms *Ousia* and *Hypostasis*," in *Histoire de l'exégèse as XVIᵉ siècle* (Geneva: Droz, 1978), pp. 351-360.

_____. "L'enseignement de la logique à l'Académie de Genève entre 1559 et 1565," in *Revue de Théologie et de Philosophie*, 111 (1979), pp. 153-63.

_____. "The Fathers in Calvinist Orthodoxy: Patristic Scholarship," in *The Reception of the Church Fathers in the West*, edited by I. Backus, vol. II, pp. 839-866.

Backus, Irena, ed. *The Reception of the Church Fathers in the West: From the Carolingians to the Maurists*. 2 vols. Leiden: E. J. Brill, 1997.

Badcock, A. John. "Aspects of the Medieval Idea of God," in *London Quarterly and Holborn Review*, 177 (1952), pp. 86-97.

Bagchi, David. "Sic et Non: Luther and Scholasticism" in *Protestant Scholasticism*, edited by Trueman and Clark, pp. 3-15.

Baillie, John. *The Idea of Revelation in Recent Thought*. New York: Columbia University Press, 1956.

Bainton, Roland. *Here I Stand: A Life of Martin Luther*. Nashville: Abingdon, 1950.

Baker, Herschel. *The Image of Man: A Study of the Idea of Human Dignity in Classical Antiquity, the Middle Ages, and the Renaissance* Cambridge, Mass.: Harvard University Press, 1947.

Baker, J. Wayne. *Heinrich Bullinger and the Covenant: The Other Reformed Tradition*. Athens, Ohio: Ohio University Press, 1980.

_____. "Heinrich Bullinger, the Covenant, and the Reformed Tradition in Retrospect," in *Calvin Studies VIII: The Westminster Confession in Current Thought*, papers presented at the Colloquium on Calvin Studies, edited by John H. Leith (Davidson College, January 26-27, 1996), pp. 58-75. Also published in *Sixteenth Century Journal*, 29/2 (1998), pp. 359-376.

_____. Also see: McCoy, Charles S.

Bakhuizen van den Brink, J. N. "Bible and Biblical Theology in the Early Reformation," in *Scottish Journal of Theology*, 14 (1961), pp. 337-352; 15 (1962), pp. 50-65.

_____. "La tradition dans l'Église primitive et au XVIᵉ siècle," in *Revue d'histoire et de philosophie religieuses*, 36 (1956), pp. 271-281.

Balázs, Mihály. *Early Transylvanian Antitrinitarianism (1566-1571): from Servet to Palaeologus.* Baden-Baden: Koerner, 1996.

Balic, C., ed. *De Doctrina Ioannis Duns Scoti.* Acta Congressus Scotistici Internationalis. 4 vols. Rome: Congressus Scotisticus Internationalis, 1968.

Bangs, Carl. *Arminius: A Study in the Dutch Reformation.* Nashville: Abingdon, 1971.

_____. "Arminius as a Reformed Theologian," in *The Heritage of John Calvin*, edited by John H. Bratt (Grand Rapids: Eerdmans, 1973), pp. 209-222.

Barnaud, Jean. *Pierre Viret, sa vie et son oeuvre.* Saint-Amans, 1911. Reprint, Niewkoop: De Graaf, 1973.

Baron, Hans. *The Crisis of the Early Italian Renaissance.* Rev. ed. 2 vols. in 1. Princeton: Princeton University Press, 1966.

Barth, Karl. *Church Dogmatics.* Edited by G. W. Bromiley and T. F. Torrance. 4 vols. Edinburgh: T. & T. Clark, 1936-1975.

_____. *The Knowledge of God and the Service of God According to the Teaching of the Reformation.* Translated by J. L. M. Haire and Ian Henderson. London: Hodder and Stoughton, 1938.

_____. *The Theology of John Calvin.* Translated by Geoffrey W. Bromiley. Grand Rapids: Eerdmans, 1995.

Barth, Karl, and Emil Brunner. *Natural Theology, comprising Nature and Grace by Emil Brunner, and the reply, No, by Karl Barth.* Translated by Peter Fraenkel. London: G. Bles, 1946.

Barth, P. Timotheus. "Die Notwendigkeit Gottes und seine Begründung bei Duns Scotus," in *De Doctrina Ioannis Duns Scoti*, edited by C. Balic, vol. II, pp. 414-425.

Bass, W. W. "Platonic Influences on Seventeenth Century English Puritan Theology as expressed in the thinking of John Owen, Richard Baxter, and John Howe." Ph.D. diss., University of Southern California, 1958.

Battles, Ford Lewis. "God was Accommodating Himself to Human Capacity," in *Interpretation*, 31/1 (January, 1977), pp. 19-38.

Baudry, Léon. *Lexique philosophique de Guillaume d'Ockham.* Paris: P. Lethielleux, 1949.

_____. *The Quarrel over Future Contingents (Louvain 1465-1475).* Unpublished texts collected by Léon Baudry, translated by Rita Guerlac. Dordrecht and Boston: Kluwer, 1989.

Bauke, Hermann. *Die Probleme der Theologie Calvins.* Leipzig: J. C. Hinrichs, 1922.

Bauman, Michael E. "Milton's Arianism: 'Following the way which is called Heresy.'" Ph. D. diss., Fordham University, 1983.

Bavinck, Herman. *Gereformeerde Dogmatiek.* 4ᵗʰ ed. 4 vols. Kampen: J. H. Kok, 1928.

Beardslee, John W., ed. *Reformed Dogmatics.* New York: Oxford University Press, 1965.

_____. "Theological Development at Geneva under Francis and Jean-Alphonse Turretin." Ph.D. diss., Yale University, 1956.

Beck, Andreas. "Gisbertus Voetius (1589-1676): Basic Features of His Doctrine of God," in *Reformation and Scholasticism*, edited by W. van Asselt and E. Dekker, pp. 205-226.

Beck, L. J. *The Method of Descartes: A Study of the Regulae.* Oxford: Clarendon Press, 1952.

Bedouelle, Guy. *Lefèvre d' Étaples et l'intelligence des Écritures.* Geneva: Droz, 1976.

Bedouelle, Guy, and Bernard Roussel, eds. *Le temps des Réformes et la Bible.* Vol. 5 of *Bible de tous les temps.* Paris: Beauchesne, 1989.

Beeke, Joel R. "The Order of the Divine Decrees at the Genevan Academy: From Bezan Supralapsarianism to Turretinian Infralapsarianism," in *The Identity of Geneva: The Christian Commonwealth, 1564-1864*, edited by John B. Roney and Martin I. Klauber, pp. 57-75.

Belaval, Yvon, and Dominique Bourel, eds. *Le siècle des Lumières et la Bible*. Vol. 7 of *Bible de tous les temps*. Paris: Beauchesne, 1986.

Bell, Michael Daniel. "*Propter Potestatem Scientiam, ac Beneplacitum Dei*: The Doctrine of Predestination in the Theology of Johannes Maccovius." Ph.D. diss., Westminster Theological Seminary, 1986.

Bellucci, Dino. *Science de la Nature et Réformation: La physique au service de la Réforme dans l'enseignement de Philippe Mélanchthon*. Rome: Edizioni Vivere, 1998.

Belmond, Séraphin. "La connaissance de Dieu d'après Duns Scot," in *Revue de philosophie*, 10, vol. XVII (1910), pp. 496-514.

_____. *Études sur la philosophie de Duns Scot. Dieu, existence et cognoscibilité*. Paris: Beauschesne, 1913.

_____. "L'existence de Dieu d'après Duns Scot," in *Revue de philosophie*, 8, vol. XIII (1908), pp. 241-268, 364-381.

Bennett, Jonathan. "Spinoza's Metaphysics," in *Cambridge Companion to Spinoza*, edited by Don Garrett, pp. 61-88.

Benoit, Jean-David. "The History and Development of the *Institutio*: How Calvin Worked," in *John Calvin*, edited by G. E. Duffield (Grand Rapids: Eerdmans, 1966), pp. 102-117.

Benoit, Pierre. "Revelation et inspiration selon la Bible, chez Saint Thomas et dans les discussions modernes," in *Revue Biblique*, 70/3 (July 1963), pp. 321-370.

Bente, F. *Historical Introductions to the Book of Concord*. St. Louis: Concordia, 1921. Reprint, 1965.

Bentley, Jerry H. *Humanists and Holy Writ: New Testament Scholarship in the Renaissance*. Princeton: Princeton University Press, 1983.

Berger, Samuel. *La Bible an seizième siècle; étude sur les origines de la critique*. Paris: Sandoz & Fischbacher, 1879.

Bergerson, M. *La Structure du concept latin de personne*. Études d'histoire littéraire et doctrinale du XIII᷒ siécle, first series, vol. II. Paris and Ottawa: Pontifical Institute of Medieval Studies, 1932.

Bernus, Auguste. *Richard Simon et son Historie critique du vieux testament: la critique biblique au siècle de Louis XIV*. 1869. Reprint, Geneva: Slatkine Reprints, 1969.

Berthaud, Auguste. *Gilbert de la Porrée, évêque de Poitiers, et sa philosophie, 1070-1154*. Poitiers, 1892; Frankfurt: Minerva Verlag, 1985.

Betts, C. J. *Early Deism in France: From the So-Called 'Déistes' of Lyon (1564) to Voltarie's 'Letres philosophiques' (1734)*. Den Haag: Martinus Nijhoff, 1984.

Beumer, Johannes. *Die Inspiration der Heiligen Schrift*. Vol. 1/3b of *Handbuch der Dogmengeschichte*. Freiburg: Herder, 1968.

_____. "Das Katholische Schriftprinzip in der theologischen Literatur der Scholastik bis zur Reformation," in *Scholastik*, 16 (1941), pp. 24-52.

_____. *Die theologische Methode*. Vol. 1/6 of *Handbuch der Dogmengeschichte*. Freiburg im Breisgau: Herder, 1972.

Beyssade, Jean-Marie. "The Idea of God and the Proofs of His Existence," in *Cambridge Companion to Descartes*, edited by John Cottingham, pp. 174-199.

Bible de tous les temps. 9 vols. Collection dirigée par Charles Kannengiesser. Paris: Beauchesne, 1984-. [Also see: Riché, Pierre; Bedouelle, Guy; Armogathe, Jean-Robert; and Belaval, Yvon.]

Bie, J. P., de and J. Loosjes. *Biographisch Woordenboek van Prot. Godgeleerden in Nederland.* 6 vols. Den Haag, 1905-49.

Bierma, Lyle D. "Federal Theology in the Sixteenth Century: Two Traditions?" in *Westminster Theological Journal*, 45 (1983), pp. 304-21.

————. *German Calvinism in the Confessional Age: The Covenant Theology of Caspar Olevian.* Grand Rapids: Baker Book House, 1996.

————. "The Role of Covenant Theology in Early Reformed Orthodoxy," in *Sixteenth Century Journal*, 21/3 (1990), pp. 453-462.

Bizer, Ernst. *Frühorthodoxie und Rationalismus.* Zurich: EVZ Verlag, 1963.

————. "Die reformierte Orthodoxie und der Cartesianismus," in *Zeitschrift für Theologie und Kirche* (1958), pp. 306-372.

Blench, J. W. *Preaching in England in the Late Fifteenth and Sixteenth Centuries: A Study of English Sermons, 1450-c.1600.* Oxford: Basil Blackwell, 1964.

Bloomfield, Morton W. "Joachim of Flora: A Critical Survey of his Canon, Teachings, Sources, Biography, and Influence," in *Traditio*, 13 (1957), pp. 249-311.

————. "Recent Scholarship on Joachim of Fiore and his Influence," in *Prophecy and Millennarianism* (Essex: Longman, 1980), pp. 23-52.

Blumenberg, Hans. *The Legitimacy of the Modern Age.* Translated by Robert M. Wallace. Cambridge, Mass.: MIT Press, 1983.

Boehner, Philotheus. *Collected Articles on Ockham.* Edited by Eligius M. Buytaert. St. Bonaventure, New York: Franciscan Institute, 1958.

Boersma, Hans. *A Hot Peppercorn: Richard Baxter's Doctrine of Justification in Its Seventeenth-Century Context of Controversy.* Zoetermeer: Boekencentrum, 1993.

Boh, Ivan. "Divine Omnipotence in the Early Sentences," in *Divine Omniscience and Omnipotence in Medieval Philosophy*, edited by T. Rudavsky, pp. 185-211.

Bohatec, Josef. *Budé und Calvin: Studien zur Gedankenwelt des französischen Frühumanismus.* Graz: Herman Böhlaus, 1950

————. *Die cartesianische Scholastik in der Philosophie und reformierten Dogmatik des 17. Jahrhunderts.* Leipzig: Deichert, 1912.

————. "Gott und die Geschichte nach Calvin," in *Philosophia reformata* (1936), pp. 129-161.

————. "Die Methode der reformierten Dogmatik," in *Theologische Studien und Kritiken*, 81 (1908), pp. 272-302, 383-401.

Boisset, Jean. *Calvin et la souverainéte de Dieu. Présentation, choix de textes, bibliographie.* Paris: Seghers, 1964.

Bolgar, R. R., ed. *Classical Influences on European Culture A.D. 1500-1700.* Cambridge: Cambridge University Press, 1976.

————. *Isaac La Peyrère (1596-1676): His Life, Work, and Influence.* Leiden: Brill, 1987.

Bonansea, Bernardino M. "Duns Scotus and St. Anselm's Ontological Argument," in *De Doctrina Ioannis Duns Scoti*, edited by C. Balic, vol. II, pp. 461-475.

————. *God and Atheism: A Philosophical Approach to the Problem of God.* Washington, D.C.: Catholic University of America, 1979.

_____. *Tomasso Campanella: Renaissance Pioneer of Modern Thought*. Washington: Catholic University of America Press, 1969.

Bornkamm, Heinrich. *Luther and the Old Testament*. Translated by Eric W. and Ruth C. Gritsch. Philadelphia: Fortress, 1969.

_____. *Martin Bucers Bedeutung für die europäische Reformationsgeschichte*. Gütersloh: Gerd Mohn, 1952.

Bos, E. P., and H. A. Krop, eds. *Franco Burgersdijk (1590-1635): Neo-Aristotelianism in Leiden*. Amsterdam: Rodopi, 1993.

Botte, Petrus Chrysologus. "Ioannis duns Scoti doctrina de constitutivo formali personae Patris," in *De Doctrina Ioannis Duns Scoti*, edited by C. Balic, vol. III, pp. 85-104.

Bougerol, J. Guy. *Introduction to the Works of Bonaventure*. Translated by José de Vinck. Paterson: St. Anthony Guild, 1964.

Boughton, Lynne Courter. "Supralapsarianism and the Role of Metaphysics in Sixteenth-Century Reformed Theology," in *Westminster Theological Journal*, 48 (1986), pp. 63-96.

Bouveresse, Jacques. "Leibniz et le problème de la 'Science Moyenne,'" in *Revue Internationale de la Philosophie*, 48 (1994), pp. 99-126.

Bouwsma, William J. "The Two Faces of Humanism: Stoicism and Augustinianism in Renaissance Thought," in *Itinerarium Italicum: The Profile of the Italian Renaissance in the Mirror of its European Transformations*, edited by Thomas A. Brady and Heiko A. Oberman (Leiden: E. J. Brill, 1975), pp. 3-60.

Bowman, John. "A Forgotten Controversy," in *Evangelical Quarterly*, 20 (1948), pp. 46-68.

Boyle, Marjorie O'Rourke. *Erasmus on Language and Method in Theology*. Toronto: University of Toronto Press, 1977.

Brady, I. C., J. E. Gurr, and J. A. Weisheipl. "Scholasticism" in *New Catholic Encyclopedia*, vol. 12, pp. 1153-1170.

Brampton, C. K. "Scotus and the Doctrine of the 'potentia Dei absoluta,'" in *De Doctrina Ioannis Duns Scoti*, edited by C. Balic, vol. II, pp. 567-574.

Brandmüller, W. "*Traditio scripturae interpres*. The Teaching of the Councils on the Right Interpretation of Scripture up to the Council of Trent," in *Catholic Historical Review*, 73 (1987), pp. 523-540.

Bray, John S. *Theodore Beza's Doctrine of Predestination*. Nieuwkoop: DeGraaf, 1975.

Brecht, Martin. *Martin Luther: His Road to Reformation, 1483-1521*. Translated by James Schaaf. Philadelphia: Fortress, 1985.

Breen, Quirinus. *Christianity and Humanism: Studies in the History of Ideas*. Grand Rapids: Eerdmans, 1968.

_____. "The Terms 'Loci Communes' and 'Loci' in Melanchthon," in *Christianity and Humanism*, pp. 93-105.

Bréhier, Émil. *The History of Philosophy*. Translated by Wade Baskin and Joseph Thomas. 7 vols. Chicago: University of Chicago Press, 1965.

Brémondy, François. "Affection," in *Encyclopédie philosophique universelle*, II/1, pp. 49-50.

Breward, Ian. "The Life and Theology of William Perkins, 1558-1602." Ph.D. diss., University of Manchester, 1963.

_____. "The Significance of William Perkins," in *The Journal of Religious History*. IV (1966-67). pp.113-128.

_____. "William Perkins and the Origins of Reformed Casuistry," in *Evangelical Quarterly*, 20 (1968), pp. 3-20.

Bridges, Geoffrey G. *Identity and Distinction in Petrus Thomae, O. F. M.* St. Bonaventure, New York: Franciscan Institute, 1959.

Brink, Gijsbert van den. *Almighty God: A Study of the Doctrine of Divine Omnipotence.* Kampen: J. Kok, 1993.

Brink, Gijsbert van den, and Marcel Sarot, eds. *Understanding the Attributes of God* [Contributions to Philosophical Theology, vol. 1]. Frankfurt: Peter Lang, 1999.

Broeyer, Frits G. M. "Traces of Reformed Scholasticism in the Polemical Theologian William Whitaker (1548-1595)," in *Reformation and Scholasticism*, edited by W. van Asselt and E. Dekker, pp. 141-154.

Brom, Luco Johan van den. *Divine Presence in the World, a Critical Analysis of the Notion of Divine Omnipresence.* Kampen: Kok Pharos, 1993.

Broglie, G. de. "La vraie notion thomiste des 'praeambula fidei,'" in *Gregorianum*, 34 (1953), pp. 341-389.

Brook, Benjamin. *The Lives of the Puritans: Containing a Biographical Account of those Divines who Distinguished Themselves in the Cause of Religious Liberty, from the Reformation under Queen Elizabeth, to the Act of Uniformity, in 1662.* 3 vols. London: James Black, 1813. Reprint, Pittsburgh: Soli Deo Gloria, 1994.

Brown, Raymond E. *The Sensus Plenior of Sacred Scripture.* Baltimore, MD: St. Mary's University, 1955.

Brown, Stephen. "Scotus' Univocity in the Early Fourteenth Century," in *De Doctrina Ioannis Duns Scoti*, edited by C. Balic, vol. IV, pp. 35-41.

Brown, Stuart. "The Critical Reception of Malebranche, from His Own Time to the End of the Eighteenth Century," in *The Cambridge Companion to Malebranche*, edited by Nadler, pp. 262-287.

_____. "Locke as Secret 'Spinozist': the Perspective of William Carroll," in *Disguised and Overt Spinozism*, edited by W. van Bunge, pp. 213-234.

Brühls, Alfons. *Die Entwicklung des Gotteslehre beim jungen Melanchthon, 1518-1535.* Bielefeld: Luther Verlag, 1975.

Brunner, Emil. *The Christian Doctrine of God. Dogmatics: Vol. I.* Translated by Olive Wyon. Philadelphia: Westminster, 1950.

_____. *Revelation and Reason: The Christian Doctrine of Faith and Knowledge.* Translated by Olive Wyon. Philadelphia: Westminster, 1946.

Bryar, William. *St. Thomas and the Existence of God: Three Interpretations.* Chicago: Henry Regnery, 1951.

Buckley, George T. *Atheism in the English Renaissance.* New York: Russell and Russell, 1965.

Buckley, Michael J. *At the Origins of Modern Atheism.* New Haven: Yale University Press, 1987.

Bunge, Wiep van. "Balthasar Bekker's Cartesian Hermeneutics and the Challenge of Spinozism," in *The British Journal for the History of Philosophy*, 1 (1993), pp. 55-79.

Bunge, Wiep van, and Wim Klever, eds. *Disguised and Overt Spinozism Around 1700.* Leiden: E. J. Brill, 1996.

Burchill, Christopher. "Le dernier théologien réformé: Girolamo Zanchi, *De officio docentium et discernentium in scholis*," in *Bulletin de la Société de l'Histoire du Protestantisme français*, 135 (1989), pp. 54-63.

Burnett, Stephen George. "The Christian Hebraism of Johann Buxtorf (1564-1629)." Ph.D. diss., University of Wisconsin, Madison, 1990.

_____. From Christian Hebraism to Jewish Studies: Johannes Buxtorf (1564-1629) and Hebrew Learning in the Seventeenth Century. Leiden: E. J. Brill, 1996.

Burrell, David B. Knowing the Unknowable God: Ibn-Sina, Maimonides, Aquinas. Notre Dame, Ind.: University of Notre Dame Press, 1986.

Burtt, Edwin A. The Metaphysical Foundations of Modern Science. Revised ed. New York: Humanities Press, 1951.

Busson, H. La pensée religieuse

Butin, Philip W. Revelation, Redemption, and Response: Calvin's Trinitarian Understanding of the Divine-Human Relationship. New York: Oxford University Press, 1995.

Butterworth, Joseph. "The Doctrine of the Trinity in St. Thomas Aquinas and St. Bonaventure." Ph.D. diss., Fordham University, 1985.

Buytaert, Eligius M. "Abelard's Trinitarian Doctrine," in Peter Abelard, edited by E. Buytaert (Den Haag: Nijhoff, 1974), pp. 127-152.

Byrne, James M. Religion and Enlightenment: From Descartes to Kant. Louisville, KY: Westminster/John Knox, 1997.

Byrne, Peter. Natural Religion and the Nature of Religion: the Legacy of Deism. London: Routledge, 1989.

Cadix, Marcel. "Le Dieu de Calvin," in Bulletin de la Société calviniste de France, November 1929, pp. 2-15.

Callan, Charles J. "The Bible in the Summa Theologica of St. Thomas Aquinas," in The Catholic Biblical Quarterly, 9 (1947), pp. 33-47.

Calvinus Reformator: His Contribution to Theology, Church and Society. Potchefstroom: Potchefstroom University, Institute for Reformational Studies, 1982.

The Cambridge History of the Bible. 3 vols. Edited by P. R. Ackroyd and C. F. Evans (I), G. W. H. Lampe (II), and S. L. Greenslade (III). Cambridge: Cambridge University Press, 1963-70.

Cameron, Richard. "The Attack on the Biblical Work of Lefèvre d'Etaples, 1514-1521," in Church History, 38 (1969), pp. 13-24.

_____. "The Charges of Lutheranism Brought Against Jacques Lefèvre d'Etaples (1520-1529)," in Harvard Theological Review, 63 (1970), pp. 119-149.

Cannon, Charles K. "William Whitaker's Disputatio de Sacra Scriptura: A Sixteenth-Century Theory of Allegory," in Huntington Library Quarterly, 25 (1962), pp. 129-138.

Caplan, Harry. "The Four Senses of Scriptural Interpretation and the Medieval Theology of Preaching," in Speculum, 4 (1929), pp. 282-290.

Carter, Charles S. The Reformers and Holy Scripture. London: C. J. Thymme and Jarvis, 1928.

Cassirer, Ernst. The Philosophy of the Enlightenment. Translated by Fritz Koelln and James Pettegrove. Princeton: Princeton University Press, 1951.

_____. The Platonic Renaissance in England. Translated by James P. Pettegrove. Edinburgh: Nelson, 1953.

Catania, F. L. "Divine Infinity in Albert the Great's Commentary on the Sentences of Peter Lombard," in Medieval Studies, 22 (1960), pp. 27-42.

Chalker, William H. "Calvin and Some Seventeenth-Century Calvinists: A Comparison of their Thought through an Examination of their Doctrines of the Knowledge of God, Faith and Assurance." Ph.D. diss., Duke University, 1961.

Chenu, Marie-Dominique. La théologie au douzième siècle. Paris: Vrin, 1957.

_____. "La théologie comme science au XIIIe siècle," in *Archives d'Histoire Doctrinale et Littéraire du Moyen Age*, 2 (1927), pp. 31-71.

_____. *La théologie comme science au XIIIe siècle.* 3rd ed. Paris: Vrin, 1957.

Childs, Brevard S. "Hermeneutical Reflections on C. Vitringa, Eighteenth-Century Interpreter of Isaiah," in *In Search of True Wisdom: Essays in Old Testament Interpretation in Honour of Ronald E. Clements*, edited by Edward Ball, in *Journal for the Old Testament*, supplement Series, 300 (1999), pp. 89-98.

_____. "The *Sensus Literalis* of Scripture: An Ancient and Modern Problem," in *Beiträge zur alttestamentlichen Theologie*, edited by Donner, Hanhart, and Smend (Göttingen: Vandenhoeck & Ruprecht, 1977), pp. 80-93.

Chollet, A. "Aristotélisme de la scolastique," in *Dictionaire de théologie catholique*, vol 1/2, cols. 1869-1887.

Chossat, M. "Dieu. Sa nature selon les scholastiques," in *Dictionnaire de théologie catholique*, vol. 4/1, cols. 1152-1243.

Clark, David W. "Voluntarism and Rationalism in the Ethics of Ockham," in *Fransiscan Studies*, 31 (1971), pp. 72-87.

Clark, Robert Scott. "The Authority of Reason in the Later Reformation: Scholasticism in Caspar Olevian and Antoine de La Faye," in *Protestant Scholasticism: Essays in Reassessment*, edited by C. Trueman and R. Clark, pp. 111-126.

_____. "*Duplex Beneficium*: Caspar Olevian's Trinitarian, Protestant, Calvinist, Federal Theology." Ph.D. diss., Oxford University, 1998.

Clausen, Sara Jean. "Calvinism in the Anglican Hierarchy, 1603-1643: Four Episcopal Examples." Ph.D. diss., Vanderbilt University, 1989.

Coffey, P. *Ontology or the Theory of Being: An Introduction to General Metaphysics.* New York: Peter Smith, 1938.

Colie, Rosalie. *Light and Enlightenment: A Study of the Cambridge Platonists and the Dutch Arminians.* Cambridge: Cambridge University Press, 1957.

Colish, Marcia L. *Peter Lombard.* 2 vols. Leiden: E. J. Brill, 1994.

Colker, Marvin L. "The Trial of Gilbert of Poitiers, 1148: A Previously Unknown Record," in *Medieval Studies*, 27 (1965), pp. 152-183.

Colligan, J. H. *The Arian Movement in England.* Manchester: Manchester University Press, 1913.

Cologny, L. *L'antitrinitarisme a Genève au temps de Calvin: étude historique.* Geneva: Taponnier & Studer, 1873.

Congar, Yves M.-J. *A History of Theology.* Translated by Hunter Guthrie. Garden City: Doubleday, 1968.

_____. *Tradition and Traditions: An Historical and a Theological Essay.* Translated by M. Naseby and T. Rainborough. New York: Macmillan, 1967.

Constantin, C. "Rationalisme," in *Dictionnaire de théologie catholique*, vol. 13/2, cols. 1688-1778.

Copleston, Frederick. *A History of Philosophy.* 9 vols. Westminster, Md.: Newman Press, 1946-1974. Reprint, Garden City: Image Books, 1985.

Corbin, Michel. *Le chemin de la théologie chez Thomas d'Aquin.* Paris: Beauschesne, 1974.

Costello, William T. *The Scholastic Curriculum at Early Seventeenth-Century Cambridge.* Cambridge, Mass.: Harvard University Press, 1958.

Cottingham, John, ed. *The Cambridge Companion to Descartes.* Cambridge: Cambridge University Press, 1992.

_____. "Cartesian Dualism: Theology, Metaphysics, and Science," in *Cambridge Companion to Descartes*, edited by J. Cottingham, pp. 236-257.

_____. "A New Start? Cartesian Metaphysics and the Emergence of Modern Philosophy," in *The Rise of Modern Philosophy*, edited by Tom Sorrel, pp. 15-32.

Coughenour, Robert A. "The Shape and Vehicle of Puritan Hermeneutics," in *Reformed Review*, 30 (1976), pp. 23-34.

Courtenay, William J. *Capacity and Volition: A History of the Distinction of Absolute and Ordained Power*. Bergamo: P. Lubrina, 1990.

_____. *Covenant and Causality in Medieval Thought: Studies in Philosophy, Theology, and Economic Practice*. London: Variorum Reprints, 1984.

_____. "The Dialectic of Omnipotence in the High and Late Middle Ages," in *Divine Omniscience and Omnipotence in Medieval Philosophy*, edited by T. Rudavsky, pp. 243-269.

_____. John of Mirecourt and Gregory of Rimini on whether God can undo the Past," in *Recherches de théologie ancienne et médiévale*, 39 (1972), pp. 244-56; 40 (1973), pp. 147-74.

_____. "Necessity and Freedom in Anselm's Conception of God," in *Analecta Anselmiana*, 4/2, edited by H. Kohlenberger (1975), pp. 39-64.

_____. "Nominales and Nominalism in the Twelfth Century," in *Lectionum Varietates: Hommage à Paul Vignaux (1904-1987)*, edited by Jean Jolivet, et al. (Paris: J. Vrin, 1991), pp. 11-48.

_____. "Nominalism and Late Medieval Thought: A Bibliographical Essay," in *Theological Studies*, 33 (1972), pp. 716-734.

_____. "Nominalism in Late Medieval Religion," in *The Pursuit of Holiness*, edited by Trinkaus and Oberman, pp. 26-59.

Courth, Franz. *Trinität. In der Scholastik*. Vol. 1/1b of *Handbuch der Dogmengeschichte*. Freiburg: Herder, 1985.

_____. *Trinität. Von der Reformation bis zur Gegenwart*. Vol. 2/1c of *Handbuch der Dogmenge-schichte*. Freiburg: Herder, 1996.

Courthal, Pierre. "Karl Barth et quelques points des confessions de foi Reformées," in *La Revue Reformée*, 9 (1958), pp. 1-29.

Courtine, Jean-François. "Le projet suarézien de la métaphysique: pour une étude de la thèse suarézienne du néant," in *Archives de Philosophie*, 42 (1979), pp. 234-274.

Courvoisier, Jacques. *Zwingli: A Reformed Theologian*. Richmond: John Knox Press, 1963.

Cousins, Ewert H. "St. Bonaventure, St. Thomas, and the Movement of Thought in the 13th Century," in *International Philosophical Quarterly*, 14 (1974), pp. 393-409.

Craig, William L. *The Problem of Divine Foreknowledge and Human Freedom from Aristotle to Suárez*. Leiden: Brill, 1980.

_____. "Middle Knowledge: A Calvinist-Arminian Rapprochement?" in *The Grace of God and the Will of Man*, edited by Clark H. Pinnock (Grand Rapids: Zondervan, 1989), pp. 141-64.

Craigie, P. C. "The Influence of Spinoza in the Higher Criticism of the Old Testament," in *The Evangleical Quarterly*, 50 (1978), pp. 23-32.

Cremeans, Charles D. *The Reception of Calvinistic Thought in England*. Urbana: University of Illinois Press, 1949.

Cress, Donald A. "Duns Scotus, Spinoza and the Ontological Argument," in *Regnum Hominus et Regnum Dei* (Rome: Societas Internationalis Scotistica, 1978), pp. 389-399.

Crooks, George R. and Hurst, John F. *Theological Encyclopedia and Methodology on the Basis of Hagenbach*. Rev. ed. New York: Hunt and Eaton, 1894.

Cross, Richard. *Duns Scotus*. New York: Oxford University Press, 1999.

_____. "Duns Scotus on Eternity and Timelessness," in *Faith and Philosophy*, 14/1 (January 1997), pp. 3-25.

Cunningham, William. *Historical Theology*. 3rd ed.. 2 vols. Edinburgh: T. & T. Clark, 1870.

_____. *The Reformers; and the Theology of the Reformation*. Edinburgh: T. & T. Clark, 1862.

Curley, E. M. *Descartes Against the Sceptics*. Cambridge, Mass.: Harvard University Press, 1978.

_____. "Spinoza as an Expositor of Descartes," in *Speculum Spinozanum, 1677-1977* (London: Routledge and Kegan Paul, 1977), pp. 133-142.

Curtis, Mark H. *Oxford and Cambridge in Transition 1558-1642*. Oxford: Clarendon Press, 1959.

Curtius, E. R. *European Literature and the Latin Middle Ages*. New York: Harper & Row, 1953.

Daane, James. *The Freedom of God: A Study of Election and Pulpit*. Grand Rapids: Eerdmans, 1973.

Dales, Richard C. *Medieval Discussions of the Eternity of the World*. Leiden: E. J. Brill, 1990.

D'Amico, John F. "Humanism and Pre-Reformation Theology," in *Renaissance Humanism: Foundations, Forms, and Legacy*, edited by Albert Rabil, vol. 3, pp. 349-379.

Dán, Róbert. *Matthias Vehe-Glirius: Life and Work of a Radical Antitrinitarian, with his Collected Writings*. Translated by Imre Gombos; revised, L. S. Domonkos. Budapest: Akadémiai Kiadó; Leiden: E. J. Brill, 1982.

Dán, Róbert, and Antal Pirnát. *Antitrinitarianism in the Second Half of the 16th Century*. Budapest: Akadémiai Kiadó; Leiden: E. J. Brill, 1982.

Dantine, Johannes. "Das christologische Problem in Rahmen der Prädestinationslehre von Theodor Beza," in *Zeitschrift für Kirchengeschichte*, LXXVII (1966), pp. 81-96.

_____. "Les Tabelles sur la doctrine de la prédestination par Théodore de Bèze," in *Revue de théologie et de philosophie*, XVI (1966), pp. 365-377

Dausch, P. *Die Schriftinspiration, eine biblischgeschichtliche Studie*. Freiburg im Breisgau: Herder'sche Verlagshandlung, 1891.

Davies, Brian. "Classical Theism and the Doctrine of Divine Simplicity," in *Language, Meaning and God: Essays in Honor of Herbert McCabe, OP*, edited by B. Davies (London: Cassell, 1987), pp. 51-74.

_____. *The Thought of Thomas Aquinas*. Oxford: Clarendon Press, 1992.

Davies, Rupert E. *The Problem of Authority in the Continental Reformers: A Study in Luther, Zwingli, and Calvin*. London: Epworth, 1946.

Davis, Edward B. "God, Man and Nature: The Problem of Creation in Cartesian Thought." *Scottish Journal of Theology* 44, No. 3 (1991): 325-348.

Dear, Peter. "Method and the Study of Nature," in *Cambridge History of Seventeenth-Century Philosophy*, edited by Daniel Garber and Michael Ayers, vol. I, pp. 147-177.

Deferrari, Roy Joseph, and Mary Inviolata Barry. *A Lexicon of St. Thomas Aquinas based on the Summa theologica and selected passages of his other works, by Roy J. Deferrari and M. Inviolata Barry, with the collaboration of Ignatius McGuiness*. Washington: Catholic Univ. of America Press, 1948.

De Jong. Peter Y., ed. *Crisis in the Reformed Churches: Essays in commemoration of the Great Synod of Dort, 1618-1619*. Grand Rapids: Reformed Fellowship, 1968.

Dekker, Eef. "Does Duns Scotus Need Molina? On Divine Foreknowledge and Co-causality," in *John Duns Scotus (1265/6-1308): Renewal of Philosophy*, edited by E. P. Bos (Amsterdam: Rodopi, 1998), pp. 101-111.

_____. "Jacobus Arminius and his Logic: Analysis of a Letter," in *Journal of Theological Studies*, ns. 44 (1993), pp. 118-142.

_____. "The Reception of Scotus' Theory of Contingency in Molina and Suárez," in *Via Scoti*, edited by L. Sileo, pp. 445-54.

_____. *Rijker dan Midas: Vrijheid, genade en predestinatie in de theologie van Jacobus Arminius, 1559-1609*. Zoetermeer: Boekencentrum, 1993.

_____. "The Theory of Divine Permission According to Scotus' *Ordinatio* I 47," in *Vivarium*, 37/2 (2000), pp. 231-242.

_____. "Was Arminius a Molinist?" in *Sixteenth Century Journal*, 27/2 (1996), pp. 337-352.

DeLubac, Henri. *Augustinianism and Modern Theology*. Translated by Lancelot Sheppard. London: Geoffrey Chapman, 1969.

_____. *Exégèse mediaevale: les quatre sens de l'Ecriture*. 4 vols. Paris: Aubier, 1959-1964.

Dennison, James T. "The Twilight of Scholasticism: Francis Turretin at the Dawn of the Enlightenment," in *Protestant Scholasticism*, edited by C. Trueman and R. Clark, pp. 244-255.

Denzinger, Heinrich. *Enchiridion Symbolorum, Definitionum et Declarationum de Rebus Fidei et Morum*. 32nd ed. Edited by Adolfus Schönmetzer. Barcinone: Herder, 1963

De Rijk, Lambertus Marie. "Semantics and Metaphysics in Gilbert of Poitiers: A Chapter of Twelfth Century Platonism," 2 parts, in *Vivarium*, 26 (1988), pp. 73-112 and *Vivarium*, 27 (1989), pp. 11-35.

Desharnais, Richard P. "Reason and Faith, Nature and Grace: A Study of Luther's Commentaries on the *Sentences* of Lombard," in *Studia Int. Filosof.*, 3 (1971), pp. 55-64.

_____. "Reassessing Nominalism: A Note on the Epistemology and Metaphysics of Pierre D'Ailly," in *Franciscan Studies*, 34 (1974), pp. 296-305.

DeWulf, Maurice. *An Introduction to Scholastic Philosophy, Medieval and Modern*. Translated by P. Coffey. New York: Dover, 1956.

Deyon, Solange. "Les Académies protestantes en France," in *Bulletin de la Société de l'Histoire du Protestantisme français*, 135 (1989), pp. 77-85.

Dibon, Paul. *La philosophie Néerlandaise au siècle d'or. Tome I: L'Enseignement philosophique dans les Universités néerlandaises à l'époque précartesienne (1575-1650)*. Amsterdam: Elsevier, 1954.

_____. "L'influence de Ramus aux universités néerlandaises du 17e siècle," in *Actes du XIème congrès Internationale de Philosophie*, 14 (1953), pp. 307-311.

Dickson, Donald R. "The Complexities of Biblical Typology in the Seventeenth Century," in *Renaissance and Reformation / Renaissance et Réforme*, n.s. 3 (1987), pp. 253-272.

Dictionnaire de la Bible, contenant tous les noms de personnes, de lieux, de plantes, d'animaux mentionnés dans les Saintes Écritures, les questions théologiques, archéologiques. Edited by F. Vigouroux et al. 5 vols. Paris: Letouzey et Ané, 1907-12.

Dictionnaire de théologie catholique, contenant l'exposé des doctrines et de la théologie catholique. Edited by A. Vacant et al. 23 vols. Paris: Letouzey et Ané, 1923-50.

Diem, Hermann. *Dogmatics*. Translated by Harold Knight. Edinburgh and London: Oliver and Boyd, 1959.

Diestel, Ludwig. *Geschichte des Alten Testamentes in der christlichen Kirche.* Jena: Mauke's Verlag, 1869.

_____. "Studien zur Föderaltheologie," in *Jahrbücher für deutsche Theologie,* 10 (1865), pp. 209-276.

Dillenberger, John. *Protestant Thought and Natural Science.* New York and Nashville: Abingdon, 1960.

Dockrill, D. W. "Authority of the Fathers in the Great Trinitarian Debates of the Sixteen Nineties," in *Studia Patristica,* 18/4 (1983), pp. 335-347.

Dodds, M. "St. Thomas and the Motion of Motionless God," in *New Blackfriars,* 68 (1987), pp. 233-42.

Dods, Marcus. *Forerunners of Dante: An Account of Some of the More Important Visions of the Unseen World, from the Earliest Times.* Edinburgh: T. & T. Clark, 1903.

Dogma in History and Thought: Studies by Various Writers. London: Nisbet, 1929.

Dolnikowski, Edith Wilks. *Thomas Bradwardine, a View of Time and a Vision of Eternity in Fourteenth-Century Thought.* Leiden: E. J. Brill, 1995.

Donnelly, John Patrick. *Calvinism and Scholasticism in Vermigli's Doctrine of Man and Grace.* Leiden: E. J. Brill, 1975.

_____. "Calvinist Thomism," in *Viator,* 7 (1976), pp. 441-455.

_____. "Italian Influences on the Development of Calvinist Scholasticism," in *The Sixteenth Century Journal,* 7/1 (1976), pp. 81-101.

Dorner, Isaac A. *History of Protestant Theology Particularly in Germany.* Translated by George Robson and Sophia Taylor. 2 vols. Edinburgh: T. & T. Clark, 1871.

Doumergue, Émile. "Calvin, an Epigone of the Middle Ages or an Initiator of Modern Times?" in *Princeton Theological Review,* 7 (1909), pp. 52-104.

_____. *Jean Calvin, les hommes et les choses de son temps.* 7 vols. Lausanne: G. Bridel, 1899-1917.

Dourley, John P. "The Relationship between Knowledge of God and Knowledge of the Trinity in Bonaventure's *De mysterio trinitatis,*" in *San Bonaventura Maestro,* edited by A. Pompei, vol. II, pp. 41-48.

Dowdell, Victor Lyle. *Aristotle and Anglican Religious Thought.* Ithaca: Cornell University Press, 1942.

Dowey, Edward A. *The Knowledge of God in Calvin's Theology.* New York: Columbia University Press, 1952.

Doyle, John P. "Suárez on the Analogy of Being," in *The Modern Schoolman,* 46 (1969), pp. 219-249, 323-341.

_____. "The Suárezian Proof for God's Existence," in *History of Philosophy in the Making: A Symposium of Essays to Honor Professor James D. Collins on his 65th Birthday,* edited by Linus J. Thro (Washington, D.C.: University Press of America, 1982), pp. 105-117.

Duclow, Donald F. "Gregory of Nyssa and Nicholas of Cusa: Infinity, Anthropology and the Viz Negativa," in *Downside Review,* 92 (1974), pp. 102-108.

_____. "Pseudo-Dionysius, John Scotus Eriugena, Nicholas of Cusa: An Approach to the Hermeneutic of Divine Names," in *International Philosophical Quarterly,* 12 (1972), pp. 260-278.

Dumont, Paul. *Liberté humaine et concours divin d'après Suárez.* Paris: Beauchesne, 1936.

Dumont, Stephen D. "Theology as Science and Duns Scotus's Distinction between Intuitive and Abstractive Cognition," in *Speculum* 64 (1989), pp. 579-599.

Ebeling, Gerhard. "The Hermeneutical Locus of the Doctrine of God in Peter Lombard and Thomas Aquinas," in *Journal for Theology and the Church*, 3 (1967), pp. 70-111.

_____. "The Meaning of 'Biblical Theology,'" in *Word and Faith*, translated by J. Leitch (London: SCM, 1963), pp. 79-97.

_____. *The Study of Theology*. Translated by Duane Priebe. Philadelphia: Fortress, 1978.

_____. "The Word of God and Hermeneutics," in *Word and Faith*, pp. 305-332.

Echternach, Helmut. "The Lutheran Doctrine of the *Autopistia* of Holy Scripture," in *Concordia Theological Monthly*, (April, 1952), pp. 241-271.

Eldredge, Laurence. "The Concept of God's Absolute Power in the Later Fourteenth Century," in *By Things Seen: Reference and Recognition in Medieval Thought*, edited by David L. Jeffrey (Ottawa: University of Ottawa Press, 1979), pp. 211-226.

Elert, Werner. *The Structure of Lutheranism: the Theology and Philosophy of Life of Lutheranism Especially in the Sixteenth and Seventeenth Centuries*. Vol. I. Translated by Walter A. Hansen. St. Louis: Concordia, 1962.

Elorduy, Elutherius, "Duns Scoti influxus in Francisci Suárez doctrinam," in *De Doctrina Ioannis Duns Scoti*, edited by C. Balic, vol. IV, pp. 307-337.

Emerson, Roger L. "Latitudinarianism and the English Deists," in *Deism, Masonry, and the Enlightenment*, edited by J. A. Leo Lemay (Newark: University of Delaware Press, 1987), pp. 19-48.

The Encyclopedia of Philosophy. Edited by P. Edwards. 8 vols. New York: Macmillan, 1972.

Encyclopédie philosophique universelle, publié sous la direction d'André Jacob. 4 parts in 5 vols. Paris: Presses Universitaires de France, 1989-98.

Engelbrecht, B. "Is Christ the Scopus of the Scriptures?" in *Calvinus Reformator*, pp. 192-200.

_____. "The Problem of the Concept of the 'Personality' of the Holy Spirit according to Calvin," in *Calvinus Reformator*, pp. 201-216.

Engelsma, David J. "Calvin's Doctrine of the Trinity," in *Protestant Reformed Theological Journal*, 23 (1989), pp. 19-37.

Ermatinger, Charles J. "Richard Fishacre's 'Commentarium in librum I Sententiarum' (Dist. 2, Cap. 1), Text and Introduction," in *The Modern Schoolman*, 35 (1958), pp. 213-235.

Eschweiler, Karl. "Die Philosophie der spanischen Spätscholastik auf dem deutschen Universitäten des siebzehnten Jahrhunderts," in *Gesammelte Aufsätze zur Kulturgeschichte Spaniens*, vol. I, edited by H. Finke (Münster: Aschendorff, 1928), pp. 251-325.

Esser, Hans, "Hat Calvin eine 'leise modalisierende Trinitätalehre'?" in *Calvinus theologus*, edited by W. Neuser, pp. 113-129.

Etzkorn, Girard J. "John Reading on the Existence and Unicity of God, Efficient and Final Causality," in *Franciscan Studies*, 41 (1981), pp. 110-221.

Evans, Gillian R. *Anselm and Talking About God*. Oxford: Clarendon Press, 1978.

_____. *The Language and Logic of the Bible: the Road to Reformation*. New York: Cambridge University Press, 1985.

Faber, Jelle. "Nominalisme in Calvijns preken over Job," in *Een sprekend Begin*, edited by R. ter Beek, et al. (Kampen: Uitgeverij van den Berg, 1993), pp. 68-85.

Fallon, Stephen M. "'To Act or Not': Milton's Conception of Divine Freedom," in *Journal of the History of Ideas*, 49 (1988), pp. 425-453.

Farmer, Craig S. *The Gospel of John in the Sixteenth Century: The Johannine Exegesis of Wolfgang Musculus*. New York: Oxford University Press, 1997.

Farrar, Frederic W. *History of Interpretation*. New York: Dutton, 1886. Reprint, Grand Rapids: Baker Book House, 1961.

Farthing, John L. "The Problem of Exemplarity in St. Thomas," in *The Thomist*, 49/2 (April, 1985), pp. 183-222.

Fatio, Olivier. *Méthode et théologie. Lambert Daneau et les débuts de la scholastique reformée*. Geneva: Droz, 1976.

_____. "Présence de Calvin à l'époque de l'orthodoxie réformée: Les abrégées de Calvin à la fin du 16e et au 17e siècle," in *Calvinus Ecclesiae Doctor*, edited by W. Neuser, pp. 171-207.

Fatio, Olivier, and Pierre Fraenkel, eds. *Histoire de l'exégèse an XVIᵉ siècle: textes du colloqui international tenu á Genève en 1976*. Geneva: Droz, 1978.

Faulenbach, Heiner. "Johannes Cocceius," in *Orthodoxie und Pietismus*, edited by Martin Greschat (Stuttgart: W. Kohlhammer, 1982), pp. 163-176.

_____. *Die Struktur der Theologie des Amandus Polanus von Polansdorf*. Zurich: EVZ Verlag, 1967.

_____. *Weg und Ziel der erkenntnis Christi. Eine Untersuchung zur Theologie des Johannes Cocceius*. Neukirchen: Neukirchner Verlag, 1973.

Faust, A. "Die Dialektik R. Agricolas: Ein Beitrag zur Charakteristik des deutschen Humanismus," in *Archiv für Geschichte der Philosophie* 34 (1922), pp. 118-135.

Fay, Thomas A. "Bonaventure and Aquinas on God's Existence: Points of Convergence," in *The Thomist*, 41 (1977), pp. 585-595.

Febvre, Lucien. *The Problem of Unbelief in the Sixteenth Century: The Religion of Rabelais*. Translated by Beatrice Gottlieb. Cambridge, Mass.: Harvard University Press, 1982.

Feckes, Carl. *Die Rechtfertigungslehre des Gabriel Biel und ihre stellung innerhalb der nominalistischen Schule*. Münster: Aschendorff, 1925.

Félice, Paul de. *Lambert Daneau de Baugency-sur-Loire. Pasteur et professeur en théologie (1530-1595)*. Paris: G. Fischbacher. 1882.

Fernàndez Garcèa, Mariano. *Lexicon scholasticum philosophico-theologicum in quo termini, definitiones, distinctiones et effata a Joanne Duns Scoto*. Quaracchi: Collegium S. Bonaventura, 1910. Reprint, Hildesheim: Olms, 1974.

Fey, Thomas A. "Bonaventure and Aquinas on God's Existence: Points of Convergence," in *The Thomist*, 41 (1977), pp. 585-595.

Fienberg, Stanley P. "Thomas Goodwin's Scriptural Hermeneutics and the Dissolution of Puritan Unity," in *The Journal of Religious History*, 10 (1978-79), pp. 32-49.

Finkenzeller, Josef. *Offenbarung und Theologie nach der Lehre des Johannes Duns Skotus*. Vol. 38/5 of *Beiträge zur Geschichte der Philosophie und Theologie des Mittelalters*. Münster: Aschendorff, 1961.

Firth, Katharine R. *The Apocalyptic Tradition in Reformation Britian, 1530-1645*. New York and Oxford: Oxford University Press, 1979.

Fischer, Konrad. *De Deo Trino et Uno: das Verhältnis von productio und reductio in seiner Bedeutung für der Gotteslehre Bonaventuras*. Göttingen: Vanderhoeck and Ruprecht, 1978.

_____. "Hinweise zur Gotteslehre Bonaventuras," in *San Bonaventura Maestro*, edited by Alphonso Pompei, vol. I, pp. 513-525.

Fisher, George Park. "The Theology of Richard Baxter," in *Bibliotheca Sacra and American Biblical Repository*, 9 (1852), pp. 135-169.

_____. "The Writings of Richard Baxter," in *Bibliotheca Sacra and American Biblical Repository*, 9 (1852), pp. 300-329.

Fitzgerald, Allan D., ed. *Augustine Through the Ages: An Encyclopedia*. Grand Rapids: Eerdmans, 1999.

Fitzpatrick, Noel A. "Walter Chatton on the Univocity of Being: A Reaction to Peter Aureoli and William Ockham," in *Fransiscan Studies*, 31 (1971), pp. 88-177.

Fix, Andrew. "Angels, Devils, and Evil Spirits in Seventeenth-Century Thought: Balthasar Bekker and the Collegiants," in *Journal of the History of Ideas*, 50 (1989), pp. 527-547.

Flage, Daniel E. "The Essences of Spinoza's God," in *History of Philosophy Quarterly*, 6 (1989), pp. 147-160.

Flesseman-van Leer, E. "The Controversy about Scripture and Tradition between Thomas more and William Tyndale," in *Nederlands Archief voor Kerkgeschiedenis*, 43 (1959), pp. 143-164.

Flier, Albertus van der. *Specimen historico-theologicum de Johanne Cocceijo anti-scholastico*. Utrecht: Kemink en Zoon, 1859.

Floor, L. "The Hermeneutics of Calvin," in *Calvinus Reformator*, pp.181-191.

Fontan, P. "Dieu, premier ou dernier connu, de Spinoza á St. Thomas d'Aquin," in *The Thomist*, 74 (1974), pp. 244-278.

Force, James E. "Biblical interpretation, Newton and English Deism," in *Scepticism and Irreligion*, edited by R. Popkin and A. Vanderjagt, pp. 282-305.

_____. *Essays on the Context, Nature, and Influence of Isaac Newton's Theology*. Dordrecht and Boston: Kluwer, 1990.

_____. *Newton and Religion: Context, Nature, and Influence*. Dordrecht and Boston: Kluwer, 1999.

Force, James E., and Richard H Popkin, eds. *The Books of Nature and Scripture: Recent Essays on Natural Philosophy, Theology, and Biblical Criticism in the Netherlands of Spinoza's Time and the British Isles of Newton's Time*. Dordrecht and Boston: Kluwer, 1994.

Forstman, H. J. *Word and Spirit: Calvin's Doctrine of Biblical Authority*. Stanford, CA: Stanford University Press, 1962.

Fortman, Edmund J., ed. *The Theology of God: Commentary*. Milwaukee: Bruce, 1967.

_____. *The Triune God: A Historical Study of the Doctrine of the Trinity*. New York: Hutchinson/Corpus, 1972. Reprint, Grand Rapids: Baker Book House, 1982.

The Foundation of Biblical Authority. Edited by James Montgomery Boice. Grand Rapids: Zondervan, 1978.

Fraenkel, Peter. *De l'Ecriture à la dispute: le cas de l'Académie de Genève sous Théodore de Bèze*. Cahiers de la Revue de théologie et de philosophie, 1. Lausanne: Revue de théologie et de philosophie, 1977.

_____. *Testimonia Patrum: The Function of Patristic Argument in the Theology of Philip Melanchthon*. Geneva: Droz, 1961.

Franks, R. S. *The Doctrine of the Trinity*. London: Duckworth, 1953.

_____. "Dogma in Protestant Scholasticism," in *Dogma in History and Thought*, pp. 111-141.

Freedman, Joseph S. "Aristotle and the Content of Philosophy Instruction at Central European Schools and Universities during the Reformation Era (1500-1650)," in *Proceedings of the American Philosophical Society* 137/2 (1993), pp. 213-53.

_____. "The Career and Writings of Bartholomew Keckermann," in *Proceedings of the American Philosophical Society*, 141 (1997), pp. 305-364.

_____. *European Academic Philosophy in the Late Sixteenth and Early Seventeenth Centuries: The Life, Significance, and Philosophy of Clemens Timpler (1563/4-1624).* 2 vols. Hildesheim and New York: Olms, 1988.

_____. "Philosophy Instruction within the Institutional Framework of Central European Schools and Universities during the Reformation Era," in *History of Universities*, 5 (1985), pp. 117-66.

Frei, Hans W. *The Eclipse of Biblical Narrative: A Study in Eighteenth- and Nineteenth-Century Hermeneutics.* New Haven: Yale University Press, 1974.

Freiday, Dean. *The Bible, its Criticism, Interpretation and Use in 16ᵗʰ and 17ᵗʰ Century England.* Manasquan, N.J.: Catholic and Quaker Studies, 1979.

Freitas, Emmanuel. "De argumentatione Duns Scoti pro infinitate Dei," in *De Doctrina Ioannis Duns Scoti,* edited by C. Balic, vol. II, pp. 427-433.

Friedman, Jerome. *Michael Servetus: A Case-Study in Total Heresy.* Geneva: Droz, 1978.

_____. *The Most Ancient Testimony: Sixteenth-Century Christian-Hebraica in the Age of Renaissance Nostalgia.* Athens, Ohio: Ohio University Press, 1983.

_____. "Servetus and Anti-trinitarianism: à propos Antonio Rotondo," in *Bibliothèque d'Humanisme et Renaissance,* 35 (1973), pp. 543-545.

Friedmann, R. "The Encounter of Anabaptists and Mennonites with Anti-Trinitarians," in *Mennonite Quarterly Review,* XXII (1948), pp. 139-162.

Fritz, G., and A. Michel. "Scholastique," in *Dictionnaire de théologie catholique,* vol. 14/2, cols. 1691-1728.

Frost, Ronald N. "Aristotle's *Ethics*: The *Real* Reason for Luther's Reformation," in *Trinity Journal,* NS 18 (1997), pp. 223-41.

Fuerst, Adrian. *An Historical Study of the Doctrine of the Omnipresence of God in Selected Writings between 1220-1270.* Washington, D.C.: Catholic Univ. of America Press, 1951.

Fullerton, Kemper. *Prophecy and Authority: A Study in the History of the Doctrine and Interpretation of Scripture.* New York: Macmillan, 1919.

Funkenstein, Amos. "The Body of God in 17ᵗʰ Century Theology and Science," in *Millenarianism and Messianism in English Literature and Thought, 1650-1800,* edited by R. Popkin (Leiden: Brill, 1988), pp. 149-175.

_____. *Theology and the Scientific Imagination from the Middle Ages to the Seventeenth Century.* Princeton: Princeton University Press, 1986.

Gabbey, Alan. "'A disease incurable': scepticism and the Cambridge Platonists," in *Scepticism and Irreligion,* edited by R. Popkin and A. Vanderjagt, pp. 71-91.

Gaberel, J. *Histoire de l'Église de Génève depuis le commencement de la Reformation jusqu'a nos jours.* 3 vols. Geneva, 1858-1862.

Gamble, Richard. "*Brevitas et facilitas*: Toward and Understanding of Calvin's Hermeneutic," in *Westminster Theological Journal,* 47 (1985), pp. 1-17.

_____. "Calvin as Theologian and Exegete: Is there Anything New?" in *Calvin Theological Journal,* 23 (1988), pp. 178-194.

_____. "Exposition and Method in Calvin," in *Westminster Theological Journal,* 49 (1987), pp. 153-165.

Gane, Erwin R. "The Exegetical Methods of Some Sixteenth-Century Anglican Preachers: Latimer, Jewel, Hooker, and Andrews," in *Andrews University Seminary Studies,* 17 (1979), pp. 23-38, 169-188.

_____. "The Exegetical Methods of Some Sixteenth-Century Puritan Preachers: Hooper, Cartwright, and Perkins," in *Andrews University Seminary Studies* 19 (1981), pp. 21-36, 99-114.

_____. "The Exegetical Methods of Some Sixteenth-Century Roman Catholic Preachers: Fisher, Peryn, Bonner, and Watson," in *Andrews University Seminary Studies*, 23 (1985), pp. 161-180, 259-275.

Ganoczy, Alexandre. *Calvin, théologien de l'église et du ministére*. Paris: Editions du Cerf, 1964.

_____. *The Young Calvin*. Translated by David Foxgrover and Wade Provo. Philadelphia: Westminster, 1987.

Ganoczy, Alexandre, and Stefan Scheld. *Die Hermeneutik Calvins: Geistesgeschichtliche Voraussetzungen und Grundzüge*. Wiesbaden: F. Steiner, 1983.

Garber, Daniel. "How God Causes Motion: Descartes, Divine Sustenance, and Occasionalism," in *The Journal of Philosophy*, 84 (1987), pp. 567-580.

Garber, Daniel, and Michael Ayers, eds. *The Cambridge History of Seventeenth-Century Philosophy*. 2 vols. Cambridge: Cambridge University Press, 1998.

Gardeil, A. "Lieux théologiques," in *Dictionnaire de théologie catholique*, 9/1, cols. 712-747.

_____. "La notion du lieu théologique,' in *Revue des Sciences Philosophiques et Théologiques* (1908), pp. 51-73, 246-276, 484-505.

_____. "La topicité," in *Revue des Sciences Philosophiques et Théologiques* (1911), pp. 750-757.

Garrett, Don, ed. *The Cambridge Companion to Spinoza*. Cambridge: Cambridge University Press, 1996.

Garrigou-Lagrange, Reginald. *God: His Existence and His Nature: A Thomistic Solution of Certain Agnostic Antinomies*. Translated by Dom Bede Rose. 2 vols. St. Louis: B. Herder, 1946.

_____. *Predestination*. Translated by Dom Bede Rose. St. Louis: B. Herder, 1939.

_____. "Thomisme," in *Dictionnaire de théologie catholique*, vol. 15/1, cols. 823-1023.

Gass, Wilhelm. *Geschichte der protestantischen Dogmatik in ihrem Zusammenhange mit der Theologie*. 4 vols. Berlin: Georg Reimer, 1854-67.

_____. "Recension von Schneckenburger, *Darstellung des lutherischen und reformirten Lehrbegriffs*," in *Theologische Studien und Kritiken*, 1857, pp. 115-149.

Gay, Peter. *The Enlightenment: an Interpretation*. 2 vols.: I. *The Rise of Modern Paganism*; II. *The Science of Freedom*. New York: Alfred A. Knopf, 1966-1969. Reprint, New York: Norton, 1977.

Geiger, L.-B. "Abstraction et séparation d'après S. Thomas in de Trinitate, q. 5, a. 3," in *Revue des Sciences Philosophiques et Théologiques*, 31 (1947), pp. 3-40.

_____. "Les idées divines dans l'oeuvre de S. Thomas," in *St. Thomas Aquinas, 1274-1974; Commemorative Studies*. Foreword by Etienne Gilson, 2 vols. (Toronto, Pontifical Institute of Mediaeval Studies, 1974), vol. I, pp. 175-209.

Geisler, Norman L., ed. *Inerrancy*. Grand Rapids: Zondervan, 1979.

Gelber, Hester Goodenough. "Logic and the Trinity: A Clash of Values in Scholastic Thought, 1300-1335." Ph.D. diss., University of Wisconsin, 1974.

Gelder, H. A. Enno van. *The Two Reformations of the Sixteenth Century*. Den Haag: De Graaf, 1961.

Genderen, J. van. *Herman Witsius: Bijdrage tot de Kennis der Gereformeerde Theologie*. Den Haag: Guido de Bres, 1953.

Genest, Jean-François. *Prédétermination et liberté creé à Oxford au XIVe siècle: Buckingham contre Bradwardine*. Paris: J. Vrin, 1992.

George, Timothy. "'A Right Strawy Epistle': Reformation Perspectives on James," in *Review and Expositor*, 83 (1986), pp. 369-382.

Gerrish, Brian A. "Biblical Authority and the Continental Reformation," *Scottish Journal of Theology*, 10 (1957), pp. 337-360.

_____. "'To the Unknown God': Luther and Calvin on the Hiddenness of God," in *The Journal of Religion*, 53 (1973), pp. 263-292.

Gerstner, John H. "The Church's Doctrine of Biblical Inspiration," in *The Foundation of Biblical Authority*, edited by J. M. Boice, pp. 23-58.

_____. "The View of the Bible held by the Church: Calvin and the Westminster Divines," in *Inerrancy*, edited by N. Geisler, pp. 385-410.

Geymonat, Jean. *Michel Servet et ses idées religieuses*. Geneva: Carey, 1892.

Gibbs, Lee W. "Puritan Natural Law Theory in William Ames," in *Harvard Theological Review*, 64 (1971), pp. 37-57.

_____. "William Ames's Technometry," in *Journal of the History of Ideas*, 30 (1972), pp. 615-624.

_____. *William Ames's Technometry*. Philadelphia: University of Pennsylvania, 1979.

Gilbert, Neal W. *Renaissance Concepts of Method*. New York: Columbia University Press, 1960.

Gill, J. *The Council of Florence*. Cambridge: Cambridge University Press, 1959.

Gillett, E. H. *God in Human Thought; or, Natural Theology Traced in Literature, Ancient and Modern, to the Time of Bishop Butler*. 2 vols. New York: Scribner, Armstrong, 1874.

Gilson, Etienne. "Boéce de Dacie et la double vérité," in *Archives d'histoire doctrinale et littéraire du moyen age*, 30 (1955), pp. 81-99.

_____. *The Christian Philosophy of Saint Augustine*. Translated by L. E. M. Lynch. New York: Vintage, 1960.

_____. *The Christian Philosophy of Saint Thomas Aquinas*. Trans L. K. Shook. New York: Random House, 1956.

_____. "La doctrine de la double vérité," in *Etudes de philosophie médiévale* (Strasbourg: Commission des publications de la Faculté des lettres, 1921), pp. 50-69.

_____. *Etudes sur le r ole de la pensée médiévale dans la formation du système cartésien*. Paris, J. Vrin, 1930.

_____. "Humanisme médiévale et Renaissance," in *Les idées et les lettres*. 2nd ed. Paris: J. Vrin, 1955.

_____. *Jean Duns Scot: Introduction à ses positions fondamentales*. Paris: J. Vrin, 1952.

_____. *The Philosophy of St. Bonaventure*. Translated by Dom Illtyd Trethowan and Frank J. Sheed. Paterson: St. Anthony Guild, 1965.

_____. *Reason and Revelation in the Middle Ages*. New York: Scribner, 1938.

_____. *The Spirit of Medieval Philosophy*. Translated by A. H. C. Downes. New York: Scribner, 1936.

Girardin, Benoit. *Rhetorique et théologie. Calvin: L'Epître au Romains*. Paris: Beauchesne, 1979.

Glunz, H. *The Vulgate in England from Alcuin to Roger Bacon*. Cambridge: Cambridge Univ. Press, 1933.

Godet, P. "Durand de Saint-Pourçain," in *Dictionnaire de théologie catholique*, IV, col. 1964-1966.

Godfrey, W. Robert. "Biblical Authority in the Sixteenth and Seventeenth Centuries: A Question of Transition," in *Scripture and Truth*, edited by D. A. Carson and John D. Woodbridge (Grand Rapids: Zondervan, 1983), pp. 225-243.

Gomes, Alan, "De Jesu Christo Servatore: Faustus Socinus on the Satisfaction of Christ," *Westminster Theological Journal*, 55 (1993), pp. 209-231.

Goris, Harm J. M. J. *Free Creatures of an Eternal God: Thomas Aquinas on God's Infallible Foreknowledge and Irresistible Will*. Leuven: Peeters, 1996.

_____. "Thomism and Zanchi's Doctrine of God," in *Reformation and Scholasticism*, edited by W. van Asselt and E. Dekker, pp. 125-126.

Gorkom, Gerardus van. *Specimen theologicum inaugurale de Joanne Cocceijo, s. codicis interprete.* Utrecht: Kemink en Zoon, 1856.

Goshen-Gottstein, Moshe. "Foundations of Biblical Philology in the Seventeenth Century: Christian and Jewish Dimensions," in *Jewish Thought in the Seventeenth Century*, edited by Isadore Tweersky and Bernard Septimus (Cambridge, Mass.: Harvard University Press, 1987), pp. 77-94.

_____. "The Textual Criticism of the Old Testament: Rise, Decline, Rebirth," in *Journal of Biblical Literature*, 102 (1983), pp. 365-399.

Gostwick, Joseph. *German Culture and Christianity: their Controversy in the Time 1770-1880.* London: Frederic Norgate, 1882.

Goudriaan, Aza. *Philosophische Gotteserkenntnis dei Suárez und Descartes in Zusammenhang mit die niederländischen reformierten Theologie und Philosophie des 17, Jahrhunderts.* Leiden: E. J. Brill, 1999.

_____. "Die Rezeption des cartesianischen Gottesdankens bei Abraham Heidanus," in *Neue Zeitschrift für systematische Theologie und Religionsphilosophie*, 38/2 (1996), pp. 166-197.

Gouhier, Henri. *La pensée religieuse de Descartes.* Paris, 1924.

Graafland, C. "De Gereformeerde Orthodoxie en het Piëtisme in Nederland," in *Nederlands Theologisch Tijdschrift*, 19 (1964-65), pp. 466-479.

_____. "Gereformeerde Scholastiek V: De Invloed van de Scholastiek op de Gereformeerde Orthodoxie," in *Theologia Reformata*, 30 (1987), pp. 4-25.

_____. "Gereformeerde Scholastiek VI: De Invloed van de Scholastiek op de Nadere Reformatie," in *Theologia Reformata*, 30 (1987), pp. 109-131; 313-340.

_____. *Het vaste verbond: Israel en het Oude Testament bij Calvijn en het gereformeerd protestantisme.* Amsterdam: Bolland, 1978.

_____. *Van Calvijn tot Barth: oorsprong en ontwikkeling van de leer der verkiezing in het Gereformeerd Protestantisme.* 's-Gravenhage: Boekencentrum, 1987.

_____. *De zekerheid van het geloof: een onderzoek naar de geloofsbeschouwing van enige vertegenwoordigers van reformatie en nadere reformatie.* Wageningen: Veenman, 1961.

_____. *Van Calvijn tot Comrie: oorsprong en ontwikkeling van de leer van het verbond in het Gereformeerd Protestantisme.* 3 vols. Zoetermeer: Boekencentrum, 1992-1994.

Graham, W. Fred, ed. *Later Calvinism: International Perspectives.* Sixteenth Century Essays & Studies, vol. 22. Kirksville, MO: Sixteenth Century Journal Publishers, 1994.

Grant, Edward. "The Condemnation of 1277, God's Absolute Power and Physical Thought in the Late Middle Ages," in *Viator*, 10 (1979), pp. 211-244.

Grant, Robert M. "History of the Interpretation of the Bible: I. Ancient Period," in *The Interpreters Bible*, 12 vols. (Nashville: Abingdon, 1951-57), vol. 1, pp. 106-114. [See also: McNeill, John T. and Terrien, Samuel]

Grant, Robert M., and David Tracy. *A Short History of the Interpretation of the Bible*. 2nd ed., revised and enlarged. Philadelphia: Fortress, 1984.

Graves, F. P. *Peter Ramus and the Educational Reformation of the Sixteenth Century*. New York: Macmillan, 1912.

Gray, Edward McQueen. *Old Testament Criticism, Its Rise and Progress from the 2nd Century to the end of the 18th Century: A Historical Sketch*. New York and London: Harper, 1923.

Greene, Donald. "Latitudinarianism and Sensibility: The Genealogy of the 'Man of Feeling' Reconsidered," in *Modern Philology*, 75 (1977), pp. 159-183.

Greig, Martin. "The Reasonableness of Christianity? Gilbert Burnet and the Trinitarian Controversy of the 1690s," in *Journal of Ecclesiastical History* 44 (1993), pp. 631-651.

_____. "The Thought and Polemic of Gilbert Burnet, c. 1673-1704. Ph.D. diss., Cambridge University, 1991.

Greijdanus, S. *Schriftbeginselen ter Schriftverklaring en historisch Overzicht over Theorien en Wijzen van Schriftuitlegging*. Kampen: J. H. Kok, 1946.

Grene, Marjorie Glicksman. *Descartes Among the Scholastics*. Milwaukee: Marquette University Press, 1991.

Grene, Marjorie Glicksman, and Roger Ariew, eds. *Descartes and his Contemporaries: Meditations, Objections, and Replies*. Chicago: University of Chicago Press, 1995.

Grenier, Henri. *Thomistic Philosophy*. Translated by J. P. E. O'Hanley. 3 vols. Charlottestown: St. Dunstan's University, 1948.

Grierson, Herbert. *Cross-Currents in 17th Century English Literature: The World, the Flesh, and the Spirit, Their Actions and Reactions*. New York: Harper & Brothers, 1958.

Groot, Aart de. "L'antitrinitarisme socinien," in *Études theologiques et religieuses*, 61 (1986), pp. 51-61.

Grossmann, Maria. *Humanism in Wittenberg, 1485-1517*. Nieuwkoop: De Graaf, 1975.

Gründler, Otto. *Die Gotteslehre Girolami Zanchis und ihre Bedeutung für seine Lehre von der Prädestination*. Neukirchen: Neukirchner Verlag, 1965.

_____. "Thomism and Calvinism in the Theology of Girolamo Zanchi (1516-1590)." Th.D. diss., Princeton Theological Seminary, 1961.

Guelluy, Robert. *Philosophie et théologie chez Guillaume d'Ockham*. Louvain: University of Louvain, 1947.

Gueroult, Martial. *Descartes' Philosophy Interpreted According to the Order of Reasons*. Translated by Roger Ariew. 2 vols. Minneapolis: University of Minnesota Press, 1984.

Gundry, Stanley N. "John Owen on Authority and Scripture," in *Inerrancy and the Church*, edited by John D. Hannah, pp. 189-221.

Gurr, John. *The Principle of Sufficient Reason in Some Scholastic Systems, 1750-1900*. Milwaukee: Marquette University Press, 1959.

Guttmann, Julius. *Philosophies of Judaism: A History of Jewish Philosophy from Biblical Times to Franz Rosenzweig*. Translated by David Silverman. New York: Schocken Books, 1973.

Gwatkin, Henry Melvill. *The Knowledge of God in its Historical Development*. 2 vols. 2nd ed. Edinburgh: T. & T. Clark, 1907.

Gysi, Lydia. *Platonism and Cartesianism in the Philosophy of Ralph Cudworth*. Bern: Herbert Lang, 1962.

Haar, J. van der. *Schatkamer van de Gereformeerde Theologie in Nederland (c. 1600-c. 1800)*. Veenendaal: Antiquariat Kool, 1987.

Haentjens, Antonie Hendrik. *Hugo de Groot als godsdienstig denker*. Amsterdam: Ploegsma, 1946.

————. *Remonstrantsche en calvinistische dogmatiek: in verband met elkaar en met de ontwikkeling van het dogma*. Leiden: A.H. Adriani, 1913.

————. *Simon Episcopius als apologeet van het Remonstrantisme in zijn leven en werken geschetst*. Leiden: A.H. Adriani, 1899.

Hagen, Kenneth. *A Theology of Testament in the Young Luther: the Lectures on Hebrews*. Leiden: E. J. Brill, 1974.

————. "What did the term *Commentarius* mean to sixteenth century theologians?" in *Théorie et practique de l'exégèse*, edited by I. Backus and F. Higman, pp. 13-38.

Hagenbach, Karl R. *German Rationalism, in its Rise, Progress, and Decline, in Relation to Theologians, Scholars, Poets, Philosophers, and the People: A Contribution to the Church History of the Eighteenth and Nineteenth Centuries*. Edited and translated by William Leonard Gage and J. H. Stuckenberg. Edinburgh: T. & T. Clark, 1865.

————. *A History of Christian Doctrines*. Translated by Plumptre. 3 vols. Edinburgh: T. & T. Clark, 1880-81.

————. "Zur Beantwortung der Frage über das Princip des Protestantismus. Sendschreiben an Herrn D. und Professor Schenkel in Heidelberg," in *Theologische Studien und Kritiken*, 1854, pp. 7-49.

Hägglund, Bengt. *History of Theology*. Translated by Gene Lund. St. Louis: Concordia, 1968.

Hailperin, Herman. *Rashi and the Christian Scholars*. Pittsburg: University of Pittsburg Press, 1963.

Hall, Basil. "Biblical Scholarship: Editions and Commentaries," in *Cambridge History of the Bible*, III, pp. 38-93.

————. "Calvin Against the Calvinists," in *John Calvin*, edited by Gervase Duffield (Grand Rapids: Eerdmans, 1966), pp. 19-37.

————. "Calvin and Biblical Humanism," in *Huguenot Society Proceedings*, 20 (1959-64), pp. 195-209.

Hallam, Henry. *Introduction to the Literature of Europe in the 15th, 16th, and 17th Centuries*. 3 vols. 1873. Reprint, New York: Ungar, 1970.

Haller, William. *Liberty and Reformation in the Puritan Revolution*. New York and London: Columbia University Press, 1955.

————. *The Rise of Puritanism: or, the Way to the New Jerusalem as set forth in Pulpit and Press from Thomas Cartwright to John Lilburne and John Milton, 1570-1643* (New York: Harper and Row, 1957).

Halleux, André de, "Dieu le Père tout-puissant," in *Revue Théologique de Louvain*, 8 (1977), pp. 401-22.

Hankey, W. J. *God in Himself: Aquinas' Doctrine of God as Expounded in the Summa theologiae*. New York: Oxford University Press, 1987.

Hannah, John D., ed. *Inerrancy and the Church*. Chicago: Moody Press, 1984.

Haring, N. M. "The Case of Gilbert de la Porreé," in *Medieval Studies*, 13 (1951), pp. 1-40.

————. "A Commentary on the Pseudo-Athanasian Creed by Gilbert of Poitiers," in *Mediaeval Studies*, 27 (1965), pp. 23-53.

————. "Notes on the Council and Consistory of Rheims (1148)," in *Medieval Studies*, 28 (1966), pp. 39-59.

_____. "Simon of Tournai and Gilbert of Poitiers," in *Mediaeval Studies*, 27 (1965), pp. 325-330.

Harman, Allan. "Speech About the Trinity: With Special Reference to Novatian, Hilary, and Calvin," in *Scottish Journal of Theology*, 26 (1973), pp. 385-400.

Harris, C. R. S. *Duns Scotus.* 2 vols. Oxford: Clarendon, 1927.

Harris, Victor. "Allegory to Analogy in the Interpretation of Scripture," in *Philological Quarterly*, 45 (1966), pp. 1-23.

Hartvelt, G. P. "Petrus Boquinus: Een bijdrage tot de geschiedenis van de gereformeerde dogmatiek," in *Gereformeerde Theologisch Tijdschrift*, 62 (1962), pp. 49-77.

_____. "Over de methode der dogmatiek in de eeuw der Reformatie. Bijdrage tot de geschiedenis van de gereformeerde dogmatiek," in *Gereformeerde Theologisch Tijdschrift*, 62 (1962), pp. 97-149.

Hastie, William. *The Theology of the Reformed Church in its Fundamental Principles.* Edinburgh: T. & T. Clark, 1904.

Hausammann, Susi. *Römerbriefauslegung zwischen Humanismus und Reformation: Eine Studie zu Heinrich Bullingers Römerbriefvorlesung von 1525.* Zürich: Zwingli Verlag, 1970.

Hayen, A. "Le Concile de Reims et l'erreur théologique de Gilbert de la Porreé," in *Archives d'histoire doctrinale et littéraire de moyen-âge* (1936), pp. 24-37.

Hayes, Zachary. *The Hidden Center: Spirituality and Speculative Christology in St. Bonaventure.* New York: Paulist Press, 1981.

Haykin, Michael A. G., ed. *The Life and Thought of John Gill (1697-1771): A Tercentennial Appreciation.* Leiden: E. J. Brill, 1997.

Hays, John H., and Frederick Prussner. *Old Testament Theology: Its History and Development.* Atlanta: John Knox, 1985.

Hazard, Paul. *The European Mind: The Critical Years (1680-1715).* New Haven: Yale University Press, 1953.

_____. *European Thought in the Eighteenth Century: From Montesquieu to Lessing.* Cleveland: World, 1963. Reprint, Gloucester, Mass.: Peter Smith, 1973.

Headley, J. M. "Tomasso Campanella and the End of the Renaissance," in *Journal of Medieval and Renaissance Studies* 20 (1990), pp. 157-74.

_____. "Tomasso Campanella and Jean de Launoy: The Controversy over Aristotle and his Reception in the West," in *Renaissance Quarterly* 43 (1990), pp. 529-50.

Hefelbower, Samuel G. *The Relation of John Locke to English Deism.* Chicago: University of Chicago Press, 1918.

Heilemann, P. A. *Die Gotteslehre des Ch. Wolff.* Leipzig, 1907.

Heim, Karl. "Zur Geschichte des Satzes von der doppelten Wahrheit," in *Studien zur systematischen Theologie: Theodor von Haering zum 70. Geburtstag* (Tübingen: J. C. B. Mohr, 1918), pp. 1-16.

Heim, S. Mark. "The Powers of God: Calvin and Late Medieval Thought," in *Andover Newton Quarterly*, n.s. 19 (1978/79), pp. 156-166.

Helm, Paul. *Calvin and the Calvinists.* Edinburgh: Banner of Truth, 1982.

_____. "Calvin, English Calvinism and the Logic of Doctrinal Development," in *Scottish Journal of Theology*, 34 (1981), pp. 179-185.

Helmer, Christine. *The Trinity and Martin Luther: a Study on the Relationship between Genre, Language and the Trinity in Luther's Works, 1523-1546.* Veröffentlichungen des Instituts für Europäische Geschichte Mainz, Bd. 174. Mainz: P. von Zabern, 1999.

Hendrix, Scott H. *Tradition and Authority in the Reformation*. Brookfield: Ashgate, 1996.

Henry, Paul. "On Some Implications of the 'Ex Patre Filioque tamquam ab uno Principio,'" in *The Eastern Churches Quarterly* (1948), Supplement 19, pp. 16-31.

Heppe, Heinrich. *Die Bekenntnisschriften der altprotestantischen kirche Deutschlands*. Cassel: T. Fisher, 1855.

_____. *Die Bekenntnisschriften der reformirten Kirche Deutschlands*. [*Schriften zur reformirten Theologie*, Band I] Elberfeld: R. L. Friederichs, 1860.

_____. "Der Charakter der deutsch-reformirten Kirche und das Verhältniss derselben zum Luthertum und zum Calvinismus," in *Theologische Studien und Kritiken*, 1850 (Heft 3), pp. 669-706.

_____. *Die confessionelle Entwicklung der altprotestantischen Kirche Deutschlands, die altprotestantische Union und die gegenwärtige confessionelle Lage und Aufgabe des deutschen Protestantismus*. Marburg: Elwert, 1854.

_____. *Die Dogmatik der evangelisch-reformierten Kirche*. Neu durchgesehen und herausgegeben von Ernst Bizer. Neukirchen: Moers, 1935. [Originally published as *Schriften zur reformirten Theologie*, Band II.]

_____. *Die Dogmatik des Protestantismus im sechzehnten Jahrhundert*. 3 vols. Gotha: Perthes, 1857.

_____. *Geschichte des deutschen Protestantismus*. 4 vols. Marburg: Elwert, 1852-1859.

_____. *Geschichte des Pietismus und der Mystik in der reformierten Kirche namentlich in der Niederlande*. Leiden: E. J. Brill, 1879.

_____. *Reformed Dogmatics Set Out and Illustrated from the Sources*. Revised and edited by Ernst Bizer. Translated by G. T. Thomson. London, 1950. Reprint, Grand Rapids: Baker Book House, 1978.

_____. *Das Schulwesen des Mittelalters und dessen Reform im sechszehnten Jahrhundert*. Marburg: Elwert, 1860.

_____. *Theodor Beza: Leben und ausgewählte Schriften*. Elberfeld: R. L. Friederichs, 1861.

Heyd, Michael. *Between Orthodoxy and the Enlightenment: Jean-Robert Chouet and the Introduction of Cartesian Science in the Academy of Geneva*. Den Haag: De Graff, 1982.

_____. "Cartesianism, Secularism, and Academic Reform: Jean-Robert Chouet and the Academy of Geneva, 1669-1704." Ph.D. diss., Princeton University, 1974.

_____. "From a Rationalist Theology to a Cartesian Voluntarism: David Derodon and Jean-Robert Chouet," in *Journal of the History of Ideas*, 40 (1979), pp. 527-542.

Hill, Eugene D. *Edward, Lord Herbert of Cherbury*. Boston: Twayne, 1987.

Hobbs, Gerald. "Exegetical Projects and Problems: A New Look at an Undated Letter from Bucer to Zwingli," in *Prophet, Pastor, Protestant: The Work of Huldrych Zwingli after Five Hundred Years*, edited by E. J. Furcha and H. Wayne Pipkin (Allison Park, PA: Pickwick, 1984), pp. 89-107.

_____. "How Firm a Foundation: Martin Bucer's Historical Exegesis of the Psalms," in *Church History*, 53 (1984), pp. 477-491

_____. "Zwingli and the Old Testament," in *Huldrych Zwingli, 1483-1531: A Legacy of Radical Reform*, edited by E. J. Furcha (Montreal: McGill University Press, 1985), pp. 144-178.

Hodge, Archibald A. *The Confession of Faith: A Handbook of Christian Doctrine Expounding the Westminster Confession*. 1869. Reprint, London: Banner of Truth, 1978.

_____. *Outlines of Theology*. 1860. Reprint, Grand Rapids: Zondervan, 1976.

Hodge, Charles. *Systematic Theology*. 3 vols. 1871-73. Reprint, Grand Rapids: Eerdmans, 1975.

Hodl, L. "Die philosophische Gotteslehre des Thomas von Aquin, O.P. in der Diskussion der Schulen um die Wende des 13. zum 14. Jahrhundert," in *Rivista di Filosofia Neo-scholastica*, 70 (1978), pp. 113-134.

Hoenen, M. J. F. M. *Marsilius of Inghen: Divine Knowledge in Late Medieval Thought*. Leiden: E. J. Brill, 1993.

Hof, W. J. Op't. "Gisbertus Voetius' Evaluatie van de Reformatie: Een voorlopig Onderzoek," in *Theologia Reformata*, 32 (1989), 211-249.

Höffding, Harald. *A History of Modern Philosophy: A Sketch of the History of Philosophy from the Close of the Renaissance to our own Day*. Translated by B. E. Meyer. 2 vols. London: Macmillan, 1935.

Hoffmann, Manfred. "Rhetoric and Dialectic in Erasmus' and Melanchthon's Interpretation of John's Gospel," in *Philip Melanchthon (1497-1560) and the Commentary*, edited by Timothy J. Wengert and M. Patrick Graham (Sheffield: Sheffield Academic Press, 1997), pp. 65-72.

Hohlwein, H. "Rationalismus. II. Rationalismus und Supranaturalismus, kirchengeschichtlich," s.v. in *Religion in Geschichte und Gegenwart*, dritte Auflage.

Holeczek, Heinz. *Humanistische Bibelphilologie als Reformproblem bei Erasmus von Rotterdam, Thomas More, und William Tyndale*. Leiden: Brill, 1975.

Holl, Karl. *Gesammelte Aufsätze*. 3 vols. Tübingen: J. C. B. Mohr, 1928.

Holopainen, Toivo J. *Dialectic and Theology in the Eleventh Century*. Leiden: E. J. Brill, 1996.

Holzhey, Karl. *Die Inspiration der heiligen Schrift in der Anschauung des Mittelalters: von Karl der Grosser bis zum Konzil von Trient*. Munich: J. J. Lentner, 1895.

Honders, H. J. *Andreas Rivetus: als Invloedrijk Gereformeerd Theoloog in Holland's Bloeitijd*. Den Haag: Nijhoff, 1930.

Hoopes, Robert. *Right Reason in the English Renaissance*. Cambridge, Mass.: Harvard University Press, 1962.

Hopkins, Jasper. *A Companion to the Study of St. Anselm*. Minneapolis: University of Minnesota Press, 1972.

Hotson, Howard. *Johann Heinrich Alsted, 1588-1638: Between Renaissance, Reformation, and Universal Reform*. Oxford: Clarendon Press, 2000.

Howell, Wilbur Samuel. *Eighteenth-Century British Logic and Rhetoric*. Princeton: Princeton University Press, 1971.

_____. *Logic and Rhetoric in England, 1500-1700*. Princeton, Princeton University Press, 1956.

Hudson, A., and M. Wilks, eds. *From Ockham to Wyclif*. Oxford: Oxford University Press, 1987.

Hughes, Gerard, ed. *The Philosophical Assessment of Theology: Essays in Honour of Frederick C. Copleston*. Washington, D.C.: Georgetown University Press, 1987.

Hughes, Philip E. *The Theology of the English Reformers*. New edition. Grand Rapids: Baker Book House, 1980.

Hulme, Edward M. "Lelio Sozzini's Confession of Faith," in *Persecution and Liberty: Essays in Honor of George Lincoln Burr* (New York: Century, 1931), pp. 211-225.

Hunt, John. *Religious Thought in England, from the Reformation to the End of Last Century, a Contribution to the History of Theology*. 3 vols. London: Strahan & Co., 1870-73.

Hunter, A. Mitchell. *The Teaching of Calvin: a Modern Interpretation*. London: James Clarke, 1950.

Hunter, W. B., Jr. "Milton's Arianism Reconsidered," in *Harvard Theological Review*, 52 (1959), pp. 9-35.

————. "Some Problems in John Milton's Theological Vocabulary," in *Harvard Theological Review*, 57 (1964), pp. 353-365.

Hunter, W. B., Jr., C. A. Patrides, and J. H. Adamson. *Bright Essence*. Salt Lake City: University of Utah Press, 1971.

Hurst, John Fletcher. *History of Rationalism*. New York: Eaton & Mains, 1901.

Huth, Harry. *Gospel and Scripture: the Interrelationship of the Material and Formal Principles in Lutheran Theology*. St. Louis: Concordia, 1972.

Hutton, Sarah. "Edward Stillingfleet and Spinoza," in *Disguised and Overt Spinozism*, edited by W. van Bunge, pp. 261-274.

————. "The Neoplatonic Roots of Arianism: Ralph Cudworth and Theophilus Gale," in *Socinianism and its Role in the culture of the XVIth to XVIIth Centuries*, edited by Lech Szczucki, Zbigniew Ogonowski, and Janusz Tazbir (Warsaw: PWN, Polish Scientific Publisher, 1983), pp. 139-145.

————. "Thomas Jackson, Oxford Platonist, and William Twisse, Aristotelian," in *Journal of the History of Ideas*, 39 (1978), pp. 635-52.

Immink, Frederik Gerrit. *Divine Simplicity*. Kampen: Kok, 1987.

————. "The One and Only: The Simplicity of God," in *Understanding the Attributes of God*, edited by Brink and Sarot, pp. 115-127.

Inge, William Ralph. *The Platonic Tradition in English Religious Thought. The Hulsean Lectures at Cambridge, 1925-1926*. London & New York: Longmans, Green, 1926.

Inspiration and Interpretation. Edited by John Walvoord. Grand Rapids: Eerdmans, 1957.

Israel, Jonathan I. *Radical Enlightenment: Philosophy and the Making of Modernity, 1650-1750* Oxford: Oxford University Press, 2001.

Itterzon, G. P. van. *Francis Gomarus*. Den Haag: Nijhoff, 1930.

————. "De 'Synopsis purioris theologiae': Gereformeerd Leerboek der 17de Eeuw," in *Nederlands Archief voor Kerkgeschiedenis*, 23 (1930), pp. 161-213, 225-259.

Ives, Robert B. "The Theology of Wolfgang Musculus (1497-1562)." Ph.D. diss., University of Manchester, 1965.

Jacob, Edmond. "L'Oeuvre exégétique d'un théologien strasbourgeois du 17e siècle: Sébastien Schmid," in *Revue d'histoire et de philosophie religieuses*, 66 (1986), pp. 71-78.

Jacobs, Henry E. "Scholasticism in the Lutheran Church," in *The Lutheran Cyclopedia*, pp. 434-435.

Jalabert, Jacques. *Le Dieu de Leibniz*. Publications de la Faculté des lettres et sciences humaines, Université de Grenoble, vol. 23. Paris: Presses Universitaires de France, 1960. Reprint, New York: Garland, 1985.

James, Frank A., III. "Peter Martyr Vermigli: At the Crossroads of Late Medieval Scholasticism, Christian Humanism and Resurgent Augustinianism," in *Protestant Scholasticism*, edited by C. Trueman and R. Clark, pp. 62-78.

James, Susan. "Spinoza the Stoic," in *The Rise of Modern Philosophy*, edited by Tom Sorrel, pp. 289-316.

Jansen, Reiner. *Studien zu Luther's Trinitätslehre*. Bern and Frankfurt: Lang, 1976.

Janz, Denis R. *Luther and Late Medieval Thomism: A Study in Theological Anthropology.* Waterloo: Wilfrid Laurier University Press, 1983.

Jardine, Lisa. "Inventing Rudolf Agricola: Cultural Transmission, Renaissance Dialectic, and the Emerging Humanities," in *The Transmission of Culture in Early Modern Europe,* edited by A. Grafton and A. Blair (Philadelphia: University of Pennsylvania Press, 1990), pp. 39-86.

_____. "Ghosting the Reform of Rhetoric: Erasmus and Agricola Again," in *Renaissance Rhetoric,* edited by Peter Mack (London: St. Martin's Press, 1994), pp. 27-45.

Jellema, Dirk W. "God's 'Baby Talk': Calvin and the 'Errors' of the Bible," in *Reformed Journal,* 30 (1970), pp. 25-47.

Jocher, Chr. G. *Allgemeines Gelehrten Lexikon.* 11 vols. Leipzig: J. F. Gleditsch, 1750-1897. Reprint, Hildesheim: Olms, 1960.

John Calvin's Institutes: His Opus Magnum. Proceedings of the Second South African Congress for Calvin Research, July 31-August 3, 1984. Potchefstroom: Potchefstroom University, Institute for Reformational Studies, 1986.

Johnson, John F. "Biblical Authority and Scholastic Theology" in *Inerrancy and the Church,* edited by John D. Hannah, pp. 67-97.

Johnson, Robert Clyde. *Authority in Protestant Theology.* Philadelphia: Westminster, 1959.

Jolivet, Jean. "Trois variations médiévales sur l'universel et l'individu: Roscellin, Abélard, Gilbert de la Porrée," in *Revue de métaphysique et de morale,* 97 (1992), pp. 97-155.

Jolley, Nicholas. *The Light of the Soul: Theories of Ideas in Leibnitz, Malebranche, and Descartes.* Oxford: Oxford University Press, 1995.

_____. "The Reception of Descartes' Philosophy," in *Cambridge Companion to Descartes,* edited by John Cottingham, pp. 393-423.

_____. "The Relation Between Theology and Philosophy," in *Cambridge History of Seventeenth-Century Philosophy,* edited by Daniel Garber and Michael Ayers, vol. I, pp. 363-392.

Jones, Howard. *The Epicurean Tradition.* London: Routledge, 1980.

Jones, Richard Foster. *Ancients and Moderns: A Study of the Rise of the Scientific Movement in Seventeenth-Century England.* 1961. Reprint, New York: Dover, 1982.

Jonge, H. J. de. *De Bestudering van het Nieuwe Testament aan de Noordnederlandse Universiteiten en het Remonstrants Seminarie van 1575 tot 1700.* Amsterdam: Noord-Hollandse Uitg. Mij., 1980.

_____. *Daniel Heinsius and the Textus Receptus of the New Testament: A Study of his Contributions to the Editions of the Greek Testament Printed by the Elzeviers at Leiden in 1624-1633.* Leiden: E. J. Brill, 1971.

_____. "Hugo Grotius: exégète du Nouveau Testament," in *The World of Hugo Grotius (1583-1645)* (Amsterdam: APA, Holland University Press, 1984), pp. 97-115.

_____. "The Study of the New Testament," in *Leiden University in the Seventeenth Century,* edited by Scheurleer and Posthumus Meyjes, pp. 64-109.

Jorissen, Hans. "Zur Struktur des Traktates De Deo in der Summa theologiae des Thomas von Aquin," in *Im Gespräch mit dem dreieinen Gott,* edited by M. Boehnke and H. Heinz (Düsseldorf: Patmos Verlag, 1985), pp. 231-257.

Jourdain, Charles. *La philosophie de saint Thomas d'Aquin.* 2 vols. Paris: Hachette, 1858.

Kaiser, Christopher B. *The Doctrine of God: an Historical Survey.* Westchester, Ill.: Crossway, 1982.

Kantzer, Kenneth. "Calvin and the Holy Scriptures," in *Inspiration and Interpretation*, pp. 115-155.

Karpp, Heinrich. "Zur Geschichte der Bibel in der Kirche des 16. und 17. Jahrhunderts," in *Theologische Rundschau*, N.F., 40 (1983), pp. 128-155.

Katchen, Aaron L. *Christian Hebraists and Dutch Rabbis: Seventeenth Century Apologetics and the Study of Maimonides' "Mishneh Torah"*. Cambridge, MA: Harvard University Press, 1984.

Katz, David S. "Isaac Vossius and the English Biblical Critics," in *Scepticism and Irreligion*, edited by R. Popkin and A. Vanderjagt, pp. 142-184.

Kautsch, Emil. *Johannes Buxtorf der Ältere*. Basel: Detloff, 1879.

Keane, Kevin P. "Why Creation: Bonaventure and Thomas Aquinas on God as Creative Good," in *The Downside Review*, 93 (1975), pp. 100-121.

Keller, Rudolf. *Der Schlüssel zur Schrift, Die Lehre vom Wort Gottes bei Matthias Flacius Illyricus*. Hannover: Luther Verlagshaus, 1984.

Kelley, Maurice, "Milton and the Trinity," in *Huntington Library Quarterly*, 33 (1970), pp. 317-318.

————. "Milton's Arianism Again Considered," in *Harvard Theological Review*, 54 (1961), pp. 195-205.

Kelly, Douglas F. "A Rehabilitation of Scholasticism? A Review Article on Richard A. Muller's *Post-Reformation Reformed Dogmatics*, Vol. I, *Prolegomena to Theology*," in *Scottish Bulletin of Evangelical Theology*, 6/2 (1988), pp. 112-122.

Kelly, J. N. D. *Early Christian Doctrines*. New York: Harper & Row, 1960.

Kelly, Matthew J. "Power in Aquinas," in *The Thomist*, 43 (1979), pp. 474-479.

Kendall, R. T. *Calvin and English Calvinism to 1649*. Oxford: Oxford University Press, 1979.

Kennedy, Leonard A. "Divine Omnipotence and the Contingency of Creatures, Oxford, 1330-1350 A.D.," in *The Modern Schoolman*, 61 (1983/84), pp. 249-258.

————. "Early Fourteenth-Century Franciscans and Divine Absolute Power," in *Franciscan Studies*, 50 (1990), pp. 197-233.

Kennedy, Leonard A. and Romano, Margaret E. "John Went, O.F.M. and Divine Omnipotence," in *Franciscan Studies*, 47 (1987), pp. 138-170.

Kennedy, Rick. "The Alliance Between Puritanism and Cartesian Logic at Harvard, 1687-1735," *Journal fo the History of Ideas*, 51 (1990), pp. 549-572.

Kevan, Ernest F. *The Grace of Law: A Study of Puritan Theology*. London: Carey Kingsgate Press, 1963.

Kickel, Walter. *Vernunft und Offenbarung bei Theodore Beza*. Neukirchen: Neukirchner Verlag, 1967.

Kiecker, James George. "The Hermeneutical Principles and Exegetical Methods of Nicholas of Lyra, O. F. M. (ca. 1270-1349). Ph.D. diss., Marquette University, 1978.

Kirby, Ethyn W. "'The Naked Truth': a Plan for Church Unity," in *Church History*, 7 (1935), pp. 45-61.

Kirste, Reinhard. *Das Zeugnis des Geistes und das Zeugnis der Schrift: das testimonium spiritus sancti als hermeneutisch-polemischer Zentralbegriff bei Johann Gerhard in der Auseinandersetzung mit Robert Bellarmins Schriftverständnis*. Göttingen: Vandenhoeck und Ruprecht, 1976.

Klauber, Martin I. "Between Protestant Orthodoxy and Rationalism: Fundamental Articles in the Early Career of Jean LeClerc," in *Journal of the History of Ideas*, 54 (1993), pp. 611-36.

_____ . *Between Reformed Scholasticism and Pan-Protestantism: Jean-Alphonse Turretin (1671-1737) and Enlightened Orthodoxy at the Academy of Geneva*. Selinsgrove: Susquehanna University Press, 1994.

_____ . "Calvin on Fundamental Articles and Ecclesiastical Union," in *Westminster Theological Journal*, 54 (1992), pp. 341-48.

_____ . "The Context and Development of the Views of Jean-Alphonse Turrettini (1671-1737) on Religious Authority." Ph.D. diss., University of Wisconsin-Madison, 1987.

_____ . "Continuity and Discontinuity in Post-Reformation Reformed Theology: An Evaluation of the Muller Thesis," in *Journal of the Evangelical Theological Society*, 33 (1990), pp. 467-475.

_____ . "The Drive Toward Protestant Union in Early Eighteenth-Century Geneva: Jean-Alphonse Turretini on the 'Fundamental Articles' of Faith," in *Church History*, 61 (1992), pp. 334-349.

_____ . "The Eclipse of Scholasticism in Eighteenth-Century Geneva: Natural Theology from Jean-Alphonse Turretin to Jacob Vernet," in *The Identity of Geneva: The Christian Commonwealth, 1564-1864*, edited by John B. Roney and Martin I. Klauber, pp. 129-42.

_____ . "Family Loyalty and Theological Transition in Post-Reformation Geneva: the Case of Bénédict Pictet (1655-1724)," in *Fides et Historia*, 24/1 (1992), pp. 54-67.

_____ . "Francis Turretin on Biblical Accommodation: Loyal Calvinist or Reformed Scholastic?" in *Westminster Theological Journal*, 55 (1993), pp. 73-86.

_____ . "The Helvetic Consensus Formula (1675): An Introduction and Translation," in *Trinity Journal*, 11 (Spring 1990), pp. 103-123.

_____ . "Jean-Alphonse Turrettini and the Abrogation of the Formula Consensus in Geneva," in *Westminster Theological Journal*, 53 (1991), pp. 325-338.

_____ . Jean-Alphonse Turrettini (1671-1737) on Natural Theology: The Triumph of Reason over Revelation at the Academy of Geneva," *Scottish Journal of Theology*, 47/3 (1994) pp. 301-325.

_____ . "Reason, Revelation, and Cartesianism: Louis Tronchin and Enlightened Orthodoxy in Late Seventeenth-Century Geneva," in *Church History*, 59 (1990), pp. 326-339.

_____ . "Reformed Orthodoxy in Transition: Bénédict Pictet (1655-1724) and Enlightened Orthodoxy in Post-Reformation Geneva," in *Later Calvinism*, edited by W. Fred Graham, pp. 93-113.

_____ . "Theological Transition in Geneva from Jean-Alphonse Turretin to Jacob Vernet," in *Reformed Scholasticism*, edited by C. Trueman and R. Clark, pp. 256-70.

_____ . "The Use of Philosophy in the Theology of Johannes Maccovius (1578-1644)," in *Calvin Theological Journal*, 30 (1995) pp. 376-391.

Klauber, Martin I., and Glenn S. Sunshine. "Jean-Alphonse Turrettini on Biblical Accommodation: Calvinist or Socinian?" in *Calvin Theological Journal*, 25 (1990), pp. 7-27.

Klein, Joseph. *Der Gottesbegriff des Johannes Duns Scotus*. Paderborn: Schöningh, 1913.

Klinck, Dennis R. "*Vestigia Trinitatis* in Man and His Works in the English Renaissance," in *Journal of the History of Ideas*, 42 (1981), pp. 13-27.

Klug, Eugene F. *From Luther to Chemnitz; on Scripture and the Word*. Grand Rapids: Eerdmans, 1971.

Kluge, Eike-Henner. "Roscellin and the Medieval Problem of Universals," in *Journal of the History of Philosophy*, 16 (1976), pp. 404-414.

Knapp, Henry M. "Understanding the Mind of God: John Owen and Seventeenth-century Exegetical Methodology." Ph. D. diss., Calvin Theological Seminary, 2002.

Knappen, Marshall. *Tudor Puritanism: A Chapter in the History of Idealism.* Chicago and London: University of Chicago Press, 1939.

Knebel, Sven K. "Leibniz, Middle Knowledge and the Intricacies of World Design," in *Studia Leibnitiana*, 28 (1996), pp. 199-200.

_____. "Scientia Media. Ein diskursarchäologisher Leitfaden durch das 17. Jahrhundert," in *Archiv für Begriffsgeschichte*, 34 (1991), pp. 262-94.

Knott, John Ray. *The Sword of the Spirit: Puritan Responses to the Bible.* Chicago: University of Chicago Press, 1980.

Knowles, David. *The Evolution of Medieval Thought.* New York: Vintage Books, 1962.

Koepf, Ulrich. *Die Anfänge der theologischen Wissenschaftstheorie im 13. Jahrhundert.* Tübingen: J. C. B. Mohr, 1974.

Kolb, Robert A. *Luther's Heirs Define His Legacy: Studies in Lutheran Confessionalism.* Brookfield, Vt.: Ashgate / Variorum, 1996.

_____. *Martin Luther as Prophet, Teacher, and Hero: Images of the Reformer, 1520-1620.* Grand Rapids: Baker Book House, 1999.

_____. "The Ordering of the *Loci Communes Theologici*: The Structuring of the Melanchthonian Dogmatic Tradition," in *Concordia Journal*, 23/4 (1997), pp. 317-37.

_____. "Teaching the Text: The Commonplace Method in Sixteenth Century Lutheran Biblical Commentary," in *Bibliothèque d'Humanisme et Renaissance*, 49 (1987), pp. 571-585.

Köhler, Walther. *Ulrich Zwingli und die Reformation in der Schweiz.* Tübingen: J. C. B. Mohr, 1919.

_____. "Zwingli als Theologe," in *Ulrich Zwingli: Zum Gedächtnis der Zürcher Reformation, 1519-1919* (Zürich: Theologischer Verlag, 1919), pp. 9-74.

Kooiman, Willem Jan. *Luther and the Bible.* Translated by John Schmidt. Philadelphia: Muhlenberg Press, 1961.

Kors, Alan Charles, "Scepticism and the Problem of Atheism in Early-Modern France," in *Scepticism and Irreligion*, edited by R. Popkin and A. Vanderjagt, pp. 185-215.

Köstlin, Julius. "Calvin's Institutio nach Form und Inhalt, in ihrer geschlichtlichen Entwicklung" in *Theologische Studien und Kritiken*, 41 (1868), pp. 7-62, 410-486.

_____. *The Theology of Luther in its Historical Development and Inner Harmony.* 2 vols. Translated by Charles E. Hay. Philadelphia: Lutheran Publication Society, 1897. Reprint, St. Louis: Concordia, 1986.

Kot, Stanislaw. *Socinianism in Poland; the social and political ideas of the Polish Antitrinitarians in the sixteenth and seventeenth centuries.* Translated by Earl Morse Wilbur. Boston, Starr King Press, 1957.

Kraus, Hans Joachim. "Calvin's Exegetical Principles," in *Interpretation* 31 (1977), pp. 329-341.

Krempel, A. *La doctrine de la Trinité chez Saint Thomas: Exposé historique et systematique.* Paris: J. Vrin, 1952.

Krentz, Edgar. *The Historical-Critical Method.* Philadelphia: Fortress, 1975.

Kretzmann, Norman, Anthony Kenny, Jan Pinborg, and Eleanore Stump, eds. *The Cambridge History of Later Medieval Philosophy: Form the Rediscovery of Aristotle to the Disintegration of Scholasticism, 1100-1600.* Cambridge: Cambridge University Press, 1982.

Kristeller, Paul Oskar. "Augustine and the Early Renaissance," in *Studies in Renaissance Thought and Letters*, 2 vols. Rome, 1956-85), vol. 1, pp. 355-372.

_____. "Humanism," in *The Cambridge History of Renaissance Philosophy*, edited by C. Schmitt, Q. Skinner, and E. Kessler, pp. 113-137.

_____. *Medieval Aspects of Renaissance Learning*. Edited by E. P. Mahoney. Durham, N.C.: Duke University Press, 1974.

_____. "Renaissance Humanism and Classical Antiquity," in *Renaissance Humanism: Foundations, Forms, and Legacy*, edited by A. Rabil, vol. I, pp. 5-16.

_____. *Renaissance Thought: The Classic, Scholastic, and Humanist Strains*. New York: Harper & Row, 1961.

_____. "Thomism and the Italian Thought of the Renaissance," in *Medieval Aspects of Renaisssance Learning*, pp. 29-91.

Kristeller, Paul Oskar and P. P. Wiener, eds. *Renaissance Essays from the Journal of the History of Ideas*. New York: Harper & Row, 1968.

Krivocheine, Basil. "Simplicité de la nature divine et les distinctions en Dieu selon S. Grégoire de Nysse," in *Studia Patristica* 16/2 (1985), pp. 389-411.

_____. "Simplicity of the Divine Nature and Distinctions in God, according to St. Gregory of Nyssa," in *St. Vladimir's Quarterly*, 21 (1977), pp. 76-104.

Kroner, Richard. *Speculation and Revelation in the Age of Christian Philosophy*. Philadelphia: Westminster, 1969.

Krook, Dorothea. *John Sergeant and his Circle: A Study of Three Seventeenth-Century English Aristotelians*. Edited with an introduction by Beverley C. Southgate. Leiden: E. J. Brill, 1993.

Kropatscheck, Friedrich. *Das Schriftprinzip der lutherischen Kirche. Geschichte und dogmatische Untersuchungen. I. Die vorgeschichte. Das Erbe des Mittelalters*. Leipzig: Deichert, 1904.

Krusche, Werner. *Das Wirken des Heiligen Geistes nach Calvin*. Göttingen: Vandenhoeck & Ruprecht, 1957.

Kuizenga, Henry. "The Relation of God's Grace to His Glory in John Calvin," in *Reformation Studies: Essays in Honor of Roland H. Bainton*, edited by Franklin H. Littell (Richmond: John Knox, 1962), pp. 95-105.

Kümmel, Werner Georg. *The New Testament: The History of the Investigation of Its Problems*. Translated by S. McLean Gilmour and Howard C. Kee. Nashville: Abingdon, 1972.

Künzli, Edwin. "Quellenproblem und mystischer Schriftsinn in Zwinglis Genesis- und Exoduskommentar," *Zwingliana* 9 (1950-51): 185-207, 253-307.

_____. "Zwingli als Ausleger des Alten Testament," in *Huldreich Zwinglis Sämtliche Werke*, edited by Emil Egli, Georg Finsler, et al., 14 vols. (Zürich: Berichthaus, 1959), XIV, pp. 871-99.

Kurtz, J. H. *Church History*. Translated by John Macpherson. 3 vols. New York: Funk & Wagnalls, 1890.

Kürzinger, Josef. *Alfonsus Vargas Tolentanus und seine theologishe Einleitungslehre. Ein Beitrag zur Geschichte der Scholastik in 14. Jahrhundert*. Beitrage zur Geschichte der Philosophie und Theologie des Mittelalters, XXII/5, 6. Munich: Aschendorff, 1930.

Kusukawa, Sachiko. *The Transformation of Natural Philosophy: the Case of Philip Melanchthon*. Cambridge and New York: Cambridge University Press, 1995.

Kuyper, Abraham. *Johannes Maccovius*. Leiden: D. Donner, 1899.

Kyle, Richard. "The Divine Attributes in John Knox's Concept of God," in *Westminster Theological Journal*, 48/1 (1986), pp. 161-172.

————. "John Knox: The Main Themes of his Thought," in *The Princeton Seminary Bulletin*, 4/2 (1983), pp. 101-112.

Lagree, Jacqueline. "Leibnitz et Spinoza," in *Disguised and Overt Spinozism*, edited by W. Van Bunge, pp. 137-155.

Laistner, M. L. W. "Antiochene Exegesis in Western Europe During the Middle Ages," in *Harvard Theological Review*, 40 (1947), pp. 19-31.

Lampros, Dean George. "A New Set of Spectacles: The *Assembly's Annotations*, 1645-1657," in *Renaissance and Reformation*, 19/4 (1995), pp. 33-46.

Lane, A. N. S. *Calvin and Bernard of Clairvaux*. Princeton: Princeton Theological Seminary, 1996.

————. "Calvin's Use of the Fathers and the Medievals," in *Calvin Theological Journal*, 16 (1981), pp. 149-205.

————. "Did Calvin Use Lippoman's *Catena in Genesim?*" in *Calvin Theological Journal*, 31/2 (1996), pp. 404-19.

————. *John Calvin: Student of the Church Fathers*. Grand Rapids: Baker Books, 1999.

————. "Scripture, Tradition and Church: An Historical Survey," in *Vox Evangelica*, 9 (1975), pp. 37-55.

————. "The Sources of Calvin's Citations in his Genesis Commentary," in *Interpreting the Bible: Historical and Theological Studies in Honour of David F. Wright*, edited by A. N. S. Lane (Leicester: Apollos, 1997), pp. 47-97.

Lang, Albert. *Heinrich Totting von Oyta: Ein Beitrag zur Entstehungsgeschichte der ersten deutschen Universitäten und zur Problemgeschichte der Spätscholastik*. Münster: Aschendorff, 1937.

————. *Die Loci theologici des Melchior Cano und die Methode des dogmatischen Beweises: Ein Beitrag zur theologischen Methodologie und ihrer Geschichte*. Münchener Studien zur historischen Theologie, 6. Munich: Kösel & Pustet, 1925.

————. *Die theologische Prinzipienlehre der mittelalterlichen Scholastik* Freiburg: Herder, 1964.

————. *Die Wege der Glaubensbegründung bei den Scholastikern des 14. Jahrhunderts*. Münster: Aschendorff, 1930.

Lang, August. *Puritanismus und Pietismus*. Neukirchen: Neukirchner Verlag, 1941.

Langston, Douglas C. *God's Willing Knowledge: the Influence of Scotus' Analysis of Omniscience*. University Park, Pa.: Pennsylvania State U.P., 1986.

Laplanche, François. "Débats et combats autour de la Bible dans l'orthodoxie réformée," in *Le Grand Siècle de la Bible*, edited by Armogathe, pp. 117-140.

————. *L'Écriture, le sacré et l'historie: Érudits politiques protestants devant la bible en France au XVIIᵉ siècle*. Amsterdam and Maarssen: APA-Holland University Press / Lille: Presses Universitaires, 1986.

————. *L'Évidence du dieu chrétien. Religion, culture et société dans l'apologétique protestante de la France classique (1576-1670)*. Strasbourg: Association des Publications de la Faculté de Théologie Protestante, 1983.

La Serviére, Joseph de. *La théologie de Bellarmin*. Paris: Beauchesne, 1909.

Lau, F. "Orthodoxie, altprotestantische," s.v. in *Religion in Geschichte und Gegenwart*, dritte Auflage.

Laurent, François. *La philosophie du XVIIIe siècle et le Christianisme*. Paris, 1866. Reprint, Geneva: Slatkine, 1972.

Lea, Thomas D. "The Hermeneutics of the Puritans," in *Journal of the Evangelical Theological Society*, 39 (1996), pp. 271-284.

Le Bachelet, X. "Dieu. Sa nature d'après les pères," in *Dictionnaire de théologie catholique*, vol. 4/1, cols. 1023-1152.

————. "Baius, Michel," in *Dictionnaire de théologie catholique*, vol. 2/1, col. 37-111.

Lebram, J. H. C. "Hebräische Studien zwischen Ideal and Wirklichkeit an der Universität Leiden in den Jahren 1575-1619," in *Nederlands Archief voor Kerkgeschiedenis*, 56 (1975), pp. 317-357.

Lebreton, Jules. *History of the Dogma of the Trinity*. Translated by A. Thorold. New York and Chicago: Benziger: 1939.

Le Brun, Jacques. "Meaning and Scope of the Return to Origins in Richard Simon's Work," in *Trinity Journal*, n.s. 3 (1982), pp. 57-70.

Lechner, Joan Marie. *Renaissance Concepts of the Commonplace*. New York: Pageant Press, 1962.

Lecky, William Edward Hartpole. *History of the Rise and Influence of the Spirit of Rationalism in Europe*. 2 vols. Rev. ed. London: Longmans, Green, 1910.

Lecler, Joseph. "Littéralisme bibligue et typologie au XVIᵉ siècle," in *Recherches de Science Religieuse*, 51 (1953), pp. 76-95.

————. "Protestantisme et 'libre examen': Les étapes et le vocabulaire d'une controverse," in *Recherches de science religieuse*, 57 (1969), pp. 321-374.

Leeuwen, A. van. "L'Église, règle de foi, dans les écrits de Guillaume d'Occam," in *Ephemerides theologicae lovaniensis*, 11 (1934), pp. 249-288.

Leeuwen, Henry G. van. *The Problem of Certainty in English Thought, 1630-1690*. Pref. by Richard H. Popkin. Den Haag: Nijhoff, 1963.

Leff, Gordon. *Bradwardine and the Pelagians: A Study of His "De causa Dei" and its Opponents*. Cambridge: Cambridge University Press, 1957.

————. *The Dissolution of the Medieval Outlook: An Essay on the Intellectual and Spiritual Change in the Fourteenth Century*. New York: New York University Press, 1976.

————. *Gregory of Rimini: Tradition and Innovation in Fourteenth Century Thought*. Manchester: Manchester University Press, 1961.

————. *Medieval Thought: St. Augustine to Ockham*. Baltimore: Penguin, 1958.

————. *William of Ockham: The Metamorphosis of Scholastic Discourse*. Manchester: Manchester University Press, 1975.

Le Guillou, Marie J. "Le Dieu de Saint Thomas," in *Il pensiero di Tommaso d'Aquino*, edited by A. Lobato (Rome: Herder, 1974), pp. 161-171.

Lehmann, Paul L. "The Reformers' Use of the Bible," in *Theology Today*, vol. 3 (October, 1946), pp. 328-344.

Leijenhorst, Cees. "Hobbes's Theory of Causality and its Aristotelian Background," in *The Monist*, 79 (July, 1996), pp. 426-447.

Leijssen, L. "Martin Bucer und Thomas von Aquin," in *Ephemerides Theologiae Lovaniensis*, 55 (1979), pp. 266-296.

Leinsle, Ulrich G. *Das Ding und die Methode. Methodische Konstitution und Gegenstand der frühen protestantischen Metaphysik*. 2 vols. Augsburg: Maro Verlag, 1985.

————. *Einführung in die scholastische Theologie*. Paderborn: Schöningh, 1995.

Leith. John. *Assembly at Westminster: Reformed Theology in the Making*. Richmond: John Knox, 1973.

Leithart, Peter J. "Stoic Elements in Calvin's Doctrine of the Christian Life," in *Westminster Theological Journal*, 55/1 (1993), pp. 31-54; 55/ 2 (1993), pp. 191-208; 56/1 (1994), pp. 59-85.

Lemaigre, B. M. "Perfection de Dieu et multiplicité des attributs divins. Pourquoi S. Thomas a-t-il inséré la dispute des attributs divins (I Sent., d. 2, q. 1, a. 3) dans son commentaire des Sentences," in *Revue des sciences philosophiques et théologiques*, 50 (1966), pp. 198-277.

Lennon, Thomas M., John M. Nicholas, and John W. Davis. *Problems of Cartesianism*. Kingston and Montreal: McGill-Queen's University Press, 1982.

Letham, Robert W. A. "Amandus Polanus: A Neglected Theologian?" in *Sixteenth Century Journal*, 21/3 (1990), pp. 463-476.

————. "The *Foedus Operum*: Some Factors Accounting for its Development," in *Sixteenth Century Journal*, 14 (1983), pp. 457-467.

————. "Saving Faith and Assurance in Reformed Theology: Zwingli to the Synod of Dort." 2 vols. Ph.D. diss., University of Aberdeen, 1979.

————. "Theodore Beza: A Reassessment," in *Scottish Journal of Theology*, 40 (1987), pp. 25-40.

Levi, A. H. T. "The Breakdown of Scholasticism and the Significance of Evangelical Humanism," in *Philosophical Assessment of Theology*, edited by Gerard Hughes, pp. 101-128.

————, ed. *Humanism in France*. Manchester: Manchester University Press, 1970.

Lewalski, Barbara K. *Protestant Poetics and Seventeenth-Century Religious Lyric*. Princeton: Princeton University Press, 1979.

Lewalter, Ernst. *Spanisch-jesuitisch und deutsch-lutherische Metaphysik des 17. Jahrhunderts*. Hamburg, 1935. Reprint, Darmstadt: Wissenschaftliche Buchgesellschaft, 1968.

Leyden, W. von. *Seventeenth Century Metaphysics: An Examination of Some Main Concepts and Theories*. London: Duckworth, 1968.

Lienhard, Marc. "Les Controverses entre Luthériens et Catholiques à Strasbourg entre 1682 et 1688," in *Bulletin de la Société de l'Histoire du Protestantisme français*, 132 (1986), pp. 132-237.

Lim, Won Taek. *The Covenant Theology of Francis Roberts*. Ph. D. diss., Calvin Theological Seminary, 1999.

Lindbeck, George. "Nominalism and the Problem of Meaning as Illustrated by Pierre D'Ailly on Predestination and Justification," in *Harvard Theological Review*, 52 (1959), pp. 43-60.

Linde, S. van der. "Gereformeerde Scholastiek IV: Calvijn," in *Theologia Reformata*, 29 (1986), pp. 244-266.

————. "Het 'Griekse' Denken in Kerk, Theologie en Geloofspraktijk: Een eerste Inleiding," in *Theologia Reformata*, 28 (1985), pp. 248-268. [The first article in a series on Reformed theology and scholasticism, "Gereformeerde Scholastiek," by van der Linde, van 't Spijker, and Graafland, all cited here by author.]

Liston, R. T. L. "John Calvin's Doctrine of the Sovereignty of God." Ph.D. diss., University of Edinburgh, 1930.

Lloyd, G. E. R. *Aristotle: The Growth and Structure of His Thought*. Cambridge: Cambridge University Press, 1968.

Locher, Gottfried W. *Die Theologie Huldrych Zwinglis im Lichte seiner Christologie, I, Die Gotteslehre*. Zürich: EVZ Verlag, 1952.

Lods, Adolphe. "Astruc et la critique biblique de son temps," in *Revue d'histoire et de philosophie religieuses*, 4 (1924), pp. 109-139, 201-227.

Loemker, Leroy E. "Leibniz and the Herborn Encyclopedists," in *Journal of the History of Ideas*, 22 (1961), pp. 323-338.

_____. *Struggle for Synthesis: The Seventeenth Century Background of Leibniz's Synthesis of Order and Freedom*. Cambridge, Mass.: Harvard University Press, 1972.

Loewe, Raphael J. "The Medieval Christian Hebraists of England: The *Superscriptio Lincolniensis*," in *Hebrew Union College Annual*, 28 (1957), pp. 205-252.

_____. "The Medieval History of the Latin Vulgate," in *Cambridge History of the Bible*, II, pp. 102-154.

Loewenich, Walter von. *Luther's Theology of the Cross*. Translated by W. Bouman. Minneapolis: Augsburg, 1976.

Lohr, Charles H. "Jesuit Aristotelianism and Sixteenth-Century Metaphysics," in *Paradosis: Studies in Memory of Edwin A. Quain*, edited by G. Fletcher and M. B. Schuete (New York: Fordham University press, 1976), pp. 203-220.

_____. "Medieval Latin Aristotle Commentaries," in *Traditio*, 23 (1967), pp. 313-413; 24 (1968), pp. 149-245; 26 (1970), pp. 135-216; 27 (1971), pp. 251-351; 28 (1972), pp. 281-396; 29 (1973), pp. 93-197.

_____. "Metaphysics," in *The Cambridge History of Renaissance Philosophy*, edited by C. Schmitt, Q. Skinner, and E. Kessler, pp. 537-638.

_____. "Renaissance Latin Aristotle Commentaries," in *Studies in the Renaissance*, 21 (1974), pp. 228-289; *Renaissance Quarterly*, 28 (1975), pp. 689-741; 29 (1976), pp. 714-745; 30 (1977), pp. 532-603; 31 (1978), pp. 532-603; 32 (1979), pp. 529-580; 33 (1980), pp. 623-734; 35 (1982), pp. 164-256.

Loonstra, Bert. "De leer van God en Christus in de Nadere Reformatie," in Th. Brienen, et al. *Theologische Aspecten van de Nadere Reformatie* (Zoetermeer: Boekencentrum, 1993), pp. 99-150.

Lortz, Josef. *The Reformation in Germany*. 2 vols. Translated by Ronald Walls. London and New York: Herder & Herder, 1968.

Lotz, David W. "Sola Scriptura: Luther on Authority," in *Interpretation*, 35 (1981), pp. 258-273.

Lovejoy, Arthur O. *The Great Chain of Being*. Cambridge, Mass.: Harvard University Press, 1936.

Lund, Roger D., ed. *The Margins of Orthodoxy: Heterodox Writing and Cultural Response, 1660-1750*. Cambridge: Cambridge University Press, 1995.

The Lutheran Cyclopedia. Rev. ed. Edited by Erwin L. Lucker. St. Louis: Concordia Publishing House, 1975.

Lütgert, Wilhelm. "Calvins Lehre vom Schöpfer," in *Zeitschrift für systematische Theologie*, 1931, pp. 421-440.

MacClintock, Stuart. *Perversity and Error, Studies on the "Averroist" John of Jandun*. Bloomington, Indiana: University of Indiana Press, 1956.

Mack, Peter. *Renaissance Argument: Valla and Agricola in the Traditions of Rhetoric and Dialectic* Leiden: E. J. Brill, 1993.

Mahieu, Léon. "L'eclectisme Suarézien," in *Revue Thomiste*, VIII (1925), pp. 250-285.

_____. *François Suárez: sa philosophie et les rapports qu'elle a avec sa théologie*. Paris: Desclée, de Brouwer, 1921.

Mahoney, Edward P. "Albert the Great and the *Studio patavino* in the late Fifteenth and Early Sixteenth Centuries," in *Albertus Magnus and the Sciences: Commemorative Essays, 1980*, edited by J. A. Weisheipl (Toronto: Pontifical Institute of Medieval Studies, 1979), pp. 537-563.

_____. "Aristotle as 'The Worst Philosopher' (*pessimus naturalis*) and 'The Worst Metaphysician' (*pessimus metaphysicus*): His Reputation among Some Franciscan Philosophers (Bonaventure, Francis of Meyronnes, Antonius Andreas, and Joannes Canonicus) and Later Reactions," in *Die Philosophie im 14. Und 15. Jahrhundert: In Memoriam Konstanty Michalski (1879-1947)*, edited by Olaf Pluta (Amsterdam: Grüner, 1988), pp. 261-273.

_____. "Metaphysical Foundations of the Hierarchy of Being According to Some Late-Medieval and Renaissance Philosophers," in *Philosophies of Existence, Ancient and Modern*, edited by Parviz Morewedge (New York: Fordham University Press, 1982), pp. 165-257.

_____. "St. Thomas and the School of Padua at the End of the Fifteenth Century," in *Proceedings of the American Catholic Philosophical Association*, 48 (1974), pp. 277-285.

Maieru, Alfonso. "À propos de la doctrine de la supposition en théologie trinitaire au XIVe siècle," in *Medieval Semantics and Metaphysics*, edited by E. Bos (Nijmegen: Ingenium, 1985), pp. 221-238.

_____. "Logique et théologie trinitaire: Pierre D'Ailly," in *Preuve et raisons*, edited by Z. Kaluza and P. Vignaux (Paris: J. Vrin, 1984), pp. 253-268.

Malet, Nicole. *Dieu selon Calvin: des mots à la doctrine*. Lausanne: Editions L'Age d'homme, 1977.

Mallard, William. "John Wyclif and the Tradition of Biblical Authority," in *Church History*, 30/1 (March, 1961), pp. 50-60.

Mandonnet, Pierre. "Bañez, Dominique," in *Dictionnaire de théologie catholique*, vol. 2/1, col. 140-145.

_____. "Chronologie des écrits scriptuaires de Saint Thomas d'Aquin," in *Revue Thomiste*. 33 (1928), pp. 25-45, 116-166, 211-245; 34 (1929), pp. 53-66, 132-145, 489-519.

_____. "Dominicains (Travaux des) sur les Saintes Écritures," in *Dictionnaire de la Bible*, 2/2 , cols. 1463-1482.

_____. "L'Enseignement de la Bible selon l'usage de Paris," in *Revue Thomiste*, NS 12 (1929), pp. 489-519.

Mangenot, Eugène. "Allégoires bibliques," in *Dictionnaire de théologie catholique*, 1/1, cols. 833-836.

_____. "Concordances," in *Dictionnaire de la Bible*, vol. 2/1, cols. 892-905.

_____. "Correctoires de La Bible," in *Dictionnaire de la Bible*, vol. 2/1, cols. 1022-1026.

_____. "Hugues de St Cher," in *Dictionnaire de théologie catholique*, vol. 7/1, cols. 221-239

_____. "Inspiration de l'Écriture," in *Dictionnaire de théologie catholique*, vol. 7/2, cols. 2068-2266.

_____, and Rivière, J. "Interprétation de l'Écriture," in *Dictionnaire de théologie catholique*, vol. 7/2, cols. 2290-2343.

Mann, William. "Divine Simplicity," in *Religious Studies*, 21 (1982), pp. 451-471.

_____. "Simplicity and Immutability in God," in *The Concept of God*, edited by Thomas V. Morris (Oxford and New York: Oxford University Press, 1987), pp. 253-267.

Manschreck, Clyde. *Melanchthon: The Quiet Reformer*. New York and Nashville: Abingdon, 1958.

_____. "Reason and Conversion in the Thought of Melanchthon," in *Reformation Studies: Essays in Honor of R. H. Bainton*, edited by Franklin H. Littell (Richmond: John Knox, 1962), pp. 168-180.

Margerie, Bertrand de. *The Christian Trinity in History*. Translated by Edmund J. Fortman. Still River, Mass.: St. Bede's, 1975.

Margival, Henri. *Essai sur Richard Simon et la critique biblique en 17ᵉ siècle*. Paris, 1900. Reprint, Geneva: Slatkine, 1970.

Marion, Jean-Luc. "The Idea of God," in *Cambridge History of Seventeenth-Century Philosophy*, edited by Daniel Garber and Michael Ayers, vol. I, pp. 265-304.

Masai, François. "L'enseignement d'Aristote dans les collèges du XVIᵉ siècle," in *Platon et Aristote à la Renaissance*, pp. 147-154.

Massaut, Jean-Pierre, "Lefèvre d'Etaples et l'exègèse au XVIᵉ siècle," in *Revue d'Histoire Ecclésiastique*, 78 (1983), pp. 73-78.

Masson, David. *The Life of John Milton: Narrated in Connexion with the Political, Ecclesiastical, and Literary History of his Time*. 7 vols. 1877-96. Reprint, New York, Peter Smith,1946.

Masson, Françoise. "Scolastique," in *Encyclopédie philosophique universelle*, II/2, pp. 2328-9.

Maurer, Armand. "Boetius of Dacia and the Double Truth," in *Medieval Studies*, 17 (1955), pp. 233-239.

_____. "John of Jandun and the Divine Causality," in *Medieval Studies*, 17 (1955), pp. 185-207.

_____. *Medieval Philosophy*. New York: Random House, 1962.

_____. *The Philosophy of William of Ockham in the Light of its Principles*. Toronto: Pontifical Institute of Mediaeval Studies, 1999.

Maurer, Armand, ed. *St. Thomas Aquinas "On Being Essence."* Toronto: Pontifical Institute of Medieval Studies, 1968.

McComish, William A. *The Epigones: A Study of the Theology of the Genevan Academy at the Time of the Synod of Dort, with special reference to Giovanni Diodati*. Allison Rark, Pa.: Pickwick Publications, 1989.

McCosh, James. "Introduction to Charnock's Works," in *The Complete Works of Stephen Charnock, B.D.*, 5 vols. (Edinburgh: James Nichol, 1864), I, pp. vii-xlviii

McCoy, Charles S. "The Covenant Theology of Johannes Cocceius," Ph.D. diss., Yale University, 1956.

_____. "Johannes Cocceius: Federal Theologian," in *Scottish Journal of Theology*, XVI (1963), pp. 352-370.

McCoy, Charles S., and J. Wayne Baker. *Fountainhead of Federalism: Heinrich Bullinger and the Covenantal Tradition*. Louisville, KY: Westminster/John Knox Press, 1991.

McCulloh, Gerald O., ed. *Man's Faith and Freedom: The Theological Influence of Jacobus Arminius*. New York and Nashville: Abingdon, 1962.

McDonald, H. D. *Theories of Revelation: An Historical Study, 1700-1860*. Grand Rapids: Baker Book House, 1979.

McGahagan, Thomas Arthur. "Cartesianism in the Netherlands, 1639-1676; the New Science and the Calvinist Counter-Reformation." Ph.D. diss., University of Pennsylvania, 1976.

McGiffert, A. C. *Protestant Thought Before Kant*. London, 1911. Reprint, New York: Harper & Row, 1961.

McGiffert, Michael. "Grace and Works: the Rise and Division of Covenant Divinity in Elizabethan Puritanism," in *Harvard Theological Review*, 75/4 (1982), pp. 463-502.

_____. "From Moses to Adam: the Making of the Covenant of Works," in *Sixteenth Century Journal*, 19/2 (1988), pp. 131-155.

McGowan, Andrew T. B. "Federal Theology as a Theology of Grace," in *Scottish Bulletin of Evangelical Theology*, 2 (1984), pp. 41-50.

McGrath, Alister E. "John Calvin and Late Medieval Thought. A Study in Late Medieval influences upon Calvin's Theological Development," in *Archiv für Reformationsgeschichte*, 77 (1986), pp. 58-78.

_____. *The Intellectual Origins of the European Reformation*. Oxford: Blackwell, 1987.

_____. *A Life of John Calvin*. Oxford: Blackwell, 1990.

_____. *Luther's Theology of the Cross: Martin Luther's Theological Breakthrough*. Oxford: Blackwell, 1985.

_____. *Reformation Thought: An Introduction*. Oxford: Blackwell, 1993.

_____. "Reformation to Enlightenment," in *The Science of Theology*, edited by Paul Avis, (Grand Rapids: Eerdmans, 1986), pp. 158-160.

McKane, W. "Calvin as an Old Testament Commentator," in *Nederlands Gereformeerde Teologiese Tydskrift*, 25 (1984), pp. 250-259.

McKeon, Richard. *The Philosophy of Spinoza: The Unity of His Thought*. Woodbridge, Conn.: Ox Bow Press, 1987.

McKim, Donald K. "The Functions of Ramism in William Perkins' Theology," in *Sixteenth Century Journal*, 16 (1985), pp. 503-517.

_____. "John Owen's Doctrine of Scripture in Historical Perspective," in *The Evangelical Quarterly*, 45/4 (Oct.-Dec. 1973), pp. 195-207.

_____. *Ramism in William Perkins' Theology*. New York and Bern: Peter Lang, 1987.

_____. "William Perkins' Use of Ramism as an Exegetical Tool," in William Perkins, *A Cloud of Faithful Witnesses: Commentary on Hebrews 11*, edited by Gerald T. Sheppard, *Pilgrim Classic Commentaries*, vol. 3 (New York: Pilgrim Press, 1990), pp. 32-45.

McLachlan, Herbert J. *Socinianism in Seventeenth-Century England*. London: Oxford University Press, 1951.

McLelland, Joseph C., ed. *Peter Martyr Vermigli and Italian Reform*. Waterloo: Wilfrid Laurier University Press, 1980.

_____. "Peter Martyr Vermigli: Scholastic or Humanist?" in *Peter Martyr Vermigli and Italian Reform*, edited by J. McLelland, pp. 141-151.

McNally, Robert E. *The Bible in the Early Middle Ages*. Woodstock Papers, 4. Westminster, Md.: Newman Press, 1959.

_____. "Christian Tradition and the Early Middle Ages," in *Perspectives on Scripture and Tradition*, edited by Joseph F. Kelly, pp. 37-59.

_____. "The Council of Trent and Vernacular Bibles," in *Theological Studies*, 27 (1966), pp. 204-207.

_____. "Medieval Exegesis," in *Theological Studies*, 22 (1961), pp. 445-454.

_____. "Tradition at the Beginning of the Reformation," in *Perspectives on Scripture and Tradition*, edited by Joseph F. Kelly, pp. 60-83.

McNeill, John T. *The History and Character of Calvinism*. New York: Oxford University Press, 1954.

_____. "History of the Interpretation of the Bible: II. Medieval and Reformation Period," in *The Interpreters Bible*, 12 vols. (Nashville: Abingdon, 1951-1957), Vol. I, pp. 115-126. [See also Grant, Robert M. and Terrien, Samuel.]

_____. "The Significance of the Word of God for Calvin," *Church History*, 28/2 (June 1959), pp. 131-146.

Meeter, H. Henry. *The Fundamental Principle of Calvinism*. Grand Rapids: Eerdmans, 1930.

Meijering, E. P. "The Fathers in Calvinist Orthodoxy: Systematic Theology," in *The Reception of the Church Fathers in the West*, edited by I. Backus, II, pp. 867-88.

_____. *Reformierte Scholastik und patristische Theologie: die Bedeutung des Vaterbeweises in der Institutio theologiae elencticae F. Turretins: unter besonderer Berucksichtigung der Gotteslehre und Christologie*. Nieuwkoop: De Graaf, 1991.

Menges, Matthew C. *The Concept of Univocity regarding the Predication of God and Creature according to William Ockham*. St. Bonaventure, New York: Franciscan Institute, 1952.

Merrill, Eugene H. "Rashi, Nicholas de Lyra and Christian Exegesis," in *Westminster Theological Journal*, 38 (1975/76), pp. 66-79.

Mersch, E. "L'objet de la théologie et le 'Christus totus'," in *Recherches de science religieuse*, 26 (1936), pp. 129-157.

Metzger, Bruce M. *The Text of the New Testament: Its Transmission, Corruption, and Restoration*. 3rd ed., enlarged. New York: Oxford University Press, 1992.

Mews, Constant J. "Nominalism and Theology before Abelard: New Light on Roscellin of Compiègne," in *Vivarium*, 30 (1992), pp. 4-33.

Meyer, Carl S. "Erasmus on the Study of the Scriptures," in *Concordia Theological Monthly*, 40 (1969), pp. 734-746.

Meylan, Edward F. "The Stoic Doctrine of Indifferent Things and the Conception of Christian Liberty in Calvin' s *Institutio Religionis Christianae*," in *Romanic Review* 28 (1937), pp. 135-145.

Michel, A. "Essence," in *Dictionnaire de théologie catholique*, vol. 5/1, cols. 831-850.

_____. "Noms divins," in *Dictionnaire de théologie catholique*, vol. 11/1, cols. 784-793.

_____. "Processions divines," in *Dictionnaire de théologie catholique*, vol. 13/1, cols. 645-662.

_____. "Relations divines," in *Dictionnaire de théologie catholique*, vol. 13/2, cols. 2135-2156.

_____. "Trinité. La théologie latine du VI au XX siècle," in *Dictionnaire de théologie catholique*, vol. 15/2, cols. 1702-1830.

Mildenberger, Friedrich. *Theology of the Lutheran Confessions*. Translated by Erwin L. Lueker, edited by Robert C. Schultz. Philadelphia: Fortress, 1986.

Minges, Parthenius. *Der Gottesbegriff des Duns Scotus*. Vienna, 1907.

_____. *Ioannis Duns Scoti Doctrina Philosophica et Theologica*. 2 vols. Quaracchi: Collegium S. Bonaventurae, 1930.

_____. *Das Verhältnis zwischen Glauben und Wissen, Theologie und Philosophie nach D. Scotus*. Paderborn: Schöningh, 1908.

Moldaenke, Günther. *Schriftverständnis und Schriftdeutung im Zeitalter der Reformation*. Stuttgart: W. Kohlhammer, 1936.

Moltmann, Jürgen. "Zur Bedeutung des Petrus Ramus für Philosophie und Theologie in Calvinismus," *Zeitschrift für Kirchengeschichte*, LXVII (1956-57), pp. 295-318.

Montgomery, John Warwick. "Sixtus of Siena and Roman Catholic Biblical Scholarship in the Reformation Period," in *Archiv für Reformationsgeschichte*, 55 (1964), pp. 214-233.

Moreall, John. "The Aseity of God in St. Anselm," in *Studia Theologica: Scandinavian Journal of Theology*, 36/1 (1982), pp. 37-46.

Moreau, Joseph. "De la concordance d'Aristote avec Platon," in *Platon et Aristote à la Renaissance*, pp. 45-58.

Moreau, Pierre-Francois "Le Stoicisme aux XVII et XVIII siecles: Calvin et le Stoicisme," in *Cahiers de Philosophie Politique et Juridique* (Caen: Centre de publications de l'Universitae de Caen, 1994), pp. 11-23.

Muehlen, Karl Heinz. "Zur Gotteslehre M. Luthers auf dem Hintergrund der mittelalterlichen Theologie," in *Zeitschrift der Luther-Gesellschaft*, 59/2 (1988), pp. 53-68.

_____. "Keckermann, Bartholomäus," in *RE*, X, pp. 195-196.

Mueller, J. Theodore. "Luther and the Bible," in *Inspiration and Interpretation*, pp. 87-114.

Müller, E. F. Karl. *Die Bekenntnisschriften der reformierten Kirche. In authentischen Texten mit geschichtlicher Einleitung und Register.* Leipzig: Deichert, 1903.

Müller, Johannes. *Martin Bucers Hermeneutik.* Gütersloh: Gerd Mohn, 1965.

Muller, Richard A. *Ad fontes argumentorum: The Sources of Reformed Theology in the 17th Century.* Belle van Zuylenleerstoel Inaugural Address, delivered 11 May, 1999, Universiteit Utrecht. *Utrechtse Theologische Reeks*, deel 40. Utrecht: Faculteit der Godgeleerdheid, 1999.

_____. *After Calvin: Studies in the Development of a Theological Tradition.* New York: Oxford University Press, 2003.

_____. "Arminius and the Scholastic Tradition," in *Calvin Theological Journal*, vol. 24, no.2 (November 1989), pp. 263-277.

_____. "The Barth Legacy: New Athanasius or Origen Redivivus? A Response to T. F. Torrance," in *The Thomist*, 54/4 (October 1990), pp. 673-704.

_____. "Biblical Interpretation in the Era of the Reformation: The View From the Middle Ages," in *Biblical Interpretation in the Era of the Reformation*, edited by Muller and Thompson pp. 3-22.

_____. *Christ and the Decree: Christology and Predestination in Reformed Theology from Calvin to Perkins.* Durham, N.C.: Labyrinth Press, 1986. Reprint, Grand Rapids: Baker Book House, 1988.

_____. "Christ in the Eschaton: Calvin and Moltmann on the Duration of the *Munus Regium*," in *The Harvard Theological Review*, 74/1 (1981), pp. 31-59.

_____. "Christ — the Revelation or the Revealer? Brunner and Reformed Orthodoxy on the Doctrine of the Word of God," in *Journal of the Evangelical Theological Society*, vol. 26/3 (Sept. 1983), pp. 307-319.

_____. "The Christological Problem in the Thought of Jacobus Arminius," in *Nederlands Archief voor Kerkgeschiedenis*, vol. 68 (1988), pp. 145-163.

_____. *Dictionary of Latin and Greek Theological Terms: Drawn Principally from Protestant Scholastic Theology.* Grand Rapids: Baker Book House, 1985.

_____. "The Dogmatic Function of St. Thomas' Proofs: a Protestant Appreciation," in *Fides et Historia*, XXIV (1992), pp. 15-29.

_____. "*Duplex cognitio Dei* in the Theology of Early Reformed Orthodoxy," in *Sixteenth Century Journal*, X/2 (1979), pp. 51-61.

_____. "The Federal Motif in Remonstrant Theology from Arminius to Limborch," in *Nederlands Archief voor Kerkgeschiedenis*, 62/1 (1982), pp. 102-122.

_____. "Found (No Thanks to Theodore Beza): One 'Decretal' Theology," in *Calvin Theological Journal*, 32/1 (April, 1997), pp. 145-51.

_____. "The Foundation of Calvin's Theology: Scripture as Revealing God's Word," in *The Duke Divinity School Review*, 44/1 (1979), pp. 14-23.

_____. *God, Creation and Providence in the Thought of Jacob Arminius: Sources and Directions of Scholastic Protestantism in the Era of Early Orthodoxy*. Grand Rapids: Baker Book House, 1991.

_____. "God, Predestination, and the Integrity of the Created Order: A Note on Patterns in Arminius' Theology," in *Later Calvinism*, edited by W. Fred Graham, pp. 431-446.

_____. "Grace, Election, and Contingent Choice: Arminius's Gambit and the Reformed Response," in *The Grace of God and the Bondage of the Will*, edited by Thomas Schreiner and Bruce Ware, vol. II, pp. 251-78.

_____. "The Hermeneutic of Promise and Fulfillment in Calvin's Exegesis of the Old Testament Prophecies of the Kingdom," in *The Bible in the Sixteenth Century*, edited, with an introduction by David C. Steinmetz (Durham, N.C.: Duke University Press, 1990). pp. 68-82.

_____. "J. J. Rambach and the Dogmatics of Scholastic Pietism," in *Consensus: A Canadian Lutheran Journal of Theology*, 16/2 (1990), pp. 7-27.

_____. "John Gill and the Reformed Tradition: A Study in the Reception of Protestant Orthodoxy in the Eighteenth Century," in *The Life and Thought of John Gill (1697-1771): A Tercentennial Appreciation*, edited by Michael A. G. Haykin (Leiden: E. J. Brill, 1997), pp. 51-68.

_____. Joseph Hall — Rhetor, Theologian, and Exegete: His Contribution to the History of Interpretation," in Joseph Hall, *Salomons Divine Arts*, edited by Gerald T. Sheppard, *Pilgrim Classic Commentaries*, vol. 4 (New York: Pilgrim Press, 1992), pp. 11-37.

_____. "'The Only Way of Man's Salvation': Scripture in the Westminster Confession," in *Calvin Studies VIII: The Westminster Confession in Current Thought*, papers presented at the Colloquium on Calvin Studies (Davidson College, January 26-27, 1996), pp. 14-33.

_____. "*Ordo docendi*: Melanchthon and the Organization of Calvin's *Institutes*, 1536-1543," in *Melanchthon in Europe: His Work and Influence beyond Wittenberg*, edited by Karin Maag (Grand Rapids: Baker Book House, 1999), pp. 123-140.

_____. "Perkins' A Golden Chaine: Predestinarian System or Schematized Ordo Salutis?" in *Sixteenth Century Journal*, IX/1 (1978), pp. 69-81.

_____. "The Problem of Protestant Scholasticism — A Review and Definition," in *Reformation and Scholasticism*, edited by W. van Asselt and E. Dekker, pp. 45-64.

_____. "Scholasticism Protestant and Catholic: Francis Turretin on the Object and Principles of Theology," in *Church History*, 55/2 (1986), pp. 193-205.

_____. "The Spirit and the Covenant: John Gill's Critique of the *Pactum Salutis*," in *Foundations: A Baptist Journal of History and Theology*, 24/1 (January-March, 1981), pp. 4-14.

_____. "The Starting Point of Calvin's Theology: An Essay-Review," in *Calvin Theological Journal*, 36/2 (2001), pp. 314-341.

_____. "Theodore Beza: His Life, Work, and Contribution to the Reformed Tradition," in *The Reformation Theologians: An Introduction to Theology in the Early Modern Period*, edited by Carter Lindberg (Oxford: Blackwell, 2001), pp. 213-224.

_____. *The Unaccommodated Calvin: Studies in the Formation of a Theological Tradition*. New York: Oxford University Press, 2000.

_____. "The Use and Abuse of a Document: Beza's *Tabula praedestinationis*, the Bolsec Controversy, and the Origins of Reformed Orthodoxy," in *Protestant Scholasticism: Essays in Reappraisal*, edited by Carl Trueman and Scott Clark (Carlisle: Paternoster Press, 1999), pp. 33-61.

_____. "William Perkins and the Protestant Exegetical Tradition: Interpretation, Style and Method in the Commentary on Hebrews 11," in William Perkins, *A Cloud of Faithful Witnesses: Commentary on Hebrews 11*, edited by Gerald T. Sheppard, *Pilgrim Classic Commentaries*, vol. 3 (New York: Pilgrim Press, 1990), pp. 71-94.

Muller, Richard A., and John L. Thompson. *Biblical Interpretation in the Era of the Reformation: Essays Presented to David C. Steinmetz in Honor of His Sixtieth Birthday*. Grand Rapids: Eerdmans, 1996.

Muller, Richard A., and John L. Thompson, "The Significance of Precritical Exegesis: Retrospect and Prospect," in *Biblical Interpretation in the Era of the Reformation*, edited by Muller and Thompson, pp. 335-45.

Murphy, J. L. *The Notion of Tradition in John Driedo*. Milwaukee: Bruce, 1959.

Murray, Michael V. "The Theory of Distinctions in the Metaphysics of Francis Suárez." Ph.D. diss., Fordham University, 1944.

Nachbar, Bernard A. "Ideality and Reality in the Proofs of God's Existence," in *San Bonaventura Maestro*, edited by Alphonso Pompei, vol. II, pp. 41-48.

Nadler, Steven, ed. *The Cambridge Companion to Malebranche*. Cambridge: Cambridge University Press, 2000.

Nash, Ronald H. *The Concept of God: An Exploration of Contemporary Difficulties with the Attributes of God*. Grand Rapids: Zondervan, 1983.

Nauert, Charles G., Jr. "The Clash of Humanists and Scholastics: An Approach to Pre-Reformation Controversies," in *The Sixteenth Century Journal*, 4 (1973), pp. 1-18.

Nauta, D. et al. *Biografisch Lexicon voor de geschiedenis van het Nederlandse protestantisme*. 5 vols. to date. Kampen: J. Kok, 1978-.

Neal, Daniel. *The History of the Puritans, or Protestant Nonconformists; from the Reformation in 1517, to the Revolution in 1688*. 2 vols. New York: Harper, 1844.

Neander, Johann August Wilhelm. *Lectures on the History of Christian Dogmas*. Translated by John Ryland. 2 vols. London: Bohn, 1858.

Neele, Adriaan Cornelis. *A Study of Divine Spirituality, Simplicity, and Immutability in Petrus van Mastricht's Doctrine of God*. Th.M. thesis: Calvin Theological Seminary, 2002.

Nellen, H. J. M., and E. Rabbie, eds. *Hugo Grotius Theologian: Essays in Honour of G. H. M. Posthumus Meyjes*. Leiden: E. J. Brill, 1994.

Neuner, J., and J. Dupuis, eds. *The Christian Faith in the Doctrinal Documents of the Catholic Church*. 2nd ed. Dublin: Mercier Press, 1976.

Neuser, W. H., ed. *Calvinus Ecclesiae Doctor*. Die Referate des Internationalen Kongresses für Calvinforschung vom 25 bis 28 September 1978 in Amsterdam. Kampen: J. H. Kok, 1978.

_____, ed. *Calvinus Ecclesiae Genevensis Custos*. Die Referate des Internationalen Kongresses für Calvinforschung. Vom 6 bis 9 September 1982 in Genf. Frankfurt am Main: Peter Lang, 1984.

_____, ed. *Calvinus Servus Christi*. Die Referate des Internationalen Kongresses für Calvinforschung vom 25 bis 28 August 1986 in Debrecen. Budapest: Presseabteilung des Ráday Kollegiums, 1988.

_____, ed. *Calvinus Theologus*. Die Referate des Internationalen Kongresses für Calvinforschung vom 16 bis 19 September 1974 in Amsterdam. Neukirchen: Neukirchner Verlag, 1976.

The New Catholic Encyclopedia. Edited by William J. McDonald, et al. 15 vols. New York: McGraw-Hill, 1967.

The New Schaff-Herzog Encyclopedia of Religious Knowledge. Edited by Samuel Macauley Jackson, et al. 12 vols. New York: Funk & Wagnalls, 1908–14. Reprint, Grand Rapids: Baker Book House, 1952.

Niesel, Wilhelm. *The Theology of Calvin*. Translated by Harold Knight. London: Lutterworth, 1956. Reprint, Grand Rapids: Baker Book House, 1980.

Niemeyer, H. A., ed. *Collectio confessionum in ecclesiis reformatis publicatarum*. 2 parts. Leipzig: J. Klinkhardt, 1840.

Niewöhner, Friedrich and Olaf Pluta, eds. *Atheismus im Mittelalter und in der Renaissance*. Wiesbaden: Harrassowitz, 1999.

Nineham, Dennis E., ed. *The Church's Use of the Bible Past and Present*. London: S. P. C. K., 1963.

Nobbs, Douglas. *Theocracy and Toleration: a Study of the Disputes in Dutch Calvinism from 1600 to 1650*. Cambridge: Cambridge University Press, 1938.

Noble, T. A. "Our Knowledge of God According to John Calvin," in *The Evangelical Quarterly*, 54 (1982), pp. 2-13.

Normore, Calvin G. "Scholasticism," in *The Cambridge Dictionary of Philosophy*, edited by R. Audi (Cambridge: Cambridge University Press, 1995), pp. 716-17

Nuovo, Victor Lawrence. "Calvin's Theology: A Study of its Sources in Classical Antiquity." Ph.D. diss., Columbia University, 1964.

Nuttall, Geoffrey F. *The Holy Spirit in Puritan Faith and Experience*. Oxford: Basil Blackwell, 1946.

Oakley, Francis. "Absolute and Ordained Power of God in Sixteenth- and Seventeenth-Century Theology." *Journal of the History of Ideas*, 59(1998), pp. 437-461.

_____. *Omnipotence, Covenant, & Order: an Excursion in the History of Ideas from Abelard to Leibniz*. Ithaca and London: Cornell University Press, 1984.

_____. "Pierre D'Ailly and the Absolute Power of God: Another Note on the Theology of Nominalism," in *Harvard Theological Review*, 56 (1963), pp. 59-73.

Oberman, Heiko A. *Archbishop Thomas Bradwardine: A Fourteenth-century Augustinian. A Study of his Theology in its Historical Context*. Utrecht: Kemink en Zoon, 1957.

_____. *The Dawn of the Reformation: Essays in Late Medieval and Early Reformation Thought*. Edinburgh: T. & T. Clark, 1986.

_____. "*Facientibus Quod in se est Deus non Denegat Gratiam*: Robert Holcot O.P. and the Beginnings of Luther's Theology," in *The Reformation in Medieval Perspective*, edited by Stephen Ozment, pp. 119-141.

_____. *Forerunners of the Reformation*. New York: Holt, Rinehart and Winston, 1966.

_____. "Fourteenth-Century Religious Thought: A Premature Profile," in *Speculum*, 53 (1987), pp. 80-93; also in *Dawn of the Reformation*, pp. 1-17.

_____. *The Harvest of Medieval Theology: Gabriel Biel and Late Medieval Nominalism*. Rev. ed. Grand Rapids: Eerdmans, 1967.

_____. *Masters of the Reformation: Emergence of a New Intellectual Climate in Europe*. Translated by Dennis Martin. Cambridge University Press, 1981.

_____. *The Reformation: Roots and Ramifications*. Translated by Andrew C. Gow. Grand Rapids: Eerdmans, 1994.

_____. "The Shape of Late Medieval Thought: the Birthpangs of the Modern Era," in *The Pursuit of Holiness*, edited by Trinkaus and Oberman, pp. 3-25; also in *Dawn of the Reformation*, pp. 18-38.

_____. "Some Notes on the Theology of Nominalism with Attention to Its Relation to the Renaissance," in *Harvard Theological Review*, 53 (1960), pp. 47-76.

_____. "Via Antiqua and Via Moderna: Late Medieval Prolegomena to Early Reformation Thought," in *From Ockham to Wyclif*, edited by Hudson and Wilks, pp. 445-63.

Oberman, Heiko A., and Thomas Brady, eds. *Itinerarium Italicum: The Profile of the Italian Renaissance in the Mirror of its European Transformations*. Leiden: Brill, 1975.

O'Connor, Edward D. "The Scientific Character of Theology According to Scotus," in *De Doctrina Ioannis Duns Scoti*, edited by C. Balic, vol. III, pp. 3-50.

Oehler, K. "Rationalismus. I. Philosophisch," s.v. in *Religion in Geschichte und Gegenwart*, dritte Auflage,

Olivier, Paul. "Études historiques sur le problème de Dieu," in *Recherches de Science Religieuses*, 67 (1979), pp. 125-144.

O'Mahony, James E. *The Desire for God in the Philosophy of St Thomas Aquinas*. Toronto: Longmans, Green, 1929.

O'Malley, John W. "Erasmus and Luther, Continuity and Discontinuity as Key to their Conflict," in *The Sixteenth Century Journal*, 5/2 (1974), pp. 47-65.

_____. "A Note on Gregory of Rimini: Church, Scripture, Tradition," in *Augustinianum*, (1965), pp. 365-378.

Ong, Walter J. *Ramus: Method and the Decay of Dialogue: From the Art of Discourse to the Art of Reason*. Cambridge, Mass.: Harvard University Press, 1958.

Oort, Johannes van. "John Calvin and the Church Fathers," in *The Reception of the Church Fathers in the West*, edited by Irena Backus, vol. II, pp. 661-700.

Oosterom, C. "Johannes Hoornbeeck als Zendingstheoloog," in *Theologia Reformata*, 13 (1970), 80-98.

Orr, Robert R. *Reason and Authority in the Thought of William Chillingworth*. Oxford: Clarendon Press, 1967.

Osler, Margaret J. *Divine Will and the Mechanical Philosophy: Gassendi and Descartes on Contingency and Necessity in the Created World*. Cambridge: Cambridge University Press, 1994.

_____. "Eternal Truths and the Laws of Nature: the Theological Foundations of Descartes' Philosophy of Nature," in *Journal of the History of Ideas*, 46 (1985), pp. 349-362.

Ostdiek, Antonellus G. *Scotus and Fundamental Theology*. Teutopolis: St. Joseph Seminary, 1967.

Osterhaven, M. Eugene. "The Experimental Theology of Early Dutch Calvinism," in *Reformed Review*, 27 (1974), pp. 180-189.

Overfield, James H. *Humanism and Scholasticism in Late Medieval Germany*. Princeton, New Jersey: Princeton University Press, 1984.

_____. "A New Look at the Reuchlin Affair," in *Studies in Medieval and Renaissance History*, 8 (1971), pp. 165-207.

_____. "Scholastic Opposition to Humanism in Pre-Reformation Germany," in *Viator*, 7 (1976), pp. 391-420.

Owens, Joseph. *St. Thomas Aquinas on the Existence of God: Collected Papers of Joseph Owens, C. Ss. R.* Edited by John R. Catan. Albany: State University of New York Press, 1980.

Ozment, Stephen. *The Age of Reform, 1250-1550: An Intellectual and Religious History of Late Medieval and Reformation Europe.* New Haven and London: Yale University Press, 1980.

_____. "Luther and the Late Middle Ages: The Formation of Reformation Thought," in *Transition and Revolution: Problems and Issues of European Renaissance and Reformation History,* edited by Robert M. Kingdon, (Minneapolis: Burgess, 1974), pp. 109-129.

Ozment, Stephen, ed. *The Reformation in Medieval Perspective.* Chicago: University of Chicago Press, 1971.

Packer, James I. "John Calvin and the Inerrancy of Holy Scripture," in *Inerrancy and the Church,* edited by John D. Hannah, pp. 143-188.

Pailin, David A. "Herbert of Cherbury and the Deists," in *Expository Times,* 94 (1983), pp. 33-42.

Pannenberg, Wolfhart. *Theology and the Philosophy of Science.* Translated by R. McDonagh. Philadelphia: Westminster, 1976.

Parker, T. H. L. *Calvin: An Introduction to His Thought.* Louisville: Westminster/John Knox, 1995.

_____. *Calvin's New Testament Commentaries.* Grand Rapids: Eerdmans, 1971.

_____. *Calvin's Old Testament Commentaries.* Edinburgh: T. & T. Clark, 1986.

_____. "Calvin the Exegete: Change and Development," in *Calvinus Ecclesiae Doctor,* Die Referate des Internationalen Kongresses für Calvinforschung vom 25 bis 28 September 1978 in Amsterdam, edited by W. H. Neuser (Kampen: J. H. Kok, 1978), pp. 33-46.

_____. *The Doctrine of the Knowledge of God: A Study in Calvin's Theology.* Rev. ed. Grand Rapids: Eerdmans, 1959.

Partee, Charles. *Calvin and Classical Philosophy.* Leiden: E. J. Brill, 1977.

Pascoe, Louis B. "The Council of Trent and Bible Study: Humanism and Scripture," in *Catholic Historical Review,* 52 (1966-67), pp. 18-38.

Patterson, Robert L. *The Conception of God in the Philosophy of Aquinas.* London: Allen & Unwin, 1933.

Paulus, J. *Henri de Gand: Essai sur les tendances de sa métaphysique.* Paris: J. Vrin, 1938.

Payne, John B. "Erasmus and Lefèvre d'Étaples as Interpreters of Paul," in *Archiv für Reformationsgeschichte,* 65 (1974), pp. 54-83.

_____. "Erasmus: Interpreter of Romans," in *Sixteenth Century Studies and Essays* II, edited by Carl S. Meyer, (St Louis: Foundation for Reformation Research, 1971), pp. 1-35.

_____. "Toward the Hermeneutics of Erasmus," in *Scrinium Erasminianum: Mélanges historiques,* edited by Joseph Coppens, 2 vols. (Leiden: E. J. Brill, 1969), vol. 2, pp. 13-49.

Pegis, Anton. "The Bonaventurean Way to God," in *Medieval Studies,* 29 (1967), pp. 206-242.

_____. "Four Medieval Ways to God," in *Monist,* 54 (1970), pp. 317-358.

_____. "Molina and Human Liberty," in *Jesuit Thinkers of the Renaissance,* edited by Gerald Smith, pp. 75-131.

_____. "Toward a New Way to God: Henry of Ghent," in *Medieval Studies,* 30 (1968), pp. 226-247; 31 (1969), pp. 93-116.

Pégues, T. M. "Theologie Thomiste d'après Capraeolus: De la voie rationelle que nous conduite à Dieu," in *Revue Thomiste,* vol. 8 (1900), pp. 288-309.

Pelikan, Jaroslav. *The Christian Tradition: A History of the Development of Doctrine.* 5 vols. Chicago: University of Chicago Press, 1971-1989.

_____. *Luther the Expositor: Luther's Works Companion Volume*. St. Louis: Concordia Publishing House, 1959.

Pernoud, M. A. "The Theory of the *Potentia Dei* according to Aquinas, Scotus and Ockham," in *Antonianum*, 47 (1972), pp. 69-95.

Perrottet, Luc. "Chapter 9 of the Epistle to the Hebrews as Presented in an Unpublished Course of Lectures by Theodore Beza," in *Journal of Medieval and Renaissance Studies*, 14/1 (1984), pp. 89-96.

Persson, Per Erik. *Sacra Doctrina: Reason and Revelation in Aquinas*. Translated by R. Mackenzie. Philadelphia: Fortress, 1970.

Pesch, Otto Hermann. *The God Question in Thomas Aquinas and Martin Luther*. Translated by Gottfried Kroedel. Philadelphia: Fortress, 1972.

Pestalozzi, Carl. *Heinrich Bullinger: Leben und ausgewählte Schriften. Nach handschriftlichen und gleichzeitigen Quellen*. Elberfeld: Friedrichs, 1858.

Peter, J. F. "The Place of Tradition in Reformed Theology," in *Scottish Journal of Theology*, 18 (1965), pp. 294-307.

Petersen, Peter. *Geschichte der aristotelischen Philosophie im protestantischen Deutschland*. Leipzig, 1921. Reprint, Stuttgart: F. Frommann, 1964.

Peyer, Etienne de. "Calvin's Doctrine of Divine Providence," in *Evangelical Quarterly*, 10 (1938), pp. 30-44.

Pfeiffer, R. *History of Classical Scholarship from 1300 to 1850*. Oxford: Oxford University Press, 1976.

Pfizenmaier, Thomas C. *The Trinitarian Theology of Dr. Samuel Clarke (1675-1729): Context, Sources, and Controversy*. Leiden: E. J. Brill, 1997.

_____. "Was Isaac Newton an Arian?" in *Journal of the History of Ideas*, 58 (1997), pp. 57-80.

Phillips, R. P. *Modern Thomistic Philosophy: An Explanation for Students*. 2 vols. New York: Newman Press, 1959.

Phillips, Timothy R. "The Dissolution of Francis Turretin's Vision of *Theologia*: Geneva at the End of the Seventeenth Century," in *The Identity of Geneva: The Christian Commonwealth, 1564-1864*, edited by John B. Roney and Martin I. Klauber, pp. 77-92.

_____. "Francis Turretin's Idea of Theology and Its Impact upon His Doctrine of Scripture." Ph.D. diss., Vanderbilt University, 1986.

Picavet, François. *Roscelin, philosophie et théologien*. Paris: Alcan, 1911.

Pinard, H. "Création," in *Dictionnaire de théologie catholique*, vol. 3/2, col. 2034-2201.

Pitassi, Maria-Cristina. "Un manuscrit genevois du XVIIIᵉ siécle: la 'Refutation du système de Spinoza par Mr. Turrettini,'" in *Nederlands Archief voor Kerkgeschiedenis*, 68 (1988), pp. 180-212.

Platon et Aristote à la Renaissance. XVIᵉ Colloque International de Tours. Paris: J. Vrin, 1976.

Platt, John. "The Denial of the Innate Idea of God in Dutch Remonstrant Theology from Episcopius to Limborch," in *Protestant Scholasticism*, edited by C. Trueman and R. Clark, pp. 213-226.

_____. *Reformed Thought and Scholasticism: The Arguments for the Existence of God in Dutch Theology, 1575-1650*. Leiden: Brill, 1982.

Plantinga, Alvin. *Does God Have a Nature?* Milwaukee: Marquette University Press, 1980.

Plantinga, Cornelius, Jr. "Gregory of Nyssa and the Social Analogy of the Trinity," in *The Thomist*, 50/3 (July 1986), pp. 325-352.

_____. "The Threeness/Oneness Problem of the Trinity," in *Calvin Theological Journal*, 23/1 (April 1988), pp. 37-53.

Ploeg, J. van der. "The Place of Holy Scripture in the Theology of St. Thomas," in *The Thomist*, 10 (1947), pp. 398-422.

Poel, M. G. M. van der. *Cornelius Agrippa, the Humanist Theologian and His Declamations*. Leiden: E. J. Brill, 1997.

Pollet, J. V. "L'image de Zwingli dans l'historiographie contemporaine," in *Bulletin de la Société de l'Histoire du Protestantisme français*, 130 (1984), pp. 435-469.

Pompei, Alphonso. *San Bonaventura Maestro di Vita Francescana e di Sapienza Cristiana*. 3 vols. Rome: Pontifica Facolta Teologica San Bonaventura, 1976.

Poole, Reginald Lane. *Illustrations of the History of Medieval Thought and Learning*. 2nd ed. London: S. P. C. K., 1920.

Pope, Hugh. "Article on the Scholastic View of Inspiration," in *Irish Theological Quarterly* (July, 1911).

_____. "St. Thomas as an Interpreter of Holy Scripture," in *St. Thomas Aquinas*, edited by Aelred Whitacre (Oxford: Blackwell, 1925), pp. 111-144.

_____. *St. Thomas as Interpreter of Scripture*. Manchester: University of Manchester Press, 1924.

Popkin, Richard H. "Cartesianism and Biblical Criticism," in T. Lennon et al., *Problems of Cartesianism*, pp. 61-81.

_____. "The Development of Religious Scepticism and the Influence of Isaac La Peyrère's Pre-Adamism and Bible Criticism," in *Classical Influences on European Culture A.D. 1500-1700*, edited by R. R. Bolgar (Cambridge: Cambridge University Press, 1976), pp. 271-280.

_____. *The History of Scepticism from Erasmus to Spinoza*. 2nd ed. Berkeley: University of California Press, 1979.

_____. "Introduction: Scepticism and Irreligion in the Seventeenth and Eighteenth Centuries," in *Scepticism and Irreligion*, edited by R. Popkin and A. Vanderjagt, pp. 1-11.

_____. "The Religious Background of Seventeenth-Century Philosophy," in *The Third Force in Seventeenth-Century Thought*, edited by Popkin, pp. 268-84.

_____. "Theories of Knowledge," in *The Cambridge History of Renaissance Philosophy*, edited by C. Schmitt, Q. Skinner, and E. Kessler, pp. 668-684.

Popkin, Richard H., ed. *Millenarianism and Massianism in English Literature and Thought, 1650-1800*. Leiden: Brill, 1988.

_____, ed. *The Third Force in Seventeenth-Century Thought*. Leiden: E. J. Brill, 1992.

Popkin, Richard H., and Arjo Vanderjagt, eds. *Scepticism and Irreligion in the Seventeenth and Eighteenth Centuries*. Leiden: E. J. Brill, 1993.

Posset, Franz. "John Bugenhagen and the Comma Johanneum," in *Concordia Theological Quarterly*, 49 (1985), pp. 245-251.

Postema, Gerald J. "Calvin's Alleged Rejection of Natural Theology," in *Scottish Journal of Theology*, (1971), pp. 423-434.

Prenter, Regin. *Luther's Theology of the Cross*. Philadelphia: Muhlenberg, 1971.

Prentice, Robert. "The Evolution of Scotus' Doctrine of the Unity and Unicity of the Supreme Nature," in *De Doctrina Ioannis Duns Scoti*, edited by C. Balic, vol. II, pp. 377-408.

Prestige, G. L. *God in Patristic Thought*. 2nd ed. London: S.P.C.K., 1952.

Preus, James S. *From Shadow to Promise: Old Testament Interpretation from Augustine to the Young Luther*. Cambridge, Mass.: Harvard University Press, 1969.

_____. "Old Testament *Promissio* and Luther's New Hermeneutic," in *Harvard Theological Review*, 60 (1967), pp. 145-161.

Preus, Robert D. "Biblical Authority in the Lutheran Confessions," in *Concordia Journal*, 4 (1978), pp. 16-24.

_____. *The Inspiration of Scripture: a Study of the Theology of the Seventeenth Century Lutheran Dogmaticians*. Edinburgh: Oliver and Boyd, 1955.

_____. "Luther and Biblical Infallibility," in *Inerrancy and the Church*, edited by John D. Hannah, pp. 99-142.

_____. *The Theology of Post-Reformation Lutheranism*. 2 vols. St. Louis: Concordia, 1970-72.

_____. "The View of the Bible held by the Church: the Early Church through Luther," in *Inerrancy*, edited by N. Geisler, pp. 357-382.

Puckett, David L. *John Calvin's Exegesis of the Old Testament*. Louisville: Westminster John Knox Press, 1995.

Pünjer, Bernhard. *History of the Christian Philosophy of Religion from the Reformation to Kant*. Translated by W. Hastie. Edinburgh: T. & T. Clark, 1887.

Quinn, Dennis. "John Donne's Principles of Exegesis," in *Journal of English and Germanic Philology*, 61 (1962), pp. 313-329.

_____. "John Donne's Sermons on the Psalms and the Traditions of Biblical Exegesis," Ph.D. diss., University of Wisconsin, 1958.

Rabaud, Edouard. *Histoire de la doctrine de l'inspiration des Saintes Écritures dans les pays de langue française*. Paris: Fischbacher, 1883.

Rabil, Albert Jr. *Erasmus and the New Testament: The Mind of a Christian Humanist*. San Antonio: Trinity University Press, 1972.

_____, ed. *Renaissance Humanism: Foundations, Forms, and Legacy*. 3 vols. Philadelphia: University of Pennsylvania Press, 1988.

Raedy, Gerard. *The Bible and Reason: Anglicans and Scripture in late Seventeenth Century England*. Philadelphia: University of Pennsylvania Press, 1985.

Raitt, Jill. "Calvin's Use of *Persona*," in *Calvinus Ecclesiae Genevensis Custos*, pp. 273-87.

_____. *The Eucharistic Theology of Theodore Beza: Development of the Reformed Doctrine*. Chambersburg, PA: American Academy of Religion, 1972.

_____. "The Person of the Mediator: Calvin's Christology and Beza's Fidelity," *Occasional Papers of the Society for Reformation Research*, I (Dec., 1977), pp. 53-80.

Randall, John Herman. "The Development of Scientific Method in the School of Padua," in *Journal of the History of Ideas*, 1 (1940), pp. 177-206.

_____. *The Making of the Modern Mind: A Survey of the Intellectual Background of the Present Age*. Rev. ed. Cambridge, Mass.: Houghton Mifflin, 1940.

Randi, E. "Ockham, John XII and the Absolute Power of God," in *Franciscan Studies*, 46 (1986), pp. 205-216.

_____. "A Scotist Way of Distinguishing between God's Absolute and Ordained Powers," in *From Ockham to Wyclif*, edited by Hudson and Wilks, pp. 43-50.

Raymond, P. "Duns Scot," in *Dictionnaire de théologie catholique*, 4/2, cols. 1865-1947.

Realencyclopaedie für protestantische Theologie und Kirche. 3rd ed. 24 vols. Leipzig: J. C. Hinrich, 1896-1913.

Reardon, P. H. "Calvin on Providence: the Development of an Insight," in *Scottish Journal of Theology* 28 (1975), pp. 517-533.

Régnon, Théodore de. *Études de théologie positive sur la Sainte Trinité*. 5 vols. Paris: Retaux, 1892ff.

Rehnman, Sebastian. *Divine Discourse: The Theological Methodology of John Owen*. Grand Rapids: Baker Book House, 2002.

————. "John Owen: A Reformed Scholastic at Oxford," in *Reformation and Scholasticism*, edited by W. van Asselt and E. Dekker, pp. 181-203.

————. *Theologia Tradita: A Study in the Prolegomenous Discourse of John Owen* (1616-1683). Ph.D. diss., Oxford University, 1997.

Reid, James. *Memoirs of the Lives and Writings of those Eminent Divines, who Convened the Famous Assembly at Westminster in the Seventeenth Century*. 2 vols. Paisley: Stephen and Andrew Young, 1811-15. Reprint, Edinburgh: Banner of Truth, 1982.

Reid, J. K. S. *The Authority of Scripture: a Study of Reformation and Post-Reformation Understanding of the Bible*. London: Methuen, 1962.

Reitsma, J. *Geschiedenis van de Hervorming en de Hervormde Kerk der Nederlanden*. 4th ed. Utrecht: Kemink & Zoon, n.d.

Die Religion in Geschichte und Gegenwart; Handwörterbuch für Theologie und Religionswissenschaft. 3rd ed. Edited by H. Campenhausen, et al. 7 vols. übingen: Mohr, 1957–65.

Reu, Johan Michael. *The Augsburg Confession: A Collection of Sources with an Historical Introduction*. Chicago: Wartburg, 1930. Reprint, St. Louis: Concordia, 1983.

————. *Luther and the Scriptures*. Columbus, Ohio: Wartburg Press, 1944.

————. *Luther's German Bible*. Columbus, Ohio: Lutheran Book Concern, 1934.

Reulos, Michel. L'Enseignement d'Aristote dans les collèges au XVIe siècle," in *Platon et Aristote à la Renaissance* (Paris: Vrin, 1976), pp. 147-154.

Reuss, Edward. *History of the Canon of the Holy Scriptures in the Christian Church*. Translated by David Hunter. Edinburgh: R. W. Hunter, 1891.

————. *History of the Sacred Scriptures of the New Testament*. 5th ed. Translated by E. L. Houghton. Edinburgh: T. and T. Clark, 1884.

Reuter, Karl. *Das Grundverständnis der Theologie Calvins*. Neukirchen: Neukirchner Verlag, 1963.

Reventlow, Henning Graf. *The Authority of the Bible and the Rise of the Modern World*. Translated by John Bowden. Philadelphia: Fortress, 1985.

————. "L'exégèse de Hugo Grotius," in *Le Grand Siècle de la Bible*, edited by Armogathe, pp. 141-155.

Rex, Walter. "Pierre Bayle, Louis Tronchin et la Querelle des Donatistes: Étude d'un document inédit du XVIIe siècle," in *Bulletin de la Société de l'Histoire du Protestantisme français*, 105 (1959), pp. 97-121.

Reynolds, Stephen. "Calvin's View of the Athanasian and Nicene Creeds," in *Westminster Theological Journal*, 23 (1960/61), pp. 33-57.

Rice, Eugene F. "Humanist Aristotelianism in France. Jacques Lefèvre d'Étaples and his Circle," in, *Humanism in France*, edited by Levi, pp. 132-149.

————. "The Renaissance Idea of Christian Antiquity: Humanist Patristic Scholarship," in *Renaissance Humanism: Foundations, Forms, and Legacy*, edited by A. Rabil, vol. I, pp. 17-28.

Richard, Robert L. *The Problem of an Apologetical Perspective in the Trinitarian Theology of St. Thomas Aquinas*. Rome: Gregorian University, 1963.

Riché, Pierre and Guy Lobrichon, eds. *Le Moyen Age et le Bible*. Vol. 4 of *Bible de tous les temps*. Paris: Beauchesne, 1984.

Rilliet, Jean. *Zwingli: Third Man of the Reformation*. Translated by H. Knight. Philadelphia: Westminster, 1964.

Ritschl, Albrecht. *Gesammelte Aufsätze*. Edited by Otto Ritschl. Freiburg: J. C. B. Mohr, 1893.

_____. *Gesammelte Aufsätze*. Neue Folge. Edited by Otto Ritschl. Freiburg: J. C. B. Mohr, 1896.

_____. "Geschichtliche Studien zur christlichen Lehre von Gott," in *Jahrbücher für deutsche Theologie*, 10 (1865), pp. 277-318; 13 (1868), pp. 67-133, 251-302 [also in *Gesammelte Aufsätze*, Neue Folge, pp. 25-64; 65-127; 128-176.]

_____. "Über die beiden Principien des Protestantismus," in *Zeitschrift für Kirchengeschichte*, 1 (1876), pp. 397-413. [Also in *Gesammelte Aufsätze* (1893), pp. 243-247.]

Ritschl, Otto. *Dogmengeschichte des Protestantismus: Grundlagen und Grundzüge der theologischen Gedanken- und Lehrbildung in den protestantischen Kirchen*. 4 vols. Leipzig: J.C. Hinrichs, 1908-12. Göttingen: Vandenhoeck & Ruprecht, 1926-27.

Rivière, J. "Les 'capitula' d'Abélard condamnés au concile de Sens," in *Recherches de théologie ancienne et médiévale*, 5 (1933), pp. 5-8.

Robertson, J. M. *A History of Freethought, Ancient and Modern to the Period of the French Revolution*. 2 vols. 4th rev. ed., 1936. Reprint, London: Dawsons, 1969.

_____. *A Short History of Freethought, Ancient and Modern* (New York: Russell & Russell, 1957.

Robinson, John F. "The Doctrine of Holy Scripture in Seventeenth Century Reformed Theology." Ph.D. diss., Strasbourg, 1971.

Rogers, Jack B. "The Church Doctrine of Biblical Authority," in *Biblical Authority*, edited by J. Rogers, pp. 15-46.

_____. *Scripture in the Westminster Confession: A Problem of Historical Interpretation for American Presbyterianism*. Grand Rapids: Eerdmans, 1967.

Rogers, Jack B., ed. *Biblical Authority*. Waco, Texas: Word Books, 1977.

Rogers, Jack B., and Donald K. McKim. *The Authority and Interpretation of the Bible: an Historical Approach*. San Francisco: Harper and Row, 1979.

Rogers, Katherin. "The Traditional Doctrine of Divine Simplicity," in *Religious Studies*, 32 (1996), pp. 165-86.

Rogerson, John, Christopher Rowland, and Barnabas Lindars. *The Study and Use of the Bible*. Grand Rapids: Eerdmans, 1988.

Rohls, Jan. *Reformed Confessions: Theology from Zurich to Barmen*. Translated by John Hoffmeyer, intro. by Jack Stotts. Louisville: Westminster John Knox Press, 1998.

Rohnert, Wilhelm. *Die Inspiration der heiligen Schrift und ihre Bestreiter. Eine biblisch-dogmengeschichtliche Studie*. Leipzig: Georg Böhme Nachfolger, 1889.

Rolston, Holmes, III. *John Calvin versus the Westminster Confession*. Richmond: John Knox, 1972.

_____. "Responsible Man in Reformed Theology: Calvin Versus the *Westminster Confession*," in *Scottish Journal of Theology*, 23 (1970), pp. 129-156.

Rooden, Peter T. van. *Theology, Biblical Scholarship and Rabbinical Studies in the Seventeenth Century: Constantijn L'Empereur (1591-1648), Professor of Hebrew and Theology at Leiden*. Translated by J. C. Grayson. Leiden: Brill, 1989.

Roney, John B., and Martin I. Klauber, eds. *The Identity of Geneva: The Christian Commonwealth, 1564-1864.* Foreword by Robert M. Kingdon. Westport, CT: Greenwood Press, 1998.

Rossouw, H. W. "Calvin's Hermeneutics of Holy Scripture," in *Calvinus Reformator*, pp. 149-180.

Roth, Cecil. "Edward Pococke and the First Hebrew Printing at Oxford," in *Bodleian Library Record*, II/27 (1948), pp. 215-19.

Rotondo, Antonio. *Calvin and the Italian Anti-Trinitarians.* Translated by John and Anne Tedeschi. *Reformation Essays and Studies*, 2. St. Louis: Foundation for Reformation Research, 1968.

Roussel, Bernard. "Histoire de l'Eglise et histoire de l'exégèse en XVIᵉ siècle," in *Bibliotheque d'humanisme et renaissance*, 37 (1975), pp. 181-192.

_____. "De Strasbourg à Bâle et Zurich: une 'école rhénane' d'exégèse (ca. 1525-ca. 1540)," in *Revue d'histoire et de philosophie religieuses*, 68 (1988), pp. 19-39.

Rousselot, Pierre. *The Intellectualism of St. Thomas.* London: Sheed and Ward, 1924.

Rudavsky, Tamar, ed. *Divine Omniscience and Omnipotence in Medieval Philosophy: Islamic, Jewish, and Christian Perspectives.* Dordrecht: Riedel, 1985.

Ruler, J. A. van. *The Crisis of Causality: Voetius and Descartes on God, Nature, and Change.* Leiden: E.J. Brill, 1995.

_____. "Franco Petri Burgersdijk and the Case of Calvinism Within the Neo-Scholastic Tradition," in *Franco Burgersdijk*, edited by Bos and Krop, pp. 37-65.

_____. "New Philosophy to Old Standards: Voetius' Vindication of Divine Concurrence and Secondary Causality," in *Nederlands Archief voor Kerkgeschiedenis*, 71 (1991), pp. 58-91.

Rumrich, John Peter. "Milton's Concept of Substance," in *English Language Notes*, 19 (1982), pp. 218-233.

Runia, Klaas. "The Hermeneutics of the Reformers," in *Calvin Theological Journal*, 19 (1984), pp. 121-152.

Rupp, E. Gordon. "The Bible in the Age of the Reformation," in *Church's Use of the Bible*, edited by D. Nineham, pp. 73-87.

_____. "Word and Spirit in the Early Years of the Reformation," in *Archiv für Reformationsgeschichte*, 49 (1958), pp. 13-26.

Saak, E. L. "Scholasticism, Late," s.v. in *Augustine Through the Ages*, edited by Allan D. Fitzgerald, pp. 754-759.

Sabean, David. "The Theological Rationalism of Moïse Amyraut," in *Archiv für Reformationsgeschichte*, 55 (1964), pp. 204-215.

Saintes, Amand. *A Critical History of Rationalism in Germany from its Origin to the Present Time.* London: Simpkin, Marshall and Co., 1849.

Saisset, Émile. "Doctrine philosophique et religieuse de Michel Servet," in *Revue des deux mondes*, 21/4 (1848), pp. 586-618.

_____. "Le procès et la mort de Michel Servet," in *Revue des deux mondes*, 21/5 (1848), pp. 818-848.

Sanchez-Blanco, Francisco. *Michael Servets Kritik an der Trinitätslehre: philos. Implicationen u. histor. Auswirkungen.* Frankfurt: Lang, 1977.

Sandys-Wunsch, John. "Spinoza — The First Biblical Theologian," in *Zeitschrift für dir alttestamentliche Wissenschaft*, 93 (1981), pp. 327-341.

Sandys-Wunsch, John, and Laurence Eldredge. "J. P. Gabler and the Distinction between Biblical and Dogmatic Theology: Translation, Commentary and Discussion of His Originality," in *Scottish Journal of Theology*, 33 (1980), pp. 133-158.

Sasse, Herman. "The Rise of the Dogma of Holy Scripture in the Middle Ages," in *The Reformed Theological Review*, 18/2 (June, 1959), pp. 45-54.

Sassen, Ferdinand. *Geschiedenis van de wijsbegeerte in Nederland tot het einde der negentiende eeuw*. Amsterdam: Elsevier, 1959.

Saxolvá, Tereza, and Stanislav Sousedík, eds. *Rodrigo de Arriaga (+1667): Philosoph und Theolog*. Prague: Univerzity Karlovy, 1998.

Schaaf, M. E. van der. "The Theology of Thomas Jackson (1579-1640): An Anglican Alternative to Roman Catholicism, Puritanism and Calvinism." Ph.D. Diss., University of Iowa, 1979.

Scapin, Pietro. "Il significato fondamentale delle libertà divina secondo Giovanni Duns Scoto," in *De Doctrina Ioannis Duns Scoti*, edited by C. Balic, vol. II, pp. 519-566.

Schäfer, Rolf. "Melanchthons Hermeneutik im Römerbrief-Kommentar von 1532," in *Zeitschrift für Theologie und Kirche*, 60 (1963), pp. 216-235.

Schaff, Philip. *The Creeds of Christendom, with a History and Critical Notes*. 3 vols. 6th ed. New York: Scribner, 1931. Reprint, Grand Rapids: Baker Book House, 1983.

_____. *History of the Christian Church*. 8 vols. 3rd ed., revised. New York: Scribners, 1907-1910. Reprint, Grand Rapids: Eerdmans, 1976.

_____. "The Reformation and Rationalism," in *History of the Christian Church*, VII, pp. 26-42.

Scharlemann, Robert. *Aquinas and Gerhard: Theological Controversy and Construction in Medieval and Protestant Scholasticism*. New Haven: Yale University Press, 1964.

Scheel, Otto. *Martin Luther: Vom Katholizismus zur Reformation*. 2 vols. Tübingen: J. C. B. Mohr, 1921.

Schmaus, Michael. "Die Schrift und die Kirche nach Heinrich von Gent," in *Kirche und Überlieferung*, edited by J. Beta and H. Fries (Freiburg: Herder, 1960), pp. 211-271

Schenkel, Daniel. "Ueber das Princip des Protestantismus. Ein Antwortschreiben auf das Sendschreiben des Hrn. Prof. D. Hagenbach in Basel," in *Theologische Studien und Kritiken*, 1855, pp. 22-74.

Scheurleer, T. H. L., and G. H. M. Posthumus Meyjes, ed., *Leiden University in the Seventeenth Century: An Exchange of Learning*. Leiden: E. J. Brill, 1975.

Schlingensiepen, H. "Erasmus als Exeget auf grund seiner Schriften zu Matthäus," in *Zeitschrift für Kirchengeschichte*, 48 (1929), pp. 16-57.

Schmid, Heinrich. *Doctrinal Theology of the Evangelical Lutheran Church*. Translated by Charles E. Hay and Henry Jacobs. Minneapolis: Augsburg, n.d.

Schmidt, Martin. "Zur Trinitätslehre der Frühscholastik: Versuch einer problemgeschichtlichen Orientierung," in *Theologische Zeitschrift*, 40 (1984), pp. 181-192.

Schmitt, Charles B. *The Aristotelian Tradition and Renaissance Universities*. London: Variorum Reprints, 1984.

_____. *Aristotle and the Renaissance*. Cambridge, Mass.: Harvard University Press, 1983.

_____. *Cicero Scepticus: A Study of the Influence of the Academica in the Renaissance*. Den Haag: Nijhoff, 1972.

_____. *A Critical Survey and Bibliography of Studies on Renaissance Aristotelianism*. Padua: Antenore, 1971.

_____. *Gianfrancesco Pico della Mirandola (1469-1533) and His Critique of Aristotle*. Den Haag: Nijhoff, 1967.

_____. "Introduction de la philosophie platonicienne dans l'enseignement des universités à la renaissance," in *Platon et Aristote à la Renaissance* (Paris: Vrin, 1976), pp. 93-104.

_____. *John Case and Aristotelianism in Renaissance England*. Montreal: McGill-Queen's University Press, 1983.

_____. "Perennial Philosophy: from Agostino Steuco to Leibniz," in *Journal of the History of Ideas*, 27 (1966), pp. 505-532.

_____. "Reappraisals of Renaissance Science," in *History of Science*, 16 (1978), pp. 200-214.

_____. "The Rise of the Philosophical Textbook," in *The Cambridge History of Renaissance Philosophy*, edited by C. Schmitt, Q. Skinner, and E. Kessler, pp. 792-804.

_____. "Towards a Reassessment of Renaissance Aristotelianism," in *History of Science*, 11 (1973), pp. 159-173.

Schmitt, Charles B., and Brian Copenhaver. *A History of Western Philosophy*, vol. 3: *Renaissance Philosophy*. Oxford: Oxford University Press, 1992.

Schmitt, Charles B., Quentin Skinner, and Eckhard Kessler, eds.. *The Cambridge History of Renaissance Philosophy*. Cambridge and New York: Cambridge University Press, 1988.

Schneckenburger, Matthias. "Die reformirte Dogmatik mit Rückblick auf: Al. Schweizer's *Glaubenslehre der evang.-reformirten Kirche*," in *Theologische Studien und Kritiken*, 1848, pp. 68-110, 600-631.

_____. "Recension von Alexander Schweizer, *Die Glaubenslehre der evangelisch-reformirten Kirche...*," in *Theologische Studien und Kritiken*, 1847, pp. 947-983.

_____. *Vergleichende Darstellung des lutherischen und reformirten Lehrbegriffs*. Edited by Edward Guder. 2 vols. Stuttgart: J. B. Metzler, 1855.

Schnedermann, Georg. *Die Contoverse des Ludovicus Cappellus mit den Buxtorfen über das Alter der hebräishen Punctation: ein Beitrag zu der Geschichte des Studiums der hebräishen Sprache*. Leipzig: J. C. Hinrichs, 1879.

Schochet, Gordon. "Samuel Parker, religious diversity, and the ideology of persecution," in *The Margins of Orthodoxy*, edited by Roger D. Lund, pp. 119-148.

Scholder, Klaus. *Ursprünge und Probleme der Bibelkritik im 17. Jahrhundert. Forschungen zur Geschichte und Lehre des Protestantismus*, X/33. Munich: Chr. Kaiser Verlag, 1966.

Schreiner, Susan E. "Exegesis and Double Justice in Calvin's Sermons on Job," in *Church History*, 58 (1989), pp. 322-338.

_____. *The Theater of His Glory: Nature and the Natural Order in the Thought of John Calvin*. Durham, N.C.: Labyrinth Press, 1991.

_____. "Through a Mirror Dimly: Calvin's Sermons on Job," in *Calvin Theological Journal*, 21 (1986), pp. 175-193.

_____. *Where Shall Wisdom be Found? Calvin's Exegesis of Job from Medieval and Modern Perspectives*. Chicago: University of Chicago Press, 1994.

Schreiner, Thomas R., and Bruce A. Ware. *The Grace of God and the Bondage of the Will*. 2 vols. Grand Rapids: Baker Book House, 1995.

Schrenk, Gottlob. *Gottesreich und bund im älteren Protestantismus vornehmlich bei Johannes Coccejus: Zugleich ein Beitrag zur Geschichte des Pietismus und der heilsgeschichtlichen Theologie*. Gütersloh: Bertelsmann, 1923.

Schüssler, Hermann. *Der Primat der heiligen Schrift als theologisches und kanonistisches Problem in Spätmittelalter*. Wiesbaden: Franz Steiner Verlag, 1977.

Schwane, Joseph. *Histoire des Dogmes*. Trs A. Degert. 5 vols. Paris: Beauschesne, 1906.

Schwartz, K. A. von. "Die theologische Hermeneutik des M. Flacius Illyricus," in *Lutherjahrbuch*, 1933, pp. 143.

Schwarz, W. *Principles and Problems of Biblical Translation: Some Reformation Controversies and their Background*. Cambridge: Cambridge University Press, 1955.

Schweibert, E. G. *Luther and His Times: The Reformation from a New Perspective*. St. Louis: Concordia, 1950.

Schweizer, Alexander. "Die Entwickelung des Moralsystems in der reformirten Kirche," in *Theologische Studien und Kritiken*, 1850, pp. 5-78, 288-327, 554-580.

_____. *Die Glaubenslehre der evangelisch-reformirten Kirche dargestellt und aus den Quellen belegt*. 2 vols. Zurich: Orell, Füssli und Comp., 1844-47.

_____. *Die protestantischen Centraldogmen in ihrer Entwicklung innerhalb der reformierten Kirche*. 2 vols. Zurich: Orell, Füssli und Comp., 1854-56.

Scorraille, Raoul de. *François Suárez de la Compagnie de Jésus, d'après ses lettres, ses autres écrits inédits et un grand nombre des documents nouveaux*. 2 vols. Paris: Lethielleux, 1912.

Secretan, Philibert. "À propos de Dieu de Leibniz," in *Freiburger Zeitschrift für Philosophie und Theologie*," 27 (1980), pp. 24-35.

Seeberg, Reinhold. *Revelation and Inspiration*. London and New York: Harper, 1909.

_____. *Text-book of the History of Doctrines*. Translated by Charles E. Hay. 2 vols. Grand Rapids: Baker Book House, 1977.

_____. *Die Theologie des Johannes Duns Scotus. Eine dogmengeschichtliche untersuchung*. Leipzig: Dieterich, 1900.

Seidl, Horst. "The Concept of Person in St. Thomas Aquinas," in *The Thomist*, 51 (1987), pp. 435-460.

Sepp, Christiaan. *Het Godgeleerd onderwijs in Nederland gedurende de 16e en 17e eeuw*. 2 vols. Leiden: De Breuk en Smits, 1873-74.

Seybold, Michel, et al. *Offenbarung von der Schrift bis zum Ausgang der Scholastik*. Freiburg: Herder, 1971.

Shepherd, Norman. "Zanchius on Saving Faith," in *Westminster Theological Journal*, 36 (1973), pp. 31-47.

Sheppard, Gerald T., "Between Reformation and Modern Commentary: The Perception of the Scope of Biblical Books," in William Perkins, *A Commentary on Galatians*, edited by Sheppard, pp. 42-66.

_____. "William Perkins' Exposition Among Seventeenth-Century Commentaries, 1600-1645," in William Perkins, *A Commentary on Galatians*, edited by Sheppard, pp. 1-7.

Shim, Jai Sung. *Biblical Hermeneutics and Hebraism in the Early Seventeenth-Century as Reflected in the Work of John Weemse (1579-1636)*. Ph. D. diss., Calvin Theological Seminary, 1998.

Shmueli, Efraim. "Thomas Aquinas' Influence on Spinoza's Concept of Attributes," in *Journal of Religious Studies*, 6-7 (1978/79), pp. 61-72.

Shuger, Debora K. *Sacred Rhetoric: The Christian Grand Style in the English Renaissance*. Princeton: Princeton University Press, 1988.

Siebrand, Heine J. *Spinoza and the Netherlanders: An Inquiry into the Early Reception of His Philosophy of Religion*. Assen: Van Gorcum, 1988.

Sileo, Leonardo, ed. *Via Scoti: Methodologica ad mentem Joannis Duns Scoti: atti del congresso Scotistico Internazionale, Roma, 9-11 marzo 1993*. Rome: Antonianum, 1995.

Singer, Charles. *A Short History of Scientific Ideas to 1900*. London: Oxford University Press, 1959.

Sinnema, Donald W. "Antoine De Chandieu's Call for a Scholastic Reformed Theology (1580)," in *Later Calvinism*, edited by W. Fred Graham, pp. 159-190.

_____. "Aristotle and Early Reformed Orthodoxy: Moments of Accommodation and Antithesis," in *Christianity and the Classics: The Acceptance of a Heritage*, edited by Wendy Helleman (Lanham, MD: University Press of America, 1990), pp. 119-148.

_____. "The Distinction between Scholastic and Popular: Andreas Hyperius and Reformed Scholasticism," in *Protestant Scholasticism: Essays in Reassessment*, edited by C. Trueman and R. Clark, pp. 125-143.

_____. "The Issue of Reprobation at the Synod of Dort (1618-19) in the Light of the History of this Doctrine," Ph.D. diss., University of St. Michael's College, Toronto, 1985.

_____. "Reformed Scholasticism and the Synod of Dort (1618-19)," in *John Calvin's Institutes: His Opus Magnum*, edited by B. J. van der Walt (Potcheftstroom: Institute for Reformational Studies, 1986), pp. 467-506.

Sleigh, Robert, Vere Chappell, and Michael Della Rocca. "Determinism and Human Freedom," in *Cambridge History of Seventeenth-Century Philosophy*, edited by D. Garber and Ayers, vol. II, pp. 1195-1278.

Sliedregt, Cornelis van. *Calvijns opvolger Theodorus Beza, zijn verkiezingsleer en zijn belijdenis van de drieënige God*. Leiden: Groen, 1996.

Smalley, Beryl. "The Bible in the Medieval Schools," in *Cambridge History of the Bible*, II, pp. 197-220.

_____. "The Bible in the Middle Ages," in *Church's Use of the Bible*, edited by D. Nineham, pp. 57-71.

_____. *English Friars and Antiquity in the Early Fourteenth Century*. Oxford: Blackwell, 1960.

_____. *The Study of the Bible in the Middle Ages*. Notre Dame: University of Notre Dame Press, 1964.

Smid, T. D. "Beza en Nederland," in *Nederlands Archief voor Kerkgeschiedenis*, 46 (1963-65), pp. 169-191.

_____. "Bibliographische Opmerkingen over de Explicationes Catecheticae van Zacharias Ursinus," in *Gereformeerd Theologisch Tijdschrift*, 41 (1940), pp. 228-243.

Smith, Gerard, ed. *Jesuit Thinkers of the Renaissance*. Milwaukee: Marquette University Press, 1939.

Solé, Jacques. "Rationalisme chrétien et foi réformée à Genève autour de 1700: les derniers sermons de Louis Tronchin," in *Bulletin de la Société de l'Histoire du Protestantisme français*, 128 (1982), pp. 29-43.

Sorell, Tom, ed. *The Rise of Modern Philosophy: The Tension between the New and Traditional Philosophies from Machiavelli to Leibnitz*. Oxford: Clarendon Press, 1993.

Sousedík, Stanislav, "Arriagas Universalienlehre," in *Rodrigo de Arriaga*, edited by Saxolvá and Sousedík, pp. 41-49.

Spence, Alan. "John Owen and Trinitarian Agency," in *Scottish Journal of Theology*, 43 (1990), pp. 157-73.

Spencer, Stephen. "Reformed Scholasticism in Medieval Perspective: Thomas Aquinas and François Turrettini on Incarnation." Ph.D. diss., Michigan State University, 1988.

Spicq, Ceslaus. *Esquisse d'une histoire de l'exégèse latine au moyen âge*. Paris: J. Vrin, 1944.

_____. "Pourquoi le Moyen Age n'a-t-il pas practiqué davantage l'exégèse littérale," in *Revue des Sciences Philosophiques et Théologiques*, 30 (1941-42), pp. 169-179.

_____. "Saint Thomas d'Aquin: VI. Saint Thomas d'Aquin exégète," in *Dictionnaire de Théologie Catholique*, vol. 15/1, cols. 694-738.

Spijker, Willem van 't "Gereformeerde Scholastiek II: Scholastiek, Erasmus, Luther, Melanchthon," *Theologia Reformata*, 29 (1986), pp. 7-27.

_____. "Gereformeerde Scholastiek III: Zwingli en Bucer," *Theologia Reformata*, 29 (1986), pp. 136-160.

_____. *Principe, methode en functie van de theologie bij Andreas Hyperius*. Apeldoornse Studies, 26. Kampen: J. H. Kok, 1990.

_____. "Reformatie tussen patristiek en scholastiek: Bucers theologische positie," in *De kerkvaders in Reformatie en Nadere Reformatie*, edited by J. van Oort (Zoetermeer: Boekencentrum, 1997), pp. 45-66.

_____. "Reformation and Scholasticism," in *Reformation and Scholasticism*, edited by W. van Asselt and E. Dekker, pp. 84-85.

Spitz, Lewis W. "Humanism and the Protestant Reformation," in *Renaissance Humanism: Foundations, Forms, and Legacy*, edited by A. Rabil, vol. III, pp. 380-411. [also in *Luther and German Humanism*]

_____. *Luther and German Humanism*. Brookfield, Vt.: Ashgate/Variorum, 1996.

_____. *The Reformation: Education and History*. Brookfield, Vt.: Ashgate/Variorum, 1997.

_____. *The Religious Renaissance of the German Humanists*. Cambridge, Mass.: Harvard University Press, 1963.

_____. *The Renaissance and Reformation Movements*. Rev. ed. 2 vols. St. Louis: Concordia, 1987.

Spitz, Lewis W., and Barbara Sher Tinsely. *Johann Sturm on Education: The Reformation and Humanist Learning*. St. Louis: Concordia, 1995.

Sprunger, Keith L. "Ames, Ramus, and the Method of Puritan Theology," in *Harvard Theological Review*, 59 (1966), pp. 133-151.

_____. *The Learned Doctor William Ames*. Chicago: University of Chicago Press, 1972.

_____. "Technometria: A Prologue to Puritan Theology," in *Journal of the History of Ideas*, 29 (1968), pp. 115-122.

Staedke, Joachim. "Die Gotteslehre der *Confessio Helvetica posterior*," in *Glauben und Bekennen: Vierhundert Jahre Confessio Helvetica Posterior, Beiträge zu ihrer Geschichte und Theologie*, edited by J. Staedke (Zürich: Zwingli Verlag, 1966), pp. 251-257.

Staehelin, Ernst. *Amandus Polanus von Polansdorf*. Basel: Helbing & Lichtenhan, 1955.

Stalker, D. M. G. "John Weemse of Lathocker, One of Scotland's Early Hebraists," in *Scottish Church History Society Records*, 5 (1944), pp. 151-66.

Stange, Karl. "A. Ritschls Urteil über die beiden Principien des Protestantismus," in *Theologische Studien und Kritiken* (1897), pp. 599-621.

Stauffer, Richard. "Le calvinisme et les Universités," in *Bulletin de la Société de l'Histoire du Protestantisme français*, 126 (1980), pp. 27-51.

_____. *Dieu, la création et la Providence dans la prédication de Calvin*. Bern and Frankfurt: Lang, 1978.

_____. *Interprétes de la Bible: Études sur les réformateurs du XVIe siécle*. Paris: Beauchesne, 1980.

Stead, Christopher. "Divine Simplicity as a Problem for Orthodoxy," in *The Making of Orthodoxy: Essays in Honor of Henry Chadwick*, edited by Rowan D. Williams (Cambridge: Cambridge University Press, 1989), pp. 255-269.

_____. *Divine Substance*. Oxford: Clarendon Press, 1977.

Steenbakkers, Piet. "Johannes Braun (1628-1708), Cartesiaan in Groningen," in *Nederlands Archief voor Kerkgeschiedenis*, 77/2 (1997), pp. 196-210.

Steenberghen, Fernand van. "Le problème de l'existence de Dieu dans la 'Somme contre les gentils,'" in *Mélanges á la memoire: C. de Konick*, edited by A. Gagne (Quebec: Presses de l'Université Laval, 1968), pp. 387-404.

_____. "Le problème de l'existence de Dieu dans le commentaire de Saint Thomas sur la 'Physique' d'Aristote," in *Sapientia*, 21 (1971), pp. 163-172.

_____. "Le problème de l'existence de Dieu dans les questions disputées 'De potentia Dei,'" in *Pensiamento*, 25 (1969), pp. 249-257.

_____. *Thomas Aquinas and Radical Aristotelianism*. Washington, D.C.: Catholic University of America Press, 1980.

Steinmetz, David C. "Calvin and the Absolute Power of God," in *Journal of Medieval and Renaissance Studies*, XVIII/1 (Spring, 1988), pp. 65-79.

_____. *Calvin in Context*. New York: Oxford University Press, 1995.

_____. "John Calvin on Isaiah 6: A Problem in the History of Exegesis," in *Interpretation*, 36 (1982), pp. 156-170.

_____. *Luther and Staupitz: An Essay in the Intellectual Origins of the Protestant Reformation*. Durham: Duke University Press, 1980.

_____. *Misericordia Dei: The Theology of Johannes von Staupitz in its Late Medieval Setting*. Leiden: Brill, 1968.

_____. "The Scholastic Calvin," in *Protestant Scholasticism: Essays in Reappraisal*, edited by C. Trueman and R. Clark, pp. 16-30.

_____. "The Superiority of Pre-Critical Exegesis," in *Theology Today*, 37 (1980), pp. 27-38.

_____. "The Theology of Calvin and Calvinism," in *Reformation Europe: A Guide to Research*, edited by Steven Ozment (St. Louis: Center for Reformation Research, 1982.

Steinmetz, David C., ed. *The Bible in the Sixteenth Century*. Durham, N.C.: Duke University Press, 1990.

Steinmann, Jean. *Richard Simon et les origines de l'exégèse biblique*. Paris: Desclée de Brouwer, 1960.

Stephen, Sir Leslie. *History of English Thought in the Eighteenth Century*. 2 vols. Preface by Crane Brinton. New York: Harcourt, Brace and World, 1962.

Stephens, W. P. *The Theology of Huldrych Zwingli*. Oxford: Clarendon Press, 1986.

Stoughton, John. *History of Religion in England from the Opening of the Long Parliament to the End of the Eighteenth Century*. Rev. ed. 6 vols. New York: Armstrong, 1882.

Strauss, Leo. *Spinoza's Critique of Religion*. New York: Schocken, 1982.

Strehle, Stephen. "Calvinism, Augustinianism, and the Will of God," in *Theologische Zeitschrift*, 48/2 (1992), pp. 221-237.

_____. *Calvinism, Federalism, and Scholasticism: A Study of the Reformed Doctrine of Covenant*. Bern: Peter Lang, 1988.

_____. *The Catholic Roots of the Protestant Gospel: Encounter Between the Middle Ages and the Reformation*. Leiden: E. J. Brill, 1995.

_____. "The Extent of the Atonement and the Synod of Dort," in *Westminster Theological Journal*, 51 (1989), pp. 1-23.

_____. "Fides aut Foedus: Wittenberg and Zurich in Conflict Over the Gospel," in *Sixteenth Century Journal*, 23/1 (1992), pp. 3-20.

_____. "Universal Grace and Amyraldianism," in *Westminster Theological Journal*, 51 (1989), pp. 345-57.

Streveler, Paul A. "The Problem of Future Contingents," in *The New Scholasticism*, 47 (1973), pp. 233-247.

Strohl, Henri. "La méthode exégétique des Réformateurs," in *Le probléme biblique dans le Protestantisme*, edited by J. Boisset, (Paris: Presses Universitaires de France, 1955), pp. 87-104.

Stump, Eleonore, and Norman Kretzman. "Absolute Simplicity," in *Faith and Philosophy*, 2 (1985), pp. 353-82.

Sweeney, Leo. "Divine Infinity, 1150-1250," in the *The Modern Schoolman*, 35 (1957-58), pp. 38-51.

_____. *Divine Infinity in Greek and Medieval Thought*. New York: Peter Lang, 1992.

_____. "Divine Infinity in the Writings of Thomas Aquinas," Ph.D. diss., University of Toronto, 1954.

_____. "Lombard, Augustine and Infinity," in *Manuscripta*, 9 (1958), pp. 24-40.

_____. "Some Medieval Opponents of Divine Infinity," in *Medieval Studies*, 19 (1957), pp. 233-245.

Sweeney, Leo, and Charles Ermatinger. "Divine Infinity according to Robert Fishacre," in *The Modern Schoolman*, 35 (1957-58), pp. 191-235.

Sykes, Norman. "The Religion of Protestants," in *Cambridge History of the Bible*, III, pp. 175-198.

Synave, Paul. "Le canon scriptuaire de saint Thomas d'Aquin," in *Revue Biblique*, 33 (1924), pp. 522-533.

_____. "Les commentaires scriptuaires de saint Thomas d'Aquin," in *La Vie Spirituelle*, 8 (1923), pp. 455-469.

_____. "La doctrine de saint Thomas D'Aquin sur le sens littéral des Ecritures," in *Revue biblique*, 35 (1926), pp. 40-65.

Tavard. George H. *Holy Writ or Holy Church: the Crisis of the Protestant Reformation*. London: Burns and Oates, 1959.

_____. "Tradition in Early Post-Tridentine Theology," in *Theological Studies*, 23 (1962), pp. 377-405.

Terrien, Samuel. "History of the Interpretation of the Bible: III. Modern Period," in *The Interpreters Bible*, 12 vols. (Nashville: Abingdon, 1951-1957), Vol. I, pp. 127-141. [see also: Grant, Robert M. and McNeill, John T.]

Thijssen-Schoute, Caroline Louise. "Le cartésianisme aux Pays-bas," in E. J. Dijksterhius, et al., *Descartes eet le cartésianisme hollandais* (Paris and Amsterdam: Editions Françaises d'Amsterdam, 1950), pp. 239-59.

_____. *Nederlands cartesianisme (avec sommaire et tables des matières en français)*. Amsterdam: Noord-Hollandsche Uit. Mij., 1954.

Thilly, Frank. *A History of Philosophy*. New York: Henry Holt, 1941.

Tholuck, Friedrich August. *Vorgeschichte des Rationalismus*. 4 vols. Halle: E. Anton, 1853-62.

Thomas, Levian. "Ulrich of Strasburg: His Doctrine of Divine Ideas," in *The Modern Schoolman*, 30 (1952), pp. 21-32.

Tillyard, E. M. W. *The Elizabethan World Picture*. New York: Vintage: 1942.

Todd, Henry John. *Memoirs of the Life and Writings of the Right Rev. Brian Walton, D.D.*, 2 vols. London: Rivington, 1821.

Tökés, István. "Bullingers hermeneutische Lehre," in *Heinrich Bullinger, 1504-1575: Gesammelte Aufsätze zum 400 Todestag*, edited by Ulrich Gäbler and Erland Herkenrath (Zürich: Theologischer Verlag, 1975), pp. 161-189.

Tolley, William Pearson. *The Idea of God in the Philosophy of St. Augustine*. New York: R. R. Smith, 1930.

Torrance, James B. "Strengths and Weaknesses of the Westminster Theology," in *The Westminster Confession in the Church Today: Papers Prepared for the Church of Scotland Panel on Doctrine*, edited by Alasdair Heron (Edinburgh: St. Andrews Press, 1982), pp. 40-53.

Torrance, Thomas F. "Calvin's Doctrine of the Trinity," in *Calvin Theological Journal*, 25/2 (November, 1990), pp. 165-193.

_____. "The Distinctive Character of the Reformed Tradition," in *Reformed Review*, 54/1 (Autumn, 2000), pp. 5-16.

_____. "The Doctrine of the Holy Trinity: Gregory of Nazianzen and John Calvin," in *Calvin Studies V*, edited by John H. Leith (Davidson, N.C.: Davidson College, 1990), pp. 7-19; also printed in *Sobornost*, 12 (1990), pp. 7-24.

_____. *The Hermeneutics of John Calvin*. Edinburgh: Scottish Academic Press, 1988.

_____. "Intuitive and Abstractive Knowledge from Duns Scotus to Calvin," in *De Doctrina Ioannis Duns Scoti*, edited by C. Balic, vol.IV, pp. 291-305.

_____. "Karl Barth and the Latin Heresy," in *Scottish Journal of Theology*, 39 (1986), pp. 461-482.

_____. "Knowledge of God and Speech about Him according to John Calvin," in *Theology in Reconstruction* (Grand Rapids, Eerdamsn, 1966), pp. 76-98.

_____. "The Legacy of Karl Barth (1886-1986)," in *Scottish Journal of Theology*, 39 (1986), pp. 289-308.

_____. "La philosophie et la théologie de Jean Mair ou Maior (1469-1550), in *Archives Philosophiques*, 33 (1970), pp. 261-294.

_____. "Scientific Hermeneutics According to St. Thomas Aquinas," *Journal of Theological Studies*, 13 (1962), pp. 259-289.

Toussaint, C. "Aséité," in *Dictionnaire de théologie catholique*, vol. 1/2 , cols. 2077-2080.

_____. "Attributs divins," in *Dictionnaire de théologie catholique*, 1/2, col. 2223-2235.

Trapp, Damasus. "Augustinian Theology of the Fourteenth Century: Notes on Editions, Marginalia, Opinions and Book-lore," in *Augustiniana*, VI (1956), 146-274.

Trechsel, Friedrich. *Die protestantischen Antitrinitarier vor Faustus Socin: Nach Quellen und Urkunden geschichtlich dargestellt*. 2 vols. Heidelberg: K. Winter, 1839-1844.

Trentman, John A. "Scholasticism in the Seventeenth Century," in *The Cambridge History of Later Medieval Philosophy*, edited by N. Kretzmann, A. Kenny, and J. Pinborg (Cambridge: Cambridge University Press, 1982), pp. 818-837.

Trinkaus, Charles. "Erasmus, Augustine and the Nominalists," in *The Scope of Renaissance Humanism*, pp. 274-301.

_____. *In Our Image and Likeness: Humanity and Divinity in Italian Humanist Thought*. 2 vols. Chicago: University of Chicago Press, 1970.

_____. "Italian Humanism and Scholastic Theology," in *Renaissance Humanism: Foundations, Forms, and Legacy*, edited by A. Rabil, vol. III, pp. 327-348.

_____. "The Religious Thought of the Italian Humanists, and the Reformers: Anticipation or Autonomy?" in *The Pursuit of Holiness*, edited by Trinkaus and Oberman, pp. 339-366.

_____. "Renaissance Problems in Calvin's Theology," in *Studies in the Renaissance*, 1 (1954), pp. 59-80. [also in *The Scope of Renaissance Humanism*, pp. 317-339]

_____. *Renaissance Transformations of Late Medieval Thought*. Brookfield, Vt.: Ashgate/Variorum, 1999.

_____. *The Scope of Renaissance Humanism*. Ann Arbor: University of Michigan, 1983.

Trinkaus, Charles E., and Heiko A. Oberman, eds. *The Pursuit of Holiness in Late Medieval and Renaissance Religion*. Leiden: Brill, 1974.

Troeltsch, Ernst. *Vernunft und Offenbarung bei Johann Gerhard und Melanchthon*. Göttingen: Vandenhoeck & Ruprecht, 1891.

Trueman, Carl R. *The Claims of Truth: John Owen's Trinitarian Theology*. Carlisle: Paternoster Press, 1998.

_____. "Faith Seeking Understanding: Some Neglected Aspects of John Owen's Understanding of Scriptural Interpretation," in *Interpreting the Bible*, edited by A. N. S. Lane (Leicester: Apollos, 1997), pp. 147-162.

_____. "John Owen's *Dissertation on Divine Justice*: An Exercise in Christocentric Scholasticism," in *Calvin Theological Journal*, 33 (1998), pp. 87-103.

_____. "Richard Baxter on Christian Unity: A Chapter in the Enlightening of English Reformed Orthodoxy," in *Westminster Theological Journal*, 61 (1999), pp. 53-71.

_____. "A Small Step Toward Rationalism: The Impact of the Metaphysics of Tommaso Campanella on the Theology of Richard Baxter," in *Protestant Scholasticism*, edited by C. Trueman and R. Clark, pp. 147-164.

Trueman, Carl, and R. Scott Clark, eds. *Protestant Scholasticism: Essays in Reassessment*. Carlisle: Paternoster Press, 1999.

Tschackert, P. *Die Entstehung der lutherischen und reformierten Kirchenlehre*. Göttingen, 1910.

_____. *Petrus von Ailli: Zur Geschichte des grossen abenländischen schisma und der Reformconcilien von Pisa und Constanz*. Gotha: Perthes, 1877.

Tukker, C. A. "Theologie en Scholastiek: De Synopsis Purioris Theologiae als Theologisch Document (II)," in *Theologia Reformata*, 18 (1975), pp. 34-49.

_____. "Vier Leidse Hoogleraren in de Gouden Eeuw: De Synopsis Purioris Theologiae als Theologisch Document (I)," in *Theologia Reformata*, 17 (1974), pp. 236-250.

Tulloch, John. *Rational Theology and Christian Philosophy in England in the Seventeenth Century*. 2 vols. Edinburgh: Blackwood, 1872.

Tylenda, Joseph. "Calvin's Understanding of the Communication of Properties," in *Westminster Theological Journal*, 38 (Fall 1975-Spring 1976).

_____. "Christ the Mediator: Calvin versus Stancaro." *Calvin Theological Journal*, VII (1973), pp. 5-16, 131-57.

_____. "Girolami Zanchi and John Calvin," in *Calvin Theological Journal*, X (1975), pp. 101-141.

_____. "The Warning that Went Unheeded: John Calvin on Giorgio Biandrata," in *Calvin Theological Journal*, 12 (1977), pp. 24-62.

Urban, Percy Linwood. "The Will of God: A Study of the Origin and Development of Nominalism and its Influence on the Reformation." S.T.D. diss., General Theological Seminary (NY), 1959.

Vansteenberghe, E. "Molina, Louis," in *Dictionnaire de théologie catholique*, vol. 10/2, cols. 2090-2092.

_____. "Molinisme," s.v. in *Dictionnaire de théologie catholique*, vol. 10/2, cols. 2094-2187.

Vasoli, Cesare. "*Loci communes* and the Rhetorical and Dialectical Traditions," in *Peter Martyr Vermigli and Italian Reform*, edited by Joseph C. McLelland, pp. 17-28.

_____. "The Renaissance Concept of Philosophy," *The Cambridge History of Renaissance Philosophy*, edited by C. Schmitt, Q. Skinner, and E. Kessler, pp. 57-74.

Veldhuis, Henri. "Duns Scotus' Theory of Synchronic Contingency in *Lectura* I 39 and its Theological Implications," in *Via Scoti*, edited by L. Sileo, pp. 571-76.

Venema, Cornelis P. "Heinrich Bullinger's Correspondence on Calvin's Doctrine of Predestination, 1551-1553," in *Sixteenth Century Journal*, 17/4 (1986), pp. 435-50.

_____. "The 'Twofold Knowledge of God' and the Structure of Calvin's Theology," in *Mid-America Journal of Theology* 4 (1988), pp. 156-82.

Verbeek, Theo. *Descartes and the Dutch: Early Reactions to Cartesianism (1637-1650)* Journal of the History of Philosophy Monograph Series. Carbondale Ill.: Southern Illinois University Press, 1992.

_____. "Descartes and the Problem of Atheism: the Utrecht Crisis," in *Nederlands Archief voor Kerkgeschiedenis*, 71/2 (1991), pp. 211-223.

_____. "From 'Learned Ignorance' to Scepticism: Descartes and Calvinist Orthodoxy," in *Scepticism and Irreligion*, edited by R. Popkin and A. Vanderjagt, pp. 31-45.

_____. *La Querelle d'Utrecht*. Texte établi et traduites avec une introduction et notes par Theodorus Verbeek. Paris: Impressions Nouvelles, 1988.

_____. "Tradition and Novelty: Descartes and Some Cartesians," in *The Rise of Modern Philosophy*, edited by Tom Sorrel (Oxford: Clarendon Press, 1993), pp. 167-196.

Verhoef, Pieter A. "Luther and Calvin's Exegetical Library," in *Calvin Theological Journal*, 3 (1968), pp. 5-20.

Vernet, F. "Lyon, Concile de," in *Dictionnaire de théologie catholique*, IX, cols. 1379ff.

Vet, J. J. V. M. de. "Jean Leclerc, an Enlightened Propagandist of Grotius' 'De Veritate Religionis Christianae,'" in *Nederlands Archief voor Kerkgeschiedenis*, 64 (1984), pp. 160-195.

Vignaux, Paul. "Etre et infini selon Duns Scot et Jean de Ripa," in *De Doctrina Ioannis Duns Scoti*, edited by C. Balic, vol. IV, pp. 43-56.

_____. *Luther, Commentateur des Sentences*. Paris: J. Vrin, 1935.

_____. "Métaphysique de l'Exode, philosophie de la religion (à partir du *De Primo Principio* selon Duns Scot)," in *Rivista di Filosofia Neo-scholastica*, 70 (1978), pp. 135ff.

_____. "Nominalisme," s.v. in *Dictionnaire de théologie catholique*, vol. 11/1, cols. 717-784.

_____. *Nominalisme au XIVe siècle*. Montreal: Institute d'études médiévales, 1948.

_____. "Philosophie et théologie trinitaire chez Jean de Ripa," in *Archives Philosophique*, 41 (1978), pp. 221-236.

_____. "*Processus in infinitum* et preuve de Dieu chez Jean de Ripa," in *Mélanges offerts á M.-D. Chenu*, edited by A. Duval (Paris: J. Vrin, 1967), pp. 467-476.

Villanova, Evangelista. *Histoire des théologies chrétiennes*. 3 vols. Paris: Éditions de Cerf, 1997.

Vischer, Wilhelm. "Calvin exégète de l'Ancien Testament," in *La Revue Reformée*, 18 (1967), pp. 1-20.

Visscher, Hugo. *William Ames: His Life and Work*. Translated by W. Horton. Cambridge, Mass.: Harvard Divinity School Library, 1965.

Visser, Derk, ed. *Controversy and Conciliation: The Reformation and the Palatinate, 1559-1583*. Allison Park, Pa.: Pickwick, 1986.

Voeltzel, René. "La Méthode théologique de Hugo Grotius," in *Revue d'histoire et de philosophie religieuses*, 32 (1952), pp. 126-133.

Von Leyden, W. *Seventeenth-Century Metaphysics: An Examination of Some Main Concepts and Theories*. London: Gerald Duckworth and Co., 1968.

Von Rohr, John. *The Covenant of Grace in Puritan Thought*. Atlanta: Scholars Press, 1986.

Vooght, Paul de. "Le rapport écriture-tradition d'après saint Thomas d'Aquin et les théologiens du XIII siècle," in *Istina*, 8 (1962), pp. 499-510.

_____. *Les Sources de la doctrine Chrétienne d'après les théologiens du XIVe siècle*. Paris: Desclée De Brouwer, 1954.

_____. "Wiclif et la *Scriptura Sola*," in *Ephemerides theologiae lovanienses*, 39 (1963), pp. 50-86.

Vos, Antonie. "Always on Time: The Immutability of God," in *Understanding the Attributes of God*, edited by G. van den Brink and M. Sarot, pp. 53-73.

_____. "Immutabilitas Dei," in *Nederlands Theologisch Tijdschrift*, 35 (1981), pp. 111-133.

_____. "De kern van de klassieke gereformeerde Theologie," in *Kerk en Theologie*, 47 (1996), pp. 106-125.

_____. *Johannes Duns Scotus*. Leiden: Groen en Zoon, 1994.

_____. "The Philosophy of the Young Duns Scotus," in *Medieval Semantics and Metaphysics: Studies Dedicated to J. M. L. de Rijk*, edited by E. P. Bos (Nijmegen: Ingenium, 1985), pp. 195-220.

_____. "Reformatorische Theologie en Metaphysica," in *Theologia Reformata*, 26 (1983), pp. 266-289.

_____. "Scholasticism and Reformation," in *Reformation and Scholasticism*, edited by W. van Asselt and E. Dekker, pp. 99-119.

_____. "De theorie van de eigenschappen en de leer van de eigenschappen van God," in *Bijdragen*, 42 (1981), pp. 81-87.

Vos, Antonie, et al., eds. *John Duns Scotus: Contingency and Freedom. Lectura I/39*. Dordrecht and Boston: Kluwer, 1994.

Vosté, James M. "Medieval Exegesis," in *Catholic Biblical Quarterly*, 51 (1948), pp. 229-246.

Vriend, David John. "Causality, Reliability and God's Foreknowledge." Ph.D. diss., UCLA, 1987.

Vries de Heekelingen, H. de. *Genève, Pepinière du Calvinisme hollandais. Tome I. Les étudiants des Pays-Bas à Genève au temps de Théodore de Bèze. Tome II. Correspondence des élèves de Théodore de Bèze apres leur départ de Genève*. 2 vols. Den Haag: Nijhoff, 1918-24.

Vuilleumier, Henri. *Histoire de l'église réformée du pays de Vaud sous le régime bernois*. 4 vols. Lausanne: Concorde, 1928.

Waddington, Charles. *Ramus, sa vie, ses écrits et ses opinions*. Paris: Ch. Meyrueis, 1855.

Walker, Daniel P. *The Ancient Theology: Studies in Christian Platonism from the Fifteenth to the Eighteenth Century*. London: Duckworth, 1972.

Walker, Williston. *John Calvin: The Organizer of Reformed Protestantism, 1509-1564*. With a bibliographical essay by John T, McNeill. 1906; rerp. New York: Schocken, 1969.

Wall, Ernestine G. E. van der. "Cartesianism and Cocceianism: A Natural Alliance?" in *De l'humanisme aux lumières, Bayle et le protestantisme: mélanges en l'honneur d'Elisabeth Labrousse*, edited by M. Magdelaine, et al. (Oxford: Voltaire Foundation, 1996), pp. 445-455.

_____. "Orthodoxy and scepticism in the early Dutch Enlightenment," in *Scepticism and Irreligion in the Seventeenth and Eighteenth Centuries*, edited by R. Popkin and A. Vanderjagt, pp. 121-141.

Wallace, Dewey. "From Eschatology to Arian Heresy: the Case of Francis Kett (d. 1589)," in *Harvard Theological Review*, 67 (1974), pp. 459-473.

_____. "The Life and Thought of John Owen to 1660: A Study of the Significance of Calvinist Theology in English Puritanism." Ph.D. diss., Princeton University, 1965.

_____. *Puritans and Predestination: Grace in English Protestant Theology, 1525-1695*. Chapel Hill: University of North Carolina Press, 1982.

Wallace, Ronald S. *Calvin's Doctrine of the Word and Sacrament*. Grand Rapids: Eerdmans, 1957.

Wallace, William A. "Traditional Natural Philosophy," in *Cambridge History of Renaissance Philosophy*, edited by C. Schmitt, Q. Skinner, and E. Kessler, pp. 201-235.

Wallman, Johannes. *Der Theologiebegriff bei Johann Gerhard und Georg Calixt*. Tübingen: J. C. B. Mohr, 1961.

Warfield, Benjamin Breckinridge. *Calvin and Augustine*. Edited by Samuel Craig. Philadelphia: Presbyterian and Reformed Publishing Company, 1956.

_____. "Calvin's Doctrine of God," in *Calvin and Augustine*, pp. 133-185.

_____. "Calvin's Doctrine of the Knowledge of God," in *Calvin and Augustine*, pp. 29-130.

_____. "Calvin's Doctrine of the Trinity," in *Calvin and Augustine*, pp. 189-284.

_____. "On the Literary History of Calvin's Institutes," in *Calvin and Calvinism*. New York: Oxford University Press, 1931.

_____. *The Westminster Assembly and Its Work*. New York: Oxford University Press, 1931. Reprint, Grand Rapids: Baker Book House, 1981.

Wass, Meldon C. *The Infinite God and the Summa Fratris Alexandri*. Chicago: Franciscan Herald Press, 1964.

Watson, Richard A. *The Breakdown of Cartesian Metaphysics*. Atlantic Highlands, New Jersey: Humanities Press, 1987.

_____. *The Downfall of Cartesianism, 1673-1712: A Study of Epistemological Issues in Late 17th Century Catresianism*. International Archives of the History of Ideas, vol. 2. Den Haag: Nijhoff, 1966.

Watts, Michael R. *The Dissenters*, 2 vols. Oxford: Clarendon Press, 1978.

Weber, Claude, "Heerboord ou Heerboort, Adriaan," in *Encyclopédie philosophique universelle*, III/1, pp. 1191-92.

Wéber, Edouard. "Passio, Passivitas," in *Encyclopédie philosophique universelle*, II/2, p. 1871.

Weber, Hans Emil. *Der Einfluss der protestantischen Schulphilosphie auf die orthodox-lutherische Dogmatik*. Leipzig: Deichert, 1908. [Pp. 19-74 of this work were published separately as *Die analytische Methode der lutherische Orthodoxie* (Naumburg, 1907).]

_____. *Die philosophische Scholastik des deutschen Protestantismus in Zeitalter der Orthodoxie*. Leipzig: Quelle & Meyer, 1907.

_____. *Reformation, Orthodoxie und Rationalismus*. 2 vols. Gütersloh, 1937-51. Reprint, Darmstadt: Wissenschaftliche Buchgesellschaft, 1966.

Weber, Otto. *Grundlagen der Dogmatik*. 2 vols. Neukirchen: Neukirchner Verlag, 1955.

_____. *Foundations of Dogmatics*. 2 vols. Translated by Darrell Guder. Grand Rapids: Eerdmans, 1981-82.

Weiler, A. "The Christian Humanism of the Renaissance and Scholasticism," in *Concilium*, 27 (1967), pp. 29-46.

Weir, David A. *The Origins of the Federal Theology in Sixteenth-Century Reformation Thought*. Oxford: Clarendon Press, 1990.

Weisheipl, J. A., "Scholastic Method," in *New Catholic Encyclopedia*, vol. 12, pp. 1145-1146.

Wendel, François. *Calvin: The Origins and Development of His Religious Thought*. Translated by Philip Mairét. New York: Harper and Row, 1963.

Wendel, François, and Pierre Scherding. "Un Traité d'exégèse pratique de Bucer," in *Revue d'histoire et de philosophie religieuses*, 26 (1946), pp. 32-75.

Werner, Karl. *Franz Suárez und die Scholastik der letzten Jahrhunderte*. 2 vols. Regensburg: G. J. Man, 1861.

_____. *Die Scholastik des späteren Mittelalters*. 4 vols. in 5. Vienna, 1881-87. Reprint, New York: Burt Franklin, n.d.

Wernle, Paul. *Der evangelische Glaube nach den Hauptschriften der Reformatoren*. 3 vols. Tübingen: J. C. B. Mohr, 1919.

Werther, David. "Leibnitz on Cartesian Omnipotence and Contingency," in *Religious Studies*, 31 (1995), pp. 23-36.

West, Delno C., and Sandra Zindars-Swartz. *Joachim of Fiore: A Study in Spiritual Perception and History*. Bloomington: Indiana University Press, 1983.

Westcott, Brooke Foss. *A General Survey of the History of the Canon of the New Testament*. 6th ed. 1889. Reprint, Grand Rapids: Baker Book House, 1980.

Westfall, Richard. "The Rise of Science and Decline of Orthodox Christianity: A Study of Kepler, Descartes, and Newton," in D. Lindberg and R. Numbers, *God and Nature*, pp. 218-237.

_____. *Science and Religion in Seventeenth Century England*. New Haven: Yale University Press, 1958.

Wetter, Friedrich. "Die Erkenntnis der Freiheit Gottes nach Johannes Duns Scotus," in *De Doctrina Ioannis Duns Scoti*, edited by C. Balic, vol. II, pp. 477-517.

_____. *Die Trinitätslehre des Johannes Duns Scotus*. Münster: Aschendorff, 1967.

Whale, J. S. *The Protestant Tradition*. Cambridge: Cambridge University Press, 1962.

White, Peter. *Predestination, Policy and Polemic: Conflict and Consensus in the English Church from the Reformation to the Civil War*. Cambridge: Cambridge Univ Press, 1992.

Wilbur, Earl Morse. *A History of Unitarianism*. 2 vols. Cambridge, Mass.: Harvard University Press, 1947-52.

Wilbur, James B., ed. *Spinoza's Metaphysics: Essays in Critical Appreciation*. Assen: Van Gorcum, 1976.

Willey, Basil. *The Eighteenth Century Background: Studies on the Idea of Nature in the Thought of the Period*. Boston: Beacon Press, 1961.

_____. *The Seventeenth Century Background: Studies in the Thought of the Age in Relation to Poetry and Religion*. Garden City: Doubleday Anchor, 1953.

Williams, Bernard. "Rationalism," in *The Encyclopedia of Philosophy*, vol. 7, pp. 69-75.

Williams, Michael E. *The Teaching of Gilbert Porreta on the Trinity as Found in His Commentaries on Boethius*. Rome: Gregorian University, 1951.

Willis, E. David. "Calvin and the Anti-trinitarians," in *Archiv für Reformationsgeschichte*, 62 (1971), pp. 279-282.

_____. *Calvin's Catholic Christology: the Function of the so-called Extra Calvinisticum in Calvin's Theology.* Leiden: E. J. Brill, 1966.

_____. "Calvin's Use of Substantia," in *Calvinus Ecclesiae Genevensis Custos*, pp. 289-301.

_____. "The Influence of Laelius Socinus on Calvin's Doctrines of the Merits of Christ and the Assurance of Faith," in *Italian Reformation Studies in Honor of Laelius Socinus*, edited by John Tedeschi (Florence: F. Le Monnier, 1965), pp. 231-241.

Willis, R. *Servetus and Calvin.* London: Henry King, 1877.

Wilson, Catherine. *Leibnitz's Metaphysics: a Historical and Comparative Study.* Princeton: Princeton University Press, 1989.

Wilterdink, Garret A. "The Fatherhood of God in Calvin's Thought," in *Reformed Review*, 30/1 (Fall 1976), pp. 9-22.

_____. "Irresistible Grace and the Fatherhood of God in Calvin's Theology." Ph.D. diss., University of Chicago, 1974.

_____. *Tyrant or Father? A Study of Calvin's Doctrine of God.* 2 vols. Bristol, IN: Wyndham Hall Press, 1985.

Wippel, John F. *The Metaphysical Thought of Godfrey of Fontaines: A Study in Late Thirteenth-Century Philosophy.* Washington: Catholic Univerisity of America Press, 1981.

Wissink, Jozephus Bernardus Maria. *The Eternity of the World, in the Thought of Thomas Aquinas and his Contemporaries.* Leiden: E. J. Brill, 1990.

Wolfson, Harry Austryn. *The Philosophy of Spinoza.* 2 vols. Cleveland and New York: World, 1958.

_____. *The Philosophy of the Church Fathers: Faith, Trinity, Incarnation.* 3rd ed., revised. Cambridge, Mass.: Harvard University Press, 1970.

_____. *Religious Philosophy: A Group of Essays.* New York: Atheneum, 1965.

_____. "St. Thomas on Divine Attributes," in *Studies in the History and Philosophy of Religion*, II, pp. 1-28.

_____. *Studies in the History and Philosophy of Religion*, 2 vols. edited by Isadore Twersky and George H. Williams (Cambridge, Mass.: Harvard University Press, 1973-77.

Wollgast, Siegfried. *Philosophie in Deutschland zwischen Reformation und Aufklärung, 1550-1650.* Berlin: Akademie Verlag, 1988.

Wolter, Allan B. "Duns Scotus on the Existence and Nature of God," in *Proceedings of the American Catholic Philosophical Association*, XXVIII (1954), pp. 94-121.

_____. "Duns Scotus on the Natural Desire for the Supernatural," in *The New Scholasticism*, XXIII (1949), pp. 281-317.

_____. "Duns Scotus on the Nature of Man's Knowledge of God," in *Review of Metaphysics*, 1/2 (Dec. 1947), pp. 3-36.

_____. *Duns Scotus on the Will and Morality.* Selected and translated, with an introduction by Allan B. Wolter. Washington, DC: Catholic University Press, 1986.

_____. "Ockham and the Textbooks: On the Origin of Possibility," in *Franziskanische Studien*, 32 (1950), pp. 70-96.

_____. "The 'Theologism' of Duns Scotus," in *Fransiscan Studies*, 7 (1947), pp. 257-273, 367-414.

_____. *The Transcendentals and their Function in the Metaphysics of Duns Scotus.* St. Bonaventure, NY: The Franciscan Institute, 1946.

Wolter, Allan B., and Marilyn McCord Adams. *The Philosophical Theology of John Duns Scotus*. Ithaca: Cornell University Press, 1990.

Wolterstorff, Nicholas. "Divine Simplicity," in *Philosophical Perspectives*, vol. 5, *Philosophy of Religion*, edited by James Tomberlin (Atascadero, CA: Ridgeview Publishing, 1991), pp. 531-552.

Woodbridge, John D. *Biblical Authority: a Critique of the Rogers/McKim Proposal*. Grand Rapids: Zondervan, 1982.

_____. "Richard Simon le 'père de la critique biblique,'" in *Le Grand Siècle de la Bible*, edited by Armogathe, pp. 193-206.

Woolhouse, R. S. *Descartes, Spinoza, Leibniz: the Concept of Substance in Seventeenth Century Metaphysics*. London and New York: Routledge, 1993.

Woolsey, Andrew Alexander. "Unity and Continuity in Covenantal Thought: A Study in the Reformed Tradition to the Westminster Assembly. 2 vols. Ph. D. diss., University of Glasgow, 1988.

Workman, Herbert B. *The Dawn of the Reformation*. 2 vols. London: Charles Kelley, 1901-2.

Woudstra, Marten H. "Calvin Interprets 'What Moses Reports': Observations on Calvin's Commentary on Exodus 1-19," in *Calvin Theological Journal*, 21 (1986), pp. 151-174.

_____. "The Synod and Bible Translation," in *Crisis in the Reformed Churches: Essays in commemoration of the Great Synod of Dort, 1618-1619*, edited by Peter Y. DeJong (Grand Rapids, 1968), pp. 95-114.

Wright, David F. "Calvin's Pentateuchal Criticism: Equity, Hardness of Heart, and Divine Accommodation in the Mosaic Harmony Commentary," in *Calvin Theological Journal*, 21 (1986), pp. 33-50.

Wright, David F., ed. *Martin Bucer: Reforming Church and Community*. Cambridge: Cambridge University Press, 1994.

Wundt, Max. *Die deutsche Schulmetaphysik des 17. Jahrhunderts*. Tübingen: J. C. B. Mohr, 1939.

Zanta, Léonine. *La Renaissance du Stöicisme au XVIᵉ siècle*. 1914; reprint, Geneva: Slatkine, 1975.

Zavalloni, Roberto. "Personal Freedom and Scotus' Voluntarism," in *De Doctrina Ioannis Duns Scoti*, edited by C. Balic, vol. II, pp. 613-627.

Zeller, Winfried. "Die Marburger Theologische Fakultät und ihre Theologie im Jahrhundert der Reformation," in *Jahrbuch der Hessischen Kirchengeschichtlichen Vereinigung*, 28 (1977), pp. 7-25.

Zuber, Roger. "De Scaliger à Saumaise: Leyde et les grands 'Critiques' français," in *Bulletin de la Société de l'Histoire du Protestantisme français*, 126 (1980), pp. 461-488.

Zuylen, W. H. *Bartholomaus Keckermann: Sein Leben und Wirken*. Leipzig: Robert Noske, 1934.

Index